Principles of Pitch Organization in Bartók's *Duke Bluebeard's Castle*

Rita Honti

Principles of Pitch Organization in Bartók's *Duke Bluebeard's Castle*

Second, revised edition

Studia musicologica Universitatis Helsingiensis XVI

2008

Studia musicologica Universitatis Helsingiensis

General Editor
Eero Tarasti

Faculty of Arts
Department of Musicology
PO Box 35
00014 University of Helsinki
Finland

http://www.helsinki.fi/taitu/musiikkitiede/esittely.htm

Second printing

Printed by Gummerus, Finland 2008

Cataloging-in-Publication Data

Honti, Rita, 1963-
Principles of pitch organization in Bartók's Duke Bluebeard's Castle / Rita Honti.—2nd, rev. ed., 2nd printing.—xii, 362 p. : ill., music, tables ; 25 cm.—(Studia musicologica Universitatis Helsingiensis, ISSN 0787-4294 ; 16).
Includes bibliographical references (p. [311]-345) and index.
ISBN 978-952-10-3837-2 (pbk)
1. Bartók, Béla, 1881-1945. Kékszakállú herceg vára. 2. Operas—Analysis, appreciation. 3. Tonality. 4. Musical intervals and scales. 5. Ethnomusicology. I. Title. II. Series.

ML410.B26 H66 2008
782.1—dc22

CONTENTS

ABSTRACT

Rita Honti
Principles of Pitch Organization in Bartók's *Duke Bluebeard's Castle*

University of Helsinki, Faculty of Arts, Department of Musicology

The topic of my doctoral thesis is to demonstrate the usefulness of incorporating tonal and modal elements into a pitch-web square analysis of Béla Bartók's (1881–1945) opera, *A kékszakállú herceg vára* (*Duke Bluebeard's Castle*). My specific goal is to demonstrate that different musical materials, which exist as foreground melodies or long-term key progressions, are unified by the unordered pitch set {0,1,4}, which becomes prominent in different sections of Bartók's opera. In *Bluebeard's Castle*, the set {0,1,4} is also found as a subset of several tetrachords: {0,1,4,7}, {0,1,4,8}, and {0,3,4,7}. My claim is that {0,1,4} serves to link music materials between themes, between sections, and also between scenes.

This study develops an analytical method, drawn from various theoretical perspectives, for conceiving superposed diatonic spaces within a hybrid pitch-space comprised of diatonic and chromatic features. The integrity of diatonic melodic lines is retained, which allows for a non-reductive understanding of diatonic superposition, without appealing to pitch centers or specifying complete diatonic collections. Through combining various theoretical insights of the Hungarian scholar Ernő Lendvai, and the American theorists Elliott Antokoletz, Paul Wilson and Allen Forte, as well as the composer himself, this study gives a detailed analysis of the opera's pitch material in a way that combines, complements, and expands upon the studies of those scholars. The analyzed pitch sets are represented on Aarre Joutsenvirta's note-web square, which adds a new aspect to the field of Bartók analysis.

Keywords: Bartók, *Duke Bluebeard's Castle* (Op. 11), Ernő Lendvai, axis system, Elliott Antokoletz, intervallic cycles, intervallic cells, Allen Forte, set theory, interval classes, interval vectors, Aarre Joutsenvirta, pitch-web square, pitch-web analysis.

ACKNOWLEDGEMENTS

The research presented in this thesis was carried out at the Department of Musicology, University of Helsinki, under the supervision of Professor Eero Tarasti and Docent Alfonso Padilla. Their kind support and guidance have been of great value in this study. Having also received my licentiate in musicology there, I opted for a further year of study at the University of Helsinki, and wrote the present thesis in 2005-2006.

I wish to express my deep and sincere gratitude to Eero for his continuous support in my Ph.D. program. His wide knowledge and open-mindedness have been of great value to me. His understanding, encouragement, and personal guidance have provided an excellent basis for the present thesis. Eero showed me different ways to approach a research problem and the need to be persistent in order to accomplish any goal: how to get into analysis and how to get out. His critical insights have been crucial in all stages of my research.

I am deeply grateful to Alfonso, as always, for his detailed and constructive comments, and for his firm support, which has continued ever since I attended his doctoral seminars. My warmest thanks to Alfonso for his unwavering help and positive attitude toward my work. Our extensive discussions and interesting analytic explorations have been very helpful to me in completing this thesis.

I wish to express my gratitude to the official reviewers of this thesis; in particular, Professor Vilmos Voigt of Eötvös Lóránd University (Budapest) and Dr. Tom Pankhurst of Liverpool Hope University College. Their detailed review and valuable comments are greatly appreciated.

No study such as this could come to fruition without the support and encouragement of many others. During this work, I have collaborated with many colleagues for whom I have great regard. I wish to extend my warmest thanks to all those who have helped me with my work in the Department of Musicology at the University Helsinki, International Doctoral and Post-Doctoral Seminars on Musical Semiotics, and International Semiotics Institute's annual summer congresses on semiotics. Several people have commented on my manuscript or sections of it, which include articles and papers related to the present research. In addition to my supervisors, I owe my most sincere gratitude to Professor Márta Csepregi (Budapest), Professor John Deely (Houston), Professor Márta Grabócz (Strasbourg), Professor Robert Hatten (Bloomington), Professor Erkki Pekkilä (Helsinki), Professor Anne Sivuoja-Gunaratnam (Helsinki), Professor Ivanka Stoïanova (Paris), and Professor Leo Treitler (New York). Their encouragement and significant scholarly comments and suggestions have been greatly appreciated and have deeply affected the substance of this book.

I would like to thank the scholarly community, my friends, and colleagues at the Department of Musicology for their interest and support during the course of my work. Special thanks go to Ph.L. Esa Lilja for many inspiring discussions, which have had a remarkable influence on my entire thesis, and for preparing the notated examples in Chapter 4.4.9. I also thank Dr. György Honti Jr. (Budapest) and Márta Schmidt for several books and for the detailed comments on Chapter 3, and Dr. Susanna Välimäki for her comments on my thesis at different stages. I am grateful also to Liisamaija Hautsalo, Reijo Jyrkiäinen, Anu Konttinen, and Eila Tarasti for the precise and illuminating comments on my analysis. Various people have helped me in many other ways. Thanks to Irma Vierimaa, Merja Hottinen, Erja Hannula, Kirsti Nymark, Sipo Vanhanen, Henrik Ruso, and Kristiina Norlamo for helping me at any time, and for solving the many unsolvable problems facing a Ph.D. student. Professor Richard Littlefield (Michigan), to whom I express my thanks for his contribution, revised the English of the present manuscript. In addition, my thanks are due to Paul Forsell, who dedicated his precious time to help me in editing the final draft of the dissertation, in the layout of the book, and in several other technical matters. A particular debt of gratitude is owed to Jaakko Tuohiniemi, who put the ball in play, helped me in countless ways in gaining my search material, and answered all my possible and impossible questions with great patience. Jaakko was always ready with whatever material or information I needed. I also thank Anna Rajala (Helsinki), for her continuous support and assistance in technical matters during the preparation of my dissertation. I thank Universal Editions, Vienna, for permission to use excerpts from the score of Béla Bartók's *Duke Bluebeard's Castle*, Op. 11, which appear as examples in this work. The financial support of the University of Helsinki is gratefully acknowledged, without which this project could not have been completed.

Last, but by no means least, I owe my loving thanks to my parents Mária and György Honti. My father lives on in the loving memory of his family and friends. Without their encouragement and understanding, it would have been impossible for me to finish this work. Special gratitude is due to my brother, Dr. György Honti Jr, for sharing his experience of the dissertation-writing endeavor with me, and for his continuous intellectual support.

Helsinki and Budapest, August, 2006

Rita Honti

1. INTRODUCTION

> Every moment is a symbol, a reduced-scale image of the whole.
>
> (Lukács 1974 [1911]: 156.)

This study concerns the incorporation of tonal and modal elements with Aarre Jout-senvirta's pitch-web square in an analysis of Béla Bartók's[1] (1881–1945) opera, *A kékszakállú herceg vára* (*Duke Bluebeard's Castle*) (Op. 11, Sz 48, BB 62,[2] 1911, rev. 1912, 1918). *Bluebeard's Castle*, one of the most significant musical works of the early twentieth century, represents Bartók's only venture into the operatic genre. Both chronologically and musically, it occupies a central position in his early career. The one-act opera, which was his first work for voice, has two singing roles, those of Bluebeard (baritone) and Judith (soprano). The "Prologue" is narrated by the "Bard", and Bluebeard's three previous wives appear only briefly in mute roles. (Bartók 1952 [1925]; and 1963 [1921].)

Bluebeard's Castle was composed to a libretto written by Béla Balázs (1884–1949), who embraced the French Symbolists as a model for his work. At the same time, the libretto also displays a strongly Hungarian, national identity. In Balázs's

---

1. According to Hungarian custom, the family name is followed, not preceded, by the baptismal name. This leads to a considerable amount of confusion in countries where the reverse custom prevails. In my study, the Western order is employed: Béla Bartók, rather than Bartók Béla, which is correct in Hungary. In citing titles of Bartók's works, I often use only the English titles as they appear in the comprehensive "List of Compositions" in *Béla Bartók: A Guide to Research* (Antokoletz 1997 [1988]: 5–43), but sometimes present the Hungarian titles as well, especially for major works such as *Duke Bluebeard's Castle* (*A kékszakállú herceg vára* – literally *The Blue-bearded Duke's Castle*). In my study, the opera is variously referred to as *Duke Bluebeard's Castle*, *Bluebeard's Castle*, or *Bluebeard*. Hungarian titles of scholarly publications are accompanied by English translations; those in French and German are given in the original languages.

2. Bartók gave opus numbers 1 to 21 to his early works. In 1898, he stopped assigning opus numbers to his compositions for six years. In 1904, with the *Rhapsody* for piano solo (Sz 26, BB 36a), Bartók began the numbering once again, giving opus numbers to compositions that he considered major works. In 1921, he assigned the opus number 21 to his *Sonata for Violin and Piano* No. 1 in C-sharp minor (*I. Szonáta hegedűre és zongorára*) (Sz 75, BB 84), dedicated to Jelly Arányi (1893–1966), after which Bartók stopped using opus numbers for good. The Sz numbers refer to András Szőllősy's (1956) catalogue of Bartók's mature works, "Bibliographie des œuvres musicales et écrits musicologiques de Béla Bartók," in Bence Szabolcsi's edition of *Bartók, sa vie et son œuvre*. In *Béla Bartók*, József Ujfalussy (1971 [1970]: 400–430) revised that list with a few corrections. In *Bartók kompozíciós módszere* (*Béla Bartók: Composition, Concepts and Autograph Sources*), the Hungarian Bartók scholar, László Somfai (2000 [1996]) clarifies matters regarding active research into sources, and the methodology used in the complete edition (BB); see also, Somfai (1995).

mystery play (*misztériumjáték*)[3] the action is reduced to a minimum, with (internal) character development being the central dramatic process.

In *Magyar Színpad* (*The Hungarian Stage*), Bartók remarks on his opera as follows:

> It may sound peculiar but I must admit that the failure of my one-act play, *Bluebeard's Castle*, prompted me to write *The Wooden Prince*. It is common knowledge that this opera of mine failed at a competition; the greatest hindrance to its stage production is that the plot offers only the spiritual conflict of two persons, and the music is confined to the description of that circumstance in abstract simplicity. Nothing else happens on the stage. I am so fond of my opera that when I received the libretto [of *The Wooden Prince*] from Béla Balázs, my first idea was that the ballet – with its spectacular, picturesque, richly variegated actions – would make it possible to perform these works the same evening. I believe it is unnecessary to stress that the ballet is just as dear to me as my opera. (*BBE* 1976 [1917]: 406.)

Duke Bluebeard's Castle was premiered on May 24, 1918, at the Magyar Királyi Operaház (Hungarian Royal Opera House) in Budapest. On that occasion, Bartók declared:

> I set the miracle play *Duke Bluebeard's Castle* from March to September 1911. It was simultaneously my first stage [work] and my first vocal work. At that time conditions were not suitable for its performance, so that I showed it to count Miklós Bánffy, and to conductor Egisto Tango only after the performance of *The Wooden Prince*. I am most grateful to them for sparing neither trouble nor pains in producing such a first-rate performance. Olga Haselbeck and Oszkár Kálmán sang their parts so perfectly that the performance completely came up to my expectations. (*BBE* 1976 [1918]: 407.)

My primary purpose in this study is to investigate the pitch organization in Bartók's opera by means of Aarre Joutsenvirta's (b. 1957) little-explored pitch-web analysis (1989). Put briefly, pitch-web analysis is a method of comparing the pitch content of different passages of music (tonal or atonal) so as to make explicit certain structural properties. A pitch-class set (PC-set) is an unordered set of pitch classes, without duplications, that are mutually related by one or more transformations (Forte 1973: 1, 3). Surface structures such as repetitions, octaves, and enharmonic spelling of individual notes are not properties of PC-sets and do not influence the identity of the set. For example, the pitch collection $\{0,3,7,12\}$ contains the repetition of a pitch

---

3. In his writings, Balázs (1968 [1913]; and 1982 [1922]) referred to *Bluebeard's Castle* variously as a "*librettó*" (libretto), "*operaszöveg*" (opera text), "*dráma*" (drama), "*dámai jelenet*" (dramatic scene), "*misztériumjáték*" (mystery play), "*színpadi ballada*" (scenic ballad) and "*költemény*" (poem). In the present study, *Bluebeard's Castle* (1979 [1910]) will also be alternatively referred to in the generic terms given by Balázs; on the context of Balázs's libretto, see Chapters 4.1–4.2, below.

class (0 = 12); hence {0,3,7,12} reduces to PC-set {0,3,7} (Forte number 3–11;[4] Interval Class Vector [ICV] 001110[5]). In my study, the interval succession is shown as a sequence of numbers separated by commas and enclosed in brackets.

Although interval succession provides useful information about the ordered relations between types of sets, a clearer and more concise representation is made possible by Joutsenvirta's *pitch-web square* (Table 1.1).

0	3	6	9	0	3	6	9	0	3	6	9
5	8	11	2	5	8	11	2	5	8	11	2
10	1	4	7	10	1	4	7	10	1	4	7
3	6	9	0	3	6	9	0	3	6	9	0
8	11	2	5	8	11	2	5	8	11	2	5
1	4	7	10	1	4	7	10	1	4	7	10
6	9	0	3	6	9	0	3	6	9	0	3
11	2	5	8	11	2	5	8	11	2	5	8
4	7	10	1	4	7	10	1	4	7	10	1
9	0	3	6	9	0	3	6	9	0	3	6
2	5	8	11	2	5	8	11	2	5	8	11
7	10	1	4	7	10	1	4	7	10	1	4

Table 1.1. The 12 x 12 pitch-web square (Joutsenvirta 1989: 95).

My analytic aim in this study is to demonstrate the existence and preponderance of set {0,1,4} in *Bluebeard*, clarified by means of Joutsenvirta's (1989) pitch-web analysis. It shows the role of the set in ordering the musical surface, without implying that the music exhibits a serial ordering. My claim is that, in Bartók's *Bluebeard*, the different musical materials are unified by the ways in which set {0,1,4} becomes prominent in different sections (Example 1.1, next page).

I shall further propose that set {0,1,4} has supplanted the tonal system in Bartók's opera, where temporary tonal centers are established by PC and intervallic centricity. In *Tonality, Atonality, Pantonality*, Rudolph Réti explains tonal centricity as follows:

---

4. Allen Forte lists the prime forms of PC-sets, and gives their interval class vectors (total interval content); for the latter, I hereinafter use Forte's abbreviation, ICV (1973: 179–181; see also, the Appendix to this study). Forte lists 208 unordered sets in the twelve-tone system. Interval classes (ICs) indicate both the interval and its inversion (ibid.: 14, 20; see also, Cook 1987: 134, 326); the prime forms of sets are discussed in Forte (ibid.: 3, 5, 11–13); and ICVs of sets in Forte (ibid.: 15–18, 30–31). More explanation of PC-sets is provided as this study goes on, especially in Chapter 2.4 (pp. 80–82).

5. The ICV (Forte 1973: 15–18, 30–31) is an array of six integers (mathematical notation) representing the IC content of a chord. The ICV exhibits the total interval content of the set. It is a practical and effective means to analyze the internal construction of a combination of PCs. The six numbered positions in the ICV stand for ICs 1 to 6. The numbers filling those positions show how many times that IC is represented in any set in the class. (Ibid.: 2–3.)

Example 1.1. Set {0,1,4}.

It is characterized by the fact that pitches, which by repetition and resumption become [prominent cornerstones] in the compositional course, can by this very quality assume a quasi-tonical role. This can help a group appear as a unit and can thus create form, even if the harmonic design of the group points to a different tonal path or to no [tonal] basis at all. (Réti 1958: 77.)

In Bartók's opera, the unordered trichord set {0,1,4}, shown in Example 1.1, has a fixed intervallic content, but not a fixed ordering. It appears in foreground melodies and in long-term progressions, a point to which I return in Chapter 4.

It is important to distinguish between ordered and unordered pitch intervals. Ordered pitch intervals are determined by subtracting the pitch number of the first pitch from the pitch number of the second pitch. This produces both positive and negative numbers, indicating ascending and descending intervals, respectively. The absolute value of the unordered pitch interval is used to determine the absolute size of an interval without regard to the order in which the pitches are presented. (Forte 1973: 3, 60–61; and Straus 2000: 7–9.)

My claim is that the unordered set {0,1,4}, sometimes embedded in tetrachords {0,1,4,7}, {0,1,4,8}, and the most typical Bartók chord {0,3,4,7}, also serve as links between certain themes, sections, and scenes. Those sets also establish large-scale, organized structural coherence in Bartók's opera (cf. pp. 195–196, Chapter 4.3).

On set-complex relations, Forte notes that:

As sets are identified, and relations are revealed, it is usually not difficult to make judgments concerning significance. The most effective basis for these judgments is provided by set-complex relations. […] These relations, properly interpreted, will often point out sets of lesser significance, which would be more correctly replaced by a superset, or further decomposed into component subsets. (Forte 1973: ix.)

The statement above shows that a central concept of Forte's brand of PC-set analysis is "inclusion" (Forte 1973: 25). The concept of complete invariance – such as "inclusion under inversion" and "inclusion under transposition" – is discussed in Chapter 2.4 (pp. 87–88). In the next quotation, Forte discusses the subset and superset relations determined by inclusion:

If all elements of a certain set X are also in a bigger set Y, then X is a subset, and Y is a superset of X. X is a proper subset of Y if the cardinal number[6] of Y is greater than the cardinal number of X, and if every element of X is an element of Y. [...] A set X is said to be a superset of a set Y if every element of Y is an element of X. X is a proper superset of Y if the cardinal number of X is greater than the cardinal number of Y, and if every element is an element of X. (Forte 1973: 211.)

In *Duke Bluebeard's Castle*, the unordered, abstract PC-set {0,1,4}, shown in Example 1.1 (previous page), is also found as a subset, e.g., in the tetrachord supersets {0,1,4,7} and {0,1,4,8}.

Because no single method is sufficient to demonstrate the relations that I propose exist in *Bluebeard*, my concern is not with a mechanical application of pitch-web analysis alone. Rather, a synthesis of pitch-web (Joutsenvirta 1989) and motivic analysis (Cook 1987: 89–115, 151, 165) best describes the rapprochement between pitch structures and dramatic expression in the opera. *Bluebeard's Castle* is especially interesting when studied from the viewpoint of pitch-web analysis, since it contains elements derived from various musical languages. These include, e.g., functional tonality, folk song modality, and symmetrical pitch combinations. I focus on harmonic constructs in terms of their intervallic properties, thus suggesting the secondary importance of traditional functional concepts. My analytical strategies produce results that are often strikingly different from those found in single-theory studies.

I integrate various types of theoretical approaches, analytical techniques, and methodologies of Hungarian scholar Ernő Lendvai, and of American theorists Elliott Antokoletz, Allen Forte, and Paul Wilson (who receives only limited attention). Through those perspectives, my study gives a detailed analysis of the musical design and thematic material of *Bluebeard's Castle*, in a way that combines, complements, and expands upon the studies of those theorists. Adding a new aspect to the field of Bartók analysis, I demonstrate the PC-sets through application of the Finnish theorist Aarre Joutsenvirta's (1989) *sävelverkko* (pitch-web) analysis and two-dimensional *sävelverkkoruutu* (pitch-web square), shown in Table 1.1 (p. 3) and described in the author's *Introduction to Pitch-Web Analysis*. In measuring PC intervals, I follow Forte in my use of closed Modulo 12 (Mod 12) arithmetic (also called Clock Math or Modulo Math), to which Joutsenvirta's ideas are closely related.

The common thread between Forte and Joutsenvirta is their reliance on theoretical concepts and systems that were developed mainly to deal with music generally labeled as "atonal." By contrast, Lendvai, Antokoletz, and Wilson are Bartók specialists *par excellence*. Those theorists' groundbreaking ideas were formulated independently of each other, and each focuses on a different phase of the analytical spectrum. An integrated analytic methodology yields fruitful results, when applied to local and global tonal centers of Bartók's opera (Chapter 4.3). I examine how Bartók displaced the functional connections of traditional tonality and created a new

---

6. Cardinal numbers, or cardinals for short, are numbers used to denote the size of a set. It means the number of elements in a set, discounting repetitions. It denotes quantity, not ordering. (Forte 1973: 3, 12, 19, 209.)

sonic universe in *Bluebeard's Castle*. My examination will show how Bartók used polymodal scale combinations (Lendvai 1968) to create a twelve-note chromatic environment with a single fixed point of reference (Wilson 1982; 1992; and 1993). This involves examination of the use of pitch-cell interval content (Antokoletz 1984: 16, 78–137), the main analytical tool for which is Joutsenvirta's pitch-web square (1989: 95; see also, Table 1.1, p. 3).

Through the analytical process, thematic and formal coherence can be established in *Bluebeard's Castle*, because the preponderance of particular intervals in the structure of set {0,1,4} automatically assures a certain homogeneity. Necessarily related sub-questions are also engaged, concerning other important structural formations that Bartók incorporated in the opera, including chordal settings and phrase structures (Chapter 4). First, however, the structure of that set and the manner in which it is employed require special consideration.

Forte's (1973) set theory operates with particular reference to three sequences of numbers:

1. The collection representing the twelve different PCs, numbered from 0 to 11, where C is designated 0.
2. The collection representing the six different ICs, numbered from 0 to 6.
3. The sequence of prime form PC-sets, which total 224, or 208 if the sets of cardinality (total number of PCs) 0, 1, 2, 10, 11, and 12 are excluded.

Forte's way of mapping certainly draws attention to various pitch-class and interval similarities among sets. Yet, a more differentiated means of comparing particular events in a musical piece is needed, if translating pitch, via PC, into number is to be justified. According to Joutsenvirta (1989: 1), to make comparisons means to observe the possible degrees of differences and similarities, so that, in the end, their relative *musical* significance may be evaluated in specific contexts.

Figures 1.1–1.4 display sets {0,1,4}, {0,1,4,7}, {0,1,4,8}, and {0,3,4,7} through Joutsenvirta's 12 x 12 pitch-web square (Joutsenvirta 1989: 95; see also, Table 1.1, p. 3). Those sets share certain characteristics; moreover, each replicates itself in inversion in Bartók's opera. The designation "set" signifies that the pitches may occur in vertical (harmonic) or horizontal (melodic) configurations, or in both.

Figure 1.1. Set {0,1,4}.

Figure 1.2. Set {0,1,4,7}.

Figure 1.3. Set {0,1,4,8}.

Figure 1.4. Set {0,3,4,7}.

In this study, the sets shown in Figures 1.1–1.4 serve as the *point de départ*. They have idiomatic differences from Antokoletz's starting point, which is based on intervallic cells (for more details, see especially, pp. 73–75, Chapter 2.3). According to Antokoletz (1984: 89–92), the musical language Bartók uses in *Bluebeard* is a fusion of tonal writing, with an emphasis on old-style Hungarian peasant songs[7], with a deliberate use of dissonance. In "Bartók's *Bluebeard*: The Sources of Its Modernism," Antokoletz (1990: 79) argues that the opera is based on the shifting relations among semitones, and on the various transformations of those relations, both of which appear to be associated with special dramatic situations. Antokoletz (1984: 89–92) takes *Bluebeard* as an illustration of Bartók's use of dissonant intervallic cells for dramatic purposes, especially the X cell, shown as set {0,1,2,3} in Figure 1.5 and as used in Example 1.2 (next page).

Figure 1.5. Set {0,1,2,3}.

The excerpt from Bartók's *Bluebeard's Castle,* shown in Example 1.2 (next page), is a prominent foreground statement of X cell (Figure 1.5). It occurs in the "Torture Chamber" scene, the first of the doors to be opened by Judith. The text at this point reveals that Judith has just noticed blood in Bluebeard's castle: "*A te várad fala vérzik*" (Your castle's walls are bleeding).[8]

I take Antokoletz's (1984: 89–92; and 1990) analysis, discussed briefly above, as a point of departure for my own. My fundamental concern is to analyze pitch relations, not on a larger-sized scale, but in terms of smaller-unit PC-sets, to show how Bartók incorporates dissonance into the music. My assumption, however, is the same as Antokoletz's: the opera develops toward "increasing dissonance" (1990: 79).

---

7. Old-style folk songs are discussed in Chapter 3.5.1.
8. For a detailed analysis of the "First Door" scene, see Chapter 4.4.4.

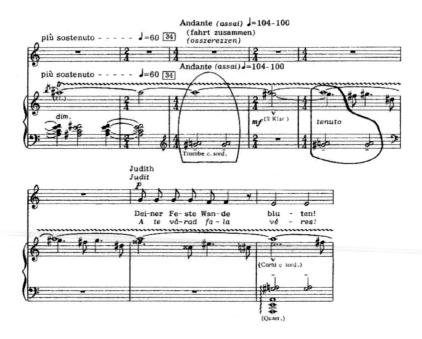

Example 1.2. Bartók, *Bluebeard's Castle*, X cell in the "Torture Chamber" scene, 34/1–6.9 © 1921 by Universal Edition A. G., Wien/UE 7026, used by kind permission.

Chapter 2 contains a general overview of crucial theoretical and analytic issues as found in relevant literature, methodologies, and analytical tools. A further theoretical distinction needs to be made, however, since one cannot discuss Bartók's musical language without touching on his own writings. The division of the chapter is guided by shifts of interest and compositional method rather than by chronology.

In Chapters 2.1.1–2.1.4, Bartók's "Harvard Lectures" (*BBE* 1976 [1943])[10] serve as the primary theoretical background. The scope of my research is limited to music of Bartók's mature style, dating from 1908[11] to 1911 (Antokoletz 1997 [1988]:

9. In the designation "34/1–6", the number on the left refers to the rehearsal number(s) in the score; the number(s) to the right of the slash refer to the measure numbers, as counted from the rehearsal number; that form of designation is used throughout this study. The rehearsal and measure numbers refer equally to the published full score (Bartók 1952 [1925]) and piano-vocal score (Bartók 1963 [1921]) of *Duke Bluebeard's Castle*.

10. Bartók's (*BBE* 1976 [1943]) four "Harvard Lectures" were given during February, 1943. The titles of the lectures are as follows: (1) 'Revolution and Evolution in Art'; (2) 'Modes and Polytonality'; (3) 'Chromaticism'; and (4) 'Rhythm'. Bartók originally planned to discuss nine topics, in the following order: (1) 'Revolution, Evolution'; (2) 'Modes and Polymodality'; (3) 'Chromaticism'; (4) 'Rhythm, Percussion Effect'; (5) 'Form'; (6) 'Scoring'; (7) 'Trend Toward Simplicity'; (8) 'Educational Works'; and (9) 'General Spirit'. Because of his illness, however, Bartók had to interrupt the lecture series after the third lesson. By that time, he had written part of the fourth lecture and a draft containing the above outline, but nothing survives of lectures 5 through 9.

11. The year 1908 saw the first expression, in a mature and individualistic style, of the synthesis of his dual experience of classical and folk music. In that same year, Bartók also composed a note-

5–43). My discussion of different conceptions of tonality and modality is wide-ranging, and synthesizes a number of interrelated theoretical views. I give an account of Bartók's theoretical premises and the fundamental relationships that exist between the diatonic folk modes and various other pitch formations. Special emphasis goes to Bartók's use of modality (bimodality, polymodality) and tonality (microtonality), and their influences on symmetrical intervallic constructions.

In Chapters 2.2–2.4, special attention is paid to the theories and analytic methods of Lendvai, Antokoletz, Wilson, Joutsenvirta, and Forte. For purposes of space, my discussion is limited to the most important and relevant aspects of their theories. I present topics sometimes in succession and sometimes simultaneously, as needed to explicate the organization of unordered abstract pitch sets (see Figures 1.1–1.4, pp. 6–7). Chapter 2.5, "An outline of integrated technique,[12]" is meant to complete the framework of theoretical references necessary to cope with the central problem of the classification of pitch structures, and to present my own, eclectic analytical framework based on ideas of the aforementioned theorists. In my view, the important thing is not so much to invent new techniques nor to endlessly refine those we already have, but rather to make the fullest possible use of them. One way in which those techniques can be made more useful is to employ them in combination with one another. My aim is to develop an analytical process using tools that could act as an interface between pitch-web analysis and more general aspects of pitch organization (such as those of traditional music theory).

An examination of Bartók's intellectual environment cannot be limited merely to looking at contemporary musical life, or his personal experiences. It is necessary to consider the ideological and intellectual trends of the period in order to gain a better understanding of Bartók's artistic world.[13] Chapter 3.1 contains a discussion of the social context and cultural background of Bartók's works from 1908 to 1911.[14] In Chapters 3.2.1 and 3.3, there is a discussion of how Bartók used Liszt as an early compositional model, one who synthesized stylistic features of Hungarian *verbunkos* (recruiting dance) music with the idioms of Romantic music. In Chapter 3.2.2, I outline a historical background of the Hungarian opera tradition. Chapters 3.4–3.5 give an account of Bartók's discovery of folk music and his subsequent ethnomusicological studies in Hungary and neighboring nations. I describe Bartók's methods of classifying material, which formed the basis of his comparative, ethnographic approach. In Chapter 3.6, I concentrate on Bartók's three-level concept of folk-music arrangement.[15]

---

worthy work, the *First String Quartet* (Op. 7, Sz 40, BB 52, 1908).

12. I thank Dr. Tom Pankhurst for suggesting the term "integrated technique" for my analytical method.

13. Bartók has been a symbol of traditional/modern and Hungarian/cosmopolitan creativity in Hungary, and the secondary literature about him and his works continues; thus, for all practical purposes, it is endless.

14. I am greatly indebted to Dr. György Honti for discussing this solution with me.

15. Somfai (2000 [1996]: 1) characterized the extant literature on Bartók as the "disturbingly uncoordinated and controversial" product of a field grappling with many obstacles: an ideologically charged language divide, geographical separation of primary sources, isolation from the musico-

Chapters 4.1–4.2 trace the history of Balázs's play, *Duke Bluebeard's Castle*, which Bartók adapted (with few changes) for his opera, and the relationship between composer and playwright. In Chapter 4.3, the global arch-form of the composition, articulated by the tonalities of the scenes, is discussed in a way that expands upon previous studies; a pitch-web analysis of the tonal construction is also provided.

Chapter 4.4 begins with a discussion of the spoken "Prologue", which traditionally has been one of the features overlooked in analyses of the opera. My primary goal is realized in Chapters 4.4.1–4.4.11. There, my analytical method and tools (set forth in Chapter 2.5) are applied to the structure of the opera, which consists of an introduction and seven scenes corresponding to the castle's seven locked doors. The analysis consists in a detailed analyses of the main themes in the opera. My decision to focus most closely on themes needs an explanation. Detailed examination of the whole opera is beyond the realm of my investigations, and my study's emphasis is on the highly complex analytical issues. I do not attempt to treat every unit or bar, measure by measure, of *Duke Bluebeard's Castle*; my aim is more modest. By breaking down the larger sections of the scenes, I can concentrate on those moments – thematic structure, motifs, and their harmonic context – that are most significant when viewed from the present theoretical perspective, and that reflect principal features and stylistic elements of the composer's style. My analysis retains the integrity of diatonic constructs and allows for an understanding of diatonic superposition, by appealing to traditional and non-traditional notions of pitch centers, and by representing pitch collections by means of the pitch-web square. Issues of larger significance to Bartók's compositional style in the opera are taken up as they arise, and I discuss briefly the formal designs of the individual scenes.

My research specially centers on the "Sixth Door" scene (Chapters 4.4.9.1–4.4.9.4). I examine the sections in terms of the progressive development of thematic material, tonal/modal aspects, chromatic elements, and the background shifts of modal centers. I investigate such as tonally meaningful chord progressions, key centers, and varying degrees of tonality and modality. I then reach the crucial point of this research: first, the segmentation of the music according to pitch structures. Concerning segmentation, Forte remarks:

> By segmentation is meant the procedure of determining which musical units of a composition are to be regarded as analytical objects. Whereas this process is seldom problematic in tonal music due to the presence of familiar morphological formations (harmonies, contrapuntal substructures, and the like), it often entails difficulties in the case of an atonal work. [...] One segmentation procedure that is often productive may be described as *imbrication*[16]: the systematic (sequential) extraction of subcomponents of some configuration. [...] Imbrication represents

---

logical mainstream, and an unwillingness to build on its own accomplishments. Yet Bartók studies also waver under the burden of investment in a composer and a repertory required to perform cultural, national, political, philosophical, and ideological labor. Thus when Somfai exhorts his colleagues to "do justice to Bartók, rather than Bartók scholarship, for the disadvantages of the past" (ibid.: 8), it is a dictum at once evident and elusive.

16. Forte's italics.

an elementary way of determining the subsegments of a primary segment. (Forte 1973: 83–84.)

In the last chapter, a summary of the study is provided, as well as some critical reflections on my unconventional combining of analytical methods, as adapted to explain the musical structure of Bartók's opera. Several consequences of that adaptation are discussed. After that chapter an Appendix has been added, which is meant to illustrate and complete the theoretical and analytical frame.

Music examples from *Duke Bluebeard's Castle* are taken from both the piano arrangement and the orchestral score (Bartók 1963 [1921]; and 1952 [1925]). The selections have been chosen for their relevance and comprehensiveness in illustrating basic principles of musical progression set forth in earlier chapters. My usage of footnotes, examples, figures, and tables is intended to be informative, while not disturbing the flow of the text. Abbreviations employed in this study are defined upon their first appearance, either in a footnote or in the body of the text. The "Glossary of Abbreviations, Basic Terms, Definitions, and Concepts" explains the musical terms used in this study.

My interest in *Duke Bluebeard's Castle* has led me to engage topics not treated at length, or at all, by previous writers on Bartók's opera. Despite the tremendously large number of theoretical writings on Bartók's music, few comprehensive studies of that opera have been made. Mine will be the first full-scale dissertation on Bartók's opera to be written in Finland.

Interested readers need not have a degree in music theory in order to understand the present study. While relying upon various theoretical concepts, I do not attempt to refine them as an end in itself. Rather, they are used to support my primary goal: to explain the music in an interesting way.

2. IN SEARCH OF A SYSTEM

2.1. Analytical problems, theoretical issues

Traditionally defined, theory undertakes to codify the various materials of a composition and to exemplify their functioning in a range of works. It insists that its methods meet explicitly stated criteria of coherence, often proclaiming aesthetic preferences – though not always directly.

In his posthumously published essay, "On the Problem of Musical Analysis" (1982), Theodor W. Adorno (1903–1969) reflects on the potential of music analysis. Reading notation, e.g., requires "an analytical act"; analysis is "the prerequisite for an adequate performance"; and aesthetic theories of music are "inconceivable without analysis" (ibid.: 170). Perhaps most importantly, analysis "has to do with the surplus in art" (ibid.: 182). This surplus being the "truth content" of a work in so far as it goes beyond the mere facts. Adorno continues his line of thought: "No analysis is of any value if it does not terminate in the truth content of the work, and this, for its part, is mediated through the work's technical structure" (ibid.: 186).

Analysis is a relatively young discipline. Although codified analytical methods date back at least to the eighteenth century, the refinement and formalization of techniques in the twentieth century depended directly on those earlier developments. In *The New Grove Dictionary of Music and Musicians*, Ian Bent describes analysis in the following way:

> Analysis is the means of answering directly 'How does it work?' Its central activity is comparison. By comparison, it determines the structural element and discovers the functions of those elements. Comparison is common to all kinds of musical analysis – feature analysis, formal analysis, functional analysis, information-theory analysis, Schenkerian analysis, semiotic analysis, style analysis and so on: comparison of unit with unit, whether within a single work, or between two works, or between the work and an abstract 'model' such as sonata form or arch form. The central analytical act is thus the test for identity. And out of this arises the measurement of amount of difference or degree of similarity. (Bent 1987 [1980]: 342.)

In *The New Oxford Companion to Music*, Arnold Whittall (1983: 58) writes that "the analytical process is two-fold: to identify the various materials of a composition, and to define the ways in which they function". Bent has defined analysis in similar terms:

The resolution of musical structure into relatively simpler constituent elements, and the investigation of the functions of those elements within that structure. In such process, the 'structure' may be part of a work, a work in its entirety, a group or even a repertory of works, in a written or oral tradition. The distinction often drawn between formal analysis and stylistic analysis is a pragmatic one, but is unnecessary in theoretical terms. Both fall within the above definition, since on the one hand any musical complex, no matter how small or large, may be deemed a 'style'; and on the other hand, all the comparative processes that characterize stylistic analysis are inherent in the basic analytical activity of resolving structure into elements. (Bent 1987 [1980]: 340–341.)

In his *Chroniques de ma vie*, Igor Stravinsky (1882–1971) declared that music is "powerless to express anything at all" (1962 [1935]: 53). In *Expositions and Developments* (Stravinsky & Craft 1981: 101), Stravinsky states "music expresses itself"; music, being both "supra-personal and super-real", is "beyond verbal meanings and verbal descriptions". The works of a composer might well embody his feelings, might express, or symbolize these feelings. Nevertheless, "consciousness of this step does not concern the composer." Stravinsky (ibid.) stresses the distinction between thinking *in* music ("perceptual") and thinking *about* music ("conceptual").

Music analysis always invokes abstract concepts that help to classify and make sense of the concrete musical experience. In *Explaining Music*, Leonard B. Meyer clarifies that:

Without some relatively rigorous and explicit criteria, there is a real danger that theoretical preconceptions will influence, if not determine, the analysis of structural versus ornamental tones. And when this occurs, analysis becomes circular and self-confirming. (Meyer 1973: 121.)

Music theory in the past few decades has explored the rich terrain of mathematical and other quantifiable aspects of twentieth-century music, while tending to neglect repertories whose interpretation may demand other, perhaps more flexible approaches. It is clear that some analytic systems are designed for a particular kind of music, but most advocates of a new strategy like to show its scope to be as wide as possible. An attempt to reduce the characteristics of a system to a minimum of features has been made in the mathematical theory of sets (cf. Cook 1987: 124–151, 231, 343; explanatory principles are also mentioned below, in Chapter 2.4).

When ideas based on the triad are no longer adequate interpretative tools for the harmonic analysis of atonal or dodecaphonic works, it may indeed be necessary to change one's notion of what the whole comprises. As Adorno properly puts it:

It is particularly in new music [...] that analysis is concerned just as much with dissociated moments [*Dissoziationsmomente*] – with the works' 'death-wish', that is to say, with the fact that there are works, which contain within themselves the tendency to strive *from* unity back into their constituent elements – as it is concerned with the opposite process. (Adorno 1982: 182.)

Forte has vigorously defended analysis based on precepts, against what he takes to be the specious dogmas of historicism. Forte points out that:

> My view [...] is that knowledge of history is totally inadequate for understanding musical documents, including musical scores as well as treatises on music. It is only now, with the development of contemporary modes of theoretical thought that scholars are beginning to understand more fully many of the classic documents of music theory. (Forte 1986: 335.)

Richard Taruskin (1986: 318) observes that Forte certainly would not deny that music theories have historical origins and contexts. Rather, Forte asserts that historical factors in and of themselves cannot provide complete understanding or logical validation of theory. This is, of course, the position of the positivist.[17]

In "How We Got into Analysis and How to Get Out", Joseph Kerman (1994 [1980]) tried to elevate his own brand of criticism to a position of privilege among the competing discourses about music. Although he recognized criticism's debt to analysis, Kerman nevertheless placed a higher premium on a research enterprise that did not terminate either in the gathering of facts or in the establishment of a work's internal relationships. In *Contemplating Music*, Kerman (1985) enabled a crystallization of the offending categories as positivism and formalism.[18]

The analysis of serial music poses problems of a different nature from those encountered in more traditionally-oriented music. Forte (1973: ix) states that pitch-class set theory reveals the "fundamental components of structure." In his *Twelve-Tone Tonality*, George Perle (1996 [1977]: 172) remarks that interval contents are "the sole objective basis for whatever connections one may wish to establish between pitch collections." What needs to be acknowledged is that Forte (1973: 124–177) raises issues that remain central to any attempt to analyze an atonal piece, not as an isolated phenomenon, but as part of a larger whole. The methods and the terminology are generally borrowed from mathematical formalization of the theory of sets (aggregates, or collections) of objects (elements, or members).

Pierre Boulez has defined "an *active* analytical method" as follows:

> [...] it must begin with the most minute and exact observation possible of the musical facts confronting us; it is then a question of finding a plan, a law of internal organization, which takes account of facts with the maximum coherence [and] finally comes the interpretation of the compositional laws deduced from

---

17. Taruskin (1986), in challenging the value of Forte's theory of pitch-class sets, applied it to the music of Stravinsky and Scriabin (1872–1915). Taruskin is skeptical about such applications of Forte's theory, since in his view, criteria for analytical statements on music "are historically delimited and must be determined by historical methods" (ibid.: 318). Forte's theory, Taruskin maintains, clearly does not meet this demand. Taruskin advocates the use of alternative theories, ones that are rooted in the same cultural soil as the music. This means, at least in the case of Stravinsky and Scriabin, modified forms of tonal (but not Schenkerian) and octatonic analysis.

18. The complex histories were subsequently suppressed in the drive to underline the limitations of theory-based analysis. The charge of formalism was made because analysts inquired only into the connections between patterns *within* a piece.

this special application. All these stages are necessary; one's studies are of merely technical interest if they are not followed through to the highest point – the interpretation of the structure; only at this stage can one be sure that the work has been assimilated and understood. (Boulez 1975 [1963]: 18.)

In my opinion, all analysts must make decisions about what strikes them as the most salient or important features of a piece, then select the formal evaluation procedure best designed to address those features. The selection and usage of theoretical tools for analysis together act as filters and constraints on the analyst and on the piece at hand. In the present case, context-sensitive criteria seem reasonable, because in Bartók's *Bluebeard's Castle* the composite segments inhabit the tonal PC-set world in very different ways. In the determination of composite segments, we find an analogy to the set-theoretical operation of union and intersection of PC-sets. Forte notes that:

Also of potential interest are segments that are formed by the interaction of more than one primary segment. These are called *composite segments*.[19] A composite segment is a segment formed by segments or subsegments that are contiguous or that are otherwise linked in some way. Like other segments, a composite segment has a beginning and an end, both of which may be determined in several ways – for example, by an instrumental attack or by a rest. (Forte 1973: 84.)

Certain segments, at various levels of formal design within Bartók's opera, may also inhabit that world in significantly different ways. On the question of using contextual criteria for determining segments, it may be pointed that rigorously systematic segmentation procedures may often produce units that are of no consequence with respect to structure, and hence may require editing (Forte 1973: 83, 92). In the next paragraph, Forte clarifies his aim:

The term contextual criteria [...] is intended to cover decisions concerning segmentation, which involve references to local context of the candidate segment or, which involve references to non-local sections of the music. If a particular segment forms a set that is represented elsewhere in the music, it is probably a legitimate structural component. On the other hand, a segment that forms a set that occurs once may have its own *raison d'être*. (Forte 1973: 91.)

During my study, several appeals are made to contextual criteria for segment determination.[20]

---

19. Forte's original emphasis.
20. I am here indebted to Dr. Alfonso Padilla, for our long conversations about various analytical problems and theoretical issues.

2.1.1. Pitch organization

In the present chapter, I confine the discussion to pitch organization considering Bartók's own writings, and reflecting them in the light of the theoretical thought by different theorists.

Before expanding on the analytical tools, and completing the framework of the theoretic references that are necessary to cope with the central problem of the classification of pitch structures, it is worth examining the various approaches, different theoretical principles, and methods that have characterized the Bartók research field. I present an overview, highlighting some of the types rather than a detailed and finely honed analysis.

As evidenced in Antokoletz's *Béla Bartók: A Guide to Research* (1997 [1988]), the complexity of Bartók's musical language have kindled intense musicological interest. Music theorists are in a heterogeneous field, where different scholars pursue their various goals in various ways. The principles that govern Bartók's musical structures have been given often contradictory interpretations: there are almost as many theories as essays on the subject. Therefore, it is not surprising that numerous technical analyses have appeared according to the Bartókian pitch organization, based on Bartók's own writings and the theorists' views. In fact, pitch organization seems to be the greatest challenge to most of the scholars and it has become the primary concern of many Bartók studies increasingly so from the 1960s on.[21] Systematic treatment of such other aspects as rhythm and meter or thematic processes has been pushed largely into the background (Little 1971[22]).

Antokoletz remarks on the subject that part of the dilemma that has existed in determining the basic means of pitch organization in Bartók's music is that:

> There has been no theory, comparable to that of the traditional tonal system, to draw together all pitch formations in his music under one unified set of principles. The significance of the evolution of Bartók's musical language from the folk modes to a highly systematic and integrated use of abstract melodic and harmonic formations lies in the growth toward a new kind of tonal system and a new means of progression. (Antokoletz 1984: xi.)

Contemporary analyses often focus on the importance of symmetrical pitch formations as a central feature of Bartók's style (from the early stages, see, e.g., Lendvai 1955). Bartók over the course of his career revolutionized virtually every concept

---

21. It is literally impossible to collect all the data necessary for Bartók's analytical research just by working on one or two guiding disciplines.

22. In the *Architectonic Levels of Rhythmic Organization in Selected Twentieth-Century Music*, Jean Little (1971) compares the rhythmic styles based on rhythmic density of number of articulations per minute in violin compositions by Bartók, Berg, Stravinsky, and Webern. It includes a study of Bartók's *Violin Concerto* No. 2. The study outlines five steps in the analytical process: (1) morphological lengths and perception (the relation of static structural lengths); (2) rhythmic form (the microrythm of rhythmic groupings at superior and primary levels); (3) rhythmic species (types of rhythmic impulse-initial, medial, terminal); (4) rhythmic structure (the macrorhythm of metric, multimetric, and non-metric organizations); (5) rhythmic patterns and accentuation.

of tonality (or lack thereof) in existence. The basic principles of the progression and the means by which tonality is established in Bartók's music remain problematical to many theorists.

Ever since the publication of Edwin von der Nüll's (1905–1945) *Béla Bartók: Ein Beitrag zur Morphologie der neuen Musik* (1930), the phenomenon of note structures that contain major and minor thirds simultaneously has been a well-known and frequently discussed topic in research on Bartók; e.g., the major-minor chord, set {0,3,4,7}. Nüll (ibid.: 74) deemed the major-minor chord a neutral sound, claiming that simultaneous sounding of the two thirds produces an "absence of mode" (*Geschlechtslosigkeit*).[23] Nüll (ibid.: 73) sees Bartók as an evolutionary phenomenon in matters of form and pitch organization alike, in contrast to Arnold Schoenberg (1874–1951), invariably starts out from precedent and goes on from there to unfold further possibilities. In *Moderne Harmonik*, as regards Bartók's pitch organization, Nüll (1932) asserts that it is tertian, tonal, and diatonic.

Ivan F. Waldbauer's (1996) essay, "Theorists' Views on Bartók from Edwin von der Nüll to Paul Wilson," is a cogent summary of the analytical responses to Bartók's music, and the history of Bartók analysis. Waldbauer opens his study by embracing of six different pitch theories directed towards Bartók's œuvre. Waldbauer summarizes theories of Edwin von der Nüll, Ernő Lendvai, Milton Babbitt, János Kárpáti, Elliott Antokoletz, and Paul Frederick Wilson among others, and examines the level of self-containment of the various theories, as well as their relationship to traditional tonal systems.[24]

Bartók's stance towards music theory and his reticence to talk about his music provide little help to theorists for choosing their analytical ends and means; they are left largely to their own devices. Characteristically, Bartók himself said little directly regarding his theoretical developments, compositional processes, and of the sonori-

---

23. Nüll's (1930) work is a study on Bartók's piano music from 1908 to 1926. The monograph is not only the first major theoretical study on Bartók, but also the only one to have at least some input from Bartók himself. Nüll compared the significance of the *Tizennégy zongoradarab* (*Fourteen Bagatelles*) for piano (Op. 6, Sz 38, BB 50, 1908) to Schoenberg's *Drei Klavierstücke* (Op. 11, 1909). On Schoenberg's pieces from this period, see Egon Joseph Wellesz's (1885–1974) remarks in "Arnold Schönberg et son œuvre" (1989 [1923]: 14–15). Bartók's *Fourteen Bagatelles* is a milestone in Bartók's development as a composer as it combined his interest in deriving new pitch structures from folk music and his own individual musical conceptions. It also coincided with his discovery of parallels between Debussy's music and folk music. In these short pieces, of varying programmatic and abstract qualities, Bartók pioneered his new style of piano writing, devoid of the embellishments and rippling excesses of late-Romantic piano figuration. (See also, Gombosi 1978 [1931]: 383.) Nüll (1930) points out that Bartók's *Bagatelle* No. 8 reveals important similarities in both style and method to the first of Schoenberg's *Drei Klavierstücke*. Both pieces employ pitch cells, which replace the traditional triad as the basic harmonic premise (Antokoletz 1984: 21). I will discuss the pitch cells ahead in Chapter 2.3. In both works, a non-symmetrical three-note cell is ultimately transformed, by means of intervallic expansion and literal inversion, into four-note symmetry. (Nüll 1930; see also, *BBE* 1976 [1920a]; and Oramo 1976; and 1977b: 71.)

24. On the tendencies of Bartók analysis, see, e.g., Somfai (1981c), *Tizennyolc Bartók-tanulmány* (*Eighteen Bartók Studies*). For a summary of Antokoletz's, Forte's, Perle's, and Babbit's analytical views on Bartók's music, see Kárpáti (2004), "Bartók analízis az óceánon túl" ("Bartók Analysis over the Ocean").

ties that govern his musical structures, and general stylistic features (see, e.g., *BBE* 1976 [1929]). However, Bartók emphasized the relations of his music to folklore, chiefly with the intention of propagating folk music (see, e.g., *BBE* 1976 [1931c]).

Bartók's references to the sources and properties of his compositional tools have been invaluable in the present theoretical interpretations. The "Harvard Lectures" (*BBE* 1976 [1943]) provide Bartók's most candid and detailed explanation of his compositional techniques. Bartók's broad view is implied in the following citation:

> I must state that all my music is determined by instinct and sensibility; no one need ask me why I wrote this or that or did something in this rather than in that way. I could not give any explanation other than I felt this way, or I wrote it down this way. I never created new theories in advance. I hated such ideas. I had of course, a very definite feeling about certain directions to take, but at the time of the work, I did not care about the designations, which would apply to those directions or to their sources. This attitude does not mean that I composed without set plans and without sufficient control. The plans were concerned with the spirit of the new work and with technical problems (for instance formal structure involved by the spirit of the work) all more or less instinctively felt, but I never was concerned with general theories to be applied to the works I was going to write. Now that the greatest part of my work has already been written, certain general tendencies appear – general formulas, which theories can be deduced. (*BBE* 1976 [1943]: 376.)

2.1.2. Synthesis of folk- and art-music sources

The principal aim of these pages is to provide a context for the discussion of Bartók's pitch-centric music, with focus on his style from 1908 to 1911.

We know a great deal about the types of music that interested Bartók in the years prior to *Duke Bluebeard's Castle*. At the time he wrote his opera, Bartók had been engaged in the study and collecting of eastern European music for over five years (Bartók's folk activities are discussed below, in Chapters 3.4–3.5). The development of Bartók's style in the years leading up to *Bluebeard* has been mapped out in detail and continued in an unbroken line by prominent Bartók scholars. More than any work written before it, *Duke Bluebeard's Castle* seamlessly blends the diverse musical threads of Bartók's earlier years (for more detail, see Chapters 2.1.3–2.1.4).

Bartók's works are generally theorized starting from either of two main points of departure. (1) His music is viewed as an extension of traditional Western art music, particularly the expanded harmonic resources that emerged during the Romantic musical period. (2) The other analytic point of departure is from Bartók's own research into folk music.[25] (Vinton 1966;[26] and Suchoff 1977[27].) In Bartók's hands, folk music gave rise to new melodic, rhythmic, and harmonic possibilities, which formed the basis of his unique style (Starr 1985–1986;[28] and Parker 1987[29]). In *The Music of Béla Bartók*, Wilson (1992: 20) notes that "Bartók achieved something that no one had before his time, the symbolic handshake between East and West: synthesis, a seamless blending of two sources into a single style." Throughout his life, Bartók was also receptive to a wide variety of Western musical influences, both contemporary (notably Debussy, Stravinsky, and Schoenberg) and historic (see especially, Kárpáti 1978; also, Demény, ed. 1976: 261–262; and A. Molnár 1931a: 96, 99, 103, 109, 111). Bartók acknowledged his shift from a more Beethovenian to a more Ba-

---

25. His Transylvanian tour of 1907 convinced Bartók that the renewal of his own style could be based on folk music; for more on this topic, see pp. 143–145, Chapter 3.4.

26. Vinton (1966) argues that Bartók's remarks on folk music were a product of scholarly research and systematic analysis, while on his own music his comments were based on informal thinking. Vinton sorts the composer's comments about his own music into those concerned with (1) melodic economy; (2) melodic and rhythmic variability; (3) tonality and modality; (4) harmonic mannerisms; (5) the use of percussion instruments.

27. If a single example from Bartók's catalogue can be regarded as representative, it is certainly the piano collection *Mikrokosmos* (1926–1939), originally intended as a progressive keyboard primer for the composer's son, Péter Bartók. Those six volumes, comprising 153 pieces, remain valuable not only as a pedagogical tool but also as an exhaustive glossary of the techniques – melodic, harmonic, rhythmic, formal – that provided a vessel for Bartók's extraordinary musical personality. Suchoff (1977) sums up the pedagogical aims of that work, including its "stylistic cosmos" (influences and parallels ranging from Bach to Debussy, Schoenberg, and Gershwin) and its "folk cosmos" (including elements of Hungarian, Arabic, Balkan, American, and other cultures), then provides a historical outline of Bartók's piano music of the 1920s, including the *Mikrokosmos*.

28. In "Melody-Accompaniment Textures in the Music of Bartók, as seen in his *Mikrokosmos*", Lawrence Starr (1985–1986) states that in such a texture, one predominant voice is the determining factor in establishing the tonal direction and coherence of the piece. Bartók's main starting point was the tonally self-sufficient, monophonic folk tune, around which the composer freely developed a wide span of textural possibilities. Starr moves from pieces of simpler texture (e.g., *Mikrokosmos* No. 68, based on an ostinato derived from important tones in the melody) to those of more complexity (e.g., *Mikrokosmos* Nos. 100 and 125).

29. In her dissertation, *Bartók's "Mikrokosmos": A Survey of Pedagogical and Compositional Techniques*, Mary Parker (1987) states that the importance of the *Mikrokosmos* lies in its comprehensive and systematic organization of both keyboard and compositional techniques. Parker provides both pedagogical and theoretical analyses of selected pieces from all six volumes. She discusses the historical background of the work and the development of Bartók's career in connection with it. The author illustrates the pedagogical value of each volume, using examples to show Bartók's approach in developing technical facility and basic musical skills. Parker provides theoretical analyses dealing with new principles of pitch organization based on the equalization of the twelve tones. These principles include analyses of pentatony and modality, which reflect the influence of folk music, post-Romantic and polymodal chromaticism, whole-tone and other single-interval cycles, the octatonic scale, and inversional symmetry, in which axes of symmetry interact with traditional modal centers. These theoretical principles are related to those discussed by Antokoletz (1984; see also, pp. 68–75, Chapter 2.3 for a brief review of his studies).

chian aesthetic stance in his works from 1926 onwards (Demény 1946: 29–30; Brelet 1955[30]; and Breuer 1975a[31]). In 1928, Bartók wrote the following to Nüll:

> In my youth, Bach and Mozart were not my ideals of the beautiful, but rather
> Beethoven. During the past years, I have been occupied with pre-Bach music and
> I think that traces of these studies are revealed in the *Piano Concerto* and the *Nine
> Little Piano Pieces*. (Quoted in Demény, ed. 1976: 359.)

The sources of his inspiration and the results that Bartók achieved in following the Baroque example were, however, quite different from those of his Western
contemporaries. Bartók assimilated what was best in Baroque style so that he experienced a renewal of his sense of responsibility as an artist. In a statement given to
The Etude (Rothe 1941: 83), we read, "As a man grows more mature, it seems that he
has a greater longing to be more economical with his means, in order to achieve simplicity." In the same interview (ibid.: 130), Bartók said: "As far as I am concerned,
I think I have developed logically and in one direction, at least beginning with 1926,
when my works became more contrapuntal and simpler in general." Indeed, it is
because of their contrapuntal artistry that the compositions dating from 1926 are so
important in relation to the structure of Bartók's works. The Bartókian stylistic synthesis is so complex that only some of its aspects can be examined here.

The uniquely Bartókian qualities are manifested not by any single feature, but
by the synthesis of a multiplicity of folk- and art-music sources into an original and
contemporary musical language and style (Bartha 1963;[32] Tarasti 1994 [1978];[33] and
Frigyesi 1989[34]). Bartók's detailed studies of the melodic and rhythmic characteristics of monodic peasant tunes led him to new sources for the formation of his musical language (Dobszay 1984: 363–374; see also, pp. 165–168, Chapter 3.6, below).
This synthesis is achieved chiefly in the areas of form, tonality, and symmetry, all of
which are interrelated. Bartók's early inclination toward synthesis and transformation of folk- and art-music sources paved the way for his systematic and integrated
use of non-traditional melodic and harmonic formations. The elements of folk music

---

30. In "L'esthétique de Béla Bartók", Gisèle Brelet (1955) emphasizes the importance of folk
music as the basis of Bartók's aesthetics, which also developed from such divergent sources as
the music of Beethoven, Liszt, Brahms, and others. Brelet states that while folkrorism is not new,
Bartók's approach to it contrasts with its usage in preceding eras.

31. In "Bach és Bartók" ("Bach and Bartók"), János Breuer (1975a) discusses Bartók's early systematic studies of Bach's music, and demonstrates the compositional (e.g., use of dissonance) as
well as the pedagogical influence on him. Breuer compares Bach's and Bartók's varied approaches
to using folk music in their compositions.

32. In "La musique de Bartók", the Hungarian musicologist Dénes Bartha (1963) examines Lendvai's theories in connection with Bartók's harmonic language, applications of Lendvai's principles
to folk-music research and jazz, as well as their connections with other theories.

33. In *Myytti ja musiikki: Semioottinen tutkimus myytin estetiikasta* (*Myth and Music: A Semiotic
Approach to the Aesthetics of Myth in Music, Especially That of Wagner, Sibelius and Stravinsky*),
Eero Tarasti (1994 [1978]: 44, 46, 58, 102, 132, 228, 240, 285) presents semiotic views on Bartók's
musical language and style.

34. On Bartók's attitude toward merging Hungarian and foreign styles, see Frigyesi (1989: 138–
139, 233).

are transmuted into richly patterned, sophisticated art music. (Adorno 1984 [1922];[35] and Breuer 1973; and 1974a;[36] see also, pp. 165–169, Chapter 3.6, below.) Bartók's opera embodies his search for a contemporary style through which he combined music and language to make a fervently Hungarian declamation (discussed further in Chapters 3.5.1 and 4.3–4.4).

In *The Music of Béla Bartók: A Study of Tonality and Progression in Twenti-eth-Century Music*, Antokoletz (1984), taking into account Bartók's influences and compositions, raises the analysis of his music to an entirely new level. Folk-music sources, concepts and analytic tools current in contemporary art music are both necessary for an adequate understanding the evolution of Bartók's musical language. Antokoletz (ibid.: 1) observes, "Fundamental relationships exist between the diatonic folk modes and various abstract pitch formations commonly found in contemporary compositions." Antokoletz shows stages of transformation from the folk-music sources to a highly abstract set of art-music principles. Further on, he points out that the fusion of folk- and art-music elements resulted in "a highly complex and systematic network of divergent chords and scales" (ibid.). Bartók himself stressed that the starting point

> [...] for the creation of the new Hungarian art music was given first by a thorough knowledge of the devices of old and contemporary Western art music (for the technique of composition); and second by this newly-discovered musical [and] rural material of incomparable beauty and perfection (this for the spirit of our work to be created). Scores of aspects could be distinguished and quoted, by which this [peasant music] material exerted its influence on us; for instance: tonal influence, melodic influence, rhythmic influence, and even structural influence. (*BBE* 1976 [1943]: 363.)

In "*Allegro barbaro*: Az új magyar zene bölcsjénél" ("*Allegro barbaro*: At the Cradle of the New Hungarian Music"), Lendvai (1974) closely examines Bartók's harmonic principles, showing how they derived from pentatonic folk-music sources. Many compositions written before the *Allegro barbaro* (Sz 49, BB 63, 1911) show ample evidence of the hurdles Bartók encountered as he attempted to reconcile the forms and language of Western musical tradition with those of Hungarian music (Lindlar 1984: 23; Ujfalussy 1971 [1970]: 115[37]; also, pp. 164–168, Chapter 3.6).

---

35. Adorno (1984 [1922]) failed to understand Bartók's art, so that he took a fundamentally distorted view of Bartók's development. Adorno was the originator of the idea that Bartók's music is distinctly divided into folk music and modern music. In Adorno's eyes, Bartók's compositional achievement depended largely on his power to suppress his nationalistic instinct.

36. In "Adorno und die ungarische Musik", Breuer (1974a) discusses Adorno's changing opinion of Bartók's music, which became more critical in his later writings. Breuer states that Adorno's re-appraisal had its source in cultural and social differences between Germany and Hungary. For further reading on Adorno's views, see Breuer's (1973) serious critical observations in "Népzene és modern zene: Adorno és a magyar zene" ("Folk Music and Modern Music: Adorno and Hungarian Music").

37. In the first half of 1910s, Bartók's fame as a composer was growing, and with that, requests for him to perform. At the Festival Hongrois concert in Paris on March 12, 1910, Bartók played

In particular, Bartók's borrowings from peasant music are generally applied on the microscopic rather than macroscopic scale. He tends to adopt the scale forms, phrasing, meters, rhythms, and/or melodic contours of folk-sources, very rarely quoting verbatim from actual melodies in his large-scale works. Bartók was stimulated compositionally by the peculiarities of peasant music; for instance, microtonality (*törpetonalitás*). (Bárdos 1974: 36–38.) In "The Folk Songs of Hungary", a lecture given in Portland, Oregon, Bartók described his transformation of folk elements into unordered abstract pitch sets:

> Through inversion, and placing these chords in juxtaposition one above the other, many different chords are obtained and with them the freest melodic as well as harmonic treatment of the twelve-tones of our present day harmonic system. [...] Of course, many other (foreign) composers, who do not rely upon folk music, have met with similar results at about the same time – only in an intuitive or speculative way, evidently, is a procedure equally justifiable. The difference is that we created through Nature, for the peasants' art is a phenomenon of Nature. (*BBE* 1976 [1928]: 338.)

It is important to note that Bartók's ideas were by no means developed in isolation from the developments in European art music. He acknowledged that his compositional style was not only limited to the new Hungarian art music, but obviously influenced also by other composers (*BBE* 1976 [1920b]; and *BÖI*[38] 1966 [1905]). The development of Bartók's musical language according to these principles is described by the composer in "The Relation of Folk Song to the Development of the Art Music of Our Time":

> [...] the early researches [...] into the youngest of the sciences, namely musical folklore, drew the attention of certain musicians to peasant music, and with astonishment, they found that they had come upon a natural treasure-trove of surpassing abundance. This exploration [...] seems to have been the inevitable result of a reaction against the ultra-chromaticism of the Wagner-Strauss period. The folk music of Eastern Europe is almost completely diatonic and in some parts, such as Hungary, even pentatonic. Curiously enough, at the same time an apparently opposite tendency became apparent, a tendency towards the emancipation of the twelve sounds comprised within our octave from any system of tonality. (This has nothing to do with the ultra-chromaticism referred to, for the chromatic notes are only chromatic in so far as they are based upon the underlying diatonic scale.) The diatonic element in Eastern European folk music does not in any way conflict

---

several of his own works, as well as pieces composed by Árpád Szendy (1863–1922) and Zoltán Kodály (1882–1967). A press comment about these "young barbarians" from Hungary probably prompted Bartók to write the *Allegro barbaro* as a kind of summing up of the most important aims of his first avant-garde period, the use of East-European folk idioms marking a bold declaration of a new style. Inspired by folk music, Bartók infused his works with asymmetrical, driving (often savage) rhythms that propel works such as *Allegro barbaro*. (Ujfalussy 1971 [1970]: 115.)

38. In *Bartók összegyűjtött írásai* (*BÖI*) (*Bartók's Collected Writings*), Szőllősy (1966) includes Bartók's essays in Hungarian, whose subjects range from autobiographical to aesthetic and musicological issues, including Bartók's ideas and opinions of other composers.

with the tendency to equalize the value of semitones. This tendency can be realized in melody as well as harmony; whether the foundation of the folk melodies is diatonic or even pentatonic, there is still plenty of room in the harmonization for equalizing the value of the semitones. (*BBE* 1976 [1921e]: 323–324.)

In "The Problem of the New Music", Bartók (*BBE* 1976 [1920c]: 455) proposed that his earliest compositions reveal the combined influence of Franz (Ferenc) Liszt, Johannes Brahms, and Richard Strauss. The influence of Liszt makes itself felt mainly in the orchestral works, and apart from that, possibly in the piano chamber music, as in the case of the *Zongoraötös* (*Piano Quintet*) (DD[39] 77, BB 33, 1903–1904) (Demény 1946: 5–6; for more extensive discussion of the matter, see also, Chapters 3.2.1 and 3.3).

The new discoveries, however, brought him no inspiration, as is recalled in Bartók's "Autobiography":

> I got rid of the Brahmsian style, but did not succeed, via Wagner and Liszt, in finding, the new way so ardently desired. (I did not at that time grasp Liszt's true significance for the development of modern music, and only saw the technical brilliance of his composition.) (*BBE* 1976 [1921a]: 410.)

We see clearly the primary difference in style that separates the youthful compositions from the first pieces in the modern style. The youthful works include such pieces as the *I. Szvit* (*Suite* No. 1) for full orchestra (Op. 3, Sz 31, BB 39, 1905, revised 1920)[40], *II. Szvit* for small orchestra (Op. 4, Sz 34, BB 40, 1905–1907, revised 1920; also arranged for two pianos 1943)[41], and the *Rhapsody,* Op. 1 (see n. 2, p. 1, Chapter 1); among the first pieces in the modern style are the *Fourteen*

---

39. The DD numbers refer to the catalogue of the Belgian musicologist and Bartók expert, Denijs Dille's (1974) *Thematisches Verzeichnis der Jugendwerke Béla Bartók, 1890–1904*. (See also, Ujfalussy 1971 [1970]: 395–399.)

40. The *Suite* No. 1 was peculiarly Hungarian in its romanticism, though still untouched by Eastern European folklore and ancient Hungarian folk music. In conservative musical circles, the style of his works was already considered too advanced. In the Rubinstein Competition, arranged in Paris in the summer of 1905, the young Bartók experienced the first painful failure of his life, for neither his performance nor his compositions were appreciated. (Yet, his whole life was enriched by his experience of Paris.) The Piano Prize was awarded to the Leipzig-born pianist Wilhelm Backhaus (1884–1969), who was appointed Professor at the Royal College of Music, in Manchester in that same year. The Composition Prize was not awarded. See especially the letters that Bartók wrote from Paris at that time, to his mother, Mrs. Béla Bartók (*née* Paula Voit) (1857–1939), and to Irmy Jurkovics (1882–1945) of Nagyszentmiklós (Demény, ed. 1971: 44–54; and 1976: 89–100). Leading the orchestra was noted Viennese conductor, Ferdinand Löwe (1865–1925), on the memorable performance of Bartók's *Suite* No. 1 in Vienna on November 29, 1905 (ibid.: 20).

41. The last movement of the *Suite* No. 2 was completed in the mountains of Csík, Transylvania. It already showed signs of the style that he was just beginning to develop earlier under the influence of his knowledge of folk music. This was the first of Bartók's orchestral compositions in which we find anhemitonic pentatonic pitch cells, e.g., F–G–B-flat–C–D, set {0,2,5,7,9}, discussed further in Chapter 3.5.1, below. (Bartók Jr, ed. 1981a: 94; and Demény, ed. 1971: 57.)

Bagatelles[42] and *Duke Bluebeard's Castle*. Bartók's first two opus-numbered works, the *Rhapsody* for piano solo (Op. 1, Sz 26, BB 36a, 1904)[43], and *Scherzo* for piano and orchestra[44] (Op. 2, DD 68, Sz 28, BB 35, 1904) are stylistic and structural amalgams of Liszt, Brahms, and Strauss. The *Rhapsody* shows Bartók emulating the Liszt *Hungarian Rhapsody* tradition, which also stems from stylized *verbunkos* (*Werbung*; *toborzás*) and *csárdás* (*czardas*) dances, popular art songs, or *cigány* (gypsy) embellishing figures (Weissmann 1980: 630; Lindlar 1984: 43, 171; and Demény 1946: 6). Bartók's *Rhapsody* and *Scherzo* are also replete with Hungarian identifiers, drawn from the patriotic compositions of Mihály Mosonyi (1815–1870) and Ferenc Erkel (1810–1893) (Kodály 1984 [1939]: 37; see also, Chapters 3.2–3.2.2). The gypsy association is evident in the use of the dulcimer-like *cimbalom* in the orchestral version of the *First Rhapsody* (Mason 1949[45]).

Especially around 1907–1908, Bartók also found stimulus in contemporary art music, primarily in its tonal aspects and its redefinition of consonance and dissonance (Reaves 1983;[46] Ujfalussy 1982;[47] see also, Chapters 2.1.1 and 2.1.3–2.1.4, be-

---

42. Bartók's earliest works, which attained modest popularity, show his command of the Romantic techniques then in vogue. By contrast, the *Fourteen Bagatelles* (1998 [1908]) are economical to the point of starkness, based on Magyar scales for melody and harmony, and show great freedom in the use of subsidiary notes, rhapsodic and insistent rhythms. They are lyrical and dramatic statements, as are Beethoven's *Bagatelles*.

43. This piece was dedicated to Mrs. Emma Gruber (1863–1958), an accomplished composer and pianist, and one of the bright lights of Budapest's cultural life. Formerly Emma Schleisinger (and later Emma Sándor), she took the name of her first husband, Henrik Gruber, until August 3, 1910 when she married Kodály, retaining his last name until her death. Mrs. Gruber's home was a meeting place for those having a more serious interest in music than did the guests at most social gatherings. On May 10, 1901, Bartók visited her salon for the first time with Felicie Fábián, and later gave Mrs. Gruber lessons in counterpoint. Ernő (Ernst von) Dohnányi (1877–1960) composed variations on one of her musical themes, which appear also in Kodály's songs and are incorporated in the works of Bartók. (Bartók Jr, ed. 1981a: 36, 47; and Demény, ed. 1971: 18; and 1976: 30, 874.)

44. This work was originally titled *Burlesque* (see n. 2, p. 1, Chapter 1).

45. Colin Mason (1949) discusses the *Three Rhapsodies*, written in different periods of Bartók's life, in terms of their different versions, the history of their publications (with an attempt at chronology of composition), Bartók's approach to form in the compositional process, and a comparative analytical study of the *Rhapsodies* (primarily in terms of form, with some reference to stylistic features).

46. In *Bartók's Approach to Consonance and Dissonance in Selected Late Instrumental Works*, Florence Ann Reaves (1983) explores parts of the *Fifth* and *Sixth Quartets*, *Divertimento*, *Violin Concerto* No. 2, and *Concerto*, with the aim of demonstrating a theory of consonance and dissonance (tension and relaxation) in Bartók's music based on evidence obtained through aural perception. The study of Bartók's tonality is supported by discussions of rhythm as a determinant of the consonant or dissonant functions of specific intervallic constructions. She provides a classification of types of sonorities, based on those investigations.

47. In his article "1907–1908 in Bartók's Entwicklung", Ujfalussy (1982) discusses the risk and yet the necessity in every historical investigation of establishing period divisions in a composer's career. The parameters according to which periods are demarcated are so manifold and overlapping, that valid periodization is difficult to assure. Ujfalussy states that the works around 1908–1911 are so new and special that this period can only be compared with the crucial turning point later in Bartók's career, in the mid 1920s. Ujfalussy examines the numerous intersecting influences

low). *Suite* No. 1 is the composition that may be said to summarize Bartók's achievements as a young composer. Bartók's originality had been most clearly displayed in shorter piano pieces. Those works were the "laboratory" in which he worked out his ideas. (Tallián 1983a: 138–139; see also, pp. 164–168, Chapter 3.6.) His formal innovations and concern with proportion are also evident in the orchestral works from 1908–1911, such as the *Két portré* (*Two Portraits*) for orchestra (Op. 5, Sz 37, BB 48b, 1907–1916). Bartók sometimes returned to the elaboration and stylized emotion of his earlier music. (Demény 1946: 9–10; and Mason 1958[48].) Lendvai summarizes the plot of the *Two Portraits* as follows:

> I would compare the first piece to a transfigured and deep sleep; but in the case of the exposition, the dream expresses a yearning, unquenchable thirst, the *reprise*, however, is the dream fulfilled. […] The Ideal theme is made into a trivial and showy waltz, turning the sensitive features of the first movement into a frantic spin. The basis of the dramatic concept [of the second movement] is that the Grotesque theme must die – with the reprise. […] The reprise brings back the main theme not as a melody, but in the form of inarticulate rattles, naturalistic imitation of sounds, only to have them burst like petards a few bars later. […] The expanding funnel motive explodes in the leading motive [*Leitmotiv*] D–F-sharp–A–C-sharp. […] The cadences harmonically destroy the leading motive, D–F-sharp–A–C-sharp. (Lendvai 1971: 74.)

In his piano works, Bartók exploited the extreme registers of the keyboard, often in the usage of tone clusters. He made use of strong asymmetrical rhythmic figures suggestive of Slavic folk music. Bartók employed melodic figures comprising the twelve different notes of the chromatic scale, but never adopted the integrative techniques of the twelve-tone method (discussed in Chapters 2.1.3–2.1.4).[49]

---

of the earlier period (Strauss's influence, study of Debussy, first folk-music explorations, etc.) that contributed to Bartók's development at that time. Ujfalussy observes the stylistic and technical features of the works of that period, as well as thematic interrelationships of certain works that developed from Bartók's relationship with the violinist Stefi Geyer (1888–1956), and from personal crises of his youth. (See also, Demény, ed. 1976: 123–128; Ujfalussy 1976: 33–34; and Kroó 1975 [1971]: 39.)

48. The two movements are entitled "Egy ideális" ("One Ideal") and "Egy torz" ("One Grotesque"). The first portrait is identical to the first movement of the *1. Hegedűverseny* (*Violin Concerto* No. 1) (Op. Posth., Sz 36, BB 48a, 1907–1908). The piece was dedicated to Geyer, and premiered in 1958. The second movement is the orchestrated version of the 14th *Bagatelle*, "Valse: Ma mie qui danse". (Demény 1946: 9–10.) In "Bartók's Early *Violin Concerto*", Mason (1958) discusses the extra-musical significance of the concerto, with regard to Bartók's love for the violinist Geyer, as may be found also in the *First String Quartet* and the *Two Portraits*. Mason gives a brief descriptive outline of formal and thematic relations, and mentions Lisztian and Straussian influences on those works.

49. Victoria Fischer (2001) observes that all these collections have a common thread in the pedagogical exploration of the limited use of technique. These pieces can be interpreted as the seeds of composition, revealing the basic constructions of Bartók's musical œuvre, which later evolved into more complexity. On one level, these works reveal Bartók's interest in a pedagogical approach to composition; and on another, they are an exposition of his early experimental ideas, which later took shape in his larger-scale compositions.

Influenced by Max Reger (1873–1916), whose works he perused in autumn 1907, Bartók experimented with post-*Tristan* chromatic melody, and with the intensive development of motifs, particularly those containing augmented or diminished intervals. Good examples include the opening movement of the *First String Quartet* (Op. 7, Sz 40, BB 52, 1908–1909)[50] and the first of the *Két elégia* (*Two Elegies*)[51] (Op. 8b, Sz 41, BB 49, 1908–1909), to name a few. The *Two Elegies* show a continuing Lisztian influence, merged with that of Debussy; influences of atonality are evident in No 2. (Lindlar 1984: 51–54, 142–143; and Demény 1967[52].)

Bartók found new inspiration in the works of Debussy, and later Stravinsky (Browne 1931;[53] and Bárdos 1974: 67, 211–231). He remarks on the effect of his encounters with the music of Debussy and Stravinsky:

> In 1907, at the instigation of Kodály, I became acquainted with Debussy's work, studied it thoroughly and was greatly surprised to find in his work 'pentatonic phrases' similar in character to those contained in peasant music. I was sure these could be attributed to influences of folk music from Eastern Europe, very likely from Russia. Similar influences can be traced in Igor Stravinsky's work. It seems therefore that in our age, modern music has developed along similar lines in countries geographically far away from each other. It has become rejuvenated under the influence of a kind of peasant music that has remained untouched by the musical creations of the last centuries. (*BBE* 1976 [1921a]: 410.)

---

50. On March 19, 1910, Bartók's debut concert was held in the Concert Hall of the Royal Hotel in Budapest. It featured the *première* of the *First String Quartet* performed by the Waldbauer-Kerpely Quartet (named after the first violinist, Imre Waldbauer [1892–1952]) as well as performances of the *Piano Quintet* and various solo piano pieces. A similar debut concert by Kodály had been held two days earlier. The two debuts constituted a "manifesto" for the new Hungarian music. (Demény, ed. 1976: 160.) Bartók's *First String Quartet* is an exceptional work of stylistic transition. Although exhibiting many disparate influences, the work is remarkably coherent. That quartet illustrates both traditional and progressive tendencies in its melodic and harmonic constructions, and in the means by which tonal areas are established. In the "Lento", the compositional technique is reminiscent of canon and fugue openings, a slow weaving of texture out of individual melodic threads. All this shows Bartók as a disciple of Reger, about whose works Bartók and Geyer had been enthusiastic (Demény 1946: 11). The "Lento" takes as its main theme the transformation of the Geyer-motif, set {0,1,4,8}, within a contrapuntal, Tristanesque mood of yearning. The second movement, in a lively triple rhythm, develops out of the first, with much variety of expression. The last movement, "Allegro vivace," has a wilder mood, expressed by a novel use of dissonance. Extensive similarities between the musical languages of Bartók and Debussy may be seen in the use of modal and whole-tone formations in the *First Sting Quartet* and his opera, *Duke Bluebeard's Castle*. (Kroó 1975 [1971]: 45–50.)

51. The two movements are titled as 1. "Grave" and 2. "Molto adagio, sempre rubato".

52. János Demény (1967) refers to Bartók's musical connections with Strauss and Debussy, as well as to Busoni, Reger, and Delius. Demény points to the late works of Liszt as the sources of some of Bartók's innovations.

53. Arthur G. Browne (1931) remarks on Bartók's economy of means and the forcefulness of his ultra-modernist approach to developmental procedures. An antithesis to Stravinsky, Hindemith, Honegger, etc., Bartók is in the line of descent from Beethoven and Brahms. Browne refers to Bartók's individualism of technique, by which transforms different genres according to the musical needs at hand.

It was not only Stravinsky's remarkable orchestration techniques, rhythms, and use of folk music or themes resembling folk music that inspired Bartók, but also the latter's spiritual side. In "Der Einfluss der Volkmusik auf die heutige Kunstmusik", Bartók highlights that aspect in Stravinsky's music as follows:

> This should be noted: it is not a question here of the mere use of folk melodies or the transplantation of single phrases from there: a deep comprehension of the spirit of the respective folk music, difficult to put into words, manifests itself in these works. (*BBE* 1976 [1920b]: 318.)

Another great and lasting influence on Bartók was Debussy.[54] It went beyond the superficial kind of influence that Debussy had on the work of all young composers of that time, for whom Debussy's music had come as a revelation and a promise of release. Paradoxically, Bartók, if he ever imitated, did so only to become original. From Debussy he learned about new possibilities inherent in simplicity of expression and texture, the importance of the individual note and of overall sonority, which together led Bartók to develop a new logic of melody and harmony, which he adapted to new types of rhythm. (Gervais 1971: 93–140.) Bartók scholars have been studying strongly related features in the art of Debussy and that of Bartók (e.g., Kodály 1957 [1918]; Kroó 1962; Ujfalussy 1971 [1970]; Antokoletz 1984: 2–8, 16–17, 320–321; 1990; and 2004; and Leafstedt 1994; 1995a; and 1999). Debussy's influences are apparent, notably in the orchestral *Két kép* (*Deux images*)[55] for orchestra (Op. 10, Sz 46, BB 59, 1910) and the *Négy zenekari darab* (*Four Orchestral Pieces*) (Op. 12, Sz 51, BB 64, piano version 1912; orchestrated 1921).[56] In *The Life and Music of Béla Bartók*, Halsey Stevens remarks on the *Four Orchestral Pieces* as follows:

> The *Four Pieces* may be considered an interruption of the direct line of Bartók's evolution; their lack of economy, their dependence upon color-devices, their tendencies to harmonic succulence, and especially the absence of any marked relation to the peasant music of Hungary, with which Bartók had been working for more than six years, stamp them as atavistic. (Stevens 1964: 269.)

Several further examples, all characterized by variability, deserve mention here. The slow movements of the *Táncszvit* (*Dance Suite*) for orchestra (1923, Sz 77, BB 86a);[57] the *Fifth String Quartet* in B-flat Major (Sz 102, BB 110, 1934); the *Sonata*

---

54. See especially, André Hodeir's (1961: 66–77, 79, 87, 105, 187) remarks on Bartók in *La musique depuis Debussy*.

55. The movements mentioned are as follows: 1. "Virágzás" ("In Full Flower") and 2. "A falu tánca" ("Village Dance").

56. These orchestral compositions not only absorbed the great achievements of Debussy, but also went beyond him and contributed, in almost complete independence of the sound pictures that Schoenberg and Stravinsky were composing at the same time, to become an *ars nova* of the twentieth century that remains one of the great inspirations of contemporary music. (Demény 1946: 14–15; and Lindlar 1984: 114.)

57. The concert was to celebrate the fiftieth anniversary of the unification of Pest and Buda on November 19, 1923. It has become an important date in the history of Hungarian music, the sym-

for Two Pianos and Percussion (Sz 110, BB 115, 1937); and *Music for Strings Percussion and Celesta* (Sz 106, BB 144, 1936)[58]. All of those works are interesting examples, in Bartók's most mature style, of the direct aesthetic influence of Debussy. (Kroó 1975 [1971]: 116–121, 177–204.) Extensive similarities between the musical languages of Bartók and Debussy may be seen in the use of modal and whole-tone scales, e.g., set {0,2,4,6,8,10} (Figure 2.1).[59]

Figure 2.1. Set {0,2,4,6,8,10}.

In Debussy's work, Bartók found pentatonic scales similar to those in Hungarian peasant music; e.g., the anhemitone pentatonic row, set {0,2,4,7,9}, displayed in Figure 2.2.

Figure 2.2. Set {0,2,4,7,9}.

Bartók (*BBE* 1976 [1921e]: 325) acknowledges the influences of East-European folk music on his own, and particularly that from Russia, and he points to Mussorgsky as a major forerunner of that compositional trend. There is evidence that Debussy acquired certain features of folk music primarily from that Russian composer

bol of the awakening of Hungarian intellectual life after the ravages of the World War I. Bartók, Dohnányi and Kodály were all commissioned to write compositions in honor of the occasion. The concert began with a performance of Dohnányi's *Ünnepi nyitány* (*Festivale Overture*), Op. 31, followed by two masterpieces of twentieth-century Hungarian music: Kodály's *Psalmus Hungaricus* (Op. 13) and Bartók's *Dance Suite*. (Bartók Jr, ed. 1981a: 211–212.) After writing the *Dance Suite*, Bartók composed nothing for three years.

58. Commissioned by Paul Sacher (1905–1999) and the Basle Chamber Orchestra.

59. A fundamental contributor to this style was Debussy's approach to harmony, which took on a new role. Rather than a means for dynamic musical motion, Debussyan harmony serves as a static means for the production of atmosphere and colorist effects. Since harmonies are chosen not only for their tension/relaxation effects, but also for their color, resonant quality and general sonority, they can logically be derived from a variety of "exotic" scale types – modes, whole tone scales, pentatonic scales. Most associated with Debussy is the whole tone scale, which differs greatly from the diatonic scale in one important area: unlike the diatonic scale, the whole tone scale is constructed of six, equal whole steps, and is therefore tonally ambiguous. (Gervais 1971: 97–104.) Although this scale was used previously by composers such as Liszt, and was especially popular in Russia, Debussy was the first to employ it with compositional determination and consistency. Even in his work, though, it is usually combined with various other scale types and integrated into larger pitch complexes. (Ujfalussy 1959: 84–91.)

(Ujfalussy 1959: 74–75). Such discoveries gave Bartók "valuable hints for future possibilities" (*BBE* 1976 [1943]: 362).

Bartók's *Duke Bluebeard's Castle* has come to be viewed as the crowning achievement of a certain period in his career, from 1908 to 1911. At that time, Bartók first began to consolidate into a truly personal and original style the multitude of influences he had absorbed as a young composer in the first decade of the twentieth century. *Bluebeard's* world of form and harmony evolves as an increasingly complex and original musical language, fusing a vocabulary of romantic tradition, impressionism, and atonality with the melodic modes and rhythmic irregularity of the most ancient Hungarian folk music (on the latter, see pp. 155–159, Chapter 3.5.1), yet without ever quoting a single original peasant melody. The pervasive interactions of modal and whole-tone material in the Symbolist and Impressionist contexts of Debussy's only completed opera, *Pelléas et Mélisande* (1893–1902)[60] and Bartók's *Bluebeard* hardly appear to be coincidental.[61] (Batta, ed. 1999: 16–17, 108–111.)

2.1.3. Bartók's tonal system

The expansion of classical tonality in the nineteenth century was marked by several related developments, the most important of which was an increasing emphasis on chromaticism that extended the range of classical tonal functions, while at the same

---

60. Debussy's numerous opera projects show the difficulties confronting an admirer of Wagner, whom Debussy revered as a musician but not as a man of the theater, since he himself abhorred all traditional operatic conceptions. Debussy has planned to compose other operas, including *Rodrigue et Chimène* (1890), with a libretto by Catulle Mendès (1841–1909) and based on the Spanish epic, *Le Cid* (1885). In 1891, presumably while working on *Rodrigue*, Debussy was asked to set the Belgian symbolist poet and playwright Maurice Maeterlinck's (1862–1949) *La Princesse Maleine*, a request that he turned down (on those works, see Grayson 1986: 17–18, 113, 156, 294 n. 37). It was his reading of Maeterlinck's drama, *Pelléas et Mélisande* (1892) that decided Debussy to embark on a dramatic work. Maeterlinck's text, with its dream-like quality, its enigmatic characters and settings in a never-never land, was admirably suited to his genius, and the resultant opera may be regarded as the central work of Debussy's career. (Ujfalussy 1959: 92–99.) The otherworldliness of the text is adapted to the subtleties of the French language, around which Debussy weaves a mysterious orchestral score in his opera of 5 acts and 12 scenes. The opera shows that Debussy retained much of his youthful infatuation with Wagner, and the vocal writing is essentially Wagnerism in French dress. There is also much of Wagner in the contrapuntal texture and the subtle use of leitmotivs. (Grayson 1986: 225–275.) The opera was premiered in Paris on April 30, 1902 (Ujfalussy 1959: 146–158); on the concert performances of it, see Grayson (1986: 44–46, 294 n. 30).

61. Debussy's new approach to harmonic resources, and to the structuring of contrasting harmonic regions and how they relate to each other, is one of the seminal achievements of early twentieth-century music. Debussy's compositional procedures altered the ways in which music could be experienced. Formerly, Western music was heard largely as a direction toward local and long-range tonal goals. As a result, listening focuses on tracking this motion from one such goal to another. Debussy's radical contribution was in the treatment of tonality in a more static, even stationary way. In this method, one large static block or harmonic area is defined and replaced by or juxtaposed with another such block. Therefore, the listener hears the musical moment more in relation to the internal, inherent properties of that moment, rather than in relationship to what has preceded and follows from such a moment. (Ujfalussy 1959: 84–91.)

time decreasing structural dependency on tonal regions that had heretofore been used to support the central tonality. From the very start, scholars and critics found pitch structures to be the most striking feature of Bartók's music. Literally countless discussions and studies have been devoted to explaining, refining, or refuting theories of Bartók's means of pitch organization (for a summary, see Antokoletz 1997 [1988]). It is not my aim to provide a genealogy of those discussions, but rather to emphasize the startling assortment of theories and analytic methods dedicated to explaining Bartók's conceptions of tonality.

As Lendvai (1971: 1–16) rightly suggests, the Bartókean tonal system grew out of functional tonal music. The evolution of pitch usage in Bartók's music can be traced, from its beginnings in the functional harmonies (I, IV, V, etc.) of Viennese classicism and musical romanticism, on up to the composer's personal innovation: the *tengelyrendszer*, or "axis system" (explained, e.g., in R. Honti 2006: 698–703; see also, pp. 58–60, Chapter 2.2.1, below).

Put simply: "tonal music" is fundamentally music in which all the pitches or tones relate to one referential tone, called variously the tonic or tonal center (see pp. 91–92, Chapter 2.5, below). Classical harmony is bound to seven-degree diatony, as is much of the harmonic world of Romanticism; in later Romantic and twentieth-century music, generally speaking, chords are related to, and begin to move within, the more expansive sphere of twelve-degree chromaticism. Classical harmony thus reflects a hierarchical mode of thought, whereas "chromatic thought" is relativistic in nature, the importance of harmonies being determined by their relationships to one another. Within the closed sphere of the diatonic circle of fifths, which generally determines harmonic root-motion in classical harmony, it is ironic to speak of harmonic "progression", given that such motion is in fact circular and hence not at all "progressive". Rather, the *effect* or *sense* of progression in classical music lies in functional attractions, whereas that of much Romantic music relies on modal or polymodal tensions.[62] (Kapst 1972; and Kárpáti 1982.)[63]

The question relevant to this study is, What does the expression "tonal system" mean in Bartók's case? The composer comments as follows: "[…] we had two different starting points for our creative work: the modes of our rural melodies and the pentatonic scale of our oldest music" (*BBE* 1976 [1943]: 364). Bartók writes elsewhere about the considerable influence that his folk-music studies had on his harmonic thinking:

---

62. Polytonality and polymodality are related to atonality, except that the two former preserve a sense of the old major and minor modes, and even of the church modes, while the chromaticism of the German school deliberately leads away from tonality. The advantage of polytonality is that it still leaves room for stylistic possibilities such as neo-classicism, and for music based on folk song. Bimodality can actually lead to panchromaticism, from a melodic point of view: an ascending Lydian scale and a descending Phrygian scale within the same octave produce the aggregate of twelve notes, with one note occurring twice and another three times. (*BBE* 1976 [1943]: 367.)

63. Erich Kapst (1972) discusses the primacy that tonality had for Bartók, focusing on pentatonic, modal, whole-tone, chromatic, and especially polymodal-chromatic combinations in the composer's works; for more on this issue, see Kárpáti (1982).

[…] the study of folk music […] freed me from the tyrannical rule of the major and minor keys. The greater part of the collected treasure, and the more valuable part, were in old ecclesiastical or old Greek modes, or based on more primitive (pentatonic) scales. […] It became clear to me that the old modes, which had been forgotten in our music, had lost nothing of their vigor. […] This new way of using the diatonic scale brought freedom from the rigid use of the major and minor keys, and eventually led to a new conception of the chromatic scale, every tone of which came to be considered of equal value and could be used freely and independently. (*BBE* 1976 [1921a]: 410.)

Bartók's statement above emphasizes a very important aspect of his harmonic language: it is not subservient to the traditional hierarchy of tonic–dominant functions (T–D), nor does it necessarily incorporate other harmonic relations that characterize art music of the Western tradition (Helm 1953;[64] Travis 1970;[65] and Starr 1973[66]). By contrast, Bartók's own tonality is often best conceived "non-harmonically", as musicologist Eino Roiha describes:

We may briefly say that we comprehend a composition melodically when the harmonic cadence-feeling does not play any role in our mind. We perceive tone-relations, but there is no latent feeling of harmony, which in its own way strengthens and leads the tonal process and its organization. (Roiha 1956: 41.)

Tonality, as the term is used most broadly in Bartók's "Harvard Lectures", refers to the domination of a single tone over a section of music; all other tones resolve to it, either in actuality or potentially (*BBE* 1976 [1943]: 365). For Bartók's music, developments taking place in new art music proved less decisive than the influence of peasant music (see pp. 168–169, Chapter 3.6); in the latter, he found new kinds of tonal structures, which he could further develop and shape into his unique personal style (ibid.: 367; and Gillies 1982[67]).

Milton Babbitt (1949: 378), writing on the *String Quartets*, suggests that Bartók was a "traditionalist" who employed "generalized functional tonal relationships",

64. Helm (1953) examines thematic relations and gives a brief overview of the movements, and concludes that tonality is present, but not in the traditional sense of tonic, dominant, and subdominant functions.

65. Roy Travis (1970) attempts to explain the pitch structures of Bartók's *Fourth String Quartet* in terms of traditional tonality, by taking a Schenkerian approach to analyzing the piece. His voice-leading graphs of foreground, middleground, and background levels are intended to show the contrapuntal prolongations of structural harmonies (scale-steps I, IV, V, I). However, Travis replaces Schenker's crucial concept of the tonic triad as *Ur-Akkord* with that of a "dissonant tonic" sonority.

66. Starr (1973) attempts to join certain features of structure and prolongation. He merges the familiar methodological approach of Schenker-Salzer-Travis with more recently established concepts of structure based on axes of symmetry.

67. Gillies (1982) advances a theory of Bartók's tonality and modality based on the composer's "Harvard Lectures" (*BBE* 1976 [1943]), the principles of which are especially applicable to the late works. Notation (e.g., E instead of F-flat) is essential for discovering the tonal and modal bases of musical passages, modulation, and pitch hierarchy. Among other means of establishing a tonal center, the author discusses encirclement/half-encirclement (leading-tone motions).

even though the "exclusive employment of unique, internally defined relationships leads to a considerable sacrifice of tonal motivation". (Also see, especially, Monelle 1970;[68] and Nordwall 1972.[69])

In *Die Tonalität im Instrumental-Schaffen von Béla Bartók*, Peter Petersen (1971: 15–30) presents almost everything that Bartók ever said about pitch organization and tonality, with the exception of a few rather sketchy analyses the composer made of some of his own works (*BBE* 1976 [1943]).[70] According to Petersen, Bartók recognized two components in tonality: a controlling pitch, and a system of relationships. The latter could be predetermined (based on modes, pentatonic structures, etc.) or constructed from all twelve pitches available in the chromatic system. As to the latter, Bartók sometimes created chromatic fields by using melodic mirror-inversion, as in *Mikrokosmos* No. 144, "Minor Seconds, Major Sevenths" (Sz 107, BB 105, 1926–1939); in the *Sonata for Two Pianos and Percussion*, by contrast, twelve-tone pitch groups are repeated in ostinato fashion.

Petersen (1971) also demonstrates that Bartók's later writings and music both develop in the direction of a new concept of tonality, which Peterson identifies as having three principal ingredients:

1. Tonality is no longer based on the traditional diatonic hierarchy, but on the total chromatic resource as afforded by polymodality[71].
2. Dominating pitches are no longer determined by their position in the scale, but by a variety of other criteria.
3. The configuration of given chords no longer indicates their tonal function *per se*, partly because their very structure is equivocal, and partly because this structure may be no more than the result of horizontal motion.

As a conclusion, Petersen remarks that "*ist Bartóks Tonalität insgesamt eher durch das Linear–Polyphone bestimmt als durch das Akkordisch–Homophone*" (1971: 179).

Malcolm Gillies (1983), in his study of the sketches of the *Sonata for Solo Violin*, argues that new insights into Bartók's use of tonality and modality are to be gained from three sources:

---

68. Raymond Monelle (1970) gives descriptive analysis of various passages of the *String Quartets*, differentiating those features that are classically derived from those that are radical, "astringent," and originating in territories removed from those of Western art-music.

69. In *Béla Bartók: Traditionalist / Modernist*, Ove Nordwall (1972) includes biographical and autobiographical materials, in addition to a study of the numbering of Bartók's works in the context of their relationship to traditional and modern features of other composers; of special interest to this study is his examination of tonal relations in *Bluebeard*.

70. *Béla Bartók Essays* (*BBE*) were compiled and edited by the leading expert on Bartók's music and writings, Benjamin Suchoff (1976). Included therein are Bartók's writings on musical folklore, book reviews, polemics, autobiographical statements, brief analyses of his own music, and discussions of other music and musicians.

71. The term essentially designates two different meanings in the case of Bartók and Messiaen. In *Technique de mon langage musical*, Messiaen (1966 [1944]: 61–63) uses "polymodality" only in reference to his own theoretical concoctions, the "modes of limited transposition".

1. the composer's ethnomusicological writings;
2. his writings on wider musical issues;
3. the compositional process: from sketch to revised published score.

According to Gillies, the sketches suggest that notation is one clue as to how the composer produced tonal centers (e.g., by half-step encirclement of a given tone).

One of the most important concepts in Bartók's harmonic thinking was the idea of polytonality, polymodality and bimodality. In *Twentieth-Century Harmony*, composer and theoretician Vincent Persichetti summarizes those terms as follows:

> Polytonal writing is a procedure in which two or more keys are combined simultaneously. If only two keys are sounded, the specific term bitonality may be used, but polytonality has come generally to imply the use of more than one tonal plane at the same time. The scales that form the different tonic centers may be intervallically identical or contrasting, traditional or synthetic. (Persichetti 1961: 255.)

In *Polymodal Chromaticism*, Lendvai (1980) points out that the basic texture of Bartók's music remained true to tonality, which he expanded to include chromatic polymodal structures and starkly dissonant chordal combinations. (For more on Bartók's adaptations of traditional tonality, see R. Honti 2006: 698–703; cf. also, pp. 58–60, Chapter 2.2.1.)

Bartók, Stravinsky, and Karol Szymanowski (1882–1937) are among those who perfected the art of writing in several keys at once: a procedure that charges the harmony with competing tonal centers, while retaining a differentiated musical space. Bartók explains:

> I used the term "bi-modality", a little-known designation. There are, however, two other very frequently used terms, I would almost say "slogans": atonality (or twelve-tone system) and pantonality (if only two parts are concerned, bi-tonality). [...] Polytonality means the use of different diatonic keys in music of two or more parts, each part in a special key. The pioneers of polytonality used to present their system as the opposite of atonality: the former doubling, tripling, or quadrupling tonality, the latter abolishing tonality, or purporting to do so. [...] Polytonality exists only for the eye, [that is to say, only] when one looks at such music. But our mental hearing will select one key as a fundamental key, and will project the tones of the other keys in relation to the one selected. The parts in different keys will be interpreted as consisting of altered tones of the chosen key. [...] Our hearing cannot perceive two or more different keys with two or more different fundamental tones, as such; it will simplify matters by reducing the maze of keys to one principal key. (*BBE* 1976 [1943]: 365–366.)

In *The Craft of Musical Composition*, Paul Hindemith gives a similar opinion on the matter:

> The game of letting two or more tonalities run along side by side and so achieving new harmonic effects is, to be sure, very entertaining for the composer, but the

listener cannot follow the separate tonalities, for he relates every simultaneous combination of sounds to a root – and thus we see the futility of the game [...] polytonality is not a particular principle of the composition. (Hindemith 1942 [1937]: 156.)

As will be shown later (Chapters 4.3–4.4), bitonality and/or polytonality alone cannot explain the pitch structures of *Bluebeard's Castle*. In that opera, the chord formations, the avoidance of traditional tonal patterns of resolution, and tendency toward bimodal textures and dissonant voice-orchestra relationships give Bartók's tonality a broader, less easily defined meaning.

To continue the present discussion: Bartók's tonality is based upon a new system, which made possible the adaptation of the diatonic modes of peasant music to a free use of the twelve notes. The new compositional devices derive from what Bartók calls "polymodality",[72] by which term he designated the simultaneous use of two or more of the Church modes, based on a common pitch, to derive extensions from the basic diatonic collection (*BBE* 1976 [1943]: 363–364; see also, Antokoletz 1984: 2, 27–28, 51–66, 204–270). Bartók's complex and variegated approach to polymodal interaction in his works is best described in the following comment by the composer, to which I shall return at several points in this study:

> In our works, as well as in other contemporary works, various methods and principles cross each other. For instance, you cannot expect to find among our works one in which the upper part continually uses a certain mode and the lower part continuously uses another mode. So if we say our art music is polymodal, this only means that polymodality or bimodality appears in longer or shorter portions of our work, sometimes only in single bars. So change may occur from bar to bar, or even from beat to beat in a bar. (*BBE* 1976 [1943]: 370.)

In his analysis of Bartók's *Fourth Quartet*, Colin Mason (1957) asserts that polymodality, based on simultaneous modes on a common tonic, is subordinate to symmetrical formations in the pitch organization. Nevertheless, tonal implications are gradually fulfilled in the course of the work, which gradually grows into the key of C. Mason draws the following, general conclusion about the composer's harmonic style:

> [...] he [Bartók] had already discovered, in the *Piano Sonata* and the first *Concerto*, what was to be his final, "tonal" solution of the problem of total chromaticism, in polymodality (i.e., a multiplicity of simultaneous modes on a common tonic). In these two works, he had used this polymodality only within a restricted and to some extent uncharacteristic linear neo-classical style.[73] Then in the *Third Quar-*

---

72. On polymodality, see also, Kárpáti (1971).

73. What, then, is Bartók's relationship to neo-classicism? It is certainly quite different from Stravinsky's. To speak of contemporary composers in terms of classicism and romanticism, as if they could be essentially either in an age that is itself neither, may seem futile. The terms are, however, useful for historical reference and for a shorthand way of drawing attention to analogies, however incomplete. In addition, "neo-classicism" forces the issue on one's attention. The term is

tet, he had tried to apply it to his most advanced expressionist style, and later, in the *Fifth Quartet,* and thereafter, he was to find in it the means of restoring to, and controlling in, his music, the lyrical richness and freedom of harmony of his early period. (Mason 1957: 195.)

On the chance that Mason has too narrowly defined Bartók's solution to the "problem of total chromaticism", it is perhaps a good idea to quote the composer himself:

One point, in particular, I must again stress: our peasant music, naturally, is invariably tonal, if not always in the sense that the inflexible major and minor system is tonal. (An "atonal" folk music, in my opinion, is unthinkable.) Since we depend upon a tonal basis of this kind in our creative work, it is quite self-evident that our works are quite pronouncedly tonal in type. I must admit, however, that there was a time when I thought I was approaching a species of twelve-tone music. Yet even in works of that period, the absolute tonal foundation is unmistakable. (*BBE* 1976 [1928]: 338–339.)

In itself, the fact that a definite tonality, which arranges movements and musical works around a single center, disappears from music, is neither a positive nor a negative development. It is inevitable: music has tended in this direction since Beethoven. (Pütz 1968;[74] and Seiber 1945[75].) The repertory of atonal music is characterized by the occurrence of pitches in novel combinations, as well as by the occurrence of familiar pitch combinations in unfamiliar environments. According to Persichetti:

Atonality is a term loosely applied to music in which a definite key feeling has been weakened or lost, and to music in which no key gravitation ever existed. Atonal writing is the organization of sound without key establishment by chordal root relationships; but tone combinations or areas may form an atonal equivalent of tonality. […] Atonal movement is often linear but may produce vertical combinations of mixed intervals, compound harmonies that are free from the power of an overbearing tonic. (Persichetti 1961: 261.)

---

intended to evoke a specialized way of writing and a certain attitude towards music, but does not necessarily have any relation to other or wider meanings of the word "classicism". Bartók is not neo-classical in this sense, nor does his espousal of eighteenth-century principles make him any the more so. However, there are phases in his development for which the labels "classical" and "romantic" are useful. In great music, the two are balanced, according to (1) whether the composer has a feeling or idea, then finds the notes to express it; or (2) whether he trusts in his own musical material. How that balance is struck is one measure of the importance of Bartók's life and work: perhaps the means he found for achieving equilibrium will be the means by which composers of the future will find it, too.

74. Werner Pütz (1968) relates Bartók's use of motivic development to that of Beethoven, and points to the folk-like materials within the contrapuntal contexts as the basis for both composers' means of expanding inherited compositional designs.

75. In *The "String Quartets" of Béla Bartók* (1945), the Hungarian-born composer and cellist Mátyás Seiber (1905–1960) approaches Bartók's string quartets as his most representative works, suggesting an analogy to Beethoven's development in his quartets.

Bartók's absorption of folk-music properties into modern music of an increasingly atonal tendency led to works that are not tonal *per se*, but rather what Bartók described as "quite pronouncedly tonal in type" (*BBE* 1976 [1928]: 338). As will be shown, *Bluebeard's Castle* falls into the latter category (Chapters 4.3–4.4).

Bartók felt that his usage of dissonance had moderated somewhat by the year 1910. In September of that year, Bartók wrote to Frederick Delius (1862–1934) in response to the Parisian composer's criticism of the "arbitrary" dissonance in his *Suite* No. 2:

> Since the piano pieces, I have become more "harmonious" again, so that I know no longer need the contradictory accumulation of dissonances to express the feeling of a mood. This may possibly be a result of my giving way more to the influence of folk music. (Quoted in Demény, ed. 1971: 105.)

Delius was not the only one to notice the "atonal" characteristics of the composer's earlier works. In "Bartók, Schoenberg, and Some Songs", Adelan Collins points out that:

> The *Five Songs* […] are not only worth study for their own sake, but are also of great value as a key to the understanding of a certain amount of Bartók's later work, and even to the nature of atonic [*sic!*] music in general. There are, of course degrees in atonality; and these songs are by no means wholly atonic. But one harmonic device is so quickly displaced by another that the same rapid adjustment of the point of view from moment to moment is required from the listener as in the understanding of any purely atonic piece of Schoenberg. (Collins 1929: 177.)

Schoenberg, of course, went on to make the transition from atonal to twelve-tone composition, which Joseph N. Straus aptly summarizes:

> The twelve tones are arranged in series, which can be inverted, reversed, and transformed in all the ways that are familiar from contrapuntal writing in the tonal tradition. Certain rules of the musical syntax are then adopted. Unlike the rules of tonal harmony, these rules have an a priori character: they are laid down in advance, as willed constrains on the composer's practice. (Straus 2000: 144.)

Carl Dahlhaus (1928–1989) reminds us that Schoenberg found the word "atonal" offensive and that the reason why he had renounced tonality, as stated in the composer's *Harmonielehre* (1911), was to enable the "emancipation of dissonance" (1987 [1968]: 120–121). The specific distinction between consonance and dissonance, the division of intervals into those two contrasting groups, was based on compositional technique, argued Schoenberg, not on the unalterable nature of the consonance/dissonance dichotomy itself.

Schoenberg preferred the term "pantonality" over atonality to describe his compositional method of using the twelve tones, and he referred to movable tonics and fluctuating harmonies (Dahlhaus 1987b [1978]: 80).[76] Réti (1958) describes pan-tonality as a distinct form of tonal organization, and the final and lasting result of the modernist experiments. Réti writes in this context of a "tonality, which does not appear on the surface but is created by the ear singling out hidden relationships between various points of a melodic or contrapuntal web" (ibid.: 65). Réti further suggests that any pitch class can function as a tonic, and a piece may keep an indefinite number of tonics in play without canceling their primary function, either as the focus of melodic organization, or as the reference point against which the harmonies must be read (ibid.).

Thus, the basic principle behind composition with twelve-tones is the even distribution of PCs such that none of them dominates the others. As Schoenberg clarifies, "the construction of the set of twelve-tones derives from the intention to postpone the repetition of every tone as long as possible" (1984: 246). This is called a twelve-tone row, or series, which is a group of PCs (usually the 12 chromatic PCs), set {0,1,2,3,4,5,6,7,8,9,10,11},[77] placed in a particular order to be so used in a composition (Figure 2.3).

2	5	8	11
7	10	1	4
0	3	6	9

Figure 2.3. Set {0,1,2,3,4,5,6,7,8,9,10,11}.

Schoenberg (1984: 127) took pains to minimize the differences between tonal and twelve-tone music, stressing that in the evolution from diatonic to chromatic there had been no break with or divergence from natural musical laws. In some of his writings, Schoenberg refuted the idea of "natural law" in music, as in the preface to his *Harmonielehre* (1978 [1911]: 8–9). There he referred to rules traditionally called "laws of harmony", such as the avoidance of parallel fifths. These Schoenberg considered mere practices, not "natural laws", but he did not question the idea that certain universal laws existed in music.[78] In *The Listening Composer*, Perle remarks that:

---

76. It is clear that this new twelve-note method of organization rescued music from the tempting dangers of the freedom it had so recently gained. Indeed, the new rules were stricter than the old rules of tonality. They are comparable in strictness with the advanced canonic techniques of tonal music, and often draw upon that style; for example, in the usage of mirror and retrograde structures. (Perle 1962: 7–8, 148–149.)

77. Forte's "List of Prime Forms and Interval Class Vectors" (see the Appendix) does not contain this set. In Joutsenvirta's pitch-web analysis (1989: 6), the 12 chromatic PCs are called "3 x 4 *kromaruudukko*" ("3 x 4 chroma-square").

78. On Schoenberg's compositional technique, see also, Wellesz (1989a [1926]); (1989b [1926]); (1989c [1926]); and (1989d [1926]).

The achievement of such a change of register through a sequential progression is a familiar procedure in the music of the "common practice". The significant distinction is that where Berg subdivides the registral span into equal, i.e., cyclic, intervals, his tonal predecessors subdivide it, in changing register through sequential transference, into the unequal intervals of the diatonic scale. [...] The qualitative transformation in the language of music, which we have experienced in our century, has a long prehistory. Beginning with Schubert, we occasionally find normal diatonic functions questioned in changes of key that progress along the intervals of the whole-tone scale, or the diminished seventh chord, or the augmented triad. An even more radical example of a cyclic progression in a tonal composition is [...] from Wagner [*Die Walküre*, Act III]. (Perle 1990a: 96.)

Later Perle observes that:

If [Alban] Berg departs so radically from tradition, through his substitution of a symmetrical partitioning of the octave for the asymmetrical portioning of the major/minor system, he departs just as radically from the twelve-tone tradition that is represented in the music of Schoenberg and Webern, for whom the twelve-tone series was *always*[79] an integral structure that could be transposed only as a unit, and for whom twelve-tone music always implied a constant and equivalent circulation of the totality of pitch classes. (Perle 1990a: 98.)

Bartók (*BBE* 1976 [1920c]) explains the principal difference between his concept of harmonic dissolution and that achieved by composers such as Schoenberg, Webern, and Berg. Bartók talks of contemporary music striving toward atonality, which is a gradual development stemming from tonality. On twelve-tone music, Bartók remarks as follows:

[...] the decisive turn toward atonality began only when [...] the need was felt for the equality of rights of the individual twelve tones of our dodecaphonic mode: when the attempt was made to avoid arrangement of the twelve tones according to certain scalar systems or to attribute to the individual tones greater or lesser value [...], so that use could be made of the individual tones in any optional combination horizontally as well as vertically irretrievable to any scalar system. It is true that certain tones in this combination also gain by this procedure a relative predominance; this difference of importance, however, is not based on a certain scale pattern but is the outcome of the occasional combination. [...] The possibilities of expression are increased in great measure, incalculable as yet, by the free and equal treatment of the twelve tones. (*BBE* 1976 [1920a]: 455.)

Bartók looks at Schoenberg's (1978 [1911]) *Harmonielehre* regarding this development, saying that atonality came from the need for equality among the twelve tones.[80] Bartók gives examples of adjacent, dissonant-note sonorities, and suggests

---

79. Perle's original emphasis.
80. Bartók (*BBE* 1976 [1920c]) gives examples of new types of chords (comprised of fourths and mixed intervals). He also discusses briefly some principles of organizing atonal material, and ends with a statement regarding notation for symbolizing the twelve tones equally.

a more varied approach to atonality than is found in the dodecaphonic methods of Schoenberg. He proposed the retention of certain features of the tonal system, such as triads and scale constructions, claiming that, as isolated occurrences, they need not imply a sense of tonality (*BBE* 1976 [1920c]; see also, Bárdos 1974: 138). Bartók never made exclusive use of dodecaphony, and made clear his intention never to sacrifice tradition merely for the sake of innovation. In his view, the proper use of twelve-tone methods was to supplement and enrich traditional musical thought. The most obvious musical embodiment of those ideas is Bartók's *Three Studies* for piano (Op. 18/3, Sz 72, BB 81, 1918), which is undoubtedly one of his most radical creations (on the latter, see Stevens 1964: 125;[81] Dille 1965;[82] and Orvis 1974[83]).

Bartók's music is by no means atonal; rather, the term tonality means something quite different in his case. The main problem lies in the tension between two apparently opposite ideas. Comparing Schoenberg and Bartók, one finds the basic difference to be that Bartók used a system combining two or more modal segments, based on a single fundamental pitch. That system enabled Bartók to use all twelve pitches of the chromatic spectrum. (*BBE* 1976 [1920c]: 455.) What is unique about the situation, is that the use of the special twelve-tone set in Bartók's works is analogous to the pre-compositional assumption of the traditional major and minor scales of tonal music, shown in Figures 2.4 and 2.5, respectively.[84] (For a different view, see Kárpáti 1969b; 2004 [1963–1964]; and 1966.)[85]

11	2	5
4	7	
9	0	

Figure 2.4. Set {0,2,4,5,7,9,11}.

2	5	8
7	10	
0	3	

Figure 2.5. Set {0,2,3,5,7,8,10}.

---

81. Stevens (1964: 125) remarks that Bartók's *Studies* deal with specific pianistic problems not engaged in the etudes of Chopin, Debussy, Stravinsky, or Prokofiev. Although they encompass a smaller range of expression, they are technically and tonally beyond anything found in his earlier piano works.

82. Dille (1965) discusses the personal connections between the two composers, and the bearing those had on their subsequent exchanges of opinion on artistic issues; see also, Demény (ed. 1976: 262).

83. In *Technical and Stylistic Features of the Piano Etudes of Stravinsky, Bartók, and Prokofiev*, Joan Orvis (1974) discusses the technical difficulty of performing Bartók's *Etudes*, which are described as displaying atonal principles.

84. Forte's (1973: 179–181) "List of Prime Forms and Interval Class Vectors" does not contain these sets.

85. Kárpáti (1966) relates Bartók's harmonic language to the twelve-tone idiom and to some of Stravinsky's techniques, concluding that Bartók provided a synthesis of those divergent trends.

Like Schoenberg, Bartók emphasizes the "natural" evolution of atonality:

> The music of our times strives decidedly toward atonality. Yet it does not seem to be right to interpret the principle of tonality as the absolute opposite of atonality. The latter is much more the consequence of a gradual development, originating from tonality, absolutely proceeding step by step – without any gaps or violent leaps. (*BBE* 1976 [1920c]: 455.)

Schoenberg (1975 [1947]: 166) justified his own innovations by appeals to (German) tradition, but spoke disparagingly of the "static treatment of folk song" (ibid.: 165).[86] Many other composers and theorists also saw art music and folk music as basically incompatible, and the merging of these styles as a serious problem that could not be conceptually resolved (Schoenberg 1984: 161–184). Bartók felt obliged to respond, saying that Schoenberg "is free from all peasant influence and his complete alienation to Nature, which of course I do not regard as a blemish, [but] is no doubt the reason why many find his work so difficult to understand" (*BBE* 1976 [1921e]: 326; see also, Demény 1946: 27–28).

Most western treatises on harmony, from Renaissance times (e.g., Zarlino) to the mid-twentieth century (e.g., Hindemith), seek to codify explanatory principles of chord construction and progression. It is commonly acknowledged that these were most lastingly codified in the theoretical works of Jean-Philippe Rameau (1683–1764). In his *Traité de l'harmonie reduite à ses principes naturels* (1971 [1722]), Rameau, as others before and after him, started from the naturally occurring acoustical phenomenon of the overtone series (as demonstrable on any vibrating body) (Example 2.1).[87]

Example 2.1. The natural overtone series.

Schoenberg (1978 [1911]), following that theoretical tradition, explains dissonances as more distant overtones, which in principle are as easy to understand as consonances. According to Schoenberg, the method of composing with twelve tones was the fruit of striving for a deeper logic. Still, for both Schoenberg and his pupil, Anton Webern, the materials of music originated in the natural phenomenon of the

86. Schoenberg (1975 [1947]) elsewhere in the article voices his belief that the use of folk music in compositions inevitably produces incoherence and stasis.

87. In the *Introduction to the Psychology of Music* (1954: 17–20), the Hungarian pioneer of experimental psychology, Géza Révész (1878–1955), offers a comprehensive overview of research in both psychology and acoustics. Révész, as many acousticians have done (e.g., Helmholtz), remarks that, in addition to the overtones (Example 2.1, above), there are also "combination tones", which can be heard when two notes sound together. Both overtones and combination tones confirm the "natural" primacy of the (major) triad.

overtone series. The notes of the diatonic scale are found among the lower overtones, and the chromatic notes as higher overtones.

In 1930, in an essay later published in his *The Path to the New Music*, Webern regarded the development of Western music over the centuries as "the ever-extending conquest of the material provided by nature" (1975 [1960]: 17). He saw no reason why the quarter-tones and other microtones among still higher overtones would not someday be used (on Bartók's use of microtones, see Nordwall 1965[88]). Viewing the overtone series as a continuum, Schoenberg saw no essential differences between intervals that formerly were differentiated as consonances and dissonances:

> What distinguishes dissonances from consonances is not a greater or lesser degree of beauty, but a greater or lesser degree of *comprehensibility*. In my *Harmonielehre*, I presented the theory that dissonant tones appear later among the overtones, for which reason the ear is less intimately acquainted with them. This phenomenon does not justify such sharply contradictory terms as concord and discord. Closer acquaintance with the more remote consonances – the dissonances that is – gradually eliminated the difficulty of comprehension and finally admitted not only the emancipation of dominant and other seventh chords, diminished seventh and augmented triads, but also the emancipation of Wagner's, Strauss's, Mussorgsky's, Debussy's, Mahler's, Puccini's, and Reger's more remote dissonances. (Schoenberg 1984: 216–217.)

Schoenberg proposed that harmonic theory be based "not on the seven tones of the major scale, but on the twelve [tones] of the chromatic scale", offering a brief outline as an initial step in that direction (1978 [1911]: 387).

Bartók described the contrast between works based on an atonal system and those fixed in a concept governed by tonal centricity as follows:

> To point out the essential difference between atonality, polytonality, and polymodality, in a final word on this subject, we may say that atonal music offers no fundamental tone at all, polytonality offers – or is supposed to offer – several of them, and polymodality offers a single tone. Therefore our music, I mean the new Hungarian art music, is always based on a single fundamental tone, in its sections as well as in its whole. And the same is the case with Stravinsky's music. He lays stress on this circumstance even in the titles of some of his works. He says, for instance, "*Concerto* in A". The designation "major" or "minor", however, is omitted; for the quality of the third degree is not fixed. (*BBE* 1976 [1943]: 370–371.)

Applied to Bartók's music, therefore, the term tonality refers to the way in which a given tone acts as a focal point for a constellation of vertical sonorities and pitch relationships, based loosely (at this point in his career) on the language of tonality, which he had inherited as a composer working in the early twentieth century.

---

88. Nordwall (1965) discusses significant differences between the original version and the published edition of the *Sonata for Violin*, the finale of which provides the clearest example of Bartók's use of microtones. On the same topic, see also, Bartók's letter to violinist Yehudi Menuhin (in Demény, ed. 1976: 696–697).

When in the 1920s Bartók looked back to what he had written ten years earlier, he re-avowed his unswerving adherence to tonality.[89] Bartók spoke of the *Three Studies*, in a letter to von der Nüll: "Even in the *Studies* there are firmly held, prominent centers of sound (masses of sound at the same pitch), as a consequence of which, regardless of anything else, an effect of tonality is evoked" (quoted in Nüll 1930: 58).

2.1.4. New chromaticism

Certain theorists at the beginning of the twentieth century, most notably Schoenberg and his followers, developed an understanding of chromaticism that was intended not only to pave the way to new compositional methods, but that also had the potential to shed new light on the music of their predecessors. Viewed in many quarters as a radical who had broken away from the natural laws, which had governed music for centuries, Schoenberg insisted all his life that, in creating the method of composition with twelve tones, he was simply carrying forward an evolutionary process that linked him with previous generations of German masters (for more on Schoenberg, see pp. 37–42, Chapter 2.1.3). Bartók remarks on his own new chromaticism as follows:

> As to the general characteristics, exactly the same can be said about my melodies as what I said already concerning the chromatic folk melodies. That is, the single tones of these melodies are independent tones having no interrelation between each other. There is in each specimen, however, a decidedly fixed fundamental tone to which the other tones resolve in the end. The main difference between the chromatic folk melodies and my own chromatic melodies is to be found in their range. The former consists exclusively of five, six, or at most seven half tones, which correspond to a range of about a fourth. My own melodies generally have at least eight half tones and cover, in some cases, the distance of an octave or more. […] The working [*sic!*] with these chromatic degrees gave me another idea, which led to the use of a new device. This consists of the change of the chromatic degrees into diatonic degrees. In other words, the succession of chromatic degrees is extended by leveling them over a diatonic terrain. (*BBE* 1976 [1943]: 381.)

---

89. The period of 1920–1926 represents a beneficial crisis in the creative life of Bartók. In those years, he struggled to find a new, more balanced style, and composed relatively few works (in 1925, he wrote nothing at all). (Bartók Jr, ed. 1981a: 175–242.) In 1926 – as in the years between 1908 and 1911 – he wrote a considerable amount of piano music: the *Sonata for Piano* (Sz 80, BB 88, 1926), *Szabadban* (*Out of Doors*) (Sz 81, BB 89, 1926), *Nine Small Pieces for Piano* (Sz 82, BB 90, 1926), the *Piano Concerto* No. 1 (Sz 83, BB 91, 1926) and the first pieces of the *Mikrokosmos* series. In those compositions his ideal of style, which in earlier years he had found in the work of Beethoven, was now enriched by the strictness of form, counterpoint, and linear technique characteristic of the music of J. S. Bach. (Demény 1946: 29–30; Brelet 1955; and Breuer 1975a.) In his extensive concertizing during the years 1920 to 1926, Bartók established relations with concert bureaus and broadcasting corporations worldwide, with foreign artists and Hungarian musicians living abroad, and with violinists and conductors. In 1928–1929, he traveled even farther abroad, giving concerts in the United States as well as in the Soviet Union. (Bartók Jr, ed. 1981a: 255–285.)

In his dissertation, *Technical Bases of Nineteenth-Century Chromatic Tonality: A Study in Chromaticism*, Gregory Proctor (1978: 149) argues that nineteenth-century composers began to move away from thinking in terms of asymmetrical, diatonic tonal space, and toward conceptions of tonality based on chromatic, symmetrical space. Schoenberg and his followers continued that line of thought, with new speculations about musical pitch space. For Schoenberg, chromaticism performed an essential function in the articulation of large-scale tonal forms:

> Whether something be a principal or subordinate idea, introduction or transition, episode, bridge, connecting link, embellishment, extension, or reduction, whether independent or dependent, and, further, at which moment it begins or ceases to express one of these formal characteristics – all this is possible for masters of form to make manifest through harmony. [...] The degree of relationship allows a graduated removal of individual parts away from the tonal center, according to the degree of their meaning: more remote digressions can thus be characterized differently from ideas that are closely related. (Schoenberg 1984: 278.)

On problems of form arising from the relativized, non-hierarchical concept of tones as found in 12-tone music, Bartók states the following:

> The fear that atonal compositions would present a shapeless mass as a consequence of relinquishing the symmetric scheme founded on the tonal system is unjustified. First of all, an architectonic or similar scheme is not absolutely necessary; the construction of the line born out of the different degrees of intensity that are inherent in the tonal succession would be completely satisfactory. (This structural method is somewhat analogous to that of works written in prose.) Secondly, the atonal music does not exclude certain exterior means of arrangement, certain repetitions (in a different position, with changes, and so forth), the previously mentioned progressions, [the] refrain-like reappearance of certain ideas, or the return to the starting point at the end. (*BBE* 1976 [1920c]: 455.)

Finally, Webern (1975 [1960]: 22–23) discussed pitch space most often in terms of the "conquest of the tonal field". Although on occasion he used this expression in discussing general compositional space, more typically his phrase seems to mean "the full explanation of the natural resources of the overtone series". That, for Webern, was the basic historical principle that had led to the equalization or relativizing of all twelve pitches of the chromatic scale.

Even in some early works, significantly in the *Fourteen Bagatelles*, *First String Quartet*[90] and *Duke Bluebeard's Castle*[91] – in which traditional triadic structures still contribute to the musical work – Bartók's innovative use of the diatonic scale led to a new conception of the chromatic one. In his introduction to the published score, the composer described the *Fourteen Bagatelles* in this way: "A new piano style appeared as a reaction to the exuberance of the Romantic piano music of the nineteenth century; a style stripped of all unessential decorative elements, deliberately using only the most restricted technical means" (*BBE* 1976 [1945]: 432). Bartók was clearly aware of the importance of those pieces in his compositional development: "The *Bagatelles* inaugurate a new trend of piano writing in my career" (ibid.: 433). Many Bartók scholars have emphasized the importance of the *Bagatelles* in the wider context of *fin-de-siècle* modernism.[92] Halsey Stevens (1964: 41–42), for

90. In the early mature works of 1908–1909, Bartók's new resources appear only in given movements or works, rather than being synthesized or transformed into a unified style. In terms of the Germanic style, the *First String Quartet*, like Strauss's *Elektra*, is historically transitional in its interaction of triadic harmonies with chromatic melodic lines that unfold according to non-functional voice-leading patterns. (Batta, ed. 1999: 594–599.) With the disappearance, in the early part of the twentieth century, of the traditional triad as the basic harmonic premise, greater importance was placed on the interval as a primary means of harmonic and melodic integration. Both his *First String Quartet* and Strauss's *Elektra* epitomize late Romantic music on the threshold of a new chromatic idiom. However, while Strauss never crossed that threshold, Bartók's *First String Quartet* was only the beginning of his new chromaticism. (*BBE* 1976 [1910]; and Antokoletz 1984: 14.)

91. In *Bluebeard's Castle*, purely triadic passages, as at the opening of the fifth door (74/19–23), co-exist with passages of markedly atonal character (for a detailed analysis of this scene, see Chapter 4.4.8). The dissonant music that accompanies the opening of the first door (30/1–31/6) gradually yields to triadic harmonies once the shock of seeing such horrors has eased for Judith (see Chapter 4.4.4). The B-flat pedal serves as an underlying tonal anchor during the opera's most shatteringly dissonant passage, the orchestral climax at the very end (136/1–137/10), directly before the return of the F-sharp pentatonic melody in 138/1–139/12 (discussed in Chapter 4.4.10). Standing in contrast to passages like these are monuments of almost serene triadic repose; for example, as occurs when a D major triad (54/1–59/10) accompanies the treasure chamber scene (see Chapter 4.4.6).

92. In early 1908, Bartók composed his *Fourteen Bagatelles*, two of which (4. "Grave" and 5. "Vivo") were obviously folk-song arrangements. He viewed those as experimental, containing many a device from folk music made to function in a new way. In the piano piece in question, Bartók has begun to engage with transforming vocal styles of folk music into instrumental melodies. The *Bagatelle* No. 1, written in two keys simultaneously, shows aspects of *parlando* style. The right hand plays in four sharps throughout (C-sharp minor), and the left hand is written in four flats, in Phrygian C minor (or the F minor scale, starting on C). The listener is made aware of the fact that the two melodies are in different keys since one is an ascending line, the other descending. Other *Bagatelles* in the set, especially numbers 10 and 13, also show combinations of two different tonalities. In the tenth, Bartók uses a technique that might be termed successive polytonality. One section of the piece, in which broken chords are combined in a striking way with an upper part, was quoted by Schoenberg in the last chapter of his *Harmonielehre* (1911). *Bagatelle* No. 13 consists of an E-flat minor ostinato in the bass. The upper part arpeggiates D major, G major, and other chords. The piece as a whole has two tonal planes: the E-flat minor ostinato is interrupted from time to time by a similar A minor ostinato, the two tonalities pressing ever closer on each other's heels. In this piece, Bartók only combines tonalities that are distantly related (in this case, a tritone apart). The tritone relation is also characteristic of Stravinsky's early uses of bitonality, notably in *Petrushka* (1911). The famous Petrushka-chord is a combination of the broken triads of C major and F-sharp

example, points out that Bartók was ahead of his contemporaries: "The piano music of 1908 shows experimentation with bitonality, dissonant counterpoint, chords in intervals other than thirds, somewhat before the works of Stravinsky and Schoenberg in which these devices first came to light." They mark an important transition, from Bartók's youthful style, to the individualism that became characteristic of his mature style, displayed in his later works.

One of the few recorded statements made by Bartók about his compositional method occurs in his third "Harvard Lecture", in the context of a discussion of twentieth-century chromaticism:

> Bimodality led towards the use of diatonic scales or scale portions filled out with chromaticized degrees, which have a totally new function. They are not altered degrees of a certain chord leading to a degree of a following chord. They can only be interpreted as the ingredients of the various modes used simultaneously and at a given time, a certain number of seemingly chromaticized degrees, [some] belonging to one mode, other degrees to another mode. These degrees have absolutely no chordal function; on the contrary, they have a diatonic-melodic function. This circumstance is clearly shown if the degrees are picked out and grouped into the modes to which they belong. (*BBE* 1976 [1943]: 376.)

The composer's comments in that lecture suggest that he viewed and used chromaticism in three basic ways (*BBE* 1976 [1943]: 376–383):

1. as restricted *bimodality*: the juxtaposition of two modal forms based on one fundamental tone, but retaining their separate modal obligations;
2. as *modal chromaticism*: elements of modes are mixed with chromatic degrees having no chordal basis or function, yet retaining diatonic melodic functions;
3. as new *melodic chromaticism*: single tones are independent, but there is one fundamental tone to which the other tones eventually resolve; such is the case in Arabian and Dalmatian folk songs, but Bartók's melodies usually have a wider range (tessitura) than those.

The uniqueness of Bartók's case lies in the fact that modality led him to a loose kind of tonality in which a melody (formal section, movement, or whole composition) can begin and end with a clear statement of a mode, but may exhibit alteration and diversity of modality along the way (*BBE* 1976 [1921c]: 61; Oramo 1977b: 21–56; 1980; and 1982a).

Bartók considered modal chromaticism, "as we will call this phenomenon henceforward, to distinguish it from the chordal chromaticism of the nineteenth century," to be the most distinctive feature of the new Hungarian music (*BBE* 1976 [1943]:

---

major. The effect is particularly striking because keys whose tonics lay a tritone apart have notes in common, e.g., the notes F (E-sharp) and B in the case of C major and F-sharp major. Sequences of chords a tritone apart are altogether characteristic of Russian music. (Ujfalussy 1971 [1970]: 85–94; and Lindlar 1984: 24–25.)

376). Moreover, polymodality can lead to interesting symmetrical formations. For example, although the C major scale is not symmetrical in itself, when it is combined with Phrygian mode on C, the result is a symmetrical scale. Lydian may be combined with Locrian, and Aeolian (natural minor) with Mixolydian, so as to obtain similar results (see Example 2.2, below). For simplicity's sake, the modes in the example are shown as having a common final. In practice, however, it is inconsequential if any two, "overlaid" modes have the same final, as long as they together produce the desired symmetrical scale.

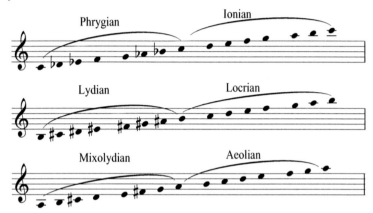

Example 2.2. Combinations of modes.

Together with Dorian and Mixolydian modes on the same note, a combination of Lydian (strongly characteristic of certain Slovak melodies) with Phrygian mode proved particularly useful, especially in Bartók's rapidly developing notion of what he called "polymodal chromaticism". Bartók (*BBE* 1976 [1943]: 367) explains: "Just as the two types of the minor scale can be used simultaneously; two different modes can be used at the same time as well." Such a combination is shown in Example 2.3.

Example 2.3. Two types of minor scale used simultaneously.

In Table 2.1 (next page), the notes of the scales shown in Example 2.3, above, are translated into pitch-class integers:

Integers	0	10	8	7	9	11	0	10	8	7	9	11	0
Minor 1.	C	Bb	Ab	G	A	B	C	Bb	Ab	G	A	B	C
Minor 2.			C	Bb	Ab	G	A	B	C	Bb	Ab	G	C
Integers			0	10	8	7	9	11	0	10	8	7	0

Table 2.1. Two types of minor scale, with corresponding integers.

Bartók describes how he combined Phrygian and Lydian modes to create a polymode comprising all twelve tones of the chromatic scale:

> As the result of superimposing a Lydian and a Phrygian pentachord with a common fundamental tone, we get a diatonic pentachord filled out with all the possible flat and sharp degrees. These seemingly chromatic degrees, however, are tonally different in their function from the altered chord degrees of the chromatic styles of the previous periods [of musical style]. A chromatically altered note of a chord is in strict relation to its non-altered form; it is a transition leading to [...] the following chord. In our polymodal chromaticism, however, the flat and sharp tones are not altered degrees at all; they are diatonic ingredients of a diatonic modal scale. (*BBE* 1976 [1943]: 367.)

Bartók's statement above provides a clear illustration of bimodality through the combination of two heptatonic modes to create a twelve-note chromatic scale. Of the seven letter-names, only two are used once, those on which the Phrygian scale and Lydian scale forms coincide (Figures 2.6–2.7).

	5	8
7	10	1
0	3	

Figure 2.6. Set {0,1,3,5,7,8,10}.

	11	2
	4	7
6	9	0

Figure 2.7. Set {0,2,4,6,7,9,11}.

C is encircled by half-steps B (Lydian) and D-flat (Phrygian); G by F-sharp (Lydian) and A-flat (Phrygian). The chromatic, Phrygian, and Lydian scales are shown in Table 2.2, along with their respective integers.

Scale	Pitch classes	Point 0	Integers
Chromatic	C–D-flat–D–E-flat–E–F–F-sharp–G–A-flat–A–B-flat–B	C	{0,1,2,3,4,5,6,7,8,9,10,11}
Phrygian	C–D-flat–E-flat–F–G–A-flat–B-flat	C	{0,1,3,5,7,8,10}
Lydian	C–D–E–F-sharp–G–A–B	C	{0,2,4,6,7,9,11}

Table 2.2. Chromatic[93], Phrygian, and Lydian scales.

Bartók has reflected on such modal combinations:

If we examine these two modes [...] we will see that the upper halves of both modes are in exactly the same relation as the upper halves of the two minor scale types. So we can declare our example shows an extension of the above-described methods of old composers to the lower of the scale. [...] But not only different modes can be superposed; the same can be done with the common major and minor scale or, to be more exact, with a major and minor pentachord. As a result, we will get a triad with a doubled third: one minor, the other major. (*BBE* 1976 [1943]: 366.)

Bartók (*BBE* 1976 [1943]: 376) asserts, "In modal chromaticism, when the modal forms are intermingled, these diatonic melodic functions are still maintained." He also mentions that, in his and Stravinsky's music, the fundamental key (tonality) cannot be called major or minor, because the quality of the third degree is not fixed.

By the way, much mischief was done in the worship of polytonality or bitonality. Some composers invented a hackneyed-sounding diatonic melody in, let us say, C, and added a very hackneyed accompaniment in F. [...] Incidentally, much of Stravinsky's music, and also of my music, looks as if it is bitonal or polytonal. Therefore, the pioneers of polytonality used to regard Stravinsky as one of their fellow polytonalist. Stravinsky, however, deliberately denies this circumstance, even in such exterior features as orthography. (*BBE* 1976 [1943]: 367.)

The diatonic and chromatic scales are all based on the assumption of a hierarchy of intervals, proceeding from the essential nature of musical tones themselves; the latter must not be disregarded if music is to result from the composing, literally the "putting together", of tones. The composer explains:

The anhemitonic pentatonic scale [Figure 2.8, next page][94], with its peculiar leaps because of the missing second and seventh degree [*sic!*], is the very opposite of the chromaticized scale used, for instance, in Wagner's music. So we took it – quite subconsciously – as the most suitable antidote for the hyperchromaticism of Wagner and his followers. (*BBE* 1976 [1943]: 364.)

---

93. It is based on the constant intervallic symmetry of the half-step.
94. Bartók explained the features of Hungarian folk art-music in numerous writings throughout his life (e.g., *BBE* 1976 [1921c]; and 1981[1924]: 12–23). Here I refer frequently to the pentatonic mode. By pentatonic, I mean the particular mode that Bartók discovered in Hungarian folk song, set {0,3,5,7,10}. Other modes are discussed in Chapter 3.5.1 (pp. 155–157).

	5
7	10
0	3

Figure 2.8. Set {0,3,5,7,10}.

Varieties of scale in Bartók's output include the pentatonic, the whole tone, ecclesiastical modes, major and minor, as well as composite forms of modal chromaticism. Along with pentatonic melodic structures, Bartók called modal chromaticism "a main characteristic of the new Hungarian art music" (*BBE* 1976 [1943]: 376; also see, especially, Antokoletz 1984: 27–28, 33–50). Bartók refers to *modal* chromaticism as that which is most prevalent in his work, which he distinguished from the *chordal* chromaticism of the nineteenth century. Bartók gives an interesting account of this discovery:

> Let us make the statement that chordal chromaticism in folk music is absolutely inconceivable; first, because folk music, apart from some exceptional areas, is monophonic music – music in unison, all over the world; and secondly because it represents, even in Western European art music, a more or less – if I may say so – artificial development, standing on a "higher" level, a level which cannot be expected in rural music. Nor is modal chromaticism possible in folk music, because this style again would presuppose a polyphonic structure of two or more parts, which does not exist in rural music. (*BBE* 1976 [1943]: 376–377.)

Bartók further developed new structural (that is, non-embellishing) types of melodic chromaticism, in which earlier modal obligations are dispensed with, though allegiance to a focal note is retained. Within that framework, Bartók applied his theory of tonal axes as the basis of tonality. His melodic chromaticism has folk parallels, in that it differs from European chromaticism based upon alteration. On this subject, Bartók remarks as follows:

> [...] very few areas where melodies, or even a melodic style, exist look as if they are based on a genuine chromatic system. Then what kind of chromatic system can it be? The single degrees generally are at a half-tone distance from each other; thus, they cannot be regarded as ingredients of various modes. As a matter of fact, they are as much independent tones as are the single degrees of the diatonic scale, and they have no interrelation except their relation to the fundamental tone. For all these chromatic scales have a fixed fundamental tone. In any case, their chromaticism very much resembles that of the new chromaticism. [...] Such a chromatic style exists in Arab areas of Northern Algeria and in Dalmatia (a district of Yugoslavia, on the Adriatic cost). (*BBE* 1976 [1943]: 377.)

In the *Dance Suite*, one finds a new synthesis of folk song and composing techniques. Bartók explains his use of melodic chromaticism in that work:

My first "chromatic" melody I invented in 1923; I used it as the first theme of my *Dance Suite*. This music has some resemblance to Arab melody. [...] This kind of melodic invention was only an incidental digression on my part and had no special consequences. My second attempt was made in 1926; on [that] occasion, I did not try to imitate anything known from folk music. I cannot remember having met [with] this kind of melodic chromaticism deliberately developed to such a degree in any other contemporary music. (*BBE* 1976 [1943]: 379–380.)

Antokoletz describes the integrative process in Bartók's music, which lies just beneath the surface of his varied melodic and harmonic constructions. He writes:

While the diatonic extensions themselves appear as one or another of the church modes in authentic folk melodies, the octatonic extensions represent abstract formations of the original non-diatonic folk sources. In addition, in certain instances in Bartók's music, whole-tone scales may be understood as abstract extensions of one or another of the folk modes. All these extensions, whether or not they can be found among the authentic peasant melodies (the completed octatonic and whole-tone scales cannot), are exploited both melodically and harmonically by Bartók as pitch sets, that is, as divorced from traditional tonal functions. (Antokoletz 1984: 204.)

Bartók referred to the principle of diatonic "extension in range" of chromatic themes, as well as the reverse, i.e., chromatic compression of diatonic themes. This bi-directional principle governs his "organic" technique shaping of melodic and harmonic materials. Bartók describes that technique as follows:

We have mostly the impression that we are dealing with an entirely new melody. And this circumstance is very good indeed, because we will get variety on the one hand, but the unity will remain intact because of the hidden relation between the two forms [of chromaticism]. [...] If, perhaps, you object that this new device is somehow artificial, my only answer will be that it is absolutely no more artificial than those old devices of augmentation, diminution, inversion, and *cancrizans* [crab inversion] of themes; in fact, *cancrizans* seems to be even much more artificial. (*BBE* 1976 [1943]: 381.)

Bartók mentions other examples that show his "extension in range" technique:

A rather surprising circumstance has been discovered in connection with the compression of diatonic into chromatic melodies. I discovered it only six months ago when studying the Dalmatian chromatic style, consisting of independent chromatic melodies. [...] The chromatic melodies of this style are, as a matter of fact, nothing other than diatonic melodies of neighboring areas, compressed into a chromatic level. There are irrefutable proofs for this theory, which, however, I will not enumerate now, but in one of my later lectures. This theory offers a very easy explanation of the queer major-second distance between the two parts. The compression simply works in two directions: in the horizontal direction for the melody, and in the vertical direction for the intervals, or distance between two [adjacent] parts. Evidently, the major or minor thirds distance, usually met with in two-part singing, is compressed into the unusual major-second distance. (*BBE* 1976 [1943]: 382–383.)

Whole-tone pitch patterns, surprisingly, play an insignificant role in Bartók's *Duke Bluebeard's Castle*, while fourth-chords (quartal chords) are much more in the foreground. That fact suggests that Bartók, at least at that time, seems to have been influenced more by folk music than by the ideas of Schoenberg (see Chapters 4.4–4.4.11, below). Bartók comments:

> When I first used the device of extending chromatic melodies into a diatonic form, or vice versa, I thought I invented something absolutely new, which never yet existed. And now I see that an absolutely identical principle exists in Dalmatia since Heaven knows how long a time, maybe for many centuries. This again proves that nothing absolutely new in the world can be invented; the most unusual-looking ideas have or must have had their predecessors. (*BBE* 1976 [1943]: 383.)

Unlike Schoenberg, Bartók fuses dense chromatic counterpoint with the modal material of peasant tunes and the transparent textures of Debussy. Schoenberg's music, by contrast, is tonally and rhythmically free from the influences such sources. A distinctive compositional signature for Bartók's contrapuntal style consists of the superposition of melodic lines, each in a different key. What is to be immediately noted here is that Bartók used homophonic pitch relations to expand his harmonic palette to all twelve-tones of the chromatic spectrum, while still remaining tonal.

With that, my discussion of analytic approaches to Bartók's music is complete. In sum: tonal theorists subsume resultant chromaticism within a pitch-centered, diatonic background; in contrast, atonal theorists cut across the diatonic strands to conceive pitch cells or motifs that move more properly in a chromatic twelve-pitch space (see, e.g., Agawu 1984;[95] and Parks 1981[96]). Both analytic approaches, however, obscure

---

95. Writing about Bartók's work for piano, *Eight Improvisations on Hungarian Peasant Songs* (Op. 20, Sz 74, BB 83, 1920), Kofi Agawu (1984) discusses previous approaches to analyzing the piece, starting with Richard Parks's atonal approach to the music of Bartók. Agawu notes, as we have done, that Bartók advocated a tonal basis as a starting point for analysis. Agawu goes on to mention Babbitt's advocation of approaching the works of Bartók from both tonal and atonal standpoints. Babbitt never put that principle to use in analysis, however. But, as Agawu mentions, Antokoletz did, by emphasizing the parallels between principles of folk-music construction and the harmonic and contrapuntal procedures used in the composing of art music. Agawu analyzes the *Improvisations* using the analytical systems of Schenker, Forte, and Lendvai (though Agawu finds fault with various aspects of Lendvai's system).

96. Richard Parks (1981), in his analysis of Bartók's piano piece "Kvartok" ("Fourths") from the *Mikrokosmos*, attempts to use atonal set theory to make sense of that brief, so-called tonal work. Parks first determines its form: nine sections defined by changes in thematic material. Parks breaks the harmonic material down into tetrachords and performs a PC-set analysis, which reveals Bartók's economical use of tetrachords. Only five different sets are used throughout: {0,3,5,8}, {0,1,5,6}, {0,1,6,7}, {0,2,5,7}, and {0,1,5,8}, each of which contains at least two perfect fourths. Parks then investigates the overall tonal plan, which he sees to comprise two key centers a third apart, E-flat and G. Parks also notes the ways in which the five sets are distributed over the nine sections, and

the individuality and coherence of perceivable diatonic strands: the first, by reducing chromaticism to diatonicism, the second, by picking apart diatonicism to show how it fits within the chromatic universe.

2.2. Lendvai's theories[97]

Presented next is a brief examination of theories advanced by Bartók analyst, Ernő Lendvai (1925–1993), whose unique contributions to the analysis of pitch and proportions in Bartók's music has generated one of the most long-lasting debates in the field. Lendvai proposed several unique concepts by which to understand Bartók's musical language, but scholars are anything but united in assessing the significance of his theories. Decades of scholarly discussion have yet to produce even an approximate re-definition of Lendvai's terms. (See, e.g., Kárpáti 1975 [1967];[98] 2000[99];

---

concludes by briefly relating Bartók's method in "Fourths" to some of his other pieces, e.g., the *Fourteen Bagatelles* (1998 [1908]). Parks argues that atonal theory provides a suitable method for analyzing and understanding Bartók's music.

97. Chapters 2.2–2.2.3 are based on my article "Bartók's Harmonic Language" (R. Honti 2006).

98. In *Bartók's String Quartets*, Kárpáti (1975 [1967]) discusses fundamental theoretical principles underlying Bartók's general musical language, along with information regarding the sources of Bartók's compositional tools: folk influences, monothematicism and variation, polymodal chromaticism, tonality, polytonality, and the phenomenon of mistuning (possibly Kárpáti's most peculiar topic; see, e.g., 1972 [1971]); and 2004 [1995]). Kárpáti (1975 [1967]) includes a detailed chronological chart of Bartók's various musical activities (folk-music research, composition, etc.), reviews the evolution of his string quartets, and discusses Bartók's forerunners and contemporaries. In addition to providing historical, thematic, motivic, tonal, scalar, phrasal, and structural details of the quartets, the author reviews the work of other scholars responding to the theories of Lendvai; see also, Kárpáti (1991 [1976]).

99. Especially pertinent in this regard is Kárpáti's (2000) article, "A Bartók-analitika kérdései: Még egyszer Lendvai Ernő elméletéről" ("Questions of Bartók Analysis: Once More about Ernő Lendvai's Theories").

Szentkirályi 1976;[100] and 1978;[101] Bachmann & Bachmann 1979;[102] Somfai 1981b; Howat 1977;[103] 1983a;[104] and 1983b;[105] and Agawu 1984.) As mentioned above, the present chapter deals with Lendvai's theoretical claims, particularly his approach to Bartók's handling of pitch, which he views through what he calls the "tonal axes system", discussed in Chapter 2.2.1, below. (Lendvai 1964: 16–24; 1971: 1–16; and 2000 [1971]: 283–288.) In his entry in *The New Grove Dictionary of Music and Musicians*, Ian Bent points out that:

> [...] the work of Ernő Lendvai on the music of Bartók should be mentioned, not so much for its theory of a tonal axis system as for its locating of proportion in musical structure. Lendvai sought to demonstrate the presence of the Golden

---

100. András Szentkirályi's dissertation (1976) presents an analysis of Bartók's *Second Sonata for Violin and Piano* (Sz 76, BB 85, 1922) based on Lendvai's theoretical principles. This piece can be considered as a landmark in Bartók's development of technique. It is at once a consolidation of his former practice and a starting-point for further explorations. The two movements are mature examples of very characteristic moods, the freely rhapsodic, and the stylized dance-movement of elaborate and violent rhythms. The violin part is purely melodic, the piano part almost entirely percussive, using what may be called chord-clusters. Free from the complexities of counterpoint, it serves as a particularly clear example of the chief features of Bartók's technique. Szentkirályi explores the tonal structure of the piece in terms of alpha-formations, distance models, the acoustic (overtone) scale, set {0,2,4,6,7,9,10}, and the pentatonic scale (e.g., set {0,2,4,7,9}), and demonstrates the structural relation of these tonal structures to the Fibonacci Series.
101. Szentkirályi (1978) bases his arguments on Lendvai's theories. He asserts that Bartók's compositional techniques cannot only be the result of intuition, but rather of conscious, systematic, and logical thinking. Szentkirályi outlines a conglomerate of diverse principles (based on folk modes, romantic chromaticism leading to equal divisions of the octave, etc.) then focuses on Lendvai's usage of the Golden Section, Fibonacci Series, and Axis System as the basis of an analysis of the first twenty measures of the *Second Sonata for Violin and Piano*.
102. Tibor Bachmann's and Peter J. Bachmann's (1979) "An Analysis of Béla Bartók's Music Through Fibonaccian Numbers and the Golden Mean" is an application of Lendvai's theories. The article explains the Golden Section and its relation to Fibonacci Series, and relates those to Bartók's interest in nature. Bachmanns show the relation of Fibonacci Series to the anhemitonic scale and the pentatonic chord, a minor triad with a minor seventh, specifically in second inversion, showing the numbers 2, 3, 5, and 8. Bachmanns also give examples from *Duke Bluebeard's Castle*, which show durational values of various passages.
103. In "Debussy, Ravel, and Bartók: Towards Some New Concepts of Form", Roy Howat (1977) explores proportional relations in the musical forms of those composers, based on an expansion of the principles of the Golden Section ratios established by Lendvai in his studies of Bartók's music. Howat applies his method in a comparative analysis of Debussy's *Reflets dans l'eau* (1905), Ravel's *Oiseaux tristes* (1905), and Bartók's *Music for Strings, Percussion and Celesta*.
104. Much has been written on the Golden Section, but one should approach the issue cautiously. In "Bartók, Lendvai, and the Principles of Proportional Analysis", Howat (1983a) concentrates on that proportion in Bartók's music, and on Lendvai's claim that Bartók organized many pieces around the Golden Section. Unlike Lendvai's, Howat's theory is more expansive, and attempts to link together intervallic structures in harmony, tonality, and melody, the use of rhythm and meter, and the organization of forms in terms of large- and small-scale proportion.
105. In *Debussy in Proportion: A Musical Analysis*, Howat (1983b: 6, 15, 22, 170, 187) evaluates the musical relevance of proportional analysis and gives a wide-ranging discussion of technical issues, in response to critical challenges to Lendvai's methods.

Section and of the Fibonacci Series [...] in Bartók's compositions. (Bent 1987 [1980]: 369.)

Lendvai's study of *Bluebeard's Castle*, in his book *Bartók's Dramaturgy: The Stage Works and the "Cantata Profana"*, is one of the cornerstones of his harmonic theories about Bartók's music (1964: 65–112). That study was revised and condensed for the major chapter on Bartók's opera in *The Workshop of Bartók and Kodály* (Lendvai 1983: 219–245); the chapter in question contains Lendvai's appraisal of the theoretical foundations of Bartók's music, but analyses of individual scenes have been omitted. Lendvai's *Poetic World of Bartók* also contains a brief analysis of the opera (2000 [1971]: 19–40). Substantial portions of Lendvai's (1960–1961) and Kroó's (1962) original researches into *Duke Bluebeard's Castle* remain untranslated, so those who do not read Hungarian cannot appreciate their work. The opera con-stitutes not so much a new departure as a consummation on a higher level. Bartók's later style does not display a single significant element that was lacking when he composed his opera, a fact emphasized by Lendvai (2000 [1971]: 21): "In *Blue-beard*, Bartók's style sprang at once into existence."

Lendvai views the various levels of Bartók's music as integrated by means of several interlocking systems. The latter are illustrated in his groundbreaking study, *Béla Bartók: An Analysis of His Music* (1971).[106] The three pillars of his theories are as follows:

1. The Golden Section (GS) as governing principle in both pitch and formal organization.[107]

---

106. Lendvai's (1971) relatively short study gives a comprehensive English presentation of his theories, including tonal principles based on the AS, formal principles based on the Golden Sec-tion and Fibonacci Series, the use of chords and intervals derived from the Golden Section as well as the chromatic, acoustic (overtone), or diatonic system. Reference is made to ancient Greek, Gothic, and Renaissance mathematical models, and a discussion given of the philosophical signifi-cance of those principles. For a summary of Lendvai's views on Bartók's music, see Szentkirályi (1976: 163–166).

107. In "Bartók and the Golden Section", Lendvai (1966a) evaluates Bartók's use of the *proportio divina*, and explains how its use brings about a fusion of Bartók's two-fold view of life: as a bond-ing of biological being (body) with the intellectual power of logic (mind). The Fibonacci Series is a number series, named after a 13th-century Italian mathematician, that is derived from a recursive formula in which each subsequent element is the sum of the previous two (e.g., 1, 2, 3, 5, 8, 13, 21, etc.). The Fibonacci Series, though infinite, has the following property: the ratio between neighbor-ing pairs of numbers increasingly approximates the Golden Mean (0.618033...), with the accuracy increasing the further one progresses along the number series. The Golden Mean, or "Golden Section", can be understood as the point on a line that divides it into two segments, such that the ratio between the segments is the same as that between the longer segment and the entire line. (See also, Bárdos 1974: 98–102; Howat 1983b: 1–4; and Kuokkala 1979; and 1992: 26, 206.) So far, however, no evidence has emerged that Bartók consciously planned his works in the ways Lendvai suggests (Howat 1983b: 6, 15, 22, 170, 187). Another striking, if contrived, image of symmetry is produced when an ascending scale based on the intervals of the Golden Section is superimposed over a descending acoustic (overtone) scale, set {0,2,4,6,7,9,10}. The second "pillar" in the list above, the axis system (AS), been dealt with by various theorists; e.g., Szentkirályi (1976), Wilson (1992: 6–8, 203–208), and Solomon (1973).

2. The axis system (AS) with its complement in the acoustic (overtone) scale.
3. Chords are based on (1) the harmonic paradigm of the α-chord, and its β, γ, δ, and ε segments; and (2) on alternating-distance scales that divide the octave, most importantly those constructed in 1–2–1 (alternating minor and major seconds), 1–3–1 (alternating minor seconds and minor thirds), and 1–5–1 (alternating minor seconds and perfect fourths).

In his "Introduction to Bartókian Forms and Harmonies", Lendvai (1968) shows that Bartók, in his early thirties, devised his own method of integrating all the elements of music. Lendvai argues that one basic principle – the Golden Section, i.e., $X:1 = (1-X):X$ – governs scales, chordal structures and their respective melodic motifs, as well as durational proportions between the movements of a multi-movement work, main divisions within a movement (such as exposition, development, recapitulation), and even the phrases within sections of movements. By means of that principle, Lendvai describes many of the scales, harmonies, and formal structures of Bartók's compositional style. Thus, the pentatonic scale, the α-chords and the modal scales all belong to this system. (See also, Bárdos 1974: 19, 98–102, 107, 133, 164, 203, 239–240.) The Fibonacci Series and the Golden Section principle form such a large part of Lendvai's theoretical writings that they have attracted the attention of other theoreticians (e.g., Kramer 1973[108]).

Lendvai is also concerned with symmetrical systems, which he believes are one of the few features common to both Eastern and Western European music. That concern is evidenced in his development of the axis theory and its deployment in Bartók's music (R. Honti 2006: 698–706; see also, pp. 58–59, Chapter 2.2.1, below).

Many of Lendvai's calculations have subsequently been discredited; for example, his measurements of the Golden Section (see, e.g., Howat 1983a; and 1983b: 6, 15, 22, 170, 187; see also, Oramo 1982b). I, too, find some of Lendvai's work questionable. Still, one suspects that his theories have been negatively criticized mostly due to the absolute lack of any comments by Bartók regarding the Golden Section (GS) or Fibonacci Series (FS).

The Golden Section can be found in the harmonies, in which the structure of the intervals sometimes mirrors the Fibonacci sequence. Such questions cannot be fully resolved, however, without consideration of musical temporality. Harmonies create an acoustic space; but what about durational, that is, temporal space? The Fibonacci series and its related sequences (e.g., the Lucas series) have long attracted the attention of composers and theorists; but their application to pitch structure has not yet been fully understood. In my opinion, neither the Golden Section nor the Fibonacci Series designate a unified and objective framework through which to view pitch organization in Bartók's œuvre.

---

108. Jonathan Kramer (1973) discusses application of the Golden Section to pitch structure by several composers. In discussing Bartók's *Music for Strings, Percussion and Celesta* (first and third movements), Kramer "corrects" some of Lendvai's findings, but generally accepts them as valid, on the condition that they be understood as approximations.

Lendvai (2000 [1971]: 291) claims that Bartók's chromatic system is based on the Golden Section and the Fibonacci Series, but that claim is questionable. Some organic formations in nature have been shown to grow according to Golden Section proportions, at least ideally (e.g., shells of certain sea creatures, foliage and fruit, trees, etc.). Lendvai and his followers (see, e.g., Szentkirályi 1976; and Bachmann & Bachmann 1979) have spent a considerable amount of energy identifying such proportions (often multiply nested) in the durational and rhythmic parameters of Bartók's music. Their work in that area rests on two assumptions: that the concept of GS in the temporal domain is similar to the one in space, and that we hear and listen linearly.

In his *L'Évolution créatrice*, Henri Bergson (1859–1941) spoke of a "natural geometry of the human intellect" in order to explain people's resistance to noticing the development of things in time (1941 [1909]). That may well be true, but an investigation of "natural geometry" lies outside the scope of the present study, and will not be pursued. If music is endowed, either consciously or unconsciously, with the same ratios that nature occasionally displays, that might validate the claim that music is linked to the natural world. But it does not mean that one should overlook fundamental flaws in Lendvai's analytic methods and calculations based on the Golden Section.

Here, however, a full-blown critique of his theories is not necessary. For my purposes, it suffices to sketch and summarize those characteristics of Lendvai's system that relate most closely to the music in question.

2.2.1. The tonal axis system

Lendvai explains Bartók's method of composition according to what he calls "the tonal axis system". What exactly does that mean? The answer is rather complex. Lendvai defines a historical tradition for Bartók's axis system (AS), and elaborates on it at length (1983).[109] The key point for Lendvai is Bartók's tonal axis (TA). The latter may be viewed as a method of assigning functional harmonic significance to the pitch classes (PCs) operating within his particular diatonic and chromatic scales. Lendvai, in the course of his investigation, concludes that Bartók's art represents a logical continuation and, in a certain sense, conclusion of the development of European music. The circles of harmonic development are fused into a single, coherent, closed unit in Bartók's sound system: the tonal axis (TA). (See also, Lendvai 1947; 1971; and 1993.)

---

109. Lendvai (1983) analyzes many of Bartók's major works according to the composer's theories. Lendvai's discussions have a common thread: the principle of duality. The latter is represented in chromatic (Golden Section) *versus* acoustic (diatonic) systems, in the principles of the polar-axis system, as well as in more musically abstract juxtapositions, such as instinctive/intellectual, masculine/feminine, emotional/sensuous, etc. Lendvai's ultimate aim is to demonstrate by means of analysis how these opposing principles are integrated in Bartók's music.

Before discussing that system in detail, it is appropriate to consider in a general way the term "tonality". Traditional tonality depends upon scale and chord relationships for its organization. Vincent Persichetti remarks on tonality:

> The tonal meaning of an isolated chord is indefinite; it may be a crucial, or an ornamental chord of many keys, or it may belong to no key. When surrounded by other chords its meaning may be restricted to a single tonality, to two, or more wavering tonalities; or if it has atonal intentions, the fact can be made obvious. Tonality does not exist as an absolute. It is implied through harmonic articulation and through the tension and relaxation of chords around a tone, or chords base. A particular style or period is not always limited to a predilection for a single kind of tonality. Twentieth-century music makes use of many degrees of tonality and employs many means for establishing them. (Persichetti 1961: 248.)

To make the concept clear, consider a circle of fifths[110], which is a general presupposition for the development of Bartók's harmonic system. In classical harmony, the cycle of fifths F–C–G–D–A–E–B (notes in the C major scale) corresponds to the functional series S–T–D–S–T–D, respectively. If continued, that circle returns to its starting point F, producing a diminished fifth between B and F. However, if the circle is extended by all *perfect* fifths (here, B to F-sharp, etc.), it will eventually cover all twelve chromatic tones. In that case, the scheme of the axis system (AS) becomes apparent, as shown in Figure 2.9.

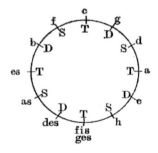

Figure 2.9. The Axis System (Lendvai 1971: 2).

The question arises, can the axis system be considered as a functional system in the true sense of the word? Lendvai believes so. In his article (1957), "Einführung in die Formen- und Harmoniewelt Bartóks", Lendvai points out that the pitch axis

---

110. The term "Circle of Fifths" was coined by the German composer and theorist, Johann David Heinichen (1683–1729), in his treatise *Der Generalbaß in der Composition* (1967 [1728]). Heinichen's visualization of the circle is somewhat hard to decode immediately, because the major-key (odd numbers, *ma*) and minor-key (even numbers, *mi*) cycles are interleaved. Heinichen did not anticipate today's convention of representing minor keys by lower-case letters, but the letters associated with even numbers should be read that way; e.g., A (a) is the relative minor of C major ("relative" because it has the same key signature as the latter).

(PA) may be viewed as a method of assigning functional harmonic significance to PCs.[111]

Lendvai's axis system (Figure 2.9) affirms the presence of tonic–subdominant–dominant chord functions, if not traditional ones, among the tonal relationships in Bartók's music (Table 2.3 and Figure 2.10).

Axis	Pitch classes	Point 0	Set	Forte number	ICV
Tonic	C–E-flat–F-sharp/G-flat–A	C	{0,3,6,9}	4–28 (3)	004002
Subdominant	F–A-flat/G-sharp–B–D	F	{0,3,6,9}	4–28 (3)	004002
Dominant	G–B-flat–D-flat/C-sharp–E	G	{0,3,6,9}	4–28 (3)	004002

Table 2.3. The tonal axis system.

0	3	6	9

Figure 2.10. Set {0,3,6,9}.[112]

This threefold functioning in the classical sense (T, S, D, etc.) is not typical of the small-scale harmonic progressions of any of Bartók's mature music. Still, Lendvai's axis system, in which those three functions are fulfilled by the three diminished seventh groupings, is undeniably operative in the composer's music. In essence, it functions as an organizing principle of tonal levels or centers in movements or large sections thereof, as a structure in which all 12 notes are strictly related to one center. (Lendvai 1964: 16–24; 1971: 1–16; and 2000 [1971]: 283–288.)

For example, Bartók's augmented fourth/diminished fifth is based almost entirely on an octatonic collection formed by joining two {0,2,3,5} sets six semitones apart (Figure 2.11).

Figure 2.11. Set {0,2,3,5}.

The relations of the AS (Figure 2.9, previous page) differ from those of traditional tonality in that they are essentially symmetrical and relative; that is to say,

---

111. Lendvai's (1957) article also contains two examples from *Music for Strings, Percussion and Celesta* as well as a chart showing the formal middle point of the movement (according to the Golden Section proportions), where the tonality has moved from the opening key of A (which also closes the movement) to its polarized area at the tritone (E-flat).

112. Milton Babbitt (1986) has revealed the startling persistence of {0,3,6,9} and {0,4,8} symmetry as governors of centricity in music constructed according to Stravinsky's technique of hexachordal transposition and cyclic permutation ("rotation").

their definition depends solely on context (Gervers 1969[113]). Taking into account how those properties affect Bartók's harmonic language, Lendvai's (1971) polar axis system is founded on the following premises:

1. A tonic (T) is interchangeable with its parallel mode.
2. Any major or minor triad built on one of the pitches belonging to the circle of minor-third relations with the tonic (T), can be substituted for the other, such that no change of function is considered to take place; the same holds for the remaining functions (S, D), each determined by its respective circle of minor thirds and resultant scales and harmonies.

Ujfalussy (1969), in "The Basic Harmonic Conception of *Allegro barbaro* and Bartók Scales", seems to have been the first to discover the role and significance of harmonic and tonal relationships of the common third in Bartók's music. The piece starts with the tonal duality of F-sharp minor–F major revolving around the melodic A, the axis-note in *Allegro barbaro*.

2.2.2. The α-chord structures

It is time to consider the characteristic features of Bartókean α-chord structures. The most innovative aspects of that harmony become part of the sound world of the more mature Bartók: (1) the distinctive use of major-minor chords, or set {0,3,4,7}; and of (2) chords derived from the overtone series. (Lendvai 1957: 114; see also, Kárpáti 2004 [1977].[114]) On the major-minor third, Bartók remarks that it

> […] is very interesting to note that we can observe the simultaneous use of major and minor third even in instrumental folk music. Folk music is generally music in unison; there are areas, however, where two violins are used to perform dance music; one plays the melody and the other plays accompanying chords.

---

113. Hilda Gervers (1969) discusses the *Five Songs* (Sz 61, BB 71, 1915–1916) in terms of their formal and tonal properties, pointing up the expressionistic style of the texts. The analyses are based on Lendvai's polar-axis system rather than classical key relations. Gervers notes the scarcity of solo song in the composer's overall output, and relates the *Five Songs* to Bartók's later stylistic development. (See also, Demény 1946: 22–23; and Lindlar 1984: 103–104.)

114. In "Alternative Structures in Bartók's *Contrasts*", Kárpáti (2004 [1977]) demonstrates that Bartók, by using systematic chains of fifths with a common third, arrived at a method reminiscent of 12-tone serialism. The *Contrasts* for violin, clarinet and piano (Sz 111, BB 116, 1938) was commissioned by Benny Goodman (1909–1986), and represents Bartók's only music featuring solo clarinet (Demény, ed. 1976: 605; and Lindlar 1984: 93). In his article, Kárpáti (ibid.) discusses triads with major-minor structures, e.g., set {0,3,4,7}, as dual or alternative structures, by which he means that they still can be justified separately, and, when appearing together, preserve their original modal content. Kárpáti discusses the meaning of this structure also in the context of Nüll's as well as Lendvai's theoretical concepts (e.g., Lendvai's 1:3 models). Kárpáti explains that if the two equivalent kinds of third appear within the stable frame of a fifth, then one arrives logically at the dual root and fifth situated around the stable third. In *Contrasts*, the motif of the Lydian fourth becomes equivalent to the dual third-structure of sound. See also, Kárpáti (2004 [1995]), "Perfect and Mistuned Structures in Bartók's Music."

And rather queer-sounding chords may appear in these pieces. (*BBE* 1976 [1943]: 369–370.)

Bartók at first placed the minor third on top; e.g., C–D-sharp/E-flat–E–G, set {0,3,4,7} (C = 0). After a time, the chord appeared consistently only in inversion, stacked as minor third, perfect fourth, and minor third. Often a minor seventh is added above the root: C–D-sharp/E-flat–E–G chord with B-flat, set {0,3,4,7,10} (Figure 2.12).

4	7	10
	0	3

Figure 2.12. Set {0,3,4,7,10}.

The function remains unchanged when the C major mode comprised by the above chord is replaced by the parallel E-flat major: A minor – C major-minor – E-flat major. Those substitution chords may also be employed in major-minor form, which brings the system to a close, because the parallel keys of A major / F-sharp minor and E-flat minor / G-flat major conjoin enharmonically, F-sharp = G-flat. (See Figure 2.9, p. 58, Chapter 2.2.1.) The major-minor chord has a number of synonymous forms.

Lendvai (1964: 33) refers to that harmony as α, i.e., the alpha chord: C-sharp–E–G–B-flat / C–E-flat–F-sharp–A. That chord is shown in Example 2.4 (no. 1), along with harmonies derived from it (subsets): the beta chord, β and its variants β1, β2 (nos. 2–4); the gamma chord, γ and γ1 (nos. 5–6); the delta chord, δ, δ1, δ2 (nos. 7–9); and no. 10, the epsilon chord, ε. (See also, Bárdos 1974: 71–76, 105.)

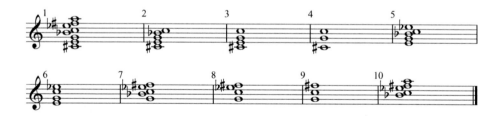

Example 2.4. The α-chord and its segments (after Lendvai 1964: 33).

According to Lendvai, the α-chord and its segments, displayed in Example 2.4, are derivatives of the tonic axis and the dominant axis (1964: 33; 1971: 35–66; and 2000 [1971]: 291–299). Table 2.4 and Figures 2.13–2.22 (next page) show the α-chord and its subsets as pitch classes and integers, as well as the chord's polar functions in the axis system.

α-chord and its segments	**Pitch classes**	**Point 0**	**Integers**	**Tonal axis (TA) references**
α	C-sharp–E–G–B-flat–C–E-flat–F-sharp–A	C-sharp	{0,2,3,5,6,8,9,11}	D–D–D–D–T–T–T–T
β	C-sharp–E–G–B-flat–C	C-sharp	{0,3,6,9,11}	D–D–D–D–T
β1	C-sharp–E–G–C	C-sharp	{0,3,6,11}	D–D–D–T
β2	C-sharp–G–C	C-sharp	{0,6,11}	D–D–T
γ	E–G–B-flat–C–E-flat	E	{0,3,6,8,11}	D–D–D–T–T
γ1	E–G–C–E-flat	E	{0,3,8,11}	D–D–T–T
δ	G–B-flat–C–E-flat–F-sharp	G	{0,3,5,8,11}	D–D–T–T–T
δ1	G–C–E-flat–F-sharp	G	{0,5,8,11}	D–T–T–T
δ2	G–C–F-sharp	G	{0,5,11}	D–T–T
ε	B-flat–C–E-flat–F-sharp–A	B-flat	{0,2,5,8,11}	D–T–T–T–T

Table 2.4. The α-chord and its segment, shown in relation to the tonal axis (TA).

0	3	6	9
5	8	11	2

Figure 2.13. Set {0,2,3,5,6,8,9,11}.

0	3	6	9
		11	

Figure 2.14. Set {0,3,6,9,11}.

0	3	6
		11

Figure 2.15. Set {0,3,6,11}.

0		6
		11

Figure 2.16. Set {0,6,11}.

0	3	6
	8	11

Figure 2.17. Set {0,3,6,8,11}.

0	3	
	8	11

Figure 2.18. Set {0,3,8,11}.

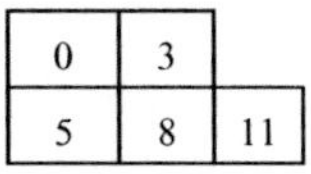

Figure 2.19. Set {0,3,5,8,11}.

Figure 2.20. Set {0,5,8,11}.

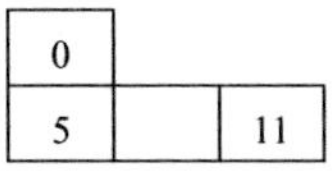

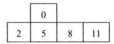

Figure 2.21. Set {0,5,11}.

Figure 2.22. Set {0,2,5,8,11}.

Lendvai discusses two crucial harmonies: the hypermajor (*hyperdúr*) and the hyperminor (*hypermoll*) chords (1964: 68, 284; also see, especially, Bárdos 1974: 64). Table 2.5 and Figures 2.23–2.24 display those chords and their properties:

Chords	Descriptive names	Point 0	Set	Forte number	ICV
Hypermajor	major triad with major seventh	C	{0,4,7,11}	4–20	101220
Hyperminor	minor triad with major seventh	C	{0,3,7,11}	4–19	101310

Table 2.5. Hypermajor and hyperminor chords described in traditional terms and as set types (with corresponding Forte numbers and ICVs).

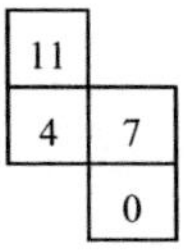

Figure 2.23. Set {0,4,7,11}.

Figure 2.24. Set {0,3,7,11}.

The hyperminor chord (Figure 2.24) and its inversions have special significance in Bartók's harmonic vocabulary, as used, for example, in the "Secret Garden" scene of *Duke Bluebeard's Castle* (60/1–74/18; see Chapter 4.4.7 for a detailed analysis of the "Fourth Door" scene).

2.2.3. Alternating-distance scales

Another crucial structure in Bartók's tonality is that of scales, which have no fixed final (or "tonic") and which contain repeating fragments within the octave. Such pitch formations are basic elements of certain folk music.[115] Bartók, however, did not become aware of their usage in specific folk music until his field-trip to Biskra (an area in North Africa) in June 1913, where he collected songs of nomadic Arab tribes (*BÖI* 1966 [1917]; and Kodály 1974 [1921]: 433).[116] Bartók used those kinds of scales in, e.g., the *Piano Suite* (Op. 14) and the *Second Quartet*[117]. Lendvai (1971: 51), using terminology based on interval formations, calls them "model 1:2",[118] "model 1:3", and "model 1:5"[119] divisions (Table 2.6 and Figures 2.25–2.27). Lajos Bárdos (1974: 38), in his *Ten Recent Essays, 1969–1974*, calls them "alternating-distance scales".

Model	Pitch classes	Point 0	Set	Forte number	ICV
1:2	C–C-sharp–D-sharp–E–F-sharp–G–A–B-flat	C	{0,1,3,4,6,7,9,10}	8–28	448444
1:3	C–C-sharp–E–F–G-sharp–A	C	{0,1,4,5,8,9}	6–20 (4)	303630
1:5	C–C-sharp–F-sharp–G	C	{0,1,6,7}	4–9 (6)	200022

Table 2.6. The alternating-distance scales.

---

115. E.g., the Arabian "Biskra scale" consists of D, F, F# and G#. The scale contains the following intervals: minor third (D–F), major third (D–F#), and augmented fourth (D–G#). Such a structure becomes part of Bartók's melodic style; for example, in the first movement of his *Music for Strings, Percussions and Celesta*.
116. Also see, especially, Kárpáti (2004 [2000]), "Bartók in North Africa: A Unique Fieldwork and Its Impact on His Music."
117. The *Second Quartet* displays greater transformation of modal elements into abstract pitch formations than do any of Bartók's preceding works, and marks a radical break from the harmonic progressions found in the *First Quartet* (Lindlar 1984: 142–143).
118. Model 1:2 is identical with Stravinsky's octatonic scale and Messiaen's second "mode of limited transposition".
119. Antokoletz (1984: 69–72) labels the 1:5 divisions Z cell.

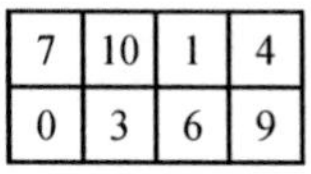

7	10	1	4
0	3	6	9

Figure 2.25. Set {0,1,3,4,6,7,9,10}.

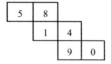

Figure 2.26. Set {0,1,4,5,8,9}.

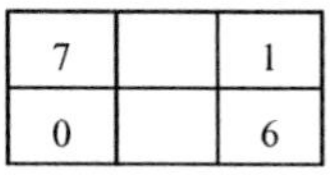

7		1
0		6

Figure 2.27. Set {0,1,6,7}.

In 1907–1908, Bartók made an important discovery in folk music. The old modal scales offered the possibility of eliminating dominant–tonic (D–T) cadences, and established a certain amount of equality among chords based on different degrees of the scales. Bartók exploited the fact that only a single step separates the relatively tonal "overtone" scale shown in Figure 2.28, set {0,2,4,6,7,9,10}, from the more "atonal" whole-tone scale, set {0,2,4,6,8,10}. (Lendvai 1957: 127; see also, Bárdos 1974: 27–30, 36, 109, 172, 190.)

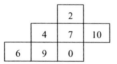

Figure 2.28. Set {0,2,4,6,7,9,10}.

In his analysis of *Bluebeard's Castle*, Kroó (1961: 335) states that the "overtone series chord" acts as the "nucleus of the treasure chamber music" (54/1–59/9, 54/4–9, and 56/1–5). In those passages, we find the acoustic (overtone) scale with D as "tonic" (D–E–F-sharp–G-sharp–A–B–C). In both Debussy's *Pelléas et Mélisande* and Bartók's *Bluebeard*, one finds syntheses of the pentatonic scale, whole-tone scale, and overtone scale (Lendvai 1983: 19–40; Frigyesi 1998: 196–294; Kroó 1993; and Lindlar 1984: 61).

Some special cases require comment. There are only two possible whole tone scales, complements of each other, together producing the total chromatic collection of twelve tones. Lendvai labels the two, complementary whole-tone hexachords as Omega 1 (ω1) and Omega 2 (ω2), as displayed in Table 2.7 and Figure 2.29 (1964: 284; see also, Bárdos 1974: 36). Lendvai observes that ω1 and ω2 proliferate in

Bartók's music of the 1920s, and become foundational to his works of the 1930s (Lendvai 1964: 284).

Scale	Pitch classes	Point 0	Set	Forte number	ICV
ω1	C–D–E–F-sharp–G-sharp–A-sharp	C	{0,2,4,6,8,10}	6–35 (2)	060603
ω2	C-sharp–D-sharp–E-sharp–G–A–B	C-sharp	{0,2,4,6,8,10}	6–35 (2)	060603

Table 2.7. The ω1 and the ω2 with the PC, set, Forte number and ICV references.

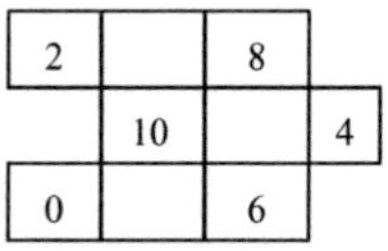

Figure 2.29. Set {0,2,4,6,8,10}.

Bartók used two fundamental scales to project his twin harmonic universes: the "diatonic" and the "chromatic" (Lendvai 2000 [1971]: 281–304). Lendvai refers to the diatonic universe as the "Golden Section system" and the chromatic universe as the "acoustic (overtone) system". Bartókian diatonicism, according to Lendvai, is virtually the opposite of chromaticism; the diatonic system includes the acoustic scale, chains of open fourths, and chords of accumulated thirds, open fifths, augmented triads and so on.

Lendvai's article (1966b [1962]), "Duality and Synthesis in The Music of Béla Bartók," provides a concise view of his theoretical ideas on the Golden Section, polar-axis system, Bartók's diatonic and chromatic scale systems, and the relationship of all those to traditional and folk-music idioms, Impressionistic music, and twelve-tone technique. Lendvai also discusses how Bartók may have used the Fibonacci Series in the pitch structure of his *Sonata for Two Pianos and Percussion*. Remaining in the framework of dualistic categorization, Lendvai states that the Golden Section scale and overtone scale mirror each other in a complementary relationship (Figures 2.30 and 2.31). As Table 2.8 shows, neither the Golden Section scale nor the overtone scale contains the integers 1 and 11.

Scale	Pitch classes	Point 0	Set
Golden Section	C–E-flat–F–A-flat	C	{0,3,5,8}
Acoustic (Overtone)	C–D–E–F-sharp–G–A–B-flat	C	{0,2,4,6,7,9,10}

Table 2.8. Golden Section scale and acoustic scale, with corresponding integers.

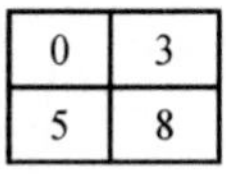

Figure 2.30. Set {0,3,5,8}.

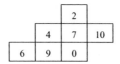

Figure 2.31. Set {0,2,4,6,7,9,10}.

Lendvai concludes that Bartók's Golden Section system was rooted in Eastern European pentatonic concepts, and that his acoustic derived from Western harmonic thinking (2000 [1971]: 281–304). He further polarizes these harmonic identities by characterizing the Golden Section system as dissonant, and the acoustic system as consonant (1966b [1962]). Lendvai states that: "An equally deep secret of Bartók's music (perhaps the most profound) is that the 'closed' world of the Golden Section system is counterbalanced by an open sphere of the acoustic system" (ibid.: 174). It can be shown that non-diatonic modes permeate much of Bartók's mature music. Lendvai provides examples of the acoustic scale in works such as *Duke Bluebeard's Castle*, the *Fourth String Quartet* (Sz 91, BB 95, 1928),[120] *Music for Strings Percussion and Celesta, Sonata for Two Pianos and Percussion* (Op. posth., Sz 115, BB 121, 1937), *Contrasts*, and *Divertimento* for string orchestra (Sz 113, BB 118, 1939). Though a close analysis of all those works is beyond the scope of this study, it can be said that, in general, they all exhibit the tendencies of Bartók's lifelong commitment to the synthesis of divergent modal material with the techniques of Western art music.

2.3. A cycle-based system for relating pitch-class sets

The purpose of the present chapter is to investigate Bartók's tendency to "symmetrize" the modal basis of folk music and project the compositional potential of basic referential elements at the levels of progression and structure. His reliance on folk or folk-derived elements is compatible with symmetrical pitch construction and rests on a methodology for the study of "progression", a dynamic approach to procedure. That is one of Antokoletz's (1984) most significant contributions to Bartók research. Because referential elements are often residuals of folk extraction, whose potential "progresses" into the purely compositional levels of pitch organization and structure, their generative role defines Bartók's creative journey. Antokoletz summarizes:

---

120. By 1928, when the *Fourth String Quartet* was completed, Bartók was using the *parlando* style more as a compositional style than for the general effect of a *parlando* imitation folk song. The nucleus of this quartet is the third movement (*Non troppo lento*) of which the main theme is a richly ornamented, instrumental-style *parlando* melody. Although the theme is mostly chromatic, beginnings and endings of phrases often consist of perfect fourth or perfect fifth intervals. The modal ascending line F–G–A–B, set {0,2,4,6} later developed as a descending motif and the often repeated ♫. and ♫ rhythms, remind us of its folk-music origins. (Lindlar 1984: 146–148; see also, Kroó 1975 [1971]: 153–159.)

[…] symmetrical configurations or progressions may be based on recurrent and clearly identifiable symmetrical cells. In such symmetrical relations, the term tonal center has a linear designation. Both the traditional and non-traditional concepts are relevant to Bartók's music. These two seemingly unrelated means of establishing a sense of pitch-class priority are often integrated by means of special interactions and transformations. (Antokoletz 1984: 138.)

Antokoletz came to realize, through systematic score analysis and scholarly research, that a coherent network of theoretical principles, based on the interaction and transformation between the diatonic folk modes and the more abstract symmetrical pitch formations, can be derived from the system of the interval cycles. The total complex of cycles consists of one cycle of minor seconds, two of whole tones, three of minor thirds, four of major thirds, one of perfect fourths, and six of tritones. Antokoletz became aware of the multiplicity of musical sources underlying the divergent, yet unified musical structures of Bartók's repertory in general. These stages include the harmonization of folk tunes, symmetrical transformation of diatonic folk modes, the construction, development, and interaction of intervallic cells. (Antokoletz 1975; 1977; and 1984: 78–137.)

Bartók's move toward ever-greater abstraction and synthesis of divergent art- and folk-music sources had reached its most intensive stage of development in the *Fourth String Quartet*. The large-scale arch form of the five-movement plan serves as a carefully constructed framework within which Bartók organizes diversified melodic, harmonic, and rhythmic formations into a systematic network of interrelationships. Despite the more abstract medium, rhythmic and structural properties of folk music are nevertheless still very prominent. Elements from Hungarian and other folk sources provide materials that contribute to the distinctive styles of the different movements. (Kroó 1975 [1971]: 153–159.)

In his dissertation, *Principles of Pitch Organization in Bartók's "Fourth String Quartet"*, Antokoletz (1975) started out from the writings of the dodecaphonist George Perle, whose articles were germinal to his theories. The strand that Antokoletz (1984: xii, 68, 271–311) sees running through the entire corpus is Bartók's preoccupation with symmetrical structures in conjunction with the complete set of interval cycles. Perle's (1955) pioneering article, "Symmetrical Formations in the *String Quartets* of Béla Bartók," gives a brief history of symmetrical pitch collections in the late nineteenth and early twentieth centuries (in Debussy,[121] and Russian

---

121. Early in his career, Debussy's music reflects the aesthetic of his primary teachers: Alexis Emanuel Chabrier (1841–1894) and Gabriel Fauré (1845–1924). In their search for freedom from the omnipresent chromatic extensions of traditional tonality, they opened the way for Debussy to explore harmonic practices that, although fundamentally diatonic, were outside the realm of traditional practice. In particular, Russian music was influential on the young Debussy. Early works, e.g., his *String Quartet* (1893), were groundbreaking in their juxtaposition of modal practices – a tradition imported from Russian sacred music – with more traditional diatonic ones. This interest in expanding the harmonic resources of music by drawing from external sources represents a radical departure from the path upon which German music was headed – expansion from internal sources, e.g., chromatic extensions of the language. (Ujfalussy 1959: 29–38, 74–75, 100–106.)

composers). Perle advances a significant discussion of the equal subdivisions of the octave into the interval cycles and the use of inversionally symmetrical relations, which together define axes as a new concept of tonal focus in the *Second String Quartet* in A minor (Op. 17, Sz 67, BB 75, 1915–1917)[122], *Fourth String Quartet*[123] and the *Fifth String Quartet* in B-flat Major (Sz 102, BB 110, 1934)[124]. In Perle's view, this tendency begins in 1908, becomes gradually stronger, and culminates in the *Fourth String Quartet* where it becomes the dominating factor in generating both the sense and substance of tonality. Thereafter, axis constructs share this role in varying measure with more traditional means of establishing modal centers. Perle identifies X cells and Y cells[125] specifically in the *Fourth String Quartet*. Perle describes symmetrical and non-symmetrical structures in Bartók's *Second* and *Fifth Quartet* as follows:

For further reading, see Françoise Gervais (1971), "Étude comparée des langages harmoniques de Fauré et de Debussy."

122. The work is dedicated to the Waldbauer-Kerpely Quartet, which premiered the piece on March 3, 1918 in Budapest. Antal Molnár's (1948) *Bartók művészete, emlékezésekkel a művész életére* (*Bartók's Art with Recollections of the Artist's Life*) is an important primary source document, since the author was a violinist in the Waldbauer-Kerpely String Quartet. The members were friends of Bartók and played the *First* and *Second String Quartets* when no one else would approach them. Molnár provides significant biographical and cultural data as well as personal insights into the composer's personality and psychology. The *Second String Quartet* reveals a greater fusion of those diverse sources found in Bartók's earlier compositions, with a tendency toward more pervasive manifestations of the folk-music sources. The first movement of that quartet is both passionate and serene. Its polyphony is even more highly developed than that of the *First String Quartet*. One is occasionally surprised to find the harmony reminiscent of Scriabin, though it is completely transformed by Bartók's very personal melodic line and mastery of texture. As for style, Bartók's *Second Quartet* is probably the most innovative one to appear since Beethoven's posthumously published quartets. The second movement is in the *Allegro barbaro* manner, and the last one ("Lento") is utterly stark, bare, lonely, and tragic. Bartók had never before written anything so uncompromising. We do not find this mood again until the slow movements of the *Piano Sonata* (Sz 80, BB 88, 1926) and the *Divertimento for Strings* (1939). (Lindlar 1984: 143; see also, Kroó 1975 [1971]: 92–97.)

123. In Bartók's wealth of piano music written in the mid-1920s and in his *Fourth String Quartet*, the transformation of his musical language into further abstractions (or at least fusions) of modal folk-music elements might have been steered toward extreme systematization by his contact with other contemporary composers and their works. In 1921, he met Ravel and Stravinsky in Paris, through the musical writer Henri Prunières (1886–1942) (Demény, ed. 1971: 160). In the summer of 1922, he joined with members of the Schoenberg School, and with Stravinsky, Milhaud, and others, in forming the International Society for Contemporary Music (ISCM), of which Bartók always remained an active member. At the ISCM concert in Baden-Baden on July 26, 1927, Bartók performed his own *Piano Sonata* on the same program as Berg's *Lyric Suite* for string quartet (1925–1926). It was Berg's first large-scale work in which employed the twelve-tone method of composition. On Berg, see Prunières (1989 [1936]), and Collaer & Weterings (1989 [1935]).

124. It was commissioned by the American patron of arts, Elisabeth Sprague Coolidge. In the *Fifth String Quartet*, the principle of symmetry is basic to both the large-scale formal design and the underlying pitch relations. (Stevens 1964: 191; and Lindlar 1984: 148–150.)

125. In sum, X cells are chromatic tetrachords that are labeled by the lowest pitch class (in normal order) in the collection. Hence, a C–C#–D–Eb collection would be X–0, since C is pitch class 0. Y cells are whole-tone tetrachords, and they are labeled in the same way. Thus, a C–D–E–F# collection is cell Y–0. (Antokoletz 1984: 69–72.)

The strict inversion of a non-symmetrical progression will, unlike that of a symmetrical progression, generate new harmonic connections, which are the complements of the original relations. Thus, the non-symmetrical detail becomes a necessary component of a larger symmetrical relationship. (Perle 1955: 311.)

Antokoletz (1977: 3) remarks that "a collection of pitches is symmetrical if the intervallic structure of one-half of it can be mapped onto the other half through mirroring, i.e., literal inversion". In order to test this point, I take the Dorian mode (Example 2.5) as an example:[126]

Example 2.5. Literal inversion in Dorian mode.

In his *Serial Composition and Atonality*, Perle (1962: 9) explains that a pitch cell is a group of pitches that "may operate as a kind of microcosmic set of fixed intervallic content, either as a chord or as a melodic figure or as a combination of both", and that "replace the triad as the basic harmonic premise". Its components, however, are not fixed with regard to order in Bartók's works (e.g., *Bagatelle* No. 8) nor in the early free-atonal works of Schoenberg (e.g., Op. 11/1). (See also, my discussion on Bartók's new chromaticism in Chapter 2.1.4.)

On the non-symmetrical diatonic elements and non-diatonic symmetrical elements, Perle makes the following remark:

This intersecting of inherently non-symmetrical diatonic elements with inherently non-diatonic symmetrical elements seems to me the defining principle of the musical language of *Le Sacre* and the source of the unparalleled tension and conflicted energy of the work. (Perle 1990a: 83.)

Antokoletz (1984: xii) sets out to demonstrate that Bartók's music is based on "an all-encompassing system of pitch relations". In "Organic Development and the Interval Cycles in Bartók's *Three Studies*, Op. 18", Antokoletz (1995) points out that both the harmonic and melodic constructions in Bartók's music include every possible combination of intervallic relations: interval cycles based on the equalization of the twelve chromatic tones, octatonic, pentatonic, whole-tone, chromatic, and modal structures.

The new means of providing coherence in an idiom based on equalization of the semitones is primarily found in the intervallic pitch cell. Bartók's music is always tonally organized around a foundational pitch (or cell or collection) or directed towards a tonal goal. In this sense, tonal centricity is vital to Bartók's melodic, har-

126. Another good example of literal inversion is the Locrian diatonic scale: 1–2–2–1–2–2–1.

monic, and formal organization (a fuller explanation and corresponding discussion of this principle may be found in Chapter 2.1.3). However, Antokoletz (1984: 138) points out that even the term "tonal center" cannot describe the pitch organization in Bartók's music unambiguously, since it carries two meanings:

1. The establishment of a given pitch class as the primary tone of a traditional mode.
2. The establishment of a given sonic area by symmetrical organization of a conglomerate of pitches around an axis of symmetry.

In other words, a tonal center in Bartók's music can be either a tonal anchor or a tonal axis.

In my earlier discussions, in Chapters 2.1–2.2, attention was given to Bartók's pitch organization. The principle of pitch organization in his works is that of symmetrical structuring. Bartók's music has been the subject of a number of disparate analytic approaches, and there is, of course, a very wide area of overlap between these investigations. Due to Bartók's intense level of musical research and his artistry as a composer, his works are open to a variety of analytic approaches. There are several kinds of symmetry; e.g., mirror symmetry, parallel symmetry, replication, inversion, and multivalent symmetry. Such symmetry is not restricted to pitch, but extends to timbre, rhythm, dynamics, texture, and more. (Antokoletz 1997 [1988]; see also, Bárdos 1974: 85–98; and Solomon 1973.[127]) Says Perle:

> By the time of his *Fourth String Quartet*, inversional symmetry had become as fundamental premise of Bartók's harmonic language as it is of the twelve-tone music of Schoenberg, Berg, and Webern. Neither he nor they ever realized that this connection establishes a profound affinity between them in spite of the stylistic features that so obviously distinguish his music from theirs. [...] Nowhere does he [Bartók] recognize the commonality of his harmonic language with that of the twelve-tone composers that is implied in their shared premise of the harmonic equivalence of inversionally symmetrical pitch-class relations. (Perle 1990a: 46–47.)

In "Space and Symmetry in Bartók", Jonathan Bernard (1986) points out that symmetry is, after all, primarily a spatial phenomenon.[128] Bernard discusses ele-

---

127. In his dissertation, *Symmetry as Determinant of Musical Composition*, Larry Solomon (1973) provides a method of analysis based on principles of symmetry in works of several composers, including movements of Bartók's *Music for Strings, Percussion and Celesta*. Solomon gives a definition of symmetry, involving operations of reflection, rotation, and translation; he also develops a concept of *quadrates*, presents a detailed analysis of the work, and speculates on its psychological implications.

128. Bernard (1986) begins his article by discussing what he sees as the major shortcoming of set theory; that it does not deal with pitches in real space (actual placement on the staves) and that by approaching Bartók's music this way, one overlooks the spatial symmetries that are on the page (vertical and horizontal). Bernard mentions that many of Bartók's symmetrical forms were based upon absolute dimensions. Bartók even mentioned that particular registrations were crucial for

ments of symmetry in Bartók's music, and how they relate to spatial organization. At least four points in his definition of symmetry should be pointed out and further elucidated:

1. Mirror symmetry, in which pitches are organized about an axis.
2. Parallel symmetry, in which the intervals, which make up a chord read the same from the top down and from the bottom up.
3. Replication and inversion, which are similar to the first two types but which take into account the temporal element.
4. Multivalent symmetry, which considers musical criteria other than pitch: timbre, rhythm, dynamics, texture, etc.

Replication and inversion are better suited to describing order of events, in which a given configuration may be said to give rise to another (Bernard 1986: 188, 190). Bernard wishes to move beyond the single-axis conception of symmetry, remarking that:

> [...] multivalent symmetry will imply a compositional emphasis upon the procedures of symmetrical progression themselves rather than upon the axes *per se*. That is, more significance will be attributed to the fact that there are axes (hence, symmetries) than to the pitches that actually constitute these axes. This system therefore will not engage the pitch (or pitch-class) identity of the axes, either at particular moments or over time. (Bernard 1986: 192.)

In "Pitch-Set Derivations from the Folk Modes in Bartók's Music", Antokoletz (1982a) investigates the symmetry in Bartók's music, not at the formal level, but in terms of the use of symmetrical horizontal and vertical (or melodic and harmonic) structures. Antokoletz (1984: 51–137) points out that symmetrical pitch collections, which tend to negate those properties of traditional major and minor scales that establish a sense of tonality, have a fundamental function in many of Bartók's works: they serve to establish a sense of PC priority.

In traditional tonal music, composers worked according to a system in which the octave was divided into unequal parts. The fundamental division was derived from the perfect fifth, which served as the basis of harmonic root function and as the primary structural interval of major and minor triads. In turn, the perfect fifth of the triad was unequally divided into major and minor thirds. Antokoletz asserts that:

> Pitch relations in Bartók's music are primarily based on the principle of *equal subdivision* of the octave into the total complex of interval cycles. The funda-

---

the desired effect. The author presents brief analyses of the *Piano Concerto* No. 1 and the *Sonata for Two Pianos and Percussion*. The *Piano Concerto* No. 1 was premiered in Frankfurt in 1927, conducted by Wilhelm Furtwängler (1886–1954), with Bartók playing the piano solo. Bernard's analyses demonstrate the principles of multivalent symmetry. Bernard concludes by saying that, while certainly not applicable to all of Bartók's music, multivalent symmetry is certainly a force to be reckoned with, especially in the piano works and in pieces with slow tempos.

mental concept underlying this equal-division system is that of *symmetry*.[129] The function and interaction of symmetrical pitch collections are significant both in the generation of the interval cycles in a given composition and in the establishment of central tonal or sonic areas. [...] All of these fundamental principles are related to a larger system that has been referred to by George Perle as "twelve-tone tonality". (Antokoletz 1984: xii.)

The same has also been noted by theorists such as Milton Babbitt (1949), Leo Treitler (1959), and George Perle (1955; 1962: 37–59; 1977[130]; and 1996 [1977]). Using principles determined by those theorists, Antokoletz (1984: 69–72; and 1995) isolates three four-note intervallic cells: the X cell, Y cell, and Z cell[131] (see Example 2.6 and Figures 2.32–2.34, below). Many would call them PC-sets, but it seems to me that a clear distinction between the two must be made if confusion is to be avoided. The Z nomenclature is not to be confused with that in the theoretical writings and apposite terminology of Forte's PC-set theory.[132]

Example 2.6. X cell, Y cell, and Z cell.

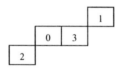

Figure 2.32. Set {0,1,2,3}.

---

129. Antokoletz's italics.
130. In "Berg's Master Array of the Interval Cycles", Perle (1977) includes a brief discussion of inversional symmetry as the basis of Bartók's use of interval cycles in his *Fourth String Quartet* and states that this principle can be traced back to as early as the second of Bartók's *Fourteen Bagatelles* (1998 [1908]). Perle demonstrates some basic properties of three cyclically derived symmetrical cells in the quartet.
131. Lendvai (1971: 51) calls the Z cell as "1:5 model".
132. Forte (1973) employs the ICVs to define an additional set relation. Two sets that share the same ICV are said to be Z-related, and the relation between them is known as a Z-relation. The representation is based on a simple extension of the system devised by Forte. Fortean set names consist of two numbers separated by a dash, with an optional up-case letter Z preceding the second number. The number following the dash simply distinguishes different PC-sets having the same cardinality. The letter Z is used to indicate that the set shares the same interval class content as some other set, Z-related sets. For example, set {0,1,4,6} (Forte number 4–Z15; ICV 111111), and set {0,1,3,7} (Forte number 4–Z29; ICV 111111) are said to be Z-related since they both exhibit the same IC content. (Ibid.: 21–22, 79.) Z-relation, or rather, "that certain pitch-class collections share the same 'interval vector' even though they are neither transpositionally nor inversionally equivalent," as pointed out by Howard Hanson (1960: 22) in his *Harmonic Materials of Modern Music*.

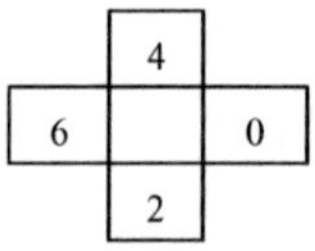

Figure 2.33. Set {0,2,4,6}.

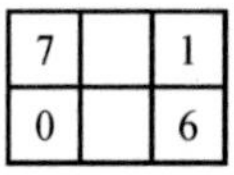

7		1
0		6

Figure 2.34. Set {0,1,6,7}.

According to Antokoletz (1977), those cells (see Example 2.6 and Figures 2.32–2.34) generate and frame the total pitch content of a Bartók work. Table 2.9 shows the symmetrical tetrachords of the X cell, Y cell, and Z cell in root formations.

Cell	Pitch classes	Point 0	Set	Forte number	ICV
X cell	C–C-sharp–D–E-flat	C	{0,1,2,3}	4–1	321000
Y cell	C–D–E–F-sharp	C	{0,2,4,6}	4–21 (12)	030201
Z cell	C–C-sharp–F-sharp–G	C	{0,1,6,7}	4–9 (6)	200022

Table 2.9. Cells: PC content, set type, Forte numbers and ICVs.

Each cycle is a series of pitches generated from the repetitions of one interval. The cycles are labeled by integer notation, measured in semitones. Cycles built from the minor second, the major second, the minor third, the major third, and the tritone, subdivide the octave without exhausting the twelve-tone chromatic collection. A symmetrical four-note cell contains two dyads such that each member of a dyad can be paired with a member of the other dyad to form two intervals with equal sums (Antokoletz 1984: 69, 75). This pair of sums is called the "sum couple" by Antokoletz (ibid.: 70).

While sets of three or more elements are clearly important in the structure of Bartók's *Bluebeard*, it is generally pairs of pitches (dyads) that first catch our attention, because they are involved in motivic recurrences throughout the opera. Most often, these pairs are related by a semitone. Certainly, the most conspicuous, or salient, chromatic dyad is the Blood motif, heard for the first time in (0)/16 (see Example 4.1, p. 204, Chapter 4.4.1). This dyad appears to take priority as the fundamental sonority of *Duke Bluebeard's Castle* (see, e.g., 11/1–3, 33/6–34/4, 45/1–5, 77/12–78/2, 112/5–113/8, etc.).

In "Harmonic Procedure in the *Fourth Quartet* of Béla Bartók", Treitler (1959) coined the term Z cell as an extension of Perle work. Treitler provides observations about the ways in which the music hovers around specific pitch-areas, and about the relationships that are imposed upon the pitch-groups that assume this central role. Treitler's study deals with the dual approach to harmonic organization in the *Fourth*

String Quartet, including traditional tonal concepts and new concepts of pitch-set relations. Treitler introduces a new Z cell, as a follow-up to Perle's (1955) X cell and Y cell in the *Fourth String Quartet*. Basically, a Z cell is a pitch collection of the doubly symmetrical PCs. Treitler points out that Bartók often uses the Z cell as a fifth (e.g., C–G), setting up two tendency tones that push outward to it by half step (e.g., D-flat–F-sharp). The Z cell in its various transpositions (Tn) receives the most attention, because of its content and symmetrical flexibility. This flexibility is the result of its dual axes of symmetry. Scholars are divided on whether Z cells are fundamentally important to Bartók in their own right, or whether they are by-products of other processes (see, e.g., Kárpáti 2004: 195–198). In any case, Z cells appear in a large number of Bartók works, often in significant places[133] (Treitler 1959).[134]

Antokoletz (1984: 51–137) states that the cell structures undermine those properties of traditional major and minor scales that establish a sense of tonality. Their axes of symmetry can act as replacements for tonal centers, and movement between them can function in a way analogous to modulation. According to Antokoletz (ibid.: 69–76, 138–203), the concept of tonal center in Bartók's music has two general meanings:

1. The establishment of a given PC as the primary tone of a traditional mode; here the term is a misnomer.
2. The establishment of a given sonic area by symmetrical organization of a conglomerate of pitches around an axis of symmetry.

In his review of Antokoletz's *The Music of Béla Bartók: A Study of Tonality and Progression in Twentieth-Century Music*, Paul Wilson (1986) suggests that Antokoletz's (1984) approach seems to lead the analyst past the individual musical structures of specific works, in search of a pre-compositional system of pitch organization that is too abstract to illuminate those individual structures. Wilson's response is to propose a hierarchical theory of pitch organization more concerned with the works as heard experiences. Wilson is skeptical concerning the possibility of a single general theory capable of fitting all of Bartók's music.

For analyzing Bartók's music, Wilson's (1984; and 1993) point of departure differs from that of Antokoletz. Like Cohn (1988; and 1991), Wilson begins with Forte's set theory. Wilson (1982) attempts to present a clear picture of Bartók's music, through several compelling analyses of deeper pitch structure, and presenting various theoretical perspectives on Bartók's music, including those of Ernő Lendvai,

---

133. As early as the *Second String Quartet* the Z cell played a significant role in establishing axes of symmetry on the background level of the work. According to Perle (1955: 306–307), symmetrical formations on the local level of each movement do not revolve, as they do in the *Fourth String Quartet* and the *Fifth String Quartet*, around stable axes that function as tonal centers, but are freely employed around constantly shifting axes of symmetry. On the local level, a sense of tonality is established by assertion of certain elements of the traditional modes. Perle does not discuss sums of complementation, a principle that is essential in understanding the special symmetrical properties of pairs of related Z cells.

134. I am indebted to Professor Leo Treitler for a private communication on his concept.

Elliott Antokoletz, Joseph N. Straus, and Roy Travis. From those Wilson develops a significant theory of his own. In Wilson's theory (1982; 1992; and 1993), the points of arrival and departure, the tonics and dominants of tonal music, are not fixed before the event by abstract models, but are dynamically assigned according to their musical context. Roiha also endorses that idea:

> The boundary zones of a shape are naturally of importance, [...] the first and last tones (time-extreme) and highest and lowest tones (pitch-extreme). [...] The tone that represents the point of rest is called final or melodic tonic, and, on the other hand, the tone, which is the most important one from the standpoint of tension, is called the melodic dominant. The relation of tonic and dominant is naturally very often that of a fifth, but it can be just as well that of a second, a third, etc. The melody tends in general to end in a point of rest, i.e., in a melodic tonic. This is in general a low tone, with which the feeling of finality is more closely associated than with a high one. One of the most important factors affecting tonality is a repeating tone. This is very often the dominant. A repeating tone has in a certain sense the [same function as] our (harmonic) tonic [has in] maintaining tonal unity; the repetition of a certain group of tones serves the same purpose. The other final points, [along with] the last one, [are] naturally also notable. (Roiha 1956: 41–42.)

According to Wilson (1982; and 1992), certain pitch collections appear consistently in Bartók's works, such as the whole-tone scale, the pentatonic scale, and the *Heptatonia seconda*, or second seven-note (*második hétfokúság*) system, set {0,1,3,4,6,8,10} (see Figure 2.35, below). Those pitch collections parallel the diatonic seven-note modes, and seem to stem more obviously from Bartók's studies of ethnic music rather than from the application of serial processes. (See also, Bárdos 1974: 30–34, 135.)

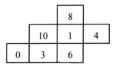

Figure 2.35. Set {0,1,3,4,6,8,10}.

In *Bluebeard's Castle*, at the end of the "First Door" scene (30/1–42/4), Bluebeard's lines unfold along another extended chain of thirds, this time based on C-sharp. The last pitch, C-sharp, coincides with the sustained C-sharp in the bass: the end has been reached. The atonal pizzicato chords act as a musical symbol for Judith's overcoming of the horror inspired by the torture chamber. In this context, the atonal chords develop a new role as ornamental flourishes over the stable open fifths projected in the orchestra. The chain of thirds in the harmony at the end of the "First Door" scene (41/1–42/3) can be reduced as follows: C-sharp–E–G-sharp–B, and B–D-sharp–F-sharp–A-sharp, forming the *Heptatonia seconda*, or second seven-note system. (A detailed analysis of the "First Door" scene may be found in Chapter 4.4.4.)

In his dissertation, *Atonality and Structure in Works of Béla Bartók's Middle Period*, Wilson (1982) argues that, although Bartók is generally regarded as a composer separate from the second Viennese school, it is important to note that he was aware of that school and its music. Wilson points out that Bartók adopted some form of atonal compositional strategies in his middle period, from 1917 to 1922. Wilson investigates ways in which Bartók's atonal configurations can give hierarchical structure to his music, and looks at the interaction of Bartók's atonality with pitch centricity and traditional tonality. The focus of Wilson's analyses is on the way in which Bartók creates music, which has characteristics of both the tonal and atonal universes and can function equally well in each.

In the years 1918–1920, Bartók embarked on what Gillies (2001: 796) calls "his most radical, Expressionist phase, during which he believed he was approaching some kind of atonal goal". In "Approaching Atonality: *Studies* and *Improvisations*", Wilson (1993: 162) points out that the products of this period – *The Miraculous Mandarin* (Op. 19, 1918–1919) and the *First* and *Second Violin Sonatas* (1921 and 1922) – "employ a harmonic language, which greatly modifies and often abandons the modal and polymodal basis of Bartók's previous and subsequent works". In the *First* and *Second Violin Sonatas*, Bartók came closer than in any of his other works to a kind of atonal chromaticism and harmonic serialization typical of the expressionistic works of the Schoenberg School. The *Violin Sonatas* stand out as bold experiments and are clearly the product of the most intense concentration. At about the same time, Schoenberg was producing his first completely serial twelve-tone works.

Some scholars have argued – with less clarity than one would wish – that Bartók's music sometimes mirrors or alludes to the investigations of Schoenberg and his disciplines (Stevens 1964; Babbitt 1949; Forte 1955; 1960; 1973: 24; and 1993; Parks 1981; Wilson 1982; 1992; and 1993; Agawu 1984; and Cohn 1988; and 1991). As Wilson (1992: 20) states, "There are select moments that reveal these [Schoenbergian] types of procedures, but overall his [Bartók's] music rarely displays the consistent vocabulary that would prove a set theory approach to be worthwhile."

After a period of experimentation with abstract, atonal chromaticism in works such as *Miraculous Mandarin*, *Three Studies,* and the *Violin Sonatas*, Bartók concentrated on modality as a primary means of organizing pitch structures. In his mature works, he assimilated his knowledge of non-diatonic folk modes into his music. Antokoletz (1984: 205–206) points out that, while interactions of diatonic, whole-tone and octatonic scale are common to many of Bartók's works, it was the *Cantata Profana: A kilenc csodaszarvas* (*Cantata Profana: The Nine Enchanted Stags*) for tenor, baritone, double chorus and orchestra (Sz 94, BB 100, 1930)[135] that was most successful in integrating non-diatonic scales into Western art music. Kárpáti (1969a:

---

135. On November 9, 1936, the Hungarian premier of the *Cantata Profana* was performed by the Orchestra of the Budapest Philharmonic Society, conducted by Dohnányi. The tenor solo was sung by Endre Rösler (1904–1963) and the baritone solo by Imre Palló (1891–1978). (Kárpáti 1969a: 10.)

10) remarks that the most prominent scale used in the *Cantata Profana* is the Romanian folk mode, better known as the acoustic (overtone) scale. This scale, characterized by its augmented fourth and flattened seventh, had its debut as early as Bartók's second piece of the *Két román tánc* (*Two Romanian Dances*) for piano (Op. 8a, Sz 43, BB 56, 1909–1910). (On the *Two Romanian Dances*, see also, Lindlar 1984: 36–40, 122; and Demény 1946: 12–13.)

In "The Music of Bartók: Some Theoretical Approaches in the USA", Antokoletz (1982b[136]) observes that, unlike the harmonic idiom of twelve-tone language, the concept of a set or series in Bartók's music is fundamentally different from that of Schoenberg's twelve-tone system, and any attempt at a direct comparison of the two seems futile. To call attention to the fact that serialism is excluded from discussion, it has become customary to refer to "free" twelve-note music. (See also, Antokoletz 1995: 249; and Perle 1990a; and 1996 [1977].)

2.4. Pitch-web analysis

In this chapter, Aarre Joutsenvirta's[137] (1989) "pitch-web" analytic method is discussed. The main analytical concepts of the method are defined and examined, then linked to PC-set structures in a systematic way. Several terms are introduced to facilitate the application of pitch-web analysis to descriptions of pitch-class relations, so as to show characteristic intervallic relationships of given pitch formations. Because pitch-web analysis is based on concepts of set theory, particularly that of Forte (1973), the latter will be explained first. It should be emphasized, however, that to combine Forte's and Joutsenvirta's concepts into a single analytic method cannot be done without many compromises. Nevertheless, the methods share enough theoretical premises (e.g., octave equivalence[138], integer notation) to make them suitable for my analysis of *Bluebeard's Castle*.

136. Antokoletz (1982b) discusses the concepts of such theorists as Roy Travis (Schenkerian), Allen Forte (serial scheme), Tibor and Peter Bachmann and Hilda Gervers (as followers of Lendvai's Golden Section and Fibonacci principles), Perle (concepts of the interval cycle and inversional symmetry), and Antokoletz (transformation of the folk modes to the system of the interval cycles and inversional symmetry). Antokoletz explores these varied approaches by moving from the more traditional concepts to those that can only belong to the present century. This high degree of individuality and divergence among theorists, which is particularly prominent in the United States, may partly be due to the versatility and complexity of Bartók's musical language.

137. Joutsenvirta teaches music theory at the Sibelius Academy in Helsinki, where he now chairs the department of composition and music theory. Since 1986, Joutsenvirta has been developing pitch-web analysis for pedagogical and practical compositional purposes. Theories of pitch space go back at least as far as the ancient Greek "Harmonists". Bacchius poses the question (quoted in Franklin 2002: 669): "And what is a diagram? A representation of a musical system. And we use a diagram so that, for students of the subject, matters which are hard to grasp with the hearing may appear before their eyes." The "Harmonists" drew geometrical pictures so that the intervals of various scales could be compared visually, thereby locating intervals spatially.

138. Forte (1973) assumes two additional types of equivalence related to collections: transpositional and inversional. By transposition, any sonority (or PC-set) can be transposed to another pitch level and retain its identity. The operation of addition, in Modulo 12 pitch space, produces transposition. Inversional equivalence is the most problematic of all of the equivalence assump-

Set theory[139] has become the dominant paradigm for analyzing certain music, particularly the atonal works of the Second Viennese School (e.g., see Babbitt 1949;[140] Forte 1955;[141] 1960;[142] 1973;[143] and 1993;[144] Wittlich 1969;[145] Parks 1981; Wilson 1982; and 1992; Agawu 1984; Cohn 1988; and 1991; and Straus 2000: 65–70, 114, 121–122, 129–131, 139–143[146]). Yet set theory alone, as will be shown, might not be the ideal means of exploring processes that are intended to be conceived, especially by the composer, as essentially tonal.

The concepts of pitch class (PC), PC-set, and others were introduced in the landmark works of the composer-theoretician Milton Babbitt (e.g., 1949; 2003 [1961]; and 2003 [1960]).[147] Babbitt's strongest influence derives from his mathematical formalization of pitch and interval relationships possible within the twelve-note system, for which he draws on a pure number-theory that models ordering and invariance relationships within the Modulo 12 (Mod 12) arithmetical system[148]. I do not attempt here a summary of the many critiques, descendants, and variations of Babbitt's system. Put generally, however, set theory may be divided into two, interrelated categories:

---

tions made so far. If the collection is flipped upside down, it retains the same interval content as before; however, the result may sound somewhat different. For example, when a major triad is inverted, it becomes a minor triad. So, in cases of inversional equivalence, the equivalence can be assumed for the purposes of identifying PC-sets, but it may often be more intuitive and useful to distinguish between a sonority and its inversion.

139. Perhaps set theory, in its rigorous and formalized mathematics, marks the most profound demarcation of differences between the American and European musicological traditions.

140. Babbitt's (1949) article, "The *String Quartets* of Bartók," is the first serious discussion of long-range structural connections in those works. According to Babbitt, the themes of each quartet are developed through the restatement and recombination of basic pitch cells.

141. Forte's (1955) article, "Béla Bartók: Number VIII from *Fourteen Bagatelles*, Op. 6," offers a detailed, Schenkerian-based analysis of various musical levels (background, middleground, foreground) and voice-leading techniques, going on to relate the *Bagatelles* (1998 [1908]) with Stravinsky's *Petrushka* (1910–1911) and Schoenberg's *Drei Klavierstücke* (1911).

142. In "Bartók's Serial Composition", Forte (1960) attempts to show the tonal centricity in the third movement of the *Fourth String Quartet*. He argues that the diatonic hexachord C–D–E–F–A, set {0,2,4,5,7,9} (C = 0) provides that center, acting as a cantus firmus that permeates the entire texture.

143. Forte (1973: 24) takes his example from the last movement of Bartók's *Suite* for piano (Op. 14, Sz 62, BB 70, 1916). He investigates the pitch set {0,1,4,5,8} and the importance of the Z-related sets {0,1,4,5,7} and {0,1,2,5,8} in structuring the work.

144. Forte (1993) has contributed to the relatively scarce stock of rhythmic analyses of the *Fourteen Bagatelles* (1998 [1908]).

145. In his dissertation, *An Examination of Some Set-Theoretic Applications in the Analysis of Non-Serial Music*, Gary Wittlich (1969) includes a detailed analysis of Bartók's *Mikrokosmos*, Nos. 91 and 109.

146. The aural perception of various set-theoretical concepts has received considerable attention; see, e.g., Rahn (1980); Morris (1987); Mitchell (1987); and Straus (2000).

147. In this work, Babbitt is mainly concerned with explaining ordered (serialized) twelve-tone rows.

148. Modular arithmetic (the "arithmetic of congruencies") was introduced by the German mathematician Carl Friedrich Gauss (1777–1855) in his *Disquisitiones arithmeticae* (*Discourses on Arithmetic*) (1965 [1801]).

1. Linear set theory deals sets according to their temporal ordering (Babbitt is the primary authority in this area).
2. Non-linear set theory deals with PC-sets in a manner in which temporal order is not relevant. It is essentially a generalization of the principles of traditional harmony to include post-tonal harmony (Forte is the primary authority in this area).

For present purposes, the second of those approaches – non-linear analytic methods – are the most pertinent ones, particularly those of Joutsenvirta and Forte.

Though adumbrated by Babbitt, the means of identifying the structural building blocks of atonal music were elaborated most fully by Forte, whose *The Structure of Atonal Music* (1973) was the first theoretical exposition to offer a systematic study of non-serialized, non-twelve-tone PC-sets. Forte's set theory provides a comprehensive terminology and method of classifying PC-sets, as well as the underlying principles, or deep structures that govern the pitch content of all possible PC combinations. (See also, Bent 1987 [1980]: 366–369; and Dunsby & Whittall 1988: 105–207.)

Forte's (1973) theory is both descriptive and prescriptive. It provides us with a means for describing the surface of atonal music, and suggests that the given description be used to explain what we hear (and should hear) on the musical surface if we are to obtain the experience of musical order. Forte's intention is "to provide a general theoretical framework, with reference to which the processes underlying atonal music may be systematically described" (ibid.: ix). His set theory[149] has inspired much fruitful and wide-ranging debate; thus, there is no need, here, to add to the body of critical evaluations of Forte's theories, the strengths and weaknesses of which are already well-known. Rather, I next address the underlying axioms of PC-set theory and some of its corollary concepts.

It is necessary to have a standardized way of ordering the pitches of a pitch collection, so that they may be referred to conveniently. The fundamental collective category is the pitch-class (PC) set, understood as an unordered set of pitch classes. The notion of "pitch class" – a pitch name, regardless of how many times it is repeated, its registral position, and/or enharmonic counterparts – is based on the axiom of octave equivalence, which reduces the possible number of pitch classes from at least 21 (or more, counting double-sharps and double-flats) to only 12 (see Table 2.10, next page). Equivalent does not mean identical, but rather conceptually equal for the purpose of analysis. Such equivalence is based on the unique property of intervals (Wilcox 1992[150]). In a PC collection, or set, matters of registral position-

---

149. Although musical set theory may be considered an application of mathematical set theory to music, there is often little coincidence between the terminology and sometimes even the methods of the two; both theories make use of sets, but in mathematical theory a set is always an unordered collection of things (Straus 2000: 7–9).

150. In "Generating Fibonacci Sequences of Pitch Classes", Howard Wilcox (1992) points out that repeated PCs have great significance in Fibonacci pitch sets; moreover, any deviation from the ordered sets would distort the Fibonacci relationship between linear adjacencies.

ing and compound intervals (those beyond the octave) are not relevant.[151] Like set theory, Joutsenvirta's pitch-web analysis uses integer notation (1989: 4), with which PCs are simply numbered from 0 to 11, as shown in Table 2.10.

Pitch classes	Integer notation
B-sharp, C, D-double-flat	0
C-sharp, D-flat	1
C-double-sharp, D, E-double-flat	2
D-sharp, E-flat	3
D-double-sharp, E, F-flat	4
E-sharp, F, G-double-flat	5
F-sharp, G-flat	6
F-double-sharp, G, A-double-flat	7
G-sharp, A-flat	8
G-double-sharp, A, B-double-flat	9
A-sharp, B-flat	10
A-double-sharp, B, C-flat	11

Table 2.10. Pitch classes and integer notation.[152]

In the equally tempered, twelve tone (chromatic) collection, any two pitches that sound the same or are only different due to octave displacement are said to belong to the same pitch class. For example, C0, C1, C2, C3, C4...; and B-sharp 4, B-sharp 5...; and D-double-flat 5..., etc., all belong to the same class of pitches: pitch class (PC) C. Integer notation facilitates systematizing the fundamental distinction between pitch and PC; and between interval and interval class (IC), the latter designation, discussed further below, referring both to an interval and its inversion as measured in semitones (e.g., minor third/major sixth = IC 3/9). In the following discussions and analyses, integer notation is used to designate pitch classes; and intervals of PC-sets are measured in semitones.

Before consideration of the pitch-web square, a discussion of Modulo 12 arithmetic is necessary, because of its close relation to Joutsenvirta's model (see Table 1.1, p. 3, Chapter 1). In the Mod 12 system, the numbers are arranged horizontally and vertically, as on a "clock face" such as the one shown in Figure 2.36 (see p. 83).

Mod 12 arithmetic shows the prime form, or "set class" (SC), of any PC-set with zero as the lowest member.[153] More explicitly, the ascending interval from PC

---

151. Marcus Castrén (1997) has suggested a partial separation of IC components, which he calls "registrally-ordered intervals". Under this scheme, the two components of each interval class are still paired, but maintain separate identities according to their functional differences in specific musical contexts. See also, Castrén & Laurson (1989).

152. The numbers 10 and 11 are often represented with letters A and B, respectively, so that they are not confused with a 1 followed by a 0, or two 1s in succession.

153. The primary aim of PC-set analysis is to produce a list of intersecting sets that emerge as especially significant – structurally, if not aurally – by virtue of containing the largest number of intersections, i.e., features held in common (Forte 1973: 3, 5, 11–13; and Cook 1987: 134; see also, the Appendix to this study).

4 to PC 11 is 4+7 = 11:7 semitones. The descending interval is 4–5 (= – 1) = 11:5 semitones. Any addition or subtraction that exceeds the modulo operator 12, or goes below 0, must take into account that, on the "clock face", 12 = 0 (see Figure 2.36, next page). The tritone is made up of two notes directly opposite each other, e.g., C = 0 and F-sharp = 6, since they divide the octave into equal halves. The notes directly across from each other make up a symmetrical chord: the doubly (fully) diminished seventh (e.g., C = 0, D-sharp = 3, F-sharp = 6, A = 9); the augmented triad C = 0, E = 4, G-sharp = 8 is symmetrical as well. (Joutsenvirta 1989: 5.) Joutsenvirta's pitch-web analysis does not presuppose tonal contexts; hence, enharmonically paired intervals are considered equivalent, and how they would traditionally "resolve" becomes irrelevant.

Without a fixed modulo, a pitch sequence would ascend or descend infinitely, quickly extending beyond the range of human hearing (Wilcox 1992). In Mod 12 arithmetic, however, the Fibonacci proportion is obscured; but the Fibonacci property – that each succeeding PC is the sum of the two previous PCs – is preserved even as it passes through the Mod 12 prism. Reducing the pitches to PCs creates a recurring sequence, beginning on number 24. Note that the same linear ordering of PCs would occur in actual Fibonacci spacing.[154]

The PC-set is an unordered set of PCs. Pitches are separated from one another by intervals, but PCs are separated from one another by ICs (mentioned above). Just as PCs 2 and 4 could be D and E in any and every octave position, so the IC 2, which separates 2 and 4, can be inverted and compounded to generate the minor seventh, major ninth, and all larger spans of actual music. The concept of octave equivalence underlies the familiar notion of interval inversion (and by extension, chord inversions). In tonal music theory, the perfect fourth and perfect fifth are said to be inverses of each other, as are the minor third and major sixth, the major second and minor seventh, etc. The same principle holds in PC-set theory; e.g., intervals of 7 and 5 semitones = IC 5/7, and so on (Forte 1973: 2, 5, 14). Table 2.11 summarizes the seven interval classes (ICs), each named after the smaller of its two PC intervals.

PC intervals	0/12	1/11	2/10	3/9	4/8	5/7	6/6
Interval classes	0	1	2	3	4	5	6

Table 2.11. Pitch-class intervals and interval classes.

To round off our overview of PC-set theory, the term "pitch space" should be mentioned. In musicological literature, it refers to all pitch relations (e.g., proximity), and is usually represented by geometric models, most often multidimensional

---

154. Unfortunately, little accurate research has been done regarding the relation of the Fibonacci series to pitch relations in music.

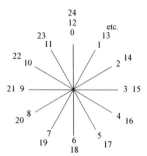

Figure 2.36. Closed Modulo 12 (Mod 12) system.

ones.[155] There are generally two dimensions, that of pitch class and that of register (i.e., the specific pitch, or frequency in Hz); but theoretically, there may be any number of them (Lerdahl 1992).

Now let us turn to Joutsenvirta's "web", the aim of which is to establish a new way to analyze music through graphic notation. As mentioned in Chapter 1, the two-dimensional pitch-web square is an abstract, visual tool for exploring intervals, chords, scales, rows, etc, giving a clear, simple, and easily comparable feature to the musical structures (see Table 1.1, p. 3, Chapter 1). Joutsenvirta limits the usage of the web to Western twelve-tone equal temperament (12-TET).[156] Simply put, the pitch web serves as a visual tool by which to conceptualize the total content of pitch space: PC-sets as integers, intervals, chords, scales, rows, etc. Such visualizations are illustrated in Figures 2.37–2.40.[157]

Figure 2.37. Set {0,4,7}.

155. The circle of fifths is one representation of pitch space, first proposed geometrically by Heinichen (1967 [1728]). In 1855, Moritz Drobisch (1802–1896) was the first to suggest a helix to represent octave equivalency and reoccurrence. These and other topics are outlined in Lerdahl (1992; and 2001: 42–43). The psychologist Roger N. Shepard (1962) played a pivotal role in drawing attention to the highly regular structure of mental representations, which he depicted as multidimensional, "representational spaces". All of his inferred mental representations have subsequently been validated (Shepard 1982; and Shepard, Kilpatrick & Cunningham 1975). Michael Tenzer (2000) suggests the use of a melodic map to represent Balinese gamelan music, since the octaves are not equivalent, as in most tonal music. In 1739, the use of a lattice was first proposed by the Swiss mathematician and physicist Leonhard Euler (1707–1783), to model just intonation using an axis of perfect fifths and another of major thirds (Lerdahl 2001: 42–43). James Tenney (1993 [1983]) has also argued in favor of multidimensional lattices, especially for just-intonation systems. Other systems of representation have been proposed by Mathieu (1997), Helmholtz (1821–1894), Oettingen (1836–1920), and others; see also, Lerdahl & Jackendoff (1983); Vogel (1966); and Deutsch & Feroe (1981).

156. Other equal temperaments do exist; some music has been written in 19-TET and 31-TET, for example; and Arab music is based on a 24-tone equal temperament.

157. On the pitch-web square, Joutsenvirta (1989: 8) remarks that the fundamental note cannot always be placed to the bottom line. This issue addressed in more detail, below.

Figure 2.38. Set {2,6,9}.

6	9
2	

Figure 2.39. Set {0,2,4,6,9}.

Figure 2.40. Set {0,2,4,6,8,9,11}.

In Joutsenvirta's system, the integers are placed horizontally and vertically, systematically arranged according to intervallic sequences (Table 1.1, p. 3, Chapter 1). As a starting point, one of the practical methods for demonstrating this model is the Cartesian coordinate system.[158] Cartesian coordinates are rectilinear, two-dimensional or three-dimensional coordinates (and therefore a special case of curvilinear coordinates), which are also called rectangular coordinates. The two dimensional rectangular coordinate-system is commonly defined by two axes. The three-dimensional Cartesian system conventionally denotes linear measurement (x axis: horizontal; y axis: vertical) and adds those a third dimension: the z axis (that of spatial measurement). The axes are commonly defined as mutually orthogonal to each other.[159]

In Joutsenvirta's model, the basic "grammatical" rules are as follows:

1. The x axis refers to a chain of minor thirds (three semitones).
2. The y axis refers to the vertical height of the circle of fifths or fourths, mapped out of the chromatic scale by multiplication (M).
3. The 3 x 4 chroma-square is repeated 12 times.

---

158. See René Descartes's (1596–1650) *Discours de la méthode pour bien conduire sa raison, et chercher la verité dans les sciences*. In part two of that study, Descartes (2000 [1637]) introduces the new idea of specifying the position of a point or object on a surface, using two intersecting axes as measuring guides. In *La géométrie* (1954 [1637]), Descartes further explores the above-mentioned concepts. Many other coordinate systems have been developed since that of Descartes. In different branches of mathematics coordinate systems can be transformed, translated, rotated, and re-defined altogether, in order to simplify calculations and to reach specialized goals.
159. The choice of letters is by convention, first part of the alphabet being used to designate known values.

Technically speaking, the horizontal x axis is obtained from doubly-diminished seventh chords. Basically, each vertical line contains a thrice repeated sequence of {0,3,6,9}, {2,5,8,11}, and {1,4,7,10}. Their further arrangement is determined by multiplication.

On the y axis, the circle of fifths (IC 7) or fourths (IC 5) is mapped from the chromatic scale by multiplication, and *vice versa* (see Table 1.1, p. 3, Chapter 1).[160] In equal temperament, twelve successive fifths equate to exactly seven octaves; after that, repetition of pitch classes begins, and the circle closes back "into" itself, as does any sequence of equal intervals. Abstractly, this circle is a cyclic group of order 12, and may be identified as residual classes of Mod 12.

To demonstrate: Joutsenvirta's basic procedure is to begin with an ordered "12-tuple" (chromatic 12-tone row) of integers {0,1,2,3,4,5,6,7,8,9,10,11}. Next, the 12-tuple is multiplied by 5: {0,5,10,15,20,25,30,35,40,45,50,55}. Then a modulo 12 reduction is applied to each of the numbers; i.e., 12 is subtracted from each number as many times as necessary until the given number becomes smaller than 12: {0,5,10,3,8,1,6,11,4,9,2,7}. Those integers are equivalent to pitch classes C–F–Bb–Eb–Ab–Db–Gb–Cb–Fb–Bbb–Ebb–Abb, which comprise the circle of fifths. Now, if the entire 12-tuple is multiplied by 7, we get {0,7,14,21,28,35,42,49,56,63,70,77}. After modulo 12 reduction, the result is {0,7,2,9,4,11,6,1,8,3,10,5}. Those integers are equivalent to pitch classes C–G–D–A–E–B–F#–C#–G#–D#–A#–E#, which also comprises the circle of fifths.

The doubly diminished seventh chain, when combined with a fourth (IC 5) and fifth (IC 7) sequence results in the "3 x 4 chroma-square", shown in Figure 2.41 as it appears in web-square form.

0	3	6	9
5	8	11	2
10	1	4	7

Figure 2.41. The 3 x 4 chroma-square.

Joutsenvirta emphasizes that the coherence of the system allows for theoretically infinite possibilities in both directions, but for practical purposes, limits his web model to 12 x 3 x 4 chroma-squares, as represented on the 12 x 12 pitch-web square (1989: 6, 13, 95; see also, Table 1.1, p. 3, Chapter 1).

One of my theses is that the unordered trichord, set class {0,1,4}, supplanted the tonal system in Bartók's opera. The set-classes (SCs) are represented by a prime-form PC-set. For example, set {0,1,4} = {3,4,7} (transposed); {8,11,0} (inverted); {5,8,9} (transposed and inverted); and {8,9,0} (transposed). All of those belong to the prime form {0,1,4}. A group of similar PC-sets like these is called a set class. (Example 2.7 and Figures 2.42–2.46.)

---

160. These are inverses of each other: PC intervals 5/7 and 7/5 both belong to IC 5.

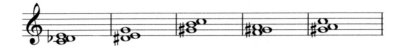

Example 2.7. Set {0,1,4} (original), set {3,4,7} (transposed), set {8,11,0} (inverted), set {5,8,9} (transposed and inverted), and set {8,9,0} (transposed).

Figure 2.42. Set {0,1,4}.

Figure 2.43. Set {3,4,7}.

Figure 2.44. Set {8,11,0}.

Figure 2.45. Set {5,8,9}.

Figure 2.46. Set {8,9,0}.

Since reordering and transposing never affects the relations described, those operations may be performed whenever convenient. The pitch-class collection D–G–B-flat, for instance, is known as set {2,7,10}. The normal order of a PC-set is its most compact representation – the set rearranged and/or reduced to within the octave as needed; that is, multiples of 12 may always be added or subtracted arbitrarily to any element of the set, to keep it within the span of semitones 0–11, such that the intervallic distance between the two extremes is as small as possible. If there is more than one possibility, the set must be rearranged again, such that it begins with the smallest interval possible (or second lowest, third lowest, etc.). The "best normal order" is either the normal order of a given set, or the normal order of its inversion:

whichever gives the most compact representation. For set {2,7,10}, the normal order is {7,10,2}; the normal order of the inversion is {10,2,7}; the best normal order is {7,10,2}. The prime form is the best normal order transposed to start with zero, in order to classify it lexically, in something like dictionary format; for example, the prime form of set {2,7,10} is {0,3,7}, as illustrated in Figure 2.47. (Forte 1973: 3, 5, 11–13, 179–181.)

Figure 2.47. Set {0,3,7}.

In set theory, the intuitive notion of a set leads to paradoxes. There is considerable mathematical disagreement on how best to refine the intuitive notion. In a set, the order of members is irrelevant, and the repetition of members is not meaningful. The inclusion may be literal: every PC of X is also a member of Y, or *vice versa*; but most often, the smaller set may be included in the larger only if one of them first is transposed (Forte 1973: 211; see also, pp. 4–5, Chapter 1). The operation of transposition, common to both tonal and atonal music, is in set theory called "inclusion under transposition". (Even literal inclusion may be described as inclusion under transposition, only that the transposition is made by zero semitones.) The relation of inclusion between two sets also includes inversion ("inclusion under inversion"), such that an ascending interval is replaced with a descending one of the same size, or *vice versa* (ibid.: 24–26).

In Forte's system, inversion always implies a subsequent transposition (Forte 1973: 62–63). According to Forte, the concepts of inclusion under transposition (ibid.: 28–37) and inclusion under inversion and transposition (ibid.: 40–41, 44) are relevant not only between a set X and a set Y, but also between set X and the complement of set Y. As in set logic, the *complement* is the rest of the universe in question. In this case, the universe comprises the twelve semitones of an octave, and the complement of a set X is thus all PCs not included in X. Forte (ibid.: 24–26) demonstrates that set X is included in set Yc (the complement of set Y) if set Y also is included in Xc (the complement of set X). Theorist Ian Bent explains:

> Forte has extended the notion of pitch-class set [...] and its relationships to include the association of sets in "set-complexes" and "subcomplexes" – a "complex" being an array of all the sets that are related by inclusion to any one given central set.[161] This additional concept establishes a type of organization, which has analogies with tonality. It makes possible the elucidation of tonal coherence in

161. Forte (1973: 93–97) defines two important kinds of inclusion: K- and Kh-relations, which play important structural roles in his system. If there is a relation of inclusion (under transposition and/or inversion) between sets X and Y, or between sets X and Yc (but not both), the sets are said to be members of the same set complex, and the relation between them is designated K. Nicholas Cook (1987: 135–138) suggests a more generous interpretation of the K- and Kh-relations, which does not exclude relations between complementary sets.

large-scale musical structures and the links between sections of structures. With this theory, Forte has provided analyses of atonal works by Berg, Schoenberg, Stravinsky, and Webern. (Bent 1987 [1980]: 367.)

A PC-set may also be characterized by its interval content: the amount of minor seconds, major thirds, perfect fifths, etc. Since octaves are not relevant in this context, any interval larger than six semitones (e.g., a tritone) may be transposed to one of the following: prime, minor second, major second, minor third, major third, perfect fourth, and tritone. The prime is analytically uninteresting; the other interval content of a given PC-set is conveniently summarized by an interval class vector (ICV). For instance, the set {0,1,3,5,6,8,10}, shown in Figure 2.48, the ICV of 254361, meaning that it contains two different minor seconds, five different major seconds, four different minor thirds, three different major thirds, six different perfect fourths, and one tritone. (Note that Joutsenvirta's pitch-web analysis does not account for ICs and ICVs of PC-sets.)

	5	8
	10	1
0	3	6

Figure 2.48. Set {0,1,3,5,6,8,10}.

To illustrate the value of such analysis, let us take a case in point. James Woodward (1981) looks to explain Bartók's complicated *Bagatelle* (Op. 9/6) through application of PC-set theory. His examination of the opening four measures reveals all of the pitch-class sets that recur throughout the work: Forte numbers 4–16, 4–26, 4–19, and 4–20. Numerous musical examples illustrate these sets and their manipulation in the piece. Woodward also addresses the placement and pitch levels (registers) of the various sets. As a result, he demonstrates that, far from an "immature" or "experimental" work, this *Bagatelle* is a carefully conceived and well-constructed atonal composition.

Of course, the secondary literature on Forte is rife with criticism of his analytic method. George Perle provides the best-known, and perfectly correct, argument against blindly using Forte's theories as an analytic tool:

> Do we really have to look these chords up in Forte's catalog in order to find a name for them? [...] I would not want you to suppose that my rejection of Allen Forte's theory of pitch-class sets implies a rejection of the notion that there can be such a thing as a pitch-class set. It is only when one defines everything in terms of pitch-class sets that the concept becomes meaningless. (Perle 1990a: 42, 67.)

If Perle is correct, then it is quite senseless to deal with the problem of *Bluebeard's* harmonic language strictly in terms of Forte's theory of pitch-class sets as such. For that reason, among others, an integrated technique is needed, which can more adequately explain, generate, and frame the pitch organization of Bartók's opera.

2.5. Outline of an integrated analytic technique

In Chapters 2.2–2.4, I briefly sketched the various theoretical views and analytic methods of Ernő Lendvai, Paul F. Wilson, Elliott Antokoletz, Aarre Joutsenvirta, and Allen Forte. There I declared my goal to combine, complement, and expand those theories in an attempt to understand all available approaches to analyzing *Bluebeard's Castle*. It turns out that all those contributions – notwithstanding their diversity – have the same primary focus: pitch structure. Now it is time to weigh those ideas, to see which ones are useful (or not) for my analytical research, and particularly for *Bluebeard's Castle*.[162] Even if I must take an untraveled route, some signposts from the Bartók analytical tradition help show the way.

New systems of describing pitch relations usually require new terms and labels, since traditional terminology inevitably carries with it traditional tonal-system implications that may no longer be relevant to the new one. In this study, wherever traditional terms can be applied without seriously distorting the non-traditional concepts, they are retained for the sake of familiarity (e.g., diatonic half-step, whole-step, etc.). Another decision must also be made, this one concerning the commonly used letter nomenclature for PCs. In traditional music, notes having the same letter name, such as C and C-sharp in the key of A, are considered to be diatonic inflections of one another, since both of those tones function as the third degree of the tonic minor and major triad, respectively. In Bartók's music, however, the twelve notes are not distinguished in terms of traditional tonal functions even where triads exist; in which case, C and C-sharp are considered as independent entities. The common nomenclature (here, "C") suggests an inherent connection between these two, otherwise independent integers of the chromatic continuum. (Forte 1973: 2–3; and Joutsenvirta 1989: 4.) Thus, such traditional nomenclature might inadvertently give rise to misconceptions regarding a progression or PC function, especially in cases of enharmonicism. As a result, certain theorists of contemporary music have substituted all numerical (integer) notation for the letter-names of PCs.[163]

From Bartók's (*BBE* 1976 [1943]: 354–392) theoretical statements and his types of notation, five guiding rules of notational analysis can be deduced:

1. The octave, filled chromatically, uses seven names for twelve pitches; five letter-names occur twice; the two letter-names used once are fundamental tones.
2. Fundamental tones can be established by an upper and/or lower "leading tone"; that is, by an encircling semitone, each with a different letter-name.

---

162. I thank Professor Anne Sivuoja-Gunaratnam for personal discussions of my integrated analytic technique.
163. E.g., Antokoletz (1984) retains traditional alphabetical nomenclature where possible, primarily for the sake of familiarity.

3. Alteration in notation signifies a change in one or both fundamentals – a change in the notation of a fundamental cancels its status.
4. Fundamental tones, of primary and/or secondary status, cannot be distinguished purely on the basis of notation.
5. Notational consistency must be sought primarily in individual melodic lines, since Bartók's chromaticism is melodic rather than harmonic in nature. Where a clash between vertical and horizontal notation occurs, preference must be given to the horizontal, melodic orientation.

In his dissertation, *Notation and Tonal Structure in Bartók's Later Works*, Gillies (1986) explores the changing role of pitch notation in the course of Bartók's compositional development. The early works display notation with a late-Romantic, chordal bias. Gillies observes that, between 1908 and the early 1920s, a change occurs. There is a conflict and gradual shift in the role of Bartók's notation: from a vertical to a horizontal emphasis. From 1926 on, the focus of the pitch notation becomes mainly horizontal. The consistency of this focus allows notation to serve as a useful tool for tonal analysis. Gillies advances eight hypotheses that are relevant to tonal analysis of Bartók's later works:

1. The notes of a tonal piece of music belong to a tonal structure in which at least one note acts as a tonal center.
2. Bartók's music is tonal.
3. Bartók strove to present the tonal structures of his music in his pitch notation.
4. Bartók's pitch notation serves as a tool for analyzing the tonal structures of his music.
5. In a number of situations, the pitch notation alone is too "impure" to serve as an important criterion for identification of tonal structures.
6. In many situations, pitch notations are not exclusive enough to be the sole criterion for identification of tonal structures.
7. Differences in pitch-spelling, in different sections or parts of the music, normally reflect differences in tonal structure.
8. On the basis of pitch notations, it is possible to provide a comprehensive account of tonal structures in works by Bartók, using the composer's analyses of his own works as models by which to propose a structural hierarchy of pitch.

The various PC-sets discovered in Bartók's *Bluebeard's Castle* can be related to each other in a number of ways. My underlying assumption is that, when an established theory conflicts with the musically most satisfying or stylistically most appropriate analysis, the theory should be examined and changed where necessary. In his "Harvard Lectures", Bartók notes that:

[...] methods and principles cross each other [...] but only one fundamental tone can operate at any one time as far as the ear is concerned, although the visual analysis of the music might suggest either atonality or polytonality. (*BBE* 1976 [1943]: 370.)

Forte's set theory has been criticized for its overly complex nature.[164] Further, his analytic method does not always provide a complete accounting of what are evidently important patterns in atonal music, and sometimes gives results that do not fit with the reality of the music described (discussed in more detail in Chapter 2.4, pp. 80–83, 85–88). The principles according to which a piece of music is constructed do not necessarily determine the structure of the piece as it is heard. For example, serial music is organized in our perception, and arguably in the same ways as other music is organized: in terms of phrasing, closure, and boundary; rhythmic patterns, harmonic tension, and movement of melodic line. Such things are difficult to hear in serial music. Even if the serialized structure can be discerned, it may form no part of the musical organization as perceived, which often arises in spite of the serial ordering, and not as a result of it. Responding to this difficulty, theorists have suggested new forms of organization that can be heard in atonal music. The music must be divided into sections that are musically coherent – that is to say, they have audible boundaries, which may be created rhythmically, melodically, harmonically, or a mix of those three parameters. Pitch-class sets become significant only if they are brought into prominence by the segmentation. One of my main points is that a completely set-theoretical analysis of Bartók's opera would prove inadequate. The problem becomes even more serious when one approaches the harmonic language of the opera.

The next point is very important: Bartók's opinions about perception lead him to insist that there is only one fundamental tone in any section of music.

> Real or 'perfect' atonality does not exist, even in Schoenberg's works, because of that unchangeable physical law concerning the interrelation of harmonics and, in turn, the relation of the harmonics to their fundamental tone. When we hear a single tone, we will interpret it subconsciously as a fundamental tone. When we hear a following, different tone, we will – again subconsciously – project it against the first tone, which has been felt as the fundamental, and interpret it according to its relation to the latter. (*BBE* 1976 [1943]: 365.)

Using an example from Bartók's *Music for Strings, Percussion and Celesta* IV, Lendvai (1966b [1962]) relates his polar-axis ideas (see pp. 58–59, Chapter 2.2.1) to Kodály's relative solmization system, which contains a movable Do[165] (see, e.g., Kodály 1974 [1961]: 127–128, 130; and 1974 [1943–1944]: 131–132, 134). In another study, one with pertinence to my own, Lendvai (1988) uses those strategies in describing the operas of Giuseppe Verdi (1813–1901) and Richard Wagner (1813–1883).

From now on, I begin to draw my own theoretical framework and analytical conclusions. The strategy I will adopt requires me to alter Lendvai's and Forte's meth-

---

164. Good examples are the reflections of Perle (1990a: 42, 67; and 1990b) and Solomon (1982).
165. Even today, this solmization system is often presented mainly in terms of major and minor keys rather than modes, with major keys having their tonic on *do* and minor keys on *la*.

ods in some ways. In essence, my analytic method diverges from that of traditional set theory, but the change is meant to be integrative rather than disruptive. In fact, and exactly according to Bartók (*BBE* 1976 [1943]: 370), I assign the "fundamental tone" as point 0 for the pitch sets, because it depends solely on context. As in systems such as Kodály's (1974 [1943]: 140–141, 143–146), here the referential tone is relative and movable. As the first step in analysis, the referential tone is determined – precisely and in every case – through its relation to the tonality (microtonality) and modality (bimodality, polymodality). (Bartók's views on these terms are discussed in Chapter 2.1.4, see especially, pp. 46–49.)

A few explanatory remarks are in order here, due to the unconventional character of my analytic method. Within that framework, I draw from the theories and terminologies of both Lendvai and Forte. True, set theory (Forte) is in many ways far-removed from Lendvai's axis system of tonality; but that gap can be bridged. Lendvai is concerned with the α-chord (Figure 2.49), and its β (Figure 2.50), β1 (Figure 2.51), β2 (Figure 2.52), γ (Figure 2.53), γ1 (Figure 2.54), δ (Figure 2.55), δ1 (Figure 2.56), δ2 (Figure 2.57), and ε (Figure 2.58) segments (Table 2.12, next page). The latter designates such elements as pitch-class sets, integers, Forte numbers, and ICV references (Forte 1973: 179–181; see also, the Appendix). At the same time, basic differences, mostly methodological and theoretical, exist between my analytical strategies and the ones of the above-mentioned theorists.

To continue: I give a brief list of Joutsenvirta's (1989) analytical tools. I use them only as they serve my purposes. This distinction is in fact crucial to make my point more precise.

1. The figures are segments of the pitch-web square.
2. The normal order of the set is in the most compact representation.
3. The most compact representation is to be understood in a way that the sets are rearranged and kept in semitones 0–11.
4. The outer distance of the sets and figures must be the smallest possible one.
5. In the figures, the sets are always explored in one, two, or three rows.
6. The referential tone is defined as point 0.
7. The referential tone depends solely on context.
8. The referential tone is movable.
9. On the figures, point 0 cannot always be situated in the bottom line because of the pitch-web square's strictly defined intervallic structure.
10. In inversional forms are marked by added letter I.

It is now time to point out the relation between the α-chord segments and PC-sets. In order to put these elements in the right relation with each other, the essential structure of the α-chord and its segments should be defined in the most compact representation (Table 2.12 and Figures 4.49–4.58).

α-chord segment	Point 0	Integers	Compact forms	Forte number	ICV
α	C-sharp	{0,2,3,5,6,8,9,11}	{0,1,3,4,6,7,9,10}	8–28	448444
β	C-sharp	{0,3,6,9,11}	{0,1,4,7,10}	–	–
β1	C-sharp	{0,3,6,11}	{0,1,4,7}	4–18	102111
β2	C-sharp	{0,6,11}	{0,1,7}	3–9	010020
γ	E	{0,3,6,8,11}	{0,1,4,7,9}	5–32	113221
γ1	E	{0,3,8,11}	{0,1,4,9} (I)	–	–
δ	G	{0,3,5,8,11}	{0,1,4,6,9}	5–32	113221
δ1	G	{0,5,8,11}	{0,1,4,9} (I)	–	–
δ2	G	{0,5,11}	{0,1,4}	3–3	101100
ε	B-flat	{0,2,5,8,11}	{0,1,3,6,9}	5–31	114112

Table 2.12. α-chord segments and their set, Forte number, ICV references.

7	10	1	4
0	3	6	9

Figure 2.49. Set {0,1,3,4,6,7,9,10}.

	10	1	4	7
0				

Figure 2.50. Set {0,1,4,7,10}.

1	4	7
		0

Figure 2.51. Set {0,1,4,7}.

1		7
		0

Figure 2.52. Set {0,1,7}.

1	4	7
	9	0

Figure 2.53. Set {0,1,4,7,9}.

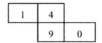

Figure 2.54. Set {0,1,4,9} (I).

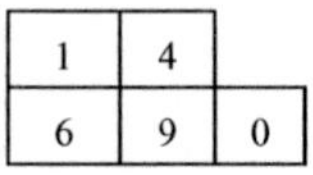

Figure 2.55. Set {0,1,4,6,9}.

Figure 2.56. Set {0,1,4,9} (I).

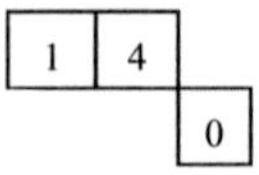

Figure 2.57. Set {0,1,4}.

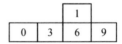

Figure 2.58. Set {0,1,3,6,9}.

Before going on, it is important to stress that set theory is "non-linear"; that is to say, it deals with PC-sets in such a way that their temporal ordering is not relevant (Forte 1973: 3, 60–61; see also, p. 80, Chapter 2.4, above). The concept of ICs will become important in examining the properties of PC-sets, which I combine with the Bartókian tonal functions in terms of α-formations. The α-chord segments may appear in inversional forms, indicated with the letter "I" (Table 2.12 and Figures 2.49–2.58, above).

From the foregoing discussion, I draw the following conclusions: the notion of an ordered inversion, as related to an ordered transposition, introduces the additional complexity of double mapping, which is necessary to compare sets. In no way does Joutsenvirta's pitch-web analysis subtract from the basic tenets of set theory, nor does it change Forte's foundational sets, which are highly relevant to this study. Instead, pitch-web analysis adds information that is lost in Forte's theory, when inverse sets are subsumed under the same set form (prime form). The pitch-square also has the additional benefit of simplifying the determination of the set form by elimination of the step that defines the inverse. The discussions in this chapter, and the analytical tools illustrated above, together constitute the main framework through which to examine the music of *Duke Bluebeard's Castle* in Chapter 4.

3. BÉLA BARTÓK AS FOLK-MUSIC RESEARCHER

3.1. Some cultural aspects of turn-of-the-century Hungary

One of the main achievements of the Hungarian War of Independence, 1848–1849, was the abolition of the emergence of a new social ideology. The Compromise of 1867 established a dual division of power between the Hungarian nobility and the Hapsburg monarchy. In the dual Austro-Hungarian monarchy, Hungary was permitted self-governance over local and national affairs. That situation created a new constitutional order, which was controlled by the aristocracy and mid-level nobility. (Gergely & Szász 1978: 7–39.)[166]

---

166. On March 7, 1849, the Imperial Diet was dissolved. Emperor Franz Joseph I (1848–1916) imposed a new, centralist constitution, based on neo-absolutist principles. The new system was backed by the army, the administration, and the Catholic Church. Liberal efforts were weakened until the military defeat of Prussia at Königgrätz in 1866, which led to a loss of political power and forced the Emperor to return to a constitutional form of government. (Gergely & Szász 1978: 29, 63, 115–129.) Hungary obtained far-reaching concessions, and the parliament was granted extensive powers of participation. The Austro-Hungarian Compromise 1867 replaced the Austrian Empire with what was called the Austro-Hungarian Dual Monarchy. The central figure of this era was Ferenc Deák (1803–1876). Foreign, military and financial matters, and from 1878 the administration of Bosnia and Herzegovina, were placed under the authority of shared ministries of domestic affairs. The railroad system, trade and customs policies, the common national debt, central banks and the issuing of currency were handled separately, as dualistic affairs. (Merényi 1978: 20–27, 51, 129–135.) In December 1867, the *Reichsrat* adopted the *Staatsgrundgesetz*, which deemed all citizens equal in the eyes of the law. They were granted the right to privacy, to move about freely, to acquire real estate, to practice gainful activities; also permitted were freedom of assembly and association, freedom of opinion and the press, freedom of belief and conscience, and more. The December Constitution entailed no changes in electoral law; for forty more years, voting rights remained based on ownership of property. From 1867 to 1918, the *Reichsrat* represented the peoples of the Austrian part (Cisleithania) of the Austro-Hungarian monarchy. That body of representatives consisted of two parts: (1) the *Herrenhaus* (Upper Chamber), whose members came from the nobility and the Church, and were appointed by the emperor; and (2) the *Abgeordnetenhaus* (House of Deputies), the members of which were elected and served six-year terms. Until 1873, members of the House of Deputies were indirectly elected through provincial diets, then directly, by majority vote. Taxes were levied according to four *curiae*: (1) the curia of the big landowners; (2) that of towns, marketplaces and industrial municipalities; (3) that of chambers of commerce and trade; (4) that of agricultural parishes. In 1873, the demand for direct elections to the House of Deputies was met, and in 1882, taxes were lowered. The reform in 1896 introduced a new electoral body, wherein the right to vote was not linked to property. It created a more general class of voters, which in turn led to the representation of the Social Democrats in the *Abgeordnetenhaus*. The only requirement for voting was to have resided in an Austrian municipality for at least six months. This reform increased the number of voters from about 1.7 million to 5.3 million. Direct, universal, equal and secret suffrage was introduced for men in 1907, and for women in 1918. (Gergely & Szász 1978: 34–39, 52–54; see also, Merényi 1978: 30–31, 53–54.) More historical information

Hungarian musicologist Judit Frigyesi (1994) points out that, as a result of the abolition of feudal privileges, the landless gentry dominated the bureaucracy of local government, adopting a patriotic ideology that regarded the nobility as the true embodiment of the Hungarian nation (see also, Merényi 1978: 7, 39, 44, 53; and Szerb 1982 [1934]: 433–434). Frigyesi remarks: "[…] out of an almost mystical belief in the legitimizing power of the conquest of Hungary arose the idea that the supremacy of the nobility was in accordance with the Hungarian spirit" (1994: 259). This mode of government preserved a quasi-feudal economic and social system, which maintained a polarized society between the nobility on the one hand, and a largely underprivileged peasant class on the other.[167] (See also, Romsics 1982: 9–19.)

Towards the end of the nineteenth century, Hungarian society was influenced by a rising tide of national consciousness, which expressed itself in an increasing anti-Austrian sentiment.[168] Frigyesi points out that it was the middle nobility, or *dzsentri* (gentry), who monopolized concepts of patriotism, proclaiming itself the true pro-

---

on dual empire period may be found in P. Ignotus (1972), Kosáry (1944 [1941]), May (1951), and Hanák (1971).

167. In order to express the suffering and feelings of abandonment of the underprivileged, Endre Ady (1877–1919) revived and stylized Hungarian poems about the partly historical, partly legendary figure of the *kuruc*, the poor fugitive (*bújdosó*). Ady modeled his poems on those found in Kálmán Thaly's (1839–1909) editions of real and pseudo-*kuruc* poetry (Szerb 1982 [1934]: 504–510). The *kuruc* claimed descent from the peasant army of György Dózsa (1470–1514), who in 1514 led the greatest peasant uprising of the sixteenth century. Soldiers who practiced guerrilla warfare against the Hapsburgs were viewed as carrying on the *kuruc*'s legendary cause (ibid.: 26, 150, 152, 156, 183–186).

168. The Austro-Hungarian Empire comprised a dozen nationalities, all speaking different languages. In the western half (Cisleithania) the dominance of the German-speaking majority was a perennial source of discontent. In the Hungarian part (Transleithania), a rigorous policy of Magyarization also suppressed other nationalities after the Austro-Hungarian Compromise was struck. Hungarians used their power to prevent similar privileges being granted any other nationalities. Czechs, especially, were disappointed by the priviledges enjoyed by Hungarians. In their view, the Bohemian crown lands were entitled to equal treatment. Czech deputies reacted by boycotting the imperial diet. At the same time, local Czech organizations (e.g., educational associations) were competing against their German counterparts. Slovaks had to face a rather similar situation with respect to Hungary. Slovakian and Czech nationalism developed along the same lines, making them natural allies, which would later lead to the foundation of Czechoslovakia. The Poles followed a different strategy. While their goal also was an independent and united Poland, they cooperated actively with central authorities of the monarchy, and produced some leading politicians, e.g., Prime Minister Kasimir Badeni (1895–1897). As a result, they managed to achieve a certain degree of autonomy for Galicia. In the southern part of the monarchy, the Yugo-slavism movement sought a common state for Slovenians, Croats, and Serbs, either as part of the Hapsburg Empire and having autonomous rights similar to Hungary, or in union with the independent Kingdom of Serbia. Like the Serbs, the Italians also wanted to develop an independent state. The Irredentist movement strove to free Italians that were still under Hapsburg rule. In the end, there were no clear frontlines in the conflicts just described. Each group envied the others for any privileges they might have. Enormous regional economic differences further heated the conflict. Tensions continued to mount, and the nationalities became more and more inconsolable, which led to a number of crises within the dual monarchy. (Gergely & Szász 1978: 8–9, 47–48; and Merényi 1978: 21–47; see also, Gratz 1934; and Galántai 1985.)

totype of the Hungarian people (1998: 52–55, 59–60; see also, Szerb 1982 [1934]: 433, 448–452; and Gergely & Szász 1978: 12–14, 89–92). To quote Frigyesi:

> Instead of the peasantry, the gentry passed for the best guardians of national identity. The real character of the peasants had no place in this concept of Hungarianness. As a class, the peasants were of little importance in public life, and the peasant question was believed to have been solved forever with the abolition of serfdom. Yet, in reality, the lifestyle and standard of living of the peasantry had hardly changed. (Frigyesi 1994: 263.)

Such self-aggrandizing nationalism dominated official art and literature, creating a hierarchical and chauvinist social order. Against this background, a younger generation of artists made a radical break with the past, to embrace modernist ideals, which they viewed as essential for continued artistic creativity.

Social change at the turn of the century was influenced not only by nationalism, but also by the rapid rate of industrialization, urbanization, and population growth[169] (Gergely & Szász 1978: 104–108; and Merényi 1978: 3–8). In "The Intellectual and Cultural Background of Bartók's Work", Mary Gluck observes that Bartók came to maturity in a "society undergoing rapid even cataclysmic, social, economic, and political transformation" (1987: 10). Lackó comments on the intellectual environment of Bartók and Kodály:

> Despite Hungary's dependent status within the Austro-Hungarian Monarchy, she also derived advantages from dualism. Between 1890 and 1910 the population of the country grew by almost 20 percent; during this period the number of people employed in agriculture increased by a scant 6 percent, while the industrial population soared by nearly 75 percent, so that as opposed to the 75 percent in 1870, in 1910 only – but still – 62 percent of all inhabitants found employed in agriculture. Urbanization also made considerable progress: in 1867 only 14 percent, but by 1913 nearly one quarter of the populations were town dwellers – Budapest had expanded into a metropolis. As is well known, Hungary was a multinational country, but the composition of her inhabitants was shifting to the advantage of the Hungarians, a condition more favorable for bourgeois development. [...] Besides the predominantly peasant ethnic groups (Romanians, Slovaks, and South Slavs), the territory of Hungary was also inhabited by other national minorities who had not belonged to the feudal framework. One of these groups was the Germans, who had begun settling in the Carpathian Basin already in medieval times, but most of whom were recent immigrants; the other group was the Jews. Accelerated bourgeois development around the turn of the century obviously favored these strata. As a consequence, their rise into the middle class involved their large-scale assimilation, and their adoption of Hungarian customs. It is estimated that between 1880 and 1910 more than one million people were assimilated. It is important to

---

169. On working-class life, see Ferge (1986), *Chapters from the History of Hungarian Politics Concerning the Poor*. Agricultural servants normally worked sixteen hours a day for little pay, and might also be required to work at night and on holidays. For an informative account of their lives, see the autobiographical novel by Gyula Illyés (1902–1983), *The People of the Puszta* (1967 [1936]).

note that perhaps with the exception of Berlin and Germany in general, nowhere in Eastern Europe were the Jews so apt to assimilate as in Hungary. (Lackó 1987: 26–27.)

During most periods of Hungarian history, to be Hungarian meant simply to be an inhabitant of the Hungarian state and had no ethnic implications: a *hungaricus* was not necessarily of *Magyar* (Hungarian) ethnicity (Gergely & Szász 1978: 108). For some intellectuals of the twentieth century, including Bartók, such a traditional image of the state remained an ideal (Frigyesi 1989[170]). Hungary, at the *fin de sciècle*, was a multi-ethnic society, in which Hungarian speakers were the largest of a number of distinct ethnic groups. Hungary's rural provinces contained large Romanian, Slovak, and Slavic peasant groups. Jews and Germans integrated themselves into Hungary's urban society, rising into the middle classes and undergoing a large-scale assimilation, which often involved adopting Hungarian nationality. (Lackó 1987: 26–27; J. Lukács 1988: 84–107[171]; Gergely & Szász 1978: 108–114, 198–219; Romsics 1982: 11, 14, 251; and Frigyesi 1993a[172].) That assimilation furthered the division between the urban middle classes and the rural population, who occupied what Lackó (1987: 27) calls the "under nation" position in society. The writer and journalist Hugó Veigelsberg (1869–1949), using the pen-name Ignotus, wrote as follows:

It would be useful to collect how many things were deemed non-Hungarian in the past decade. […] Budapest is not Hungarian. The dialect of Pest is not Hungarian. The stock exchange is not Hungarian. Socialism is not Hungarian. Internationalism is not Hungarian. The organization of agricultural workers is not Hungarian. Capital is not Hungarian. Secession and symbolism are not Hungarian. It is not a Hungarian idea to exclude the religious institutions from public education, or to eliminate religion from the curriculum. Caricature is not Hungarian. Greater tolerance toward love is also not Hungarian. General suffrage is not Hungarian. Materialism is not Hungarian, and it is not Hungarian to suppose that people may change their institutions […] rationally, according to their needs. But most of all:

---

170. Frigyesi (1989) discusses the political development of nationalism in the early years of the twentieth century, and its effects on the Hungarian outlook.

171. The social history of Jews and Germans in Hungary is discussed in J. Lukács (1988: 84–107); see also, Romsics (1982: 11, 213–214); Lackó (1987: 26–27); and Szerb (1982 [1934]: 433–434, 448, 466). Béla Balázs and György Lukács (Löwinger) both came from German-Jewish families who had settled in Hungary during the great influx of German homesteaders in the nineteenth century. Lukács's parents were Adele Wertheimer (1860–1917) and József Lukács (József Löwinger) (1855–1928). József Lukács was a self-made man who came from a poor family; he rose to become a wealthy and influential director of the Anglo-Hungarian Bank in Budapest and was an enthusiastic Hungarian patriot. Balázs – German on his mother's side and Jewish on his father's – came from the world of the provincial Jewish intelligentsia. In 1913, Balázs formally changed his name from Herbert Bauer to Béla Balázs. See Willam McCagg (1972), *Jewish Nobles and Geniuses in Modern Hungary*.

172. Frigyesi (1993a) notes that in the domain of bourgeois life and culture there was a strong alliance between Jews and Hungarians. The spiritual ideal of the Hungarian-Jewish bourgeoisie of the early twentieth century outlived its creators and, according to Frigyesi, remains an important ingredient of the Hungarian psyche to this day.

whoever is not satisfied with the existing situation is certainly not a Hungarian and such a person should have the sense to leave the country with which he is unsatisfied. (Quoted in Frigyesi 1998: 83.)

Bourgeois revolution and social transformation made a strong impact on Hungarian culture. The *fin de sciècle* was characterized by the widening of horizons on many levels. Modernist ideas entered into prose, poetry, plastic arts, and music. It was inevitable that reformist ideas would extend to all of the "new" arts, as shown by the example of Hungarian poetry (Szerb 1982 [1934]: 495). At the beginning of the new century, those reformist ideals were adopted by champions of the new music (Gy. Lukács 1972: 11). In *fin-de-sciècle* Hungary, the attitude of the members of the radical circles was shaped by the difficult and controversial position of the intelligentsia within the society as a whole[173]

On this topic, see also, especially, Gluck (1985: 44–48); P. Ignotus (1972: 122–123[174]); Bodnár (1963[175]); and B. Horváth (1974[176]).

173. There were tensions even among what may seem to be a fairly homogeneous group. For instance, the young intellectuals who rallied around Lukács, becoming known as the *Vasárnapi kör* (Sunday Circle), were mostly assimilated Jews; among them, too, there were significant differences in wealth, rank, and ideology. The Sunday Circle was a regular gathering of intellectuals, including the philosopher and literary critic Bernát Alexander (1850–1927), writer Béla Balázs, philosopher Béla Fogarasi (1891–1959), printer and publisher Imre Kner (1890–1944), writer Anna Lesznai (Seghers) (1885–1966), sociologist Karl Mannheim (1893–1947), writer Emma Ritoók (1868–1945), philosopher Leo Popper (1886–1911), art historian and philosopher Lajos Fülep (1885–1970), art historian Arnold Hauser (1892–1978), writer Ernő Lorsy (1889–1961), philosopher Béla Zalai (1882–1915), and more. They met to discuss the contradictions and crises of liberal bourgeois society. (On the Lukács circle, see Gluck 1985: 44–48.) During this time, Bartók spent his afternoons – at one point, almost every other afternoon – with Emma Gruber and Kodály, who were not only musicians but also well-read intellectuals. Through them Bartók came into contact with a broad circle of musicians and intellectuals, among them Balázs, who was in turn a link with the Sunday Circle.

174. Paul (Pál) Ignotus (1901–1978) took as his surname the pseudonym of his famous father, Hugo Veigelsberg. In his monograph, *Hungary*, Ignotus wrote the following about the literary journal *Nyugat* (*West*), which had been founded in 1908: "The *Nyugat* guard were determined to a totally European Hungary, free of fervent patriotism, but at the same time asserting the national personality that had grown out of the rich Magyar heritage of images, concepts, and melodies, but had become degraded by effects of time and foreign influences. Thus *Nyugat* not only went one step further than its predecessors in making Hungarian literature metropolitan: it also brought a synthesis of that metropolitan spirit and pre-urban, primordial Hungary – a synthesis, which today's Western audience can probably apprehend more clearly through Bartók's and Kodály's music than through any other medium" (P. Ignotus 1972: 122–123). See also, Szerb (1982 [1934]: 468–469, 483–486, 516–529).

175. In "Bartók et le mouvement *Nyugat*", György Bodnár (1963) discusses the connections between Bartók and the great Hungarian writers of his epoch – connections already noted by Hungarian essayists and critics during the interwar period. Among the contemporaries of Bartók was the poet Ady, the most prominent member of the *Nyugat* movement. For more on the Ady-Bartók connection, see Gluck (1987: 17–18), Dille (1981), Frigyesi (1998: 168–195), and Birnbaum (1987).

176. In painting, the break with conservative ideas took place in 1896. Simon Hollósy (1857–1918) left the Academy of Arts and, together with his pupils, opened the Nagybányai iskola (Nagybánya School of Painting); among his students were important figures of modern Hungarian art, such as János Thorma (1870–1937), Béla Iványi Grünwald (1867–1940), Károly Ferenczi (1862–1917),

In *Béla Bartók and Turn-of-the-Century Budapest*, Frigyesi (1998) describes the two decades prior to World War I as a period of tremendous vitality in the creative arts in Hungary. In many respects, the issues dealt with by Hungarian artists paralleled those engaged by creative artists all over Europe (Gy. Lukács 1971;[177] and Glatz 1987: 70–71). Yet, Hungary, because of its language, geographical position, and lack of economic and strategic power, has for the most part remained outside the European cultural mainstream (Merényi 1978: 21–27). After a long tradition of pervasive Germanic influence, however, Hungarian culture began to be influenced by that of France (see, e.g., *BBE* 1976 [1938];[178] and Cross 1967[179]). Given the reaction against prevailing Germanic influences in Budapest at the *fin de sciècle* and the search for new sources of artistic inspiration, it is curious that many of Bartók's compositions continued to show certain characteristics of the Germanic musical tradition (Glatz 1987: 71–73; and Weiss-Aigner 1982.[180])

and Pál Szinyei Merse (1845–1920), who joined the group later. This development was followed in 1906 by the creation of the Magyar Impresszionisták és Naturalisták Köre (MIÈNK) (Circle of Hungarian Impressionists and Naturalists), which included István Csók (1865–1961), Béla Czóbel (1883–1976), Adolf Fényes (1867–1945), Károly Ferenczi, Károly Kernstock (1873–1940), and József Rippl-Rónai (1861–1927), under the leadership of Szinyei. A year later, those painters who found the association of MIÈNK insufficiently separated from the group to form the Eight (Nyolcak). In "Bartók és a Nyolcak" ("Bartók and the Eight"), Béla Horváth (1974) provides information regarding Bartók's connections with a group of avant-garde Hungarian painters in 1911, some whom with he had already been associated as early as 1905. The members of the Nyolcak were Károly Kernstok, Róbert Berény (1887–1953), Bertalan Pór (1880–1964), Lajos Tihanyi (1885–1938), Dezső Czigány (1883–1937), Béla Czóbel and Ödön Márffy (1878–1959). Márffy, Pór and Berény all studied art in Paris before returning to Budapest, drawing personal inspiration from the works of Paul Cézanne (1839–1906), Henri Matisse (1869–1954), Paul Gauguin (1848–1903), and the impressionists, a pattern followed to some extent by virtually all painters of their generation. Horváth reports that Berény published an article, "The Case of Béla Bartók" in *Nyugat* (1911), and in the spring of 1913, he painted a portrait of Bartók. On those groups, see also, István Deák (1991), "Hungary: A Brief Political and Cultural History."

177. In "Béla Bartók: On the Twenty-Fifth Anniversary of his Death", Lukács (1971) observes the significance of Bartók's work from the point of view of political and cultural history. Lukács asks, "What does it mean to be Hungarian?" The author (ibid.: 43) advocates that "Hungarian culture must have the courage and social and moral basis to say: 'Bartók has opened for us the historical way to true Hungarian culture'."

178. In "The Influence of Debussy and Ravel in Hungary", Bartók (*BBE* 1976 [1938]) examines the musical dominance of Germany in Europe for several hundred years, but the Hungarian musicians of the century decisively turned toward France. Bartók observes that the Latin spirit (especially the French spirit) is nearer to the Hungarian genius than is the German one.

179. Cross (1967) discusses Bartók's turn toward France and Debussy as a replacement of the Germanic influence. Cross gives a history of the first decade of the century and documents sources of Bartók's literary interests, housed at the Budapest Bartók Archive. Cross (ibid.: 126) remarks that, between 1907 and 1911, Bartók purchased Debussy's *String Quartet,* Op. 10 (1893) and a number of piano pieces, including *Pour le piano* (1902), *L'Isle joyeuse* (1904), *Images I* (1905), *Images II* (1907), and *Douze Préludes I* (1910). Cross points to influences that both composers have in common, and how each they used those influences in individual ways.

180. Günter Weiss-Aigner (1982) presents a detailed study of the elements of Bartók's early works in terms of their Classical and Romantic sources, especially those of Beethoven and Liszt. As one instance, the octatonic scale already appears in such works as Liszt's Symphonic Poem, *Tasso* (1849, rev. 1854).

In "The Years of Béla Bartók's Artistic Development", Demény (1955b) gives a comprehensive summary of the composer's encounters with other artists and members of the intelligentsia. The latter included Bartók, the Marxist philosopher and literary critic György Lukács (1885–1971), the major literary figure Ady[181], and Béla Balázs[182]. In the works from this period, we find evidence of the strong sense of Hungarian national identity that began to emerge at the end of the nineteenth century as a result of sociopolitical tensions in that land.[183] (See also, Frigyesi 1998: 89–115.[184]) As Mihály Babits recalls:

181. Ady spent some years in Paris before publishing his first mature volume of poems, the *Új versek* (*New Poems*) in 1906. Those poems drew heavily on the work of Charles Baudelaire (1821–1867), Paul Verlaine (1844–1896), and other French symbolists. Ady's radically innovative symbolist poems ushered in a new age in Hungarian literature. They provided a new language and a new style for expressing the complex inner landscape of the artist's consciousness. (Szerb 1982 [1934]: 294, 486–510.)

182. Balázs's poems were published, together with those of the best of his contemporaries, Ady and the outstanding representative of modern intellectual poetry, Mihály Babits (1883–1941), in the pioneer anthology, *Holnap* (*Tomorrow*).

183. Bartók started his career in the first decade of the twentieth century, which saw the appearance of many Hungarian men of talent, even by European standards. Pioneers in the humanities included the dominant personality of the Hungarian avant-garde literature, the poet, writer, artist Lajos Kassák (1887–1967), the philosophers Leo Popper and Béla Zalai, Lajos Fülep, and the art historian Károly (Charles de) Tolnay (1899–1981). Other talented men of modern radical political thinking were such as the syndicalist Ervin Szabó (1877–1918), the bourgeois radical Oszkár Jászi (1875–1957) (founder of the Social Science Association), the economist Jenő Varga (1879–1964), as well as sociologists and social theorists such as Karl Polányi (1886–1964) and several others who achieved European distinction between the two world wars. (Gergely & Szász 1978: 236–248; and Merényi 1978: 106–125.)

184. Frigyesi (1998) has much to say about Bartók's credentials as the kind of modernist whose work involves attempting to impose a unity on materials whose most natural state is divergence, dissociation. Frigyesi proceeds from the claim that coherence manifested itself not in consistency and continuity but in polar oppositions. She states that it became the foundation of Bartók's conceptualization of modern style. Frigyesi declares that for Bartók and the poet Ady, each work was a challenge to create a framework in which the unity of the most polarized elements becomes inevitable. (Ibid.: 168–195.) Frigyesi (ibid.: 27–28, 295, 297) contrives the formulation that, in Bartókian modernism, wholeness is not uniformity, nor is harmony without tension. In my opinion, her position is not acceptable. I think that unity in art means the capacity to make transparent the presence of the inner governing force that unites all elements in spite of their fragmentary nature, even opposition. In my view, the crucial sense in which this formula unites Bartók's mature modern classicism is not brought out. Frigyesi (ibid.: 196–298) focuses on Bartók's earlier years. She creates a kaleidoscope rather than the clear-cut portrayals of personalities and purposes that the subject requires. Crucially, Frigyesi (ibid.: 69, 95, 311 n. 21) does not attempt to flesh out those aesthetic points concerning unity and modernity, treating each relevant work in chronological sequence. Rather, she aims to describe the early twentieth-century Hungary: the architecture and art, social studies and politics, aesthetics, psychology, literature, journalism, music, poetry, popular culture, and other parallel and seemingly independent domains, the subject of wholeness or its absence fascinated the intellectual modernist circles and oriented their activities. Frigyesi's study may indeed be the first attempt to discuss the artistic world of Ady and Bartók together (ibid.: 7–8, 170–172, 204, 213–215, 322 n. 4, 327 n. 37) and to superpose the discussion on current theories in aesthetics and on social and cultural history, it seems by that very claim to be far from the final word on the subject.

Our teachers saw barely anything else in the great Hungarian works than some patriotic or folkloristic "content". And whatever modern poets we had access to seemed to regard this aspect as the most important in poetry. We, the critical young people, had a rather straightforward judgment of all this contemporary literature. In our eyes, it was nothing but the empty rhetoric of cheap sentimentalism. From the one side we got preaching, on the other we were bombarded by *magyar nóta*. But the public was not even looking for anything else in literature besides phrases and *nóta*. [...] Whoever was chased by the decadent thirst for real literature looked toward the West. He raved about English and French poets, about modern and postmodern poems, in order to keep himself ostentatiously away from the banal truisms of the poetry of empty phrases and the *nóta* of incriminating simplicity. The names of Baudelaire and Verlaine, Poe and Swinburne, Mallarmé and Rilke circulated among the fuzzy-haired youth of the *Nyugat* circle. (Babits 1997 [1939]: 96–97.)

By 1906, Bartók had shifted towards a more politically radical and aesthetically cosmopolitan stance. He was interested in combining symbols of Hungarian identity with modernist approaches to art, as were taking place in Berlin, Vienna, and Paris (P. Ignotus 1972[185]). Balázs has a very special place in the ranks of Hungarian artists of the twentieth century, for he alone assumed responsibility for the development of modern Hungarian music from its beginnings. He considered it his personal duty to provide modern librettos of high quality to promote the music of Bartók and Kodály. He was among those who were disappointed by the aestheticism of German intellectual circles in Berlin.[186] Consider the quotation below, which appears in Balázs's *Diary* on January 11, 1910:

This entire cultural milieu in which I find myself appears somehow outdated. [...] I feel it to be claustrophobic. [...] Where is that famous West European culture, which is still fresh and unknown, into which I can enter and from which I can draw sustenance? [...] Everything I meet appears to consist of empty noise and verbosity; I feel decadent weakness here, not the freshness of spiritual energy. (Cited in Gluck 1985: 117.)

---

185. The members of the "generation of 1900", as they have sometimes been called, reacted in various ways to the society that surrounded them, often voicing dissatisfaction with the cultural values held by the bourgeois, industrial society of which they were a part. Romanticism's enormous force underpinned the modernist movement and gave its ideology a sharper focus. Paul Ignotus (1972) describes the War for Freedom of 1848–1849, the Reform generation of poets and thinkers in the 1830s, the social advancement of the last fifty years of the Hapsburg Empire, and the Second Reform Generation of the early 1900s. See also, Zoltán Horváth (1961), *Turn-of-the-Century Hungary: The History of the Second Reform Generation, 1896–1914*.

186. In 1907, Balázs spent an extended period in Berlin attending the renowned philosopher Georg Simmel's (1858–1918) famous seminar on the philosophy of culture. On this trip abroad, Balázs was still imbued with the traditional, almost axiomatic, assumption and expectation of East European intellectuals that the West offered newer, more advanced cultural patterns and forms than those available back home. Balázs's sense of disenchantment was overwhelming when he found that even Simmel could offer little beyond the hyper-individualistic aestheticism of the *fin de sciècle*. (Leafstedt 1999: 34.)

By bringing together the political, cultural and musical issues of the day, we can shape the sphere in which Bartók and his colleagues worked and the scope of their challenge to the traditional, conservative notions of "Hungarian-ness" and Hungarian music. Bartók clarifies the situation:

> It was the time of a new national movement in Hungary, which also took hold of art and music. In music, too, the aim was set to create something specifically Hungarian. When this movement reached me, it drew my attention to studying Hungarian folk music, or, to be more exact, what at that time was considered Hungarian folk music. (*BBE* 1976 [1921a]: 409.)

In *Béla Bartók compositeur hongrois*, Jean Gergely (1975) provides an extensive examination of Hungarian history and art as an influence on music of the past and present. The new Hungarian school, formed in the first half of the twentieth century by Bartók, Kodály, and their disciples, represented the greatest intellectual synthesis realized in Hungary to date. Subsequently, Bartók and Kodály created a varied musical idiom from the world of folk melodies, sometimes in almost contradictory ways, but with equal intensity (Kodály 1974 [1921][187]). Lajos Vargyas (1982: 44) observes, "They found not only interesting music but also an independent human universe, which captured their imagination as creative artists and the spirit of which they transplanted into their own work." Gergely (1975) argues that Bartók, in his personal style, created a historical, ethnic, and sociological synthesis by transferring elements of the musical language, style, and variety of popular music into the realm of art music.[188] The heritage of nineteenth-century Hungary, the political environment of early twentieth-century Hungary, the resulting polarization of intellectual and cultural groups, and the progressive musicians with whom Bartók associated, all had an impact on his views and his artistry (Gy. Lukács 1972[189]).

---

187. In his article "Béla Bartók", Kodály (1974 [1921]) outlines a history leading to the rebirth of the Hungarian spirit, and the creation of contemporary Hungarian intellectual culture. Kodály provides a history of influences and sources of Bartók's works in Bach, Debussy, and others.

188. Gergely (1975) further remarks that the *parlando* rhythms give Bartók's music an unlimited dimension that, like its folk models, is shaped by the Hungarian language. From the Hungarian point of view, Bartók's music is made up of a historical part, which is the heritage of the style of *verbunkos*, and another part modeled on folk music. As early as 1905, the year of his first collecting tours, Bartók employed the orchestral *parlando* style in the *Suite for Orchestra* No. 2, Op. 4 (rev. 1920, 1943). Although the work was not completed until 1907, the first three movements were finished in November of 1905. A long bass clarinet solo that contains the rhythmic freedom and the rhythm of *parlando*, with the appropriate lack of anacrusis, opens the third movement. (See also, Chapters 3.2.1 and 3.4–3.5, below.)

189. Lukács's essay, "Bartók und die ungarische Kultur," was written in the late sixties and published in 1972. It is the Marxist philosopher's last major pronouncement on Hungarian culture, and in it, he discusses Bartók's significant impact on the latter. He contends, for example, that after 1848 Hungarian literature followed the "Prussian path"; i.e., even some of its best poets shared what Lukács calls, after Thomas Mann (1875–1955), a "power-sanctioned intimacy" with the establishment (ibid.: 11). Ideologically, even János Arany (1817–1882) and Babits were conservatives at heart, who upheld, however reluctantly, the established order. (See also, Szerb 1982 [1934]: 399–418, 510–522.) According to Lukács (ibid.), only poets like Mihály Csokonai Vitéz

3.2. Hungarian musical tradition: Whose heritage?

This discussion of Hungarian musical tradition is not meant to be exhaustive, but selective: the topics considered here were chosen because they are intimately connected with the musical style of *Bluebeard's Castle*.

In *The New Grove Dictionary of Music and Musicians*, John Weissmann (1980: 629) presents the following definition: "*Verbunkos*, or 'Recruiting,' was a Hungarian dance that served as a method of enlistment during the imperial wars of the eighteenth century." Bálint Sárosi describes how *verbunkos* music was used to embody a sense of "nation" that excluded other layers of society:

> The representative of this period largely did not recognize the music of the Hungarian people as being characteristic of the Hungarian nation – that is, the noble and very slender upper class layer – indeed; they simply refused to consider the existence of folk music. (Sárosi 1978: 90.)

Frigyesi (1994: 260) remarks that the Hungarian nobility "transmitted the cultural-ideological trends of the West, while at the same time it developed a distinct 'national' culture". In "Bartók and Folk Music", Stephen Erdely (2001: 26) shows how dissimilar types of music corresponded to different layers of Hungarian society:

1. the upper classes (which included the nobility, the urban financiers, industrialists, and bourgeoisie) turned to the West for their needs;
2. the gentry and the urban middle classes found satisfaction in the music of gypsy bands and *magyar nóta* (Hungarian song), *népies műdal* (folk-like art songs, or urban folk songs), *műdal* (art song);
3. agrarian folk, with their *népdal* (folk song) and other musical customs, which were isolated from the rest of the country.

The gypsy music that was adopted by the gentry can be divided, roughly and generically, into two main forms: *verbunkos* and Hungarian song (*magyar nóta*) (Dob-

---

(1773–1805), Sándor Petőfi (1823–1849), Ady, Attila József (1905–1937), and a composer like Bartók can be considered truly revolutionary artists. Their works reflect what Lukács calls "indefinite objectivization": that quality in art, which conveys most profoundly, most dramatically, and most completely a change in man's perception of his world. (See also, Szerb 1982 [1934]: 8, 283–290, 376–393, 486–510.) Lukács (ibid.: 12) states that Bartók, like other European artists, protested the alienation taking place in modern capitalist society and culture, and this is the essence of his music. In general, Lukács views Bartók's research into folk music as a protest against the alienating effects of modern capitalist society. Lukács states that, despite the plebeian, folkloric elements in his works, Bartók could only have chosen the modern idiom he did in fact choose. Bartók's rejection of the world around him reaches its apogee, according to Lukács, in the folk-based *Cantata Profana* (1974 [1930]). In that work, the Bartókian peasants – the young men who have been turned into stags – show their revulsion by refusing to return to a corrupt and inhuman world. Lukács argues that what makes Bartók an outstanding figure, in both the Hungarian and total European context, is that he dared to be different, and created a musical idiom, which though rooted deeply in folk art, became suggestive of the dangers and possibilities of the new age.

szay 1984: 276–283, 325–331; and Szekfű 1939: 335, 517). Those forms permeated the Hungarian musical traditions of the eighteenth and nineteenth centuries.

3.2.1. *Verbunkos* and *Magyar nóta*

The *verbunkos* sources, not yet completely known, include some of the traditions of old Hungarian popular music (Heyduck dance,[190] swineherd dance), certain Balkan and Slavic elements, probably through the intermediaries of the gypsies, and elements of Viennese-Italian music, coming, no doubt, from the first cultivators of the *verbunkos*, the urban musicians of German culture. Sárosi (1978: 86–89) notes that in earlier times *verbunkos* was known as the *Magyar* (Hungarian), which was also linked to civilian dance forms such as the *allemande, anglaise, française* and *polonaise*. In his seminal *Hungarian Folk Music*, Kodály (1976 [1960]: 7) observes that "[*Verbunkos*] was town art-music, in essence nothing but dance music; at first it was even written by foreigners and immigrants, and like its later counterpart, was to be found in print." (For more on *verbunkos* sources, see Bónis 1972; Dobszay 1984: 264–270[191]; Kodály 1974 [1951]: 274, 279; and Szabolcsi 1951: 151–308.)

The *verbunkos* very soon developed a complete set of characteristic elements. In "Gypsy Music or Hungarian Music?" Bartók (*BBE* 1976 [1931a]: 206) summarizes the stereotypical features of the *verbunkos* style, which include the following:

1. use of the so-called "Gypsy" or "Hungarian" scale (Figure 3.1, below);
2. an abrupt, cambiata-like cadential figure, *bokázó* (clicking of heels);
3. a wide-ranged melody with flamboyant decorations;
4. alternation between *lassú* (slow) and *friss* (fast) tempi.

8	11	2
	4	7
6		0

Figure 3.1. Set {0,2,4,6,7,8,11}.

---

190. Hungary fought first against the Ottoman then the Hapsburg oppression; thus, the character of her dances was defined by those of the military. The virtuoso forms of the *hajdú* or 'heyduck-dance' (performed with swords) survived in the herdsmen's *botoló* dances (performed with crooks in the hand) and in male solo dances. The national movements of Romanticism used features of the recruiting dance and of the two types of *csárdás*: slow and fresh. The *Szatmár* dance, with its three-part articulation, is a beautiful example of this national dancing style, which still vividly keeps the nineteenth-century atmosphere alive. (Balassa & Ortutay 1984: 449–450.)

191. Dobszay (1984: 264–270) observes that the antecedents of the *verbunkos* are the Ungaresca dances, played in Europe throughout the sixteenth and seventeenth centuries, and preserved in collections both within and outside of Hungary. The continuous existence of the type was attested in later written sources, e.g., in the *Lányi Zsuzsanna-féle kézirat* (1729) and *Apponyi kézirat* (1730). A few early *verbunkos* publications, and the peculiar melodic patterns found in the instrumental music of all peoples in the Danube valley, show clearly that the new style owed its unexpected appearance to some older popular tradition.

Bartók clarifies that the so-called "Gypsy" or "Hungarian" minor scale, C–D–E-flat–F-sharp–G–A-flat–B–C (Figure 3.1) points to a southern oriental (Arabic) origin and may possibly have reached Hungary through the gypsies. Peasants never used the augmented intervals of the Gypsy scales (*BÖI* 1966 [1917]). Figure 3.2 displays the Hungarian major scale, C–D-sharp–E–F-sharp–G–A–B–C, set {0,3,4,6,7,9,11}.

Figure 3.2. Set {0,3,4,6,7,9,11}.

In addition to Bartók's reflections, other variables must be considered, to provide a wider comprehension of the *verbunkos* style. The *verbunkos* style was usually characterized by instrumental flexibility, a Western conception of form-building, with sharp divisions but widely arched melodic patterns, and a striking and extensive set of rhythms. It should be added that, from the beginning, this music could count on powerful allies in the form of musicians who found it irresistible to play. Jonathan Bellman (2001: 425–426) writes: "Although the *verbunkos* is sometimes considered to be Gypsy music, it was actually Hungarian, often derived ultimately from the song repertory, but played in a fashion characteristic of the gypsy musician." Members of the provincial, lesser nobility amused themselves by listening to the *hallgató-nóta* (melody without words), and later some *csárdás*, performed by Gypsy bands, who played them with free and capricious sprinklings of extemporaneous ornamentation and paraphrases (Nettl 1965: 77; and Kodály 1976: 81–82).

In *Gypsy Music*, Sárosi (1978: 85) points out that, the term *verbunkos* was applied later "as a musical indicator of the whole period". The eighteenth-century *verbunkos* shared certain features with contemporary Western music, such as periodic structure, triadic harmonies, tonic-dominant functions. Nevertheless, it had some unique characteristics as well, such as the predominance of dotted rhythms, descending note-pairs, cadential syncopation, ornaments attached to long notes. The foreign elements of the early *verbunkos* were absorbed, and their foreign roots quickly forgotten, it seems. Around 1800, the leading role of the new dance music was taken over by János Bihari (1764–1827), János Lavotta (1764–1820), Antal Csermák (1774–1822), and the Jewish composer Márk Rózsavölgyi (1789–1848); its melodic and rhythmic richness were found to be so appealing that the *verbunkos* immediately became the most important expression of Hungarian musical Romanticism. It even assumed the role of the representative art of nineteenth-century Hungary, when it took on the role of national music. (Dobszay 1984: 276–283; see also, pp. 113–118, Chapter 3.2.2.) *Verbunkos* was also transplanted into nineteenth-century art-music of Hungarian Romantics such as Ferenc Erkel and Mihály Mosonyi. Liszt's *Hungarian Rhapsodies* No. 1–15 (1847–1853), No. 16–19 (1882–1885),[192] and Brahms's *Hun-*

---

192. Sárosi (1978: 115) demonstrates how Liszt adapted a well-known popular song for the first theme of his *Hungarian Rhapsody* No. 8. In his composition, Liszt imitated all the mannerisms of

garian Dances (1873) are probably the most familiar examples of the transplantation of the *Verbunkos* tradition into nineteenth-century art music.[193]

In regard to Gypsy music, I cannot avoid mentioning the milestone work of Liszt (1861 [1859]), *Des Bohémiens et de leurs Musique en Hongrie*. In that publication, Liszt interprets literally the use of the term "Gypsy music" to describe folk-based Hungarian popular music, and he regards the popular Hungarian musical idiom of the nineteenth century as the work of the Gypsies. That part of Hungary's oral musical tradition, which had been rendered suitable for consumption by the middle classes was considered by Liszt to be the invention of the Gypsies. He and his contemporaries, highly educated but unfamiliar with folk traditions, were ignorant of traditional Gypsy music. (For more on the latter, see Demény, ed. 1976: 521; Kodály 1974 [1923a]: 438; Dobszay 1984: 311, 317–318; and Bárdos 1974: 24–27.)

Another article worthy of mention is Bartók's (1956 [1936]) "Liszt a miénk", which deals with four issues regarding Liszt and his compositional output:

1. the degree to which the present generation understands Liszt's works: those which they like most, and those they like least;
2. the degree of influence that Liszt's music has had on the general development of the art of music;
3. Liszt's (1861 [1859]) writings on gypsy music;
4. reasons for classifying Liszt as a Hungarian composer.

Bartók blamed Liszt for propagating a number of misconceptions about folk music. He explains that Liszt credited the gypsies with originating Hungarian music, and characterized the rural folk-music tradition as being a modification of Gypsy music (see also, Demény, ed. 1955a: 410–411; and 1976: 521). Though Bartók spoke on what appeared to be a historical subject, there were both political and personal implications in what he added:

> Finally, I would again mention the controversy of the last few years, to some extent deliberately fostered in the columns of the press, in which the dilettante protagonists of popular art music – who are unfortunately in the majority among

---

Gypsy performance, which he regarded as the source of Hungarian music. The *Rhapsody* No. 8 uses all the musical clichés of *Verbunkos* performance: cimbalom-like arpeggiations, interruptions of the vocal melody, emphatic dotted rhythms, grace notes, trills, and chromatic runs. Sárosi (ibid.) points out that "[I]n the original melody there is no augmented second: here on the other hand there is." With his primary aim being to notate the improvisatory practices of the Gypsy musicians, Liszt was less concerned with preserving the original character of the source material.

193. The geographical origin of the *verbunkos* style is difficult to locate, because when we first learned of its existence, it was already gaining ground in the towns, in Gypsy bands, and in the hands of Western musicians. Mozart's *Violin Concerto in A Major* may be mentioned here, as well as Beethoven's *König Stephan*, and some parts of his *Third* and *Seventh Symphonies*, Schubert's *Divertissement*, Haydn's and Weber's *Hungarian Rondos*, Diabelli's *Hungarian Dances*, etc. All of those are memorable events in the history of Hungarianism in the music of Western composers. (Kodály 1974 [1921]: 426; and 1984 [1939]: 9, 37; see also Dobszay 1984: 269.)

the upper classes – do their best to disparage the music of the peasants. (Bartók 1956 [1936]: 234.)

The other subtopic of this chapter is the *magyar nóta* (Hungarian song), which was a mid-nineteenth-century phenomenon that was largely the creation of middle-class composers of noble descent. The *magyar nóta* developed from a similar type of German urban folk song, known as *Volkstümlichlieder*. Those songs, usually accompanied by piano, are generally strophic and in reprise (ABA) structure. Numerous Hungarian imitations were composed by amateurs from the educated classes and disseminated along with the *verbunkos* and *csárdás* by urban gypsy bands (Kodály 1976: 10, 15; and Dobszay 1984: 275, 325–331). In *Folk Music: Hungarian Musical Idiom*, Sárosi (1986: 57) describes the *magyar nóta* as follows: "Its main distinctive feature is its strong harmonic basis: the turns of melody virtually dictate the accompanying chords – the chord sequences and accompaniment clichés well known from gypsy orchestras." In the preface to the English edition of *Folk Music of Hungary*, Kodály (1971 [1960]: 6) points out that "[T]he tunes became common property soon after their appearance, and nobody inquired into their origin." The common misconception of the origin of Hungarian music at the turn of the century was that the *magyar nóta* represented the indigenous culture of both the Hungarian and the Gypsy peoples. It was not until the twentieth century that these claims were invalidated, and the extreme confusion of terms brought to light, by Kodály and Bartók's ethnomusicological research (Kodály 1976: 9, 13). From the deep layers of popular culture and oral peasant tradition, the two composers unearthed a dramatic, colorful, and varied heritage, which had been buried beneath romantic national illusions. Kodály describes the situation as follows:

> Generally speaking, Hungarian folk music is still identified with gypsy music, and folksong is confused with popular art-music. Yet in its narrower sense, Hungarian folk music has little or nothing in common with the music offered [...] as "Hungarian folk tunes" or [...] as "gypsy melodies". Performed by gypsy orchestras or in other popular arrangements, such music has been the basis of all generalizations about Hungarian music for nearly a hundred years. (Kodály 1971 [1960]: 5.)

In spite of its urban origins, the *magyar nóta* permeated the music of rural villages, where it was assimilated into an orally transmitted folk tradition (Dobszay 1984: 325–331). Bartók described the project of collecting and classifying folk melodies, which in the first instance led to a realization that the ideal musical expression was to be found in the peasant village, rather than the pseudo-folk tradition of the urban cultural center:

> In my studies of folk music, I discovered that what we had known as Hungarian folk songs until then were more or less trivial songs by popular composers and did not contain much that was valuable. I felt an urge to go deeper into this question and set out in 1905 to collect and study peasant music unknown until then. (*BBE* 1976 [1921a]: 409.)

In "La musique populaire hongroise", Bartók drew a distinction between the collective art of the peasant and the contrived art of urban culture:

> The latter are composed mainly by dilettante musicians who have a certain musical culture generally imported from the city; therefore, in the melodies of their invention, they blend certain Western commonplaces with certain exotic particularities of their own folk music. Consequently, even if these melodies preserve some faint exotic traces, they are too vulgar to have any intrinsic value. In contrast, we find in the folk melodies properly so-called, generally, a truly perfect purity of style. (*BBE* 1976 [1921c]: 59.)

The basis for Bartók's construction of a musical expression was fundamentally different from the gypsy idiom that constituted the accepted Hungarian national tone:

> This phenomenon is but a variant of the types of music that fulfill the same function in Western European countries; of the song hits, operetta airs, and other products of light music as performed by salon orchestras in restaurants and places of entertainment. [...] That this Hungarian popular art music, incorrectly called gypsy music, has more value than [much similar] foreign trash is perhaps a matter of pride for us, but when it is held up as something superior to so-called "light music" [...] we must raise our voices in solemn protest. The role of this popular art music is to furnish entertainment and to satisfy the musical needs of those whose artistic sensibilities are of a low order. (*BBE* 1976 [1931a]: 206–207.)

Erdely (2001: 25) observes that such ditties were intended "to provide the growing urban population with songs resembling folk songs but 'on a higher level'". The public regarded these songs "as being the true Hungarian song and gypsy music tradition" (ibid.: 26). In the nationalist ideology, music was exploited to promote the patriotism of the gentry and urban middle classes, who were completely unconcerned with the musical tradition of the Hungarian peasant.[194] Sándor Kovács (1993: 5) describes how "[T]he composer Bartók found the [urban] melodies less than inspiring, while the patriot Bartók found himself obliged to cherish them."

3.2.2. Hungarian national opera

The establishment of great musical institutions was a decisive step in the direction music was to take in Hungary. The Hungarian Royal Academy of Music was

---

194. In his "New Results of Folk Song Research in Hungary", Bartók (1932) discusses how, through his folk-music studies in Hungary, he found that so-called gypsy music, also widely known as such in foreign countries, is incorrectly called by that name. Bartók explains that it is none other than popular Hungarian art music that was disseminated by urban gypsy bands. Furthermore, the village gypsies have their own folk songs that differ from the repertoire of the city gypsy bands. The Hungarian music of the village gypsies sparked the beginning of contemporary Hungarian, high-art music.

founded in Budapest in 1875, with Liszt as its president and Erkel as director.[195] That institution has been the center of Hungarian musical education ever since that time, and together with the Budapest Philharmonic Society (1853) and the Operaház (1884), has formed the workshop of Hungarian artistic interpretation (Dobszay 1984: 320–325).

The early history of opera in Hungary is exemplified by the works of Joseph Haydn at Eszterháza, which were written in German or Italian for the Hapsburg nobility (Batta, ed. 1999: 216–217; see also, *BBE* 1976 [1943]: 361). Stage music was the domain in which the great results, and even greater problems, of Hungarian music of the nineteenth century unfolded. Along with addition *magyar nóta*, stage music was the genre that could reach wide strata of the Hungarian public in the most direct way, and it promised the first solution to problems of content and form in Hungarian music (Batta, ed. 1999: 325–331; on such problems, see also, pp. 110–111, Chapter 3.2.1).

The issue such as national opera deserves more than a general scrutiny I give it in this chapter. Opera histories have difficulties with accounting for national operas (Batta, ed. 1999: 143, 165, 245, 286, 296). The *New Grove Dictionary of Music and Musicians* includes the definition of national opera in the chapter about "Slavonic and National Opera" (Norris 1980: 615), claiming that national operas satisfied the hunger for national heritage with folk music and libretto based on national history, myth, legend, history and idealized peasant life.[196] If we examine more closely nineteenth-century Hungarian music and the contemporary written documents about the nature of this music, a problem emerges, what do we call national music? The question thus seems to be highly problematic, although it is once more impossible to explore every argument, as it deserves. Still, it is valuable to illustrate some crucial points and theories. On a very general level, we have to face a discrepancy between the musical material and the discourses on music. While the musical texture is still very much linked to the European musical trends and styles (mainly to German and

---

195. Several talented masters, composers and pedagogues of German origin or German culture worked in Hungary at that time. They played a decisive role in the musical education of the new Hungarian generation. On the other hand, violinist and composer Josef Joachim (1831–1907), Hans Richter (1843–1916), Arthur Nikisch (1855–1922), Leopold Auer (1845–1930), all natives of Hungary, worked at the same time as leading pedagogues in foreign countries. Robert Volkmann (1815–1883) was working from 1858 onwards in Pest, and he supported the contemporary romantic tendencies with his work as a composer. His successor, Hans (János) Koessler (1853–1926), enjoyed great authority as pedagogue. One of the most famous cellists of the time, David Popper (1843–1913), taught at the Budapest Academy of Music from 1886 onward, and the violinist and composer Victor Herzfeld (1856–1919) from 1888. (Herzfeld succeeded Koessler as the Chair of Musical Composition.) As Dobszay describes it (1984: 336–342), Hungarian composers and pedagogues learned much from German Romanticism, which introduced into Hungary not only an advanced professional ability but, at the same time, the music and the "cult" of contemporary German masters as well.

196. In most of European countries, opera had general esteem as the most representative work of a composer and of national style. It was the musical repertoire's best candidate to express nationalism. To compose a dramatic piece for stage was among the highest aspirations of those composers who hoped to establish themselves as national composers. (Batta, ed. 1999: 142–143.)

partly to Italian music) the discourses on music are in search of and try to establish the national music. Within such a framework, national operas emerged at the beginning of the nineteenth century. They were closely linked to the national awakenings of this period. These awakenings were also behind the re-institutionalization of the opera, which resulted in building new opera houses in many cities, and creating national companies. The success of these operas was largely due to their textual component: the use of vernacular. In Hungary, the emergence of national operas was closely tied to *nyelvújítás* (language reform) that started in the eighteenth century, and to the striving for a national theater and drama. These were reactions against the use of German and Latin language on stage and in the institutions of everyday life in general, which lingered on until the late nineteenth century in East-Central Europe. (Szerb 1982 [1934]: 261, 268–270, 312.)

After 1820, increasing experiments were made to create Hungarian opera.[197] With the appearance of the regular Hungarian theater, the Pesti Magyar Színház in 1837 and of an extraordinary artistic personality (Erkel) as well, the earlier endeavors seemed to reach their goal. (Szerb 1982 [1934]: 311–312, 348.) Added to this impetus was given to Hungarian opera through the close and organic connection with the ideas of national freedom, powerfully unfolding in the "reform era",[198] and of bourgeois progress (Dobszay 1984: 283–295; and Németh 1967: 37–52). I shall not deal with every single Hungarian opera related to the "reform era", but some are unavoidable. Quite well known is that Erkel was the first to consciously create a Hungarian opera language. Erkel's themes described the conflicts of the Hungarian reform era, of the War of Liberation and of Absolutism, and the historical background, revived in his works, spoke to the great masses of the audience. For Erkel the relation to the people was not the central problem, the invigorating power; for him the people represented an idyll, reconciliation, not an obligation, but a comforting background. The success of his operas is much indebted also to their librettos, which were canonized texts of Hungarian literature. József Katona's (1791–1830) *Bánk Bán* came to be regarded as the national drama and in 1848, when it was first performed during the Hungarian revolution, had a huge success. (Szerb 1982 [1934]: 100, 291, 294–299.) Nearly ten years later, Erkel's opera with the same title had a

197. A good example is e.g., the *Béla futása* (1822) by József Ruzitska (1775–1823).
198. In the Reform Era of 1820–1848, the aristocratic leadership of Hungary, in its struggle against Austrian oppression, played at least temporarily, a truly liberal and forward-looking political role. It learned then that only Hungary's industrial, commercial, and legal development would enable her to withstand foreign encroachment. (Gergely & Szász 1978: 5–6.) Counts István Széchenyi (1791–1860), Lajos Battyhány (1807–1849), and Baron József Eötvös (1813–1871) were representatives of this early liberal tendency in the Hungarian ruling class (Szerb 1982 [1934]: 313, 315–322, 340–348, 361–366; see also, Gergely & Szász 1978: 56). Széchenyi called for the Western political and social orientation of Hungary, as well as her systematic industrialization. Battyhány was executed for his leadership of the democratic revolutionary government in the war of independence of 1848–1849. Baron Eötvös was the father of Hungary's liberal educational system and perhaps the foremost advocate in Eastern Europe of the emancipation of Jews. (Ibid.: 192–193.) The favorable atmosphere created by this development was instrumental in opening up to the Jews the field of economic initiative, particularly after the middle of the nineteenth century (Szekfű 1939: 315; see also, Gergely & Szász 1978: 83–85).

similar success (Kodály 1974 [1960]: 412; and Batta, ed. 1999: 142–143). Erkel's exceptionally expressive melodies, forceful dramatic imagination, and the dramatic *recitativo* itself were first introduced into the Hungarian opera.[199] He composed eight operas – or nine, if we include *Erzsébet* (*Elizabeth*) (1857), written in collaboration with Ferenc Doppler (1821–1883), and Károly Doppler (1825–1900). (Dobszay 1984: 291–295; see also, Table 3.1.)

Librettist(s)	Title	Year
Béni Egressy	*Bátori Mária* (*Mária Bátori*)	1840
Béni Egressy	*Hunyadi László* (*László Hunyadi*)	1844
Béni Egressy	*Erzsébet* (*Elizabeth*)	1857
Béni Egressy	*Bánk bán*	1861
József Czanyuga	*Sarolta*	1862
Mór Jókai and Ede Szigligeti	*Dózsa György* (*György Dózsa*)	1867
Lehel Ódry and Ferenc Ormai	*Brankovics György* (*György Brankovics*)	1874
Ede Tóth	*Névtelen hősök* (*Unknown Heroes*)	1880
Antal Várady	*István király* (*King Stephen*)	1885

Table 3.1. Ferenc Erkel's operas.

Erkel's life work – the national opera – found its organic continuation in the monumental musical forms created by Liszt[200] and Mosonyi. All three composers ap-

199. Erkel may be thus justly ranked with the contemporary composers of the Spring of the Nations, of the European awakening around 1848, with the musician-heralds of the ideals of national and social progress, with Mihail Ivanovics Glinka (1804–1857), Stanislaw Moniuszko (1819–1872), Bedřich Smetana (1824–1884), and to a certain extent with Verdi (Batta, ed. 1999: 162–169, 572–573, 666–753). Verdi's best Italian operas were written within the framework of a national tradition that tolerated basic changes only in the contents of the plot. Yet, Verdi was a fertilizing influence on the *verismo* school from Amilcare Ponchielli (1834–1886) to Giacomo Puccini (1858–1924), and on modern Italian opera until Luigi Dallapiccola (1904–1975). The dramatic force of *Bánk bán*, *Dózsa György* or *Brankovics György*, and the lyrical richness of *Névtelen hősök*, could not be reached by any of Erkel's Hungarian contemporaries. I mention some examples indicating the issue. Mosonyi's *Szép Ilonka* (*Beautiful Nelly*) (1861) was created under the influence of popular national purism, and was quite a noteworthy experiment in the domain of the Hungarian fairytale opera. Mosonyi's *Álmos* (1862) was a monumental Hungarian drama of the period. (Bónis 1960: 163–218.) Other opera composers of Erkel's time, however, were inferior to his example, e.g., Károly Thern, Ferenc Doppler, Károly Doppler, György Császár. Gusztáv Böhm's (1823–1878) and Gusztáv Fáy's (1824–1866) theatrical work introduced new elements for the most part only inasmuch as they gave – beside Italian and Hungarian elements – a bigger play to German and possibly to French influences. (Dobszay 1984: 295–308, 319.)

200. Liszt was active in the world of opera. Yet the only one he wrote, *Don Sanche ou Le château d'amour* (1824–1825), was a youthful work, performed when Liszt was fourteen years old. Liszt was most important, in this context, for his unflagging support of contemporaneous opera, particularly those of Wagner. Part of this support was manifested by Liszt's many piano transcriptions of opera works. From 1843 to the end of his life Liszt conducted opera, the first being a performance of *The Magic Flute* at Breslau. Liszt also wrote an oratorio, *Die Legende von der heiligen Elisabeth* (1857–1867), which was performed as an opera, against his wishes, at Weimar in 1881, and several times later. (Gárdonyi 1984: 427–428, 433.)

proached Hungarian music as *aficionados* of foreign musical cultures, who were en-deavoring to raise the music of their own country to a high artistic level.[201] They drew inspiration not from within, but from without, giving it musical expression in roman-tic-idealistic ways.[202] Erkel, for instance, transplanted the idiom of Western opera in-to the Hungarian milieu without completely abandoning Italian melodic styles (e.g., *bel canto*) and treatment of the libretto. The operas that Erkel wrote before Wagner (1984 [1852]) published his theories of *Musikdrama* and *Gesamtkunstwerk* (total art-work)[203] were immediately received with enthusiasm by the public, and became recognized as the national operas (see Table 3.1, previous page). Wagner believed that his *Gesamtkunstwerk* had superseded all earlier phases of artistic development, making the former redundant. Doubtless, the intellectualization of the creative proc-ess was an advance on methods that relied merely on vague intuition. (A. Molnár 1931b: 241–242; and Heiniö 1989: 67; for more on Wagner, see also, Tarasti 1994 [1978].) Erkel's writing in *Bátori Mária*, *Hunyadi László*, and the *Hunyadi Nyitány* (*Hunyadi Overture*) (1845) was based on the *verbunkos* style and *csárdás* dance music, which were, and still are, the stereotypes of Hungarian music (Németh 1967: 52–59, 72–85). Erkel's operas displayed a romanticized and progressive conception of history and humanity; in them, the "young", developing nation could see itself as wearing a crown of romantic-historical glory (ibid.: 67–100, 123–236). Be that as it may, his works do in fact represent the crowning achievement of Hungarian musical drama in the nineteenth century.[204]

201. Erkel's Italianate melodies and theatrical work went a long way towards the creation of Hun-garian heroic opera. In contrast, the revolutionary spirit of French Romanticism, in its attempts to reform symphonic, church, and piano music, inspired Liszt. (Kodály 1974 [1921]: 428.) Mosonyi worked with classical forms when composing; at other times, he engaged in profound and diverse educational activities. The influences of those composers on Hungarian music remains unsurpassed even by their successors, because in addition to their individual abilities, they brought about an unprecedented artistic intensification of the Romantic musical idiom. (Bónis 1960: 219–266.)
202. The composers who realized the romantic ideals of Erkel's time in the field of instrumental music were the representatives and (in Liszt's case) leading figures of European Romanticism. Hungarian stage-singing could not yet draw upon a rich tradition, in spite of the experiments of Ruzitska, András (Endre) Bartay (1799–1839), and others. However, composers for the Hungar-ian stage had forms readily at hand: those of Italian and French opera literature (Rossini, Bellini, Donizetti, Verdi, Auber, and Meyerbeer) and those of the *verbunkos* and popular Hungarian songs. (Kodály 1984 [1939]: 22, 34–35; see also, Chapters 3.2–3.2.1.)
203. Wagner believed that the future of music, music theater, and all the arts relied on acceptance of the *Gesamtkunstwerk*, a fusion of the arts that had not been attempted on this scale since clas-sical Greek drama. In his essay, "The Art-Work of the Future," Wagner (1993 [1949]) prescribed a synthesis in which opera served as a vehicle for the unification of all arts into a single medium of artistic expression. The Festspielhaus Theater opened in 1876 in Bayreuth, and there Wagner applied his theatrical innovations: darkening the house, surround-sound reverberation, and the re-vitalization of Greek amphitheater seating to focus audience attention on the stage. This approach to opera foreshadowed contemporary experiments in virtual reality, by immersing the audience in the imaginary world of the stage.
204. By the 1860s, when the first Hungarian musical review (*Zenészeti Lapok*) appeared, a strong Wagnerian influence dominated Hungarian musical discourse. Mosonyi compared Erkel to Wag-ner, though we cannot detect in Erkel's music of that time any sign of Wagner's influence. (Kodály 1974 [1921]: 427; and 1974 [1960]: 413.) The *Zenészeti Lapok* canonized Erkel as the Hungarian

Later, Erkel worked along two lines. On the one hand, he concerned himself with closed, *arioso* forms; on the other, his objective was the creation of Hungarian dramatic *recitativo*. In the former, he relied on Italian operatic techniques and aspects of Hungarian popular song (*Bánk bán, Sarolta, Névtelen hősök*); later, Erkel was inspired by Wagner (*Dózsa György, Brankovics György, István király*).[205] (Németh 1967: 153–236.) There are some indications that Erkel considered his dramatic *recitativo* to be Hungarian in character, but he did not take the *recitativo* of the Hungarian folk song as his compositional starting point, as Bartók did a quarter of a century later (Kodály 1974 [1946a]: 180). Indeed, in all Hungarian opera literature of the nineteenth century – despite its great promise and important results – one senses an atmosphere of experimentation. The operas of Erkel and his contemporaries nevertheless provide a glimpse of the possibilities of Hungarian stage music, if not a final solution. It was no accident that those composers worked so hard to attain such results in the name of romantic national ideas.[206] (Batta, ed. 1999: 142–143.)

---

national composer. Wagner's theories were embraced by Mosonyi (1984 [1852]), who at the same time criticized Hungarian musical life for being too much under the influence of German music. When vilification of foreign composers was a common occurrence in the press, he urged that music be taught by Hungarian music teachers, not by Germans (Bónis 1960: 142–162). On the one hand, Mosonyi wanted to establish Hungarian music criticism and the idea of Hungarian music on Wagnerian foundations; on the other, he also took great care to avoid being affected by the influence of German music (Dobszay 1984: 324). Bartók faced a similar situation, as can be observed in his early writings, which date from the first years of the twentieth century (see p. 124, Chapter 3.3).

205. Wagner had an immense effect on Hungarian musical life. Though the concept of a national opera is older than Wagner's theories, he used this term in a specific sense. Wagner (1984 [1852]) connected the idea of the musical drama with the reification of the truly national character of a nation. Wagner found inspiration in old Nordic sagas and German mythology. However, one must keep in mind that German mythology was in vogue as early as the time of the Grimm brothers, which tied in very well with the struggle for a national literary history. (Voigt 1990c: 100–101; and Batta, ed. 1999: 242–243, 432, 776.) Attempts at discovering, re-constructing, and making national mythologies took place all over Europe, and were characteristic of nineteenth-century literary and musical pursuits. Yet, those so-called pure national elements turned out to be not so pure after all. In Eastern Europe, for example, where different peoples intermingled or lived very close to each other, we can easily see the hybridization of national cultural traditions. The same is true of national musics, which have their roots mainly in folk music. Today, it is clear that much music and literature of the nineteenth and twentieth centuries was composed and received within the context of this or that national discourse. (Norris 1980.) Most important for the present study is the impact that the major trends of European romanticism, along with Wagner's theoretical essays and musical dramas, had on Hungarian culture (Bónis 1960: 142–162).

206. Musical artists worked zealously to build systematic schools, co-operatives, and cultural forums for their work. Kornél Ábrányi (1822–1903), Mosonyi's comrade-in-arms in heading up the *Zenészeti Lapok* (*Musical Journal*), worked tirelessly on behalf of the centralization of Hungarian musical life. Ábrányi made his mark in the 1870s with the foundation of the Országos Magyar Daláregyesület (National Hungarian Choral Society) and ten years later, the Hungarian Music Academy (Bónis 1960: 142–162), Károly Huber (1828–1885), piano virtuoso, composer of songs and piano pieces, author, editor, pedagogue, and social agitator, propagated Erkel's and Mosonyi's ideals while also furthering the cause of violin playing and male-choir literature. In the 1860s, Ede Reményi (1828–1898), the well-known violinist, was one of the chief promoters of musical life in the capital city. Imre Székely (1823–1887), composer of Hungarian fantasies, rhapsodies and folk-song paraphrases, was one of the most celebrated pianists in the country after 1852.

The principal works of Erkel's day soon belonged to the past, and Liszt's symphonic poems and piano works would have no sequels. Still, the zealous work of lesser artists and of educators could have grown into a movement of national significance, if the historic and social contradictions of the post-Compromise period had not become increasingly obvious.[207] (*BBE* 1976 [1921b];[208] and Szabolcsi 1960;[209] for more on this topic, see pp. 99–103, Chapter 3.1.)

A turning point came when the romantic-national tendency was pushed into the background after 1880. The national tendency of the romantic school changed during this period, deteriorating into works written by salon composers, into the genre of stylish Hungarian fantasies, arrangements of gypsy music, and so on. The exhausted Hungarian-romantic generation was revived by the new "school" of Late Romanticism, which was again nurtured by foreign musical influences, only more one-sidedly and more exclusively than its predecessors had been. (Kodály 1984

Székely's artistic development was influenced greatly by the atmosphere and culture of Paris, as was that of two representatives of the Liszt-school, Sándor Bertha (1843–1912) and Károly Aggházy (1855–1918). All three of them traveled widely, and in their works endeavored to adapt Hungarian romantic musical language to West-European forms. Bertha and Aggházy also wrote for the stage: Bertha's opera *Mátyás király* (*King Matthias*) was first performed in Paris in 1883; Aggházy's opera, *Maritta*, written during his stay in Berlin and Budapest, was premiered in 1897. Not surprisingly, experiments in creating characteristically Hungarian sonata forms also began, carried out by Ábrányi, Bertha, Attila Horváth (1862–1921) and Henrik Gobbi (1842–1920), a pupil of Volkmann and Liszt; Reményi tried his hand at developing a distinctly Hungarian, multi-movement string quartet. Antal Siposs (1839–1923) and Aladár Juhász (1856–1922), followed by Szendy (appointed a Professor at the Academy of Music in 1890) and István Thomán (1862–1941), continued Liszt's tradition in the domain of piano playing and pedagogy. Around them were a great many composers whose influence remained within a narrower compass, e.g., Imre Elbert (1860–1897), Ferenc Sárosi (1855–1913), Ödön Farkas (1851–1921), and others. They were partly followers of Western musical traditions, and partly followers of Erkel's, Mosonyi's, and Liszt's romantic-national styles. (Dobszay 1984: 305–308, 336–342.)

207. Károly Goldmark (1830–1915) was a popular opera composer at the end of the nineteenth century. He followed in the steps of contemporary Viennese masters in his effective stage works, e.g., *Die Königin von Saba* in 1875, and *Merlin* in 1885. (Batta, ed. 1999: 178–179; and Dobszay 1984: 342.) Ödön Mihalovich (1842–1929), a dominant figure who for more than three decades was the director of the Budapest Academy of Music, composed his stage works under Wagner's influence, as is particularly evident in *Eliána* (1885–1887) and *Toldi* (1888–1889, rev. 1893–1894). Mihalovics, when young, had met both Liszt and Wagner, and from the 1860s onwards, he promoted the Wagner cult in Hungary. Jenő Hubay (Huber) (1858–1937) was Mihalovich's successor at the Budapest Academy of Music, where he worked as director, composer, and founder of the world-famous Hungarian violin school; he composed in the style of French and German instrumental musical culture of the nineteenth century, particularly that of Jules Massenet (1842–1912) and Henri Vieuxtemps (1820–1881). (Lindlar 1984: 70; and Dobszay 1984: 338.)

208. In his essay "On Modern Music in Hungary", Bartók (*BBE* 1976 [1921b]) gives political and geographic reasons for the lack of a truly Hungarian composer until the nineteenth century. He based his argument on information gathered while collecting folk music, as well as on source-studies of Liszt's music, the modern French school, and some German sources. (See also, Kodály 1974 [1960]: 413.)

209. In "Liszt and Bartók" (1960), the Hungarian musicologist Bence Szabolcsi (1899–1973) discusses the fraternal homage of one great master to another, and the decisive impact Liszt's music had on Bartók, who was impressed by Liszt's virtuosity, composing skills, thought (prose), and humanism, as well as his impact on the contemporary public.

[1939]: 37–38.) Now only "European culture", not indigenous musical roots, set the program for the new romantic composers of Hungary. In consequence, the duality of Hungarian musical life became more and more pronounced. The antagonism between the urban public (imitators of the West) and the provincials (cultivators of Gypsy music) deepened, forcing a choice between two alternatives: culture or Hungary. (Dobszay 1984: 275; see also, pp. 108–109, Chapter 3.2.1.) Such an alternative could only result in deception: by semi-education on the one hand, and by superficial nationalism on the other.[210]

The gulf between members of the generation born after 1900 was widening; neither was unity to be found between members of the older generation. The great millennial celebrations (1896) were held in Budapest in the spirit of national chauvinism, and slogans were intended to encourage members of the *petit-bourgeoisie* to support the Hungarian ruling classes.[211] The coming of the new millennium refocused the attention of many Hungarians on something they had previously undervalued: the indigenous peasant culture of their own land.[212] Not just members of the older musical generation, but also highly cultured writers and men of public life, professionals and amateurs alike, began to sense a vacuum under the surface of life.[213] (Kodály 1974 [1950]: 451; see also, Gergely & Szász 1978: 212–216.) The Hungarian public, which in the first half of the nineteenth century had responded to Italian and French opera music, was now enthralled by Germanic musical trends, as

---

210. The school of Volkmann consisted of several well-known musicians, among them Gyula J. Major (1858–1925) and Mór Vavrinecz (1858–1913), both of whom composed stage and symphonic works. They were joined by two of Liszt's pupils, Count Géza Zichy (1849–1924) and Henrik Gobbi, and by one of Mosonyi's pupils, János Végh (1845–1918). In the last third of the nineteenth century, Hungarian music flourished once again; e.g., in the church music of Mátyás Engeszer (1812–1885) and in the symphonies of Gyula Beliczay (1835–1893), both of whom adapted the formal tradition of German late-Romanticism. (Dobszay 1984: 336–342.)

211. The situation became even graver, with the strengthening of financial capital and rise of the bourgeoisie, who were feeling an urgent need for independence in order to purse their form of Hungarian capitalism.

212. Around the turn of the century, architecture was the domain in which the idea of creating a modern and national style by the stylistic integration of folk art proved most fruitful. Ödön Lechner (1845–1914), the leading figure of the secessionist movement, along with Sándor Baumgarten (1864–1928), designed the Posta-takarékpénztár (Postal Savings Bank) in 1896 (built 1900–1901) and the Földtani Intézet (Institute of Geology) (designed 1896, built 1897–1899). Erected in Budapest, both buildings mingled decorative motifs from Hungarian folk art with the secessionist style. Several members of the following generation continued on the path of Lechner. Among them was architect Károly Kós (1883–1977), who used Székely's architectural patterns in the geometrical shapes of his buildings. (Gergely & Szász 1978: 212–216.)

213. Pessimism ran high among the younger generation of composers at the turn of the century. The older composers, e.g., Béla Szabados (1867–1936) and Ede Poldini (1869–1957), were still absorbed in the national traditions of the last century, the younger composers, even those schooled in French and German musical culture or who settled abroad, had lost faith in the pathos of Romanticism. They were largely interested developing a more modern Hungarian musical idiom, but realized that the barriers to doing so were insurmountable; among them were Albert Siklós (1878–1942), Emil Ábrányi Jr. (1850–1920), Tivadar Szántó (1877–1934), Ervin Lendvai (1882–1949), and Jenő Zádor (1894–1977). (Dobszay 1984: 319–325.)

promoted by Hans Koessler[214] and his circle. An academic bias toward Late Romanticism began to appear, playing a dominant role around 1900, and creating a deep gulf between the academic composers of German culture and the increasingly dilettantish epigones of national Hungarian romanticism. (Demény, ed. 1976: 59; and Lindlar 1984: 92–93.)

How to continue? That was the predicament facing all composers, both major figures and lesser lights. Around 1905, members of the younger musical generation were becoming conscious of the fact that the romantic artists of the last century belonged to the past, and that their work had presented only a transitional solution. The problems were more profound and more complicated than could be seen at the time, amid the prosperity of the national era and the enthusiasm of the musical pioneers.

The change in Bartók's style took place precisely in those years, when the first modernist developments occurred in other spheres of Hungarian cultural life, and when his social researches and literary experiences were the most intense (see also, pp. 103–105, Chapter 3.1). In his article "On Modern Music in Hungary", Bartók (*BBE* 1976 [1921d]: 474) refused to consider the music of Erkel, and even of Liszt, as Hungarian art music. Bartók maintained that the heterogeneous combination of elements found in their pieces not only failed to produce great music but also hindered the development of a national style, a view shared also by Kodály (1974 [1950]: 451; and 1976: 11). This raises questions as to the place of *Bluebeard's Castle*. Bartók, planning to create an art that was specifically Hungarian but free from the conventions of political nationalism, had no model to rely on. He thus needed to reinvent the genre of national opera in Hungary. Bartók's *Bluebeard* illustrates his search for a contemporary style, which was nevertheless rooted in popular sources and through which he could combine music and language to make a fervently nationalistic declaration. As emphasized by Frigyesi:

> Bartók's stylistic inventions in *Bluebeard Castle* fall roughly into two categories. The orchestral music is essentially a large-scale, one-movement, symphonic form that creates a stylistic synthesis similar to [that of] Bartók's later music. The vocal style, however, had no continuation either in the pieces of Bartók or in others, even though this invention was no less original and was, in fact, the only attempt to create a modern Hungarian vocal style. (Frigyesi 1998: 235.)

As it turned out, *Duke Bluebeard's Castle* failed to set a new course for other composers to follow. Bartók clearly based his approach to writing opera on the more

---

214. After Volkmann's death (1883), Koessler became the Professor of Composition at the Budapest Academy of Music. He retired in 1908, but later resumed working, as head of the Composition Department of the Academy of Music from 1920 to 1925.

recent works of Strauss[215] and Debussy[216], while also looking back to Wagner (A. Molnár 1931b: 229, 231, 246–247). Nevertheless, the range of Bartók's resources, and the skill and freedom with which he employs them, are evident throughout the opera.

3.3. Bartók and nationalism

A full account of nationalism cannot reasonably be given in this chapter. Thus, my aim here is to consider some previous accounts of the phenomenon, in a way that is fitting and useful to the theoretical and analytical aims of the present study.

How does one approach the topic of nationalism? The study of nations and nationalism has been treated by a variety of disciplines, including history, sociology, and political science.[217] The history of music, too, can make a considerable contribution to the study of nations and nationalism, both as a source of information and a view (and possible problematizing) of musicological debates on the subject. Traditionally, musicology has been reluctant to consider the possible role and importance of nationalism.[218] Richard Taruskin's article on the subject lays out some problems that musicologists face when engaging with nationalism, the first of which is defining the topic: "Definitions of nationalism depend, of course, on definitions of the nation. It is not likely that consensus will ever be reached on their precise meaning,

---

215. In "Common Nietzschean Symbols in Bartók and R. Strauss", András Batta (1982) discusses the influence of Strauss's music (e.g., *Also sprach Zarathustra*) on that of Bartók. Batta states that Strauss's enchantment with Nietzsche's delirium took root in the aesthetic views of the young Bartók. The result was complete and consistent, preserved in Bartók's dramatic concepts in durable and perceptible form. (See also, Demény, ed. 1976: 84, 86, 130; and Batta 1984.)

216. Composition on more than one tonal plane was prefigured in both Debussy and Strauss. In *Pelléas et Mélisande* and his later piano music, Debussy often writes parallel, non-functional chord progressions, in a style very close to the successive polytonality of Bartók. Strauss, in *Also sprach Zarathustra*, frequently combines the keys of C major and B major. Indeed, the work closes with a high pianissimo B major triad answered by a C in the bass. In *Salome*, triads belonging to different tonalities often appear in rapid succession or simultaneously. (Batta, ed. 1999: 588–599.)

217. This multiplicity of disciplines has prompted the interdisciplinary approach to the issue taken by many scholars. The history of music has been employed as a source in the study of nations and nationalism, but not to the same extent as, for example, architecture and art history. (Taruskin 2001: 670.)

218. While there are usually multiple historical accounts of the music in a country, region or locality, musicology has largely treated musical nationalism under the category of "national schools" and as a divergence from a universal norm. The national has been considered the particular, and has been associated with genres such as symphonic poems, rhapsodies, dance suites, and other character pieces of Hungarian, Norwegian or similarly peripheral origins. Such pieces have been seen as the "lighter" side of the concert repertory and/or as salon music (see above, p. 118, Chapter 3.2.1). In the early twentieth century, Guido Adler's "school" emphasized musicology as a science, and took as its point of departure Eduard Hanslick's (1825–1904) ideas about "absolute music"; applying those ideas to musical composition, Adler and his followers developed a concept of style that was considered universal – i.e., "classical" – and beyond national differences. For example, the Palestrina style was not considered Italian, but as classical vocal polyphony; J. S. Bach's style was viewed as the culmination of the linear counterpoint; and Viennese classicism was not necessarily seen as "Viennese", but as the peak of the symphonic style. (Taruskin 2001: 690–694.)

since different definitions serve different interests" (2001: 689). Different definitions emphasize linguistic, ethnic, religious, cultural, or historical communities that are considered to constitute the foundations of the nation. It appears that musical nationalism has its roots in cultural communities that preceded the modern nation (see also, Samson, ed. 2001[219]).

In a letter dated January 10, 1931 and addressed to the Romanian ethnographer Octavian Beu (1893–1964), Bartók writes, "I consider myself a Hungarian composer" (quoted in Szabolcsi, ed. 1957: 261). It is one of many statements that has contributed to an image of Bartók as a distinctively national composer. For example, Bartók had written a letter to his mother about twenty-eight years earlier, criticizing her for speaking German rather than Hungarian[220] (Demény, ed. 1971: 30; and 1976: 61–62). Bartók stated his own position on the national question: *"Ich meinerseits werde auf allen Gebieten meines Lebens immer und in jeder Weise nur einem Zwecke dienen: den Wohle der ungarischen Nation und des ungarischen Vaterlandes"*[221] (quoted in Szabolcsi, ed. 1957: 262). After Bartók's death, Hungarian musicologists, most notably Szabolcsi, Demény, and Ujfalussy, considered nationalism to have been a constant factor in his life.[222]

In "Gastronomy or Geology? The Role of Nationalism in the Reconstruction of Nations", Anthony Smith has this to say:

---

219. Jim Samson's (ed. 2001) analysis of nationalism deals with it in at least two ways: (1) as a predominantly political type, with roots in Western European and American liberalism; (2) as a predominantly cultural type, with roots in German philosophy. In *The Idea of Nationalism: A Study in Its Origins and Background*, Hans Kohn (1945) developed the distinction between a Western and Eastern nationalisms. For more on national identity and cultural nationalism, see Smith (1991) and Hutchinson (1987).

220. Bartók's mother, Paula Voit, and his aunt Irma Voit (1849–1941), like most of the educated people in Pozsony (otherwise Pressburg, now Bratislava, Slovakia), tended to speak German or at least to employ German words and idioms. Bartók's long letter (Demény, ed. 1971: 28–31) contains his noblest expression of his credo, to which he remained loyal throughout his life. Later in the years 1904–1905, Bartók became increasingly frustrated with the musical culture of Budapest. Bartók's nationalist pronouncements should be understood as being entirely motivated by his frustration with the conventional forms of musical expression, and necessitated by his rejection of the German dominated tradition. (Ibid.: 35–54; and 1976: 73–102.)

221. "For my own part, I will in all my doings and in every way serve only one purpose: the completion of the Hungarian nation and the Hungarian fatherland" (quoted in Demény, ed. 1971: 201).

222. The term "canonization" applies to Bartók in both senses of the word. First, he is one of the most performed and most studied composers of the twentieth century and a landmark figure in the history of ethnomusicology. Second, because of the potent combination of his nationalist rhetoric, advocacy of the peasant music of Hungarians and other groups in the region, and international prominence as a composer, he has proved an ideal candidate for "musical sainthood", in the words of Malcolm Gillies (2000: 293). Recent scholarship has shown how Bartók's work was interpreted and reinterpreted as the model for whatever direction any given writer espoused for the country, from the 1940s to the 1980s (cf. Fosler-Lussier 2001; and Gal 1991). Since Bartók was transformed into a symbol through which political meaning could be contested, writings about him have often taken on a reverential tone.

Perhaps the central question in our understanding of nationalism is the role of the past in the creation of the present. This is certainly the area in which there have been the sharpest divisions between theorists of nationalism. Nationalists, perennialists, modernists, and post-modernists have presented us with very different interpretations of that role. The manner in which they have viewed the place of ethnic history has largely determined their understanding of nations and nationalism today. (Smith 1994: 18.)

Bartók's development into a mature, modern composer has been well documented (e.g., Bartók Jr, ed. 1981a;[223] and Suchoff 1987[224]). In particular, American musicology has shown that Bartók's nationalism changed with his stylistic development and ultimately brought him into conflict with official Hungarian nationalism (Taruskin 2001). In the nineteenth and early twentieth centuries, several conflicting musical forces became evident in Europe, the most prominent of which were German late Romanticism, French Impressionism, and the folk music of Eastern Europe. Increasing nationalist demands during the decades of international tension prior to World War I contributed to the independent development of those "-isms" (see also, Chapters 2.1.2 and 3.1–3.2).

Bartók ardently embraced the nationalist spirit, but his musical training and knowledge were rooted in the Germanic tradition (Frigyesi 1989[225]). His youthful Hungarian nationalism helps explain why in 1899 he chose to study at the Budapest Academy of Music rather than at the relatively more prestigious Academy in

---

223. In his *Chronicle of My Father's Life*, Béla Bartók Jr. (1981a) gives a day-by-day account of the composer's musical pursuits. This chronology is grouped into periods of several years, each according to specific activities.

224. In the "Ethnomusicological Roots of Béla Bartók's Musical Language", Suchoff (1987) presents a brief history of the development of Bartók's musical language in his early years. Suchoff begins with late-nineteenth-century Romantic influences on the composer, such as his imitation of Liszt's Hungarianism in *Kossuth* and other works written between 1902 and 1905; after that period, Bartók drew more on folk-music sources from various nations. Suchoff also describes the structure of Hungarian, Slovak, Romanian, Ruthenian, Bulgarian, Yugoslav, Arab, and Turkish folk materials. (See also, *BBE* 1976 [1937a].)

225. The Brahmsian style of Bartók's music, written during the early 1890s when he was in Pozsony, was transformed during his student days at the Budapest Academy of Music (1899–1903) by his intense study of the chromatic scores of Wagner. Between May 17 and June 9, 1900, he made no fewer than twelve visits to the Opera House. The season included four works by Wagner: *Siegfried, Tannhäuser, Lohengrin* and *Die Walküre* (Bartók Jr, ed. 1981a: 32–33). His letters speak steadily about his study of Wagner. *Das Rheingold* and *Die Walküre* are mentioned several times, and he even transcribed parts of the scores for his family to look at (Demény, ed. 1971: 30, 40, 55, 76, 78, 82, 97, 146; and 1976: 17). In his autobiography, other works by Wagner are mentioned, such as the *Ring*-Cycle, *Tristan*, and *Die Meistersinger* (*BBE* 1976 [1921a]: 408). It is clear from the list of operas planned for the season that Budapest was one of the strongholds of Wagnerian opera. In August 1904, a Wagner scholarship enabled Bartók to make a pilgrimage to Bayreuth, the Mecca of all Wagnerians (Bartók Jr, ed. 1981a: 67).

Vienna, which had offered him a scholarship[226] (Demény 1954[227]). It permeates his earliest compositions, which were inspired by both Liszt and *verbunkos*, and was recognized as an expression of the Hungarian national identity (Bónis 1972;[228] and Oramo 1977a [1976];[229] see also, Chapters 3.2–3.2.2). The discovery of folk music liberated Bartók from not only "the stylized gypsy music of contemporary popular entertainment, but also from the forms and restrictions of nineteenth-century classical music" (Gluck 1987: 10). Another writer observes that Bartók's "program was to create a new type of music that would overthrow the centuries-old dominance of German music" (Glatz 1987: 77).

From 1899 to early 1902, Bartók's zeal for composition ebbed between 1892 and 1902, maybe because Bartók found his teacher, Koessler, too traditionalist, and hence a stumbling block rather than an inspiration[230] (Demény, ed. 1976: 16, 32, 35; Kodály 1974 [1921]: 428; and 1974 [1950]: 450). Bartók (*BBE* 1976 [1921a]: 410)

---

226. In his first year at the Academy, he worked assiduously at many subjects; but his second year was interrupted by pulmonary illness, and he had to spend several months at Meran (November 15, 1900 to April 1, 1901), which completely restored him to health. Mrs. Róza Zsigmond Gárdony was the patron of the young Bartók, and paid the costs for him to go to Meran. In his third year at the Academy (1901–1902), he first attracted notice as a pianist, and as a composer found stimulation in the scores of Strauss's symphonic poems. In his last year at the Academy, he made frequent public appearances, both as a soloist and as a member of a chamber ensemble. It was during this period he gave his first solo recital in Nagyszentmiklós. He had his first success abroad in Vienna, after which he began to give more public performances. In 1903–1904, he spent much of the winter season in Berlin, but as his career began to develop, he visited many other cities, too. The most important work from this period was the symphonic poem *Kossuth*. (Bartók Jr, ed. 1981a: 26–63.)

227. Demény (1954) gives an account of the composer's student years at the Budapest Academy of Music (1899–1903). In January 1899, Bartók left Pozsony for Budapest, where Professor Thomán gave him an audition. For the first time he lived far from his widowed mother, whom he had reluctantly left in Pozsony. The letters he wrote to his mother during the early years of his career are of such significance that they have been given almost exclusive priority (Demény, ed. 1971: 11–54; and 1976: 13–71). Demény (1954) includes an account of the following years, up to 1905 (in which Bartók turned to the Romantic influence of Liszt) and of his nationalistic period, during which he composed *Kossuth*.

228. Ferenc Bónis (1972) provides a brief history of the *verbunkos* as it developed since the latter part of the eighteenth century and discusses its influence on the development of Hungarian art music in the nineteenth century. Bónis investigates Bartók's usage of the *verbunkos* style in his early compositions and how that usage evolved in his later works (ibid.: 146–153).

229. Oramo (1977a [1976]) explores the stylistic and formal characteristics of the *verbunkos* style in the late works of Bartók, starting with the two *Rhapsodies* for violin (1928). Oramo presents a comparison of the "Marcia" and "Burletta" of the *Sixth Quartet* with the *verbunkos* and *sebes* (fast) movement of *Contrasts*. (See also, Lindlar 1984: 93.)

230. Koessler did not consider Bartók his best composition pupil. Koessler's school (around 1900) was approaching the Hungarian style more conspicuously and was more inclined to accept reform tendencies. In his compositions, Dohnányi, one of great pianists of his time, was a follower of the German masters of Romanticism; at the same time, he often "colored" his works with Hungarianism; e.g., in his *Ruralia Hungarica* of 1924 (Lindlar 1984: 47–48). Leó Weiner (1885–1960) was the most important representative of classical chamber-music culture in the first half of the twentieth century. As the writer of such orchestral pieces as *Csongor and Tünde* (1915), a piano concertino, string quartets and divertimenti, he had great influence on composers of the succeeding generation (Lányi 1978 [1916]).

remarks, "I did no independent work for two years, and at the Budapest Academy of Music was considered only a first class pianist." Bartók continues:

> From this stagnation, I was aroused as by a flash of lightning, by the first Budapest performance of *Thus Spake Zarathustra*. [...] This work, received with shudders by musicians here, stimulated the greatest enthusiasm in me; at last, I saw the way that lay before me. Straightway I threw myself into a study of Strauss's scores, and began again to compose. (*BBE* 1976 [1921a]: 410.)

Later in 1902, Bartók transcribed Strauss's tone poem *Ein Heldenleben* (*A Hero's Life*) for solo piano (Op. 40, 1897–1898), and on January 26, 1903 performed it at the Viennese Tonkünstlerverein to considerable public acclaim[231] (Bartók Jr, ed. 1981a: 50; and Demény, ed. 1976: 34–37). The polychromatic orchestral textures of Strauss had an immediate effect upon Bartók's own instrumental sense. His own compositions began to reveal the harmonic, tonal, and motivic influences of Strauss. (Leafstedt 1999: 57, 68.) From there he was guided toward the creation of a new type of chromatic melody, later exemplified in such works as the first movement of his *First String Quartet*[232] (Antokoletz 1984: 14).

---

231. On December 22, 1902, at a private session of the professors of the Academy of Music, Bartók performed the piano transcription of *Ein Heldenleben*, to such effect that news of his feat reached Vienna, where shortly afterwards he was invited to play this contemporary modern work to the conservative music-lovers of Austria (Demény, ed. 1971: 19–20). The performance was acclaimed in true Viennese style, though the critics did not miss the opportunity of denouncing Strauss's music. Theodor Otto Helm (1843–1920) referred to the performance in the "Vienna Music Letters" column of *Pester Lloyd* (a German newspaper issued in Budapest) on February 24, 1903. In the same paper, on March 28, 1903, he discussed the unsuccessful first performance of Strauss's *Macbeth*, adding that it would be useful if Bartók were to prepare an illuminating piano transcription of this work, as he did with *Heldenleben*. (Demény, ed. 1976: 40–41, 45.) Even Hanslick was moved to comment: "He [Bartók] must be a genius, but it is a pity that he spends his time on Strauss" (cited in Ujfalussy 1971 [1970]: 38; see also, Demény, ed. 1976: 40). In his early symphonic poems, *Macbeth* (1888), *Don Juan* (1889), *Till Eulenspiegel* (1895) and *Ein Heldenleben*, Strauss continued the tradition of Liszt. He expanded the sphere of chromatic harmony to fuse two or three tonalities, and widened the scope of the orchestral color so that instruments lost their individual autonomy. Hanslick's opinions on Strauss's tone poems performed before 1900 demonstrate the prevailing view of program music in *fin-de-siècle* Vienna. Concerning the tone poems of Strauss, Hanslick (1950 [1892]: 308–309) believed that the composer misunderstood completely the nature of music. He was of the opinion that Strauss had substituted poetic content for musical content in the tone poems, which resulted in a series of virtuosic sound effects. Since 1904, in letters to Lajos Dietl (1873–1945), the piano teacher of the Vienna Conservatoire, Bartók had been expressing his unreserved admiration for the Strauss songs (see e.g., Demény, ed. 1971: 38). By 1905, Bartók had become less interested in Strauss and was rediscovering the works of Liszt. (See pp. 23–27, Chapter 2.1.2.)

232. Bartók's freer tonality, largely achieved by major-minor combinations, and almost continuously dissonant texture (based on pervasive use of appoggiaturas and sevenths) may be primarily associated with the more daring harmonic fabric of Strauss's works, e.g., *Elektra* (Batta, ed. 1999: 594–599). In my view, this relationship should not be construed to mean that the quartet is influenced by the opera but, rather, that they demonstrate parallel developments. Strauss's opera is based on triadic harmonies; but the constant shifting tonalities frequently result in polytonal relations. (See also, *BBE* 1976 [1910].)

In the spring of 1903, resurgent patriotic movements emerged throughout Hungary.[233] This tremendous outburst of national feeling had its origins in the preceding period of Hungarian history, when, economically and politically, the country was moving towards imperialism (see pp. 99–102, Chapter 3.1). The emotional atmosphere of that time of national fervor is evoked vividly in the memoirs of Kodály:

> For our generation, 1849 [the Hungarians' defeat in the War of Independence] was still a grim and living memory. Old men who had taken part in the uprising and who still wore their beards in the style of Kossuth, were still to be seen frequently in the streets. Bartók may even have met some of them. And in the newspapers, when they died, one read the invariable refrain of the obituaries: "[T]hey witnessed great times." The house, in which I myself lived, had been hit by a cannon [shot]. When I was a schoolchild, it was decreed that instead of observing March 15 [the day on which the Hungarian revolution and War of Independence broke out]; we had to celebrate April 11, the date when the April Laws were passed. Young people defied the decree and secretly organized a procession to the Patriot's statue, to take place at night. (Kodály 1974 [1946]: 444.)

In "Bartók the Folklorist", Kodály wrote:

> This nation-wide longing for independence reached its climax just after the turn of the century. People demanded that everything be strictly Hungarian, the coat of arms, the language used in the army; and they demanded that the Hungarian anthem be sung instead of the *Gott erhalte*. Kuruc songs reviling the Germans reverberated throughout the land. (Kodály 1974 [1950]: 451.)

Bartók supported those aspirations with the ardent faith of a radical. He wrote to his mother, describing the political situation that had arisen because of parliamentary obstructionism (Glatz 1987: 77). He inveighed with violence against the foreign monarch, and took to wearing national costume. "Only a Hungarian can be the king of Hungary," he wrote in June 1903 (Demény, ed. 1971: 31). Bartók's discomfort with the predominance of German influences in Budapest's musical life was one factor in his sharp turn towards nationalism in 1903.[234] The opposition Independence Party, Kossuth, used a brazenly reactionary style of rhetoric (Demény, ed. 1976: 50–52; and Lindlar 1984: 97–100). As a patriotic gesture, between April

---

233. Towards the end of 1902, the Defense Minister, Géza Fejérváry (1833–1914), submitted to Parliament a bill proposing a substantial increase of Hungary's contribution to the Imperial Army. Parliamentary opposition centered round such issues as national sovereignty, independence of the Hungarian army, whether the latter should be required to speak Hungarian, wear new coats of arms and insignias, and whether it should pledge an oath to the Hungarian constitution. The longing for independence reached fever pitch throughout the country. The singing of the *Gott erhalte* was a constant incitement to unrest, and there were almost daily clashes with the police, when people refused to sing the Imperial Austrian anthem. (Kodály 1974 [1950]: 451.)

234. Bartók spoke Hungarian rather than German, and dropped the prefix "von" from his family name (some of his early compositions were signed "Béla von Bartók"). In letters to his sister, Elza Bartók (1885–1955), in fall of 1903, Bartók addressed her by her Hungarian pet name, "Böske" (Bess). (See, e.g., Demény, ed. 1971: 31.)

and August 1903, under the influence of Strauss, Bartók wrote his first major work, the ten-section *Kossuth Symphonic Poem* (DD 75a, Sz 21, BB 31, 1903). The piece honors Lajos Kossuth (1802–1894), leader of the Hungarian War of Independence in 1848–1849, and Bartók's overtly nationalist agenda is projected in both the thematic program and musical material of the work. (Ujfalussy 1971 [1970]: 48;[235] also, Kroó 1975 [1971]: 9–16; Markowsky 1970;[236] and Fodor 1970.[237]) In commenting on the *Kossuth Symphony*, Glatz (1987: 77) argues that Bartók was not a nationalist in an "ethnic" sense, but "was guided primarily by musical motives". Bartók outlines the ten closely related sections of the work, each with a description based on historical events (*BBE* 1976 [1904]). One may well wonder, on a superficial reading of the facts, how this period in Bartók's long creative life may be classified as a manifestation of something new. Bartók himself had grown dissatisfied with the compositional technique of *Kossuth*. He began to find the exaggerations of Post-Romanticism increasingly unbearable and argued, "there is no other solution than a complete break with the nineteenth century" (*BBE* 1976 [1931]: 340).

Bartók's letters contain a number of complaints about the use of German at social gatherings or the prevalence of German speakers, including a substantial number of

235. Ujfalussy (1971 [1970]: 48) remarks that in *Kossuth* the public thought they had at last discovered a new Hungarian symphonic art. The work was premiered on January 13, 1904, in Budapest, performed by the Philharmonic Society under the baton of István Kerner (1867–1929). (See also, Bartók Jr, ed. 1981a: 64.) The performance caused a political storm, which made the name of the young composer known throughout the country. Some Austrian members of the Philharmonic Society reportedly protested against the work's travesty of the Austrian anthem, *Gott erhalte*. Hungarian musicians and critics raved about the work, however, praising the piece as filled with Hungarian-ness. (Demény, ed. 1976: 54; Kodály 1974 [1921]: 427–428; and 1974 [1950]: 451.) That satisfaction was reflected in the reviews. Pongrácz Kacsóh (1873–1923) wrote in the *Zenevilág* (*Music World*): "When the name of Bartók appears once again on our front page we are stirred to the depth of our souls by a pleasant blend of lofty sentiments – satisfaction, pride and patriotism." In the columns of the *Budapesti Hírlap* (*Budapest News*), the composer and music critic Aurél Kern (1871–1928) hailed the emergence of a "new musical genius" (cited in Ujfalussy 1971 [1970]: 48). On 17 January 1904, the aesthetician and critic Géza Molnár (1964 [1904]), titled his article in *A Hét* "Musica Militans", while on the same day, in the *Ország-Világ* (*Country, World*) (1964 [1904]), Zsigmond Falk (1870–1935) announced a "new Hungarian musical genius". The reviews of the first performance of *Kossuth* by the Halle Orchestra in Manchester (on February 18, 1904, conducted by the Austro-Hungarian conductor Richter) were decidedly more objective and restrained than the patriotic notices that had appeared in Budapest. (See also, Demény, ed. 1976: 56, 101; Kodály 1974 [1921]: 429; and Bartók Jr, ed. 1981a: 65.)

236. In "Béla Bartók – a Great Humanist and Democrat", Liesel Markowsky (1970) discusses Bartók's humanistic and democratic attitudes, and their manifestations in his music. Those include his involvement in the patriotic movement for Hungarian independence as well as his studies and championing of Hungarian folk music.

237. Ilona Fodor (1970) traces Bartók's nationalism to the nineteenth-century patriotic movements and struggles for liberation as stemming from the Revolution of 1848. Bartók endorsed the progressive nationalist movement, rather than the reactionary ruling classes of the Austro-Hungarian Empire (see pp. 102–105, Chapter 3.1). His compositions of this period have a distinctively Hungarian tone: the *Four Pósa Songs* for voice and piano (DD 67, BB 24, 1902), the *Violin Sonata* (1903), the symphonic poem *Kossuth* and the *Piano Quintet* (1903–1904). In the *Rhapsody, Op. 1* (1904) and the *Scherzo* for Piano and Orchestra, Op. 2 (1904), Bartók continued to use *verbunkos* as the basic ingredient of his musical expression (discussed in Chapter 2.1.2, above).

Jews, in musical circles (Demény, ed. 1976: 33; see also, Bartók Jr, ed. 1981a: 90; and Kodály 1984 [1939]: 48). In a letter dated April 1905, to Irmy Jurkovics (a childhood acquaintance in Nagyszentmiklós), Bartók wrote:

> The intelligentsia comes, almost exclusively, from foreign stock (as shown by the excessively large number of Hungarians with foreign names); and it is only amongst intellectuals that we find people capable of dealing with art in a higher sense. A real Hungarian music can originate only if there is a real Hungarian gentry. This is why the Budapest public is so absolutely hopeless. The place has attracted a haphazardly heterogeneous, rootless group of Germans and Jews; they make up the majority of Budapest's population. (Quoted in Demény, ed. 1971: 50.)

In December of 1906, Károly Rozsnyai published the collection of *Magyar népdalok* (*Hungarian Folksongs*) (Sz 33, BB 42, 1970 [1906]).[238] Bartók had earlier informed his mother, in a postcard dated September 10, 1906, that for "three days I have been conferring with Kodály about the proposed book of songs. [...] We are writing a preface in which we have some harsh things to say about Hungarian audiences" (quoted in ibid.: 67). Bartók had already felt alienated from the Germans and Jews so prominent in Budapest's musical life (Voigt 1988: 393)[239].

Non-Germanic composers began to react against the ultra-chromaticism of the Wagner-Strauss period as they turned away from the long tradition of German musical hegemony toward new spheres of influence in France and Eastern Europe.[240]

238. Those pieces were simple settings of twenty songs for voice and piano, collected by Béla Vikár (1859–1945), along with Bartók and Kodály, the first ten arranged by Bartók and the remainder by Kodály. Before immigrating to the United States in 1938, Bartók revised these pieces. (Dobszay 1984: 345.) See also, Olsvai (1997: 91), who remarks that Vikár was the first in Europe to record folk songs and instrumental folk tunes on a mechanical device, the phonograph. That brought about the inception of a new way of studying musical folklore, and inspired composers to develop a new style of musical arrangement. The folk music collected by Vikár and his phonograph showed a broad diversity in geographical and generic distribution. The material, some 1,500 pieces, was transcribed by László Lajtha (1892–1963), Bartók, and Kodály (see also, Voigt 1990b: 3). Olsvai (1997: 92–96) points out that Vikár's collection influenced the compositions of Kodály and Bartók in two ways: (1) The tunes of folk songs, and often the lyrics as well, were used as themes around which the composer wrote polyphonic accompaniments and, in many cases, added an overture and a dénouement. (2) The theme itself was not a tune collected directly from the people but a creation of the artist, who used his musical mother tongue freely to create a piece displaying the style and atmosphere of folk music. In instances of the former type, we find 19 tunes collected by Vikár in Bartók's music and 17 in Kodály's, who also wrote the music to some parts of Vikár's *Kalevala* translations, suffusing the piece with Finnish melodies (ibid.: 96). Olsvai points out that the influence of Vikár's folk-music collecting and *Kalevala* translation are evident in three of Attila József's poems: *Regös ének, Szól a szája szólítatlan,* and *Áradat* (ibid.: 96–97).

239. I am grateful to Professor Vilmos Voigt for informing me of his study "Bartók találkozik a folklórral" ("Bartók Meets Folklore") (1988).

240. German developments of increased chromaticism and heightened expression ran counter to the French sensibility and to the history of French music, which was less firmly established in the traditions of functional tonality. Thus, when post-Romantic music took a turn towards more chromaticism and emotional intensity, the French sensibility was destined to find another route. The influence of Wagner, chromaticism, expressionism and program music all had enormous influence

Those conditions served as the social and musical framework from which Bartók's art was to emerge. (*BBE* 1976 [1921e]: 323–324.) Bartók did not take the obvious route, toward an international (French, German) modernism. Instead, he sought a new musical expression for the Hungarian identity, which he combined with compositional techniques inspired by his contemporaries, most notably Debussy, Schoenberg, and Stravinsky. (Frigyesi: 1998: 61–88;[241] see also, pp. 25–30, Chapter 2.1.2.) Bartók's discovery of folk music led him to re-evaluate completely his views on Hungarian music, as discussed above, in Chapters 3.1–3.2 (see also, Voigt 2005 [1970]).[242]

In the words of Carl Dahlhaus (1980 [1974]: 86), Bartók used the melodic forms and rhythms he discovered in folk music as a basis for "an artificial music exploring the novel". Bartók was aware that he was alone in his views, yet was able to find similar ideas among composers, above all, in the works of Kodály and in Stravin-

---

throughout Europe. In France, a group of composers (Chabrier, Saint-Saëns and Fauré) formed the Société Nationale de Musique (1871) for the purpose of reviving the aesthetic goals and historical successes of French music. Namely, it was a return to absolute music, and to the attendant principles of order, clarity, and restraint, which were considered the distinguishing traits of musical masterpieces of France's past. However, the pervasive hold that Wagner's aesthetics had over European music proved too strong for that group to overcome. Nevertheless, the group, which disbanded in the 1880s, did succeed in laying the groundwork for a different future for French music. Debussy matured in that environment, and would prove to be the catalyst for a "rebirth" of French music. Further, he laid the primary groundwork for music, by French and non-French composers alike, that was increasingly radical in its departure from Germanic aesthetic principles. (Grayson 1986: 30, 50, 184, 229–275, 297 n. 7.)

241. Frigyesi (1998: 61–88) argues, in "The Romantic Roots and Political Radicalism of Hungarian Modernism", that the aesthetics of Ady and Bartók were animated by a central tenant: an art work has to point toward a positive acceptance of life, with full awareness (and in spite) of life's tragic realities. The author, however, does not establish strong enough connections between that view and the technical specifics of *Bluebeard's Castle* or the *Concerto* No. 1. The persistent lack of fit between Frigyesi's aesthetic-historical pronouncements and her technical narratives is particularly noticeable when she "proves" her points in a cursory manner, by attaching great weight to works that she mentions only in passing (e.g., the *Second String Quartet* and *Cantata Profana*).

242. In that study, the Hungarian folklorist, anthropologist, comparative philologist, and semiotician Voigt (2005 [1970]) makes a distinction between nineteenth-century and twentieth-century folklorism, using as one of his examples Bartók's changing attitude towards tradition (ibid.: 190–191). In *A folklorizmusról* (*On Folklorism*), Voigt (1990a) outlines research problems in dealing with the topic. In "Folklore and Folklorism Today", Voigt (1979) suggests that "folklore" should not need further clarification, if one understands the term in a broad sense, as including folk music, dance, poetry, art, ritual, beliefs, and the like. In "Neofolklorism: Why Is It a Neglected Topic in the Study of Counter-Culture in Nordic Literatures?" the author explains: "If we contrast folklore with non-folklore, we can assume that a two-way correlation exists always between folklore and non-folklore. Folklorism begins with folklore and moves in the direction of non-folklore, whereas folklorization begins with non-folklore and moves in the direction of folklore. [...] On both ends (i.e., in folklore and non-folklore) the process involved could be characterized by adaptation and spread (usually with modifications) of different styles, motifs, and formulas" (Voigt 1993b: 340). I thank Professor Voigt for calling my attention to this issue and to his views on it.

sky's "Russian" pieces from the years prior to 1920.[243] Somfai remarks as follows about Bartók's *Dance Suite* (1923):

> The thematic material of all the movements is an imitation of peasant music. The aim of the whole work was to put together idealized peasant music – you could say an invented peasant music – in such a way that the individual movements of the work should introduce particular types of music. Peasant music of all nationalities served as a model: Magyar [Hungarian], Wallachian [Romanian], Slovak, and even Arabic. In fact, [one occasionally finds] a hybrid of those species. Thus, for example, the melody of the first subject of the first movement is reminiscent of primitive Arabic peasant music, whereas [the] rhythm is [that] of East European folk music. (Somfai 2000 [1996]: 17–18.)

It may be illuminating, at this point, to quote from another of Bartók's letters, this one written on May 20, 1925:

> Not long ago I received from Prague a copy of an article, which had appeared in a Czech newspaper and which expressed wonder and enthusiasm at the idea that it should have been possible for me, a Hungarian composer living in Horthy's Hungary, to publish my own collections of genuine Slovak folk music under a Czech title and including Czech songs. (Book Three and Book Four of *For Children*, which actually did appear in that manner, but in 1912, so that this extraordinary occurrence took place before Horthy's time.) (Quoted in Ujfalussy, ed. 1980 [1958]: 299–300.)

Yet, it was neither such political provocation nor narrow-mindedness that most disheartened him, but rather the negative aspects of ultra-nationalism. Bartók writes that the "impulse to begin folk song research, as well as any folklore science in general, is attributable to the awakening of national feeling" (*BBE* 1976 [1937b]: 25), then goes on to consider research issues (ibid.: 26–28). In his view, folklore researchers should be as objective as possible (in terms of national feelings) when investigating the music of foreign nations. Bartók concludes bitterly that, "though musical folklore owed a great deal to nationalism, today, it is so harmed by ultra-nationalism that the damage now exceeds the former benefits" (ibid.: 28; see also, Cooper 2001).

Throughout his life, Bartók felt a deep personal commitment to the principles of national independence and artistic freedom. In 1930, Bartók composed the *Cantata Profana*, one of three planned cantatas meant to express his ideals concerning fellowship with neighboring nations, Hungary, Romania, and Slovakia (Demény, ed. 1971: 203; and 1976: 190; see also, Moreaux 1949: 81[244]). Bartók made those plans known in a letter that he wrote in the early 1930s to Sándor Albrecht (1885–1958):

---

243. On Bartók's relationship to Stravinsky, see Schneider's (1995) essay, "Bartók and Stravinsky: Respect, Competition, Influence and the Hungarian Reaction to Modernism in the 1920s."

244. In *Béla Bartók: Sa vie, ses œuvres, son langage*, Serge Moreaux (1949: 81) has suggested that the *Cantata Profana* was a protest against the restrictions of the Regent of Hungary, Miklós Horthy (1868–1957).

As for the oratorio – in fact, it is no oratorio but a cantata, and baritone and tenor solo (I wrote it back in 1930!); *c.* 18 minutes. The choral and solo parts are very difficult but not the orchestral parts. However, it is not going to be published (or performed) for the time being because I am planning to add to it three [*sic!*] more pieces[245] of similar length in such a way that, while they will be linked together by some connecting idea, it would be possible to perform each of the three separately. It will be one year or two at least before I can see whether there is any likelihood of my achieving this. (Quoted in Demény, ed. 1971: 440.)

Stylistically, the *Cantata* reveals a neoclassical influence in its use of earlier forms and procedures, which include canon, fugue, aria, cadenza, *turba* and double choruses, as well as an orchestral introduction resembling the opening of Bach's *St. Matthew Passion*. In the *Cantata,* one finds an intense and complex synthesis of various Transylvanian folk-music elements. Bartók derived both the text and modal material from the Romanian *kolinda* (Christmas song), which was sung by boys or young men. (Kárpáti 1969a: 9–10; Tallián 1981b[246]; and Lindlar 1984: 42.) The fusion of all those features into a highly systematic network of relationships constitutes one of Bartók's most personal expressions (Gy. Lukács 1972: 12; and Lendvai 1964: 225–266[247]). In "Romanian Peasant Music", as a follow-up of his earlier articles on Hungarian and Slovak folk music, Bartók discusses vocal (e.g., *colinde*) and instru-

---

245. Ujfalussy (1971 [1970]: 283) remarks that the expression "three more pieces of similar length" was a slip of the pen, and should read "two more pieces of similar length" – a lapse corrected in the concluding part of the sentence.

246. Tallián (1981b) presents an in-depth anthropological (ethnomusicological) study of the symbolic meaning of the original *colinde* on which Bartók based his *Cantata Profana* (1974 [1930]). *Colinda* (plural: *colinde*) is a Romanian word for *Christmas carol*. The article explores the meaning of the text in its relationship to rites of separation, imitation, and transition. For more on the *Cantata Profana*, see Tallián's (1983b) dissertation on the subject, and F. László's (1980) account of the work's genesis.

247. Around 1930, Bartók, in an extension of his concern for things "natural", began to react against the mechanization and greed of civilization, which seemed to be destroying primordial values and becoming alienated from nature. Against this background, he composed his major work for chorus and orchestra, the *Cantata Profana* (Bartók 1974 [1930]), in which he stated explicitly his desire for a return to nature, to the "*tiszta forrás*", or "clean source". (Demény, ed. 1955a: 197.) The *parlando* style of this work is not particularly salient until the sons, out hunting, get lost in the forest. With their transformation into stags, a simple unornamented *parlando* melody is suddenly heard. From this point onward, the melodic lines, particularly the solo lines, become more *parlando* in character, climaxing in the tenor solo in which the best-loved son pleads with his father not to shoot his own children (see Tallián 1981b, for a detailed account of the symbolism of the stags). For Bartók, determined to find the primeval world in the twentieth century, the sons' return to nature as stags was a return to freedom, and his use of the *parlando* style was his symbolic effort to return to an ancient world uncontaminated by the shams of civilization (Lendvai 1964: 225–266).

mental music of the Romanians[248] (1970 [1920]); see also, Bartók (1935b[249]); and Breuer (1975b[250]).

Bartók stopped performing his own works in Budapest, where the political atmosphere was growing increasingly repressive (Romsics 1982: 244–246).[251] In 1931,

248. Extreme right-wing circles initiated a violent press campaign against Bartók. Polemics about Bartók's collecting of Romanian folk songs appeared in the pages of *Nemzeti Újság, Új Nemzedék,* and *Szózat* from May 19 until May 28, 1920. (Ujfalussy, ed. 1980 [1958]: 249–258.) In the *Nemzeti Újság,* Hubay falsely claimed that Bartók intended to trace back all of their Hungarian Transylvanian tunes to Romanian origin, thereby maliciously accusing Bartók of unpatriotic conduct. Bartók (ibid.: 195–197) gives contrary evidence, showing that he was actually serving the cause of the Hungarian nation. In 1924, the extreme right wing in Hungary continued its attacks and even urged that disciplinary action be taken against Bartók because of his Transylvanian concert tour.
249. Bartók's (1935b) *Melodies of the Romanian Colinde* contains 484 colinde transcriptions as well as text material and notes; see also, Demény (ed. 1971: 238; and 1976: 326–328, 331–334, 393, 404–406, 432–433).
250. Breuer (1975b) argues that the rhythmic-metric roots of Bartók's music have received too little attention, noting that the frequent changes of meter and complicated rhythmic structures are typical of colinda melodies. On the stanza structure of colinda melodies and the classification of colinda texts, see Suchoff (2002: 182–185).
251. From his letters we know that around 1912 Bartók made no public appearances in Budapest (Demény, ed. 1971: 113–119). The great success he enjoyed as a concert artist in the 1920s was offset somewhat by difficulties that arose from the tenuous political atmosphere in Hungary, a situation exacerbated by the composer's frank manner. In the years 1930–1934, Bartók gave no concerts in Budapest and for a few more years played no composition of his own at his recitals. His programs featured chiefly the works of Bach, Mozart, and Beethoven. Hungarian official organizations and musical associations behaved offensively towards Bartók on a number of occasions. One scandalous episode involved the cancellation of a performance of *The Miraculous Mandarin,* planned for his fiftieth birthday. In 1935, he was to be officially honored for the *First Suite for Orchestra* written thirty years earlier, in a youthful, romantic style. Bartók refused this honor in an open letter to the Kisfaludy Társaság (Kisfaludy Society) (Demény, ed. 1971: 245). As the specter of fascism in Europe in the 1930s grew ever more sinister, he refused to play in Germany. In those years, he undertook still more extensive concert tours. He frequently visited England, France, Switzerland, the Netherlands, and on several occasions, even Italy. (Bartók Jr, ed. 1981a: 285–418.) In letters addressed to Frau Professor Dr. Oscar Müller-Widmann (1893–1964), however, he acknowledged that the political system of the latter country was distasteful to him (Demény, ed. 1971: 257). Bartók did not allow radio broadcasts of his music in Germany and Italy. In the October 10, 1937 edition of the *Pesti Napló,* he explained why he refused to permit the Hungarian Radio to transmit his public performances to Germany and Italy. (Bartók Jr, ed. 1981a: 386.) The reason, he wrote, "is quite simple; namely, I have never given broadcast performances for the radio networks of either Italy or the Third Reich; what is more, I have never even been asked by those two broadcasting corporations to perform directly for them. Under the circumstances, I thought it would be unfair to allow the Hungarian Radio to offer these two broadcasting corporations my recital performances on Radio Budapest as a sort of gift" (quoted in Demény ed. 1971: 425–426). In March 1938, certain newspapers returned to that theme, even adding that Bartók had written to the German authorities on the subject. This new development induced Bartók to make a statement for the daily *Az Est* (Bartók Jr, ed. 1981a: 393; see also, Demény, ed. 1971: 266). On March 11, 1938, after Hitler's occupation of Austria, Bartók began to safeguard his works by sending them away, first to Switzerland and later to England. With many other Hungarian composers, he protested against the racist regulations of the German Copyright association, and together with Kodály, transferred to the English association. In 1927–1928, he had paid his first visit to America, and he stayed there again in April and May of 1940. His mother's death strengthened his resolve to leave

Bartók wrote that "*die Verbrüderung der Völker*" (brotherhood of peoples) was the ethical ideal that motivated his music, rather than visions of a Hungarian nation and Hungarian fatherland, which had seemed to guide his efforts in 1903 (quoted in Szabolcsi, ed. 1957: 262; see also, Demény, ed. 1971: 201).

In his collection of essays, *Between Romanticism and Modernism*, Dahlhaus (1980 [1974]) recommends that musical nationalism be studied in the context of political nationalism and its deep-rooted relation to structural history. He emphasizes that the national element in nineteenth-century music arose, above all, from the political and sociological function of music, rather than from the music itself: "*Erst im 20. Jahrhundert, bei Bartók und Stravinsky, ging die Vermittlung zwischen Folklore einerseits und einer nach Neuheit suchende artifizielle Musik anderseits von der Rhythmik und von der Melodik aus*" (ibid.: 86).[252]

Though the preceding statement is questionable in some respects, it contains a possible explanation for the contradiction between Bartók's music and the view of him as a nationalist. That contradiction is quite pronounced in a letter he wrote to Beu, in which it appears that Bartók's statement about being a Hungarian nationalist is not an absolute claim. Instead, it is a reaction against Beu's wish to regard him as a "Romanian" composer, by reference to the many Romanian folk songs that Bartók used in his works[253] (see also, Kodály 1974 [1950]: 452). Bartók replies to Beu that, if such is the case, then he is also a Slovak composer and thus a composer of three nationalities. Bartók draws this remarkable conclusion from their exchanges:

> *Eigentlich kann man mein kompositorisches Schaffen, eben weil es aus dieser 3-fachen (ungar, rumän, slowak). [...] Quelle entspringt, als eine Verkörperung jener Integritäts-Idee betrachten, die heute in Ungarn so sehr betont wird Meine eigentliche Idee aber, deren ich mir seitdem ich mich als Komponist gefunden habe vollkommen bewusst bin, ist die Verbrüderung der Völker, eine Verbrüderung*

Europe. On October 8, 1940, Bartók, together with his wife, Ditta Pásztory (1903–1982), gave his farewell concert in Budapest and at the end of the same month arrived in the United States, where he remained until his death (Bartók Jr, ed. 1981a: 255–260, 420–422). On the latter years of the composer's life, see Fassett (1958); some particulars of the end of Bartók's life may also be found in Walter Kring's (1917–1999) *Safely Onward: The History of the Unitarian Church of All Souls, New York City* (1991).

252. "Only in the twentieth century, with Bartók and Stravinsky, did a mediation based on rhythm and melody begins, between folklore, on the one hand, and an artificial music exploring novelty, on the other."

253. Examples of arrangements of Romanian folk melodies include the following: (1) the fifth of the *Seven Sketches* for piano (Op. 9b, Sz 44, BB 54, 1908–1910, rev. January 19, 1945); (2) *Romanian Folk Dances* (Sz 56, BB 68, 1915, transcribed for small orchestra 1917); (3) *Romanian Christmas Carols* (Sz 57, BB 67, 1915); (4) *Sonatina* (BB 69, 1915). The following are examples of works partially utilizing certain characteristics of Romanian folk melodies: *Rhapsody* No. 1 and *Rhapsody* No. 2. Examples of works with original thematic material, but completely Romanian in character are (1) No. 6 of the *Sketches*, Op. 9 for piano; and (2) *Two Romanian Folk Dances* (Op. 8a, Sz 43, BB 56, 1909–1910). An example of original thematic material that is partly Romanian in character may be found in passages of the third movement of the *Dance Suite* (Antokoletz 1997 [1988]: 5–43; Lindlar 1984: 122–124); and, as already mentioned, Bartók chose a Romanian text for his *Cantata Profana* (1974 [1930]).

trotz allem Krieg und Hader. Diese Idee versuche ich soweit es meine Kräfte ges-
tatten – in meiner Musik zu dienen. [...] *Infolge meiner sagen wir geographischen*
Lage ist mir die ungarische Quelle am nächsten, daher der ungarische Einfluss
am stärksten. Ob nun mein Stil ungeachtet der verschiedenen Quellen – einen un-
garischen Charakter hat (und daraus kommt es ja an), müssen andere beurteilen,
nicht ich.[254] (Quoted in Szabolcsi, ed. 1957: 262–263.)

Of one thing, we may be absolutely certain: in the early 1930s, that statement
must have appeared extremely utopian. Therefore, Bartók warns Beu against publishing it: *"So was ist ja nichts für die rumänische Presse"* (Such things are not for
the Romanian press) (Szabolcsi, ed. 1957: 263; see also, Demény, ed. 1971: 201).

Up to a point, of course, the past has always played a role in every composer's
music. There is no doubt that in his early years Bartók engaged in the musical construction of nationalism, for example, by drawing upon *verbunkos* music. To do so
was in line with the official Hungarian nationalism of the time (discussed in Chapters
3.2–3.2.2). Following his ethnomusicological studies, however, Bartók developed a
musical style that involved peasant songs from a variety of ethnic communities,
which he placed in an international context (Kodály 1974 [1950]: 452; see also, pp.
144–149, Chapter 3.4). Bartók's Hungarian nationalism thus seems to have developed beyond national borders only in the sense that it considers particular nations in
their relation to a higher, universal community. In my view, however, the composer's
perspective may be labeled "inter-national", because it begins with the national and
emphasizes the unification of nations as a desirable aim. The nation that Bartók had
in mind was the multi-ethnic Hungary that disappeared with the Trianon Treaty in
1920 (Macartney 1937; and Romsics 1982: 90–98) and that, in the eyes of Bartók,
was a union of people straddling Eastern and Western Europe[255] (see also, p. 100,

254. "Actually, you can consider my work as a composer as an embodiment of the vision of integration so clearly expressed in present-day Hungary, because it springs from three sources (Hungarian, Romanian and Slovak). [...] However, my own vision, which I have pursued ever since
I found myself a composer, is the brotherhood of peoples, a brotherhood despite war and hatred.
I seek to the best of my efforts to serve this idea in my music. [...] Following my – let us call it
geographical – situation, the Hungarian source is the closest, and consequently the Hungarian
influence the strongest. However, the question as to whether my style has a particularly Hungarian
character (and this is the question), despite its different sources, that is for other people to decide,
not me." (Quoted in Demény, ed. 1971: 201.)
255. With the short Romanian occupation, and the White terror that replaced the Red one, a national assembly was convened as a result of elections, which formally restored the kingdom and
elected Horthy as regent. In June 1920, the new regime signed the terms dictated by the victorious
great powers at the Treaty of Versailles (Trianon Treaty), a move that represented the de facto
acknowledgement of the dissolution of historical Hungary. The Hungary of the Austro-Hungarian
Monarchy, with its nationality problems and political conservatism, became things of the past; the
new order sanctioned by the Versailles recipe for peace did nothing to resolve the ethnic tensions
in the region, but it did dissolve a well-operating economic and cultural unit that had played a
major role in the European balance of power. The equitable principle of national self-determina-
tion as specified in the Trianon Peace Treaty was unilaterally applied to the detriment of Hungary.
Hungary lost two-thirds of its original territory, and more than half of its population. As opposed
to its new neighbors, Hungary became a virtually homogenous nation-state, while one-third of
the Hungarian population, totaling more than three million, became an ethnic minority in several

Chapter 3.1). In a letter to his mother, Bartók admitted that "the most pleasant place for me to go to would be Transylvania – it would feel more or less like Hungary to me; of all the territories that lay within the former boundaries of Hungary, that was the one I liked best, anyway" (quoted in Demény, ed. 1971: 144).

Returning to theoretical aspects, one finds the term "construction" used extensively studies of nations and nationalism, where it has a variety of meanings. Many scholars that specialize in nationalism consider the nation as a construction, particularly modernist writers, who are the most numerous in the field. Recent research into the origins of nations and national identities, as we know them today, have put forward three, more or less overlapping explanations. The Czech-British anthropologist and philosopher Ernest Gellner (1925–1995) interprets the latter as direct products of modernization, such as the transition from agrarian to industrial societies. Within the modernist paradigm there are various degrees and interpretations of construction, ranging from Gellner's (1983)[256] view of nations and nationalism as products of the demands of industrial society, to the so-called strong forms of social constructionism that are often associated with the political scientist Benedict Anderson and the historian Eric Hobsbawm.

---

neighboring states. That situation not only undermined any hopeful prospects for an already disrupted national economy, but also determined political events: no political faction hoping for domestic success could renounce revisionist claims in the era between the two world wars. Reforms introduced by the staunchly conservative Horthy regime, which retained the most crucial parliamentary positions, did little to modernize the backward social structure. By the late 1920s, some particularly outstanding politicians, such as Pál Teleki (1879–1941), managed to achieve domestic consolidation, slight economic growth, some changes in the isolationist foreign policy. On the threshold of the 1930s, however, the world economic depression restricted Hungary's opportunities. The Great Depression concluded the process started by the Versailles plan, which had resulted in breaking the economic, social and cultural unity of the Danube states by encouraging national seclusion, political extremism, and the resulting power vacuum. Hungary blamed its difficulties on the Trianon Treaty, and yearned for its revision; this meant closer ties with Germany and Italy. (Macartney 1937; and Romsics 1982: 90–98.) The loss of nation-hood was also a personal tragedy for Bartók: the severed territories were no longer open to the Hungarian folk-music collector. He was forced to shift his activities during this period more toward composition and intensive concertizing (see n. 89, p. 43, Chapter 2.1.3). That change of activity is partly evident in his approach to writing compositions that continued to include folk melodies, an approach now best described as composing with folk song rather than folk-song arranging (see p. 165, Chapter 3.6). The significance of Bartók's change of activities in the 1920s can also be seen in his increased contact with international composers and their works (see n. 123, p. 69, Chapter 2.3).

256. In *Nations and Nationalism*, Gellner (1983: 6) describes nations as follows: "[…] nations, like states, are a contingency, and not a universal necessity. Neither nations nor states exist at all times and in all circumstances. Moreover, nations and states are not the same contingency. Nationalism holds that they were destined for each other, that either without the other is incomplete, [which] constitutes a tragedy. However, before they could become intended for each other, each of them had to emerge, and their emergence was independent and contingent. The state has certainly emerged without the help of the nation. Some nations have certainly emerged without the blessings of their own state. It is more debatable whether the normative idea of the nation, in its modern sense, did not presuppose the prior existence of the state."

Anderson (1991 [1983]: 24)[257] has stressed the image of a national "character" grew out of the interaction between capitalism, new technologies of communication, and diversity of human languages. In *Nations and Nationalisms since 1780*, Hobsbawm (1990) has analyzed nations and nationalism as a consequence of the political and social transformations that followed the American and French Revolutions. Not all such modernist images of the nation rule out the existence of some "proto-national", "cultural", "linguistic or ethnic ties and sentiments that facilitated the later formations of nations" (Smith 1991: 17). Still, writers on the subject all insist that these ties and sentiments are substantially transformed in the nation-building process; if need be, national languages and national histories were re-written, to provide a more or less unbroken continuity to a medieval or ancient past. This does not mean that the formation of nations is an arbitrary process; no one nation is exclusively based on an imagined, constructed, or invented past. Gellner insists that nationalism, not nationalists, has created nations (1983: 45, 124). According to his analysis, it is clear that, for modern industrial states to exist, they must have homogeneity, a free market, qualified labor, and political ideas. Nationalists are mere pawns in that process, led by the invisible hand of modernization.

If one accepts that premise, other considerations can be proposed. For example, a key problem of the modernist perspective was (and is) that it fails to account for the passions generated by nationalism. Modernist writers have been criticized for that failure by ethnologists such Smith (2000), who has proposed what he calls an "ethno-symbolic" approach to the study of national identity and nationalism[258].

---

257. Anderson's (1991 [1983]) *Imagined Communities* has become one of the standard texts on the topic of nations and nationalism. His definition of "nation" is one of those most commonly used by scholars in the field: "In an anthropological spirit, then, I propose the following definition of the nation: it is an imagined political community – and imagined as both inherently limited and sovereign. [...] It is *imagined* because the members of even the smallest nation will never know most of their fellow-members, meet them, or even hear of them, yet in the minds of each lives the image of their communion" (ibid.: 5). Renan refers to this imagining, when he writes that "[...] *l'essence d'une nation est que tous les individus aient beaucoup de choses en commun, et aussi que tous aient oublié bien des choses*" (quoted in ibid.: 6). With a certain ferocity, Gellner (1983: 6) makes a comparable point in his judgment that "[N]ationalism is not the awakening of nations to self-consciousness: it invents nations where they do not exist." The drawback to that formulation, however, is that Gellner (ibid.) is so anxious to show that nationalism masquerades under false pretences that he equates "invention" with "fabrication" and "falsity", rather than with "imagining" and "creation". In doing so, he can imply that "true" communities do exist, which can be advantageously juxtaposed to nations. In fact, all communities larger than primordial villages of face-to-face contact (and perhaps even those) are imagined. Communities are to be distinguished, not by whether they are genuine or false, but by the ways in which they are imagined. (Anderson 1991 [1983]: 5–7.)

258. Smith was a student of Gellner and as such attempts to overcome the key flaws and inconsistencies in the modernist perspective. In *The Nation in History*, Smith (2000) provides an incisive critique of the debate between modernists, perennialists, and primordialists over the origins, development and contemporary significance of nations and nationalism. Smith provides a probing account of historians' assumptions and explanations of nationalism in different historical epochs. Ranging broadly over the contributions and divergent perspectives of historians, political scientists, sociologists, anthropologists, and others who have contributed to these fundamental debates, Smith codifies the most cogent responses that have been offered to three defining issues in this

Smith points out the fact that there exists a "great variety of historical and symbolic components of particular nationalisms at specific historical junctures. Most of all perhaps, an ethno-symbolic approach can help us to understand both the durability and the transformations of ethnicity in history" (ibid.: 77).

Smith argues that the nation should not be considered as a construction but rather a reconstruction that builds on existing cultural material.

> For the modernist, in contrast, the past is largely irrelevant. The nation is a modern phenomenon, a product of nationalist ideologies, which themselves are the expression of modern, industrial society. The nationalist is free to use ethnic heritage, but nation-building can proceed without the aid of an ethnic past. Hence, nations are phenomena of a particular stage of history, and embedded in purely modern conditions. For the post-modernist, the past is more problematic. Though nations are modern and the product of modern cultural conditions, nationalists who want to disseminate the concept of the nation will make liberal use of elements from the ethnic past, where they appear to answer to present needs and preoccupations. The present creates the past in its own image. So modern nationalist intellectuals will freely select, invent, and mix traditions in their quest for the imagined political community. None of these formulations seems to be satisfactory. History is not a candy store, in which children may "pick and mix"; but neither is an unchanging essence or succession of superimposed strata. Nor can history be simply disregarded, as more than one nationalism has found to its cost. The challenge for scholars as well as nations is to represent the relationship between ethnic past and modern nation more accurately and convincingly. (Smith 1994: 18–19.)

In Smith's view (1994: 19), nationalism draws on the pre-existing history of the "group" and attempts to fashion that history into a sense of common identity and shared experience. This is not to say that such a history should be academically valid or cogent. Quite the contrary: many nationalisms are based on historically flawed interpretations of past events and tend to inflate small, inaccurate parts of their history in efforts at mythologizing. Nationalism, according to Smith (ibid.: 18), does not require that members of a "nation" should all be alike, only that they should feel an intense bond of solidarity to the nation and other members of their nation. A sense of nationalism can inhabit and be produced from whatever dominant ideology exists in a given locale. Nationalism builds on pre-existing kinships and on religious

---

area: (1) the nature and origin of the nation and nationalism; (2) the antiquity or modernity of nations and nationalism; and (3) the role of nations and nationalism in historical, and, especially recently, social change. Using the examples of Persia, Israel, and Greece as long-term illustrations, Smith also discusses ethnic and national identities in France, Germany, England, Yugoslavia, and elsewhere. Drawing on a wide range of examples from antiquity, medieval times, and the modern world, he develops a distinctive ethno-symbolic account of nations and nationalism. Smith asserts that nationalism is something "real". Social Constructionists have faulted Smith for overestimating the permanence of nationalism and failing to recognize that nationalism is an embedded discourse held up by a mutually supportive set of theories arising from northern Enlightenment culture.

and other shared belief systems. (For an ethnosemiotic view of this issue, see Voigt 1976.)

For present purposes, Smith's unique theoretical framework calls attention to yet another possible area of research: a re-defining of Bartók's relation to nationalism that starts from an ethno-symbolic point of view (see also, Smith 1991; 1994; 2000; and 2001). More precisely, in the case of Bartók, we confront a type of construction that seeks a foundation in a scientifically-investigated peasant music derived from various ethnic communities with roots in the pre-modern period. Through the stylization of these sources and their elaboration by contemporary composition techniques, Bartók sought to establish an original and organically coherent musical form.

3.4. Fieldwork

In ethnomusicological hagiography, Bartók is still revered as one of the founding fathers of the systematic study of folk music. Bartók was a collector and analyst of folk music who wrote and lectured about indigenous music of Europe in general and of Hungary in particular.[259] Bartók's immersion in that music lasted for decades, and the intricacies he discovered therein, from plaintive modality to fiercely aggressive rhythms, exerted immeasurable influence on his own musical language. Hence, it seems proper to present here an overview of his ethnomusicological researches.

In *Folk and Traditional Music of the Western Continents*, Bruno Nettl explains "folk music", "national music," and "universal language" as follows:

> The idea that folk music is closely associated with a people, a nation, or a culture and its characteristics has long been widely accepted. In some languages, the words for "folk music" and "national music" are the same. This popular notion is, of course, quite opposed to that which deems music a "universal language". Neither is really correct nor objective. Of course, it is possible to identify music as music, whether it is in a style or not. Music is a universal phenomenon, but each culture does have its own, and learning to understand another culture's music is in many ways like learning a foreign language. No culture can claim a body of music as its own without admitting that it shares many characteristics and probably many compositions with other neighboring cultures. Balancing the idea of traditional music as a national or regional phenomenon against the concept of folk music as a supranational kind of music is one of the fascinations of this field. (Nettl 1965: 6.)

Defining "folk music" is clearly not an easy task, for several criteria can be used, each of which is unsatisfactory if applied in isolation from others. Still, the most universal aspect of all folk music is the transmission of learned patterns by oral

259. *Béla Bartók's Studies in Ethnomusicology* (Suchoff, ed. 1997) contains fifteen publications by Bartók that were previously scattered in specialized journals in four different languages. All are concerned with that branch of musicology in which Bartók was most influential and for which he is best known: ethnomusicology. The volume includes an informative preface by the editor, who examines the development of Bartók's views on the folk-music traditions of Hungary, Romania, Slovakia, and the Arab world.

tradition, usually for a very long time, and usually within a given community. In its native setting, folk music is not written down. (Nettl 1964: 7; and Kodály 1976: 9.) The next quotations bring out more clearly the extent to which folk music appears to be a unique phenomenon. In "What is Folk Music?" Bartók clarifies his notion of peasant music:

> The term peasant music, broadly speaking, connotes all the melodies which endure within the peasant class of any nation, in a more or less wide area and for a more or less long period, and which constitute a spontaneous expression of the musical sentiments of that class. (*BBE* 1976 [1931c]: 6.)

In "Why and How Do We Collect Folk Music?" Bartók observes that: "folk music is not an individual art but is essentially a collective manifestation" (*BBE* 1976 [1936]:[260] 10). Both Bartók and Kodály recognized the organic basis of musical development in the culture of the people. In "Hungarian Peasant Music", Bartók explains:

> Peasant music, to use the term comprehensively, is the complex of melodies, which, in the peasant class – that is, in a class more or less removed from the culture of the town – now exist, or at any other period have existed, in whatever region or length of time, as a spontaneous gratification of the musical instinct or impulse. Or in a narrower sense, [peasant music is] the complex of melodies so existing among the peasants and exhibiting a certain uniformity of style. (*BBE* 1976 [1933]: 81.)

László Eősze (1987 [1980]: 137) writes that, along with Bartók, "Kodály was one of the creators of a new Hungarian art music based on folk sources, and he established in Hungary a broad-based and high-level musical culture." Although the two composers shared many ideas, however, the social significance of their work differed in several ways. My concern is exclusively with the formation of Bartók's style and views, hence the development of other Hungarian modern composers such as Kodály and Weiner must be put aside in this study.

Bartók has no recollection of any childhood experience with folk music: "Neither at Nagyszentmiklós [Sînnicolau Mare, Romania since 1920] nor at Beszterce [now Bistrita, Romania] nor Nagyszőllős [now Vinogradov, Ukraine] did I receive any folkloristic musical impressions" (cited in Demény, ed. 1971: 200).[261] Although his

---

260. Bartók (*BBE* 1976 [1936]: 9–10) gives some history of the awakening of interest in collecting folk songs in Europe, and the attempt to uncover their original. He talks about the gradually changing aims in that area of research, about his own experience with music of various nations, and about the means by which he collected folk music (ibid.: 11–24).

261. At the time of Bartók's birth, Nagyszentmiklós was in the north part of the ethnically diverse, southern Hungarian province of Torontál. When two-thirds of Hungarian territory was distributed among Romania, Yugoslavia, and Czechoslovakia after the signing of the Treaty of Trianon in June 1920 (Macartney 1937; and Romsics 1982: 90–98), Bartók's birthplace was absorbed into the western tip of Romania and renamed Sînnicolau Mare. A comprehensive account of the history of Hungary may be found in the opening chapters of Halsey Stevens's *The Life and Music of*

musical upbringing was purely German, his background also included exposure to and endorsement of Hungarian nationalism, as discussed in Chapter 3.3 (see also, Tallián 1983a: 136–137[262]).

In 1904, quite by chance, Bartók first encountered Hungarian folk music. While on holiday in the northern resort town of Gerlicepuszta (now Hrlica in Slovakia[263]), Bartók heard a peasant girl named Lidi Dósa singing a popular art song with modal inflections and attenuated stanza structure. (Kodály 1974 [1950]: 451; see also, Voigt 1988: 391.) Her rendition was remarkably different from the gypsy-styled versions, which he originally thought, as did Liszt and Brahms, to be the authentic folk music of his country (F. László 1978;[264] and Kodály 1984 [1939]: 9, 11–12; see also, pp. 108–110, Chapter 3.2.1). One writer describes how "this chance discovery brought

---

Béla Bartók (1964: vii–xi). The Bartók family did not originate in Eastern Hungary. Dille (1996 [1977]), in his *Généalogie sommaire de la famille Bartók*, discovered that Bartók's forbears came from Borsodszirák in the far north of Hungary. His father, Béla Bartók Sr. (1856–1888), was headmaster of an agricultural school in the countryside; in him, the composer could find a model of the traditional Hungarian middle class. His mother, Paula Voit, who was German by origin, taught in the public school system and transmitted the ideal of a somewhat rigid morality and devotion to work. Both parents were keen amateur musicians, who encouraged the young Bartók's musical development. Impressions of a summer visit to Radegund, Austria, in 1887 led to one of his first compositions, *Echo of Radegund* (Op. 16, DD 16, BB 1/16, 1891). After his father's death, responsibility for the family rested on his mother. Bartók's first compositions, from the early 1890s, were frequently dance pieces: waltzes, ländler, mazurkas, and, especially, polkas, which he often named after friends or family members. Good examples include his *Ländler* for piano No. 1 (DD 14, BB 1/14, 1891) and No. 2 (DD 18, BB 1/18, 1891); *Katinka Polka*, for piano (DD 9, BB 1/9, 1891; *Jolán Polka* for piano (DD 11, BB 1/11, 1891); *Gabi Polka*, for piano (DD 12, BB 1/12, 1891); and *Irma Polka*, for piano (DD 15, BB 1/15, 1891). Also among his first volume of 31 piano compositions (1890–1894) were occasional programmatic works, such as *A Gymnastic Contest in Budapest* (DD 4, BB 1/4, 1890), and some early attempts in sonatina and theme-and-variation forms. Bartók's piano skills rapidly increased during the early 1890s. On May 1, 1892, he made his first public appearance, in Nagyszőllős, performing a program of works by Alfred Grünfeld (1852–1924), Joseph Joachim Raff (1822–1882), Beethoven, and his own ten-part *The Course of the Danube* (DD 20, BB 1/20a, 1890–1894). It was on this occasion that the boy's remarkable gifts were noticed by Keresztély Altdörfer (1825–1898), an organist from Sopron. (Lampert & Somfai 1980: 197–225; see also, Lindlar 1984: 72–78.)

262. Bartók was soon appointed chapel organist at the Catholic Gymnasium in Pozsony, as successor to Dohnányi. We learn from Tóth (1930: 75) that Bartók received regular musical tuition from László Erkel (1845–1896), one of the sons of Ferenc Erkel. Bartók received instruction from Anton Hyrtl after Erkel's death. During his later years at Pozsony, Bartók composed songs and chamber music, under the tutelage of János Batka (1845–1917).

263. From the letters (Demény, ed. 1976: 78–79, 82, 112), we learn that Bartók stayed in the village of Ratkó, in Gömör County, for a period of more than six months, starting in March. There he formed a friendship with Kálmán Harsányi (1876–1929), later a noted poet, some of whose poems he set to music; e.g., *Est* (*Evening*) for solo voice and piano (DD 73, BB 29, 1903), and *Est* for four-part male chorus (DD 74, BB 30, 1903). The texts are identical in both works, but the music is entirely different.

264. Ferenc László (1978) examines the events surrounding Bartók's relationship with Lidi Dósa, whose tunes he recorded. László points out that this initiated Bartók's folk-music investigations, though the tunes that she sang for Bartók were not actual folk songs and did not represent the oldest Hungarian folk-song style. László also discusses Bartók's arrangement and publication of Dósa's melodies.

to Bartók the realization that there was *Magyar* (Hungarian) music of which he, like most of his compatriots, was entirely unaware" (Stevens 1964: 22). In the words of Kovács (1993: 51), "[I]t led to a change in his entire artistic outlook." Bartók felt compelled to investigate the musical repertory of Lidi Dósa's native Transylvanian village and its environs, as a new and important source for his own compositions.

Denijs Dille (1990) provides documentary evidence, in the form of letters, about the first meeting of Bartók and Kodály at the home of Emma Gruber. In October 1905, at the time of their meeting, Kodály was in the process of finishing his dissertation, *A magyar népdal strófa-szerkezete* (*The Stanza Structure of Hungarian Folksong*) (1906). (See also, Bartók Jr, ed. 1981a: 71; Kodály 1974 [1946b]: 2; and Voigt 1988: 391.) So began an enduring artistic, scholarly, and personal relationship, which sometimes rivaled that of the Schoenberg–Webern–Berg school in intensity, but without the master-disciple aspect. Their contact was to prove extremely productive to Bartók's folk-music research.[265]

---

265. Kodály and Bartók both attended the Budapest Academy of Music; Bartók entered in 1899, Kodály in 1900. Yet they did not meet until 1905. Prior to that time, they had nurtured separate interests in Hungarian folk music. (Dille 1990.) Kodály introduced Bartók to Edison phonograph cylinders, which had already become an indispensable piece of equipment for collecting folk songs. In Hungary, the ethnographer Béla Vikár pioneered the use of that equipment as a means of preserving folk song, and during the years 1896–1910 recorded some 1,500 examples of Hungarian peasant music. With the help of that instrument, it became possible to check the notes, and to process and store the material. Bartók's transcriptions, based on recordings, differ greatly from those presented in commercial folk song collections. (Demény, ed. 1971: 88, 103, 108–109, 231, 244, 259–260.) He began to publish his scientific studies of Hungarian and other Eastern European folk music (Demény 1946: 7; and 1976: 146, 188–189, 202, 305). For further reading, see specially Voigt's (1997) paper, "Solved and Unsolved Problems Concerning the Beginnings of Sound Recording: The Changing Techniques for Audio and Video Recording in Ethnographical Research." Voigt remarks that Hungarian ethnography has always taken pride in the fact that it was the first to use the phonograph for ethnographical research, as carried out by Vikár, whose finding were received with great enthusiasm at the 1900 folklore conference in Paris (ibid.: 103). Voigt (ibid.: 104) points out that a subsequent exhibition, held in 1905 at the Néprajzi Múzeum (Museum of Ethnography), provided still more information about fieldwork, and that the technical quality of data obtained by that means may be decisive in their later interpretation. The American inventor, Thomas Alva Edison (1847–1931), and his coworkers spent many years developing the methods for the mechanical recording of sound, and Jesse Fewkes (1850–1930) was recording songs and speech by Native Americans as early as 1890 (ibid.: 104–105). In 1900, the French presented their own linguistics-related recordings in Paris. That event included a presentation of Vikár's paper on phonograph-based collecting efforts before the Millennial Festivities of 1896 in Hungary. According to Voigt (ibid.: 105–106), indirect sources tell us that Vikár started his collecting efforts in 1895. Even earlier, in 1892, Gábor Veress (1869–1937) of Transylvania had also made recordings, in Csík, Maros-Torda and Brassó Counties. Voigt emphasizes that, while we can clearly see the problems to be tackled, further research is necessary to find the right answers (ibid.: 107).

On this subject, see also especially Dobszay (1982[266]); Ujfalussy (1972[267]); and Breuer (1974b[268]). It was Kodály who, by personal example, advice, and through his writings, launched Bartók into his life work: the systematic, scientific collection of folk music. As Bartók freely acknowledged:

> It was my great good fortune to meet Zoltán Kodály, who was outstanding as a musician and as a teacher. He had a sharpness of perception and a critical judgment, which were of inestimable help to me: he guided me in my study of every kind of music. (*BBE* 1976 [1921a]: 409.)

Kodály's studies encompassed broad literary and historical aspects of Hungarian folklore, the result being that his music evokes centuries of Hungarian history. By contrast, Bartók's interests tended to be more musical- and class-related (*BBE* 1976 [1933]: 81; see also, Lindlar 1984: 90–92).

In 1905, Bartók secured a grant to collect folk songs in the remote villages of Transylvania. His priority was to collect in areas near the periphery of the country where he felt society was less influenced by urban culture. In doing so, Bartók discovered more evidence of an ancient musical culture.

It is impossible to assess the fieldwork of any individual without knowing the culture that he set out to study. Nettl (1965: 6) clarifies: "At the root of the problem of uniting nation and musical style is the idea that a nation's folk music must somehow reflect the inner characteristics of that nation's culture, the essential aspects of its emotional life – its very self." That attitude is well illustrated in the following statement by Bartók:

---

266. László Dobszay (1982: 303) asks the question, "If Bartók and Kodály derived their composing styles from Hungarian folk music, why do their styles, in their developed form, differ so widely from one another?" Dobszay goes on to discuss the role of folk song in Bartók's compositions. Paradigmatic of that usage are the *Forty-Four Duos* for two violins (Sz 98, BB 104, 1931), which can guide us in understanding other compositions and works that go beyond the direct use of folk song. Bartók wrote his *Forty-Four Duos* in 1932 for inclusion in a violin-methods text written by Freiburg music teacher and musicologist Erich Doflein (1900–1977). Doflein advocated a form of progressive musical education, which would introduce the violin student to the grammar of new music and older music, as well as to contemporary playing techniques. The *Forty-Four Duos* increased awareness of the idiosyncrasies of folk music. Bartók based all but two of them on original folk tunes having a wide variety of ethnic origins: Romanian, Ruthenian, Serbian, Ukrainian, and Arabic, as well as Slovakian and Hungarian. (Demény 1946: 32–33; and 1976: 429–430; see also, Lindlar 1984: 49–51.) The folk song chosen by Dobszay (1982) is from Transylvania, which he analyzed thoroughly in terms of pitch structure and Bartók's adaptation of the latter for bitonal purposes.

267. Ujfalussy reveals differences between Bartók's and Kodály's works, and also detects certain influences of Kodály on Bartók's music (1972: 156–157).

268. In "Bartók and Kodály", Breuer (1974b) speaks of their role in revitalizing Hungarian music in the twentieth century. Breuer outlines common features between the two composers, including the collecting of Hungarian folk music and the use of folk tunes in their compositions. There were differences between them, too: Kodály's primary interest lay in vocal music, and he limited his ethnomusicological activities to Hungarian folk music; in contrast, Bartók wrote primarily orchestral music and expanded his ethnomusicological research to other Eastern-European nations, as well as Turkey and North Africa.

It was of the *utmost*[269] consequence to us that we had to do our collecting [of folk songs] ourselves, and did not make the acquaintance of our melodic material in written or printed collections. The melodies of a written or printed collection are in essence dead materials. It is true though – provided they are reliable – that they acquaint one with the melodies, yet one absolutely cannot penetrate into the real, throbbing life of this music by means of them. In order to really feel the vitality of this music, one must, so to speak, have lived it – and this is only possible when one comes to know it through direct contact with the peasants. [...] I should, in fact, stress one point: in our case, it was not a question of merely taking unique melodies in any form whatsoever, and then incorporating them – or fragments of them – in our works, there to develop them according to the traditionally established custom. This would have been mere craftsmanship, and could have led to no new and unified style. What we had to do was to grasp the spirit of this hitherto unknown music and to make this spirit (difficult to describe in words) the basis of our works. (*BBE* 1976 [1928]: 332–333.)

Following his initial investigations of Hungarian folk music in 1906, Bartók soon became interested in the peasant music of ethnic minorities.[270] In "Die Volkmusik der Völker Ungarns", Bartók (1970 [1921]) stressed the importance of an ethnographic approach to studying the music of neighboring peoples. Unlike Kodály, whose folk-music activities remained limited to Hungarian villages, Bartók's increasingly international interests led him to collect Slovakian melodies in the autumn of 1906, Romanian ones in the summer of 1909[271] (Kodály 1974 [1921]: 432; Voigt 1988:

---

269. Bartók's emphasis.

270. The year 1906 was an eventful one for Bartók. In the spring, he went to Spain on his last tour as a young pianist; he was already engrossed in plans to edit a new collection of folk songs jointly with Kodály. However, publication was dependent on there being a sufficient number of subscribers. In the summer of that year, he went on his first extensive quest for folk songs, mostly in Békés County, in the neighborhood of Vészt, Dobos, and Gyula, and also in the nearby districts of Csanád and Csongrád. He also collected from Pest County, Tura, Tápiószele, and elsewhere, even from places as far away as Hajdúsámson. Of the places mentioned in the Balaton region and the counties of Zala and Somogy, the name that occurs most frequently is Felsőireg (now Ireg-Szemcse) in Tolna County. (Bartók Jr, ed. 1981a: 78–89.)

271. In 1910, Bartók made his first attempts to collaborate with Slovaks and Romanians in a project for the publication of their respective scientific studies of folk-music (Demény, ed. 1976: 165–166, 172–174, 184, 188, 190, 195). Bartók's first significant publication of folk song transcriptions, *The Romanian Folksongs of Bihor County*, was published in 1913 by the Academia Româna in Bucureşti. The work contained 371 melodies with an introduction, texts and notes. (See also, Demény, ed. 1976: 200, 204, 209, 211–215.) The facsimile edition (1967 [1932]) of that study appeared with the slightly altered title, *Romanian Folk Songs from the District of Bihor*. In it, Bartók incorporated the Bihor material into the three volumes that represent his last and greatest work on Romanian musical folklore (see also, Kodály 1974 [1950]: 452).

392; and Burlas 1972[272]). Benjamin Suchoff describes Bartók's interest in the mutual musical influences of minorities in pre-Trianon Hungary[273]:

> He not only unearthed ancient pentatonic melodies still in vogue but also discovered completely different genres as well as Hungarian influences in the music of neighboring villages inhabited by Romanians. He therefore decided that he would further extend his research to the folk music of the Transylvanian Romanians, in order to determine the nature and extent of reciprocity between Hungarian peasant music and minorities of people living in greater Hungary. (Suchoff 2000: 17–18.)

In January 1907, Bartók was appointed Professor of Piano at the Budapest Academy of Music, an event that was to prove important for his development as a scholar and composer. Firstly, it permitted him to settle in Hungary and continue his investigations of folk music. Secondly, at the instigation of Kodály, who was also on faculty at the Academy, he began a thorough study of Debussy's music. (Bartók Jr, ed. 1981a: 91; see also, p. 27, Chapter 2.1.2.) Kodály wrote: "Transylvania gave him no rest. He applied and was granted a scholarship (worth sixteen hundred crowns) to study Székely folk music, and in the summer of 1907 he set out for Csík County" (1974 [1950]: 452). Bartók wandered for weeks, not just in Csík but also in the counties of Gyergyó and Kolozs (Rácz 1972;[274] see also, Bartók Jr, ed. 1981a: 94–95). As reported in Demény (ed. 1976: 123; and 1971: 74–75), on August 17, 1907, Bartók sent a picture postcard to the pianist Etelka Freund (1879–1977), on which he wrote: "*Megtaláltam a székely dallamtípusokat, amiről nem hittem, hogy léteznek*" (I have made a rather strange discovery while collecting folk songs. I have found examples of *Székely* tunes, which I had believed lost). Kodály described Bartók's return from his 1907 field trip: "He came back with such a pile of pentatonic melodies that, in conjunction with my own simultaneous findings in the north, the fundamental im-

---

272. Ladislav Burlas (1972) gives a detailed outline of Bartók's interest in Slovakian folk songs, providing dates, places, and number of tunes collected. Burlas also presents the results of Bartók's research, a list of his Slovakian folk song arrangements, and a detailed modal and harmonic analysis of them (ibid.: 181–185). Burlas shows how Bartók treated material derived from Slovak folk music, e.g., harmonization of Lydian melodies by the use of parallel motion. Burlas (ibid.: 184–186) also describes pitch structures comprised of fourth, tritone, and fifth as transmutations rather than chromatic alterations, arguing that such structures led Bartók to make specific changes to his own conceptions of tonality.

273. See also, Carlisle Macartney (1937), *Hungary and Her Successors: The Treaty and Its Consequences, 1919–1937* and Romsics (1982: 90–98), *Counterrevolution and Consolidation*.

274. In "Béla Bartók's Collection of Pentatonic Tunes in Csík County, 1907", Ilona Rátz (1972) examines Bartók's realization of the importance of pentatony during his early collecting tour in the Csík district. Of the 458 melodies he collected from ten villages, 47 were pentatonic. As a result of their studies, both Bartók and Kodály (who was collecting Hungarian peasant melodies in the north during that time) hypothesized that the pentatonic scale was the basis of the oldest strata of Hungarian folk music. Rátz also discusses Bartók's methodological approach to classification, and how in 1938 he re-classified the pentatonic melodies, which were originally placed in a group by themselves, as part of the larger category of old-style Hungarian melodies ("Class A"). (See pp. 155–157, Chapter 3.5.1.)

portance of this hitherto unnoticed scale suddenly became obvious" (1974 [1950]: 452). Erdely points out that this was "Bartók's first proof of the survival of an ancient musical tradition" (2001: 30). Bartók attributed that fact to geographical isolation and inadequate means of communicating with other Hungarian-speaking areas (*BBE* 1976 [1933]: 91).

Erdely (2001: 28) describes the many hardships that Bartók faced during field trips to remote areas that were located far from modes of transport. Numerous cases of such difficulties have been documented.[275] In a letter to his mother, dated July 5, 1907, Bartók described some of the primitive conditions he witnessed in a village in the Kolozs County (in Demény, ed. 1976: 118).[276] Moreover, getting the locals to sing was a feat of persuasion, as Bartók illustrated in the next passage:

> It would probably be difficult for you to imagine the great amount of toil and labor connected with our work of collection. In order to secure musical material uninfluenced by urban culture, we had to travel to villages as far as possible removed from urban centers and lines of communication. There were many villages at that time in Hungary. In order to obtain older songs – songs perhaps centuries old – we had to turn to old people, old women in particular, whom, quite naturally, it was difficult to get to sing. They are ashamed to sing before a strange gentleman; they were afraid of being laughed at and mocked by the villagers; and they were also afraid of the phonograph (with which we did most of our work), as they had never in their life seen such a "monster". We had to live in the most wretched villages, under the most primitive conditions, as it were, and to make friends of the peasants and win their confidence. And this last, in particular, was not always easy, for in previous times the peasant class had been too thoroughly exploited by the gentry, and, in consequence, was full of suspicion where those who appeared to belong to this class were concerned. Yet despite all this, I must admit that our arduous labor in this field gave us greater pleasure than any other. Those days, which I spent in villages among the peasants, were the happiest days of my life. (*BBE* 1976 [1928]: 332.)

In 1912, Bartók collected Ruthenian melodies, as well as Serbian and Bulgarian materials from the Bánát area (*BBE* 1976 [1921c]; and Demény, ed. 1971: 233, 237, 244, 277, 281, 306). Halsey Stevens observes that Bartók's work sheets of this period demonstrate the meticulous accuracy with which he applied himself to the process of transcription (1964: 36). That observation is confirmed by a careful look

---

275. See, e.g., Bartók's letter from Gyergyó, addressed to Stefi Geyer and dated August 16, 1907, describes his ordeals in writing out, in dialogue form, a fruitless conversation between himself and a peasant woman (Demény, ed. 1971: 70–74).

276. "*Bánffyhunyad (Huedin) uccáin marokkói piszok, rendetlenség, csak éppen az európaiak kedvéért ott behozott kényelem hiányzik*" (In the streets of Bánffyhunyad [Huedin] the filth and litter is quite Moroccan, without any of the amenities imported there for the sake of the Europeans) (quoted in Demény, ed. 1971: 69).

at studies such as Bartók & Lord (1951 [1943]),[277] Bartók (1955),[278] and Kodály (1974 [1950]: 454–455).

Bartók was concerned with finding the ancient origins of Hungarian music, which was a task that also required the examination of other folk-music cultures. That task led him to consider the influence of Persian-Arab music on the folk music of Eastern Europe. In 1912, Bartók visited the Máramaros (Maramureş) region and discovered an unusual style of vocal elaboration called the *cantec lung*, or *hora lunga*. (*BBE* 1976 [1937b]: 27; see also, Kodály 1974 [1923a]: 436–437; Kárpáti 1969a: 10; and F. László 1981.)[279] That "long melody", or "long dance", which he later identified in Arabic, Ukrainian, and Persian music, was strongly instrumental in character, improvisational, highly ornamented, and of indeterminate structure.[280] Bartók later wrote: "One could and should disclose the ancient cultural connections of peoples who are now far from each other; one could clarify problems of settlement, history;

277. In *Serbo-Croatian Folk Songs* (Bartók & Lord 1951 [1943]), Bartók discusses his method of transcription: placement of bars, choice of rhythmic values, determination of melodies, methods in systematic grouping of folk melodies, problem of variants, ornaments (grace notes), and more. The main discussion concerns the morphology of the vocal folk melodies, including stanza structure, scales, etc., followed by the transcriptions of the melodies. Bartók's descriptive notations, which are exceedingly difficult to comprehend, can at the same time be used as prescriptive notation. There seem to be times when Bartók was conscious of the phonetic-phonemic distinction. In at least one of his works Bartók gives detailed transcriptions in which he places less detailed versions of the melody, which presumably represent the songs' first impressions on the listener. Bartók remarks that "the transcription of recordings of folk music should be as true as possible. [...] [Pitch] deviations, since they show a certain system and are subconsciously intentional, must not be considered faulty, off-pitch singing. [...] The first problem with which we have to deal is with what degree of exactitude we shall transcribe these deviations in pitch" (ibid.: 3–4). His feelings about the effectiveness of arrow-notation seem ambivalent, as regards their accuracy in identifying quarter-tones (ibid.: 4): "An arrow pointing downward means lowered pitch, almost reaching the quarter tone below; pointing upwards it means raised pitch, not quite or almost reaching the quarter tone above. These arrows may be used in conjunction with both flats and sharps, too, where they will conceivably be used for differences of exactly one-quarter tone. They were almost never employed here because of the great difficulty in determining by ear whether the difference is exactly a quarter tone or only approximately. Obviously these arrows, and comparable symbols used by others, are signs of approximate value, and are, perhaps, the only practical means to be used [for indicating] pitch deviations in Eastern European folk music." Nevertheless, Bartók used the arrows quite often. Nettl observes that Bartók was aware of, but did not use the system of cents notation, which indicates more precisely than arrows any deviations from standard (Western) equal temperament (1964: 16, 115–117). On Serbo-Croatian folk music, see also, Demény (ed. 1971: 229–233, 244, 289, 299–301, 310, 317, 324–325, 340).

278. János Bartók (1955) gives a historical outline of Bartók's ethnomusicological research and of his publications based on transcriptions of folk melodies from various nations, as well as the composer's descriptions of those investigations.

279. For additional reading, see Frigyesi's article (1993b), "Maramaros: The Lost Jewish Music of Transylvania."

280. The German voice physiologist and ethnographer, Erich Moritz von Hornbostel (1877–1935), was assistant lecturer under Professor Karl Stumpf (1848–1936) at Berlin University. From 1922 on, he cooperated with Stumpf in editing the series, *Sammelbände für vergleichende Musikwissenschaft*, the fourth volume (1923) of which consisted of Rumanian folk songs that Bartók collected in the Máramaros district. (Demény, ed. 1971: 152, 251; and 1976: 188, 260, 305, 436, 528.)

one could point to the form of contact, to the relationship or contrast of spiritual complexion of neighboring nations" (*BBE* 1976 [1936]: 12).

In June 1913, Bartók's collecting took him to the Biskra District of Algeria, where he recorded Arab folk music (Demény, ed. 1971: 57, 120–123; and 1976: 207; see also, p. 64, Chapter 2.2.3).[281] That activity prompted him to adopt a pan-national, comparative approach to his work in ethnomusicology.[282] In "Arab Folk Music in the Biskra District", Bartók argues that various Arab music publications are not folk music, but rather music of the urbanized Arabs on remnants of old art music (*BÖI* 1966 [1917]). That study reveals differences between instrumental scales of Eastern Europe (in which all the notes refer to the steps of the seven-tone scale) and those of the North Africans (in which additional tones within the octave cannot be regarded as a chromatic alteration of the diatonic scale). Bartók further states: "It is quite conceivable that they may have influenced my works (following that year) with their chromaticism" (*BBE* 1976 [1943]: 377). In what follows, Bartók compares the Dalmatian and Arab styles:

> This Dalmatian style is by far more important than the [...] Arab style because of its unity, higher development, and unusual effect on listeners. This extraordinary effect is enhanced further by the fact that the Dalmatians perform such melodies in two parts. The two parts go generally in parallel, but the distance between them is approximately a major second. (*BBE* 1976 [1943]: 377–378.)

Stevens concludes that Bartók discovered two opposing tendencies in peasant music: "The first [was] to preserve their old traditions and customs without change and the second to imitate at least the external signs of upper-class culture" (1964: 25). Where the imitative tendency becomes greater than the preservationist instinct, the music is varied and transformed. Bartók explains that this phenomenon was not so much the invention of peasants, but "the outcome of changes wrought by a natural force whose operation is unconscious in men who are not influenced by urban culture" (*BBE* 1976 [1931c]: 6). Bartók emphasizes the fundamental importance of that aspect of peasant music:

> Peasant music, in the strict word, must be regarded as a natural phenomenon; the form in which it manifests itself is due to the instinctive transforming power of a community entirely devoid of erudition. It is just as much a natural phenomenon as, for instance, the various manifestations of Nature in fauna and flora. [...] Peasant music is naive and oblivious. (*BBE* 1976 [1921e]: 321.)

---

281. The influences from his Arab folk-music research in 1913 are evident in movement III of his *Piano Suite*, Op. 14 (1916) and in the *Second String Quartet*. See also, Kárpáti's "Arab Folk Music Influences in Bartók's *Second String Quartet*" (1956); and "Béla Bartók et la Musique arabe" (1962).

282. Bartók (*BBE* 1976 [1912]) defines ethnomusicology as a young science straddling the border between musicology and folklore. Progress in the field was obstructed by the outbreak of World War I. (See also, Kodály 1974 [1923b]: 97.)

The association between peasant music and forces of nature appears in another of Bartók's writings of 1931: "We profess ourselves to be scientists who have chosen as the subject of their study a certain product of nature, peasant music" (quoted in Szabolcsi 1976b: 67). Whether one agrees with him or not, it should be underlined that Bartók considered folk culture as being an equal to the organic, natural life of the countryside and, in that sense, analogous to many other aspects of nature.

In November 1936, Bartók visited Turkey, where for the last time he collected folk music. During this short visit, he collected 87 folk songs, of which a surprisingly large number (20, i.e., forty per cent) were related to Hungarian folk songs (Saygun 1976[283]). Bartók considered his discovery to be of international significance, in showing that Turkish and Hungarian music have a common origin in Central Asia and the surrounding area (Demény, ed. 1955a: 407–408). Bartók remarks that "I first traced Finn-Ugrian-Turkish resemblances to the people of the Volga region, and from there finally to Turkey" (quoted in Rothe 1941: 130; see also, Demény, ed. 1971: 181, 243, 254–255, 259–261, 289; and Bartha, ed. 1974: 15–16, 289–290).

Bartók wanted to expand his research into the origins of the Hungarians, and planned trips further east, to the Csángó people of Moldavia and to the *csuvas* (Chuvash) and *tatár* (Tatar) peoples living along the Volga River. But World War I and the succeeding years of political and economic collapse put an end to his hopes of making such trips.[284] (Kodály 1974 [1950]: 453; and 1976: 17–36.) Further tours to Transylvania were prevented by Romania's entry into the war in 1916. During the period of the *Tanácsköztársaság* (Republic of Councils), Bartók, like Kodály and Dohnányi, was an advisory member of the Music Committee headed by the composer Béla Reinitz (1878–1943).[285] The counter-revolutionary regime suspend-

283. In *Béla Bartók's Folk Music Research in Turkey* (1976), the Turkish composer and folklorist Adnan Ahmed Saygun (1907–1991) – one of the party that accompanied Bartók on his collecting tour in Turkey – includes Bartók's original intabulation of the melodies and the autograph of Bartók's introduction to the collection. In the latter, the composer discusses the structure of the melodies, special performance characteristics, as well as the texts and their setting in relation to the melodies.

284. World War I suspended the process of democratization that had started during the nineteenth century. Emergency acts legalized the control of trade and the economy by repressive measures. Union power was seriously curtailed, censorship was re-introduced, and factories were placed under military control. After the defeat of the Central Powers in November 1918, the Monarchy started to fall apart. In October 1918, a state comprised of Slovenes, Croats, and Serbs (the SHS-state, later to become Yugoslavia) was proclaimed in Zágráb (Zagreb); and in Prague, the Republic of Czechoslovakia. Hungary was declared to be a republic on November 16, 1918. Emperor Karl Hapsburg, who had followed Franz Joseph in 1916, was forced to transform the Monarchy into a federal state. On November 12, 1918, the Provisional National Assembly declared Austria a republic. (Merényi 1978: 217–228.)

285. A revolution broke out in Budapest in October 1918, and a republic was proclaimed, headed by Count Mihály Károlyi (1875–1955). The trauma caused by the defeat, the disruption of the economy, and the attack by the small Entente countries, however, could not stifle the pushes toward democratic social reform that were already underway. The discontent of the masses was fomented further by Bolshevik agitators freshly trained and just back from Russian prison camps. Károlyi found himself in an impossible situation, and finally handed over power in March 1919 to the Communist Hungarian Republic of Councils headed by the Bolshevik Béla Kun (1886–1937).

ed Dohnányi, Director of the Academy of Music at the time of the revolution, and his deputy, Kodály. Teachers who demonstrated their support for that regime were brought under disciplinary action.[286] Bartók considered settling abroad, and an extract from one of his letters, dated October 23, 1919, gives evidence of his anxiety at that time:

> For the next ten years, at least, it will not be possible to do any work, i.e., the kind of work I am interested in (studying folk music). In other words, if I have a chance to do this kind of work abroad, I see no point in staying here; and [even] if it is [not] possible to make a living from this kind of work abroad either, it would still be better to teach music in, say, Vienna [rather] than in Budapest; for there at least they have good musical institutions (orchestras, opera, etc.), whereas everything is being ruined here because our best musicians, our only ones – Tango, Dohnányi, etc. – are being hounded out of their posts. (Quoted in Demény, ed. 1971: 144.)

To judge from the following quotation, it would seem that Bartók eventually became resigned to his changed circumstances:

> The situation even today makes it impossible for me to think of continuing my folk-music research. Our own resources do not permit us this "luxury", and besides, research work in territories now torn away from the former Greater Hungary, has become impossible for political reasons as well. […] And anyway, there is no genuine interest in this branch of musicology anywhere in the world – so perhaps it does not have the importance that some fanatics attribute to it. (*BBE* 1976 [1921a]: 411.)

After his fieldwork ceased, Bartók's engagement with folk song entered a more analytical phase (Erdely 1987).[287] He became fascinated not just with the transcription, analysis, and classification of the many tunes he collected, but also with the comparison of different peasant musics, each with its peculiar dialect (Bartók 1981

During its short rule (three months), the Republic of Councils aimed to implement its social programs through nationalization and revolutionary terror, while continuing its struggle for territorial integration of the country. It was Czech and Romanian intervention that elicited the collapse of the Republic, not the counter-revolution organized under Horthy. (Merényi 1978: 200–216.) Following the downfall of the Republic, Reinitz was imprisoned and subjected too much vilification in the press. These were circumstances in which Bartók dedicated his *Ady Songs* (Op. 16, Sz 63, BB 72, 1920) to Reinitz, "with true friendship and affection". Reinitz was the first to set some of Ady's poems to music (1907). As a critic, he was one of the first to recognize the significance of Bartók's and Kodály's art. Later Reinitz went into exile in Vienna, but returned to Hungary at the end of the 1920s.

286. On January 10, 1920, disciplinary action was instituted against Kodály, because of his membership in the Music Committee of the Republic of Councils; in his defense, Dohnányi and Bartók protested that Kodály was not alone in joining that group (Demény, ed. 1971: 144).

287. Erdely (1987: 83) states that by the end of World War I, both Bartók and Kodály had together accumulated in the neighborhood of 8,000 Hungarian folk melodies. Bartók's fieldwork alone consisted of a further 3,200 Slovakian melodies, 3,500 Romanian melodies, 200 Ruthenian, South Slavic and Bulgarian tunes, and 69 Arabian melodies.

[1924]; Demény, ed. 1971: 128–129, 146, 342; and 1976: 262; see also, Lampert 1976[288]). Examples of such studies are discussed in upcoming chapters.

3.5. Classification

If simple at first glance, the problem of folk-song classification has been dealt with extensively in ethnomusicological literature since the late nineteenth century, when that discipline first began, then under the appellation "*vergleichende Musikwissenschaft*" (comparative musicology). No ideal process of classification has yet been found, as witnessed by the constant appearance of new endeavors to find one. (Nettl 1964: 1–5; and *BBE* 1976 [1912].)

Obviously, one requirement of a classification system is to place a given song within a large collection. A second, equally important requirement is that of underscoring similarities and relationships among tunes, in order to assemble them into groups, or what folk-song scholars call "tune families". For the purpose of comparative analysis, the investigator should have at his/her disposal, in easily accessible form, the entire "family tree" of a given melody-group, including every known variant and derived melodic form. The variants should be arranged to permit study that will explain how each one of them is related to all the others. Hence, the primary and most urgent task is to create a system whereby a large number of melodies can be indexed in a way in which they can be readily compared with (and, at the same time, distinguished from) each other on the basis of particular criteria. Such goals are not easy to achieve, especially because criteria for classification are theoretically infinite in number. For that reason, many different methods of classification have been devised, adopted, modified, and improved (no single method is satisfying in all respects; each has its advantages and disadvantages). Given the huge number of studies on the subject, and the primary purpose of the present study, my review of classification methods in this chapter is limited to those, which are essentially analytical and/or theoretical in nature.

Toward the end of the nineteenth century, with the gradual emergence of musicology as a discipline and musicians taking over from folklorists the task of studying folk song, the necessity of thematic indexing soon became apparent. The Finnish folklorist and composer Ilmari Krohn (1867–1960) was the first to demonstrate the practical use of lexicographic indexing, applying it to the body of Finnish folk materials with which he was most familiar. Many other scholars, including Bartók and Kodály, later adapted his approach to indexing to the material they were examining (e.g., *BBE* 1976 [1912]; Bartók & Kodály 1921: 196; and Kodály 1974 [1923a]: 437; see also, Demény, ed. 1976: 214). In applications of lexicographic models, one sees a kind of rebound phenomenon: in earlier times, analysis of folk song had dealt almost exclusively with their lyrical (verbal, literary) content. Following the work of

---

288. Lampert's (1976) comprehensive study, *Béla Bartók (1881–1945)*, includes a discussion of his methodological approach to transcribing and classifying thousands of peasant melodies from various countries in Eastern Europe. Lampert also gives an account of Bartók's work at the Hungarian Academy of Sciences after his retirement from teaching.

scholars mentioned above, research took a swing in the other direction, by focusing almost solely on the music.[289]

The lexicographic method, as conceived by Krohn, was later taken over by Bartók and, to an even greater extent, by Kodály (*BBE* 1976 [1912]; and Kodály 1976: 315–328; and 1974 [1923a]: 437; also see, especially, Járdányi 1963[290]). Generally speaking, the method consisted in ordering a body of tunes according to their interval content, as words in a dictionary or lexicon are listed according to alphabetical content (Demény, ed. 1971: 128–129, 146, 342; Erdely 1965; and Domokos 1982[291]). To the lexicographic method, Bartók and Kodály added the following characteristics by which folk-songs may be classified: (1) number of lines; (2) pitch of the final note of each line; (3) number of syllables per line; (4) melodic range (Bartók 1913; and 1967 [1932]; see also, Kodály 1971 [1960]: 315–328).

Later on, Bartók devised an even more profound adaptation and improvement on the lexicographic means of classification, which he called the "grammatical method", because it singles out formal and structural characteristics of a given repertoire in ways that earlier musical lexicography did not do. Using his new method, Bartók classified bodies of music into style groups, which he linked to hypotheses about their genetic and historical development. The grammatical method was formulated when he was dealing with Serbo-Croatian material, and was used by Bartók from that time on (Bartók & Lord 1951). In contrast, Kodály always favored the lexicographic method (1976: 315–328), which does not imply that one method was "better" than the other.[292] Rather, the grammatical method simply suited Bartók's aim

289. A large musical repertoire, and ways of classifying it, already existed. That repertoire consisted primarily of music from Northern Europe (Scandinavia), Germany and German-speaking countries, Hungary and Eastern Europe and, last but not least, Britain and the USA. (Nettl 1965: 53–101.) But as scholars began to realize that European folk music showed modal characteristics, modality itself came to serve as a criterion for classification. During the first part of the twentieth century, a considerable amount of literature on this subject appeared, as well as systems of classification to be used for archival purposes (Herzog 1950: 1048–1049).

290. Pál Járdányi (1963) examines how Bartók developed his system of style-classification, after first following Krohn's model, which was useful only for comparing types of melodies (see also, Voigt 1990b: 4). Járdányi classified stylistic traits principally on the basis of the melodic contours and register peaks of strophic Hungarian folk songs. The first version of the Járdányi system, completed in 1960, was used in the two volumes of *Magyar népdaltípusok* (*Types of Hungarian Folksong*) for classifying some 60,000 tunes. As the number of tunes continued to rise, Járdányi had to revise his system, and in 1965 applied his modified system to around 100,000 tunes. In 1975–1978, Janka Szendrei and László Dobszay worked out yet another system, purportedly based on "style", which posed other, non-musical criteria of categorization (such as "shepherd songs" and other pragmatic designations) and which was used to classify tunes in their *Catalogue of Hungarian Folksong Types* (1992).

291. Mária Domokos (1982) discusses Bartók's deviation from Krohn's method of classification (see also, Kodály 1974 [1923a]: 437).

292. In one of Kodály's most significant studies, "The Song of Árgirus" (1974 [1920]), he closely examines the relationship between verse-chronicles and folk-music tradition, i.e., at the historical crossroads of literature and music. In contrast, Bartók attempted to explore the, as it were, "horizontal" or ethnographic aspects of folk song as part of the living organism of folklore (*BBE* 1976 [1921e]: 321), and to systematize such music within the context of peasant conditions (e.g., Bartók 1981 [1924]). Bartók had already become deeply immersed arranging and processing his material

for precise analyses, by adding new criteria to the melodic ones of the lexicographic system. The new criteria for classification included the following: (1) section structure; (2) metric structure (metric units or number of syllables per line); (3) rhythmic character of the lines (e.g., *parlando-rubato*, *tempo giusto*); (4) cadential structure of strophes; (5) range (tessitura); (6) types of scale; (7) motivic-melodic content of the sections.

It should be emphasized that those two broad methods of categorization – the lexicographic and the grammatical – include variant "sub-methods", and that other researchers besides Bartók and Kodály, particularly László Vikár and Lajos Vargyas, adopted the lexicographic and grammatical methods for their own ends.[293]

Finally, it should be noted that classification of a repertory may itself function as a kind of style analysis, as Bartók came to realize:

> Within peasant music in the broader sense there is a distinctly separate layer [group], at least in Eastern Europe, which we may call peasant music in the narrow sense. […] Taken in this narrower sense, peasant music includes those melodies that belong to one or more coherent styles. In other words, peasant music in the narrower sense consists of a large repertoire of melodies of similar structure and character. […] Peasant music of this kind actually is nothing but the outcome of changes wrought by a natural force whose operation is unconscious in men who are not influenced by urban culture. The melodies are therefore the embodiment of an artistic perfection of the highest order; in fact, they are models of the way in which a musical idea can be expressed with utmost perfection in terms of brevity of form and simplicity of means. […] A melody of this kind is a classic example of the expression of a musical thought in its most conceivably concise form, with the avoidance of all that is superfluous. (*BBE* 1976 [1931c]: 5–6.)

Bartók emphasized the heterogeneity of folk music: "There is considerable confusion about the concepts of folk music and folk song. The public at large generally believes that a country's folk music is something homogeneous although this is by no means the case" (*BBE* 1976 [1931c]: 5–6). Understood (or perhaps, misunderstood) as a collective artistic phenomenon of "homogenous style", folk music had taken on an almost mythical aura[294]:

---

when the shock of political events opened his eyes to the possibility of a more far-reaching project that would also embrace the study of other peoples (cf. pp. 144–147, Chapter 3.4). Kodály, on the other hand, focused on the "vertical" relationships of our musical heritage as a whole: he tried to broaden folk-music research to include historical-national aspects, and to ensure the perpetuation of folk music.

293. In Western Europe, folk-song scholarship has thus far developed in a much less systematic fashion than it has in the Eastern countries of the continent. In the west, the problem of classification was felt to be less pressing than the task of collecting and documenting the existing traditions. Nevertheless, there have been some attempts to adapt the Bartók system to classifying local national repertoires of Western Europe, the United Kingdom, and the Americas (see, e.g., Herzog 1938: 307–308).

294. Bartók describes how unfamiliar elements could penetrate the music of the peasant class, but they "are transformed to the extent that they finally appear to be homogenous in musical struc-

It offers something absolutely uncommon, in perfect shape, and it exhibits not the slightest tinge of vulgar phraseology. It has an especially refreshing effect on the Western European ear, because of the complete lack of a melody line pointing to the tonic-dominant combination. (After all, we meet this combination in other Eastern European peasant music, too.) (*BBE* 1976 [1920d]: 304.)

In Bartók's early source studies of Hungarian peasant music, certain musical consistencies came to light. For example, he found that the peasants, in their oral musical tradition, naturally tended to improvise and transform aspects of melodies, which gave rise to numerous variants (*BBE* 1976 [1933]: 81). In addition, some peasant groups who had been minimally exposed to outside cultural influences tended to preserve their old traditions without change.[295] Other peasant groups, having had communication with surrounding tribes and with urban centers, absorbed foreign elements into their existing music, creating a new style that probably began its development only at the turn of the eighteenth century. Thus, Bartók found older and newer styles existing alongside one another in some nations (e.g., Moravia and Slovakia), while a single, homogeneous style several centuries old was preserved in other nations.

Bartók's early investigations culminated in many articles and in his classic study, *A magyar népdal* (*The Hungarian Folk Song*) (1981 [1924]).[296] Instead of grouping music according to its functional, pragmatic role, Bartók established three basic stylistic divisions (*BBE* 1976 [1933]: 84; see also, *BBE* 1976 [1921c]: 63–64; and Kodály 1974 [1923a]: 437; and 1976: 37):

1. old style folk song (*régi stílusú népdal*);
2. new style folk song (*új stílusú népdal*);

---

ture and other features, [though] they are very divergent from the infiltrated original" (*BBE* 1976 [1921c]: 59).

295. Bartók was attracted not just by the melodies, but also by the inherent logic of folk music. He acknowledged the need to derive structures by which to control these influences. The folk melodies of Eastern European cultures feature a variety of styles and modal possibilities within the tonal framework: that is one of their most basic properties. In the oldest Hungarian folk tunes, the principal pitches outline a pentatonic collection containing one tone as the final pitch. The absence of minor seconds and leading tones reduces the opportunities for hierarchization of the pitches comprising the tonal system of that music, in which pitches are weighted more equally (see pp. 155–157, Chapter 3.5.1).

296. The basic study of Hungarian folk music by Bartók (1981 [1924]) sets in perspective the morphological aspects of Hungarian musical folklore. In October 1921, Bartók completed that comprehensive work, which was published by Rózsavölgyi in 1924. Hungarian folk-song styles are dealt with in terms of scalar, syllabic, and formal structures, as well as social function. The song texts and translations are followed by the musical examples, which include 320 melodies organized according to Hungarian folk-song styles, with an emphasis on the kinship between folk songs based on content and style. That principle superseded any formal, glossary arrangement. Bartók added three Cheremis songs, to illustrate their melodic similarities to the Hungarian songs (see also, Kodály 1976: 12).

3. mixed style folk song (*vegyes stílusú népdal*).[297]

Finally, in his dictionary article, "Hungarian Folk Music," Bartók (1935a) determined the percentages of those three classes of Hungarian peasant music to be as follows: 9% old style; 30% new style; and 61% mixed style. It has been claimed that the melodies of the largest group are subdivided, in a way that is primarily intended to show their evolution (Kovács 1993: 57).

3.5.1. Old-style folk song

However cozy it might be as a memory, the idea of a "Golden Age" of folk music remains vague, since one is often not certain whether it refers to individual songs or to musical styles (see, e.g., *BBE* 1976 [1933]: 74). Nevertheless, the folk music of the Hungarians, like their ancient language, has maintained its basic structure through centuries of migrations, and for more than a thousand years of statehood in Central Europe.

Of course, the structure of their folk music has undergone certain superficial changes during those centuries. Ornamentation, richer and newer tonalities, western scales, and rhythm patterns have been added to the original pentatonic scale and simple formal structures, but without obliterating their distinctly ancient characteristics. Those melodies can be traced from China to the Danube, from the Arctic Sea to Mesopotamia, mirroring the influences and contacts that shaped the racial, cultural, and artistic character of the Hungarian people during their long migrations, before their final settlement in the Carpathian Basin. Thus, the evolution of Hungarian folk music began in the prehistoric mist of antiquity, somewhere on the immense Euro-Asian plain, where a multi-racial group of tribes amalgamated into a more or less united people of heterogeneous racial and cultural composition. That composite ethnic structure accounts for the various sources of inspiration in their folk art in general, and particularly in folk music. (Kodály 1974 [1934]; and 1976: 17–36.)

Generally speaking, probably the most common among the superficial changes made to folk music of that descent is that of transposition:

> There seems to be a broad belt of "transposing cultures" stretching from Western Europe across Northern Asia into North America. Some peoples outside this belt, such as the Torres Straits Islanders, are represented in our examples as well, but on the whole, the area given includes those cultures most obviously characterized by transposition. Furthermore, some cultures near the center of this area, including the Czechs, Hungarians, other Finno-Ugric peoples living in Russia, and Mongols, make more use of this technique than the others. Thus, it is possible that transposition as a specific technique originated at one point, perhaps in Central Asia, and became diffused in all directions, affecting some cultures more than others, but decreasing in intensity from the center of distribution. On the other

---

297. Bartók (*BBE* 1976 [1921c]) discusses the variegated folk-music styles of Hungary before 1918, then a country made up of inhabitants split into different nationalities. He found that to be a basic motive for vigorous research into musical folklore of the country.

hand, the notion of transposition is so simple and so widely encountered […] that multiple origin seems likely. (Nettl 1958: 61–62.)

In his book *On the Hungarian Folk Music*, Kodály (1971 [1960]: 17) argues that what came to be Hungarian folk songs were brought by the Ugrian tribes when they moved westward in the early Middle Ages (see also, *BBE* 1976 [1943]: 363–364). Kodály compares Hungarian folk music with 13 Mari folk songs, 11 Chuvash folk songs, and one Tartar folk song, and uses their common similarities to help prove his conclusion. However, Kodály never explains that the Chuvash and the Tartar are a Turkish people, and that the Mari, who were Finno-Ugrian, lived under a strong Turkish influence some 1,000 to 1,500 years ago. As a result, Mari folk songs are similar to Turkish ones.[298] Bartók describes the old-style melodies as being specifically Hungarian cultural products, because of their radical divergence from the melody types of neighboring countries (*BBE* 1976 [1920d]: 305). Bartók notes further that, although we have no direct proof, it is reasonable to assume that those melodies are quite old, to judge by the ornamentation, pentatonicism, ancient style of text underlay, and the like (*BBE* 1976 [1933]: 74).

The oldest know Hungarian peasant music descends mainly from certain isolated regions of Transylvania. As described by Kodály (1976: 17–38, 51–59), that "ancient stratum" consists of songs for special occasions (marriage, funerals, harvest time, and so on) as well as for general usage in children's games, for dancing, ballads, and *regös* songs (on the latter, see Sebestyén 1902b; also, n. 398, p. 203, Chapter 4.4.1). Bartók established the salient characteristic features of these songs as follows (1981 [1924]; see also, *BBE* 1976 [1921c]):

1. much *parlando-rubato* rhythm;
2. small melodic compass;
3. four isometric text lines, each consisting of anywhere from 6 to 12 syllables;[299]
4. the pentatonic scale;
5. variable structuring of the four lines; e.g., A–B–C–D, A5–B5–A–B, or A5–A5v–A–Av (= repetition of the first two lines at the fifth below).[300]

---

298. Hundreds of other melodies exist that show remarkable similarities to the folk music of peoples as far apart as the Western Siberian Ostyaks and the Voguls; the Central Asian Tartars, Eastern European Bashkirs, and the Anatolian Turks; all of which seem to have had contact with Ugrian, Turkish and Central Asian cultures. The extent of the Caucasian or Mesopotamian influence on Hungarian music is less clear (Nettl 1964: 237, 261), but quite evident in decorative folk art and other aspects of Hungarian culture. Kodály suggested the possibility of "pre-Gregorian" influences on the music of the Magyars' ancestors (Proto-Hungarians), prior to their occupation of the Carpathian Basin (1971 [1960]: 17; and 1976: 63–70). Antecedents to Gregorian music came from cultures of the Mesopotamian region: Sumerian, Babylonian, and Semitic (Nettl 1965: 34, 38). For further reading on the pre-history of Hungary, see Voigt (1982: 448, 450–452).

299. The six-, eight-, and twelve-syllable *parlando* tunes are the oldest (Kodály 1976: 37–38).

300. A5 = line A at the interval of a fifth higher; Av = variant of line A (Kodály 1976: 25).

Also characterizing Hungarian old-style folk music is a type of pentatonicism based on an anhemitonic scale.[301] Bartók speaks about that characteristic:

> Even at the beginning of our exploration of Hungarian peasant music we were rather surprised to find the common major and minor scales absent for the most part, especially in what seemed to us to be the most genuine folk melodies. Instead, we found the five most commonly used modes of the art music of the Middle Ages, and besides these, some others absolutely unknown from modal music, and furthermore, scales with seemingly oriental features (that is, having augmented second steps): G–A–B-flat–C–D-flat–E-flat–F; G–A-flat–B-flat–C-flat–D-flat–E-flat–F; G–A–B-flat–C-sharp–D–E–F. None of these scales [...] can be expressed as octave segments of the diatonic scale; wherever they begun on the keyboard, black keys will occur. (*BBE* 1976 [1943]: 363–364.)

The scales mentioned in the quote above are show in Table 3.2 and Figures 3.3–3.5, below, as both notes and integers.

Pitch classes	Point 0	Integers
G–A–B-flat–C–D-flat–E-flat–F	G	{0,2,3,5,6,8,10}
G–A-flat–B-flat–C-flat–D-flat–E-flat–F	G	{0,1,3,4,6,8,10}
G–A–B-flat–C-sharp–D–E–F	G	{0,2,3,6,7,9,10}

Table 3.2. Scales containing augmented seconds.

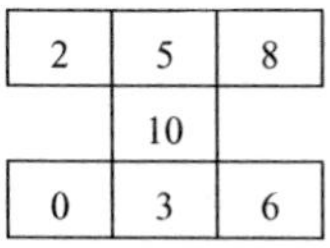

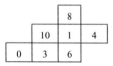

Figure 3.3. Set {0,2,3,5,6,8,10}.

Figure 3.4. Set {0,1,3,4,6,8,10}.

---

301. The pentatonic scale, probably the oldest melodic structure used by mankind, is found in the folk music of peoples who, according to generally accepted archaeological and historical thought, could not possibly have had cultural contacts with each other, such as the Celts, the Chinese, the Incas, etc. Nevertheless, comparison of Hungarian and Central Asian, Northern European (Ugrian) and Caucasian folk music reveals other similarities of melodic structure, rhythm, and other parameters, which exclude the possibility of sheer coincidence or natural development along the same lines. Magyar folk music represents the western-most advance of a great Euro-Asian musical heritage. (Kodály 1976: 17–36; and Nettl 1958: 61–62.) Moreover, it shows no similarity to the folk music of any of Hungary's central European neighbors (Slovaks, Serbs, and Rumanians) and no influence from their melodic types. If anything, the music of Hungary has influenced that of her neighbors, especially the Rumanians (Bartók 1967a: 25–27).

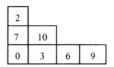

Figure 3.5. Set {0,2,3,6,7,9,10}.

Bartók continues:

In addition, in the seemingly oldest Hungarian material, we found a "defective" scale as a main characteristic, [which is] combined with a special melodic structure, called the descending structure: F–G–B-flat–C–D–F–G–B-flat. The former is [comprised of two] anhemitonic pentatonic scales [anhemitonic = without half steps]. Just as there are seven modes according to the seven octave-segments of the diatonic scale, there are five pentatonic modes according to the five octave segments of the anhemitonic pentatonic row of [scale] degrees. (*BBE* 1976 [1943]: 364.)

There follows a summary of the five pentatonic rows described in the quote (Table 3.3 and Figures 3.6–3.10).

Pitch classes	Point 0	Integers
C–D–E–G–A	C	{0,2,4,7,9}
D–E–G–A–C	D	{0,2,5,7,10}
E–G–A–C–D	E	{0,3,5,8,10}
G–A–C–D–E	G	{0,2,5,7,9}
A–C–D–E–G	A	{0,3,5,7,10}

Table 3.3. The anhemitone pentatonic rows with integers.

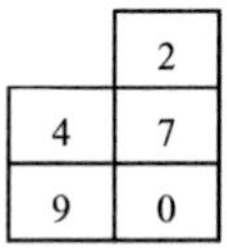

	2
4	7
9	0

Figure 3.6. Set {0,2,4,7,9}.

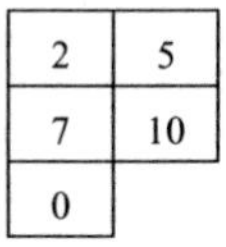

2	5
7	10
0	

Figure 3.7. Set {0,2,5,7,10}.

Figure 3.8. Set {0,3,5,8,10}.

Figure 3.9. Set {0,2,5,7,9}.

Figure 3.10. Set {0,3,5,7,10}.

Bartók explains: "The first scale[302] […] is very well known from Chinese music, and the last[303] is the only one used in 'Old' Hungarian melodies. The rest[304] are found in the music of various peoples of Eastern Russia and Central Asia" (*BBE* 1976 [1943]: 364).

Bartók divided Hungarian folk singing into two types, which he calls "*parlando-rubato*" and "*tempo-giusto*".[305] The distinction between these two ways of singing involves the singer's interpretation of rhythm and tempo. (Although that distinction was made for describing Hungarian folk music, it applies also to singing in other countries, especially those of Northern and Eastern Europe.) *Parlando-rubato* singing emphasizes the words, frequently uses elaborate ornamentation such as trills and glissandos, puts heavy stress on certain tones and considerable tension on the vocal chords, and, as its name suggests, strays freely from established rhythmic and metric patterns (Bartók & Kodály 1921: 7). Nettl comments on this style of singing:

> Hungarian peasants of an earlier kind of music than the *parlando-rubato* style would not allow us blandly to state that this style has been with the Hungarians from the dawn of human history. It is quite possible that the ancestors of these people learned and forgot various other kinds of music [which is] either more or less complicated than that which they sing today. We can make no general state-

---

302. See Table 3.3 and Figure 3.6.
303. See Table 3.3 and Figure 3.10.
304. See Table 3.3 and Figures 3.7–3.9.
305. In Hungarian ethnomusicological convention, folk songs that are not performed *parlando-rubato* have the tempo marking *giusto*, which indicates performance with minimal flexibility in the execution of beats and rhythmic patterns (Bartók & Kodály 1921: 7; and *BBE* 1976 [1921c]: 70).

ments about the history of folk music except to say that there must be a history, and that the kinds of changes in orally transmitted music are probably not too different from the kinds of changes that make up human history at large. (Nettl 1965: 10.)

By contrast, *tempo giusto* singing sticks more closely to meter and tempo, and has less ornamentation (Kodály 1984 [1939]: 25–26).

The *parlando* music of the old style derives its rhythmic characteristics from the Hungarian language, in which the vowels may be divided into short and long, the latter being approximately twice the length of the former. Each word is accented on the first vowel, since there is no anacrusis in the Hungarian language. As a result, there are two distinctive rhythms in Hungarian folk music: ♩♪ and ♪♩. The rhythm ♪♩ is the most important one; according to Bartók, it "gives that well-known, rugged rhythm" that is characteristic of many Hungarian pieces (1981 [1924]: 17). By employing the *parlando* aspect of peasant music, Bartók not only resolved the question of expressing the primeval, but also achieved a synthesis of the four basic ideas that Szabolcsi (1976b) viewed as the core of the composer's overall philosophy: nature, man, freedom, and the world of instincts.

The work of Frigyesi (1982) points up a special problem in ethnomusicology: often the analytic point of departure is not the music itself. For example, in trying to give an interpretation of rhythmical asymmetry in Bartók's music, the author's point of departure is not from the folk music itself. Frigyesi writes:

> [...] folk performances employ an infinite variety of transitional stages between rigid rhythm and free *rubato*. There are examples of partly *rubato* performance in a basically *giusto* melody while [...] a series of fixed elements can be discovered in the rhythm of *parlando* melodies. It is in this ambiguous sphere of performance that free rhythm often becomes fixed in asymmetrical forms. (Frigyesi 1982: 328.)

For Bartók and Kodály, however, the term *parlando-rubato* was not simply a performing instruction calling for some kind of speech-like performance, but a specific performing style. It was this style, which Bartók hoped to transfer – obviously with substantial modifications – to his opera.[306] Bartók felt that the declamatory style of folk song offered a potential model for an innovative style of vocal art music in which the rhythms of gypsy-inspired Hungarian music would be replaced by a freer style of singing that followed the natural rhythms and inflections of the Hungarian language. (*BBE* 1976 [1920d]; see also, n. 187, p. 105, Chapter 3.2.)

---

306. Much of the dramatic energy in *Bluebeard* derives from the vocal lines. Yet, Bartók drew a sharp separation between the music of the actors on stage from the music of the orchestra, thereby limiting the expressive potential of the singers and the interaction between vocal and orchestral lines. The old-style Hungarian songs were performed in a matter-of-fact style, not a dramatic one, as is common in most operas. Although transformed for the sake of dramatic expression, the vocal parts still strike us as stylized folk melodies, which leave little room for virtuosic display expected of opera. Such limitations embody the dramatic ideal that Balázs was particularly attached to, and that evidently was meaningful to Bartók as well (see Chapters 4.1–4.2).

Bartók's choice of Hungarian old-style songs as the model for the vocal parts created an almost insurmountable problem, which helps to explain the relative neglect
of *Duke Bluebeard's Castle* outside of Hungary. The raw strength of Bartók's opera,
particularly the rhythmic drive of the fast movements, derives in large part from his
contacts with and affinity for Hungarian folk music (Stevens 1964: 285–293). What
Bartók envisioned in *Bluebeard* was a revolutionary new style of operatic singing
based on the accentuation patterns of the Hungarian language.

3.5.2. New- and mixed-style folk song

The analysis of new- and mixed-style folk songs raises methodological questions
similar to those concerning old-style ones. During the last two centuries, the Magyar
people have developed a new style of folk music, while preserving the basic features
of the old style. The new style has maintained the pentatonic scale in many melodies,
and short pentatonic passages in others, along with Dorian, Mixolydian, and Aeolian
modes as well as minor and major scales. Transpositions at the interval of the perfect
fifth are still common, and the rhythm is as free as in the old-style songs. The new
style in question is a purely Hungarian creation; nothing similar to it has been found
in the Central European region. (Kodály 1976: 47–50.)

The new-style melodies show more Western influences than the old ones do.
Among the Hungarian peasants, the newer style developed in the nineteenth century
side by side with the older traditions, gradually replacing them. Peasants imitated certain cultural activities of upper-class town dwellers, thus absorbing and transforming
aspects of that culture into their own. As means of communication among various
areas improved, foreign elements from neighboring peoples infiltrated Hungarian
villages. Musically speaking, that process of acculturation resulted in melodies displaying heterogeneous ethnic characteristics. (Dobszay 1984: 332–336; and Kodály
1976: 60–62.) Adducing pentatonicism and transposition-by-fifth as evidence, Erdely contended, in his *Methods and Principles of Hungarian Ethnomusicology*, that
the "new style folk song is a derivative of the old style songs" (1965: 134; see also,
p. 154, Chapter 3.5.1). For his part, Bartók argued that the fundamental difference
between Eastern European and Western European folk music was that it "generally
avoids allusions to the dominant triad in its melodic structure" and in that way avoids
conventional cadence structures (*BBE* 1976 [1941]: 353). Despite the impact that
Western European music had on folk songs, their fundamental characteristics, as just
described, have remained intact.

Bartók collected and, using the grammatical method discussed in Chapter 3.5
(pp. 150–151), classified songs representing the main folk-styles of the Slovakian,
Romanian, Ruthenian, and Hungarian peoples (*BÖI* 1966 [1934]; see also, Demény,
ed. 1955a: 11–18, 217–226, 325–335; and 1976: 286). According to Erdely (1965:
98), Bartók used three analytic criteria for determining whether a song was borrowed
by or indigenous to a given people: (1) geographical distribution; (2) percentile representation in the entire tradition; (3) musical characteristics.

Kodály conceived of folk music as an intrinsic part of culture: "part of its social heritage, of learned traditions and acquired customs" (quoted in Erdely 1965: 102). Erdely himself observes that the folk-song repertory, as it presently exists, is a record stratified into historical layers, with the oldest traditions embodying the oldest and most characteristic features of "ethnomusical style". Bartók points out that many of the new-style folk songs still preserved the characteristic pentatonic phrases of the old style (see p. 154, Chapter 3.5.1), while others were in the Dorian, Mixolydian, or Aeolian modes (*BBE* 1976 [1920d]: 304–305; see also, Kodály 1976: 42–46). The new-style songs exhibited a much greater cross-fertilization with the folk music of neighboring countries than had been evident in the older songs. Also, the new-style repertoire is much larger: 7,000 different basic songs (excluding hundreds of variants), of which the most representative type is repetitive in design, with the first line heard again at the end. (Bartók 1935a.)

Bartók and Kodály established characteristics of the new-style folk songs as follows (1981 [1924]; *BBE* 1976 [1921c]; and 1976: 39–42):

1. *tempo giusto* rhythm predominates;
2. sectional designs: A–A5–A5–A, A–B–Bv–A, A–A5–B–A, A–A–B–A, A–B–Bv–A, or A–A5–A5v–A;[307]
3. "arch" form melodic contours;
4. melodic compass ranging from one octave up to the tredecima;
5. Dorian, Mixolydian, Aeolian and major scales equally common; Phrygian less frequent, but important;
6. isometric and heterometric lines;
7. number of syllables to a line varies from 6 to 25;
8. ornamentation: maximum of one or two notes are typically sung melismatically, as opposed to intricate ornamentation of the old style.[308]

Since Bartók believed that the new-style folk songs derived from the *verbunkos* (see p. 107, Chapter 3.2.1), he was able to draw connections among virtually all (*giusto*) rhythmic schemes of Hungarian music. Bartók considered the old and new styles far more significant than the mixed (heterogeneous) style, which is sometimes problematic by definition (*BBE* 1976 [1921c]), and the former two pervade his own compositions (see Chapter 4).[309]

---

307. The most well known Hungarian songs belong to one of these types. The A–B–Bv–A, or A–A5–A5v–A form is considered a particularly Hungarian structure in Western European literature. (Kodály 1976: 39.)

308. Note that, in addition to the old- and new-style songs there is an additional, equally significant group of miscellaneous content, in which no unity of style is discernible (*BBE* 1976 [1921c]).

309. Bartók's ethnomusicological work continued throughout his entire life. In 1913, Bartók and Kodály jointly submitted a "Draft of the New Universal Folk Song Collection" to the Kisfaludy Társaság (which did not respond); they were proposing a rigorously critical and monumental collection: a Hungarian *Corpus musicae popularis*. In the 1920s, Bartók did extensive work on two important Slovakian and Romanian collections, neither of which was published in his lifetime. His work on Hungarian folk music continued at the Hungarian Academy of Sciences from 1934

In "The Folk Songs of Hungary", Bartók points out that the Dorian, Phrygian, Mixolydian, and Aeolian modes (Table 3.4 and Figures 3.11–3.14, below), which are found in abundance in Hungarian folk music, generally lack a dominant harmonic function for the fifth degree (*BBE* 1976 [1928]: 334).

Scale	Pitch classes	Point 0	Integers
Dorian	G–A–B-flat–C–D–E–F	G	{0,2,3,5,7,9,10}
Phrygian	G–A-flat–B-flat–C–D–E-flat–F	G	{0,1,3,5,7,8,10}
Mixolydian	G–A–B–C–D–E–F	G	{0,2,4,5,7,9,10}
Aeolian	G–A–B-flat–C–D–E-flat–F	G	{0,2,3,5,7,8,10}

Table 3.4. Heptatonic folk modes and corresponding integers.

	2	5
	7	10
9	0	3

Figure 3.11. Set {0,2,3,5,7,9,10}.

	5	
7	10	1
0	3	

Figure 3.12. Set {0,1,3,5,7,8,10}.

to 1940, where he worked to prepare *A magyar népzene tára: Corpus musicae popularis hungaricae* (*CMPH*) (*The Complete Edition of Hungarian Folksongs*) (Bartók & Kodály et al, eds. 1951–1997). The folk-music collections edited by Bartók and Kodály constitute the base of a continually expanding stock of tapes and transcriptions, the archiving and systematizing of which is ongoing. In 1933, the leaders of the Academy contracted Kodály and Bartók to prepare a collection of Hungarian folk songs covering the entire Hungarian-speaking territory. Bartók's job was to prepare the folk-song collection for publication; Kodály's was to explore comparable sources of folk-music materials in libraries and archives. Bartók revised the material recorded by phonograph and arranged the collection according to the system he elaborated in his book *Hungarian Folk Song* in 1924. In October 1940, on the eve of his emigration, he gave the collection over to Kodály. Consisting of 13,500 items, the collection is arranged according to what is called the Bartók System; it, too, was not published in his lifetime (see also, Voigt 2005 [1970]: 88). The final chapter of Bartók's ethnomusicological research occurred during his American years, when he transcribed recordings of South Slavic melodies, made in the mid-1930s at Columbia University (Demény, ed. 1976: 666; Nettl 1965: 90–91; Kodály 1974 [1950]: 455; and Voigt 1990b: 18). Both Bartók and Kodály made their transcriptions in several copies, exchanging them and forming their individual collections as they deemed fit. In 1949, an editorial board was set up under Kodály's guidance for the publication of *CMPH*; it was later converted into the Folk-Music Research Group of the Hungarian Academy of Sciences, which existed until 1974. In 1974, that group was merged with the Institute for Musicology of Hungarian Academy of Sciences. Since then, its directors have been József Ujfalussy (1974–1979), Zoltán Falvy (1979–1998), and Tibor Tallián (since 1998). Between 1951 and 1966, five volumes (*CMPH* I–V) of tunes were published, grouped according to various calendar events and life-experiences: *Children's Games* (1957 [1951]); *Calendar Days* (1953); *Wedding* (1955–1956); *Coupling Songs* (1959); and *Laments* (1966). Later publications in the series contain strophic songs, grouped in a more general fashion: *CMPH* VI–X (1973–1997).

	2	5
4	7	10
9	0	

Figure 3.13. Set {0,2,4,5,7,9,10}.

2	5	8
7	10	
0	3	

Figure 3.14. Set {0,2,3,5,7,8,10}.

It is important to stress the fact that in scales not containing the leading tone (major-seventh above the scale tonic), the conventional dominant–tonic resolution cannot occur; e.g., in Table 3.4 and Figures 3.11–3.14 (above), the "absent" leading-tone is F-sharp. Bartók remarks that the Hungarian pentatonic scale functions in a similar way: "since the second degree (A) and major seventh (F-sharp) are missing, the trite dominant–tonic cadence is not possible" (*BBE* 1976 [1928]: 334). Figure 3.15 illustrates the pentatonic scale, G–B-flat–C–D–F as a set type; the second and sixth diatonic degrees are missing.[310]

	5
7	10
0	3

Figure 3.15. Set {0,3,5,7,10}, (G = 0).

In Bartók's works, the minor-seventh chord, constructed from degrees of the pentatonic scale, takes on a consonant character, and is frequently used at points of rest – even final cadences. Bartók derived new harmonic materials from the pentatonic scale, but did not limit himself to its limited triadic resources: apart from the minor-seventh-chord, the pentatonic scale contains only two other triads and their inversions. Given the limitations of that scale-material, Bartók frequently employed non-diatonic notes and chords to decorate and support essential melodic tones.

From his studies of folk music, Bartók also came to realize the important structural role that the tritone could play in his own compositions (*BBE* 1976 [1928]: 334). He claimed that his usage of that interval was prompted from his study of Romanian and Slovakian folk music in the Lydian mode (see pp. 47–49, Chapter 2.1.4).

In the encounters with folk music, Bartók uncovered tonal and rhythmic structures, such as modal scales, pentatonicism, *rubato* rhythm, and rhythmic ostinato. In

---

310. They may appear in ornamentations, however, in the form of unaccented passing tones.

making those discoveries, Bartók sensed a new relation between musical structure and its content:

> According to the way I feel, a genuine peasant melody of our land is a musical example of perfected art. I consider it quite as much a masterpiece, for instance, in miniature, as a Bach fugue or a Mozart sonata movement is a masterpiece in larger form. A melody of this kind is a classic example of the expression of a musical thought in its most conceivably concise form, with the avoidance of all that is superfluous. It is true that this pitiless terseness, as well as the unfamiliar mode of expression of these melodies, results in their not appealing to the average music lover. […] In a peasant melody […] all that is incidental is entirely missing – we have only what is fundamentally essential. […] So, above all, from this music we have learned how best to employ tenseness of expression, the utmost excision of all that is non-essential – and it was this very thing, after the excessive grandiloquence of the Romantic Period, which we eagerly sought to learn. (*BBE* 1976 [1928]: 333.)

3.6. Three-level concept of folk-music arrangement

In his desire to move away from traditional Western influences, Bartók was seeking to derive new pitch structures with which to harmonize original folk melodies, as well as folk-based melodies of his own invention. It has been mentioned more than once that the originality of Bartók's music lies in the fact that he absorbed folk influences into his own, personalized compositional process (Bárdos 1974: 102–104, 107–114), not by assimilating the surface features of folk music, but by what Bartók often referred to as its "spirit" or "essence" (*BBE* 1976 [1920b]: 318; *BBE* 1976 [1928]: 332–333; and *BBE* 1976 [1943]: 376). Folk music was not just a fertile field for musical arrangements; it also introduced a wealth of melodic, rhythmic, textural, and formal models that could be transformed for use in composition (Demény, ed. 1971: 198, 201–203, 220, 248–249; see also, pp. 23–24, Chapter 2.1.2).[311]

On December 26, 1904, Bartók wrote to his sister Elza Bartók about a new project that was taking shape in his mind:

> I have a plan now, to collect the finest examples of Hungarian folk song and to raise them to the level of works of art with the best possible piano accompaniment. Such a collection would serve the purpose of acquainting the outside world

311. While traveling in Transylvania, Bartók worked on the fourth movement of his *Second Suite*, the melody of which is pentatonic. Before the year ended, he had completed settings of *From Gyergyó: Three Folk Songs from the Csík District* for recorder and piano (Sz 35a, BB 45a, 1907) and the first five of his *Eight Hungarian Folksongs* for voice and piano (Sz 64, BB 47, 1907–1917). Of the latter, the first five were collected in 1907 during his folk-song expedition to the Csík District of Transylvania. (Bartók Jr, ed. 1981a: 94–95.) The last three were collected from Hungarian soldiers in 1916–1917, when expeditions to the villages were severely restricted by ongoing war. Both sets of songs were joined in one volume and published in 1922; of the six old-style songs in the collection, four are exclusively pentatonic, and pentatonic segments are prominent in the vocal lines of the other two.

with Hungarian folk music. Our own good Hungarians [...] are much more satisfied with the usual gypsy slop. (Quoted in Griffiths 1984: 17.)

During World War I, folk-song arrangements and composition in its own right
seemed to form two separate streams in Bartók's œuvre. The arrangements generally continued the kinds of adaptation that Bartók had used in 1907–1908, which
were based on harmonic and modal patterns and directly influenced by Kodály, and
indirectly by Debussy (see pp. 27–30, Chapter 2.1.2). During the war years, the folk-
song arrangements developed gradually into larger, cyclical forms. By contrast, in
the compositions bearing opus numbers, Bartók sought inspiration from folk-music
sources that blended well with the "atonal" musical idioms of his Viennese contemporaries, primarily Schoenberg (discussed above, in Chapters 2.1.3–2.1.4).

In this chapter, our aim is to provide an overview of Bartók's folk-music arrangements. The first fruits of his work in that area were published in February 1905:
Székely Folksong: The Red Apple Has Fallen in the Mud, arranged for solo voice and
piano (DD C8, Sz 30, BB 34, 1904), and the self-descriptive collection, *Hungarian
Folksongs* (Sz 29, BB 37, 1904–1905). In those earliest settings, Bartók's piano accompaniments still retain many Romantic flourishes, but already show his inclination towards the use of simple block chords and non-traditional rhythms.

Victoria Fischer (2001: 100) estimates the number of Bartók's folk-music arrangements as nearly 200, the majority of which are settings for solo piano. His
musical arranging, an activity that spanned Bartók's entire career, was most concentrated during the years 1906 to 1918, when he was doing the vast majority of his
fieldwork (Lampert 2005 [1980];[312] see also, pp. 142–148, Chapter 3.4). In 1907,
Bartók was appointed Chair of Piano Teaching at the Budapest Academy of Music, hence his desire to write pedagogical piano pieces to fulfill his duties there; at
the same time, he was forging a new and individualistic musical language (Fischer
2001). The discoveries made on his first song-collecting tours inspired his piano arrangements, most clearly in the *Three Hungarian Folksongs from the Csík District*
(Sz 35a, BB 45b, 1907)[313], the *Four Slovakian Folksongs* (*c.* 1907), some of the
Eight Hungarian Folksongs,[314] and the piano pieces *Gyermekeknek* (*For Children*)

312. Bartók's initial *parlando* folk-music arrangements for solo piano were the first two of the
Three Folksongs from the County of Csík (1907). Based on shepherds' flute tunes, they are under-
standably more instrumental than vocal in idiom, yet the style is definitely *parlando*. The meters
change frequently (3/4, 2/4, 3/4, 3/8, 2/4, etc.), and the accompaniment rhythms are much freer
than those of the 1906 vocal arrangements. It seems that Bartók was no longer writing simple
arrangements to educate the public (Griffiths 1984: 17), and that he no longer required the singer-
accompaniment format in order attain a freer rhythmic style; as a pianist, he was naturally more
comfortable writing for his own medium (Demény 1946: 8; also see, especially, Lampert 2005
[1980]).
313. During his trip to Transylvania in 1907, Bartók recorded, among others, three vocal tunes,
performed in a richly embellished fashion on a rustic flute. Soon after he returned to Budapest,
Bartók arranged them in a very simple but inspired setting for flute and piano, then made the version for solo piano.
314. The first song, with its ornamented and free-flowing instrumental line, illustrates Bartók's
interest in variable *tempo rubato*. As in the vocal settings, he uses modally derived harmony (B-

(Sz 42, BB 53, 1908–1909)[315]. Other works of the period showing some relation to folk music include the *Fourteen Bagatelles* (1998 [1908]), *Ten Easy Pieces* (Sz 39, BB 51, 1908, rev. 1945)[316], *Three Burlesques* (Op. 8c, Sz 47, BB 55, 1908–1911),[317] and *Allegro barbaro*[318]. (Purswell 1981;[319] Somfai 1981a;[320] and Tarasti 1994 [1978]: 102.)

In "The Influence of Peasant Music on Modern Music", Bartók discusses earlier folk influences on art music, but states that the beginning of the twentieth century was a historical turning point, marked most notably by strong reactions against Romanticism (*BBE* 1976 [1931b]: 342). At that time, most Western European musicians "believed that only simple harmonizations were well suited to folk melodies" (ibid.). Such simplicity was usually achieved by bare-bones successions of tonic, subdominant, and dominant triads. In a lecture given at Columbia University, on "The Relation between Contemporary Hungarian Art Music and Folk Music", Bartók outlined three general approaches to folk-song arrangement (*BBE* 1976 [1941]: 352):

1. those, which give primacy to melody, the accompaniment taking second place;
2. those in which melody and accompaniment have equal status;
3. those that highlight the compositional treatment itself, with the melody "only regarded as a kind of motto".

Folk song entered into Bartók's musical vocabulary as an outcome of his meticulous transcription work; thus, we can view Bartók's ethnomusicological activities as part of his overall compositional training. Griffiths (1984: 47) calls Bartók's early folk-music settings "the marriage of Bartók's creative and ethnomusicological self". The harmonizations of folk-music arrangements show how Bartók's extensive analysis of transcriptions influenced his musical thinking, and illustrate his derivation of harmonic structures from modal properties (Mason 1950).[321] The development of

---

Dorian).

315. By 1908–1909, with the completion of *Gyermekeknek*, comprised of 42 Slovak and 43 Hungarian tunes, Bartók had achieved a more consistent style in his usage of folk idioms.

316. The *Fourteen Bagatelles* and the *Ten Easy Pieces* were written concurrently, in May and June of 1908.

317. The *Three Burlesques* unite both old and new aspects of Bartók's piano writing with the programmaticism seen in his earlier compositions (Lindlar 1984: 36). Other collections subsequently published by Bartók, e.g., *Ten Easy Pieces*, also illustrate various levels of compositional treatment Bartók used for the accompaniment of folk music, as well as techniques for the creation of original music (Tallián 1983a: 138–139; see also, Demény 1946: 10).

318. On the *Allegro barbaro*, see Kárpáti (1997).

319. Joan Purswell (1981) states that the appearance of Bartók's *Bagatelles*, *Burlesques*, and *Sketches* in 1908–1910 represent the influences of folk sources and music of Debussy as well as a new approach to harmony and melody.

320. Somfai (1981a) examines Bartók's recordings, with the intention of establishing an approach to analyzing them that would aid performers of those pieces.

321. Mason (1950) discusses several of Bartók's folk-song settings in terms of the development of his musical language. Mason's analysis focuses on pentatony and the modes as well as concepts of

Bartók's approach to working with folk music can be seen in his vocal arrangements of the first ten of the *Twenty Hungarian Folk Songs* (1906) and in his *Falun* (*Five Village Scenes*) for female voice and piano accompaniment (Sz 78, BB 87a, 1924). Whereas only five of his 1906 arrangements are in the *parlando* style, that rhythm appears in four of the five songs in *Village Scenes* (1924). An explanation of this discrepancy may be that, if the *Twenty Hungarian Folk Songs* were arranged for the purpose of educating the public, the latter would have found the more rigid rhythmic style (*tempo giusto*) easier to comprehend. In that collection of songs, the piano accompaniments are clearly subordinate to the folk melody, which is sometimes echoed and/or harmonized sparsely in thirds, fourths, and fifths. The accompaniment rhythms adhere strictly to those of the melody, almost as if Bartók were not yet at ease with the rhythmic spontaneity of *parlando*.

In Bartók's piano arrangements, a rough division may be made between "vocal" *parlando* and instrumental *parlando* style. In the vocal *parlando* style, the music is (1) either an unadorned folk-song arrangement or (2) it displays a melodic line that, while rhythmically free and ornamented, retains the characteristics of the original melody and is clearly in a vocal idiom: all ornamentation, melodic ranges, and rhythms are those that may be sung comfortably. In Bartók's instrumental *parlando* music, the melodic range is wider, the ornamentation freer and more extensive, and the rhythms and tonalities do not always adhere strictly to the original peasant-music style. Even so, such music retains enough nuances of the Hungarian language and enough rhythmic freedom to characterize it as *parlando* style. (Somfai 1973;[322] see also, pp. 157–159, Chapter 3.5.1.)

Lampert (1982) gives a compilation of the 313 folk melodies used by Bartók for his compositions, and pursues three main lines of inquiry: (1) why Bartók chose those 313 out of several thousand possibilities for arrangement; (2) whether his melodic preferences changed over the course of his career; and (3) Bartók's method of using folk song. Lampert intends to show the extent to which the melodies arranged by Bartók reflect the proportions of the various styles of Hungarian folk music based on the composer's classifications (see also, Lampert 1981;[323] and Voigt 1988: 394).

---

harmonic consonance and dissonance. Mason gives some reference to rhythmic and other features of certain national folk-song types (e.g., Hungarian and Slovak).

322. Somfai (1973) observes that the two recorded performances by Bartók of "Evening in Transylvania", from the *Ten Easy Pieces*, made reveal continuous and intentional deviations from the printed score. Somfai's transcription of the piece offers the best opportunity to explore the significance of Bartók's notation of *parlando* style. His meticulous instructions concerning dashes, stresses, commas, and other breathing signs, are generally either disregarded, or misread. Bartók signifies *parlando* style by articulation signs even when he does not write specifically *parlando* or *parlando rubato* at the beginning. (See also, Demény 1946: 10.)

323. Lampert (1981) discusses, among other things, the erroneous dating of the *Three Hungarian Folk Tunes*, *Fifteen Hungarian Peasant Songs*, and other arrangements. The first four of *Fifteen Hungarian Peasant Songs* for piano, all in *parlando* style, show the composer's transition from the use of folk song in piano arrangement, to folk song rewritten as art song.

In "Bartók's *Romanian Christmas Carols*",[324] Ingrid Arauco (1987) considers four sources as the basis for her study of those folk-song arrangements: (1) transcriptions from the recordings he made on location; (2) notebook entries of melodies he wrote down on the spot; (3) the versions of the carols chosen; (4) the arrangements themselves. Arauco finds the changes between sources 2 and 3 to be of special interest, and interprets them as a rapprochement with Western art music. Removal of incidental tones and ornaments, repositioning of bar lines, and alteration of notes and rhythms clarify the harmonic and motivic phrase structures – all that makes things easier for listeners familiar with the tradition of Western art music. Arauco argues that the changing of elements incidental to the essence of the folk song not only adds structural clarity, but also reinforces emotive power.

It is worth mentioning that Bartók's first vocal arrangement, the *Magyar népdalok* (1970 [1906]), contains what Bartók and Kodály called "choice pieces" intended to popularize the art of the folk song and make it more accessible to the public. In the preface, the composers say they have "cut new clothes for the melodies so as not to cramp their fresh country style", and voice their concern that the influx of "light music" and many "imitation folk songs" might render Hungarian traditional music extinct within a few decades. The collection features level-one accompaniments that simply double the vocal line. Lampert describes how the content of that collection reflects modal and rhythmic characteristics of folk music:

> There are several traces of the archaic pentatonic scale (lacking any half steps) as well as Dorian, Mixolydian and Aeolian melodies. Yet the harmonizations follow traditional paths, especially in the fast songs. The harmonization of the slow songs shows more affinities to the particular features of the melodies, although they are extremely reserved. (Lampert 1993: 392.)

The modalities of the *Twenty Hungarian Folksongs* show a weakening of traditional dominant-tonic relations. "Tonal staticism" (Antokoletz 1984: 26) is produced by sustaining a single third or fourth. From the oldest tunes based on a pentatonic scale, Bartók derived the major and minor triads, the minor seventh chord, and fourth chords. Antokoletz shows how the first four songs fall within a pentatonic frame, filled by various modal pitch content. In the fifth song, however, the E-pentatonic content is expanded "beyond the limits of the polymodal chromaticism of the preceding songs" (ibid.: 39), which he explains in terms of interval cycles. The sixth song, in E-Dorian supports, a "polymodal complex on E" (ibid.: 48). The seventh song, in F-Phrygian, elaborates "a single modal interval (tritone) rather than appearing as a balanced polymodal expansion around the basic mode or its pentatonic substructure" (ibid.: 49). That mixture allows for the progression of V7–I7 in C-flat, and modal V7–I7 in F-Phrygian.

---

324. The *Romanian Christmas Carols* were planned as a continuation of the concept of *For Children*, in which Bartók arranged Hungarian and Slovak folk music for children's hands, without octaves. This is shared by the *Sonatina*, which inhabits much the same world; see Yeomans (2000); cf. also, F. László (2005).

Bartók's *Eight Improvisations on Hungarian Peasant Songs* is generally paired with the *Three Studies*, to demonstrate the atonal traits of his folk-song arrangements (Lindlar 1984: 54–55, 71). Bartók commented on that work as follows: "In my *Eight Improvisations for Piano*, I reached, I believe, the extreme limit in adding most daring accompaniments to simple folk tunes" (*BBE* 1976 [1943]: 375). Paul Griffiths points out that, with the *Eight Improvisations*, "the distinction between arrangement and original composition is beginning to break down" (1984: 26).

Bartók introduced a method of treating folk tunes as "mottos", which are repeated against different accompaniment backgrounds (*BBE* 1976 [1941]: 352).[325] He contrasts the motto technique with those utilized in his earlier folk-melody arrangements:

> In one case, accompaniment, introductory and concluding phrases are of secondary importance, and they only serve as an ornamental setting for the precious stone: the peasant melody. It is the other way round in the second case: the melody serves as a "motto" while that which is built around it is of real importance. All shades of transition are possible between these two extremes, and sometimes it is not even possible to decide which of the elements is predominant in any given case. But in every case, it is of the greatest importance that the musical qualities of the setting should be derived from the musical qualities of the melody, from such characteristics as are contained in it openly and covertly, so that melody and all additions create the impression of complete unity. (*BBE* 1976 [1931b]: 341–342.)

Bartók distanced himself from the more restrictive dimensions of folk music by trying to overcome what Schoenberg called "the discrepancy between the requirements of larger forms and the simple construction of folk tunes" (1975 [1947]: 183). Szabolcsi draws attention to an apparent conflict in Bartók's thinking, quoting a statement that the composer made to Denjis Dille in 1937:

> The "absolute" musical forms serve as a basis for freer musical formulae, even if these formulae involve characteristic melodic and rhythmic types. It is clear, however, that folk melodies are not really suited to be forms of "pure" music, for they, especially in their original shape, do not yield to the elaboration which is usual in these forms. The melodic world of my string quartets does not differ from that of folk songs: it is only their setting that is stricter. It has probably been observed that I place much of the emphasis on the work of technical elaboration, that I do not like to repeat a musical thought unchanged, and I never repeat a detail unchanged. This practice of mine arises from my inclination for variation and for transforming themes. [...] The extreme variety that characterizes our folk music is, at the same time, a manifestation of my own nature. (Quoted in Szabolcsi 1976a: 19.)

---

325. A synthesis of Hungarian folk music with his own experiments in compositions first emerged in a novel form in the *Improvisations*, after less successful, earlier attempts (see p. 25, Chapter 2.1.2). In the *Improvisations* the underlying tunes themselves are secondary to the added material: the original tunes are systematically developed, modified, and transformed into highly abstract pitch sets and interactions.

Based on the above quotation, Szabolcsi sets out to reveal two, opposing forces in Bartók music:

> The unconscious element, which is an aspiration related to the ever-changing, transformative nature of folk music [and the] conscious element, which asserts itself as the requirement for a strict framework, the tendency toward concentration, toward unity and distillation. (Szabolcsi 1976a: 19–20.)

Szabolcsi emphasizes that both of those forces counterbalance and constantly re-shape each other (1976a: 20). Leaving behind such speculations, let us end this chapter with Bartók's own words on the subject:

> The pentatonic scale, besides melodic impulses, gave us harmonic suggestions. The tonic-dominant relations, very conspicuous in the common major and minor scales, already are less distinct or blurred in the modes. But in the pentatonic scale, they simply disappear, because there is no dominant at all in the commonly accepted harmonic sense of the word. Four of the five degrees – the fundamental tone, third, fifth, and seventh – are almost equal in their weight. The fourth degree generally appears as a passing tone, and the seventh assumes the character of a consonance. Pentatonic melodies are very well imaginable with a most simple harmonization, that is, with a single chord as a harmonic background. That kind of harmonization, reduced to the extreme limit of simplification, should be used only exceptionally, in well-chosen, appropriate portions of a work, or else its exaggerated use would lead us to a monotonous oversimplification. [...] Melodies in such an archaic style can very well be provided also with the most daring harmonies. It is an amazing phenomenon that the archaic features will admit of a much wider range of possibilities, in harmonizing and treating melodies or themes of the pentatonic kind, than would be the case with the common major or minor scale melodies. The tonic and dominant degrees in the latter, implying tonic triads and dominant chords, actually prove something of a handicap for our purposes. Although this handicap can be easily circumvented, it nevertheless exists. So-called narrow range melodies with not more than three or four degrees, very common in Serbo-Croatian and Arab rural music, provide us with some liberty precisely because of the absence of the other three or four degrees. (*BBE* 1976 [1943]: 371–372.)

Bluebeard's Castle, Bartók's first vocal work apart from his arrangements of folk songs, was the laboratory in which he experimented with new vocal style. The opera dates from the early years of Bartók's mature composing career. It was an important milestone in his musical development, for with this work he for the first time amalgamated harmonic and stylistic elements of Hungarian folk music on a larger scale, and within the context of his own personal style. Writing to the composer Delius on March 27, 1911 about his opera project, Bartók confessed: "I have never written songs before – you can imagine how much and how often – at the beginning – the text bothered me. But it is going better now. And I think the music will be rather to your liking" (quoted in Demény, ed. 1971: 111).

4. BARTÓK'S *DUKE BLUEBEARD'S CASTLE*

4.1. Balázs's symbolist drama

The *Bluebeard* legend appears in various sources and in a number of different countries. Of course, the legend varies according to the time and place in which it appears, and depending on the "authors" who give it form. My aim here is not to provide a thorough literary history of the tale, but to provide enough essentials of it to serve as an adequate basis for analyzing the opera text.[326] The history of the *Bluebeard* story in European literature is well known to Bartók scholars, thanks primarily to the works of Kroó (1961: 251–270; 1962: 9–26; 1975 [1971]: 62–63; and 1993).[327]

One view has it that the real-life historical ancestor of the Bluebeard figure was the Breton nobleman Gilles de Rais (1404–1440), also known as the Baron of Rais (or Retz) and/or Gilles de Laval. Whether or not that is true, Bluebeard is the protagonist of the tale in which a man kills a succession of wives for peering into a forbidden room. (Szalay 1974: 19; Kroó 1961: 265–266; and 1993: 349–350.)[328]

---

326. The Bluebeard topic follows one of the archetypes in European narrative (tales, poems, dramas, and more), even in contemporary times. As Voigt (1999 [1990]: 211) remarks, "[S]torytelling is *per definition* always 'contemporary'." Voigt refers to Scheiber's article (1985 [1971]), "Old Stories in New Garb," in this context; i.e., what often appears to be new is usually just new in appearance. Hence, classification according to "theme" becomes problematic. Antti Aarne (1867–1925), a Finnish folklorist, developed what was to become the Aarne-Thompson classification system for folk tales (1911; 1987 [1961]). That system was criticized by the Russian Formalist, Vladimir Propp (1895–1970), whose *Morphology of the Folk Tale* (1958 [1928]) represented a breakthrough in structural-formal studies of narrative. For further reading on Propp, see Voigt (1999 [1972]: 76–79, 82, 85); Bettelheim (1976); and R. Honti (2004c: 518–520); on the Aarne-Thompson (ATU) classification system, see Uther (2004); Voigt (1993a: 169, 171, 176, 178–179); and J. Honti (1986: 368 n. 2).

327. Kroó (1961) gives a comprehensive discussion of all the aspects of Bartók's opera, including historical and compositional information. He also writes on the symbology of the Bluebeard story (Kroó 1993: 349), which goes back as far as the ancient contrasts between Darkness and Light. According to that symbolic interpretation, the figure of Bluebeard stands for the dark and sinful Night, which slays its betrothed. The Light embodies the curiosity of women (as one finds in the biblical Genesis account).

328. The mythemes of the mysterious absent husband, the sumptuous palace, the sister who encourages illicit curiosity, and the One Forbidden Thing – all those appear in earlier literature; e.g., in the Hellenistic romance by Lucius Apuleius (*c.* A.D. 123/5–*c.* A.D. 180), *Cupid and Psyche*. On the One Forbidden Thing (a central theme), compare the story of Adam (Hebrew, "earth" or "man") and Eve (Hebrew, "living one" or "life") in the biblical book of Genesis (Chapters 1–3; *passim*). Folklorists have also sought to establish the story's lineage on the basis of the "forbidden room" and "test" motifs (e.g., Hartland 1885). Some lines of the libretto are folk-tale commonplaces of their own; e.g., "Ask me nothing" (107/3–4) and "Do not open" (90/12). For further reading, see Walter Puchner's (2000 [1995]) article, "Mädchenmörder," in *Enzyklopädie des Märchens*

Earlier versions of the story are carefully enumerated by Kroó, in *Bartók's Stage Works* (1962: 9–27).[329]

Carl Leafstedt (1999: 163, 168–175) classifies the Bluebeard saga under a category of folk tales known as "forbidden-chamber" stories, which can be found in diverse cultures the world over (ibid.: 165; see also, Kroó 1961: 262). In *The Hungarian Folk Ballad and Europe*, Vargyas (1976: 44–65) gives a bibliography of European ballads on this theme. In nineteenth-century collections, one finds a popular Hungarian variant of the Bluebeard saga, written in about 1840 in Klézse, Romania. Called the *Ballad of Anna Molnár*, it features Márton Ajgó as the Hungarian Bluebeard. The following excerpt is taken from that ballad (Kroó 1961: 264; and 1962: 19):

"Molnár Anna, édes kincsem	"Anna Molnár, my sweet treasure,
Nézz egy kicsit a fejembe."	Look into my face."
Addig nézett a fejibe	She gazed at his eyes
Míg elaludt az ölibe';	Till he sank into slumber;
Föltekintett feje föli,	Her glance rose to the tree
Barkos fának ága közi,	And among its knotty branches

Encyclopaedia, which presents the results of almost two centuries of international research into folk-narrative traditions.

329. See also, Voigt (1999 [1990]: 216), who mentions Marc Soriano's (1918–1994) subtle and original treatment of the life and work of Charles Perrault (1628–1703), *Les Contes de Perrault* (Soriano 1968). Soriano reminds us that no tale is absolutely new, but may appear as such when retold and reshaped by various tellers. "Bluebeard" (AaTh 312) was already a well-known folk tale by the time Perrault wrote it down and published it in 1697; among related folktales one finds "King Bluebeard" (Germany), "Legend of a Husband" (Estonia), "Don Firriulieddu" (Italy), "The Little Boy and His Dogs" (African-American), among many others. The Bluebeard theme made an early appearance on the musical stage, under the title *Barbe-Bleue* (1789), and was published by the Brothers Grimm as a folktale. On the Bluebeard theme in European tales, see Karlinger (ed. 1973); see also, Heckman (1930: 165–173) and Frenzel (1970). Among the nineteenth-century productions was the *opéra bouffe*, *Barbe-Bleue* (libretto by Henri Meilhac, music by Ludovic Halévy and Jacques Offenbach) dating from 1866, which is a lighter take on Duke Bluebeard's journey through multiple nuptials. In the first two decades of the twentieth century the following works were written about the legend: *Ariane et Barbe-Bleue* by Maurice Maeterlinck (1901), transformed into an opera by Dukas (1907); Herbert Eulenberg's 3-act drama, *Ritter Blaubart* (1905); Anatole France's short story, *Les sept femmes de la Barbe-Bleue* (1903); Béla Balázs's one-act play, *A kékszakállú herceg vára* (1910); Balázs's and Bartók's opera, *A kékszakállú herceg vára* (1911); and the Eulenberg-Reznicek collaboration, the opera *Ritter Blaubart* (1920). There followed many other works, in other art forms, about the same theme: Charlie Chaplin's black comedy *Monsieur Verdoux* (1947); Pina Bausch's dance version, *Blaubart: Beim Anhören einer Tonbandaufnahme von Béla Bartóks Oper "Herzog Blaubarts Burg"* (1977); Angela Carter's short story, *The Bloody Chamber* (1993 [1979]); and Kurt Vonnegut's novel *Bluebeard* (1988). In her book *Women Who Run with the Wolves,* Clarissa Estes (1992) uses the myth of Bluebeard in Chapter 2. A TV production of the opera has been made by Hungarian director, Miklós Szinetár (Bartók 1992 [1981]). In 2004, following the Hungarian Film Fest, the public was given the opportunity to see the opera film entitled *Duke Bluebeard's Castle* made by Sándor Silló for Duna Television in Hungary. The list may easily be continued. Hartwig Suhrbier's (ed. 1987 [1984]) significant anthology *Blaubarts Geheimnis* is an excellent starting point for more comprehensive study of the Bluebeard-literature; a concise survey of earlier *Bluebeards* and their folk or mythological sources may be found in Ashman (1991), and Pyrhönen (2004: 30–32).

Hát ott vagyon hat szép leány	Beheld six lovely maidens
Fölakasztva egymás után:	Hanged side by side.
Aj! Gondolá magába',	Ah me, she thought to herself,
A hetedik én leszek ma.	I am to be this day the seventh.
Könny szemiből kicsordula	Her tears, brimming over,
Ajgó Márton orcájára.	Fell on Márton Ajgó's cheeks.

Balázs began to sketch his *Bluebeard* play in Paris in mid-December 1907, a time when Bartók was composing the *Bagatelles* and the first *Violin Concerto*. His work on the play proceeded sporadically over the next few years, until the drama, as we know it was published in June 1910. On December 26, 1909, Edith Hajós (1889–1975) wrote to Lukács, "Balázs is in Szeged writing his *Bluebeard*. Just received his prologue and will send it to you" (cited in Kadarkay 1991: 143). During those years, Balázs's diaries and personal papers[330] mention the new project repeatedly (1968 [1913]; and 1982 [1922]). As Balázs later recalled: "I did not write the Hungarian original of *Bluebeard's Castle* as a libretto, but simply as poetry, as one is accustomed to writing verse in general" (1968 [1913]: 34). Balázs was influenced, as so many were throughout Europe, by the current trends of Symbolism (Szerb 1982 [1934]: 469–471, 496); in other respects, the essential spirit of the play has much in common with broader trends in early twentieth-century European theater, particularly those of French and German drama (Leafstedt 1995a).

Balázs took the skeleton of his plot from a tale by Perrault,[331] first published as "La Barbe-Bleue" in his collection *Histoires ou contes du temps passé avec des mortalités* (1920 [1697]).[332] *Synopsis*: Bluebeard's latest wife is given the keys of his household and told that she may open every door save one. She opens the forbidden door anyway, and finds hanging the severed heads of Barbe-Bleue's former wives. Facing death at the hands of her husband, she is rescued at the last minute by her

---

330. Balázs's diaries and personal papers are located in the Library of the Hungarian Academy of Sciences, Manuscript Department. A catalogue of the library's Balázs collection was published by Dóra Csanak (ed. 1966).

331. On Balázs's sources, see Szerző (1979).

332. Perrault was a member of the *Académie Française* and a leading intellectual of his time. He could have not predicted that his reputation for future generations would rest almost entirely on a slender book published in 1697 containing eight simple children's stories. Perrault chose his folk-stories well, and recorded them with wit and style, thus giving them legitimacy as "literature". (Soriano 1968.)

brothers, who slay Bluebeard, at which point the play ends.[333] (Kroó 1961: 251–253; and Hempen 1997[334].)

Balázs's most immediate source was the libretto of Maeterlinck's *Ariane et Barbe-Bleue* (1899),[335] which was set by Dukas (1907) in a luxuriantly chromatic, post-Wagnerian style. Maeterlinck gave the work a subtitle that captures the essence of his treatment of the Bluebeard story: *Ariane et Barbe-Bleue, ou la délivrance inutile.*[336] (Grayson 1986: 69, 109, 132, 300 n. 68, 311 n. 28; and Batta, ed. 1999: 17.)

In *A Comparative Analysis of Dukas's "Ariane et Barbe-Bleue" and Bartók's "Duke Bluebeard's Castle"*, Mary Heath (1988) seeks to explore the interrelation of those two retellings of the Bluebeard legend, starting from the idea of the past as a pervasive presence in Perrault's telling of it (1920 [1697]). In Balázs's version, the historical Bluebeard story is significantly changed. Although Maeterlinck's play furnished the initial inspiration for Balázs's libretto, the latter displays fundamental differences in both treatment and point of view. Despite the subtlety and profundity of its musical symbolism and the psychological depth of its rendition of the traditional story, Dukas's *Ariane et Barbe-Bleue* may have been relegated to obscurity because of unintentional competition from two other, nearly contemporary works: Bartók's *Duke Bluebeard's Castle* and Debussy's *Pelléas et Mélisande.*[337]

---

333. In Perrault's (1920 [1697]) version: "'You must die!' Then, taking hold of her hair with one hand, and lifting up the sword with the other, he prepared to strike off her head. The poor lady, turning round to him, and looking at him with dying eyes, desired him to afford her one little moment to recollect herself. 'No, no,' said he, 'commend yourself to God,' and was just ready to strike. At this very instant there was such a loud knocking at the gate that Bluebeard made a sudden stop. The gate was opened, and two horsemen entered. Drawing their swords, they ran directly to Bluebeard. He knew them to be his wife's brothers, one a dragoon, the other a musketeer; so that he ran away immediately to save himself; but the two brothers pursued and overtook him before he could get to the steps of the porch. Then they ran their swords through his body and left him dead. The poor wife was almost as dead as her husband, and had not strength enough to rise and welcome her brothers."

334. Hempen (1997) discusses "Bluebeard's female helper." The character appears in some Bluebeard stories, e.g., in the Grimms' *Kinder- und Hausmärchen* (1812). See also, McGlathery (1993: 71–72); Tatar (2003 [1987]: 156–178); and Voigt (1981 [1980]: 253). *Bluebeard* as reproduced in printed fairytale collections has mainly followed Perrault (1920 [1697]).

335. See Maurice Maeterlinck (1910), *"Sister Beatrice" and "Ariane et Barbe-Bleue": Two Plays.*

336. Balázs must have encountered the latest manifestation of this spirit of adaptation, shaping and creating versions in Paris, where the Opéra-Comique in 1907 staged Dukas's three-act *Ariane et Barbe-Bleue* (Grayson 1986: 69, 109, 132, 300 n. 68, 311 n. 28). Balázs may have gone with Kodály to see the new opera, whose libretto Maeterlinck had intended for a musical setting. The door-openings in Maeterlinck's play are of secondary importance. (Kroó 1975 [1971]: 62; and 1993; also see, 1995.)

337. For more on Dukas's opera, see Gyergyai (1978 [1935]). Debussy, Dukas, and Bartók shared the common view that none of the characters in their Bluebeard operas are real: represent states of mind, not actual people. Quite a few operas (especially French ones) of the pre-World War I period deal with characters that are more iconic than realistic; that, perhaps, is a crucial, defining trait of Symbolism.

In an article written in 1908, Balázs locates himself in the tradition of writers who found inspiration in the poet and dramatist Friedrich Hebbel[338] (1813–1863). Balázs writes:

> The last great theoretician of drama was Hebbel. That which he dreamt and thought of, the great drama of the future, he himself could not realize. [...] Yet to this day, we have not reached the goals that Hebbel the theoretician had set, which live on as unsolved problems disquieting secret thought in the souls of those contemplating the fate of drama. [...] He initiated things, which have not yet been finished. (Balázs 1908: 88.)

Leafstedt (1995a) takes up that theme, and deals with Balázs's interest in German romantic drama, especially Hebbel, who added a new psychological dimension to that genre. However, Maeterlinck's influence, often acknowledged as a significant factor in the shaping of Balázs's own dramatic style, has never been examined in detail.[339]

Balázs's one-act play was finished in spring of 1910. On April 20, 1910 Artúr Bárdos's (1882–1974) journal *Színjáték* (*Stageplay*) included the minstrel's "Prologue" (see Example 4.1, p. 204, Chapter 4.4.1), part of the mystery play *A kékszakállú herceg vára* (*Duke Bluebeard's Castle*), which was published in the following issue of the journal, on June 13, 1910 (Kroó 1961: 26, 270; and 1962: 27). Balázs offered the *Bluebeard* play to be set to music by either Bartók or Kodály.[340] Bartók took over Balázs's play in its entirety, making many small changes, but leaving the overall dramatic structure and dialogue patterns essentially intact. Balázs's intentions were similar to those of Bartók, who might have been attracted as much by the style of Balázs's symbolist stage ballad as by the substance. Undoubtedly, Bartók had very vivid memories of the personal crisis he had undergone in the years 1907–1908 (Kroó 1961: 277; and 1962: 27; see also, Ujfalussy 1976: 33). As early as 1905, Bartók had confessed: "[...] spiritual loneliness is to be my destiny. I look about me in search of the ideal companion, and yet I am fully aware that it is a vain quest. Even if I should ever succeed in finding someone, I am sure that I would soon be disappointed" (quoted in Demény, ed. 1976: 99).[341]

338. Balázs received his doctorate in German philology from the University of Budapest for a dissertation on Hebbel (on the latter, see also, Szerb 1982 [1934]: 360, 405–406, 463).

339. In January 1908, Balázs (1994 [1908]) contributed his substantial article, "Maeterlinck," to the inaugural issue of *Nyugat*.

340. Balázs began studies at the University of Budapest in 1902. Balázs had met Kodály when they were students at the Eötvös Kollégium, and it was probably through Kodály that he became acquainted with Bartók. The first documented contact between Bartók and Balázs took place in September 1906, when Bartók visited Balázs's family in Szeged, while he was on a folk-song collecting trip. Balázs accompanied him on the expedition, and wrote down his recollections of Bartók in his *Diary* (Gluck 1985: 35). According to Szabolcsi, Bartók was present when the libretto was presented for the first time (Kroó 1961: 270). Demény (1974) gives a history of Bartók's friendship with Balázs, whose relationship began in 1906 and lasted until 1919, when Balázs went into exile because of his communist views, not returning until 1945.

341. "[...] *az én sorsom lelki elhagyatottság lesz. Keresek, kutatok ugyan ideális társat, bár nagyon jól tudom, hogy mindhiába. Ha esetleg valamikor találni vélnék is valakit, rövid idő múlva*

Another feature of Balázs's drama that made it peculiarly suitable for musical transcription was the clearly articulated, easily comprehended symmetry of its structure. Balázs shared in Bartók's determination to create an opera that was both Hungarian and modern. In his diary, Balázs later reminisced about the writing of *Bluebeard's Castle*:

> I was looking for a Hungarian style of drama. [...] I wanted to magnify the dramatic *fluidum* of the *Székely* [Transylvanian] folk ballads for the stage. And I wanted to depict a modern soul in the primary colors of folk song. I wanted the same thing as Bartók. We had the same will and the same youth. In our belief, complete novelty could be derived only from what was ancient, since only primeval material could be expected to stand our spiritualization without evaporating from under our fingers. Because only that which was simple was true, and only that which was simple could be truly new. (Because all that is complicated already existed as merely complicated.) My mystery was born of the common faith of common youth. It was not prepared as a libretto. It was given without music at one of the *Nyugat matinées*.[342] This poetry was addressed to Bartók in the same way as when a weary, parched wanderer strikes up a tune to induce his still more exhausted companion to sing. Because a melody will carry you along for a while when your legs are at the point of giving way. And I contrived to trick him into music. Bartók intoned and broke into such singing as has not been heard in Europe since Beethoven. (Balázs 1982 [1922]: 7.)

Balázs's mystery play provided Bartók with an opportunity to synthesize his newly found vision for the first time in a large-scale creative work. Whereas Balázs looked mostly to the Hungarian folk ballads and the symbolist plays of Maeterlinck, Bartók's ideal was most likely speech-like, *rubato* singing, influenced by the modality and rhythmic irregularities he found both in Transylvanian music[343] and in that of Debussy. (Leafstedt 1999: 53–84; Frigyesi 1998: 192–294; Lesznai 1973 [1961]; and Antokoletz 1990: 78–79[344]; see also, pp. 157–159, Chapter 3.5.1.) Around 1915, Balázs affirmed that assessment:

úgyis beállna a csalódás."

342. A stage performance of the play alone was arranged on April 20, 1913. It was directed by Balázs, with Bartók playing selections from his piano music at intermission. *Nyugat*, the prominent Hungarian literary journal, sponsored the occasion. That performance actually marked the public stage debut of *Bluebeard*, even though Bartók's music, already written, was not heard. (Bartók Jr, ed. 1981a: 133.) Balázs (1968 [1913]: 34) recorded the details of that performance, which turned out to be fiasco: "The performance, especially of *Bluebeard* was awful. None of the actors understood a word of what they were saying. [...] I was afraid that the set would collapse during the performance like a house of cards." *Duke Bluebeard's Castle* was never again staged as a theater piece.

343. Bartók's "Székely balladák" (Székely Ballads) represents his first scholarly effort (*BÖI* 1966 [1908]). The article includes texts and tunes of fifteen songs. Bartók postulates that those old melodies are not closely bound to their texts, but rather that epic and lyric melodies and texts are interchangeable within a given rhythmic context. (See also, Szerb 1982 [1934]: 186–188, 410–411; Demény, ed. 1976: 132, 318–319; and Voigt 1988: 392.)

344. Antokoletz (1984) discusses the similarities between Bartók and Debussy's operas.

I created this ballad of mine [the *Bluebeard* play] in the language and rhythms of old Hungarian Székely folk ballads. In character these folk ballads very nearly resemble old Scottish folk ballads, but they are, perhaps, more acerbic, more simple, their melodic quality more mysterious, more naive, and more song-like. Thus, there is no "literature" or rhetoric within them; they are constructed from dark, weighty, uncarved blocks of words. In this manner, I wrote my Hungarian-language Bluebeard ballad, and Bartók's music also conforms to this. (Quoted in Leafstedt 1999: 202.)

His purpose was to form "modern, intellectual inner experiences" (cited in Mauser 1981: 71). Balázs provided a pessimistic version of the tale by reducing it to the essential conflict between Bluebeard and Judith.[345] Balázs changed the entire narrative into a cyclical pattern, without scene changes and secondary plot developments. He articulated the play in seven distinct scenes, corresponding to the seven doors that Judith opens (discussed further in Chapter 4.4). The true drama is internal, and the essential story is psychological, not picturesque.[346]

On December 27, 1906, upon receiving a self-revealing letter from Paula Hermann,[347] Balázs wrote a note that anticipated several conceptual ideas of *Bluebeard*:

It is a wonderful thing to enter a soul suddenly and yet immediately reach its deepest depth, as if opening the door into a room. Because I loved and understood her even before I knew her. To enter suddenly, no, not even as if into a room – because the soul has a past to which it is connected organically – rather to enter a life, as if into a cave and softly and carefully, walk around within its small recesses whence its water and light spring. (Balázs 1982 [1922]: 284.)

The audience must rely on Judith's descriptions, watching the reactions and interactions of both protagonists as the story unfolds. In the opera, the dialogue between Judith and Bluebeard frequently alludes to the human qualities of the castle. In the original plan, Balázs included the castle as a third character. Even though he abandoned the idea for obvious practical reasons, it indicates a fundamental aspect of the dramaturgy. Balázs explained some of the symbolic meanings he had in mind:

Bluebeard's castle is not a realistic castle. The castle is his soul. It is lonely, dark and secretive: the castle of locked doors. [...] Into this castle, into his own soul, Bluebeard admits his beloved. And the castle (the stage) shudders, weeps and

---

345. Leafstedt (1999: 222 n. 2; and 2000: 243) remarks that the figure of Judith has its source in the Old Testament apocryphal book of that name. Judith is the Jewish heroine, who saves her city, Bethulia, from the hand of the cruel Assyrian general, Holofernes.

346. Typically, *Duke Bluebeard's Castle* is paired with Schoenberg's one-act monodrama *Erwartung* (Op. 17, 1909), as prime examples of expressionism, though those two operas differ in compositional method, sonority, and texture; on Schoenberg's opera, see Dahlhaus (1987a [1978]).

347. Paula Hermann was a student in the Hungarian and German Department at the University of Budapest and later became a teacher in a gymnasium. She belonged to the small circle of Balázs, Kodály, and Aranka Bauer.

bleeds. When the woman walks in it, she walks in a living being. (Balázs 1968 [1913]: 35.)

Behind the doors lie Bluebeard's secrets. Judith is shocked to find traces of blood revealed behind the first five doors, despite having heard rumors of previous wives' mysterious disappearance. With the opening of each successive door, Judith becomes more and more convinced that she would find the murdered women within the castle walls. Balázs explains the transformation that takes place in the *Bluebeard* play:

> When, through the fifth door, a flood of light and warmth engulfs the castle, and Bluebeard – liberated, redeemed, luminous, and grateful in his happiness – wants to embrace the woman in his arms; already the daylight is no longer visible to the woman who brought it to him. She sees only the bloody shadows. (Quoted in Leafstedt 1999: 202.)

The sixth door, which opens to reveal a lake of tears, confirms her suspicion. Behind the seventh door, much to Judith's astonishment, are three former wives, who solemnly step forward, alive and resplendently garbed. Balázs comments on that scene:

> When the woman looks inside, she staggers back in alarm: Not as if, she had seen the dead women, no! The women are *alive*! From behind the seventh door the wives – who had been loved at one time by the man – rise to their feet, dreamlike, from the deep recesses of slumbering memory. And wreathed with diadems and halos they are more beautiful than all women presently living. Oh, how pained, how miserable Judith feels when Bluebeard sings in dreaming ecstasy of his past loves. (Quoted in Leafstedt 1999: 203.)

Judith then realizes that she, too, is to be entombed within the dark walls of Bluebeard's castle. She takes her place beside the other women, the door closes behind them, and Bluebeard is left alone on stage. (Bartók 1952 [1925]; and 1963 [1921]; see also, Batta, ed. 1999: 16–17; and Lindlar 1984: 60.)

Some aspects of *Bluebeard* continue to generate curiosity, no matter how much has already been written about them. Some are worth mentioning, and some are not. Symbolism is always a kind of double-edged sword: it can broaden and enrich meaning, but it can also diffuse and obscure it. It seems that no two commentators can agree on precisely what *Bluebeard's Castle* is saying. Perhaps the clearest and best explanation comes from the composer, pianist and ethnomusicologist Sándor Veress, whose opinion most scholars today share. He writes:

> Bluebeard and Judith represent the eternal tragedy of the dualism of man and woman, the heavenly and earthly perspective of their souls. Here is the drama of man's loneliness seeking complete fulfillment in woman and finding only partial satisfaction, and of woman, who, in her devotion to man, sacrifices her whole being. [...] Bluebeard will find in Judith the most beautiful one, the final fulfillment [...] whom he adorns with his most precious jewels; but he has to lose her, too,

because Judith desires the disclosure of the secret behind that last door. It is in vain that he begs her not to open it. [...] Judith insists [...] and with this, her fate is sealed. (Veress 1949: 33.)

Within the framework of the above quotation, the plot of *Bluebeard* is construed solely as a spiritual conflict between two characters; Balázs's text is merely complemented by the music of Bartók.[348]

Yet, to approach the *Bluebeard* play only as a representation of the eternal conflict between man and woman would be to oversimplify its meaning. *Bluebeard's Castle* is also an allegorical study about the individual's ultimate isolation from the rest of humanity, and about the loneliness of the human spirit (Demény 1946: 15–18; Ujfalussy 1976: 32–33; and Frigyesi 1998: 199–200). As Ujfalussy explains:

Intellectuals and artists in the disintegrating and alienated bourgeois societies of the nineteenth and twentieth centuries have been happy to identify themselves with the figures of Don Juan and Bluebeard; anguished by their own sense of isolation from society, they turned to tear asunder the established social and moral laws. Kierkegaard, whose thought in some ways anticipated existentialism, hailed Mozart's *Don Juan* as a hero whose demoniacal energy enabled him to break the cords of social bondage. In this figure, he modeled the precursor of Nietzsche's "superman". Wagner, at the time a pupil of Schopenhauer, created *Tristan and Isolde*, the lovers who in the agonizing rapture desire find fulfillment in dissolution and dissolution in fulfillment. Psychological research based on individualism sought to find in their passions that lost paradise in which society did not suppress the basic human instincts, while the symbolists bemoaned the fate of the lovers as an example of man's inevitable solitariness, a prisoner without hope of escape, the helpless victim of a tragedy decreed by Fate.[349] (Ujfalussy 1971 [1970]: 106.)

Critics usually describe Bluebeard as wise and rational, and Judith as passionate and narrow-minded (Króo 1961: 302–303, 307; and 1962: 83). That image has been complemented by views of the metaphorical representation of Judith in twentieth-century art. For instance, Leafstedt suggests that Balázs might have been consciously evoking the character of the heroine of Hebbel's play *Judith*, since "both Judiths are placed into conflict with an extremely masculine man against whom they must apply all their feminine cunning to obtain what they desire" (1999: 132).

Bluebeard's Castle is an abstract drama that, as a sequence of clashes between man and woman, symbolically projects into time the timeless, dynamic force of love.

---

348. Bartók has Duke Bluebeard sing pentatonic melodies that move mostly by step, whereas Judith's vocalizing is more varied, often containing large intervallic leaps; however, the two characters' melodies do coincide from time to time.

349. It is clear from the correspondence and writings of Bartók, Schoenberg, and Webern that they knew about the works of literary figures, musicians, and philosophers who generated the organicist discourse in aesthetics, such as Busoni, Goethe, Hanslick, Nietzsche, Schopenhauer, and Strindberg. By the early 1900s, notions of organicism had become deeply engrained in the artistic awareness of those three composers, primarily through informal conversation rather than through engagement with literature on the subject. (Demény, ed. 1976: 84, 86, 130; and Schoenberg 1987 [1958]; see also, Balázs 1982 [1922]: 548, 561–562.)

Bluebeard's story partakes of the past (it is an old tale) and the present: the ever-present moment of intimacy. The piece evolves from darkness and returns thereto; folding inward, it suggests both eternal circularity and completeness. Bluebeard, led by Judith's love, returns to his origins, where he can be at one, shut within the utter loneliness of self. Leafstedt finds biographical symbolism in the opera:

> The question immediately arises: who among the women in Bartók's life does Judith represent? The obvious answer – Stefi Geyer – is hard to reconcile with the fact that Bartók had been married to Márta [Ziegler] for two years by this time. What does seem to be certain, however, is that the operatic Judith is imbued with some form of biographical association for Bartók. (Leafstedt 2000: 243.)

Yet, in response to Leafstedt's interpretation, it should be pointed out that only the woman has a personal name – the man bears a magical, totemic one. Hence, both characters remain open to interpretation as allegorical abstractions. The Eternal Man and the Eternal Woman manifest themselves for us in this worldly drama. On that reading, the mystery-element becomes more intense, and a path is also opened to modern, depth-psychological interpretations of the opera.

4.2. The creation of modern Hungarian opera

Duke Bluebeard's Castle (1911) is a complete entity in itself, but not an isolated one in Bartók's œuvre. His "trilogy" of stage works was completed by two later ones: the ballet, *The Wooden Prince* (Op. 13, Sz 60, BB 74, 1914–1916; orchestrated 1916–1917),[350] and the pantomime, *The Miraculous Mandarin* (Op. 19, Sz 73, BB 82, 1918–1919). In the latter two works, the composer continued to experiment with compositional and conceptual issues that he had confronted in his opera.

Duke Bluebeard's Castle traveled a long and eventful path from the time of its conception in 1911 to its eventual publication in 1921. In February of 1911 Bartók started work on the opera, dedicated to his first wife Márta (Ziegler), and completed it on September 20, 1911 (Bartók Jr, ed. 1981a: 116–121). In *Bluebeard's Castle,* he achieved a convincing synthesis of all his compositional influences; as such, the work represented a significant turning point in Bartók's creative development. Kroó has called *Bluebeard* "the greatest and most perfect of his compositions from 1900 to 1915" (1981 [1969]: 109). Bartók's works of that period formed only the beginning of his new chromaticism, which, as was discussed above, can be related to certain works of his Viennese contemporaries in more ways than one might expect (see n. 23, p. 18, Chapter 2.1.1). Bartók's works are stylistically removed from those of the Schoenberg School, but his exploitation of pitch sets forms a link with them (see Chapters 2.1.1 and 2.3, for a summary of contemporary approaches to analyzing the music of Bartók).

---

350. Balázs's ballet text appeared on December 16, 1912, in the *Nyugat*. The poetic libretto was written specifically for Bartók and possibly at his request (Lindlar 1984: 64). On the history of *The Wooden Prince*, see Kroó (1972).

For *Bluebeard* the path from creation to first performance was strewn with disappointments. In 1911 and 1912, Bartók entered his opera in two separate competitions in Budapest, and on both occasions, it failed to win.[351] In October 1911, Bartók entered *Duke Bluebeard's Castle* in the Ferenc Erkel Competition sponsored by the Lipótvárosi Kaszinó (Lipótváros Casino),[352] and in July 1912, the results were announced. The jury, chaired by the conductor István Kerner, rejected it as unplayable. A terse notice in the July 1912 issue of *A Zene* reported that two operas had been submitted for the Lipótváros Casino competition and that neither was awarded a prize (the name of the other opera is not known). Another Hungarian opera competition was held in March 1912, this one sponsored by the prestigious music publisher Rózsavölgyi. Again, two operas were entered: Bartók's, with the final scene revised, and another whose title and composer are unknown. Again, no prize was given. (Leafstedt 1999: 149–150; for more on the competitions, see Stevens 1964: 47, 285; and Kroó 1981: 80, 105–109.) The opera remained unheard for six years. Due to its failure in the competitions, and the dissolution of the short-lived UMZE,[353] Bartók withdrew from public musical life in 1912 (Demény, ed. 1976: 208; Kroó 1993: 351; and Berény 1978 [1911]). In a letter dated August 22, 1913 to Géza Vilmos Zágon (1890–1918), Bartók wrote the following:

A sentence of death was officially pronounced on me as a composer. Either those people are right, in which case I am an untalented bungler; or I am right, and it is they who are the idiots. In either event, this means that between myself and them (that is, our musical leaders: Hubay, etc.) there can be no discussion of music, still less any joint action. It therefore follows that since the official worlds of music has put me to death, you can no longer speak of my "prestige". [...] Therefore, I have resigned myself to write for my writing desk only. [...] The Opera House does not want to perform my opera at all. However, they have so far defied official opinion, by asking me for an hour-long ballet. I am so disgusted with Budapest performances that I do not feel at all interested. The whole thing is hardly likely to add to my reputation, nor to my income! (Quoted in Demény, ed. 1971: 124.)

---

351. At this time, Bartók was by no means a fledgling composer. He had already written such major works as the *Allegro barbaro* and his *First String Quartet*, and had begun the systematic collecting and transcribing of folk music, which was to occupy his attention most of his life (see Chapters 3.4–3.5; and Antokoletz 1997 [1988]: 5–43). Those early works had earned him a small coterie of enthusiasts and a large contingent of hostile conservatives, which included the men who sat on the Fine Arts Commission.

352. Since its opening (1883), the Casino has excelled at patronizing the arts by organizing and funding exhibitions, concerts, competitions, and operatic performances (Romsics 1982: 254; and Gergely & Szász 1978: 127).

353. At the instigation of Bartók, Kodály and a few others, the New Hungarian Musical Society (UMZE) was formed in April 1911. The main goal of the association, in Bartók's words was "to organize an independent chorus and orchestra, which could perform competently not only the old, but also the more recent, what is more, the most innovative new music" (quoted in Gluck 1987: 19). For more on the UMZE, see Demény (ed. 1976: 180, 183); Kodály (1974 [1921]: 432); Ujfalussy (1971 [1970]: 116–120); and Dobszay (1984: 347).

In 1915, convinced that *Bluebeard's Castle* was not going to be performed in the near future, Bartók wrote to Márta:

> I would like to go to collect among my dear Romanians; I would like to go, but go far away, travel, I would like to hear some great music, but not in Budapest; I would like to go to the rehearsals of *Bluebeard*, to the performance of *Bluebeard*! Now I know that I will never hear it in this life. – You asked me to play it for you – I am afraid that I would not be able to play it through. Still I will try it once, so that we could mourn for it together. (Quoted in Bartók Jr, ed. 1981b[354]: 235–236.)

The most professionally significant of Bartók's wartime compositions was his ballet, *The Wooden Prince*, which was premiered to great critical acclaim at the Hungarian Royal Opera House on May 12, 1917 (*BBE* 1976 [1917]: 406; Bartók Jr, ed. 1981a: 157; Kroó 1972: 97; and Kodály 1974 [1921]: 433). Kerner refused an invitation to conduct the work, and on the title page Bartók (1949 [1921]) dedicated the ballet to the Italian conductor Egisto Tango[355] (1876–1951): "*Herrn Kapellmeister Egisto Tango in tiefer Dankbarkeit gewidment.*"[356] On May 6, 1917, Bartók wrote to Ion Buşiţia (1875–1953), a teacher at Belényes:

> I only just managed to finish a one-act ballet for the Opera House. It would have been a big job even in peacetime, with all these troubles. And when, with great difficulty, I had got it done, then the real struggle began: you have no idea what senseless and frustrating battles I have had with the Opera House. [...] Now the first night is May 12; and this is the last week of rehearsals. People are already sharpening their claws to attack me. (Quoted in Demény, ed. 1971: 134.)

Despite his doubts, the ballet stayed on the program, its success preparing the way for a staging of his opera, as Bartók had hoped.[357] The two *premières* strength-

---

354. Bartók's undated letter from the beginning of 1915 is included in Bartók Jr. (ed. 1981b), *Family Letters of Béla Bartók*, which is a comprehensive chronological presentation of Bartók's letters, mostly written to members of his family.
355. His name is associated with the first performances in Hungary of *The Wooden Prince* (May 12, 1917) and *Bluebeard's Castle* (May 24, 1918). About those occasions, see especially, Bartók (*BBE* 1976 [1917]: 406; and *BBE* 1976 [1918]: 407).
356. In his letters, Bartók expressed admiration for the Italian artist (Demény, ed. 1971: 133, 135, 137, 144–145; and 1976: 237, 239–242, 254). Contemporary reviews also included favorable comments about the principal dancers, Anna Pallay (1890–1970), Emília Nirschy (1889–1976), and Ede Brada (1879–1955); see Ujfalussy (1971 [1970]: 146).
357. The long period in which *Duke Bluebeard's Castle* existed only in manuscript state afforded Bartók several opportunities to reevaluate his opera. That he took advantage of that situation is confirmed by the extensive changes made to the autograph scores dating from that period (Kroó 1981: 80). A revised ending for the opera was prepared in late 1911 or early 1912, and other aspects of the score were changed as well. Yet another version of the ending was prepared in 1917–1918 (Bartók Jr, ed. 1981a: 157). The celesta and xylophone were added to the instrumentation by 1918; the music for additional scenes was revised, the vocal parts rewritten in places, and the general appearance of the score significantly modified in terms of orchestration, dynamics, and tempi (Kroó 1981: 105–109). An estimated five minutes of music had been deleted by the time Bartók finished

ened Bartók's already considerable prestige in Budapest's progressive-modernist circles. He recalls the opening night of the ballet:

> The year 1917 brought a decisive change in the attitude of the Budapest audiences towards my works. I lived to see, at last, one of my bigger works, the ballet *The Wooden Prince*, given a musically perfect performance under the leadership of the conductor, Egisto Tango. (*BBE* 1976 [1921a]: 411.)

The story of the ballet was the work of Balázs; on the surface, it is a folk-tale, but is more deeply a parable, one fraught with symbolism (1976 [1912]: 101–110). In August 1917, Bartók wrote to Buşiţia:

> I am sending you the two Balázs books[358], primarily, so that you can put in some advance study on the texts of *Bluebeard* and *The Wooden Prince*. Secondly, because the other two mystery plays are also worth reading; and thirdly, the drawings of the puppet play are good, even though I do not like the text itself very much. (I find it rather commonplace, like so many of the verses in picture books for children.) (Quoted in Demény, ed. 1971: 136.)

Bartók drew two concert suites from the complete score of *The Wooden Prince* and prepared a greatly abbreviated version of the ballet itself (Kroó 1972: 97–98). In January 1918, Bartók wrote to Buşiţia: "The first night of *Bluebeard* is about to be postponed indefinitely, perhaps till May! That is the way they always treat me at the Opera" (quoted in Demény, ed. 1971: 139). *Bluebeard* finally reached the stage on May 24, 1918, after the success of his ballet led the management of the Opera House in Budapest to request the score of the opera (*BBE* 1976 [1918]: 407; see also, Kodály 1974 [1921]: 433; and Valkó 1977[359]). The opera met with some positive appreciation, to varying degrees, about which Bartók wrote to Buşiţia:

> The reviews of *Bluebeard* were better than those of *The Wooden Prince*. With the exception of the *Pesti Hírlap* and the *Újság* all the papers wrote about it favorably, especially the two German-language papers, the *Neues Pester Journal* and the *Pester Lloyd*. (Quoted in Demény, ed. 1976: 247.)

---

his revisions. Kroó contains a useful survey of the opera's evolution in Bartók's hands during the years before it saw print.

358. The two books mentioned are Béla Balázs's *Mystery Plays* and a collection entitled *Játékok* (*Plays*); among the latter was *A fából faragott királyfi* (*The Wooden Prince*), a ballet with illustrations by Miklós Bánffy (1874–1950).

359. Valkó (1977) describes several documents kept in the Hungarian State Opera archives. They include invitations extended to Bartók and Balázs, to attend a preview of *Bluebeard's Castle*, and a contract (dated 1918) between Bartók and Sándor Bródy (1863–1924), one of the most distinguished writers of his generation, for a performance of a dance setting of *Anna Molnár*, but the latter work never came to fruition.

Duke Bluebeard's Castle enjoyed an immediate if short-lived success and was performed eight times between May 24, 1918 and January 12, 1919, in the Budapest Opera House (Bartók Jr, ed. 1981a: 161–163, 166–167)[360].

Balázs, however, held political views, which conflicted with those of the Hungarian Government,[361] which ordered that his name be suppressed at further performances of the opera. Characteristically, Bartók refused to do so and withdrew his work.[362] Balázs publicly broke his friendship with the composer in 1922, but the two men continued to communicate occasionally in the 1920s and 1930s. On November 15, 1930, Balázs wrote to Bartók:

> This is to declare that I do not wish my name to be mentioned in connection with the performances, in the Roy. Hung. Opera House of Budapest, of my ballet *The Wooden Prince* and my opera *Bluebeard's Castle*. I also relinquish the fees due to me from these performances in favor of Béla Bartók, and I am simultaneously notifying our publishers, Universal Edition, Vienna, Austria, of this fact. This surrender of the right to use my name and to claim my fee is valid until revoked; for the present, until January 1, 1933. (Quoted in Demény, ed. 1971: 198.)

Balázs's letter removed obstacles to a Budapest revival of Bartók's two stage works. *The Wooden Prince* was performed again on January 30, 1935, and nearly twenty years after its *première* the opera was staged in Budapest on October 29,

---

360. Tango, who worked with the Budapest Opera from 1912 to 1919, did in fact go to Romania. He signed a contract with the Romanian Opera of Kolozsvár, where he wanted to produce Bartók's *Bluebeard*. Tango was frustrated in his attempt and not long afterwards dissolved his contract and left Romania. He sough a new contract once in Budapest, but was refused admittance into the country by the new, nationalist regime. (Demény, ed. 1971: 144, 397, 400; see also, pp. 147–148, Chapter 3.4.)

361. Balázs's alienation from the literary establishment intensified through the war years as his political leanings moved further left. He joined the Communist Party in 1918, and together with Lukács, played an active role in overthrowing the ruling government in October 1918 and in the subsequent Communist takeover in March of 1919. In the White Terror that followed in the summer of 1919, Balázs barely escaped the violent backlash against the short-lived Communist Government. Along with many other leftist Hungarians, he escaped abroad, slipping into Austria disguised as his brother. (Zsuffa 1987: 65–68.)

362. Demény (1977) gives an account of certain events in the relationship between Bartók and his librettist; see also, István Gál's (1974) article, "Béla Balázs: Bartók's First Librettist."

1936.[363] Bartók met Balázs and paid him his royalties, after which their careers took separate paths (Bartók Jr, ed. 1981a: 288–289).[364]

Outside Hungary, *Bluebeard's Castle* has been slow in making headway on the lyric stage (Bartók Jr, ed. 1981a: 373; Demény, ed. 1976: 316). The usual explanation offered is that the plot is static and virtually nothing happens on stage (*BBE* 1976 [1917]: 406). It was performed by a Hungarian company at the Florence May Festival of 1938, and a few times in Germany; e.g., in Frankfurt am Main,[365] conducted by the Hungarian-born composer and conductor Eugen Szenkár (1891–1977). A card written to Etelka Freund on May 9, 1922, indicates that Bartók was not very pleased with the latter performance:

> Here, everything is falling apart. Impossible conditions. [...] What bad violinists and what bad opera companies to spoil my works. I can only look forward to a disastrous première. Well, thank you very much, but I do not want to have anything to do with Germany. My foretaste of the event is quite enough for me, in fact too much. There is only one man who is worth anything at all and that is Szenkár from Budapest. (Quoted in Demény, ed. 1976: 281.)

The opera went on to be performed again in Germany, both in Weimar (1925) and Berlin (1929) (Demény, ed. 1971: 161; and 1976: 270; see also, Lindlar 1984:

---

363. A basic issue in the art of music performance is that of authentic rendition, especially of works written in the distant past. The same issue obtains in more recent music, as well. *Bluebeard's Castle* has been recorded often, for the first time on October 29, 1936. Bartók followed the rehearsals with attention; hence, the recording may be deemed authentic in that regard. Sergio Failoni (1890–1948) conducted the performance, with stage direction by Kálmán Nádasdy and *décor* by Gusztáv Oláh. Ella Némethy (1895–1961) and Mihály Székely (1901–1963) sang the leading roles. Oláh (1949–1950) gives a first-hand account of Bartók's theater works. Székely, who sang the part of Bluebeard for nearly three decades, recalls that "Failoni did not sense the Hungarian rubatos in the work. He thought that whatever was in the score had to be strictly adhered to, that is, it had to be sung just as it was scored. I argued with him that this role had to be performed in a much freer manner. The argument was finally settled by Bartók – in my favor" (quoted in Várnai 1978: 1). After Failoni, János Ferencsik (1907–1984) took over conducting the work in 1942. Ferencsik, too, was familiar with Bartók's wishes, and conducted performances and recordings of the opera in that spirit; his recording of *Duke Bluebeard's Castle* (1991 [1956]) offers a living tradition, as it were, which conveys the composer's conception of the opera to later ages. Certain places in Bluebeard's role had become too high for the aging Székely to sing, so Bartók set them in a lower register. (On Mihály Székely, see Várnai 1969 [1956].) Aside from that occasion, rarely was Bartók willing to alter his work for the sake of performance. Bartók's lone opera has fared well on disc; the recording directed by István Kertész (Bartók 1999 [1965]) is one of the best, even if it lacks the full bite and snap of singers emoting in their native language. The recording directed by Antal Doráti may get closer to the spirit of Bartók's sharp-edged score (Bartók 1992 [1962]), and Sir Georg Solti's (1980) recording of *Bluebeard's Castle* has long been hailed as a classic interpretation.

364. Balázs went on to work with other composers, such as Ernst Křenek (1900–1991) and Franz Schreker (1878–1934); with the latter he completed writing a film opera for a project that never came to fruition (Hailey 1993: 237).

365. For more on that occasion, see Bartók's letters to Cecil Gray (1863–1951) and Philip Heseltine (1894–1932), as well as Márta Ziegler's letter to Géza Révész (in Demény, ed. 1976: 270, 276).

60; and Bartók Jr, ed. 1981a: 197). In a letter written in 1928, Bartók distinguished *Bluebeard* from traditional opera:

> It would be very welcome if the work were announced in Berlin as a dramatic scene rather than as an opera. [...] Unfortunately, the public expects it to be something completely different. It is therefore better if the audience is prepared [...] for something other than spectacle-opera. (Quoted in Kroó 1993: 358.)

Bartók, again concerned with issues of style and tonality, urged Ernst Latzko, conductor of the National Theater in Weimar, to stress to his performers the following features of *Bluebeard's Castle*:

> I would ask you not to overemphasize the folkloristic features of my music; to stress that in these stage works, as in my other original compositions, I never employ folk tunes; that my music is tonal throughout; it has nothing in common with the "objective" and "impersonal" manner (therefore, it is not properly "modern" at all!).[366] (Quoted in Leafstedt 1999: 78–79.)

From the late 1910s on, responses to Bartók's music became more scholarly, as it began to be championed by some of Hungary's best musical minds. Kodály wrote an enthusiastic article, "Béla Bartók's First Opera," for the *Nyugat*, which was the first report on the *première* of Duke *Bluebeard's Castle* in 1918, under the direction of Dezső Zádor (1957 [1918]). Kodály noted that *Bluebeard* represented a major development in the Hungarian recitative style, and proclaimed it the first work of Hungarian operatic theater (ibid.: 61).

Most traditional literary elements of opera were present in Balázs's text, but opera itself was continuing to evolve. Carl Dahlhaus has described one category as "literature operas" (*Literaturoper*), in which a composer adopts "a spoken play unchanged, if abbreviated, as an opera text" (1989: 347). Prominent examples of literature operas include Debussy-Maeterlinck's *Pelléas et Mélisande* (1893–1902), Strauss-Hofmannsthal's *Salome* (Op. 54, 1905) and *Elektra*[367] (Op. 58, 1908). In that operatic genre, the literary element served to counterbalance what was perceived as the increasing unintelligibility of musical language. The very term, "literary opera,"

---

366. It is apparent from his choice of words that he did not wish *Bluebeard* to earn a reputation as a folk opera along the lines of Leoš Janáček's (1854–1928) *Jenůfa* (1904) or Smetana's *The Bartered Bride* (1866) (Batta, ed. 1999: 244–245, 572–573). His distinction between "folkloristic features", which *Bluebeard* possesses, and "folk tunes", which it does not, suggests that the influence of folk music on the opera is deeper and more pervasive than can be apprehended at first glance. In this light, Bartók's claim that the opera is "tonal throughout" warrants further inquiry (quoted in Leafstedt 1999: 79).

367. The fourth opera written by Strauss opened his successful partnership with the librettist Hugo von Hofmannsthal (1874–1929) and solidified his status as a leading composer (Jász 1978 [1910]: 39–40).

suggests that investigation of the literary/dramatic aspects is just as important as analyzing the music.[368]

Historically, the libretto of *Duke Bluebeard's Castle* has had a relatively cool reception. Since the opera's *première*, the music has been recognized for its greatness (see, e.g., Kodály 1957 [1918]; and A. Molnár 1961 [1918]), while the play that inspired Bartók to compose the work has gone relatively unappreciated. Kodály implies that Balázs's libretto deserves more credit than it has received:

> The almost unanimous disapproval [Balázs's libretto] has met with […] is apt to create the impression that expectations regarding operatic librettos were in these parts rather high. Yet our writers do not take the libretto seriously, forgetting that in the golden ages of opera, the words, too, had always been the work of a competent hand. This is why it makes a sensation when a libretto is written by a genuine writer, and even more so in the case of a dramatic author. So Béla Balázs deserves particular credit for having worked up one of his finest and most poetical conceptions into an opera book, contributing thus to the birth of a genuine *chef d'œuvre*. (Kodály 1957 [1918]: 60.)

Bartók's opera received much negative criticism, but even its harshest critics acknowledged its value (Kodály 1974 [1921]: 432; and Demény, ed. 1955a: 110, 247; and 1976: 247). The modernist-minded Antal Molnár (1961 [1918]) surveyed reviews of the first performance and summarized the conservative positions with sarcasm, not failing to miss the ironic fact that many critics recognized Bartók's genius and yet rejected his opera: many conservative critics praised *Bluebeard* for what they perceived as its strong Hungarian national character, but complained about the dissonant harmonic idiom and certain decadent tendencies.

In spring of 1918, as rehearsals for *Bluebeard* were going on, Bartók was exploring possibilities for new theatrical works to be performed at the Opera House, such as a pantomime, ballet, or opera.[369] Of those three, the pantomime came to be realized, in Bartók's third stage work, *The Miraculous Mandarin* (composed from September 1918 to May 1919, and orchestrated in the summer of 1923). According to the libretto, written by Menyhért Lengyel (1880–1974), the work is a "*pantomime grotesque*" in one act.[370] At that time, musical pantomime was very fashionable

---

368. Twentieth-century opera critics, beginning with Kerman (1988 [1956]), in *Opera as Drama*, have gone beyond integration as an ideal operatic type and have become increasingly concerned with a more rarefied concept: music as drama. According to Kerman, "music can contribute to drama" by "defining character, generating action, and establishing atmosphere" (ibid.: 215). Using those standards, Kerman allows only for a handful of canonical operatic masterpieces (by Mozart, Verdi, Wagner, Berg, and Stravinsky).

369. Balázs, who took a passive role in mounting the opera, was deeply hurt by Bartók's lack of public support for his libretto, as evidenced in the composer's published statement about the opera (*BBE* 1976 [1918]: 407).

370. The text of *The Miraculous Mandarin* was printed in *Nyugat* on January 1, 1917. Lengyel (1963 [1917]) provides an in-depth description as well as a setting of the tale, which was originally intended for Sergei Diaghilev's troupe, *Les Ballets Russes*. Diaghilev commissioned the work from the author on the occasion of the ballet ensemble's appearance in Budapest in 1912. For a synopsis of the story, see Szabolcsi (1955: 519).

– Stravinsky owed his fame in Europe to it (Milloss 1972). Bartók set the narrative in a mosaic-like way, using brief motivic passages of variable tonal clarity, as well as shifting densities of texture, to parallel the fluctuating sense of tension in the tale. After being twice postponed, the premier of the *The Miraculous Mandarin* took place on November 27, 1926 in Cologne, conducted by Szenkár. The work so shocked the audience that further performances of it were forbidden by the mayor of the city, Konrad Adenauer (1876–1967). *The Miraculous Mandarin* met with a similar fate in Prague in 1927, and again in Milan in 1942 (Lindlar 1984: 109–111). In March 1931, the reactionary domestic climate again prevented the Budapest *première* of the pantomime, which was not to reach the Hungarian stage until December 1945, ten weeks after Bartók's death.[371] On the technical and aesthetic merits of *The Miraculous Mandarin*, see Szabolcsi (1955[372]); Persichetti (1949); Kroó (1963); and Lampert (1995).

All three of Bartók's stage works are concerned with the relationship between man and woman, each proposing a different solution, which in turn determines the musical form. The balladic tragedy of *Bluebeard's Castle* depicts the opening and closing of the man's castle: his soul. The story of *The Wooden Prince* exhibits folktale optimism: the man forgives, nature provides release, and the work returns to the lush atmosphere of its beginning. *The Miraculous Mandarin* returns to tragedy, but in contrast to that of the opera, this one provides spectators with a catharsis: man's desire and the woman's purification in love are consummated at the moment of death.

After composing his of stage works, Bartók never returned to the world of musical theater, a decision no doubt facilitated by the difficulties and frustrations he had undergone in securing staged performances for his opera and pantomime. *Bluebeard* was not generally recognized as a major classic until after World War II, despite its place as Bartók's only opera (Lindlar 1984: 63). In addition to being the major work of the composer's early maturity, *Duke Bluebeard's Castle* continues to hold its status as an outstanding and unique masterpiece of Hungarian Symbolism.

4.3. Pitch-web analysis of tonal construction

The means by which Bartók achieves a sense of tonal integration in a context of emergent tonality must be viewed as part of a historical transition between two chromatic tonal systems. The chromatic (but still somewhat functional) voice-leading properties found in late nineteenth-century Romantic music are mingled with more

---

371. The Philharmonic Society, conducted by Dohnányi, performed *The Miraculous Mandarin Suite* in Budapest on October 15, 1928. The score calls for two flutes and piccolo (doubling third flute), three oboes (third doubling English horn), three clarinets and bass clarinet, three bassoons and contrabassoon (doubling fourth bassoon), four horns, three trumpets, three trombones and bass tuba, timpani, large and small side drum, bass drum, cymbals, triangle, tam-tam, xylophone, celesta, harp, piano, organ, and strings (a mixed chorus, offstage, is necessary for the full pantomime, but not for the suite).

372. Szabolcsi (1955) gives a history of the composition and the story, as well as a descriptive-stylistic analysis of the music; see also, Tarasti (1994 [1978]: 101).

radical chromatic configurations that defy analysis based on traditional hierarchical tonal functions. For example, traditional chord progressions based on tonic-dominant relations are juxtaposed with progressions of alternating major and minor triads; these last form types of symmetrical pitch collections, as described in Chapters 2.1–2.4. Such interrelationships of traditional (functional) and non-traditional (symmetrical) pitch constructs in *Bluebeard's Castle* contribute to establishing the tonality, as will be shown below (Chapters 4.4–4.4.11). About this moment in music history, George Perle observes:

> The crucial and monumental development in the art music of our century has been the qualitative change in the foundational premises of our musical language – the change from a highly chromaticized tonality whose principal functions and operations are still based on a limited selection, the seven notes of the diatonic scale, from the universal set of twelve pitch classes to a scale that comprehends the total pitch-class content of that universal set. We can point to the moment of that change with some precision. It occurs most obviously in the music of Scriabin and the Vienna circle, Schoenberg, Webern, and Berg, in 1909–1910, and very soon afterwards, though less obviously, in the music of Bartók and Stravinsky. I think it is safe to say that nothing of comparable significance for music has ever occurred, because the closing of the circle of fifths gives us a symmetrical collection of all twelve pitch classes that eliminates the special structural function of the perfect fifth itself, which has been the basis of every real musical system that we have hitherto known. (Perle 1990a: 42–43.)

Accepting Perle's general assessment (above) of musical style at that time, I now turn to specifics as regards the tonal construction of *Bluebeard*. The score of *Bluebeard* features great surface variety (in terms of orchestration, characteristic music for each scene, etc.), yet at a deeper level a common bond unifies the harmonic and melodic properties of the work (Bartók 1952 [1925]). The music includes many well-known romantic harmonies, such as chromatic-third related chords, second-inversion chords used as stable sonorities, and frequent appearances of the traditional perfect (V-I) and plagal (IV-I) cadences. The free use of sevenths and ninths recalls the influence of Debussy,[373] while the pervasive tritone key relationships point to the harmonies of Strauss's popular and influential operas, *Salome* and *Elektra* (see Chapters 4.4–4.4.11).

If, as one writer puts it, a "musical composition is a metaphor" in which "the composer relates a tonal construction with a specific aesthetic idea" (Mosley 1990:

---

373. In contrast to traditional, functional tonal music, Debussy's music displays more emphasis on static blocks of harmony. As a result, texture, instrumental color and dynamic nuance are all promoted to a more prominent position. Those sonorous blocks of harmonies are ever undulating, on shifting planes comprised of finely-hued instrumental combinations. (Grayson 1986: 21, 33, 73, 102, 274, 310 n. 8.) In traditional tonal music, the harmonies *progress* towards a structural goal and architectural trajectory, in Debussy's music, the harmonies are more static, and proceed in *successions* of chords of similar quality and structure (Gervais 1971: 105–114). One of Debussy's harmonic techniques is that of "planing", understood as strata of chords proceeding in parallel motion, a technique much used by both Bartók and Stravinsky.

1), in *Bluebeard* the dramatic tensions of the story are faithfully reflected in the internal logic and formal rigor of the opera's music. There has been no shortage of studies focusing on the formal design of *Bluebeard* (e.g., Antokoletz 1990; 1984: 89–92; and 2004[374]; Frigyesi 1998;[375] Mauser 1981; Nordwall 1972; and Leafstedt 1990; 1994; 1995a; 1995b; and 1999: 55–61). Such specialized studies of *Duke Bluebeard's Castle* explore issues of formal articulations, tonal scheme, and music-dramatic symbolism.[376]

Bartók's sectioning of the opera is extremely complex.[377] *Bluebeard* is through-composed, and housed within a symmetrical arch form articulated into seven distinct scenes (see Table 4.1, next page), in a manner similar to that of the *Music for Strings Percussion and Celesta* (Lindlar 1984: 111–114). Bartók comments on the latter piece:

> Thus, the entire work [*Music for Strings Percussion and Celesta*] is symmetrical: first movement, adagio, scherzo (the central point), and variation of the first movement. This is the same construction that I used in my *Fourth* and *Fifth String Quartets*, too. (Bartók 1963 [1939]: 7.)

The opera's large-scale symmetry becomes even more evident in the dichotomous emotional states of the two characters, Bluebeard and Judith. Moreover, the seven door scenes are centered on a particular visual image (stage lighting), as the colored light of the seven rooms is integrated with the prevailing keys. The contents of the doors are symbolized by the color of the light that emanates from an opening in the wall.[378] The lighting steadily brightens with the opening of each door up to the fifth ("Bluebeard's Domain"), after which the castle gloom gradually returns.

---

374. Antokoletz (2004) presents a deeper understanding of the radical changes in the traditional tonal language that occurred in the early twentieth century, relating them to the then-pervasive aesthetic of Symbolism.

375. Frigyesi (1998) is concerned with the increasingly problematic relations between society and art during the period. In her treatment of *Bluebeard's Castle* (ibid.: 230–294), there is no in-depth discussion of such musical factors as the functioning of consonance and dissonance within the world of extended tonality. She is much more effective when discussing the psychological and situational paradoxes confronting her main characters; what made the situation of the Hungarian modernists especially uncomfortable was that they wanted to break away from the traditional lifestyle of their parents but felt skeptical about modernization as well.

376. I thank Professor Ivanka Stoianova for our detailed conversation about *Bluebeard's* music-dramatic symbolism.

377. Several scholars have dealt with the complex articulation of *Duke Bluebeard's Castle* (e.g., Ujfalussy 1971 [1970]: 112–113; and 1976; Lendvai 1983: 219–224; and Leafstedt 1999). The general understanding of *Bluebeard's* dramatic and musical features was first laid out by Veress (1949) and Kroó (1961), two Hungarian scholars whose analyses have framed discourse about the opera for several generations.

378. In *The Yellow Sound: A Stage Composition* (1982 [1912]), Wassily Kandinsky emphasizes the symbolism of colors (see also, Kandinsky 1970 [1926]).

As has been much discussed,[379] underlying the entire design of the opera is the tonal dichotomy between the beginning and ending (F-sharp), and the "Fifth Door" (key area of C). Those and other factors contributing to the opera's arch form have been investigated by scholars such as Lendvai (1983: 219–224), Kroó (1993), and Leafstedt (1990).[380] The overall form of Bartók's *Bluebeard* is shown in Table 4.1, along with the colors and stage lighting[381] as listed in the directions for the opera's staging.[382]

Scene	Tonal center	Stage lighting	Rehearsal/ measure numbers
"Prologue" of the Bard (spoken)	–	–	–
The opening "Night" scene	F-sharp	total darkness	(0)/1–2/5
"Exposition"	F-sharp	dark	2/6–29/11
Door 1. "The Torture Chamber"	C-sharp–G-sharp	blood-red	30/1–42/4
Door 2. "The Armory"	C-sharp	yellowish-red	42/5–53/9
Door 3. "The Treasure Chamber"	D	golden	54/1–59/9
Door 4. "The Secret Garden"	E-flat	bluish green	60/1–74/18
Door 5. "Bluebeard's Domain"	C	white	74/19–90/14
Door 6. "The Lake of Tears"	A–A-flat	darker	91/1–120/9
Door 7. "The Former Wives"	C	much darker, silver like the moon	121/1–137/10
The closing "Night" scene	F-sharp	total darkness	138/1–140/11

Table 4.1. The tonal organization of Bartók's *Duke Bluebeard's Castle*.[383]

379. Bartók's biographers make varying degrees of reference to earlier *Bluebeard*s, generally focusing on the Dukas-Maeterlinck opera *Ariane et Barbe-Bleue* (e.g., Haraszti 1938: 71–75; Stevens 1964: 285–294; Ujfalussy 1971 [1970]; Heath 1988; and Tallián, ed. 1989). Kroó (1995) writes about the French influences on Bartók's opera, especially that of Dukas. Kroó points out numerous similarities in the two composers' operatic versions of the tale; even the main tonalities are the same: *Ariane et Barbe-Bleue* opens and closes in F-sharp minor, as does *Bluebeard's Castle*.
380. Beneath the music's variegated surface can be perceived common threads or procedures that help establish links between the scenes and eventually result in a coherent whole. Certain scenes are dominated by dissonant harmonic centers, built up largely in fourths; others are mainly triadic in nature (Chalmers 1995: 81–118; see also, Chapters 4.4–4.4.11, below).
381. The imaginative use of stage lighting in *Bluebeard* owes much to the example of stage directors like Max Reinhardt (1873–1943), whose lighting techniques profoundly altered the theatrical experience for early-twentieth-century audiences.
382. Leafstedt (1999: 61) lists the parallels between the colors associated with each scene and the colors found in the natural spectrum of light.
383. In Perrault's (1920 [1697]) version the chambers are described in the following way: "Here, said he [Bluebeard], are the keys to the two great wardrobes, wherein I have my best furniture. These are to my silver and gold plate, which is not everyday in use. These open my strongboxes, which hold my money, both gold and silver; these my caskets of jewels. And this is the master key to all my apartments. But as for this little one here, it is the key to the closet at the end of the great hall on the ground floor. Open them all; go into each and every one of them, except that little closet, which I forbid you, and forbid it in such a manner that, if you happen to open it, you may expect my just anger and resentment."

As indicated in Table 4.1 (previous page), the great arch rests on the "Night" scene pillars in F-sharp and the Door 5 "keystone" of C. Bartók's usage of the tritone dyad, set {0,6}, i.e., F-sharp and C, to define the large-scale harmonic organization[384] stems from his desire to avoid the language of functional harmony and its ramifications for musical form (Figure 4.1).

Figure 4.1. Set {0,6}.

According to Lendvai, by choosing keys that lie the farthest possible distance from each other in traditional, chromatic pitch space, Bartók gives musical expression to the symbolic opposition of darkness and light (1964: 66). Lendvai expounds further on *Bluebeard*'s symbolic and musical ideas:

> The world concept of Bartók is dual – it is not light and not dark, but light and dark, always together in an inseparable unity – as if polarity were the only framework, in which dramatic or spiritual content could manifest itself. […] Bartók takes the thought of darkness dialectically into that of light, and vice-versa – the two presuppose and justify each other. (Lendvai 1983: 220.)

Bartók does not depart entirely from the diatonic functions of modes and their ability to assert a sense of tonic key. This dimension is elaborated and emphasized with particular attention in the following remark by Lendvai:

> The entire tonal plan of *Bluebeard's Castle* is built up of complementary relations. F-sharp minor is the key of "Night" and C major that of "Light". C major can be destroyed by means of the A-flat major key – thus the latter is associated with "Death" symbolism. On the other hand, the "Night's" F-sharp minor can be defeated by B-flat major – thus it became the symbol of "Love". (Lendvai 1988: 142.)

Those tonalities and symbolisms are pictured as pitch-web squares in Figures 4.2–4.5. Altogether, the four triads include every degree of the chromatic scale (Figure 4.6, next page).

Figure 4.2. Set {0,4,7}.

---

384. Ujfalussy (1962) analyses formal symmetry in certain genres of Bartók's works, for example, in slow movements and scherzos, as well as folk music.

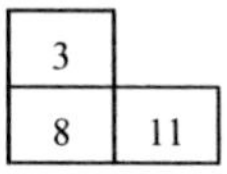

Figure 4.3. Set {3,8,11}.

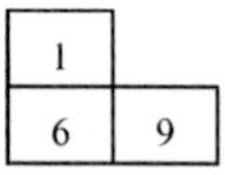

Figure 4.4. Set {6,9,1}.

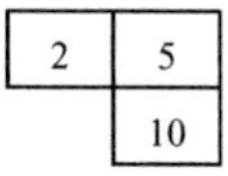

Figure 4.5. Set {10,2,5}.

2	5	8	11
7	10	1	4
0	3	6	9

Figure 4.6. Set {0,1,2,3,4,5,6,7,8,9,10,11}.

Ujfalussy (1976) points out that the tonal network of the opera, shown in Table 4.1 (p. 191), rests on a dual tonal basis: (1) on traditional relations of perfect fifths; (2) on augmented fourth/diminished fifth relations.

The opening of the fifth door marks approximately the structural center of the drama and the axis of its symmetry. The form is balanced on either side by the two arches, ascending and descending, the ascending one with its two pairs of doors. A sketch of interrelationships among door-scenes is given here. They are paired in the following, intersecting way: Door 1 (C tonality) and Door 2 (C-sharp) relate to Door 7 (G-sharp). Together, those tonal centers outline set {0,1,8}, as shown in Figure 4.7 (see also, Table 4.1, p. 191).

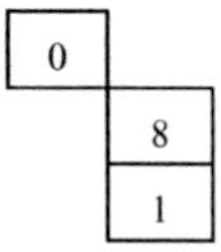

Figure 4.7. Set {0,1,8}.

Door 3 and Door 4 are related to Door 6. The tonal centers of those doors are D–E-flat–A-flat–A, which taken together form the Z cell, set {2,3,8,9}, shown in Figure 4.8 (next page).

9		3
2		8

Figure 4.8. Set {2,3,8,9}.

The five main pillars of the work are surrounded by subsidiary tonal centers (see Table 4.1, p. 191). Lendvai has observed that the initial tonalities of the fourth and sixth scenes, E-flat and A, form a tritone relationship around the pitches F-sharp and C. Taken collectively, F-sharp–A–C–E-flat form set {6,9,0,3}, as shown in Figure 4.9, thus subdividing the octave symmetrically into four minor thirds. (Lendvai 1983: 219–224.)

6	9	0	3

Figure 4.9. Set {6,9,0,3}.

When combined, the tonal centers of the individual door-scenes (Figures 4.7–4.9, above) form set {0,1,2,3,6,8,9}, shown in Figure 4.10 (see also, Table 4.1, p. 191).

	8		2
	1		
0	3	6	9

Figure 4.10. Set {0,1,2,3,6,8,9}: Combined tonal centers of the scenes.

Within the musical symmetry of the vast outer arch, the text realizes a parallel structural axis – the dramatic conflict between the two characters, which grows in intensity and culminates with the moment when they stand before the seventh door. The contradiction between the two structural principles is indicated visually when the sixth and seventh doors stay open while the castle grows darker instead of lighter (Table 4.1, p. 191). In *The Workshop of Bartók and Kodály*, Lendvai assigns positive and negative attributes to each of the seven door-scenes in *Bluebeard's Castle*, based on the nature of what lies behind each door (1983: 219–245).[385]

If, as Joseph Kerman (1988 [1956]) has claimed, there were two main types of opera at the end of the nineteenth century – "sung prose" and "vocal symphonic poems" with incidental text – then, in my view, those two types meet in *Bluebeard*. There the text itself, the dramatic form, is just as stylized and just as far removed from prose as is the strictest of musical forms. Even though Bartók presents the words in speech-song (musical prose), the music takes pride of place; and the op-

---

385. In Lendvai's analysis, the first two scenes are "negative", the middle three are "positive", and the last two are again "negative". Most observers will agree that such an analysis is acceptable, though it describes little more than a normative emotional response to things like blood, weapons, gardens, and large piles of gold and jewels (see Chapter 4.4, p. 197 ff.).

era is essentially a symphonic poem (Kroó 1961: 319–328) in its careful ordering of tonalities and motives, from the opening F-sharp minor ballad theme (0/1–16, Example 4.1, p. 204, Chapter 4.4.1) to its return at the end (138/1–140/11, Example 4.26, p. 294, Chapter 4.4.11).[386]

One of my basic theses is that the scenes are linked together by the set {0,1,4},[387] but it should be stressed at the outset that analytical implementation of set theory seldom deals exclusively with large-scale structures. For example, it may happen that a particular section of a composition is not connected with respect to set-complex structure. On the other hand, it may be that the components of a section reflect the interaction of more than one set complex (see n. 161, p. 87, Chapter 2.4). This raises certain interesting and important questions that might be grouped under the general heading of "form". Consequently, the procedures of segmentation are summarized in Tables 4.2–4.4. Here I am exploring a fundamentally new explanation of the tonal relations that generate and frame *Bluebeard*. In Table 4.2, there are examples of the large-scale relationship that encompasses set {0,1,4} between the scenes.

Door scene	"Night"	1.	2.	3.	4.	5.	6.	7.	"Night"
Rehearsal/ measure numbers	(0)/1–29/11	30/1–42/4	42/5–53/9	54/1–59/9	60/1–74/18	74/19–90/14	91/1–120/9	121/1–137/10	138/1–140/11
Key center(s)	F-sharp	C-sharp–G-sharp	C-sharp	D	E-flat	C	A–A-flat	C	F-sharp
Set	4			0	1				
Set				0	1				4
Set		0 (C-sharp)					4 (A)	1	
Set		0 (C-sharp)				1	4 (A)		
Set		0 (G-sharp)					1 (A)	4	
Set		0 (G-sharp)				4	1 (A)		
Set						4	1, 0		
Set							1, 0	4	
Set			0				4 (A)	1	
Set			0			1	4 (A)		

Table 4.2. Key transitions and set {0,1,4} between the scenes.

Similarly, Table 4.3 (next page) displays key transitions and superset {0,1,4,7} relations between the scenes.

Table 4.4 (next page) shows examples of the key transitions and set {0,3,4,7} relations between the scenes.

---

386. This symphonic poem form has a symbolic aspect. In effect, the opera is like a massive slow movement, which forms a parabolic trajectory from dark, through light, then back to darkness; the circle of the action is complete.

387. For example, it is very useful to investigate other sets held in common between the door-scenes, e.g., {0,1,2}, {0,1,3}, {0,1,5}, {0,1,6}, {0,2,3}, {0,2,6}, and {0,2,7}. They are not, however, the focus of the present dissertation.

Door scene	"Night"	1.	2.	3.	4.	5.	6.	7.	"Night"
Rehearsal/measure numbers	(0)/1–29/11	30/1–42/4	42/5–53/9	54/1–59/9	60/1–74/18	74/19–90/14	91/1–120/9	121/1–137/10	138/1–140/11
Key center(s)	F-sharp	C-sharp–G-sharp	C-sharp	D	E-flat	C	A–A-flat	C	F-sharp
Set	4			0	1		7 (A)		
Set				0	1		7 (A)		4
Set		0 (C-sharp)					4 (A)	1	7
Set	7	0 (C-sharp)					4 (A)	1	
Set	7	0 (C-sharp)				1	4 (A)		
Set		0 (C-sharp)				1	4 (A)		7
Set		0 (G-sharp)			7		1 (A)	4	
Set		0 (G-sharp)			7	4	1 (A)		
Set					7	4	1, 0 (A-flat)		
Set					7		1, 0 (A-flat)	4	
Set	7		0				4 (A)	1	
Set			0				4 (A)	1	7
Set	7		0			1	4 (A)		
Set			0			1	4 (A)		7

Table 4.3. Key transitions and set {0,1,4,7} relations between the scenes.

Door scene	"Night"	1.	2.	3.	4.	5.	6.	7.	"Night"
Rehearsal/measure numbers	(0)/1–29/11	30/1–42/4	42/5–53/9	54/1–59/9	60/1–74/18	74/19–90/14	91/1–120/9	121/1–137/10	138/1–140/11
Key center(s)	F-sharp	C-sharp–G-sharp	C-sharp	D	E-flat	C	A–A-flat	C	F-sharp
Set						0	3 (A), 4		7
Set	7					0	3 (A), 4		
Set	7						3 (A), 4	0	
Set							3 (A), 4	0	7
Set	7	4 (G-sharp)				0	3 (A)		
Set		4 (G-sharp)				0	3 (A)		7
Set	7	4 (G-sharp)					3 (A)	0	
Set		4 (G-sharp)					3 (A)	0	7

Table 4.4. Key transitions and set {0,3,4,7} relations between the scenes.

Several other examples testify that those sets are also operative when formally elaborated between the themes (see Chapters 4.4–4.4.11).

4.4. Individual scenes

The musical structure of *Duke Bluebeard's Castle* is made to conform with the action on the stage, which is organized around a series of brief scenes. Veress (1949–1950) and Kroó (1961: 319–328) argue that the musical form is similar to the movements of a suite, where each movement has its own individual character and form, mostly based on the unity of specific themes and instrumental motifs. Lendvai (1983: 221) suggests a pictorial metaphor: "Each of the opening doors is a self-contained musical painting."[388] The music flows directly from one to the next door without any scene changes or interludes, although momentary pauses in the dramatic action sometimes occur between scenes (see e.g., 90/13–91/1). As each of the seven doors is opened, the music conveys the emotions and mental states of the two characters. Veress (1949–1950) observes that each scene is linked symphonically; however they are not merely placed side by side, but grow out of each other, following a dramatic plan, as do the parts of a symphony-like cycle (as discussed above, pp. 190–196, Chapter 4.3).

In *Bluebeard*, no single theme assumes particular importance in terms of occurrence, and not a single theme in the opera is developed in the same manner as a Wagnerian *Leitmotiv*. It will be recalled that Wagner's *Leitmotiv* came along with his device of *unendliche Melodie* (Heiniö 1989: 67), and such motives were modified by modulation and variation in order to explore the full semantic potential of the poetic-melodic-harmonic universe. By contrast, in *Bluebeard's Castle*, the strongest thematic link is the Blood motif, which first appears at score no. (0)/16 (see Example 4.1, p. 204, Chapter 4.4.1). It creates the impression of a symphonic construct more than a psychological-dramatic one: The Blood motif is a short, flexible orchestral theme marked by its high concentration of dissonance. It behaves structurally like the theme of a series of variations in a romantic symphony or symphonic poem (Leafstedt 1999: 74, 76). This motif, a combination of semitones, starts unobtrusively, as part of larger thematic statements, and then grows so much as to become the primary foreground event (Antokoletz 1984: 89–92).

As the scenes change from one door to the next, the plot of the drama develops by means of dialogue, music, and acting. Bartók struck a balance in the melodic types assigned to the two characters, Judith and the Duke, whose music closely resembles Wagnerian "unending melody", but interwoven with the *parlando* of Hungarian folk music, such as one finds in the *Quatre nénies* for piano[389]. Bartók worked out his

---

388. The opera's conception as series of relatively brief, individual scenes organized around changing visual images was not without precedent in Bartók's œuvre. In the years prior to 1911, many of Bartók's instrumental compositions had been conceived as collections of shorter pieces, under descriptive, often visually inspired titles; e.g., *Two Portraits* for orchestra, *Two Pictures* for orchestra, and the *Seven Sketches* for piano.

389. The *Quatre nénies* (Op. 9a, Sz 45, BB 58, 1910) are profound little miniatures in their lean simplicity – rather like late-period Liszt. They are based on Hungarian folk laments and show Bartók tapping into the Hungarian peasant folklore. The *Quatre nénies* reveals significant connections with Debussy's works, not only in the use of a French title but also in the prominent use of pentatonic formations in the "Second Dirge". (Lindlar 1984: 79; and Demény, ed. 1976: 403.)

own *parlando* style after Debussy's model, but the result is radically different in character, for Bartók's starting point was the old-style Hungarian peasant music (see especially, pp. 155–158, Chapter 3.5.1). Bartók acknowledged the debt his opera owed to the vocal style of Debussy's *Pelléas*:

> This kind of musical recitation [in *Bluebeard*] is in a certain relation to that created by Debussy in his *Pelléas et Mélisande* and in some of his songs, which were based on the old French recitative. This recitation is in the sharpest possible contrast to the Schoenbergian treatment of vocal parts, in which the most exaggerated jumps, leaps, and restlessness appear. (*BBE* 1976 [1943]: 383.)

Aladár Tóth (1898–1968), a prominent Hungarian music critic, wrote the following (1920: 743–744) in an article in the *Nyugat*: "Bartók's music is of the most intense concentration – hence its dramatic force, which often reminds us of the rhythm of ancient, awesome folk ballads (the *recitativos* of *Bluebeard's Castle*)." Frigyesi (1998: 230–294) gives a detailed survey on the relation of the two characters, Bluebeard and Judith, to Hungarian old-style peasant songs, and traces back the orchestra music of the opera to Hungarian *verbunkos* and *pastorale* traditions (see, e.g., 27/6–28/3; 28/5–29/6). In the ornamental style of *verbunkos*, Bartók found the inspiration to craft a system of rhythmic-thematic transformation based on the most elementary fragment of music: the single note. The technique distinguishes between a main note – a long and/or melodically significant one – and ornamental tones, such as those, which are shorter and/or otherwise less salient (see pp. 107–108, Chapter 3.2.1). However, through a change of emphasis or of phrasing, ornamental notes may become main notes, and *vice versa* (see, e.g., 24/1–25/2). Bluebeard's part is centered on the plainest sort of declamation, while Judith vocal line is somewhat more elaborate rhythmically. Frigyesi, speaking at a more aesthetic level about the opera's vocal lines, makes the following observations:

> First, he [Bartók] was positing a novel view of nationalism, opposing the convention that Hungarianness equaled heroism. Second, the emphasis on the pastoral meant the assertion of the primacy of lyricism, even in dramatic form, over the narrative approach. The idea of expressing drama through lyricism paralleled the modernist trend of Hungarian literature and reflected the philosophical and aesthetic attempt to condense all the related and contrasting things of the world into simple images that were at once personal and universal. Similarly, the singing style Bartók created was a sort of Hungarian recitative and thus perfectly logical in opera, but was so different from any traditional operatic style that its use challenged operatic conventions. (Frigyesi 1998: 237.)

In sum: In *Bluebeard's Castle*, Bartók tends to lock into short, repetitive melodic patterns. Those melodic fragments serve in various ways to underline the action on stage.

Scholars Lendvai (1964: 66) and Stevens (1964: 291) state that each scene consists of two sections: (1) the introduction that precedes the actual door-opening; (2)

the section (with the Blood motif[390]) featuring Judith's reaction. By contrast, Kroó (1961) and Leafstedt (1999: 90–124) argue that there may be either two or three sections in each scenes. I lean toward the latter opinion, but would add to it the view that each scene unfolds in three distinct sections:

1. a musical description of the door, including Judith's response to its contents;
2. a dialogue in which Judith and Bluebeard work out their emotional responses to the door's revelation;
3. a dialogue pertaining to the door-key and to the door that lies ahead.

The personalities of Judith and Bluebeard undergo a gradual transformation during the course of the opera, as expressed in their dialogue and accompanying orchestral music (Veress 1949; and Antokoletz 1990: 78). Initially it is Bluebeard, not Judith, who is quiet and reserved. As Judith moves farther into the castle, Bluebeard warms to her presence, as reflected in the more active role he plays in their dialogue. Judith, in turn, gets quieter and quieter, as she becomes preoccupied with thoughts about the possible significance of her discoveries.[391]

As will soon be made clear (Chapters 4.4.1–4.4.11), the structural framework of the opera also determined Bartók's choice and arrangement of sounds, the outermost layer of which closely follows events of the plot, including Judith's sighs, her pounding on doors, the creaking of locks, and the sound of footsteps. Only at a deeper, atemporal or synchronic layer of the music are the significance and symbolism of the opera revealed.

In order to achieve the visual and dramatic effects necessary for a stage work, Bartók made brilliant use of the possibilities of the large orchestra employed by Strauss. Bartók augmented his opera orchestra with a variety of unusual instruments (such as organ, celesta, and keyed xylophone), some of which were new to him at the time, and all of which are used for special moments in the opera.

By organizing the musical material around the seven "pictures" that lay behind Bluebeard's doors, Bartók did not have to sustain a given musical idea over broad spans of time as Strauss had done in *Salome* and *Elektra* (Lendvai 1983: 221; see also, 1964: 81). In those operas, the entire musical fabric of the opera is spun out from a handful of flexible motives (cf. Batta, ed. 1999: 588–599). By contrast, in

---

390. In Bartók's *Bluebeard*, various motivic features, especially the one associated with the recurrent image of blood, are deployed to lend the score a post-Wagnerian coherence and continuity. Most Bartók scholars have drawn attention to the importance of the Blood motif, among others; e.g., see Lendvai (1964), Kroó (1962; and 1963), Frigyesi (1998), Leafstedt (1994; and 1999: 69–84) and Antokoletz (1984: 89–92; and 1990); see also, Example 4.1, p. 204, Chapter 4.4.1.

391. This pattern is by no means rigorously enforced; it represents a general tendency. Judith, for example, in her requests for additional door keys, or in her reactions to seeing blood, shows a consistent capacity for forcefulness that, if provoked, results in agitated vocal lines throughout scenes 1–6 (Chapters 4.4.2–4.4.9). In the context of the entire opera, however, the pattern is clearly operative, though complicated by the emotional flux of the two characters. In the "Fifth Door" scene (74/19–90/14), the reversal is complete: Bluebeard is now the volatile, emotional character, while Judith turns inward, becoming withdrawn and taciturn (Chapter 4.4.8).

Bluebeard, every change in dramatic focus ushers in new material; but that does not preclude the presence of deeper-level intervallic and gestural resemblances among the outwardly differentiated musical ideas (see Chapters 4.4.1–4.4.11).

Wagner's harmony and melody writing had a strong influence on Bartók, but as he later recounted in the "Harvard Lectures", "the Wagnerian spirit was the absolute antithesis of anything that could be conceived of as Hungarianism in music" (*BBE* 1976 [1943]: 362). In Bartók's *Bluebeard*, the action on stage flows uninterrupted by the insertion of purely musical forms such as arias or duets. As in Wagner's music dramas, Bartók's opera does not have the characters singing arias at each other. Devotees of conventional opera may be perturbed by the prospect of a through-composed duet, without a single recognizable aria. The melodic formulas are interesting enough not to be monotonous, and Bartók occasionally obliges with lyric *ariosos* (e.g., 50/3–51/7; and 123/5–126/7).

Bluebeard is a masterful Hungarian emulation of *Pelléas et Mélisande*, in which Debussy used modern (and even postmodern) innovations.[392] Dahlhaus restricts his definition of musical modernism to progressive music in the period 1890–1910:

> The year 1890 [...] lends itself as an obvious point of historical discontinuity. The "breakthrough" of Mahler, Strauss and Debussy implies a profound historical transformation. [...] If we were to search for a name to convey the breakaway mood of the 1890s (a mood symbolized musically by the opening bars of Strauss's *Don Juan*) but without imposing a fictitious unity of style on the age, we could do worse than revert to the term "modernism" as extending (with some latitude) from 1890 to the beginning of our own twentieth-century modern music in 1910. [...] The label "late romanticism" [...] is a terminological blunder of the first order and ought to be abandoned forthwith. It is absurd to yoke Strauss, Mahler, and the young Schoenberg, composers who represent modernism in the minds of their turn-of-the-century contemporaries, with the self-proclaimed antimodernist Pfitzner, calling them all "late romantics" in order to supply a veneer of internal unity to an age fraught with stylistic contradictions and conflicts. (Dahlhaus 1989: 334.)

In his outstanding study, *The Music of Claude Debussy's Music*, Richard Parks (1989) groups evocations of *Pelléas et Mélisande* under the headings "benign" and "malignant". This distinction is associated with musical dualisms like major/minor, diatonic/chromatic, consonant/dissonant. Parks comments that the diatonic genus

---

392. On musical modernism, see Adorno (1973 [1949]), Morgan (1991) and Albright (ed. 2004). It is not feasible to summarize the extensive musicological debates on the matter. Studies written in the 1960s and 1970s essentially follow Adorno's (1973) interpretation of modernism. Daniel Albright (ed. 2004) dates musical modernism from 1894–1895, illustrating it with examples such as Debussy's *Prélude à l'après-midi d'un faune* (1894) and Strauss's *Till Eulenspiegel*, Op. 28 (1895), the main features of which he finds to be (1) comprehensiveness and depth; (2) semantic specificity and poetic density; (3) extension of functional tonality to the point of dissolution. Leaving aside issues of defining modernism, Antokoletz (2004) deepens our understanding of music drama by using the insights of psychoanalysis for a close reading of character, gender relationships, and dramatic motion as embodied by the music.

corresponds to "benign, passive" expressions, while the whole-tone genus is "malignant, active" (ibid.: 168).[393]

In *Musical Symbolism in the Operas of Debussy and Bartók*, Antokoletz (2004) points out that Debussy's *Pelléas et Mélisande* set Bartók on the path toward a modern vocal style based largely upon the inflections of centuries-old narrative cultural traditions such as the Hungarian, *parlando-rubato* folk song (discussed above, pp. 157–159, Chapter 3.5.1). In both operas, the vocal setting is syllabic and follows the rhythms of speech patterns (Grayson 1986: 228, 286–287 n. 33; Ujfalussy 1959: 92–99; and Leafstedt 1999: 65–67). Bartók's *Bluebeard* changed the course of Hungarian opera by successfully developing a form of Hungarian declamation for Balázs's ballad-like mystery play (cf. pp. 119–120, Chapter 3.2.2). The monotonous pulsation of Balázs's octosyllabic lines – the inflections of Hungarian folk song – represented one of the most difficult problems in the treatment of the lyrics. It was the influence of Debussy and of Hungarian folk-music *parlando* that enabled Bartók to create the first truly Hungarian language for stage, one that accommodated every nuance of the text.

Bluebeard's score is pervaded with the character of the native musics that Bartók had been studying intensely (see Chapters 3.4–3.6). Although the opera contains no actual folk material, many of the melodies are based on folk-music usage of the pentatonic scale (Chapters 4.4.2–4.4.11). The "Hungarian-ness" of *Bluebeard* is guaranteed by the pervasive influence of the Hungarian language on the vocal and speech rhythms; for example, in the initial stresses of melodic lines and their propensity to descend (Zs. László 1961 [1955]; and 1985),[394] as well as a metric centering around 2/4 and 4/4, with the quarter-note comprising the beat-level of the rhythms. The differences in vocal style between Debussy's and Bartók's operas can be ascribed to differences between the languages. As subtly as Debussy did in his own language, Bartók followed the natural stresses of the Hungarian tongue in his own coupling of words and music (Kodály 1974 [1918]: 380–381; and 1974 [1921]: 431–432).

---

393. Wagner's influence is evident in Debussy's music. Most notable was the ideal of vocal expression more closely tied to that of natural language. In the 1890s, Debussy began to abandon abstract music in favor of a more programmatic approach. But whereas Wagner would favor a complex system of elaborate and explicit musical references, Debussy inclined more to a generalized evocation of mood, impressions and atmospheres. The result of such a method is that a composition seems to take shape out of an opaque, atmospheric background rather than grow "organically" out of a germinal motive, as in the more traditional, Germanic manner. (Grayson 1986: 5–6, 22, 44–45, 191, 229–275.)

394. Zsigmond László (1961 [1955]) examines the Hungarian characteristics of Bartók's text declamation in *Bluebeard's Castle*. E.g., in the "Fifth Door" scene (74/19–90/14), the individual vocal lines may be grouped into folk-like quatrain structures. The beginning dialogue between Bluebeard and Judith is comprised of four-line stanzas: Bluebeard describes the vast splendor of his domains for three lines (75/1–7), and Judith responds with one (75/10); then the pattern repeats (76/7–13, 76/16). In the next four lines, Bluebeard offers his magnificent domain to Judith, assuring her of a bright future therein (77/5–10). In response, Judith perceives blood-red clouds gathering on the horizon, and a sudden change in mood occurs when her two-line interjection creates a natural break in the text (78/1–2).

Rather than compete with the melodic sophistication and variety of the orchestral material, the vocal lines in *Bluebeard* give that material sharper meaning: both musically, by clarifying or expanding tonality and by marking structural dividing points; and textually, by interpreting key sentences with orchestral themes and/or visual images. That function accorded with Balázs's view that "words can tell little of what should be said, but it is precisely for this reason that words mean more than they actually say" (Balázs 1982 [1922]: 322). The relationship between voice and orchestra in Bartók's opera reveals a close spiritual kinship to the symphonic-opera aesthetic that represented the dominant opera paradigm for central European composers after Wagner. It may be observed, in this context, that Bartók deploys an extraordinary range of orchestral colors and textures to conjure up the febrile atmosphere of Bluebeard's dark castle. The orchestration is essentially based on the timbres and color combinations developed by Wagner[395] and Strauss, but within the framework of a largely homophonic style.[396]

The characteristically percussive quality and novel tone color of Bartók's opera are achieved with traditional instruments, with some added, not so traditional ones. As we have noted before, *Bluebeard* is scored for a massive orchestra replete with organ, celesta, a large battery of percussion, and eight brass instruments.[397] Also essential to *Bluebeard* are the spaces, the silences, the interplay of loud and soft dynamics. The frequent use of the middle and lower registers is in keeping with the atmosphere of the opera, as are the solo roles accorded to the clarinet, *cor anglais*, viola, and horn. The many static harmonies, the long sustained notes, and the absence of polyphony all emphasize the static character of the opera, and stress both the abstract nature of the stage setting and the symbolism of the mystery play (further discussed in Chapters 4.4.1–4.4.11).

From here onwards, I present my analysis of the individual scenes, focusing on their key moments in terms of formal considerations, tonal/modal aspects, chromatic elements, and the background motion of the modal centers. Special emphasis is given to the "Sixth Door", where a detailed analysis of the music is presented in order to show how closely it follows the plot (Chapters 4.4.9.1–4.4.9.4).

---

395. Bónis (1981) discusses Bartók's first encounters with Wagner's music and his future relationship with it.

396. In the early part of the twentieth century, the foremost operatic composer was Strauss. Among his most successful operas are *Salome* (1905), *Elektra* (1909), *Der Rosenkavalier* (1910), *Ariadne auf Naxos* (1911–1912), and the allegorical *Die Frau ohne Schatten* (1919). Strauss's *Elektra* epitomized late Romantic music on the threshold of a new chromatic idiom. But Strauss never crossed it to enter the free-atonal idiom of Schoenberg's *Erwartung* and Berg's *Wozzeck*. (Batta, ed. 1999: 34–37, 552–553, 588–615.) Bartók found Strauss's *Elektra* to be a disappointment, especially after the new ground broken in *Salome* (*BBE* 1976 [1910]: 446).

397. Instrumentation: two vocal soloists – a baritone in the role of Duke Bluebeard, a soprano as Judith, his bride – and an orchestra of four flutes (two doubling piccolo), two oboes and English horn, three clarinets (two doubling E-flat clarinet, the other doubling bass clarinet), four bassoons (one doubling contrabassoon), four horns, four trumpets, four trombones, tuba, timpani, bass drum, snare drum, tam-tam, cymbals, xylophone, triangle, two harps, piano, celesta, and strings. (Bartók 1952 [1925].)

4.4.1. 'Prologue'

A spoken "Prologue" precedes the entire opera. A *regös*[398] – as is identified in the score – steps in front of the curtain and explains that the tale of Bluebeard is going to be retold as a parable of the inner self (Bartók 1952 [1925]: 1–2; see Example 4.1, next page).

The function of the "Prologue"[399] is to make sure that the audience gets the symbolic meaning, which is far removed from the old fairy-tale of Bluebeard and his bride (pp. 173–174, Chapter 4.1). The second stanza of the "Prologue" offers a clue to explaining that symbolism:

Szemünk, pillás függönye fent:	The curtains of our eyelids are raised:
Hol a színpad: kint-e vagy bent,	Where is the stage, within or without,
Urak, asszonyságok?	Fair ladies and lords?

Not unlike Richard Wagner before him, Balázs (re)constructs the sound and texture of a distant past when poems were recited aloud. The twenty-eight lines of the "Prologue" are divided into six stanzas: five of 5 lines and one of 3 lines (see Table 4.5, p. 205). The first five-line stanza traces a 5–6–8–8–6 line structure. The other five stanzas closely follow the 6–6–8–8–6 syllabic pattern, and they are unified by a regular *aabbc* rhyme scheme. Five stanzas contain a one-line refrain, "*Urak, asszonyságok*" (Fair ladies and lords). The last three-line verse traces a 6–7–6 syllabic structure, with an *aab* rhyme scheme. The repetition of certain words and images like *régi* (old, ancient) and *rege* (tale, myth) helps evoke the atmosphere of earlier times and places. The formulaic use of alliteration and lilting rhythm – "*Hol volt, hol nem,*" "*Régi vár, régi már,*" "*Regénket regéljük*" – recalls a mythic world whose vagueness is underscored by non-specific adjectives ("ancient", "old"). I add here the sixth stanza of the "Prologue" (see p. 205):

---

398. Balázs (and definitely Bartók) knew about the *regös*-boys, who performed a mid-winter calendar custom. Gyula Sebestyén (1902a; and 1902b) saw in the *regös* the descendants of medieval minstrels. Voigt (1997: 106) mentions that, in 1897–1898, Sebestyén used a phonograph during his tour for collecting Regös songs. I thank Professor Voigt for informing me of Sebestyén's studies in that area.

399. In most Western productions, recordings, and academic discussions, the "Prologue" of *Bluebeard's Castle* is omitted altogether. At times it is translated, but without any explanation of its import as a structural *lieu de passage*. Perhaps worse, the published German version of the libretto by Wilhelm Ziegler – based on Emma Kodály's first translation – imputes specific meaning to phrases left vague in the Hungarian. Similarly flawed, the English translation attempts to retain the poetic and rhythmic features of the Hungarian at the expense of rendering a literal equivalent. Even recent scholarship, e.g., Frigyesi (1998: 196–294) and Leafstedt (1999: 55–61), misrepresents the text, despite the declared intent to be literal (Vázsonyi 2005). Prologues are rarely encountered in the opera house, where the task of preparing the audience for the upcoming drama has traditionally fallen to the overture. Almost all operatic prologues in the history of the genre have been set to music, dating back to the Baroque era.

HERZOG BLAUBARTS BURG

A kékszakállú herceg vára

Béla Bartók, Op. 11.

Prolog

Dies begab sich einst.
Ihr müßt nicht wissen wann, auch nicht den Ort,
da es geschah, Topographie und Jahreszahl.
„Aha", sagt ihr (und es klingt recht fatal) „eine
Legende!"Und fragt– denn es ist nützlich, das vor-
her zu wissen– was in Wahrheit sie bedeute.
Liebe Leute, ich muß euch sagen: die Wahrheit
ist ein Rauch und ist ein Echo nur von eines Seufzers Hauch.

Ihr seht mich an. Ich sehe euch. Ganz offen steht
der Vorhang unserer Augenlider. Ihr sucht die Bühne?
Ja, wo ist die aufgeschlagen? In dir? In mir? Am
rost'gen Pol der Zeit? O liebe Freunde, laßt es dabei
bewenden, beginnt nicht mit Fragen, die nie und
nimmer enden.

Ein Flickwerk ist das Leben. Und was auf Erden
blüht und Frucht wird, ernten Kriege. Aber, liebe
Leute, das ist nicht, woran wir sterben. Woran wir
denn zugrunde gehn? Die Antwort hängt im Strauch,
zerfetzt, befleckt, und ist das Echo nur von eines
Seufzers Hauch.

(Der Vorhang geht auf)

Prológus

Haj regő rejtem
Hová, hová rejtsem
Hol volt, hol nem: kint-e vagy bent?
Régi rege, haj mit jelent,
Urak, asszonyságok?

Im, szólal az ének.
Ti nézték, én nézlek.
Szemünk pillás függönye fent:
Hol a színpad: kint-e vagy bent,
Urak, asszonyságok?

Keserves és boldog
Nevezetes dolgok,
Az világ kint haddal tele,
De nem abba halunk bele,
Urak, asszonyságok.

Nézzük egymást, nézzük,
Regénket regéljük.
Ki tudhatja honnan hozzuk?
Hallgatjuk és csodálkozzuk,
Urak, asszonyságok.

(A függöny szétválik a háta mögött)

Musik beginnt. Das Spiel hebt an. Hat es euch

Zene szól, a láng ég, Kezdődjön a játék.

Piano

gefallen – dann am Ende spart nicht mit Dank und regt die
Hände. Jetzt schließt den Vorhang eurer Augenlider.

Szemem pillás függönye fent.
majd ha lement, Urak,

Tapsoljatok
asszonyságok.

Auftaucht das alte Haus. Muß ich es nennen? Ihr werdet's
tief in euch erkennen. Ihr wißt den Ort und wißt den
Namen auch: das Echo nur von eines Seufzers Hauch.
Régi vár, régi már Az mese, ki róla jár, Tik is hallgassátok.

Mächtige, runde, gotische Halle. Links führt eine steile Treppe zu einer kleinen eisernen Türe. Rechts der Stiege befinden sich in der Mauer
sieben große Türen: vier noch gegenüber der Rampe, zwei bereits ganz rechts. Sonst weder Fenster, noch Dekoration. Die Halle gleicht einer finstern, düstern, leeren Felsenhöhle. Beim Heben des Vorhanges ist die Szene finster.
Hatalmas kerek gotikus csarnok. Balra meredek lépcső vezet fel egy kis vasajtóhoz. A lépcsőtől jobbra hét nagy ajtó van a falban; négy még szemben,
kettő már egész jobboldalt. Különben sem ablak, se dísz. A csarnok üres sötét, rideg, sziklabarlanghoz hasonlatos. Mikor a függöny szétválik, teljes
sötétség van a színpadon.

Example 4.1. "Prologue": Night theme (0/1–16) and Blood motif (0/16).

Régi vár, régi már	Ancient castle, ancient too is this legend
az mese ki róla jár.	Which tells about it,
Tik is hallgassátok.	You listen to it.

There is also a vagueness of space or location ("where"), that is designated very generally ("castle"). Unattached to time and space, meaning itself is rendered indeterminate and unstable, as the text itself concedes ("Oh what does it mean?"). Here, there is already an undermining of the notion of a coherent narrative, a loss compounded when the traditional location of dramatic representation – the stage – is itself placed in doubt ("where's the stage: is it outside or in?"). The absence of context, and thus of meaning, becomes even more significant later in the opera.

The preceding discussion of stanzas and syllabic structure is summarized in Table 4.5.

Stanzas of the "Prologue"	Syllabic structure	Rhyme scheme
Stanza 1.	5 –6–8–8–6	*aabbc*
Stanza 2.	6–6–8–8–6	*aabbc*
Stanza 3.	6–6–8–8–6	*aabbc*
Stanza 4.	6–6–8–8–6	*aabbc*
Stanza 5.	6–6–8–8–6	*aabbc*
Stanza 6.	6–7–6	*aab*

Table 4.5. The stanzas, the syllabic structure, and rhyme scheme of the "Prologue".

There is a general consensus among specialists that the "Prologue" represents a departure from the isometric syllable patterns that Bartók, Kodály, and other ethnomusicologists ascribed to old-style Hungarian folk-mode. Six-syllable lines are regularly found in the oldest strata of Hungarian folk song, as seen, e.g., in Transylvanian ballads, where they are typically grouped into four-line stanzas (cf. p. 154, Chapter 3.5.1).

The verse form of the "Prologue" is found nowhere else in *Duke Bluebeard's Castle*.[400] Balázs's versification of the libretto is identical in form to the old-style, octosyllabic folk songs, one of the most ancient and typical forms of Hungarian folk poetry. The octosyllabic lines divide into two halves, each half with the first syllable stressed; otherwise, there are no other restrictions or variations of meter. Balázs libretto is almost completely in trochaic tetrameters – in a form called Ancient Eight – set in four metric units of two syllables each. In imitation of the old folk ballads, Balázs wrote the entire text of the libretto using a simple and limited vocabulary of short, 2–3 syllable words. According to Bartók's folklore categorization, it is the most archaic type of Hungarian verse (1981 [1924]; and *BBE* 1976 [1921c]).

---

400. The "Prologue" has been translated into several languages. It is recommended, however, that the original Hungarian version or that one of the word-for-word translations be used, rather than any of the "free" translations.

Leafstedt (1999: 55–61) provides the most detailed description of the opera's symbolism, which in his view has been underrated. Symbols such as the castle, the two characters themselves, the lighting are highly important as bearers of meaning in staged productions of *Bluebeard*; even the opening figure of the *regös* functions symbolically within the context of the drama as a whole. Perhaps the most striking symbol is the castle itself, with its seven doors[401], each of which opens to reveal another aspect of Bluebeard's life and identity.

4.4.2. 'Night'

In the opening "Night" scene, the bard announces that the play is beginning (0/1–2/5). The curtain goes up, and he slips silently away, disappearing into the darkness.[402] The stage setting is a hall in Bluebeard's castle in legendary times. According to the score:

> It is a vast, circular, Gothic hall. Steep stairs at left lead up to a small iron door. To the right of the stairs seven enormous doors. […] The hall is empty, dark, and forbidding like a cave hewn in the heart of solid rock. (Bartók 1952 [1925]: 2.)

The opera opens with a four-line pentatonic structure that symbolizes the ancient timelessness of the Bluebeard legend. The *parlando* style of the theme is immediately apparent, reminding us of Bartók's view that the old-style melodies present "the most interesting, exciting, and valuable features" of native folk music (*BBE* 1976 [1920d]: 305–306). The opening motive (A) is shown in the list given in Table 4.6 (next page).[403]

Indeed, melodic lines throughout the opera are based largely on pentatonic and modal scales. Each syllable of the text is sung to a single tone, creating a constant recitative. Each line of the libretto follows an unvarying octosyllabic scheme: four metric units of two syllables each – in perfect relation to the "ancient eight", so-called because of the common tendency of Hungarian music and poetry to follow that pattern. Since the rhythm is generally written in long lines of quarter- and eighth-notes, an understanding of the *parlando* style of peasant music was essential for the composer and librettist, in order to reproduce the quantitative differences inherent to the Hungarian language. (Cf. pp. 176–177, Chapter 4.1.)

---

401. E.g., Bluebeard's secret garden reacts to Judith's presence as if it were human. Like the castle itself, it has animate qualities. The flowers "bow" (69/1) and "ring bells" (72/5–6) for Judith.

402. After the fourth stanza of the "Prologue", the music begins slowly and quietly in the low strings, an event noted in the first line of the next stanza: "Music sounds." When that music sounds, the "Prologue" indicates the play is to commence. Now the "drama" proper may start. The "eyelash-curtain" metaphor is repeated, but the pronoun is altered from first person plural ("our") to first person singular ("my"). The eyelash-curtain of the "Prologue", now up, draws applause when it has fallen, focusing our gaze directly into and through its eye.

403. It is a token of Bartók's affection for *Bluebeard* that the first idea of the "Introduzione" of the *Concerto for Orchestra* should bear a great similarity to the opening passage of the opera.

The "Night" scene themes (0/1–2/5) are summarized in Table 4.6, along with the corresponding key centers.

Themes	Night theme	Dolce-marcato theme	Thematic transformation of the Blood motif
Label	(A)	(B)	(B')
Rehearsal/measure numbers	(0)/1–16	(0)/16–1/5	2/1–5
Tonal center(s)	F-sharp	C–F-sharp	F-sharp
Scale	Pentatonic	Harmonic minor scale	Chromatic
Point 0	F-sharp	F-sharp	F-sharp
Set	{0,3,5,7,10}	{0,3,5,6,9,10}	{0,1,2,3,4,5,6,7,8,9,10,11}
Forte number	5–35	7–31	12–1 (1)
ICV	932140	336333	–
Synopsis	After the "Prologue", the Bard disappears (0/15)	Dark stage	Dark stage

Table 4.6. The themes of the opening "Night" scene, (0)/1–2/5.

Bartók creates a ballad-like atmosphere with the monophonic, 4 x 4 bars Night theme (0/1–16) that rolls slowly through the darkness while the bard, on stage, concludes his spoken "Prologue". This pentatonic theme is a descending stylized old-style Hungarian folk melody, an abstract idiom of folk-like-quality.[404] Theme (A) outlines a modal pentatonic substructure: the F-sharp minor pitch collection of F-sharp–A–B–C-sharp–E, set {0,3,5,7,10}. (Figure 4.11; see also, Example 4.1, p. 204, Chapter 4.4.1.)

Figure 4.11. Set {0,3,5,7,10}.

The rhythm never varies, and there is no ornamentation or change in dynamics. The melody moves in unison, in alternating fourths and major seconds, and the symmetry of the phrases is undisturbed. By repeating this opening theme at the end of the opera, Bartók creates a frame for the entire work (138/1–139/12, Example 4.26, p. 294, Chapter 4.4.11).

---

404. Bárdos (1974: 107–114) presents twelve melodies by Bartók in imitation of folk-song style. Those examples demonstrate the principal, four-line type of folk melody in closed form, with descending or stationary cadences at the first, second, and fourth caesuras, and an ascending one on the third caesura. The opening Night theme of *Bluebeard* belongs to the last type (Example 4.1, p. 204, Chapter 4.4.1).

In writing the opening music for his opera, Bartók may have taken note of the technique used by Debussy in *Pelléas et Mélisande*, for both operas begin in a similar manner (Batta, ed. 1999: 17). The Night theme vividly evokes the memory of Pelléas, Golaud, and Mélisande, and we are reminded of Debussy's forest music. Theme (A), played by the winds in the baritone range, represents the dark, mysterious, and oppressive castle. The pentatonic theme is interrupted almost immediately by a second musical idea in the Dorian mode, with whole-tone harmonies built upon it. Then comes the recurring Blood motif, based on minor seconds, which is presented in several variants throughout the opera. This half-step motif is heard at regular intervals in the orchestra, whenever tears (e.g., 96/3–97/1) or blood (e.g., 114/1–117/7) are mentioned on stage. As Leafstedt has noticed (1999: 69–84), the Blood motif appears continuously in transformations, forming the heart of thematic derivations; structurally it behaves like a theme, though changed rhythmically and/or melodically in different musical-dramatic situations. It retains its musical individuality, thereby establishing a kind of musical equilibrium. Despite its brevity, this pertinent element is strongly felt throughout the entire opera, whether it appears embedded in a longer melodic line (e.g., 42/7 and 46/1) or as a miniature figure of its own, as at the beginning (see Example 4.1, p. 204, Chapter 4.4.1).

The Blood motif, as a chilling three-note figure, first springs up in the woodwinds, and from so inconspicuous a beginning gradually permeates the entire musical texture. The *Doppelfrasiert* moment of the Night theme and Blood motif (C–E–F-sharp) forms set {0,4,6}, as shown in Figure 4.12.

Figure 4.12. Set {0,4,6}.

As Antokoletz points out (1990: 79), the opening theme (A), a folk derived diatonic construction, serves as the point of departure for the infusion of semitones as a representation of the emerging symbol of Blood, as well as for the transit into the whole-tone sphere in connection with Judith's fatalistic intrusion into Bluebeard's private world.

The second theme (B) appears as a sharp orchestral exclamation (0/16–19, Example 4.1, p. 204, Chapter 4.4.1), in the form of a mordent-like, 64th-note pattern to be played both "dolce" and "poco marcato". Frigyesi labels it the "dolce-marcato" theme (1998: 255), which enters superposed on the last note (F-sharp) of the pentatonic theme (0)/16; see also, 4/5–5/1 in the "Exposition" scene. Antokoletz has termed it the "menacing motif" (1990: 81). Based on half steps, this thematic idea is itself composed of three motivic repetitions – based on circular motion – of a long-short note pair. There is a prominent statement of C tonality at the beginning of the second theme (0/16). A C major triad is projected over its first two beats through the alternation of C–E and E–G thirds with their lower neighbors, the lower neighbors of which outline B major (0/16–17). At score no. (0)/17, the A–C third suggests

A minor or a background A–C–E–G seventh chord. The second theme (B) is developed by an expanding register, and projects the E minor harmonic minor scale, set {0,2,3,5,7,8,11}, as shown in Figure 4.13. This minor scale, with its augmented second, is often associated with *Verbunkos* and gypsy style.

2	5	8	11
7			
0	3		

Figure 4.13. Set {0,2,3,5,7,8,11}, C = 0.

Frigyesi (1998: 255) states that, ultimately, the entire opera is built around these two themes: the pentatonic theme (A), and the "dolce-marcato" theme (B). Continuous transformations yield to a complex web of thematic relationships that bring them ever closer to each other and relate all the themes of the opera to them.

The thematic transformation (B') begins immediately (1/1–2/5) after the presentation of the dolce-marcato theme (B). As the score states (2/1–2): "*Hirtelen kinyílik fent a kis vasajtó és a vakító fehér négyszögben megjelenik a Kékszakállú és Judit fekete sziluettje.*" (Suddenly the small iron door at the head of the stairs is flung wide open, and in the dazzling white opening appear the black, silhouetted figures of Bluebeard and Judith.) The bass line of 1/2–2/1, G-sharp–B-flat–D-flat, forms set {0,2,5}, as shown in Figure 4.14.

Figure 4.14. Set {0,2,5}, G# = 0.

The chord progression of the opening "Night" scene's (B') actually summarizes a number of semitone relations that occur throughout the piece. It should be noted that the exchange of chromatic dyads is a familiar occurrence in traditional tonal music, serving to prolong a single harmonic function. (See also, Chapters 4.4.3–4.4.11 for a more detailed analysis of such reasons.) In the second statement of the "menacing" motif, the pitch collection is further chromatized by the addition of C-sharp (2/4). The supporting whole-tone bass motion (1/1–2/3), D–C–B-flat/A-sharp–G-sharp, set {0,2,4,6,8} (G-sharp = 0; Figure 4.15, below) becomes chromatic (2/3–5), G-sharp–G–F-sharp, set {0,1,2} (F-sharp = 0; Figure 4.16, next page).

4				
	0		6	
2		8		

Figure 4.15. Set {0,2,4,6,8}, G# = 0.

Figure 4.16. Set {0,1,2}, F# = 0.

Frigyesi considers *Bluebeard* as the result of two main elements:

> Bartók's decision to derive the vocal lines from the old-style folk songs, and the material of the orchestra from the type of the Hungarian instrumental pastorale, solved in one stroke the problem of national music and the problem of modernity in opera. The choice of the Hungarian pastorale for the orchestral materials was a logical solution that nevertheless allowed him to create a new type of dramatic music. Transforming the pastorale from a light intermezzo-like movement to a dramatic form, thus pulling it to the center from its peripheral place in the repertoire, allowed Bartók to break with the romantic tradition in several respects. (Frigyesi 1998: 236.)

4.4.3. 'Exposition'

In *Bluebeard's Castle*, a substantial scene precedes the actual door scenes – sometimes referred as an "Exposition", "Prelude," or "Introduction" (2/6–29/11) by different scholars (Leafstedt 1999: 56; Lendvai 1964: 70; and Kroó 1993: 356). It sets forth the background information about the two characters and their relationship to each other. The three sections of the "Exposition" (Table 4.7, below) differ in tempo, texture, phrase structure, tonality, and technique of musical development, and they represent different types of dramatic events.

Section	Rehearsal/measure numbers	Synopsis
A	2/5–7/11	Arrival at the castle; ends when iron door closes
B	8/1–20/17	Judith vows loyalty to Bluebeard
C	21/1–29/11	Discovery of the castle's seven locked doors Judith obtains the first key

Table 4.7. Structure of the "Exposition", 2/5–29/11.

Section A contains the first of three dramatic actions that function as an introduction to the seven door-scenes. Bluebeard embraces Judith (7/1), and then orders the closing of the door to the outside world (7/10–11), leaving Bluebeard and Judith together in the darkness.

At Bluebeard's first words, "We have arrived" (2/5), the music melts back into F-sharp. Bluebeard's recitative (2/5–14) starts with a progressive modal elaboration of the pentatonic scale, D–F–G–A–C (Example 4.2; set type shown in Figure 4.17).

Example 4.2. Bluebeard's recitative in the "Exposition", 2/5–14.
© 1921 by Universal Edition A. G., Wien/UE 7026, used by kind permission.

	5
7	10
0	3

Figure 4.17. Set {0,3,5,7,10}, D = 0.

The music gradually introduces semitones, which are the basic means of producing tension as Bluebeard and Judith enter the castle. In the opening instrumental punctuation (2/6–7), the lower strings present the first prominent statement of isolated semitones, D–D-sharp–F–F-sharp, shown as set {0,1,3,4} in Figure 4.18.

Figure 4.18. Set {0,1,3,4}, D = 0.

The dramatic representation of two conflicting voices during the first moments is made more pronounced by the difference between pentatonic and acoustic harmonies (2/5–3/2). Judith's first lines are described schematically in Table 4.8 (below) and Figures 4.19–4.20 (next page).

Rehearsal/ measure numbers	Text	Pitch classes	Point 0	Integers	Forte number	ICV
3/1–2	"*Megyek, megyek, Kékszakállú!*" (Coming, coming, dearest Bluebeard!)	F–D-flat–A–G-flat	F	{0,1,4,8}	4–19	101310
4/3–4	"*Megyek, megyek, Kékszakállú!*" (Coming, coming, dearest Bluebeard!)	F–E-flat–D–B	F	{0,2,3,6}	4–12	112101

Table 4.8. Judith's lines, 3/1–2 and 4/3–4.

Figure 4.19. Set {0,1,4,8}.

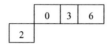

Figure 4.20. Set {0,2,3,6}.

Judith's first line is reminiscent of what some scholars have called the descending "Stefi" or "Geyer" motif (Ujfalussy 1987: 87),[405] which Bartók first developed in his *Bagatelle* (Op. 6, No. 13). That *Leitmotiv* consists of the notes C-sharp–E–G-sharp–B-sharp, which together form a hyperminor chord, or set {0,1,4,8}, B-sharp = 0 (on that chord, see pp. 63–64, Chapter 2.2.2). A letter that Bartók wrote to Stefi Geyer contains the motif bearing her name, as shown in Example 4.3 (Demény, ed. 1971: 81).

Example 4.3. Stefi motif in Bartók's *Bagatelle* (Op. 6, No. 13). "Elle est morte."

Bartók employed the Stefi motif extensively in his compositions written from 1907 on. This motif forms a basic element of *Bluebeard's Castle*, where it appears many times, in various forms and transpositions (Leafstedt 1999: 81–82; and Lindlar 1984: 102). For example, when Judith sings Bluebeard's name, "*Kékszakállú,*" for the first time (3/2), her melody outlines F–G-flat–A–D-flat, set {0,1,4,8}, F = 0 (Example 4.4).

Example 4.4. "*Kékszakállú,*" 3/2.
© 1921 by Universal Edition A. G., Wien/UE 7026, used by kind permission.

---

405. My thanks to Professor Robert Hatten for pointing out the resemblance between Judith's line and the Stefi motif. Bartók got to know and became enamored of Stefi Geyer in 1907; a child prodigy from the violin school of Hubay (a pupil of Joachim), she later became a famous virtuoso violinist. Geyer did not return his affection, however, and Bartók was so deeply shaken that he had no contact with her for many years (Demény, ed. 1976: 129–131).

Throughout the opera, Judith's motto-like repetitions of Bluebeard's name respect the stress patterns and intonation of the word in spoken Hungarian (cf. pp. 158–159, Chapter 3.5.1). The first syllable is emphasized through longer rhythmic duration and higher pitch, and the metrically unaccented second syllable commences the melodic descent from the initial pitch, often on a weak beat. The remaining syllables of the name then tumble downward stepwise or by larger intervals.[406]

Theme (B), the menacing motif, from the "Night" scene, reappears at 4/5–5/1 (see also, 25/4 and 25/6). When Judith tries to conceal her inner nervousness, she reverts to the pentatonic figures in Bluebeard's part, as displayed in Table 4.9 and Figures 4.21–4.23.

Rehearsal/ measure numbers	Character	Pitch classes	Point 0	Integers
5/1–2	Bluebeard	A–F-sharp	F-sharp	{0,3}
5/3–7	Judith	D–E–F-sharp–G–A–B–C-sharp	D	{0,2,4,5,7,9,11}
6/1–9	Judith	D–E–F-sharp–G–A–C	D	{0,2,4,5,7,10}

Table 4.9. Bluebeard's and Judith's lines, 5/1–6/9.

Figure 4.21. Set {0,3}.

11	2	5
4	7	
9	0	

Figure 4.22. Set {0,2,4,5,7,9,11}.

	2	5
4	7	10
	0	

Figure 4.23. Set {0,2,4,5,7,10}.

After the dialogue in which Bluebeard provokes Judith to express her devotion (3/6–6/14), there is a tonal development from D major (7/1–6) toward a quasi-dominant-tonic closure, C-sharp to F-sharp (7/10–11). The F-sharp acts as a pivotal pitch (common tone) to D-sharp minor pentatonic, the tonality of the first part of the following scene. At the beginning of Section B, the little iron door shuts (8/1–2); according to the stage direction, "the hall is only bright enough for the two figures and

---

406. E.g., see 4/4, 5/10, 6/9, 11/2, 12/3–4, 14/4–5, 16/7–17/4, 20/11, and 24/11 in the "Exposition" scene.

the seven huge black doors to be just visible" (8/1–7), and Judith tries to orient herself in the darkness (Example 4.5). Judith's pentatonic *parlando* line is assimilated to the D-sharp pentatonic ostinato.

Example 4.5. Judith's vocal line, 9/1–2.
© 1921 by Universal Edition A. G., Wien/UE 7026, used by kind permission.

Her vocal lines add nothing tonally or rhythmically essential to the background ostinato (Table 4.10 and Figures 4.24–4.32, below; see also, Example 4.5, above).

Rehearsal/ measure numbers	Pitch classes	Point 0	Integers
8/7–10/1	D-sharp–F-sharp–G-sharp–A-sharp–C-sharp	D-sharp	{0,3,5,7,10}
10/2	D-sharp–E-sharp–A-sharp–C-sharp	D-sharp	{0,2,7,10}
10/3	F-sharp–E-sharp–D-sharp–C-sharp–B	F-sharp	{0,1,3,5,7}
10/4	F-sharp–F–D-sharp–B	F-sharp	{0,1,3,7}
10/6–9 (= 8/7–10/1)	D-sharp–F-sharp–G-sharp–A-sharp–C-sharp	D-sharp	{0,3,5,7,10}
10/10–11	D-sharp–G-sharp–A-sharp–C-sharp	D-sharp	{0,5,7,10}
10/12	D-sharp–E-sharp–G-sharp–A-sharp–B–C-sharp	D-sharp	{0,2,5,7,8,10}
11/1–2	F-sharp–A–B–C-sharp–E-sharp	F-sharp	{0,3,5,7,11}
11/3–4	F-sharp–A–B–B-sharp–C-sharp–E-sharp	F-sharp	{0,3,5,6,7,11}
11/5–8	F-sharp–G–A-sharp–B–C-sharp–D	F-sharp	{0,1,4,5,7,8}

Table 4.10. Background ostinato, 8/7–11/8.

	5
7	10
0	3

Figure 4.24. Set {0,3,5,7,10}.

Figure 4.25. Set {0,2,7,10}.

Figure 4.26. Set {0,1,3,5,7}.

Figure 4.27. Set {0,1,3,7}.

Figure 4.28. Set {0,5,7,10}.

Figure 4.29. Set {0,2,5,7,8,10}.

Figure 4.30. Set {0,3,5,7,11}.

Figure 4.31. Set {0,3,5,6,7,11}.

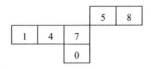

Figure 4.32. Set {0,1,4,5,7,8}.

The more emotional Judith becomes, the sharper her voice contrasts with that of Bluebeard. As long as she restricts herself to echoing the ostinato of the castle, Bluebeard remains in the background, simply repeating Judith's words (9/6, 9, 12–13). At the text "*Ki ezt látná, jaj, nem szólna, suttogó hír elhalkulna*" (Whoever sees this ought not to speak of it; whispering rumors should fade away), Judith comes forward (10/1–4), her melodic line outlining D-sharp–G-sharp–A-sharp (see Figure 4.33, below). The larger intervals and ornaments of her melody lend it an emotional quality suggestive of the dramatic presentation of a ballad.

Figure 4.33. Set {0,5,7}, D# = 0.

In the next phrase (10/8–9), Judith remarks on the darkness, "*Milyen sötét a te várad!*" (How dark is your castle!) Groping to find her way, Judith discovers that the walls are sweating. Judith's melody opens up the framework of the ostinato, by adding the note A, which leads the music toward a new tonality (Table 4.11 and Figure 4.34).

Rehearsal/ measure numbers	Pitch classes	Point 0	Integers
11/1–2	B–D–E-sharp–A	B	{0,3,6,10}
11/3–4	B–A–F-sharp–E-sharp–D–C-sharp	B	{0,2,5,6,9,10}
11/5–6	B–C-sharp	B	{0,2}
11/7–8	B–G–E–C-sharp	B	{0,4,7,10}

Table 4.11. Judith's vocal lines, 11/1–8.

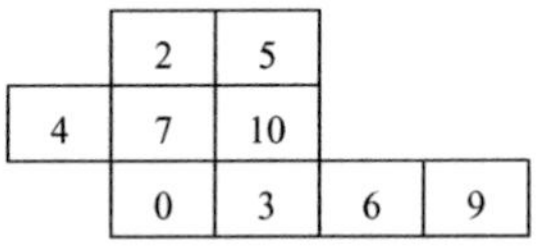

Figure 4.34. Set {0,2,3,4,5,6,7,9,10}.

Judith interprets the dampness as tears that the castle sheds in sorrow: "Your castle is weeping! Your castle is weeping!" (11/5–8), and the pentatonic melody is replaced by descending motives (Table 4.11, previous page). These melodic changes are paralleled by the gradual change of the even eighth-notes into a double-dotted rhythmic pattern (11/5, 7). For the first time, the main *Leitmotiv* of the opera, the Blood motif, is introduced in the context of tears. Its emblematic dissonance (the minor second, here, G#/A) sounds in the horns, then is repeated an octave higher in the oboes and flutes (11/1–3). In anticipation of blood, the minor seconds begin to multiply (10/1–11/3): G-sharp–A–A-sharp–B, emerging with increasing prominence from the modal thematic material and becoming a foreground event (Figure 4.35).

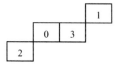

Figure 4.35. Set {0,1,2,3}, G# = 0.

When Judith's singing becomes more impassioned, Bluebeard repeatedly interrupts her, trying to pull her back to the level of simple *rubato*. When he speaks the ostinato halts, the tempo slows, and the steady flow of eighth-notes returns (11/9–16). Bluebeard's melody outlines the notes of the G-Dorian mode (Figure 4.36, below), accompanied by the orchestra playing triads in succession: G major, F major, C major, and B major (11/9–16).

2			
7	10		
0	3	6	9

Figure 4.36. Set {0,2,3,6,7,9,10}, G = 0.

Judith vows to dry the dripping stones, open up Bluebeard's castle, and let in the sun and the wind (15/2–19/4). The harmonic basis of 17/5–18/4 is a minor chord with a raised seventh (C-sharp–E–G-sharp–B-sharp), set {0,1,4,8}, B-sharp = 0. This chord connects two tonal centers, bringing them into a close relationship with the F-sharp tonality of the castle (C-sharp = V) and with C (= B-sharp), the symbol of light (Lendvai 1988: 142; see also, p. 192, Chapter 4.3)[407] – its polar opposite on the same axis. It is significant that the notes C–D–E appear on the text "light shall enter" (18/8–9), emphasizing the symbol of light in Judith's (not Bluebeard's) part. Bluebeard's response – "My castle is not bright" (19/6–7) – brings forth an ornamented variant of the clarinet melody, now played by the English horn (19/9–20/16). Both the pentatonic accompaniment and the melody emphasize the C major sonority, now

---

407. I thank Professor Eero Tarasti for informing me of Lendvai's (1988) book, *Verdi and Wagner*.

with an added G-sharp to make it even brighter (19/3). A few measures later, C becomes the pedal point of the lengthy cadence to this dramatic dialogue (20/7–13).

At the beginning of Section C (21/1–29/1), Judith discovers seven closed doors: "*Nagy csukott ajtókat látok. Hét fekete csukott ajtót!*" (Large closed doors I see. Seven black, closed doors!) She asks Bluebeard to open them, and begins pounding on the first with her fists (23/13–14).

The castle, as if a living creature, sighs four times[408] during the opera, always in the context of Judith approaching or opening a new door (23/14, 29/9–10, 90/8–9, 120/3–5). The musical passage from 24/1 to 27/2 strongly projects both hypermajor and hyperminor tonalities (see Table 4.12, next page and Figures 4.37–4.38, below).

Figure 4.37. Set {0,1,4,8}.

Figure 4.38. Set {0,1,5,8}.

The clarinet theme is a slow-moving lament, the main notes of which are encircled by shorter ornamental ones (24/3–11), a melodic type that comes from the Hungarian tradition and is associated with *verbunkos*. When that lament theme first occurs, it is superposed on the F-sharp pentatonic melody that began the opera (Example 4.1, p. 204, Chapter 4.4.1), played here by the strings. The clarinet ornaments the melodic essence of the first half of the pentatonic theme by emphasizing its main notes: by duration and/or by metrical accent (24/1–25/2): E–F-sharp–E–C-sharp–B – C-sharp, the set type of which is shown in Figure 4.39 (below). As the scene proceeds, the lament character gradually gives place to that of the pastoral (27/6–28/3, 28/5–29/6).

Figure 4.39. Set {0,2,5,7}, C# = 0.

Bartók reuses the Stefi motif (28/3), now as a D-flat hyperminor chord in first inversion, to underline Judith's exclamation, "because I love you!" (Figure 4.40).

---

408. Performed by an off-stage mixed choir.

Rehearsal/ measure numbers	Pitch classes	Chord	Point 0	Integers	Forte number	ICV
24/1	E–C–A-flat–F	Hyperminor	E	{0,1,4,8}	4–19	101310
24/2	A-flat–E–C-sharp–A	Hyperminor	A-flat	{0,1,4,8}	4–19	101310
24/11	D–F-sharp–A–C-sharp	Hypermajor	C-sharp	{0,1,5,8}	4–20 (12)	101220
26/1–2	A–C–E–G-sharp	Hyperminor	G-sharp	{0,1,4,8}	4–19	101310
26/3	F–A-flat–C–E	Hyperminor	E	{0,1,4,8}	4–19	101310
26/4	F–A–C–E	Hypermajor	E	{0,1,5,8}	4–20 (12)	101220
26/5–6	C-sharp–E–G-sharp–B-sharp	Hyperminor	B-sharp	{0,1,4,8}	4–19	101310
26/7–8	C-sharp–E–G-sharp–C	Hyperminor	C	{0,1,4,8}	4–19	101310
27/1–2	G-flat–B-flat–D-flat–F	Hypermajor	F	{0,1,5,8}	4–20 (12)	101220

Table 4.12. Sets {0,1,4,8} and {0,1,5,8}, 24/1–27/2.

Figure 4.40. Set {0,2,7,9}, B♭ = 0.

Reluctantly, Bluebeard gives her the key to the first door (29/1–11). When moments later she unlocks it, the castle heaves "deep, heavy sighs" as indicated in the stage directions. At that point (29/9–10), Bartók introduces the Sigh motif, a musical idea that will reappear several times in the opera: a rapidly oscillating pattern of four 32nd notes followed by a longer rhythmic value, all in adjacent half steps – music that embodies the effort of sighing (Table 4.13 and Figures 4.41–4.42).

Rehearsal/ measure numbers	Pitch classes	Point 0	Integers	Forte number	ICV
29/9	D–C-sharp–C	C	{0,1,2}	3–1 (12)	210000
29/10	E-flat–D-flat–C	C	{0,1,3}	3–2	111000

Table 4.13. Sigh motif, 29/9–10.

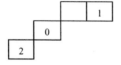

Figure 4.41. Set {0,1,2}.

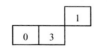

Figure 4.42. Set {0,1,3}.

4.4.4. First door: 'Torture Chamber'

The "First Door" scene may be divided into a large-scale ternary design (after Veress 1949: 34). Table 4.14 (next page) displays the structure of that scene, with subsections determined by changes in the tempo and other musical parameters; subsections are identified by lower-case letters (a, b, c).[409]

Music of the opening section, depicting the torture chamber, is brought back in condensed form to conclude the scene (Example 4.6, below). The result is a modified ternary form, represented schematically as A–B–A'.

The beginning of section A (30/1–37/3) corresponds to the dramatic action on stage, when Judith and Bluebeard describe the torture chamber and the beam of red light emanating from the door. Section B (37/4–40/4) corresponds to Judith's request that all the other doors in the castle be opened. Bartók's music traces the changing dramatic focus, away from the torture chamber, back to Bluebeard and Judith. The final section A' (40/5–42/4) begins when Bluebeard asks Judith why she wants to open the other doors: "*Judit, Judit mért akarod?*" (Judith, tell me, why do you want to do it?) She responds, "*Mert szeretlek!*" (Because I love you!) (40/6–7).

The scene opens, with a jarring, dissonant orchestral representation of the first room's content (Example 4.6).

Example 4.6. "First Door" scene's opening, 30/1–31/1.

---

409. The "First Door" scene, unlike others, was heavily revised by the composer: the woodwind figuration was altered, and a new part for keyboard xylophone was added (Leafstedt 1999: 125).

Section	Rehearsal/ measure numbers	Synopsis	Sub-sections
A	30/1–32/3	*Sostenuto.* Door opens. Orchestral "description" of torture chamber.	a
	33/1–33/7	*Più mosso.* Trills develop in melody as Judith describes the room's contents.	b
	34/1–35/7	*Andante.* Blood motif sounds, new clarinet melody, Bluebeard asks Judith if she is afraid.	c
	36/1–37/3	*Più mosso.* Discussion of the light's meaning. Music returns to previous material (b).	b
B	37/4–40/4	*Molto andante.* Clarinet melody transformed and developed at quicker tempo. Judith demands that all doors be opened.	c
A'	40/5–40/13	*Sostenuto.* Sudden return to blood motif and clarinet melody at slower tempo.	[c]
	41/1–42/4	*Più sostenuto.* Return of dissonant chords from the opening. Bluebeard warns Judith about the castle.	[a]

Table 4.14. Structure of the "First Door" scene, 30/1–42/4.

Through procedures of variation and thematic transformation, Bartók extends the opening music to cover the whole section.[410] An excruciatingly acute A-sharp/B tremolo occupies the upper strings and clarinet, combined with irregularly placed gestures in the xylophone and woodwinds (Example 4.6, previous page; see also, Table 4.15 and Figures 4.43–4.46, next page).

---

410. Raymond Monelle (1968) discusses Bartók's techniques of variation and thematic transformation in the *Fourth Quartet*, stressing the importance of the organic growth and progressive clarification of material in that work.

Rehearsal/ measure numbers	Pitch classes	Point 0	Integers
30/2	A-sharp–B–C–D–E	A-sharp	{0,1,2,4,6}
30/3	A-sharp–B-sharp–C-double-sharp–D-double-sharp–E-sharp	A-sharp	{0,2,4,6,7}
30/4	A-sharp–B–C–D–E	A-sharp	{0,1,2,4,6}
30/5	A-sharp–B-sharp–C-double-sharp–D-double-sharp–E-sharp	A-sharp	{0,2,4,6,7}
31/1	A-sharp–B–C–D–E A-sharp–G-sharp–F-sharp–E-sharp	A-sharp A-sharp	{0,1,2,4,6} {0,2,4,5}
31/2	A-sharp–B–C–D–E A-sharp–G-sharp–F-sharp–E-sharp	A-sharp A-sharp	{0,1,2,4,6} {0,2,4,5}
31/3	A-sharp–B-sharp–C-double-sharp–D-double-sharp–E-sharp A-sharp–G-sharp–F-sharp–E-sharp	A-sharp A-sharp	{0,2,4,6,7} {0,2,4,5}
31/4	A-sharp–B–C–D–E F-sharp–G-sharp–A-sharp–B A-sharp–B-sharp–C-double-sharp–D-double-sharp–E-sharp	A-sharp F-sharp A-sharp	{0,1,2,4,6} {0,2,4,5} {0,2,4,6,7}
31/5	F-sharp–G-sharp–A-sharp–B–C A-sharp–B–C–D–E	F-sharp A-sharp	{0,2,4,5,6} {0,1,2,4,6}
31/6	A-sharp–B–C–D–E F-sharp–G-sharp–A-sharp–B A-sharp–B-sharp–C-double-sharp–D-double-sharp–E-sharp	A-sharp F-sharp A-sharp	{0,1,2,4,6} {0,2,4,5} {0,2,4,6,7}

Table 4.15. Orchestral arpeggios, 30/1–31/6.

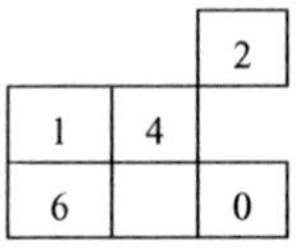

Figure 4.43. Set {0,1,2,4,6}.

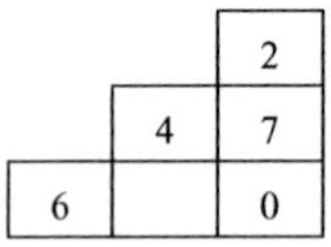

Figure 4.44. Set {0,2,4,6,7}.

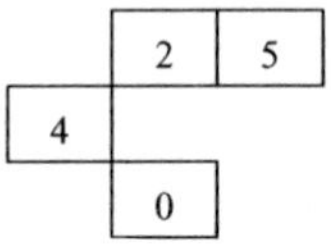

Figure 4.45. Set {0,2,4,5}.

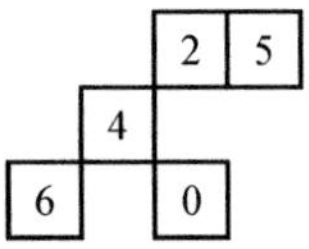

Figure 4.46. Set {0,2,4,5,6}.

The B/A-sharp tremolo and rapid gestures of the opening music combine to form a new melodic line with a contrasting rhythmic pattern. At 31/1–5, the strings and harp pluck a series of violent, atonal chord clusters whose upper pitches F-sharp–G-sharp–A-sharp–C-sharp–D-sharp trace an F-sharp pentatonic line (Figure 4.47).

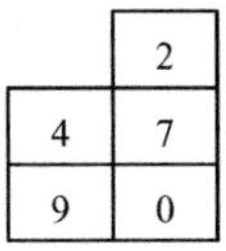

	2
4	7
9	0

Figure 4.47. Set {0,2,4,7,9}, F# = 0.

Bluebeard asks Judith (30/4, 6), "*Mit látsz? Mit látsz?*" (What do you see? What do you see?) as the Blood motif sounds in the muted trumpets (31/4–32/2). The F-sharp pentatony and the C counterpole of the Blood motif together form set {0,6}. This figure, with its underlying chordal melody, is derived from elements of "a" (30/1–32/3). Judith begins to describe the torture chamber, which is not visible to the audience (32/1–33/1): "*Láncok, kések, szöges karók, izzó nyársak*" (Shackles, daggers, racks and pincers, branding irons).

Section "b" is closely associated with the characteristic accompaniment figure (33/1–33/7), which Bartók presents as an ostinato that rises and falls repeatedly over the next few minutes of music, ceasing abruptly when the Blood motif asserts itself (34/1–35/7). Its rhythm, pitch boundaries (E-sharp/E), and orientation around a central A-sharp/B dyad reveal it to be a transformation of an earlier gesture in the winds and xylophone. Together, E–E-sharp–A-sharp–B form the set displayed in Figure 4.48.

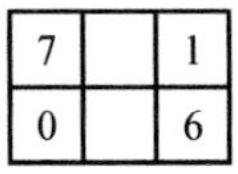

7		1
0		6

Figure 4.48. Set {0,1,6,7}, B = 0.

What was formerly foreground thematic material now moves to the background, becoming an accompaniment figure woven together by motivic gestures from the very opening of the scene. In 33/1–34/1, the whole-tone scale segment, {0,2,4,6}, which contributed to the atonal nature of the beginning, is now extended by a whole-step, creating set {0,2,6,8} in the harmony (Figures 4.49 and 4.50, respectively).

Figure 4.49. Set {0,2,4,6}, A# = 0.

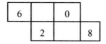

Figure 4.50. Set {0,2,6,8}.

In section "c", 34/1–35/7, a new musical idea is introduced in the quasi-pentatonic melody on the words "*A te várad fala véres! A te várad vérzik! Véres... vérzik... Félsz-e?*" (Your castle walls are blood-stained! Look, the walls are bleeding... Bleeding... bleeding... Are you afraid?) (see Example 1.2, p. 8, Chapter 1). The first explicit mention of blood in the opera occurs, not surprisingly, in the "Torture Chamber" scene, as the minor-second Blood motif is played by clarinets and muted trumpets (34/1–35/1).

At the return of the menacing motif (34/5–6), the G-sharp–A/A-sharp–B pairings of semitones, X cell, set {0,1,2,3}, appear as basic local details in the larger thematic statement (Example 1.2, p. 8, Chapter 1). The X cell, constructed of adjacent semitones, is divorced from any traditional modal construction. Antokoletz (1984: 92) remarks that in *Bluebeard's Castle*, the X cells generally appear as part of larger modal or polymodal thematic material (Figure 4.51).

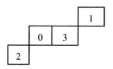

Figure 4.51. Set {0,1,2,3}.

In 36/1–37/3, the music returns to previous material (b). Judith discusses the meaning of light: "*Nem! Nem félek. Nézd, derül már. Ugye derül? Nézd ezt a fényt. Látod? Szép fénypatak!*" (No. I am not afraid. See, morning breaks! Crimson sunrise! Behold the light. Look there, lovely radiance!)[411] Judith's vocal melody outlines an E hypermajor chord: E–G-sharp–B–D-sharp, and the orchestra at 36/7 plays B hypermajor.

The scherzo-like middle of the "First Door" scene, section B (37/4–40/5), is characterized by a quicker tempo, a lighter texture, and a fleeting rhythmic diminution of the clarinet melody heard earlier in the scene.

_____

411. Christopher Hassall's translation (Bartók 1952 [1925]: 49) of this line is two syllables longer than the Hungarian phrase (36/7). In many cases, the translator does not preserve the octosyllabic content of each line.

The third and final section of the scene, A' (40/5–42/4), grows out of the moment established in section B. Nearly all the music of this final section is derived from music heard earlier in the scene. The recollection of melodic and harmonic ideas occurs in reverse order from their initial appearance, suggesting a possible symmetrical structure for the scene. In 40/1–4, a chain of tertian harmony is sustained in the orchestra: (G)–B–D–F–A–(C)–E, which forms the major-scale set {0,2,4,5,7,9,11}, with C = 0 (Figure 4.52).

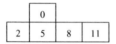

Figure 4.52. Set {0,2,4,5,7,9,11}.

The A-sharp/B tremolo returns (40/5), accompanied this time by two half-note chords that evoke the rhythm, if not the pitch content, of the Blood motif first presented in "c". The last sonority in the scene (41/10) is a solitary plucked chord, G–A–C-sharp–D-sharp–F-sharp, played under the A-sharp/B trill in the flutes; it is the same sonority with which the scene began (set type shown in Figure 4.53).

	0		
2	5	8	11

Figure 4.53. Set {0,2,5,8,11}.

The harsh world of the torture chamber lies behind Judith and Bluebeard, and the musical material that originally was presented in a strongly atonal context now develops tonal implications in section A' (40/5–42/4). The first nine measures of section A' (40/5–13) sustain a single vertical sonority constructed of interlocking major and minor thirds. Against this diatonic sound – the pitches form a gapped C major scale – a dissonant counterpoint is formed by the A-sharp/B tremolo and chromatic line of the double-dotted melody. Bluebeard's final quatrain is accompanied by a descending sequence of the open fifths on G-sharp, E, and, finally C-sharp (41/1–9). The G-sharp–E–C-sharp root motion, evident in the orchestra at this point, alludes to C-sharp minor, although it does not functionally establish that key. As Veress (1949–1950: 31) has stated, the "First Door" scene is "maintained in the tonalities C-sharp–G-sharp, but with sharp harmonic deviations". Triadic or pentatonic harmonies outlined in the vocal part reinforce the dominant–tonic relationship between G-sharp and C-sharp. By asserting the pitch C-sharp as an arrival point, Bartók gives the music a sense of tonality that, in retrospect, can be seen to govern much of the preceding music. Emphasis on G-sharp occurs in the scene, where it alternates with C-sharp to form the important structural pitches of the chord progression (36/1–37/3).

Triadic harmonies underlie the entire last section of the "First Door" scene (41/5–9): C-sharp–E–G-sharp–B–D-sharp–F-sharp–A-sharp. At the end of the scene, Judith sings: "*Szépen, halkan fogom nyitni. Szépen, halkan.*" (I will open gently, very softly.) Bartók brings back the pastoral music associated with that text, further rounding the scene's form by material from Section A. As the tremolo dies away in the flutes, woodwinds and trumpets sound a brisk tattoo (41/10–42/5). The "First Door" scene will strongly influence Judith and Bluebeard's actions as the opera proceeds.

4.4.5. Second door: 'Armory'

Scenes such as Door 1, "Torture Chamber" (30/1–42/4) and Door 2, "Armory" (42/5–53/9) may consist of outwardly unrelated materials, yet reveal themselves to have almost identical dramatic structure, such that the characters respond first to the content behind the door, and then to each other (comp. Table 4.14, p. 221, Chapter 4.4.4 and Table 4.16, below). Three distinct sections can be observed in the "Armory" scene:

Section	Rehearsal/ measure numbers	Synopsis
A	42/5–45/11	Musical description of the "Armory". Judith and Bluebeard's dialogue.
B	45/12–49/9	Judith demands additional keys. Bluebeard responds. The dialogue that ensues injects a momentary note of warmth.
C	50/1–53/9	Bluebeard's aria – a quasi-strophic passage. He offers Judith the next three keys, warning her to ask no questions.

Table 4.16. Structure of the "Armory" scene, 42/5–53/9.

When the door opens, "the aperture is of a yellowish red color, somber, and disturbing to behold. The second beam of light lies on the floor alongside the first" (42/5–6). It cuts into the darkness and reveals to Judith a hall of blood-encrusted weapons. Judith responds (42/10–43/2): "*Száz kegyetlen szörnyű fegyver, sok rettentő hadi szerszám!*" (Piles of cruel arms and armors, countless, fearful battle weapons!) Her melody outlines the set shown in Figure 4.54.

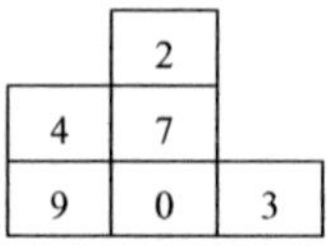

	2	
4	7	
9	0	3

Figure 4.54. Set {0,2,3,4,7,9}, F# = 0.

Numerous details reveal new ideas to be continuations of previously introduced thematic material. A tendency toward thematic concentration is discernible throughout the music of *Bluebeard's Castle*. Using small rhythmic and melodic ideas, Bartók sometimes generates entire passages of music, in something like a Lisztian thematic transformation process (Réti[412] 1951: 311–318); at other times, he has a more personalized way of creating harmonic or melodic variations of an original idea. A given musical idea, once introduced, grows and evolves over the course of the dramatic action in a scene, or across the opera as a whole. It may be repeated at different pitch levels, reharmonized, augmented or diminished rhythmically, varied in gestural shape, or its basic, unrhythmicized interval content projected onto the musical structure. One facet of this technique can be seen in Bartók's transformation of the martial principal theme (42/7) of the "Second Door" scene into an expressively lyrical melody (46/1–2):

1. mirror-motion figures in the winds;
2. a staccato theme presented first in the trumpets.

Those two ideas share certain intervallic properties (42/5–44/3), and with them Bartók depicts the tools of war by writing a march for a small complement of winds and brass. The mirror-motion decorative figure ("military theme") in the uppermost winds outlines the diatonic hexachord B–C-sharp–D-sharp–E–F-sharp–G-sharp, shown in set form in Figure 4.55.

		2	5
	4	7	
	9	0	

Figure 4.55. Set {0,2,4,5,7,9}, B = 0.

The character of the music changes when Judith requests the keys to the remaining doors. The staccato rhythms of the opening idea (42/7), A-sharp–D-sharp–C-sharp, are lengthened to even quarter-notes and condensed into legato, overlapping phrases for the English horn and other woodwinds (Figure 4.56).

Figure 4.56. Set {0,2,5}, D# = 0.

The Blood motif intervenes in an extended tertian sonority (45/2–3). Through varied repetition of ascending and descending triads, comprising B–D-sharp–F-

---

412. In *The Thematic Process in Music*, Réti (1951) developed his distinctive analytic technique, which consists of taking short melodic motifs and tracing their repetition and development throughout a piece. In Réti's opinion, there are two form-creating forces in music. One is external, based on the segmentation and grouping of units on the manifest level; the other is internal, and relates to deeper thematic structures in music (ibid.: 138). In Réti's study, rhythm is completely ignored.

sharp–A-sharp–C-sharp (Figure 4.57, below), Bartók extends the themes through the first third of the scene, until Judith turns away from the door toward Bluebeard and the Blood motif appears.

Figure 4.57. Set {0,1,3,5,8}, A# = 0.

Judith cries, "*Vér szárad a fegyvereken. Véres a sok hadiszerszám*" (Blood dries on your weapons. Your many tools of war are bloody), but the sight of blood seems to strengthen her resolve (45/4–7). Her lines outline F-sharp–G-sharp–B–D–E–F, shown as a set type in Figure 4.58.

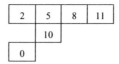

Figure 4.58. Set {0,2,5,8,10,11}, F# = 0.

The G-sharp/A dyad in 45/1–5 corresponds closely, in pitch content and rhythm, to the form it took at earlier appearances of the Blood motif.

Section B begins with Judith asking for additional keys (45/12). She follows the beam of light, rejoicing in the gradual dispelling of the castle's gloom (45/16–17). To accompany Judith's words, the orchestra recalls the dotted rhythms of the "Torture Chamber" scene (48/2–49/9, 51/7–12). The sentence "*Idejöttem, mert szeretlek*" (I came here, because I love you) is first spoken by Judith in the "Second Door" scene. Its essential clause, "*mert szeretlek*" (because I love you), recurs in various guises throughout the drama, most often as a means by which Judith obtains keys from Bluebeard.[413] Table 4.17 (below) and Figures 4.59–4.60 (next page) display the pitch content of Judith's lines in the passages just described.

Rehearsal/ measure numbers	Pitch classes	Point 0	Integers
48/3–5	C-sharp–D-sharp–A-sharp	A-sharp	{0,3,5}
51/8–9	F-sharp–A-sharp–C-sharp–D-sharp–E	F-sharp	{0,4,7,9,10}

Table 4.17. Judith's lines in 48/3–5 and 51/8–9.

---

413. See also, Judith's words before the opening of the first, second, and third doors: at 28/3, 40/6–7, and 51/9, respectively.

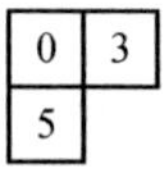

0	3
5	

Figure 4.59. Set {0,3,5}.

4	7	10
9	0	

Figure 4.60. Set {0,4,7,9,10}.

The orchestral accompaniment outlines a Dorian heptatonic scale (Table 4.18 and Figures 4.61–4.63).

Rehearsal/measure numbers	Pitch classes	Point 0	Integers
48/1	F–G–A–B–C–D–E	F	{0,2,4,6,7,9,11}
48/3–4	D-sharp–E-sharp–F-sharp–G-sharp–A-sharp–B-sharp–C-double-sharp	D-sharp	{0,2,3,5,7,9,11}
48/5–6	D-sharp–E-sharp–F-sharp–G-sharp–A-sharp–B-sharp–C-sharp	D-sharp	{0,2,3,5,7,9,10}
48/7–8	D-sharp–E-sharp–F-sharp–G-sharp–A-sharp–B-sharp–C-sharp	D-sharp	{0,2,3,5,7,9,10}
48/9–49/1	D-sharp–E-sharp–F-sharp–G-sharp–A-sharp–B-sharp–C-sharp	D-sharp	{0,2,3,5,7,9,10}

Table 4.18. Pitch content of orchestral accompaniment, 48/1–49/1.

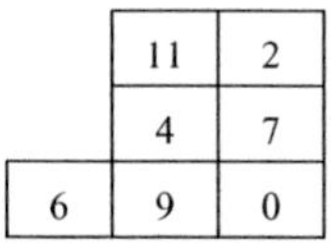

	11	2
	4	7
6	9	0

Figure 4.61. Set {0,2,4,6,7,9,11}.

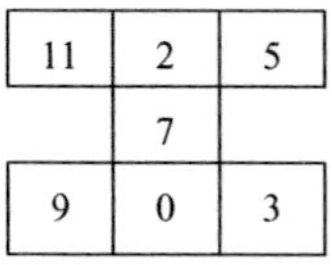

11	2	5
	7	
9	0	3

Figure 4.62. Set {0,2,3,5,7,9,11}.

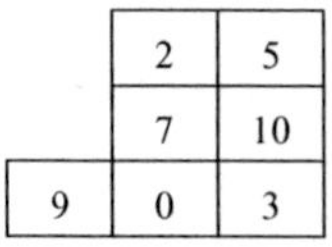

	2	5
	7	10
9	0	3

Figure 4.63. Set {0,2,3,5,7,9,10}.

Section C centers around Bluebeard's "arioso", during which he offers Judith the next three keys and warns her to ask no questions (48/1–52/13). In this quasi-strophic "arioso", accompanied by harp and solo horn, Bluebeard voices his mixed emotions of hope and uneasiness (50/3–51/5): "*Váram sötét köve reszket. Bús sziklából gyönyör borzong. Judit! Judit! Hűs és édes, nyitott sebből vér ha ömlik.*" (Through and through my castle trembles. Stones of sorrow thrill with rapture. Judith, Judith, cool and soothing is the blood that oozes freshly.) The Sigh motives of the orchestral accompaniment figures are analyzed in Table 4.19 and Figures 4.64–4.65.

Rehearsal/measure numbers	Pitch classes	Point 0	Integers
51/2	A–G–G-flat	A	{0,2,3}
51/3	C–B–B-flat	C	{0,1,2}
51/4	B-flat–A–A-flat	B-flat	{0,1,2}
51/5 (= 51/4)	B-flat–A–A-flat	B-flat	{0,1,2}
51/6 (= 51/4; 51/5)	B-flat–A–A-flat	B-flat	{0,1,2}

Table 4.19. The Sigh motif in 51/2–6.

Figure 4.64. Set {0,2,3}.

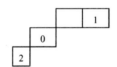

Figure 4.65. Set {0,1,2}.

Responding to Judith's urgency, reflected in her rising vocal line, Bluebeard gives her the keys to the next three doors (Table 4.20 and Figures 4.66–4.67).

Rehearsal/measure numbers	Pitch classes	Point 0	Integers
50/3–51/5	C–C-sharp–D–E–F–F-sharp–G–G-sharp–A–B-flat	C	{0,1,2,4,5,6,7,8,9,10}
52/3–10	C–C-sharp–D-sharp–E–F–G-sharp–B	C	{0,1,3,4,5,8,11}

Table 4.20. Pitch content of Bluebeard's vocal lines, 50/3–51/5 and 52/3–10.

2	5	8	
7	10	1	4
0		6	9

Figure 4.66. Set {0,1,2,4,5,6,7,8,9,10}.

	5	8	11
		1	4
0	3		

Figure 4.67. Set {0,1,3,4,5,8,11}.

Table 4.21 and Figures 4.68–4.71 display the pitch content of the brief transition section that leads to the next scene (the "Treasury").

Rehearsal/ measure numbers	Pitch classes	Point 0	Integers	Forte number	ICV
53/1–2	C–C-sharp–E–A-flat	C	{0,1,4,8}	4–19	101310
53/3–4	B–C-sharp–E-flat–F-sharp	B	{0,2,5,7}	4–23 (12)	021030
53/5–6	F–G–A–B-flat–C-sharp	F	{0,2,4,5,8}	5–26	122311
53/5–6	C-sharp–E–F-sharp–G-sharp–A	A	{0,1,3,5,8}	5–27	122230

Table 4.21. PCs, integers, Forte numbers, and ICVs; transitional passage, 53/1–9.

Figure 4.68. Set {0,1,4,8}.

2	5
7	
0	

Figure 4.69. Set {0,2,5,7}.

Figure 4.70. Set {0,2,4,5,8}.

Figure 4.71. Set {0,1,3,5,8}.

4.4.6. Third door: 'Treasury'

Bartók's greatest moments of originality in orchestration are seen in the radiance of the "Treasury" scene (54/1–59/9). In this "Third Door" scene, the D major triad, shown as a set in Figure 4.72, provides a tonal anchor for the scene's harmony, played by three trumpets, flutes, harp, celesta, and strings (54/1–59/5).

Figure 4.72. Set {0,4,7}, D = 0.

In the "Treasury" scene, small stage props provide visual confirmation of a door's contents. Bartók depicts the glittering surface qualities of the pearl, gold, and diamonds to emphasize their visual qualities. Veress (1949–1950: 32) writes that this scene has no "reflection music", only "character music" illustrating the door's content. Table 4.22 shows the structure of the "Third Door" scene, which is the shortest one in the opera.

Section	Rehearsal/ measure numbers	Synopsis
A	54/1–56/1	Judith's description of the treasury.
B	56/1–58/1	Bluebeard's response.
C	58/1–59/9	Blood on the treasures. Bluebeard urges Judith to proceed directly to the next door.

Table 4.22. Structure of "Third Door" scene, 54/1–59/9.

The audience sees only a golden beam of light emanating from behind the door (54/1–6), and against a sustained chord played by three trumpets, cello and flute tremolo (54/4–8), Judith cries out, "*Oh, be sok kincs! Oh, be sok kincs!*" (Mountains of gold! Mountains of gold!), her lines outlining the notes E–D–A (Figure 4.73).

Figure 4.73. Set {0,5,7}, A = 0.

According to the score directions, Judith "kneels down and digs into the pile of treasures, laying jewels, a crown and a luxurious cape on the threshold" (54/8–9).

Example 4.7. Judith's melodic lines, 55/2–10.
© 1921 by Universal Edition A. G., Wien/UE 7026, used by kind permission.

She describes the rich treasures that lie behind the opened door: "Golden coins and costly diamonds, lustrous jewelry encased in pearls, crowns, and splendid mantles" (Example 4.7). In describing this scene, Veress (1949–1950: 32) refers to "an effect of imaginary harmonics caused by the C–C-sharp and D–D-sharp". That X cell, shown in Figure 4.74, clashes with the other harmonies during the opening moments of the "Third Door" scene (see also, Example 4.7, above).

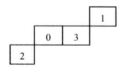

Figure 4.74. Set {0,1,2,3}.

Judith's melody, from 54/4 to 55/10, outlines the set C–C-sharp–D–D-sharp–E–F-sharp–G–A–B (Figure 4.75).

2			11
7		1	4
0	3	6	9

Figure 4.75. Set {0,1,2,3,4,6,7,9,11}, C = 0.

The individual pitches in Judith's first extended vocal line (Example 4.7, previous page) cohere into small, local patches of identifiable harmonic formations. These last are displayed in Table 4.23 and Figures 4.76–4.80.

Rehearsal/ measure numbers	Text in the score	Pitch classes	Point 0	Integers	Forte number	ICV
55/2–3	*"Aranypénz és drága gyémánt"* (Golden coins and costly diamonds)	A–C–C-sharp–E^3	A	{0,3,4,7}	4–17 (12)	102210
55/4	*Bélagyönggyel* (with pearls)	F-sharp–E–C-sharp–A	F-sharp	{0,3,7,10}	4–20 (12)	101220
55/5–6	*"fényes ékszer"* (lustrous jewelry)	C–B–E	B	{0,1,5}	3–4	100110
55/7	*"koronák"* (crowns)	C–E–G	C	{0,4,7}	–	–
55/8–10	*"és dús palástok"* (and a luxurious cape on the threshold)	B–C–D-sharp–F-sharp–A	B	{0,1,4,7,10}	–	–

Table 4.23. Local harmonic formations in Judith's line, 55/2–10.[414]

4	7

0	3

Figure 4.76. Set {0,3,4,7}.

7	10
0	3

Figure 4.77. Set {0,3,7,10}.

Figure 4.78. Set {0,1,5}.

Figure 4.79. Set {0,4,7}.

414. At 55/2–4, there is an oscillation between A major and A minor. The recurrence of certain pitches, 55/2–10, gradually asserts the bimodal triad A–C–C-sharp–E, set {0,3,4,7}, as the primary tonal focus.

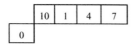

Figure 4.80. Set {0,1,4,7,10}.

Two solo violins play a substantial melodic role in this scene, acting as a third voice or refrain that echoes the dialogue between Judith and Bluebeard, just after a vocal line or partially overlapping it. The violins carry a single idea that is presented four times during the scene; it retains a consistent shape based on repeated downward gestures that expand in range upon each iteration (Table 4.24 and Figures 4.81–4.84).

Rehearsal/ measure numbers	Pitch classes	Point 0	Integers
54/8–11	C–D-sharp–E–F-sharp–G-sharp–A–B	C	{0,3,4,6,8,9,11}
55/9–56/1	C–D-sharp–E–F-sharp–G-sharp–A–A-sharp–B	C	{0,3,4,6,8,9,10,11}
56/7–57/1	C–C-sharp–D-sharp–E–F-sharp–F-double-sharp–G–G-sharp–A–A-sharp–B	C	{0,1,3,4,6,7,8,9,10,11}
57/6–10	C–C-sharp–D–D-sharp–E–F–F-sharp–F-dou-ble-sharp–G-sharp–A–A-sharp–B	C	{0,1,2,3,4,5,6,7,8,9,10,11}

Table 4.24. Instrumental refrain (violins) in "Treasury" scene.

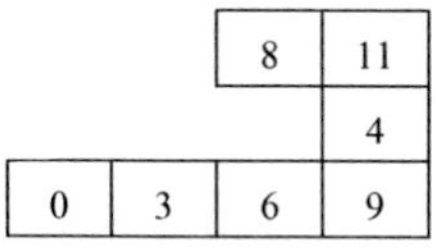

Figure 4.81. Set {0,3,4,6,8,9,11}.

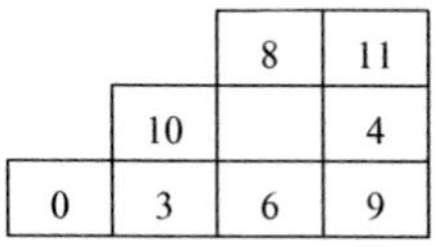

Figure 4.82. Set {0,3,4,6,8,9,10,11}.

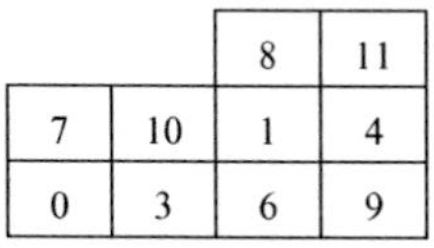

Figure 4.83. Set {0,1,3,4,6,7,8,9,10,11}.

2	5	8	11
7	10	1	4
0	3	6	9

Figure 4.84. Set {0,1,2,3,4,5,6,7,8,9,10,11}.

In 55/12, the orchestra plays D–D-sharp–F-sharp–A, set {0,1,4,7} (Figure 4.85) linking Section A and Section B.

1	4	7
		0

Figure 4.85. Set {0,1,4,7}, D = 0.

Lendvai has promulgated a hypothesis concerning the harmonic basis of the "Third Door" scene that has become absorbed into the mainstream literature about the opera. His overtone theory offers one way of explaining the modal inflections of the D major in the "Treasury" scene. According to Lendvai (1983: 223), the principal pitches in the scene are all derived from an acoustic (overtone) scale based on D, shown as a set type in Figure 4.86 (below). It is so called because a scale based on the overtone series extending through the first thirteen partials includes a sharp fourth degree (G-sharp) and a lowered (minor) seventh degree (C).

		2	
	4	7	10
6	9	0	

Figure 4.86. Set {0,2,4,6,7,9,10}, D = 0.

Lendvai's view that this altered D major provides the basic harmonic material for the "Treasury" scene seems to be substantiated by the orchestral accompaniment in Section B (56/1–58/1). When the horns enter, all the pitches combine to form part of the D-overtone series, with its characteristic raised (or "Lydian") fourth.

When Bluebeard tells Judith that all she beholds is hers (56/6–8), she replies: "*Mily gazdag vagy Kékszakállú!*" (How rich you are, Bluebeard!) Her melodic line constitutes a cadential passage that outlines the notes A–B–C–D-sharp–E–G (Figure 4.87).

2		
7	10	
0	3	6

Figure 4.87. Set {0,2,3,6,7,10}, A = 0.

At each appearance, the prevalence of certain pitches (such as G-sharp, A-sharp, B, D-sharp, and F-sharp) ambiguously implies certain keys, such as G-sharp minor or D-sharp pentatonic (56/1–58/1). Those intermingle with the main harmony, which is that of a sustained major-minor seventh chord (D–F-sharp–A–C), the set type of which is shown in Figure 4.88.

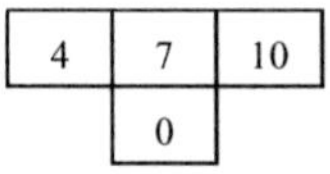

Figure 4.88. Set {0,4,7,10}, D = 0.

Over the D–F-sharp–A orchestral organ point (57/1–58/1), a canon takes place in the horns (G-sharp–E–C–A–D), altogether forming the scale C–D–E–F-sharp–G-sharp–A, shown as a set in Figure 4.89.

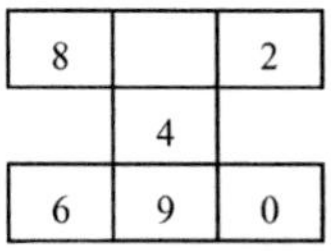

Figure 4.89. Set {0,2,4,6,8,9}, C = 0.

In Section C (58/1–59/9), the Blood motif makes an extended appearance, starting as a *sforzando* screech in the flutes and oboes. Judith notices spots of blood on the jewels and crowns (58/3–4; 59/1–2): "*Vérfolt van az ékszereken! Legszebbik koronád véres!*" (All your precious gems are blood-stained! Your brightest crown is blood-stained!) Judith's melody (B-flat–D-flat–G-flat) combines with that of the orchestral Blood motif, altogether forming the set {0,3,4,7}, as shown in Figure 4.90.

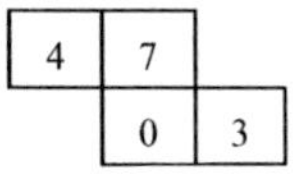

Figure 4.90. Set {0,3,4,7}, B♭ = 0.

The Blood motif intrudes again, at 58/1–59/5, where the orchestra plays D–F-sharp–A–B-flat (Figure 4.91).

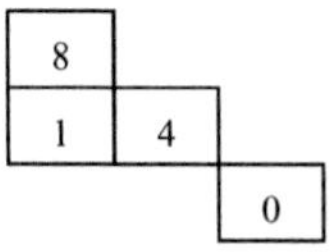

Figure 4.91. Set {0,1,4,8}, B♭ = 0.

Bluebeard sings exclusively in pentatonic modes, except at the end of the scene. Any discussion of the bloody crown's implications is forestalled when Bluebeard urges Judith to proceed directly to the next door (59/6–9). Bluebeard's last two (un-accompanied) lines are: "*Nyisd ki a negyedik ajtót. Legyen napfény, nyissad, nyissad...*" (Open now the fourth door. Bring the sunshine, open, open...) Bluebeard's melodic line there outlines yet another set featuring the raised, "Lydian" fourth: B-flat–C–D–E–F (Figure 4.92).

	2
4	7
6	0

Figure 4.92. Set {0,2,4,6,7}, B♭ = 0.

In the "Treasury" scene, Bluebeard and Judith sing some of their lines in purely anhemitonic (without semitones) pentatonic melodies, which are summarized in Table 4.25 (see also, Figure 4.93, below).

Character	Rehearsal/ measure numbers	The characters' lyrics	Scale	Set	Forte number	ICV
Judith	54/4–8	"*Oh, be sok kincs! Oh, be sok kincs!*" (Mountains of gold! Mountains of gold!)	A-pentatonic	{0,2,4,7,9}	5–35	932140
Bluebeard	56/4–6	"*Ez a váram kincsesháza.*" (This is my castle's treasury.)	D-pentatonic	{0,2,4,7,9}	5–35	932140
Bluebeard	57/1–6	"*Tiéd most már mind ez a kincs, tiéd arany, gyöngy és gyémánt.*" (Every golden crown shall be thine. All the rubies, pearls and diamonds.)	A-pentatonic	{0,2,4,7,9}	5–35	932140

Table 4.25. Bluebeard and Judith's pentatonic lines in the "Treasury" scene.[415]

	2
4	7
9	0

Figure 4.93. Set {0,2,4,7,9}.

In performance, both Judith and Bluebeard are given a high degree of rhythmic freedom in the declamation of lines. In this respect, Stevens (1964: 286) notes that *Bluebeard's Castle* reaps the harvest of Bartók's investigation of the old peasant music of Hungary. In the *parlando-rubato* tunes of the opera, the rhythms are di-

---

415. Hassall, in his English translation (score 57/2), uses the word "rubies" instead of the proper word, "*arany*" (gold), as it appears in the score (Bartók 1952 [1925]: 78).

rectly conditioned by inflections of the spoken language. By contrast, the variable *tempo-giusto* seems more or less inflexible, when heard against the irregular rhythmic groupings of the *parlando-rubato*. From this scene onwards, Judith sings exclusively in *recitative* or short *parlando* phrases. Bluebeard, on the other hand, strays little from the *parlando* style during the first third of the opera.

4.4.7. Fourth door: 'Secret Garden'

In the "Secret Garden" scene, again three sections can be delimited, based on the changing subject matter and delivery of the text (Table 4.26).

Section	Rehearsal/measure numbers	Synopsis
A	60/1–64/7	Description of the garden.
B	65/1–73/3	Dialogue about the garden.
C	73/4–74/18	Bluebeard urges Judith toward the next door.

Table 4.26. Structure of the "Fourth Door" scene, 60/1–74/18.

Section A starts with an orchestral prelude that describes what Judith sees (Example 4.8, next page). As the light glimmers blue-green (60/1–5), strings and a horn – gradually floating upward to join the higher wind instruments – represent a flowering garden in music. An A-Locrian arpeggio opens the scene: A–B-flat–C–D–E-flat–F–G (Figure 4.94).

	5	8
	10	1
0	3	6

Figure 4.94. Set {0,1,3,5,6,8,10}, A = 0.

The A-Locrian arpeggio creates a counterpole relation, set {0,6}, with the E-flat organ point of 60/2–61/7 (Figure 4.95).

Figure 4.95. Set {0,6}, A = 0.

Table 4.27 (next page) and Figures 4.96–4.99 (p. 241) display the overall harmonic shape of 60/2–62/6 (see also, Example 4.8, next page).

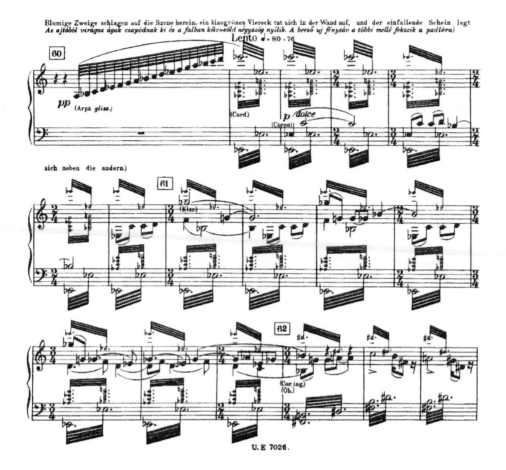

Example 4.8. "Fourth Door" scene's opening, 60/1–62/3.
© 1921 by Universal Edition A. G., Wien/UE 7026, used by kind permission.

Rehearsal/ measure numbers	Pitch classes	Point 0	Integers
60/2–61/7	A-flat–C–E-flat–G B-flat–D–F–A	A-flat B-flat	{0,4,7,11} {0,4,7,11}
62/1–3	B–D-sharp–F-sharp	B	{0,4,7}
62/4	D-sharp–F-sharp–A–C-sharp	D-sharp	{0,3,6,10}
62/5–6	E-flat–G–B-double-flat–D-flat	E-flat	{0,4,6,10}

Table 4.27. The harmonic shape of 60/2–62/6.

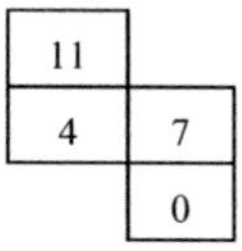

Figure 4.96. Set {0,4,7,11}.

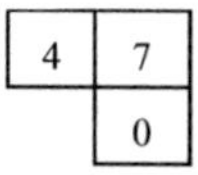

Figure 4.97. Set {0,4,7}.

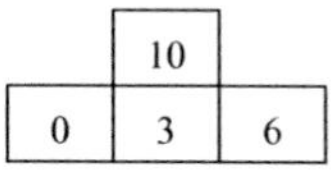

Figure 4.98. Set {0,3,6,10}.

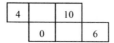

Figure 4.99. Set {0,4,6,10}.

Out of the opening (Example 4.8, previous page), there emerges a rhythmic motif that will grow increasingly prominent, eventually taking shape as a bold, repeated gesture in the orchestra after 69/1. The prosody of spoken Hungarian is evident in the motif, which issues from the horn solo starting at 60/3. Characterized by an upward leap of a major sixth, that horn melody is based on the C natural-minor scale (Figure 4.100).

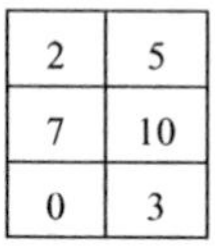

2	5
7	10
0	3

Figure 4.100. Set {0,2,3,5,7,10}, C = 0.

In the line that follows, the instrument touches on that interval repeatedly, each time to initiate phrases that explore (always diatonically) the scene's central tonality of E-flat (Example 4.8, previous page). Against the horn melody, a solo clarinet, followed by other solo wind instruments, outlines a contrapuntal line whose pitches result in chromatic clashes (61/1). At 62/1, oboe and English horn appear to echo the horn melody, with their rising sixth, but they immediately transform it into an accented figure that encompasses a descending tritone or other chromatic intervals (Table 4.28 and Figure 4.101, next page).

Rehearsal/measure numbers	Pitch classes	Point 0	Integers
62/2	C–B–F-sharp	C	{0,1,6}
62/3	A–G-sharp–D-sharp	A	{0,1,6}

Table 4.28. Accented figure, 62/2–3.

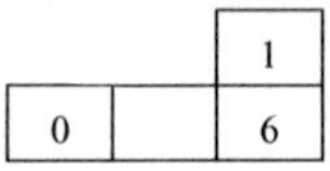

Figure 4.101. Set {0,1,6}.

At 64/2–7, a solo flute adds birdcalls, outlining all twelve chromatic pitches (Figure 4.102).

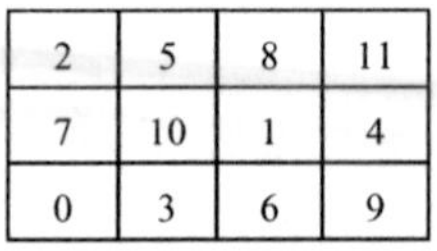

Figure 4.102. Set {0,1,2,3,4,5,6,7,8,9,10,11}, C = 0.

Section B starts with set {0,1,3,5,7,9,10} (Figure 4.103).

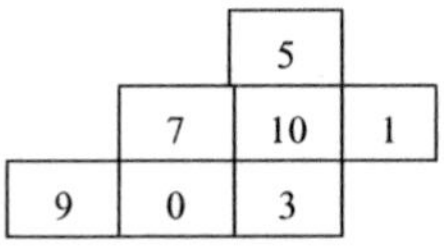

Figure 4.103. Set {0,1,3,5,7,9,10}, F = 0.

The "Fourth Door" scene is expressed by means of the Lydian-Mixolydian scale with augmented fourths, which Bartók first encountered in Debussy's works and in Romanian and Slovak folk music (see p. 47, Chapter 2.4.1). When the door opens (65/1–8), Judith reacts to the vision before her: "*Oh! Virágok! Oh! Illatos kert! Kemény sziklák alatt rejtve.*" (Ah! What lovely flowers! Sweet, fragrant garden. Hidden under rocks and boulders.) See Table 4.29 and Figures 4.104–4.105.

Rehearsal/measure numbers	Pitch classes	Point 0	Integers
65/1–4	E-flat–D–A	E-flat	{0,1,6}
65/5–6	E-flat–D–A	E-flat	{0,1,6}
65/7–8	F–G–A–B-flat–C-flat–D	B-flat	{0,1,4,7,9,11}

Table 4.29. Judith's melodic lines, 65/1–8.

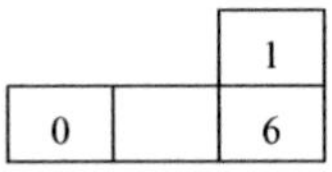

Figure 4.104. Set {0,1,6}.

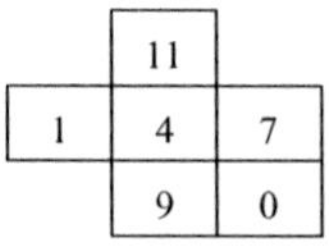

Figure 4.105. Set {0,1,4,7,9,11}.

The orchestra echoes Judith's motif, a sign of its growing thematic weight (65/1–66/2). The orchestra seizes upon the motif, leaving aside other musical ideas introduced in the opening picture, and through varied repetition, uses it to punctuate the dialogue on stage (Table 4.30 and Figures 4.106–4.115, below).

Rehearsal/measure numbers	Pitch classes	Point 0	Integers
65/1	E-flat–F-flat–G-flat–G–B-flat	E-flat	{0,1,3,4,7}
65/2	E-flat–G-flat–G–B-flat–C	E-flat	{0,3,4,7,9}
65/3	E-flat–G-flat–G–A–B-flat–D-flat	E-flat	{0,3,4,6,7,10}
65/4	E-flat–A–B-flat–D-flat	E-flat	{0,6,7,10}
65/5 (= 65/1)	E-flat–F-flat–G-flat–G–B-flat	E-flat	{0,1,3,4,7}
65/6 (= 65/3)	E-flat–G-flat–G–A–B-flat–D-flat	E-flat	{0,3,4,6,7,10}
65/7	E-flat–F–G–A–B-flat–C-flat–C–D-flat–D	E-flat	{0,1,3,5,6,7,8,9,10}
65/8 (= 65/1, 5)	E-flat–F-flat–G-flat–G–B-flat	E-flat	{0,1,3,4,7}
66/1 (= 65/1, 5, 8)	E-flat–F-flat–G-flat–G–B-flat	E-flat	{0,1,3,4,7}
66/2	E-flat–F–G-flat–G–B-flat–D-flat	E-flat	{0,2,3,4,7,10}

Table 4.30. Orchestral lines, 65/1–66/2.

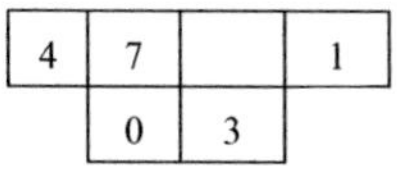

Figure 4.106. Set {0,1,3,4,7}.

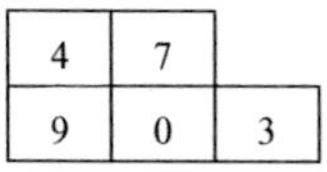

Figure 4.107. Set {0,3,4,7,9}.

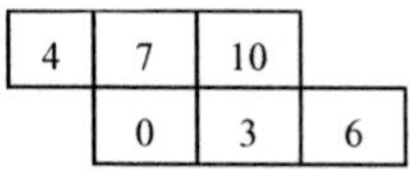

Figure 4.108. Set {0,3,4,6,7,10}.

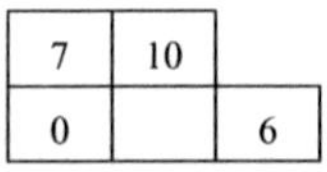

7	10	
0		6

Figure 4.109. Set {0,6,7,10}.

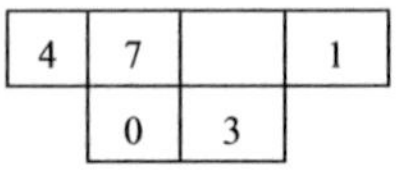

4	7		1
	0	3	

Figure 4.110. Set {0,1,3,4,7}.

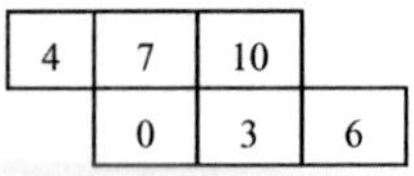

4	7	10	
	0	3	6

Figure 4.111. Set {0,3,4,6,7,10}.

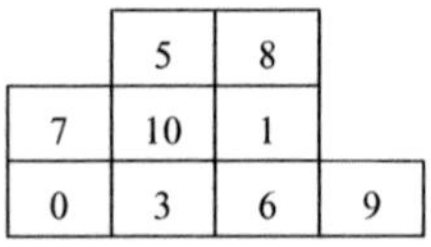

		5	8	
	7	10	1	
0	3	6	9	

Figure 4.112. Set {0,1,3,5,6,7,8,9,10}.

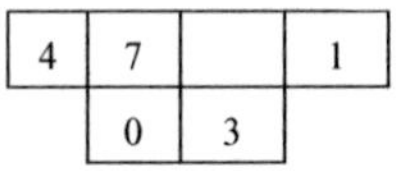

4	7		1
	0	3	

Figure 4.113. Set {0,1,3,4,7}.

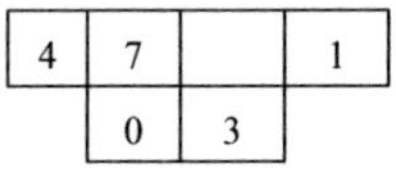

4	7		1
	0	3	

Figure 4.114. Set {0,1,3,4,7}.

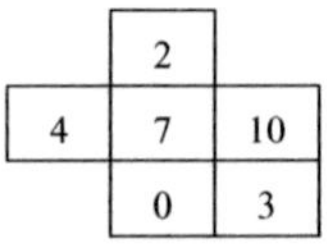

	2		
4	7	10	
	0	3	

Figure 4.115. Set {0,2,3,4,7,10}.

Bluebeard's growing ardor repeatedly induces him to step out of pentatony, for instance, in the melody, "*Minden virág neked bókol*" (Every flower bows to thee). See Table 4.31 and Figures 4.116–4.117.

Rehearsal/ measure numbers	Pitch classes	Point 0	Integers
68/10–69/1	E-flat–A-flat–B-flat–C–D	E-flat	{0,5,7,9,11}
69/3–4	E-flat–A-flat–B-flat–B–C–D	E-flat	{0,5,7,8,9,11}

Table 4.31. Bluebeard's lines, 68/10–69/1 and 69/3–4.

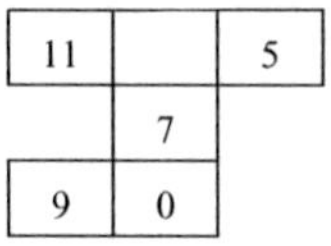

Figure 4.116. Set {0,5,7,9,11}.

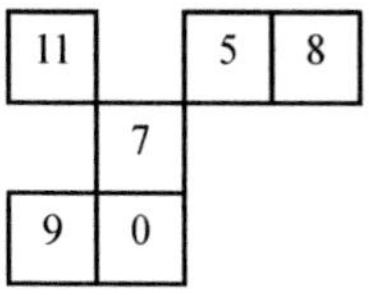

Figure 4.117. Set {0,5,7,8,9,11}.

The ensuing dialogue with Bluebeard is marked by additional, weighty pauses as the orchestra continues to sustain the opening mood. When Judith sees blood, the dramatic pace suddenly accelerates (71/2–5): "*Fehér rózsád töve véres, virágaid földje véres!*" (Your white rose is flushed with blood spots. All the soil around is blood-soaked!) The pitch set of her line is shown in Figure 4.118.

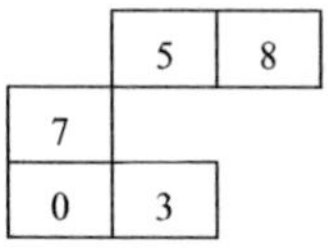

Figure 4.118. Set {0,3,5,7,8}.

Bartók's tempos reflect the changes in emotion, moving as the scene progresses from "lento" and "andante" to "agitato" and, finally, "vivacissimo".

In Section C, Bluebeard's *parlando* passages are characterized by whole-tone themes, often asserted in three-note outbursts (Table 4.32, below, and Figures 4.119–4.120, next page).

Rehearsal/ measure numbers	The characters' lines	Pitch classes	Point 0	Set
73/5–8	"*Nézd, hogy derül már a váram.*" (Look, how my castle brightens.)	D–E–F-sharp–G-sharp	D	{0,2,4,6}
74/1–3	"*Nyisd ki az ötödik ajtót!*" (Open the fifth door!)	G–B–D-sharp	G	{0,4,8}

Table 4.32. Bluebeard's lines, 73/5–8 and 74/1–3.

Figure 4.119. Set {0,2,4,6}.

Figure 4.120. Set {0,4,8}.

Table 4.33 displays the primary sets from 73/4 to 74/10 (see also, Figure 4.121, next page).

Rehearsal/ measure numbers	Pitch classes	Point 0	Set
73/4–5	B-flat–D–E–G	B-flat	{0,4,6,9}
73/6	B-flat–D–E–G	B-flat	{0,4,6,9}
	C–E–F-sharp–A	C	{0,4,6,9}
73/7	C–E–F-sharp–A	C	{0,4,6,9}
	D–F-sharp–G-sharp–B	D	{0,4,6,9}
73/8	D–F-sharp–G-sharp–B	D	{0,4,6,9}
	E–G-sharp–A-sharp–C-sharp	E	{0,4,6,9}
73/9	E–G-sharp–A-sharp–C–sharp	E	{0,4,6,9}
	F-sharp–A-sharp–B-sharp–D-sharp	F-sharp	{0,4,6,9}
73/10	D–F-sharp–G-sharp–B	D	{0,4,6,9}
	E–G-sharp–A-sharp–C–sharp	E	{0,4,6,9}
73/11	E–G-sharp–A-sharp–C–sharp	E	{0,4,6,9}
	F-sharp–A-sharp–B-sharp–D-sharp	F-sharp	{0,4,6,9}
73/12	D–F-sharp–G-sharp–B	D	{0,4,6,9}
	E–G-sharp–A-sharp–C–sharp	E	{0,4,6,9}
73/13	E–G-sharp–A-sharp–C–sharp	E	{0,4,6,9}
	F-sharp–A-sharp–B-sharp–D-sharp	F-sharp	{0,4,6,9}
74/1	F-sharp–A-sharp–B-sharp–D-sharp	F-sharp	{0,4,6,9}
	E–G-sharp–A-sharp–C–sharp	E	{0,4,6,9}
74/2	F-sharp–A-sharp–B-sharp–D-sharp	F-sharp	{0,4,6,9}
	D–F-sharp–G-sharp–B	D	{0,4,6,9}
74/3	F-sharp–A-sharp–B-sharp–D-sharp	F-sharp	{0,4,6,9}
	E–G-sharp–A-sharp–C–sharp	E	{0,4,6,9}
74/4	F-sharp–A-sharp–B-sharp–D-sharp	F-sharp	{0,4,6,9}
	D–F-sharp–G-sharp–B	D	{0,4,6,9}
74/5	F-sharp–A-sharp–B-sharp–D-sharp	F-sharp	{0,4,6,9}
	E–G-sharp–A-sharp–C–sharp	E	{0,4,6,9}
74/6	F-sharp–A-sharp–B-sharp–D-sharp	F-sharp	{0,4,6,9}
	D–F-sharp–G-sharp–B	D	{0,4,6,9}

74/7	F-sharp–A-sharp–B-sharp–D-sharp	F-sharp	{0,4,6,9}
	D–F-sharp–G-sharp–B	D	{0,4,6,9}
74/8	F-sharp–A-sharp–B-sharp–D-sharp	F-sharp	{0,4,6,9}
	D–F-sharp–G-sharp–B	D	{0,4,6,9}
74/9	F-sharp–A-sharp–B-sharp–D-sharp	F-sharp	{0,4,6,9}
	D–F-sharp–G-sharp–B	D	{0,4,6,9}
74/10	F-sharp–A-sharp–B-sharp–D-sharp	F-sharp	{0,4,6,9}
	D–F-sharp–G-sharp–B	D	{0,4,6,9}

Table 4.33. Sets, 73/4–74/10.

Figure 4.121. Set {0,4,6,9}.

The tonal centers of 73/4–74/10 outline an entire whole-tone collection, B-flat–C–D–E–F-sharp (Figure 4.122).

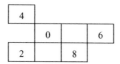

Figure 4.122. Set {0,2,4,6,8}, B♭ = 0.

Bartók sustains and intensifies this mood in the transition passage that follows (74/11–18), thus preparing the audience, and Judith, for the brilliance of the fifth door. In those final moments of the scene, the music converges onto a syncopated rhythm leads to the moment when Judith throws open the next door.

4.4.8. Fifth door: 'Bluebeard's Kingdom'

The music of *Duke Bluebeard's Castle* reaches its climatic turning point when the fifth door is opened and Bluebeard's endless domain is displayed. As one writer puts, this scene

> [...] stands in contrast to the dramatic arch of the story. The suspense in the tale continues to build beyond the opening of door six until the moment before door seven when Bluebeard finally relinquishes the last key to Judith. At this point, the music grows to another dynamic climax and aids the drama in reaching its most intense moment – the ultimate confrontation between Bluebeard and Judith. (Heath 1988: 112.)

The text divides into three, structurally equivalent sections, each comprised of 12 or 14 lines, organized through a repeating, quatrain-like pattern. Bartók's music supports a structural analysis based on that organizational pattern. Tempo and meter changes, the location of fermati, and the presence or absence of significant musical motives all suggest that Bartók used the regularity of the text structure as a point of departure for his music. The music for the "Fifth Door" scene falls into three distinct sections whose succession mirrors the changing dramatic situation (Table 4.34).[416]

Section	Rehearsal/ measure numbers	Synopsis
A	74/19–78/6	The music depicts the expanse of Bluebeard's lands.
B	79/1–84/13	Bluebeard's vainly optimistic words about the presence of light in the castle.
C	85/1–90/14	Judith again asks for permission to proceed.

Table 4.34. Structure of the "Fifth Door" scene, 74/19–90/14.[417]

The stage directions at this point read as follows:

With a sudden movement, Judith runs to the fifth door and flings it open. A lofty veranda is revealed and unbounded vistas are beyond. The light pours out in a glittering cascade. Dazzled by the radiance, Judith shields her eyes with her hand. (Bartók 1952 [1925]: 99–100.)

After the diatonic opening (Example 4.9, next page), the music steadily increases in chromatic content until ending up with triadic harmonies. A similar progression was heard in the "Secret Garden" scene (Chapter 4.4.7) and will be encountered again in the "Lake of Tears" (Chapter 4.4.9), reflecting the ebb and flow of the two characters' emotions. The tempo increases steadily throughout the scene, moving

---

416. Antokoletz (1990) provides a structural analysis of the "Bluebeard's Domain" scene, describing its overall organization as an "extended binary form". Antokoletz recognizes the quatrain-like divisions, but instead of viewing the sections as three successive, integral sections, he proposes that the third section (his Section B) acts as an "extremely expanded subsection" replacing the two missing lines at the end of his Section A2. If, unlike Antokoletz, we trace the regular, quatrain-like structure of the text itself in Bartók's musical setting, an interesting correspondence emerges: the structure of the "Fifth Door" scene directly reflects the structure of its text. When Antokoletz writes that "The symmetrical quatrain structure […] serves as the point of departure for a more complex structural development," he is suggesting that the structure of this scene becomes increasingly independent of its text (ibid.: 75). But that is not the case: Bartók's "Fifth Door" scene falls into regular, reiterated sections that exhibit essentially the same structure – from beginning to end.

417. Bartók's musical setting of the text reinforces the idea that a repeated pattern of lines (4,4,4,2) forms the structural foundation of the "Fifth Door" scene (74/19–90/14). Divisions between the three principal sections are marked unambiguously; transitions are articulated through changes of tempo, meter, and orchestration, in addition to new or transformed musical material. The transition from Section A to Section B (79/1) is marked by an abrupt shift in tempo and meter; simultaneous *ritardando molto* and *crescendo molto* in the orchestra at 78/6 emphasize the structural break. At 85/1, the transition from Section B to Section C is marked by a similar shift in tempo and meter, emphasized by a *poco ritardando* and change in dynamics; to make it clear that a structural break is intended, Bartók adds a brief fermata over the bar line at 84/12. (Leafstedt 1990: 98–102.)

from the *larghissimo* opening of Section A, to *vivace* in Section B, to *agitato* and *presto* in the conclusion, Section C.

Section A starts with the homophonic Light theme (74/19–78/1), supported by *organo pleno* and *tutti* orchestra. The organ has not been heard before the opening of this door, where its voice now lends grandeur to the proceedings. To further emphasize the splendor of Bluebeard's domains, Bartók adds a group of four trombones and four trumpets, playing behind the scenery on stage. The root-position major triads, moving in parallel motion, characterize this section and construct the Light theme.

Example 4.9. Door 5, Light theme, 74/19–24.
© 1921 by Universal Edition A. G., Wien/UE 7026, used by kind permission.

The opening of the scene exemplifies a compositional technique Bartók uses throughout *Bluebeard's Castle*, in which a musical idea is extended or varied, by the rotation of triadic harmonies around a given pitch or pitches. Following their initial statement in C major, the parallel orchestral chords are heard four more times (see Table 4.35, below, and Figure 4.123, next page).

Rehearsal/ measure numbers	Pitch classes	Point 0	Set
74/19–75/8	C–E–D–C–G–A–C	C	{0,2,4,7,9}
76/1–8	F–A–G–F–C–D–F	F	{0,2,4,7,9}
77/1–5	A-flat–C–B-flat–A-flat–E-flat–F–A-flat	A-flat	{0,2,4,7,9}
78/2–4	F minor–A minor–G minor–F minor–C minor–D minor–F minor	F	{0,2,4,7,9}

Table 4.35. Parallel orchestral chords in the "Bluebeard's Domain" scene.

Figure 4.123. Set {0,2,4,7,9}.

Antokoletz (1990: 91–94) has noted that the key of C major is established by the prominent metric placement of the major triad and by the shape of the melody itself, which, among other features begins and ends on C (74/19–75/8). Using these pitches Bartók creates variants by reinterpreting the melodic line as either the tonic mediant or the dominant in a series of parallel triads. It is striking that the diatonic substance of the "Fifth Door" scene is intersected by pentatonic projections of chordal keynotes C–E–D–C–G–A–C, surrounded by the sustained C major chord (Example 4.9, previous page). The orchestral melody outlines the previously-heard pentatonic pitch collection, C–D–E–G–A (Table 4.35, previous page, and Figure 4.123, above), which Bluebeard will pick up in his opening *parlando* line (75/1–7).

The first 14 lines form a distinct section of the text in which Bluebeard and Judith (and by extension, the audience) focus on the "Fifth Door" and its revelations. Dialogue within this section is further divisible into two- or four-line units that share a common psychological or dramatic element. Those quatrains and couplets clearly reflect the influence of Hungarian folk elements on the librettist Balázs.

Three times a *triple-forte* cataclysm of sound punctuates the scene as Bluebeard sings of his dominion (75/1–7): "*Lásd ez az én birodalmam, messze néző szép könyöklőm. Ugye, hogy szép nagy, nagy ország?*" (Now behold my vast kingdom. Gaze ye down the dwindling vistas. Is it not a noble country?) As mentioned above, his melody outlines the C–D–E–A–G pentatonic scale (Figure 4.124).

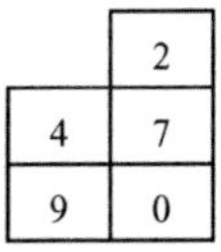

	2
4	7
9	0

Figure 4.124. Set {0,2,4,7,9}, C = 0.

Standing in great contrast is Judith's unaccompanied line of eighth-notes (75/10): "*Szép és nagy a te országod!*" (Fair and spacious is your country!) The line emphasizes the contradiction between major and minor pentatonic sounds, due to the effect of a minor second shift, as indicated in Table 4.36 and Figures 4.125–4.126.

Rehearsal/ measure numbers	Judith's lines	Pitch classes	Point 0	Set
75/10	*"Szép és nagy a te országod!"* (Fair and spacious is your country.)	A-flat–G-flat–E-flat–D-flat	A-flat	{0,2,5,7}
76/16	*"Szép és nagy a te országod!"* (Fair and spacious is your country.)	D-flat–F-flat–G-flat–C-flat	D-flat	{0,3,5,10}

Table 4.36. Judith's lines, 75/10 and 76/16.

```
2  5
7
0
```

Figure 4.125. Set {0,2,5,7}.

```
   5
  10
0  3
```

Figure 4.126. Set {0,3,5,10}.

Bluebeard's melody (76/7–13) on the words *"Selyemrétek, bársonyerdők, hosszú ezüst folyók folynak, és kék hegyek nagy messze"* (Silken meadows, velvet forests, tranquil streams of winding silver. Lofty mountains blue and hazy)[418] outlines the Dorian scale: D–E–F–G–A–B–C (Figure 4.127).

```
  2  5
  7  10
9 0  3
```

Figure 4.127. Set {0,2,3,5,7,9,10}, D = 0.

The vocal part of minor tonality is joined to E major harmony (77/5). At 77/5–10, Bluebeard's melodic line, on the words *"Most már Judit mind a tied"* (Henceforth, Judith, all is yours), outlines B–A–E–D (Figure 4.128).

```
  2
  7
9 0
```

Figure 4.128. Set {0,2,7,9}, B = 0.

---

418. The official English translation (Bartók 1952 [1925]) of *"és kék hegyek nagy messze"* as "lofty mountains blue and hazy" is one syllable longer than the Hungarian phrase (76/12–13).

Section A ends with Judith's observation of blood (Table 4.37 and Figures 4.129–4.130).

Rehearsal/ measure numbers	Judith's lines	Pitch classes	Point 0	Set
78/1–2	"*Véres árnyat vet a felhő!*" (Yonder cloud throws blood-red shadows.)	A–G–F–E-flat–D–C	C	{0,2,3,7,9}
78/5–6	"*Milyen felhők szállnak ottan?*" (What do these grim clouds portend?)	G-sharp–F-sharp–E–C-sharp	G-sharp	{0,2,4,7}

Table 4.37. Judith's lines, 75/10 and 76/16.

Figure 4.129. Set {0,2,3,7,9}.

Figure 4.130. Set {0,2,4,7}.

The minor seconds of the Blood motif reappear subtly, in the clashing harmony of trombones against tremolo strings (78/1–6). From the fifth door forward, the Blood motif begins to infect the melodic contours and harmonic content of the music at many levels.

Section B[419] opens with alternating C major and E-flat major harmonies beneath a surging melodic line in the orchestra (79/1–84/13), the pitches of which form incomplete, whole-tone scale segments in each measure, each of them reducing to set {0,2,4,6}: C–(D)–E–F-sharp at 79/1; E-flat–(F)–G–A at 79/2, and so on (Figure 4.131).

Figure 4.131. Set {0,2,4,6}.

The musical structure points up the opposition between Bluebeard and Judith's emotional states: Judith's duple meter clashes with Bluebeard's waltz (in 82/3–4 and

419. The basic pattern of 4,4,4,2 lines in the first section is confirmed by its reiteration in the second section.

81/1–8, respectively). A similar rhythmic clash occurs a few measures later (83/5–8), when Judith sings four-quarter groups over Bluebeard's music in 5/4 meter (Table 4.38 and Figures 4.132–4.133).

Rehearsal/measure numbers	Judith's lines	Pitch classes	Point 0	Set
82/3–4	*"Nyissad ki még a két ajtót."* (Let the last two doors be opened.)	A–B-flat–D-flat–E	A	{0,1,4,7}
83/5–8	*"Nyissad ki még a két ajtót."* (Let the last two doors be opened.)	F–A–B-flat–C-sharp	C-sharp	{0,3,4,8}

Table 4.38. Judith's lines in 75/10 and 76/16.

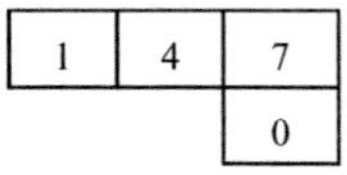

Figure 4.132. Set {0,1,4,7}.

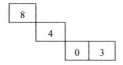

Figure 4.133. Set {0,3,4,8}.

Table 4.39 and Figures 4.134–4.138 summarize the pitch content of the orchestra's ostinato-like figures from 83/1 to 84/12.

Rehearsal/measure numbers	Pitch classes	Point 0	Set
83/1–10	B–D–E-flat–F	B	{0,3,4,6}
83/11–84/5	B–D–E-flat–F–G–A	B	{0,3,4,6,8,10}
84/6–7	B–E-flat–E–F–G–A	B	{0,4,5,6,8,10}
84/8–10	B–E-flat–F–G–A–B-flat	B	{0,4,6,8,10,11}
84/11–12	G–A–B–C-sharp–D–E–F	G	{0,2,4,6,7,9,10}

Table 4.39. Ostinato-like orchestral figures, 83/1–84/12.

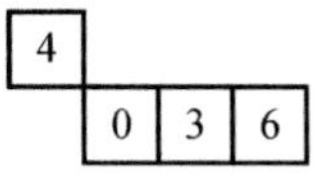

Figure 4.134. Set {0,3,4,6}.

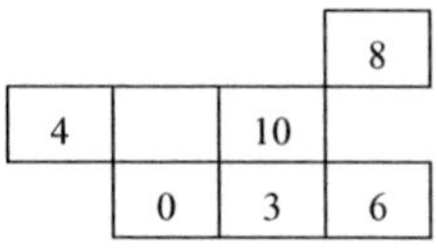

Figure 4.135. Set {0,3,4,6,8,10}.

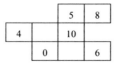

Figure 4.136. Set {0,4,5,6,8,10}.

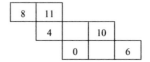

Figure 4.137. Set {0,4,6,8,10,11}.

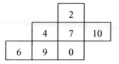

Figure 4.138. Set {0,2,4,6,7,9,10}.

Bluebeard begs Judith to pry no further – already the hall is bright with the light of the five open doors (84/1–13): "*Azt akartad, felderüljön; nézd, tündököl már a váram!*" (You begged for sunlight. See how the sun has filled my house!) The set type of Bluebeard's melody, D–E-flat–E–F–A, is shown in Figure 4.139.

Figure 4.139. Set {0,1,2,3,7}, D = 0.

At the beginning of Section C^{420} (85/1–5), a chromatic melody undermines the tonal focus of the music (Table 4.40 and Figures 4.140–4.144, next page). The chromatic Blood motif starts to develop into a self-standing entity, which will dominate the musical material until the opening of the seventh door (Chapter 4.4.9).

---

420. The third section (85/1–90/14) is distinguished from the second section by its gradual shift in emphasis to the unopened "Sixth Door" and by a notable psychological change in Bluebeard's character. In the third section, the 4+4+4+2 pattern is present, but partially obscured, reflecting the fractured nature of Judith and Bluebeard's dialogue. Because of two absent lines, the structure here may be more accurately rendered as 4,4,[4],2 lines. It is possible that the two "missing" lines are symbolically represented in the orchestra. At the end of Section C, starting at 89/8–9, Bluebeard gives Judith the key to the sixth door. As he does so, sixteen muffled rhythmic pulsations are heard in the orchestra (89/1–90/13), in the pattern: 8+7+1 beats. (Leafstedt 1990: 100–102.)

Rehearsal/ measure numbers	Pitch classes	Point 0	Set
85/1–2	A-flat–A–B-flat	A-flat	{0,1,2}
	A-flat–A–B-flat–D-flat	A-flat	{0,1,2,5}
85/3–4	F-flat–E-flat–D-flat–B-flat	F-flat	{0,1,3,6}
	A-flat–A–B-flat–D-flat	A-flat	{0,1,2,5}
85/5	A-flat–A–B-flat–F-flat	A-flat	{0,1,2,8}
	A-flat–A–B-flat–G	A-flat	{0,1,2,11}

Table 4.40. Sets in development of Blood motif, 85/1–5.

Figure 4.140. Set {0,1,2}.

Figure 4.141. Set {0,1,2,5}.

Figure 4.142. Set {0,1,3,6}.

Figure 4.143. Set {0,1,2,8}.

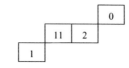

Figure 4.144. Set {0,1,2,11}.

At 87/1–6 the orchestral harmonies are C minor and B minor, both of which constitute set {0,3,7}, as shown in Figure 4.145 (next page).

Figure 4.145. Set {0,3,7}.

The sets of the orchestral melody are displayed in Table 4.41 and Figures 4.146–4.149.

Rehearsal/measure numbers	Pitch classes	Point 0	Set
87/1	G-sharp–F-sharp–E G-sharp–A-sharp–B–C-sharp	G-sharp G-sharp	{0,2,4} {0,2,3,5}
87/2	A-flat–G-flat–F-flat A-flat–A–B-flat–D-flat	A-flat A-flat	{0,2,4} {0,2,4,6}
87/3	E-flat–D A-flat–B-flat–C–D	E-flat A-flat	{0,1} {0,2,4,6}
87/4	E-flat–D A-flat–B-flat–C–D	E-flat A-flat	{0,1} {0,2,4,6}
87/5	E-flat–D	E-flat	{0,1}
87/6	E-flat–D	E-flat	{0,1}

Table 4.41. Set content, orchestral melody, 87/1–6.

Figure 4.146. Set {0,2,4}.

Figure 4.147. Set {0,2,3,5}.

Figure 4.148. Set {0,2,4,6}.

Figure 4.149. Set {0,1}.

Table 4.42 and Figures 4.150–4.154 (next page) display the sets at 88/2–13.

Rehearsal/ measure numbers	Pitch classes	Point 0	Set
88/2	D–E–F-sharp–G-sharp–A	D	{0,2,4,6,7}
88/3	B–D–F-sharp–A-sharp	B	{0,3,7,11}
	C–E–G-sharp–B	C	{0,4,8,11}
88/4	A–B–C-sharp–D-sharp–E	A	{0,2,4,6,7}
88/5	G–B-flat–D–F-sharp	G	{0,3,7,11}
	A-flat–C-flat–E-flat–G	A-flat	{0,3,7,11}
88/6	F–G–A–B–C	F	{0,2,4,6,7}
88/7	D–F–A–C-sharp	D	{0,3,7,11}
88/8	B–C-sharp–D-sharp–E–F-sharp	B	{0,2,4,6,7}
88/9	A–C–E–G-sharp	A	{0,3,7,11}
	B-flat–D-flat–F–A	B-flat	{0,3,7,11}
	G–A–B–C-sharp	G	{0,2,4,6}
88/10	E–G–B–D-sharp	E	{0,3,7,11}
	F–A-flat–C–E	F	{0,3,7,11}
	D–E–F-sharp–G-sharp	D	{0,2,4,6}
88/11	B–D–F-sharp–A-sharp	B	{0,3,7,11}
	C–E-flat–G–B	C	{0,3,7,11}
	A–B–C-sharp–D-sharp	A	{0,2,4,6}
88/12–13	A–C–E–G-sharp	A	{0,3,7,11}
	F-sharp–A–A-sharp–C-sharp	F-sharp	{0,3,4,7}
	A–B–C-sharp–D-sharp	A	{0,2,4,6}

Table 4.42. Sets, 88/2–13.

Figure 4.150. Set {0,2,4,6,7}.

Figure 4.151. Set {0,3,7,11}.

Figure 4.152. Set {0,4,8,11}.

Figure 4.153. Set {0,2,4,6}.

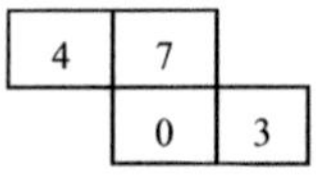

Figure 4.154. Set {0,3,4,7}.

Table 4.43 (next page) and Figure 4.155 (below) summarize the occurrences of set {0,3,4,7} in the orchestral accompaniment, 89/1–90/13.

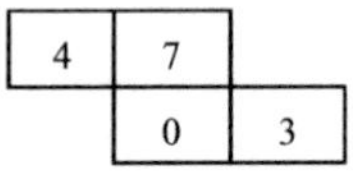

Figure 4.155. Set {0,3,4,7}.

Judith insists, there must be no secrets between her and Bluebeard (85/3–7): "*Nem akarom, hogy előttem csukott ajtóid legyenek!*" (Not one of your great doors must stay shut fast against me!) Her melody outlines A-flat–G-flat–E-flat–D-flat (Figure 4.156).

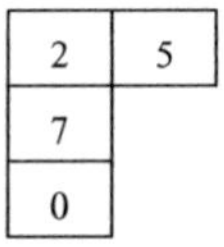

2	5
7	
0	

Figure 4.156. Set {0,2,5,7}, A♭ = 0.

Bluebeard (89/8–9) answers with an unaccompanied melodic line of just two notes, C-sharp–E (Figure 4.157): "*Adok neked még egy kulcsot.*" (Come, I grant thee one more key.)[421]

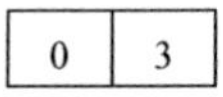

0	3

Figure 4.157. Set {0,3}, C# = 0.

The sixth door creaks on its hinges, and a moaning comes from beyond it (90/9). Bluebeard makes one last attempt to turn Judith's attention away from the remaining two doors. He hands her the key to the sixth door (90/11–12), with the plea: "*Judit! Judit! Ne nyissad ki!*" (Judith! Judith! Do not open it!) His melody outlines A–F–D-flat–B-flat (Figure 4.158, next page).

---

421. The 4+4+4+2 pattern is suggested, however, at the beginning and end of the section. The first four lines form a subsection based on the dialogue between Judith and Bluebeard; the last two lines of the scene (89/8–9), "*Adok neked még egy kulcsot*" (One more key is all I give you) and "*Judith, Judith, ne nyissad ki*" (Judith, Judith, leave its secret!) (90/11–12) are analogous to the final couplet in the two preceding sections (78/1–2, 5–6, 84/1–6, 9–12). With these two groups of lines anchoring both beginning and ending, it is thus a matter of combining intermediate lines and half-lines into recognizable groups. (Leafstedt 1990: 98–100.)

Rehearsal/measure numbers	Pitch classes	Point 0	Set
89/1–3	F-sharp–A–A-sharp–C-sharp	F-sharp	{0,3,4,7}
89/4–5	A–C–C-sharp–E	A	{0,3,4,7}
	F-sharp–A–A-sharp–C-sharp	F-sharp	{0,3,4,7}
89/6, 9 (= 89/1–3)	F-sharp–A–A-sharp–C-sharp	F-sharp	{0,3,4,7}
90/1 (= 89/4–5)	A–C–C-sharp–E	A	{0,3,4,7}
	F-sharp–A–A-sharp–C-sharp	F-sharp	{0,3,4,7}
90/2, 3, 5, 7, 13 (= 89/1–3) (= 89/6, 9)	F-sharp–A–A-sharp–C-sharp	F-sharp	{0,3,4,7}

Table 4.43. Set {0,3,4,7}, 89/1–90/13.

Figure 4.158. Set {0,4,8,11}, A = 0.

4.4.9. Sixth door: 'The Lake of Tears'[422]

With the opening of the sixth door, the stage grows darker. The wide expanse of a lake, pale and motionless, confronts Judith. Bluebeard thrice explains in broken accents (94/3–6): "*Könnyek, Judit, könnyek, könnyek*" (Tears, Judith, tears, tears). This scene symbolizes sad, silent, buried memories. The Duke swears that the last door will remain shut (101/1–4): "*Az utolsót nem nyitom ki. Nem nyitom ki.*" (I do not open the last door! I do not.)

Judith, curiously softened, pleads gently with him. She asks if there was anyone before her. Bluebeard answers evasively (106/5–107/4): "*Te vagy váram fényessége, csókolj, csókolj, sohse kérdezz.*" (Thou who art my castle's daylight, kiss me, kiss me. Ask me nothing.) Then Judith pulls away (111/9–10), and the minor seconds of the Blood motif hurtle against one another in the orchestra (112/5–117/7). Judith accuses Bluebeard of murdering his former wives and hiding their bodies in the seventh room (115/5–116/4): "*Ott van mind a régi asszony legyilkolva, vérbefagyva. Jaj, igaz hír, suttogó hír. Igaz! Igaz!*" (All your former wives have suffered. Suffered murder, brutal, bloody. Ah, those rumors, truthful rumors! True! True!)[423] Bluebeard gives up the last key (118/1–4): "*Fogjad, fogjad! Itt a hetedik kulcs.*" (Take it, take it. Here is the seventh key.)

---

422. See R. Honti (2004b), "Tone patches, mosaics, and motives in Béla Bartók's *Duke Bluebeard's Castle*'s 'Sixth Door' scene 'The Lake of Tears'." See also, Chapter 4 of my Licentiate thesis (R. Honti 2004a: 86–116).

423. In Perrault's version (1920 [1697]), "il avait déjà épousé plusieurs femmes, et qu'on ne savait ce que ces femmes étaient devenues" (he already had been married to several wives, and nobody knew what had become of them).

Analysis of "The Lake of Tears" (91/1–120/9) reveals how Bartók incorporated chromatic elements into the music, and also how he articulated what was happening on the stage. As Heath (1988: 112) observes, the "most intense moment" of the opera, the "Sixth Door"[424] scene has its unique place as a turning point or denouement of the tale.[425] This scene ushers in the *epilogue* of the whole opera. From here, the light loses its glamour; Judith's doom is accomplished; Bluebeard no longer has hope, but eternal loneliness.

"The Lake of Tears" scene (91/1–120/9) merits discussion not only for its clearly delimited sections, but also the consummation of the Blood motif (Example 4.1, p. 204, Chapter 4.4.1). The half-step Blood motif never loses its original association with tears, and eventually resurfaces in that context in the "Sixth Door" scene. The motif's ambiguity is fully recognized when Judith, standing before the lake of tears, inquires about the liquid's identity. The stillness of Door 6 is interrupted only by an occasional cascade of notes heard against the muffled sounds of the orchestra. The music at this point recalls folk music, especially the "freedom" and "nature" implied by the parlando-like melodies that occur throughout the opera.

As has been noted, the opera has an arch-like form, such that Door 6 corresponds to Door 4, "The Secret Garden" scene (60/1–74/18). There are many parallel features between those scenes. According to the tonal axis (TA), the tonality of Door 4 is E-flat, and that of Door 6 is A–A-flat. Both E-flat and A tonalities belong to the tonic axis (see Figure 2.9, p. 58, Chapter 2.21). Another link between the two scenes is that the rather dark, hymperminor (minor triad + major seventh) of "The Lake of Tears" (91/1–120/9) "balances" (or negates) the bright-sounding, hypermajor (major triad + major seventh) of "The Secret Garden" (60/1–74/18). (Lendvai 1964: 68, 284; see also, pp. 63–64, Chapter 2.22.)

At the end of the "Fifth Door" scene (80/1–15), Judith is determined to look behind the remaining two doors: "*Életemet, halálomat, Kékszakállú, nyisd ki még a két ajtót, Kékszakállú!*" (Be it my life, or my death, Bluebeard, open the last two doors!) The castle sighs when Judith turns the key in the sixth door lock (90/8–10). As the stage directions read, it is "As if a shadow had passed through the hall. It becomes slightly darker" (91/1). Judith perceives a still, silent lake (91/12–93/1), and Bluebeard tells her that tears form the water (94/3). He takes Judith in his arms, and tells her the seventh door must remain forever closed (101/1–4), confirming Judith's growing suspicion (105/3) that Bluebeard has had previous wives who have met with a tragic end (112/1–116/8). Realizing that Judith must know all his secrets, Bluebeard hands her the last key (118/1–4).

The Door 6 scene can be divided into three sections,[426] according to the three major events that happen on stage. Section A is associated with the lake of tears

424. On the special that the number six has in Hungarian folklore, see Voigt & Szemerkényi (1984).

425. By the time the sixth and seventh doors are opened, we have a very good idea of the nature of Judith's fate. The only remaining question is whether the former wives have been murdered or imprisoned. Balázs's dramatic thrust, therefore, is almost the reverse of Maeterlinck's. (Kroó 1975 [1971]: 62; and 1993; also see, 1995.)

426. Lendvai (1964: 66) states that each of the scenes can be divided into two sections.

(91/1–99/8); section B contains the dialogue about Bluebeard's former wives (100/1–111/11), section C begins when Judith separates from the embrace and demands that Bluebeard opens the last door (112/1–120/9). In Table 4.44 (below) the main sectional divisions are shown (A, B, C), with their internal themes indicated as follows: (A), (B), etc.

Sections A and B are characterized by the rapid alternation of musical ideas, which yields in section C to a development of the chromatic half-step motif.

4.4.9.1. Section A

The "Lake of Tears" scene relies more heavily on verbal repetition than does any other scene in the opera. Repetition is partly a way to depict inner psychological development through emotionally charged variations of the same thought. At other times, repetition serves to strengthen the characters' resolve and/or to reinforce their intentions.

Bartók streamlines the conclusion to "The Lake of Tears" scene and shapes it into a unified dramatic moment for Judith: her first, blunt request is followed by sharpening accusations, which terminate in her climactic demand that Bluebeard open the last door. Bartók's reasons for making minor textual revisions become clearer on examination of the musical score (Leafstedt 1999: 114). Bartók deleted certain stage directions given in the play, indicated by asterisks (*) in Table 4.45 (p. 263). Also shown on the Table are the specific musical ideas associated with Judith, Bluebeard, and the lake of tears; lower-case letters indicate the themes in section A (after Leafstedt 1999: 117).

The music of section A is, for the most part, quiet and emotionally restrained, reflecting the lake of tears and Judith's reaction to seeing it (Leafstedt 1999: 113–114). Bartók's orchestration depicts this gray and lifeless lake of tears with tremolo and harp arpeggios, joined by flute, clarinet, and celesta (Table 4.45 and Example 4.10, p. 263).

Section	Rehearsal/ measure numbers	Synopsis	Themes	Rehearsal/ measure numbers of themes
A	91/1–99/8	Lake of tears	Arpeggio theme (A) Theme (B) Theme (C)	91/1–4 92/4–7 93/1–7
B	100/1–111/11	Judith and Bluebeard speak about his former wives.	Theme (D) Theme (E)	101/9–102/4 105/1–4
C	112/1–120/9	Judith separates from Bluebeard's embrace, accuses Bluebeard of killing his former wives, and demands the last key.	Development of Theme (E) Theme (F)	113/4–8 118/4–119/1

Table 4.44. Structure of "The Lake of Tears" scene, 91/1–120/9.

In this section are two modally conceived melodies, labeled here as themes (B) and (C). Theme (B), 92/4–7, is Judith and Bluebeard's song-dialogue about the tears.

Judith's theme (Example 4.11, p. 264), a dirge-like "folk-tune" of Bartók's invention, begins this way: "*Csendes fehér tavat látok, mozdulatlan fehér tavat. Milyen víz ez Kékszakállú?*" (I can see a sheet of water. White and tranquil sleeping water. What is this mysterious water?) The pentatonic melody is built of two descending fourths, outlining the A minor pentatonic scale and E minor pentatonic scales. Peasant dirges represent the most urgently-delivered form of this "mother tongue," *parlando* style.[427] The pre-eminent violinist of the time, Szigeti, relates his experience of hearing Bartók's recordings of such dirges:

> When Bartók played for me some records he had made of improvised lamentation songs, or rather orations, it was a gripping revelation. Sorrowing peasant women who had lost some dear one – a child, or a grown-up son – had been induced somehow to face the (to them) terrifying recording machine, chant into it their names and ages, describe their grievous loss in unrhymed song (or rather *Sprechgesang*); they would sometimes break down sobbing, in the middle of the record. (Szigeti 1967: 268.)

Kodály (1976: 55–59) points out that the dirges can be grouped with the general *œuvre* of ceremonial songs. As such, they can tend to degenerate into frozen formulas, though originally an expression of spontaneous feelings. Bartók (1967b: xcvi) claims, however, that the "sobbing, which inevitably goes with the performance of the mourning songs by the near female relatives is usually genuine". Bartók gives a detailed description of the structure, text and significance of mourning songs (1967a: 25–27). He makes a clear differentiation between those of Rumanian and those of Hungarian origin, with particular reference to the elements of melody, mode, and text. Rumanian peasant dirges consist of improvised texts:

> [...] using certain traditional patterns; the metrical structure is the well-known acatalectic or catalectic quaternary, with *aa*, *bb* rhymes. [...] On the whole, major thirds occur as frequently as minor in these mourning song melodies. These [...] and many other [...] examples prove that in Eastern European folk music, no standard connections exist between the use of minor scale and expression of sorrow on the one hand, and the use of major scale and expression of merriment or joy on the other. Such connections are purely Western European conceptions. The four-section structure is frequently unstable, changing from stanza to stanza by way of alternating with three-section structure. Very characteristic features include the ending of some of the sections in which the shortened final tones, produced with a break of the voice, give the effect of stylized sobs. [...] The well-known Hungarian mourning-song melodies represent a completely different

---

427. For probing discussions of bridal laments, see Voigt (1991 [1987]), and (1983). Voigt (1991 [1987]: 96) lists three genres of lament: (1) burial laments; (2) wedding laments; (3) occasional laments (emigration, soldier recruitment, catastrophes, etc.). For more on laments, see also, Dobszay (1983).

Characters	Text	Music	Rehearsal/measure numbers
	(After a long pause*)	a	91/1–92/3
Judith	*"Csendes fehér tavat látok, mozdulatlan fehér tavat."* (I see a silent, white lake A motionless white lake.)	b	92/4–93/1
Bluebeard	(Does not respond*)	c	93/2–9
Judith	*"Milyen viz ez Kékszakállú?"* (What sort of water is this, Bluebeard?)	b	94/1–2
Bluebeard	*"Könnyek, Judit, könnyek, könnyek."* (Tears, Judith, tears, tears.) (Judith shudders.)	c / a	94/3–9 95/1–6
Judith	*"Milyen néma, mozdulatlan."* (How deathly silent, motionless.)	b	96/1–2
Bluebeard	*"Könnyek, Judit, könnyek, könnyek"* (Tears, Judith, tears, tears.) (She bends down and scrutinizes the water.)	c / a/[c]	96/3–7 97/1–6
Judith	*"Sima fehér, tiszta fehér."* (Calm white – pure white.)	b	98/1–3
Bluebeard	*"Könnyek, Judit, könnyek, könnyek"* (Tears, Judith, tears, tears.)	[c]	98/4–6
Judith	(She slowly turns and silently faces Bluebeard.) (Long pause*)	a	99/1–8

Table 4.45. Door 6: "The Lake of Tears," section A, 91/1–99/8
(after Leafstedt 1999: 117).

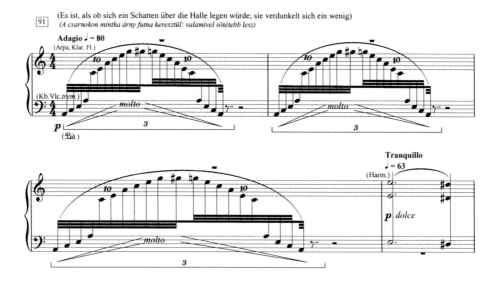

Example 4.10. Arpeggio theme (A), 91/1–4.
© 1921 by Universal Edition A. G., Wien/UE 7026, used by kind permission.

Csen - des fe - hér ta - vat lá - tok, Moz - du - lat - lan fe - hér ta - vat.

Example 4.11. Theme (B), 92/4–7.
© 1921 by Universal Edition A. G., Wien/UE 7026, used by kind permission.

type. First of all, the texts are improvisations in prose: there are no rhymes and no metrical structure of the lines. Accordingly, the melodies have a rather free stanza structure – if one is allowed to call them stanzas at all. (Bartók 1967a: 24.)

Theme (C) is an orchestral melody that is heard beneath and after the dialogue (see Example 4.12, next page). All of these themes, (A), (B), and (C), are based on the key of A.

The music associated with Bluebeard in section A (91/1–99/8) differs markedly from that which represents him in section B (100/1–111/11). Similarly, Judith's music in section A (91/1–99/8) is superseded by new musical material for her in section B (100/1–111/11).

4.4.9.2. Section B

After the tranquil section A, Judith starts to ask about Bluebeard's past loves (105/3–5): *"Mondd meg nekem Kékszakállú, kit szerettél én előttem?"* (Tell me, tell me, dearest Bluebeard, tell me whom you loved before me?) There are two characteristic themes in section B. The first is a modally based theme, shown as (D) in Example 4.13 (p. 266).

The other theme (E) sounds when Judith urges Bluebeard to tell her the secret of the seventh door (Example 4.14, p. 266).

Theme (E) has a high degree of dissonance, with vertical clashes of minor seconds and linear articulation of the same, the latter of which is a greatly expanded unfolding of the original Blood motif (comp. Example 4.1, p. 204, Chapter 4.4.1).

Both of the themes in this section, (D) and (E), show a tendency to increase in chromaticism. The result is a destabilization of the modality achieved in the previous section.

4.4.9.3. Section C

This final, climactic section of the scene depicts Judith's confrontation of Bluebeard and her demand to have the key of the final door. The section begins with a monologue, as Judith voices her sure knowledge that Bluebeard has killed his former wives, as the music develops theme (E). In her monologue, Judith accuses Bluebeard (113/4–5 and 114/6–115/2): *"Tudom, tudom, Kékszakállú, mit rejt a hetedik ajtó.*

Example 4.12. Theme (C), 93/1–7.
© 1921 by Universal Edition A. G., Wien/UE 7026, used by kind permission.

[…] *Tudom, tudom, Kékszakállú, fehér könnytó kinek könnye.*" (I have guessed your secret, Bluebeard. I can guess what you are hiding. Now I know it all, oh, Bluebeard, I know whose weeping filled your white lake.) Judith's determination to open the last door and overcome Bluebeard's resistance is expressed musically by her measured, insistent repetitions of a single tone or tones. Here, too, however, a subtle *rubato* broadens or shortens the rhythmic values. The musical ideas of the Stefi motif (Figure 4.159, below) and its half-step subset, the Blood motif, come together at the end of the "Sixth Door" scene, during the symphonic development of the latter.

Figure 4.159. Set {0,1,4,8}.

During this passage the moving parts in the strings, bassoons, and horns spell out a steady succession of major seventh chords (the first two eighth-notes produce the vertical sonorities F–A–C–E and G–B–D–F-sharp), while above, dissonant half steps are sustained as overlapping waves of sound. Bluebeard gives Judith the final door key, and shows her his former wives (119/6–8): "*Nyisd ki, Judit. Lássad őket. Ott van mind a régi asszony.*" (Open now the door and see them. All my former wives await thee.) At this point we hear Theme (F), shown in Example 4.15 (p. 267), or what Leafstedt calls "sorrow music" (1999: 115; see Table 4.46, p. 267).

Example 4.13. Theme (D), 101/9–102/4.
© 1921 by Universal Edition A. G., Wien/UE 7026, used by kind permission.

Example 4.14. Theme (E), 105/1–4.
© 1921 by Universal Edition A. G., Wien/UE 7026, used by kind permission.

The score directions at this point read as follows:

Far a while she stands motionless then she takes the key with a faltering hand, and goes, her body swaying slightly, to the Seventh Door. When the lock snaps, the Fifth and Sixth Doors swing to with a gentle sighing sound. It becomes much darker. Only the opposite four open doorways illuminate the hall with their beams of colored light. […] And now the Seventh Door opens, and a long, tapering beam of silvery moonshine reaches out from the aperture and bathes the faces of Judith and Bluebeard in its silvery light. (Bartók 1952 [1925]: 153–154.)

The Sigh motif, moving in half-steps, is heard when the seventh door opens (120/5–6, 8).

In Table 4.46, I have added Leafstedt's distribution of musical ideas across the "Lake of Tears" scene.

Section	A	B	C
Rehearsal/measure numbers	91/1–99/8	100/1–111/11	112/1–120/9
Lake of tears	(A)		
Judith	(B)	(D)	development of (D)
Bluebeard	(C)	(E)	
Sorrow music			(F)

Table 4.46. "The Lake of Tears" scene, 91/1–120/9 (after Leafstedt 1999: 115).

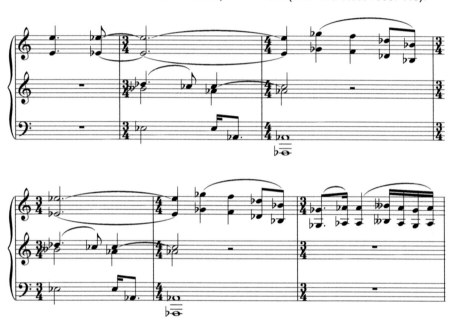

Example 4.15. Theme (F), 118/4–119/1.
© 1921 by Universal Edition A. G., Wien/UE 7026, used by kind permission.

The themes of this scene are summarized in Table 4.47 with corresponding modal/tonal key centers.

Themes	Rehearsal/ measure numbers	Property	Center
(A)	91/1–92/3	Modal	A-Aeolian (A minor)
(B)	92/4–7	Modal	A-Aeolian (A minor)
(C)	93/1–7	Modal	A-Phrygian
(D)	101/9–102/4	Modal melody with a complex harmonic background	F-Aeolian (F minor)
(E)	105/1–4	Chromatic	(F–center)
(F)	118/4–119/1	Modal	A-flat-Dorian

Table 4.47. "Lake of Tears" scene: Summary of thematic modal centers.

4.4.9.4. Pitch-web analysis of the scene

The music of the "Sixth Door" scene provides a summation-in-miniature of the overall symmetry of the opera: tonally stable beginning – chromatic middle section – tonally stable ending. As shown in Table 4.47 (previous page), themes (A), (B), (C), (D), and (F) are relatively stable tonally; by contrast, theme (E) is chromatic. At first glance, all these themes seem to be unrelated. However, a set-theoretical analysis of this scene shows its coherence, with focus on a particular pitch-class set that persists in the modal themes, chromatic elements, and in the background motion of the modal centers.

Like a shiver down the spine, an A minor arpeggio begins the scene (Example 4.16). Its uppermost notes, G–G-sharp, form the fatal interval of the Blood motif at 91/1–92/3, atop the mirror-symmetrical arpeggio with G-sharp as center. The combination results in an A minor 7th harmony and an A hyperminor 7th (A minor + major seventh), the latter comprehending the Stefi motif, superset {0,1,4,8}. (Lendvai 1964: 93.) Both C–E–G–G-sharp and G-sharp–G–E–C appear in mirror symmetry, and form set {0,1,4,8} at 91/1–3 (see Example 4.16, next page, and Figure 4.160).

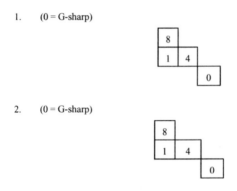

1.   (0 = G-sharp)

2.   (0 = G-sharp)

Figure 4.160. Sets in Theme (A), 91/1–4.

The Sigh motif at 91/4, so-called by scholars, is primarily a dramatic idea, and only secondarily a musical one (Example 4.16, next page). This motif, played by *oboi*, *corno inglese*, and *fagotti*, can be explained based on the tonal axis system. The notes E and D-sharp sound here; the E is the chord fifth of the Am7, and the D-sharp is the counterpole of A, on the axis system. This viewpoint is supported also at 95/1, where the Sigh motif sounds again, but in a different rhythm: after the Am7 and AmM7 arpeggio, we hear E–E-flat. The E, again, is understood as the chord fifth and E-flat (= D-sharp) as the counterpole of A on the tonal axis (TA), as explained in Chapter 2.2.1 (see especially, Figure 2.9, p. 58).

E–D-sharp–A (the last note of the Arpeggio theme) makes up the set {0,1,6}. Here can be found another mirror symmetry between the notes A: as last note of the arpeggio theme (91/3), E–D-sharp (Sigh motif at 91/4), A as first note of the arpeggio theme, when it returns in its original form at 91/5. A–E–D-sharp–A form a

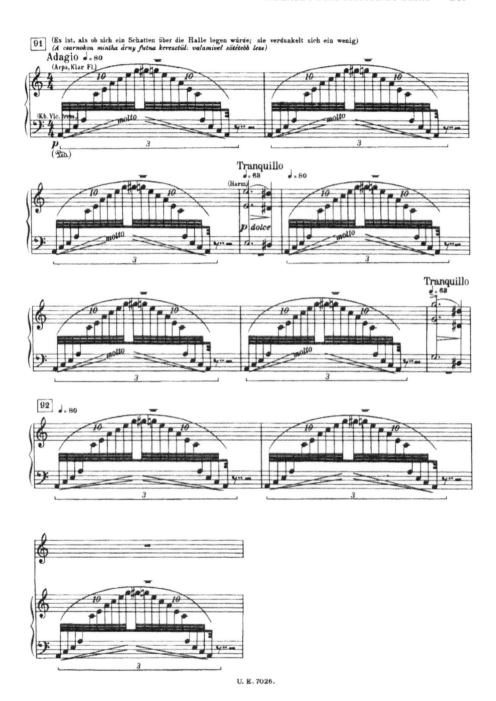

Example 4.16. "Sixth Door" scene, Section A, 91/1–92/3.

melodic mirror of set {0,1,6}; 91/5–7 is identical with 91/1–3 (Example 4.16, previous page).

Table 4.48 displays a sketch of the pitch structure in 91/1–92/3.

Rehearsal/ measure numbers	Theme/motif	Harmonies, sets, and ICVs
91/1–3	Arpeggio theme / Stefi motif	A minor seventh and A-hym seventh {0,1,4} (IC 1; Forte number 3–3; ICV 101100)
91/4	Sigh motif	Tonal axis (TA) Am7's fifth to D-sharp
91/5–7	Arpeggio theme / Stefi motif Softened image of Blood motif	Am7 and Ahym7 {0,1,4} (IC 1; Forte number 3–3; ICV 101100)
91/8	Sigh motif	Tonal axis (TA) Am7's seventh to D-sharp,{0,2,6} (Forte number 3–8; ICV 010101)
92/1–3	Arpeggio theme / Stefi motif Blood motif	Am7 and Ahym7 {0,1,4} (IC 1; Forte number 3–3; ICV 101100)

Table 4.48. The structure of section A, 91/1–92/3.

It is interesting to note that a third Sigh motif is missing. Instead, Judith's great dirge begins (at 92/4; Example 4.11, p. 264, Chapter 4.4.9.1).[428]

Set {0,1,4} first gains importance at the end of themes that may be conceived as "modal". For example, the ending of Theme (B) is re-harmonized in a way that produces the set {0,1,4}, at 98/4–6 (see Example 4.17, below; see also, Example 4.11, p. 264, Chapter 4.4.9.1). That set is made more apparent by Figure 4.161 (next page); inversions of the set are marked with the letter "I".

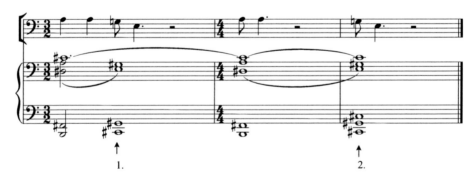

Example 4.17. Theme (B), re-harmonized, 98/4–6.
© 1921 by Universal Edition A. G., Wien/UE 7026, used by kind permission.

---

428. "Dirge" is the generally accepted term with which scholars refer to Judith's pentatonic theme (e.g., Kroó 1961: 281). Kroó's seminal article on *Duke Bluebeard's Castle* remains by far the most thorough appraisal of the opera and its dramatic text.

1.   (0 = G-sharp/I = Inversion)

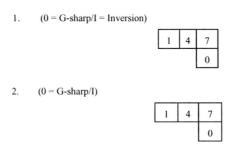

2.   (0 = G-sharp/I)

Figure 4.161. Sets of Theme (B) re-harmonized, 98/4–6.

Theme (D), score 101/9–102/4, is re-harmonized in its last appearance near the end of section B, at 110/5–111/5 (Example 4.18, below; comp. Example 4.13, p. 266, Chapter 4.4.9.3). In that re-harmonization, set {0,1,4} is a subset of the three tetrachords shown in Table 4.49.

Set	Pitch classes	Point 0	Forte number	ICV
{0,1,4,7}	C-sharp–E–G–C	C	4–18	102111
{0,1,4,8}	C–C-sharp–E–G-sharp/A-flat	C	4–19	101310
{0,3,4,7}	C–E-flat–E–G	C	4–17 (12)	102210

Table 4.49. Sets in the re-harmonized Theme (D), 110/5–111/5.

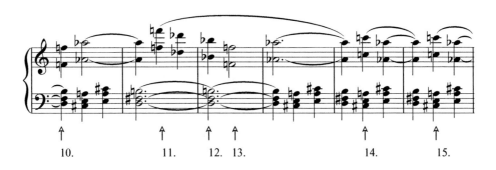

Example 4.18. Theme (D) re-harmonized, 110/5–111/5.
© 1921 by Universal Edition A. G., Wien/UE 7026, used by kind permission.

1. (0 = E)

2. (0 = C/I)

3. (0 = D)

4. (0 = G-sharp/I)

5. (0 = G-sharp/I)

6. (0 = C)

7. (0 = B-flat)

8.   (0 = F-sharp)

9.   (0 = B-flat)

10. (0 = F-sharp/I)

11. (0 = F-sharp)

12. (0 = B-flat)

13. (0 = F-sharp/I)

14. (0 = A)

15. (0 = A)

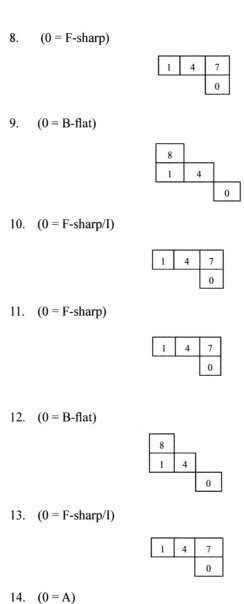

Figure 4.162. Instances of {0,1,4} as subset of Theme (D) re-harmonized, 110/5–111/5.

In addition to the endings, other parts of the modal themes are influenced by the prevalent {0,1,4} set, as shown in Example 4.19 and Figure 4.163.

Example 4.19. Theme (F), 118/4–6.[429]
© 1921 by Universal Edition A. G., Wien/UE 7026, used by kind permission.

1.   (0 = G-flat)

Figure 4.163. Set type of Theme (F).

Theme (D) is a special case. It begins with clear melodic instances of {0,1,4} with the accompanying harmony featuring that set as well (101/9–102/4, Example 4.13, p. 266, Chapter 4.4.9.3). Theme (D) makes its appearance during increases of dramatic tension (Example 4.20, below, and Figure 4.164, next page; see also Example 4.13, p. 266, Chapter 4.4.9.3).

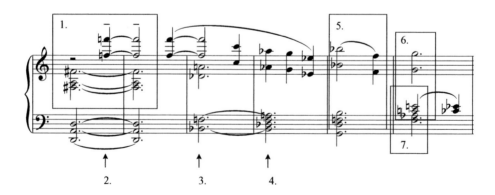

Example 4.20. Theme (D), 101/9–102/4.
© 1921 by Universal Edition A. G., Wien/UE 7026, used by kind permission.

---

429. The first part of Theme (F) has a clear Aeolian character; the theme itself is A-flat-Dorian.

1.   (0 = F)

2.   (0 = D)

3.   (0 = A)

4.   (0 = A)

5.   (0 = B-flat)

6.   (0 = A-flat/I)

7.   (0 = E)

Figure 4.164. {0,1,4} sets in Theme (D), 101/9–102/4.

The chromaticism, deriving from set {0,1,4} in these modal themes, reaches its peak in Theme (E), shown in Example 4.14 (p. 266, Chapter 4.4.9.3). In addition to the linear minor seconds in the upper-voice melody, the notes G and F on downbeats clash harmonically with the F-sharp pedal in the middle. The clearly profiled, lower-voice melody of Theme (E) in 105/1–4 unfolds the superset {0,1,4,7}; see Example 4.21 and Figure 4.165.

Example 4.21. Theme (E), lower-voice melody, 117/1.
© 1921 by Universal Edition A. G., Wien/UE 7026, used by kind permission.

1.   (0 = F/I)

Figure 4.165. Set {0,1,4,7}, lower-voice melody in Theme (E), 117/1.

The linear unfolding of superset {0,1,4,7} intrudes into the originally chromatic upper-voice melody of Theme (E), at 105/1–4. As shown in Example 4.22 (below), superset {0,1,4,7} is superimposed in the upper-voice melody. In the last bars of the example, the *stretto* of that superimposed tetrachord produces a vertical instance of the same set (Figure 4.166, next page).

Example 4.22. Theme (E), climax, 117/1–6.
© 1921 by Universal Edition A. G., Wien/UE 7026, used by kind permission.

1.   (0 = F/I)

2.   (0 = F/I)

3.   (0 = F/I)

4.   (0 = E/I)

5.   (0 = F-sharp)

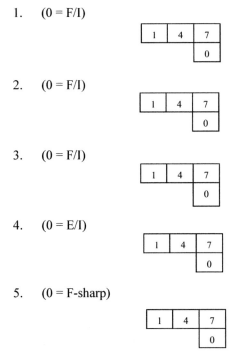

Figure 4.166. Instances of superset {0,1,4,7} in Theme (E), climax, 117/1–6.

At the beginning of section C, the upper-voice melody of the Theme (E) is developed in 105/1–4. In Example 4.23 (next page), the composer's mastery of the set-vocabulary of the opera is strikingly evident, both melodically and harmonically (see also, Figure 4.167, next page).

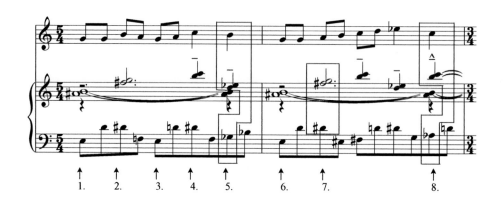

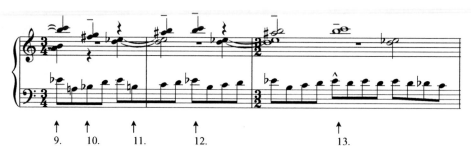

Example 4.23. Section C, development of Theme (E), 113/4–8.
© 1921 by Universal Edition A. G., Wien/UE 7026, used by kind permission.

1.   (0 = B/I)

2.   (0 = G/I)[430]

3.   (0 = B/I)

4.   (0 = B)

---

430. Without the Blood motif.

5. (0 = B)

6. (0 = B)

7. (0 = G)

8. (0 = C)

9. (0 = B)

10. (0 = F-sharp)

11. (0 = E-flat)

12. (0 = B)

13. (0 = B)

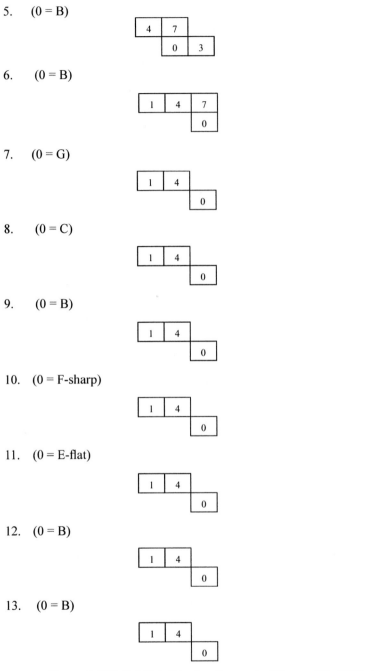

Figure 4.167. Set {0,1,4} in development of Theme (E), 113/4–8.

Imbrication (overlapping of melodic segments) represents an elementary way of determining the subsegments of a primary segment.[431] We find here an early, interesting example of linear imbrication in Judith's extended melody in 114/1–4, shown in Example 4.24 (see also, Figure 4.168, below): "*Vér szárad a fegyvereken, legszebbik koronád véres, virágaid földje véres, véres árnyat vet felhő!*" (Bloodstains on your warrior's weapons, blood upon your crown of glory. Red the soil around your flowers. Red the shade your cloud was throwing!)

Example 4.24. Judith's melody, 114/1–4.
© 1921 by Universal Edition A. G., Wien/UE 7026, used by kind permission.

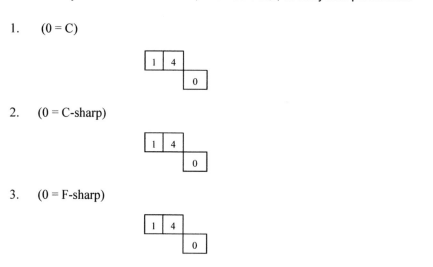

Figure 4.168. Sets of Judith's melody, 114/1–4.

In addition to the themes and harmony of the scene, the set {0,1,4} might also have influenced the choice of tonal centers, well as that scene's interconnection with others. Leafstedt (1999: 115) points out that the "Sixth Door" scene has a half-tone bimodal structure of A/A-flat. The A minor beginning leads through a chromatic internal passage, ending in A-flat "sorrow music". This long-term disposition of pitch centers is influenced by set {0,1,4}. The A/A-flat bimodality is clear, and the middle section is chromatic, without a modal center in the traditional sense. As in Theme

---

431. In his dissertation, *The Trichord: An Analytic Outlook for Twentieth-Century Music*, Steven Gilbert (1970) gives a detailed and systematic treatment of imbrication, with special emphasis on overlapping trichord segments.

(E), a lower-voice melody appears in 105/1–4, starting on the note F (Example 4.14, p. 266, Chapter 4.4.9.3; see also, Example 4.21, p. 276). As the melody stubbornly attached to the entire (E) theme in 105/1–4, here the note F is always found on the bass downbeat, whenever Theme (E) is heard in its entirety. During the development, where Theme (E) is not heard in its original form but instead varied (113/4–8), the note F still recurs as the downbeat of the bass. From rehearsal number 115 to the climax of the scene (at 117–118), each measures of music begin on F in the bass (115/1–117/4). If we accept F as the tonal center of the middle of the scene, the result is a total of three key areas formed in this passage, and the progression of centers A–F–A-flat is a inverted, linear unfolding of subset {0,1,4}.

Those key areas are not arbitrary. As the themes are comfortably fitted into those centers, the latter articulate dramatic events as well. The key area in A minor (Example 4.11, p. 264, Chapter 4.4.9.1), on which Themes (B) and (C) are based, signifies the lake of tears in 92/4–7 and 93/1–7 (Example 4.12, p. 265, Chapter 4.4.9.3). The key area of F, at 105/1–4, on which Theme (E) and its development (113/4–8) are based, signifies Judith's quest for Bluebeard's last key and the confrontation between the two protagonists. The "sorrow music," in A-flat, signifies Bluebeard's giving up the key to the last of his forbidden doors.

The outer key areas, A and A-flat, connect also to the key areas of preceding and subsequent scenes in the same fashion as they connect internally. In the "Fifth Door" scene ("Bluebeard's Domain") the key of C (74/19–90/14) connects with the two modally stable key areas, A and A-flat, with set {0,1,4}. The same set connects the C minor of the "Lake of Tears" scene (91/1–120/9) with that of "The Former Wives" (121/1–137/10), as shown in Table 4.50 and Figure 4.169.

Door Scene	"Fifth Door" scene: "Bluebeard's Domain"	"Sixth Door" scene: "The Lake of Tears"	"Seventh Door" scene: "The Former Wives"
Rehearsal/ measure numbers	74/19–90/14	91/1–120/9	121/1–137/10
Key centers	C	A–A-flat	C
Sets	4	1, 0	4

Table 4.50. Key transitions between the three last scenes.

1.   (0 = A-flat)

2.   (0 = A-flat)

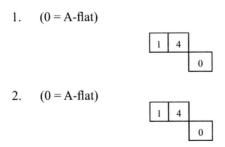

Figure 4.169. Sets of key transitions between the three last scenes.

In the "Lake of Tears" scene (91/1–120/9), the deliberate and sometimes exaggerated use of chromaticism obscures the relationship among musical materials. In the light of pitch-web analysis, it is revealed that different musical materials, which exists as foreground melodies or long-term key progressions, are unified in the sense that set {0,1,4} becomes prominent in different sections of the scene. Set {0,1,4} links the music materials between themes, between sections, and between scenes.

The set {0,1,4} appeared in different ways in different themes. The themes of the scene can be categorized into two main kinds: (1) the modal themes, which display clear tonal centricity; and (2) Theme (E) at 105/1–4, which forms its own category, since it is built from the chromatic scale. The {0,1,4} set found its place in Theme (E), mostly in the linear unfoldings of set {0,1,4,7}. By contrast, the set {0,1,4} appears in a different fashion in the modal themes.

According to Forte, the number of intervals formed by its cardinal number and the number of intervals is fixed for all PC-sets (1973: 3, 12, 19, 179, 209). That issue was dealt with in Chapter 1 (see especially, n. 4, p. 3), so here I add just the following quotation from Forte, who views the intervallic content of PC-sets

> [...] as the fundamental basis of the [pitch-class] genera, which provides a foundation independent of the vicissitudes of pitch-class constituency, it seems most fruitful to take the trichord as the set of least cardinal number, which, unlike the dyad, offers more than one representative of an interval class and which therefore is capable of being compared meaningfully with others of its kind. (Forte 1988a: 188.)

Given a PC-set of two members (cardinality 2), the number of intervals is 1.[432] If an element is added to it, the cardinal number or "cardinality" of the set rises to 3 (Forte 1973: 3, 12, passim; see also, n. 132, p. 73, Chapter 2.3), and the addition of the new element forms a new interval (Tables 4.51–4.52 and Figures 4.170–4.174, next page).

---

432. Forte's decision includes only sets of cardinality 3 to 9 in his definitive list (1973: 179–181; see also, the Appendix). It is the result of his general view of atonal compositional techniques, and indicates among other things that small-scale motivic factors are not in his judgment the most essential in determining the structure of atonal music. The domain of all PC-sets may be partitioned into types or equivalence classes based on cardinality or number of PCs, or other criteria. There are thirteen cardinalities from 0–12: the null set (Forte number 0–1; ICV 000000), monad, dyad, trichord, tetrachord, pentachord, hexachord, septachord, octachord, nonachord, decachord, undecachord, and aggregate or dodecachord. (See also, n. 6, p. 5, Chapter 1.)

Cardinal number	Number of intervals
1	0
2	0 + 1
3	0 + 1 + 2
4	0 + 1 + 2 + 3
5	0 + 1 + 2 + 3 + 4
6	0 + 1 + 2 + 3 + 4 + 5
7	0 + 1 + 2 + 3 + 4 + 5 + 6
8	0 + 1 + 2 + 3 + 4 + 5 + 6 + 7
9	0 + 1 + 2 + 3 + 4 + 5 + 6 + 7 + 8
10	0 + 1 + 2 + 3 + 4 + 5 + 6 + 7 + 8 + 9
11	0 + 1 + 2 + 3 + 4 + 5 + 6 + 7 + 8 + 9 + 10
12	0 + 1 + 2 + 3 + 4 + 5 + 6 + 7 + 8 + 9 + 10 + 11

Table 4.51. Cardinal number and number of intervals.

Set	Number of intervals	Forte number	IC	ICV	Descriptive name
{0,1,2}	0 + 1 + 2	3–1 (12)	1	210000	chromatic trimirror
{0,1,3}	0 + 1 + 2	3–2	1	111000	Phrygian trichord
{0,1,4}	0 + 1 + 2	3–3	1	101100	major-minor trichord
{0,1,5}	0 + 1 + 2	3–4	1	100110	incomplete major seventh
{0,1,6}	0 + 1 + 2	3–5	1	100011	tritone fourth

Table 4.52. Sets {0,1,2}, {0,1,3}, {0,1,4}, {0,1,5}, {0,1,6}, and the Cardinal numbers, Forte numbers, ICVs and descriptive name/properties.

Figure 4.170. Set {0,1,2}.

Figure 4.171. Set {0,1,3}

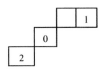

Figure 4.172. Set {0,1,4}.

Figure 4.173. Set {0,1,5}.

Figure 4.174. Set {0,1,6}.

Among all chromatic trichords, the {0,1,4} trichord is the most apparent one in the scene. Set {0,1,4} reveals its importance in various ways, both in and between the themes, and can serve as a link to all the musical material that follows. The trichord contributes chromaticism to the music in the scene, since set {0,1,4} contains one minor second (or interval class 1). Compared to other trichords with at least one instance of interval class 1, {0,1,4} is the most remote from the traditional major scale. Table 4.53 lists several possibilities of chromatic and traditional scales in which sets {0,1,2}, {0,1,3}, {0,1,4}, {0,1,5}, and {0,1,6} may be found.

Set	Forte number	ICV	Found in traditional scale	Sets of traditional scale
{0,1,2}	3–1 (12)	210000	Chromatic scale	{0,1,2,3,4,5,6,7,8,9,10,11}
{0,1,3}	3–2	111000	Major scale (7, 1, 2)	{0,2,4,5,7,9,11}
{0,1,3}	3–2	111000	Major scale (3, 4, 5)	{0,2,4,5,7,9,11}
{0,1,3}	3–2	111000	Dorian scale (2, 3, 4)	{0,2,3,5,7,9,10}
{0,1,3}	3–2	111000	Dorian scale (6, 7, 1)	{0,2,3,5,7,9,10}
{0,1,3}	3–2	111000	Phrygian scale (1, 2, 3)	{0,1,3,5,7,8,10}
{0,1,3}	3–2	111000	Phrygian scale (5, 6, 7)	{0,1,3,5,7,8,10}
{0,1,3}	3–2	111000	Lydian scale (7, 1, 2)	{0,2,4,6,7,9,11}
{0,1,3}	3–2	111000	Lydian scale (4, 5, 6)	{0,2,4,6,7,9,11}
{0,1,3}	3–2	111000	Mixolydian scale (3, 4, 5)	{0,2,4,5,7,9,10}
{0,1,3}	3–2	111000	Mixolydian scale (6, 7, 1)	{0,2,4,5,7,9,10}
{0,1,3}	3–2	111000	Aeolian scale (2, 3, 4)	{0,2,3,5,7,8,10}
{0,1,3}	3–2	111000	Aeolian scale (5, 6, 7)	{0,2,3,5,7,8,10}
{0,1,3}	3–2	111000	Harmonic minor scale (2, 3, 4)	{0,2,3,5,7,8,11}
{0,1,3}	3–2	111000	Harmonic minor scale (7, 1, 2)	{0,2,3,5,7,8,11}
{0,1,3}	3–2	111000	Melodic minor scale (2, 3, 4)	{0,2,3,5,7,9,11}
{0,1,3}	3–2	111000	Melodic minor scale (7, 1, 2)	{0,2,3,5,7,9,11}
{0,1,3}	3–2	111000	Locrian scale (1, 2, 3)	{0,1,3,5,6,8,10}
{0,1,3}	3–2	111000	Locrian scale (4, 5, 6)	{0,1,3,5,6,8,10}
{0,1,4}	3–3	101100	Chromatic scale (1, 2, 5)	{0,1,2,3,4,5,6,7,8,9,10,11}
{0,1,4}	3–3	101100	Chromatic scale (2, 3, 6)	{0,1,2,3,4,5,6,7,8,9,10,11}
{0,1,4}	3–3	101100	Chromatic scale (3, 4, 7)	{0,1,2,3,4,5,6,7,8,9,10,11}
{0,1,4}	3–3	101100	Chromatic scale (4, 5, 8)	{0,1,2,3,4,5,6,7,8,9,10,11}
{0,1,4}	3–3	101100	Chromatic scale (5, 6, 9)	{0,1,2,3,4,5,6,7,8,9,10,11}
{0,1,4}	3–3	101100	Chromatic scale (6, 7, 10)	{0,1,2,3,4,5,6,7,8,9,10,11}
{0,1,4}	3–3	101100	Chromatic scale (7, 8, 11)	{0,1,2,3,4,5,6,7,8,9,10,11}
{0,1,4}	3–3	101100	Chromatic scale (8, 9, 1)	{0,1,2,3,4,5,6,7,8,9,10,11}
{0,1,4}	3–3	101100	Chromatic scale (9, 10, 2)	{0,1,2,3,4,5,6,7,8,9,10,11}
{0,1,4}	3–3	101100	Chromatic scale (10, 11, 3)	{0,1,2,3,4,5,6,7,8,9,10,11}
{0,1,4}	3–3	101100	Chromatic scale (11, 1, 4)	{0,1,2,3,4,5,6,7,8,9,10,11}

{0,1,4}	3–3	101100	Harmonic minor scale (5, 6, 7)	{0,2,3,5,7,8,11}
{0,1,4}	3–3	101100	Harmonic minor scale (7, 1, 3)	{0,2,3,5,7,8,11}
{0,1,4}	3–3	101100	Melodic minor scale (7, 1, 3)	{0,2,3,5,7,9,11}
{0,1,5}	3–4	100110	Major scale (3, 4, 6)	{0,2,4,5,7,9,11}
{0,1,5}	3–4	100110	Major scale (7, 1, 3)	{0,2,4,5,7,9,11}
{0,1,5}	3–4	100110	Dorian scale (2, 3, 5)	{0,2,3,5,7,9,10}
{0,1,5}	3–4	100110	Dorian scale (6, 7, 2)	{0,2,3,5,7,9,10}
{0,1,5}	3–4	100110	Phrygian scale (1, 2, 4)	{0,1,3,5,7,8,10}
{0,1,5}	3–4	100110	Phrygian scale (5, 6, 1)	{0,1,3,5,7,8,10}
{0,1,5}	3–4	100110	Lydian scale (4, 5, 7)	{0,2,4,6,7,9,11}
{0,1,5}	3–4	100110	Lydian scale (7, 1, 3)	{0,2,4,6,7,9,11}
{0,1,5}	3–4	100110	Mixolydian scale (3, 4, 6)	{0,2,4,5,7,9,10}
{0,1,5}	3–4	100110	Mixolydian scale (6, 7, 2)	{0,2,4,5,7,9,10}
{0,1,5}	3–4	100110	Aeolian scale (2, 3, 7)	{0,2,3,5,7,8,10}
{0,1,5}	3–4	100110	Aeolian scale (5, 6, 1)	{0,2,3,5,7,8,10}
{0,1,5}	3–4	100110	Harmonic minor scale (2, 3, 5)	{0,2,3,5,7,8,11}
{0,1,5}	3–4	100110	Harmonic minor scale (5, 6, 1)	{0,2,3,5,7,8,11}
{0,1,5}	3–4	100110	Melodic minor scale (2, 3, 5)	{0,2,3,5,7,9,11}
{0,1,5}	3–4	100110	Locrian scale (1, 2, 4)	{0,1,3,5,6,8,10}
{0,1,5}	3–4	100110	Locrian scale (4, 5, 7)	{0,1,3,5,6,8,10}
{0,1,6}	3–5	100011	Major scale (3, 4, 7)	{0,2,4,5,7,9,11}
{0,1,6}	3–5	100011	Major scale (7, 1, 4)	{0,2,4,5,7,9,11}
{0,1,6}	3–5	100110	Dorian scale (6, 7, 3)	{0,2,3,5,7,9,10}
{0,1,6}	3–5	100110	Lydian scale (4, 5, 1)	{0,2,4,6,7,9,11}
{0,1,6}	3–5	100110	Mixolydian scale (3, 4, 7)	{0,2,4,5,7,9,10}
{0,1,6}	3–5	100110	Aeolian scale (2, 3, 6)	{0,2,3,5,7,8,10}
{0,1,6}	3–5	100110	Harmonic minor scale (2, 3, 6)	{0,2,3,5,7,8,11}
{0,1,6}	3–5	100110	Melodic minor scale (7, 1, 4)	{0,2,3,5,7,9,11}
{0,1,6}	3–5	100110	Locrian scale (1, 2, 5)	{0,1,3,5,6,8,10}

Table 4.53. Comparison of chromatic trichords.[433]

Subsets {0,1,2} and {0,1,4} are absent from the major scale or mode. {0,1,2} can only be found inside a chromatic scale, whereas {0,1,4} can only be perceived in a modified minor scale. Set {0,1,4} can be thought of as both remote from major tonalities and, more importantly, from the (mostly pentatonic) modes on which the opera is based.

433. This list could be continued with several examples of {0,1,4}, such as {0,1,4,5}, {0,1,4,6}, {0,1,4,7}, {0,1,4,8}, {0,1,4,5,6}, {0,1,4,5,7}, {0,1,4,5,8}, {0,1,4,6,7}, {0,1,4,6,8}, {0,1,4,6,9}, {0,1,4,7,8}, {0,1,4,7,9}, {0,1,4,5,6,7}, {0,1,4,5,6,8}, {0,1,4,5,7,8}, {0,1,4,5,8,9}, {0,1,4,6,7,8}, {0,1,4,6,7,9}, {0,1,4,5,6,7,8}, and {0,1,4,6,7,8,9}. See also, Solomon (1982) and the Appendix to the present study.

4.4.10. Seventh door: 'Former Wives'

The "Seventh Door" scene fulfills the expectations that one has had about Judith's fate. The entire drama has been converging on this point, which forms the opera's second climax (Mauser 1981: 77; [434] see also, pp. 247–249, Chapter 4.4.8). Table 4.54 shows the structure of this scene.

Section	Rehearsal/measure numbers	Synopsis
A	121/1–126/11	The former wives step alive, splendidly adorned with jewels and rich fabrics.
B	127/1–130/10	Each wife is associated with a time of day: morning, noon, evening.
C	131/1–137/10	Bluebeard symbolically links Judith with night. She steps forward to assume her place next to Bluebeard's former wives.

Table 4.54. Structure of the "Seventh Door" scene, 121/1–137/10.[435]

Bartók sets the music of the opening, Section A, in C-minor (see Example 4.25, next page).

---

434. Siegfried Mauser (1981: 77) notes a resemblance between the opera's dramatic form, one act articulated around two distinct dramatic peaks, and general tendencies in early modern and expressionist theater.

435. In Perrault's (1920 [1697]) version: "Etant arrivée à la porte du cabinet, elle s'y arrêta quelque temps, songeant à la défense que son mari lui avait faite, et considérant qu'il pourrait lui arriver malheur d'avoir été désobéissante; mais la tentation était si forte qu'elle ne put la surmonter: elle prit donc la petite clef, et ouvrit en tremblant la porte du cabinet. D'abord elle ne vit rien, parce que les fenêtres étaient fermées. Après quelques moments, elle commença à voir que le plancher était tout couvert de sang caillé, et que dans ce sang, se miraient les corps de plusieurs femmes mortes et attachées le long des murs: c'était toutes les femmes que la Barbe-Bleue avait épousées, et qu'il avait égorgées l'une après l'autre. Elle pensa mourir de peur, et la clef du cabinet, qu'elle venait de retirer de la serrure, lui tomba de la main. Après avoir un peu repris ses sens, elle ramassa la clef, referma la porte, et monta à sa chambre pour se remettre un peu; mais elle n'en pouvait venir à bout, tant elle était émue. Ayant remarqué que la clef du cabinet était tachée de sang, elle l'essuya deux ou trois fois; mais le sang ne s'en allait point: elle eut beau la laver, et même la frotter avec du sablon et avec du grès, il demeura toujours du sang, car la clef était fée, et il n'y avait pas moyen de la nettoyer tout à fait: quand on ôtait le sang d'un côté, il revenait de l'autre." (Having come to the closet door, she made a stop for some time, thinking about her husband's orders, and considering what unhappiness might attend her if she was disobedient; but the temptation was so strong that she could not overcome it. She then took the little key, and opened it, trembling. At first, she could not see anything plainly, because the windows were shut. After some moments she began to perceive that the floor was all covered over with clotted blood, on which lay the bodies of several dead women, ranged against the walls. These were all the wives whom Bluebeard had married and murdered, one after another. She thought she should have died for fear, and the key, which she pulled out of the lock, fell out of her hand. After having somewhat recovered her surprise, she picked up the key, locked the door, and went upstairs into her chamber to recover; but she could not, so much was she frightened. Having observed that the key to the closet was stained with blood, she tried two or three times to wipe it off; but the blood would not come out; in vain did she wash it, and even rub it with soap and sand. The blood still remained, for the key was magical and she could never make it quite clean; when the blood was gone off from one side, it came again on the other.)

Example 4.25. Folk-song theme,121/1–9.
© 1921 by Universal Edition A. G., Wien/UE 7026, used by kind permission.

The recitative tune, in 5/4 meter, is the third "folk-song" of the opera invented by Bartók (see also, Example 4.1, p. 204, Chapter 4.4.1, and Example 4.11, p. 264, Chapter 4.4.9.1). At 121/3–122/4, an English horn melody (B-flat–B–C–C-sharp–E–F-sharp–G–A-flat) weaves contrapuntal arabesques around the clarinet tune (set type shown in Figure 4.175).

2		8	
	10	1	
0	3	6	9

Figure 4.175. Set {0,1,2,3,6,8,9,10}, B♭ = 0.

The English horn motif is a four-note figure curling upward around the pitch E-flat with motions of a minor third to G-flat. Suchoff (1995: 66–67) has remarked on the resemblance between that motif and a similar melodic figure in the arioso "Ach,

Golgotha" from Bach's *St. Matthew Passion*.[436] Table 4.55 and Figures 4.176–4.177 summarize the pitch-content of Bluebeard and Judith's lines in 122/1–5.

Rehearsal/ measure numbers	Character	Text	Pitch classes	Point 0	Set
122/1–3	Bluebeard	"*Lásd a régi asszonyokat! Lásd akiket én szerettem.*" (Hearts that I loved and cherished! See, my former loves.)	C–E-flat–G	C	{0,3,7}
122/4–5	Judith	"*Élnek*, élnek, itten élnek!" (Living, breathing. They live here!)	E-flat–E–A	E-flat	{0,1,6}

Table 4.55. Pitch content of Bluebeard and Judith's lines, 122/1–5.

Figure 4.176. Set {0,3,7}.

Figure 4.177. Set {0,1,6}.

According to the score:

---

436. Bartók in 1911 was certainly not in the habit of making quiet reference to Christian theology in his music, but this oblique commentary may be his way of underlining the larger meaning of Judith and Bluebeard's final actions on stage. Judith is killed in an emotional or psychological sense. Bónis (1981) points out that Bartók's compositions contain numerous "hidden autobiographical elements," quotations from his own and from other composers' works. These can often be revealed only through careful analysis. In *Bluebeard's Castle*, Bartók quotes an ostinato motive from Bach's *St. Matthew Passion* and also uses the motive B-A-C-H. *The Wooden Prince* begins with an evocation of nature modeled upon the one that begins Wagner's *Das Rheingold*, except in Bartók the first seven harmonics are combined (as opposed to the first five in the Wagner) to create the "Bartók chord". Other examples noted include reference to Ravel's "Scarbo" in Bartók's *Allegro barbaro* and the reformulation of the slow movement of Beethoven's *String Quartet* in A Minor, Op. 132, in the second movement of Bartók's *Third Piano Concerto*. Bónis (1963) remarks that Bartók's quotations have never been completely examined. His quotations are rarely made for "effect," but are instead hidden away and are of personal significance. Many examples are noted with reference to folk melodies and to the works of Haydn, Liszt, Wagner, Bach, Beethoven, Debussy, Ravel, Kodály, and Stravinsky. Bartók also quotes music from his own earlier works. The quotations discussed are divided into four groups: (1) reference to the music of other composers, often inspired by similar compositional situations; (2) programmatic and autobiographical quotations; (3) quotations of a humorous or ironic nature; and (4) "shopwork" quotations, themes that recur in several works and are molded to "final perfection". Bartók is viewed as an innovator who at the same time is a great synthesizer of disparate influences.

Through the seventh door, his former wives come forth. They are three in number. They wear crowns on their heads, and their bodies are ablaze with priceless gems. Pale of face, but with proud and haughty gait, they step forward, one after the other, and stand before Bluebeard, who sinks to his knees in homage. (Bartók 1952 [1925]: 156.)

When Bluebeard holds out his arms to address the wives (123/4–124/1), the upper strings enter at 124/1 (and begin the melodic lines, yielding a more string-dominated sound that, in the opera, is often heard in the context of his vocal lines.

In Section B, Bluebeard explains that these are his former wives. The melody, after symbolizing dawn and midday, turns to begin its descent, leading symbolically toward of evening time. The tonal centers of Section B are outlined in Table 4.56 and Figure 4.178.

Rehearsal/ measure numbers	Synopsis	Tonality
127/1–16	"*Hajnalban az elsőt leltem...*" (I met the first in the red dawn...)	B-flat major
128/1–129/11	"*Másodikat délben leltem...*" (I met the second one at noon...)	C major
129/12–130/10	"*Harmadikat este leltem...*" (I met the third in the evening...)	D minor

Table 4.56. "Seventh Door" scene, Section B.

Figure 4.178. Set {0,2,4}.

The orchestral accompaniment of the first two wives is made more dramatic by the frequent change of harmony.

In Section C, the three wives step back behind the seventh door (130/7–10), and Bluebeard turns to Judith (131/2–3). At that moment, the timbre reverts to the woodwind-dominated sound heard at the scene's opening. Along with these changes comes an oscillation between the chromatically inflected realms associated with Judith throughout the opera, and the diatonic/pentatonic music to which Bluebeard sings the majority of his lines. At 130/8–10, the Stefi motif, D–F–A–C-sharp (Figure 4.179, next page) provides a dramatic pause in the "Seventh Door" scene before Bluebeard turns to Judith to tell her that she will be the fourth of his entombed wives (131/2–132/10): "*Negyediket éjjel leltem. Csillagos, fekete éjjel.*" (The fourth I found at midnight. Starry, ebon-mantled midnight.)

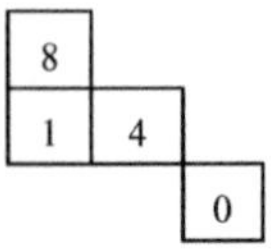

Figure 4.179. Set {0,1,4,8}, C# = 0.

The fourth door slowly closes (131/2–3). While passages of minor seconds return in lengthy repetition, from the threshold of the third door Bluebeard takes mantle, crown, and jewelry and adorns Judith with them (132/10–133/3). Judith protests, and her vocal line in 133/4–134/7 is confined to the interval of a minor second (Table 4.57 and Figures 4.180–4.184).

Character	Rehearsal/ measure numbers	Character's lines	Pitch classes	Point 0	Integers
Bluebeard	133/4–7	*"Tied csillagos palástja."* (Thine is now the starry mantle.)	G–A-flat–C-flat– D-flat–E-flat	G	{0,1,4,6,8}
Judith	133/4–7	*"Kékszakállú, nem kell, nem kell."* (Bluebeard, spare me! Spare me!)	A-flat–G-flat	G-flat	{0,2}
Bluebeard	134/1–4 (=133/4–7)	*"Tied gyémánt koronája,"* (Thine is now the crown of diamonds,)	F–F-sharp–A–B– C-sharp	F	{0,1,4,6,8}
Judith	134/1–3	*"Jaj, jaj, Kékszakállú vedd le."* (Oh, it is too heavy!)	C-sharp–D–E	C-sharp	{0,1,3}
Bluebeard	134/5–7	*"Tied a legdrágább kincsem."* (Thine is the wealth of my kingdom.)	E–G–A–B	E	{0,3,5,7}
Judith	134/5–7	*"Jaj, jaj, Kékszakállú vedd le."* (Oh, it is too heavy!)	B–C	B	{0,1}

Table 4.57. Bluebeard and Judith's lines, 133/4–7.

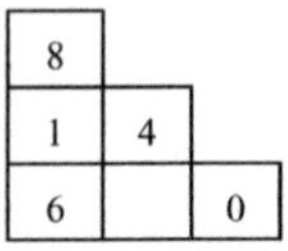

Figure 4.180. Set {0,1,4,6,8}.

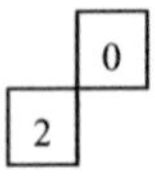

Figure 4.281. Set {0,2}.

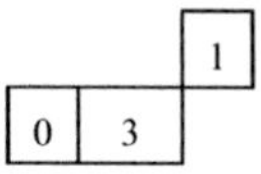

Figure 4.182. Set {0,1,3}.

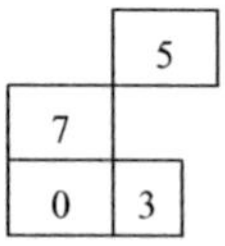

Figure 4.183. Set {0,3,5,7}.

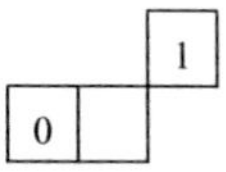

Figure 4.184. Set {0,1}.

The farewell is accompanied by the orchestra playing in intervals of seconds and thirds (135/1–19). Beginning diatonically, in a Lydian-inflected B-flat major, the six-note figures rise higher to incorporate chromatic tones that move in half-step motion. The dialogue returns to focus on Judith, whom Bluebeard addresses in the chromatic harmonic environment of the Blood motif (135/1–10). Bluebeard's line, "*Szép vagy, szép vagy, százszor szép vagy*" (You are beautiful, beautiful, a hundred times beautiful), outlines D–E–F–G–A–B–C, the Dorian heptatonic scale, given as a set in Figure 4.185. It then leads to an orchestral climax over a B-flat pedal tone (136/1–137/10).

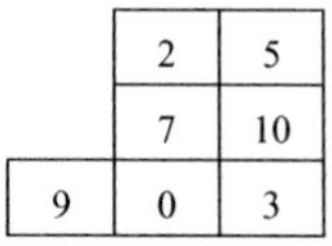

	2	5
	7	10
9	0	3

Figure 4.185. Set {0,2,3,5,7,9,10}, D = 0.

The orchestral music becomes increasingly dissonant as Bluebeard sings his last line to Judith (135/5–10): "*Te voltál a legszebb asszony*" (You were the most beautiful wife), culminating in the mighty crash of dissonance in 136/1–137/10. As the score states:

> They gaze into each other's eyes. Bowed down by the weight of the cloak, her head dropping, Judith goes the way of the other women, walking along the beam of moonlight toward the seventh door. She enters, and it closes after her. (Bartók 1952 [1925]: 171–172.)

The organ reappears, supporting the final orchestral surge over a B-flat pedal point (136/1–137/10) and subsequently provides a brief transition (138/1–140/11) back to the opera's opening F-sharp melody (comp. also, Example 4.1, p. 204, Chapter 4.4.1).

4.4.11. Closing 'Night' scene

In the closing "Night" scene, also called "Epilogue"[437], the circle of the composition is closed with a recapitulation of material from the beginning of the opera (0/1–16; Example 4.1, p. 204, Chapter 4.4.1). Bluebeard is left alone on the stage, where he sings the following lines, which are additions that Bartók made to the original text: "*És mindég is éjjel lesz már... éjjel... éjjel...*" (Henceforth all shall be darkness... darkness... darkness...) His melody outlines C–C-sharp–D–E-sharp–F-sharp–G–A, displayed as a set in Figure 4.186 (see also, Table 4.58, below).

2	5	
7		1
0		6	9

Figure 4.186. Set {0,1,2,5,6,7,9}, C = 0.

Section	Rehearsal/measure numbers	Synopsis
A	138/1–139/12	Bluebeard's last lines.
B	139/13–140/11	Bluebeard disappears; total darkness on stage.

Table 4.58. Structure of the closing "Night" scene, 121/1–137/10.

The F-sharp pentatonic theme, F-sharp–A–B–C-sharp–E (Figure 4.187) from the beginning of the opera (0/1–16; Example 4.1, p. 204, Chapter 4.4.1), is harmonized with chords based on that pentatonic minor, including minor triads and other tonal harmonies.

	5
7	10
0	3

Figure 4.187. Set {0,3,5,7,10}, F# = 0.

Fragments of the menacing motif from the opening "Night" scene (0/16–19) reappear in 138/4–5, 9–10; 139/4–5, 9–11; and 140/1–2, 4. The horn lines of those passages are explored in Table 4.59 and Figure 4.188 (next page).

Rehearsal/measure numbers	Pitch classes	Point 0	Set
138/4–5	C-sharp–D-sharp–E-sharp–F-sharp	C-sharp	{0,2,4,5}
138/9–10	C-sharp–D-sharp–E-sharp–F-sharp	C-sharp	{0,2,4,5}
139/4–6	C-sharp–D-sharp–E-sharp–F-sharp	C-sharp	{0,2,4,5}

Table 4.59. Horn lines, 138/4–139/6.

---

437. It is based on the constant intervallic symmetry of the half-step.

Figure 4.188. Set {0,2,4,5}, C# = 0.

The F-sharp melody is harmonized with chords that grow in dissonance, while Bluebeard sings the last word on an oscillating tritone/diminished fifth (Table 4.60 and Figure 4.189, below).

Rehearsal/ measure numbers	Text	Pitch classes	Point 0	Set	Forte number	ICV
139/4–5	"*éjjel*" (night)	G–C-sharp	C	{0,6}	2–6 (6)	000001
139/9–10	"*éjjel*" (night)	F-sharp–C	C	{0,6}	2–6 (6)	000001

Table 4.60. Bluebeard's lines, 139/4–5 and 139/9–10.

0		6

Figure 4.189. Set {0,6}, C = 0.

In this context, the F-sharp tonality regains it dramatic association with darkness (Example 4.26, next page).

The Night is a symbolic center into which everything collapses, an emblem of stillness and cold. Bluebeard found Judith at night. Before she came to the castle, and now that she has departed from Bluebeard, all the doors are locked, and, again, there is darkness. (Lendvai 1988: 142; see also, Table 4.1, p. 191, Chapter 4.3.) Leafstedt observes that:

> The idea of bringing back the opening music at the end was Bartók's own, a ges-
> ture inspired perhaps by the stage direction prescribing "total darkness" for the
> final moments – a return to the stage lighting of the beginning – and by his firm
> grasp of the play's inherent symbolic dimension. (Leafstedt 1999: 58.)

The four-line pentatonic melody ends, and the curtain closes over the tragedy. The harmonic resolution remains vague. The dissonant Blood motif makes its last appearance in the clarinets, as F-sharp–G (140/6–8). Then the music softly dies away, ending with an imperfect cadence (140/9–11).

Bartók extensively revised *Bluebeard's Castle*, both after composing it and prior to its performances, often at the last moment. In February 1912, Bartók made a few musical changes in the manuscript, and composed a new ending to the opera (Example 4.26, next page). He struggled throughout his career with the large-scale form of his pieces, and especially with the problem of endings. Unlike Stravinsky or Webern, Bartók did not like to leave his pieces "open" – ending with a question mark or with unresolved contrasts. Nor did he want the resolution to come about in a simple or

Example 4.26. Closing Night theme, 138/1–140/11.
© 1921 by Universal Edition A. G., Wien/UE 7026, used by kind permission.

easy manner. In several cases, he changed the shape of the finale at the suggestion of performers, as in the *Sonata for Solo Violin* (the last movement of which exists in two versions) and the *Concerto for Orchestra* (Sz 116, BB 123, 1944).[438] Bartók made major cuts in the finale of the *Sonata* (1926) during the compositional process, and discarded his entire conception of the last movement of the *Sixth String Quartet* (Sz 114, BB 119, 1939)[439] at a relatively late stage of composition.

Bartók composed three versions of the ending of the opera, from 1911 to 1918, all focusing on Bluebeard and Judith's last words to each other, and on the return of the opening F-sharp-pentatonic theme to conclude the work[440] (Leafstedt 1999: 125–158; 2000: 226; and Kroó 1981). Leafstedt remarks on some of those changes:

> By 1918, the extramusical associations of the major-seventh chord must have no longer been very strong for Bartók. What had seemed to him, in 1911, such a perfect symbol of the emotional heartache of love – a symbolic relationship worthy of emphasis at the opera's conclusion – must have now appeared unnecessarily obvious. He therefore made little effort to retain this feature of the original. As he went back to revise the opera, he removed the major sevenths from the final version of the ending and rewrote Bluebeard's pentatonic lines. Of the former musical symbolism, only the melodic half-step remains in Judith's vocal part to remind us of the opera's tragic conclusion: that the fulfillment of love also brings the death of love. The original ending of *Duke Bluebeard's Castle* brought that symbolism sharply into focus. (Leafstedt 2000: 243.)

---

438. On Bartók's concertos, see Schneider (1997) and Suchoff (1995).

439. The *Sixth String Quartet* was completed in November 1940, just before Bartók immigrated to the United States (Abraham 1942). The *Sixth String Quartet*, to some extent, represents a return to the lyrical, Romantic style of the *First Quartet* (see pp. 26–27, Chapter 2.1.2, and n. 90, p. 45, Chapter 2.1.3). See also, Abraham (1945); and Kárpáti (1975).

440. Kodály's first wife, Emma, had made a German translation of the libretto (Demény, ed. 1976: 313). Bartók continued to revise the opera, making alterations for the published vocal score in 1921, and changes in vocal declamation during the 1930s. Six complete manuscript scores of *Bluebeard's Castle* and one six-page fragment survive. Five of those scores date from the years 1911–1912; the other two date from 1917–1918 and ca. 1922, respectively. On Bartók's revisions, a detailed listing of source material is provided in Kroó (1981) and Leafstedt (1999: 125–158). Kroó traces the progress of Bartók's revisions from 1911 to 1921 and even further, when the composer condoned minor changes in the vocal parts for stage and radio performances in the 1920s and 1930s. Kroó, using source materials held in Hungary and the United States, compares various endings of the opera, giving us insight into Bartók's approach to composition and dramaturgy. Kroó establishes dates for Bartók's revisions and presents the revised vocal parts of *Bluebeard* that were written after publication of the work. Leafstedt (1999: 128–130) lists the principal sources of the opera in chronological order, beginning with Bartók's autograph draft.

5. CONCLUSIONS

Bluebeard's Castle has long been considered one of the most significant masterpieces of the international music canon, and the opera occupies a central place in Hungarian culture, as a historical landmark of the nation's musical consciousness. To this day, it remains the subject of many spirited and impassioned analyses. As such, one might assume that Bartók's opera has been so thoroughly analyzed that any future work in that area would be redundant. Yet, the results of my study suggest that that many facets of the work remain to be investigated.

The analyst is in a precarious position when attempting to establish unifying relationships among elements separated by intervening events, especially in music based on melodic and harmonic conventions unlike those of traditional functional harmony. In the present study, I have proposed a combined analytic model to deal with such problems, drawing primarily from set theory (Forte), pitch-web analysis (Joutsenvirta), axis-system tonality (Lendvai), and Bartók's own views of compositional method as related to bitonality, modes, tonal focus, and other matters, as evidenced in the evolution of his personal musical style.

As discussed in Chapters 1 and 2.4, pitch-set theory was evolved by Allen Forte to provide insight into the underlying structure of atonal music in a way that Schenkerian analysis does for tonal music (Schenker 1956 [1935]; see also, Forte & Gilbert 1982). As Forte puts it, his theory "establishes a framework for the description, interpretation and explanation of any atonal composition" (1973: 93). Though often criticized as an analytic method – because of its lack of rigor in musical segmentation rules and its non-compliance with aural experience – the importance of Forte's work cannot be denied. If nothing else, the theory presents an exact accounting and labeling of pitch collections and their interrelationships (see the Appendix).

It is obvious, however, that Bartók's music rarely displays the consistent atonal vocabulary that would make it suitable for only a set-theory approach (Chapters 4.4–4.4.11). Theorists have long known that, in one way or another, tonal direction is always discernible in Bartók's music. The means whereby it is achieved and the patterns in which it results are a constantly varying amalgam of Western and folk-traditions joined with novel, non-traditional tonal procedures (Chapter 2.1.1). The evolution of Bartók's works can be understood as a complex of folk-music influences (Chapters 2.1.2 and 3.6). In his early works, Bartók began to rely increasingly on harmonic characteristics of folk melodies to provide a new means of musical expression and to play a unifying role in his more abstract compositions (Chapters 2.1.3–2.1.4).

The central focus of my analysis was to explore the unifying micro- and macro-relationships involving set {0,1,4} in *Duke Bluebeard's Castle*. That set cannot be derived from the major scale nor from ecclesiastical modes; and even thought it appears as a segment in various kinds of scales (e.g., the octatonic scale), there is insufficient evidence to suggest that Bartók conceived it as such. Rather, the source of set {0,1,4} in his music is better understood as arising from a note being added to a triad, such that it forms at least one half-step between itself and a member of the triad (Example 5.1).

Example 5.1. *Duke Bluebeard's Castle*: Harmonic configurations based on major and minor triads.

Example 5.2 (next page) shows all the possible tetrachord sets formed by the addition of a chromatic note to major and minor triads. Figure 5.1 (next page) displays those sets in terms of Joutsenvirta's 12 x 12 pitch-web square (see also, Table 1.1, p. 3, Chapter 1). The addition of a note forming a minor second above or below a member of major and minor triads results in 12 possibilities (see Example 5.2 and Figure 5.1, below). Among them, chords 3 and 10 are identical; nos. 1 and 12 are, in traditional terms, chords with an added major seventh above the root position triad. As a result, only ten distinct tetrachords are generated in this operation.

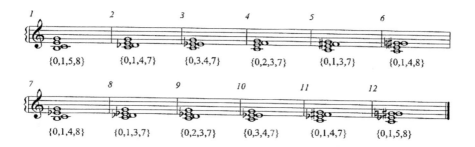

Example 5.2. Major and minor triads with added chromatic notes.

1.   (0 = C)

2.*   (0 = C)

3.*   (0 = C)

4.   (0 = C)

5.   (0 = C)

6.*   (0 = C)

7.*   (0 = C)

8.   (0 = C)

9.*   (0 = C)

10.* (0 = C)

11.* (0 = C)

12.   (0 = C)

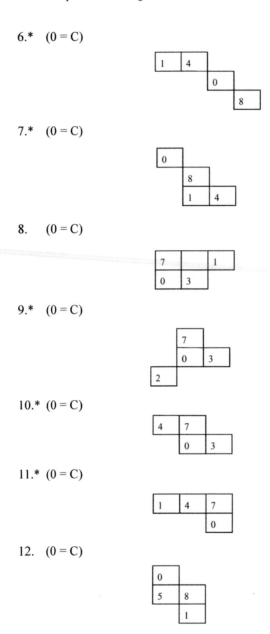

Figure 5.1. Added chromatic note to major and minor triads explored through the pitch web.

Adding a note that forms a minor second above or below the members of the major and minor triads results in 12 possibilities. A closer look shows that the chords labeled 3 and 10 are identical, and that chords 1 and 12 are, in traditional terms, major seventh chords (i.e., chords with a major seventh added above the major triad). As a result, only ten different tetrachords are generated in this operation (Example 5.2 and Figure 5.1, previous page).

Set {0,1,4} appears as a subset in the chords marked with asterisks, resulting in five tetrachords in three sets, {0,1,4,7}, {0,1,4,8}, and {0,3,4,7}. All of the asterisked tetrachords can be rewritten to show that they are made up of two triads. This type of superimposing one triad over another may generate, in traditional terms, a seventh chord like no. 8 in Example 5.2 and Figure 5.1 (p. 299), which is a minor triad with a major seventh. Such superimpositions may also generate tetrachords that cannot be notated as seventh chords upon inversion. Example 5.3 and Figure 5.2 display those sets through Joutsenvirta's 12 x 12 pitch-web square (1989: 95; see also, Table 1.1, p. 3, Chapter 1).

Example 5.3. Sets {0,1,4,7}, {0,1,4,8}, and {0,3,4,7}.

1. (0 = C)

1	4	7
		0

2. (0 = C)

4	7	
	0	3

3. (G-sharp = 0)

8		
1	4	
		0

4. (B = 0)

8		
1	4	
		0

5. (G = 0)

1	4	7
		0

Figure 5.2. Pitch-web squares representing sets {0,1,4,7}, {0,1,4,8}, and {0,3,4,7}.

The concept of added-note chords cannot completely explain how Bartók composed the music for his opera, in which tonal centers are produced by chordal structures in addition to those based on the sets. Still, the appearances of {0,1,4}, often found as a subset of the tetrachords formed by adding one triad to another, are basic to the growth and structural coherence of *Bluebeard*. As demonstrated in Chapters 4.3–4.4.11, the organic transformation of sets appears to be a fundamental means of providing unity in Bartók's opera, both at local levels and across wider spans of music.

In Bartók's opera, the usage of sets as structural units represents a non-tonal procedure; still, the melodies, and the tertian harmonies they generate, are almost fully traditional. The resulting harmonic design is partly traditional, partly non-traditional. The interpretation of Bartók's opera within a set-theoretical, pitch-web analytical framework need not slight its tonal underpinnings. Rather, in the method proposed in this study, the tonal aspects of the work are simply generalized in terms of a larger, more capacious system. Coherent harmonic relationships are achieved through the employment of certain sets in the opera. Sets {0,1,4}, {0,1,4,7}, {0,1,4,8}, and {0,3,4,7} point to a strong link between the similarity relations among those sets and the set-complex structure governing the overall span of *Bluebeard*'s music. To judge from the published literature on Bartók's opera, most of those relations have gone unrecognized until the present study.

To place *Bluebeard* in historical context, it has been necessary to trace the evolution of Bartók's tonal practices: from the principle of the "unresolved passing note," from which follows the unresolved passing-chord and, more important still, the unresolved neighboring tonality. In harmonizing music of folk-origin, Bartók had always drawn his harmonies from the scale of the tune. In original compositions, however, he would often use modal mixture (Chapter 3.6); of course, the same can be said of other "neo-modalists" of his time, but Bartók stands alone in his innovations in that area. At a more advanced stage, his music could be analyzed in terms of polytonality (Chapters 2.1.3–2.1.4), and even later, his pitch structures seemed almost indistinguishable from those of the so-called atonalists. In reality, however, they are strongly anchored to a definite tonality, defined most strongly by melody. The superficial appearance of atonality is due to the fact that the ear does not at first easily perceive the subsidiary tonalities within the principal one. That anchorage, however, is essentially diatonic, and the triad remains the basis of Bartók systematic usage of pitch.

Bartók is of course primarily a melodic composer and a great contrapuntist. Harmony as such is subordinate: it points up the rhythms, gives relative emphasis in phrasing, and strengthens the tonality, by clarifying the melodic lines with clean-cut, vigorous articulations. As did other composers, Bartók saw that there were possibilities for compositional development derived from eighteenth-century practices, other than those taken by the Romantics, who tended toward adding more and more chromaticism to a traditionally functional harmonic system. From 1923 on Bartók consciously developed his technique according to eighteenth-century principles, but with all the resources and experience of a twentieth-century composer (Chapters 2.1.2 and 2.5).

Duke Bluebeard's Castle, like many of Béla Bartók's compositions, invites a host of theoretical explanations of its unique position within the composer's total musical output. The present dissertation in no way constitutes a theoretical examination of all the analytical possibilities inherent to this work, and it is certainly not the last word on the subject. As long as Bartók's compositions remain at the heart of the modern repertoire, they, as well as his scholarly writings and folk-music studies, will continue to inspire new generations of scholars and musicians. A complete explanation of Bartók's general principles of pitch structure might be a long way off. Yet, in this writer's opinion, further progress along that path may be accomplished through more thorough investigations of individual works, as has been attempted here in the case of *Bluebeard*.

GLOSSARY OF ABBREVIATIONS, BASIC TERMS, DEFINITIONS, AND CONCEPTS

Symbol	Meaning
A	Section A.
(A)	Theme (A).
(A')	Variant of the theme (A).
a	Subsection a.
[a]	Fragment of subsection a.
AaTh	Aarne-Thompson Tale Type Index.
Acoustic scale	Set {0,2,4,6,7,9,10}; also called overtone scale.
A5	Melodic line A sounded a perfect fifth interval higher.
A5v	Variant of line A5.
α	Alpha chord. Integers {0,2,3,5,6,8,9,11}, Forte number 8–28, ICV 448444.
AS	Axis System.
AT	Aarne-Thompson Tale Type Index.
ATU	Aarne-Thompson & Hans-Jörg Uther Tale Type Index.
Av	Variant of line A.
Axis	A point or line used as a divider in symmetrical operations.
B	Section B.
(B)	Theme (B).
(B')	Variant of theme (B).
b	Subsection b.
BB	Thematic catalogue numbers of Béla Bartók's works.
β	Beta chord. Integers {0,3,6,9,11}.
β1	First segment of the β-chord. Integers {0,3,6,11}, Forte number 4–18, ICV 102111.
β2	Second segment of the β-chord. Integers {0,6,11}, Forte number 3–9, ICV 010020.
B5	Melodic line B sounded a perfect fifth higher.
B5v	Variant of line B5.
Bimodality	Two keys combined simultaneously.
C	Section C.
(C)	Theme (C).
c	Subsection c.
[c]	Fragment of subsection c.
γ	Gamma chord. Integers {0,3,6,8,11}, Forte number 5–32, ICV 113221.
γ1	First segment of the γ-chord. Integers {0,3,8,11}.
Cardinal number	Set classification in the Table of Set Classes (see the Appendix).

Cardinality	The number of PCs in a PC-set, e.g., C–E–G–C–G is a set of cardinality 3 since there are only three different pitch classes.
Chord	Three or more PCs considered simultaneously or as an unordered set. A chord is a non-linear PC-set with a minimum cardinality of 3.
Chromatic scale	Set {0,1,2,3,4,5,6,7,8,9,10,11}, Forte number 12–1 (1).
Combinatoriality	The special property of combining tone rows simultaneously, without duplication of PCs.
Complement	(1) All PCs not in a given set; (2) the interval that when added to a given interval will complete an octave (interval inversion).
Composite segment	Pitch segments formed by the interaction of more than one primary segment.
D	Dominant.
(D)	Theme (D).
DA	Dominant Axis. E.g., G–B-flat–D-flat/C-sharp–E, set {0,3,6,9}, Forte number 4–28 (3), ICV 004002.
DD	Refers to the catalogue of Denijs Dille (1974).
δ	Delta chord. Integers {0,3,5,8,11}, Forte number 5–32, ICV 113221.
δ1	First segment of the Delta chord. Integers {0,5,8,11}.
δ2	Second segment of the Delta chord. Integers {0,5,11}, Forte number 3–3, ICV 101100.
Derived set	A PC-set that is constructed by operations (transposition, inversion, etc.) upon a given source set.
(E)	Theme (E).
ε	Epsilon chord. Integers {0,2,5,8,11}, Forte number 4–27, ICV 012111.
(F)	Theme (F).
FS	Fibonacci Series. An infinite number series derived from a recursive formula in which each subsequent element is the sum of the previous two, e.g., 1, 2, 3, 5, 8, 13, 21, etc.
GS	Golden Section (*proportio divina*), also called Golden Mean; X:1 = (1–X):X. In practical terms, approximately 0.618... of any given quantity.
GS scale	Set {0,3,5,8}, Forte number 4–26 (12), ICV 012120).
Gypsy scale	Set {0,2,4,6,7,8,11}.
Heptatonia seconda	Set {0,1,3,4,6,8,10}, Forte number 7–34, ICV 254442; also called second seven-note system.
Hypermajor	Major triad with major seventh, e.g., C–E–G–B. Set {0,1,5,8}, Forte number 4–20, ICV 101220.
Hyperminor	Minor triad with major seventh, e.g., C–E-flat–G–B. Set {0,1,4,8}, Forte number 4–19, ICV 101310.
I	Inversion.
IC	Interval Class. One of the seven Interval Classes designated by the integers 0 through 6.
ICV	Interval Class Vector. An ordered array of numerals enclosed

	in square brackets that represents the interval content of a PC-set. The first numeral gives the number of intervals of Interval Class 1; the second gives the number of intervals of Interval Class 2, and so on.
Imbrication	Sequentially overlapping subcomponents of some linear configurations.
Inclusion relation	Two sets so related that one is included in the other (also called the superset/subset relation).
Index number	The transposition number, in semitones, above a referential PC. E.g., P5 = P0 transposed up 5 semitones.
Integer notation	PCs numbered from 0 to 11, C = 0.
Intersection	For two sets A and B, the intersection C of A and B is the set of elements common to A and B. This is written $C = * (A, B)$.
Interval	If a and b are PC integers, then the interval formed by a and b is the absolute (positive) value of the difference of a and b ($[a–b]$).
Interval content	Refers to total interval content: the collection of Interval Class representatives formed by taking the absolute value differences of all pairs of elements of a PC-set.
Invariant subset	When a set S undergoes transformation (transposition or inversion), some subset T of S remains unchanged, or invariant; subset T may be null (empty).
Interval succession	The intervals formed by successive elements of an ordered PC-set. If, for example, the set is {0,1,6,7}, Forte number 4–9 (6), ICV 20002, the interval succession is [1–5–1].
Inverse	If a is a PC integer and a' represents the inverse of a, then $a' = 12–a$ (modulo 12).
Inversion	In Mod 12 arithmetic, the process by which each element e of a PC-set is replaced by 12-minus-e.
Inversional equivalence	Refers to two PC-sets related by the operation of inversion followed by transposition, such that the two sets are reducible to the same prime form.
IS	Inversional symmetry.
K	Set complex. A set of sets associated by virtue of the inclusion relation.
Kh	A special subcomplex of the set complex K.
Linear set	A set ordered in time, as a temporal array, e.g., a tone row.
M	Multiplication.
Mapping	One-to-one vs. many-to-one; onto vs. into.
Mirror or mirror set	A PC-set that is symmetrical by reflection around a PC axis. A minor-seventh chord is a mirror because if its intervals are projected in the opposite direction the same chord results.
Mirroring	Reflecting a set around an axis of time or pitch.
Modality	The use of modes other than major/minor.
Mod 12	Modulo 12. In order to ensure that a pitch member j is reduced to a PC integer, it is necessary to replace j by the remainder of j divided by 12 if j is greater than or equal to

12.

Nexus set	A referential set for a particular set complex.
No.	Number.
Non-linear set	A set in which linear order is irrelevant, as in chords; see also, unordered set.
Normal order	A particular circular permutation of a PC-set in ascending order.
Nos.	Numbers.
Octave displacement	Presentation of a pitch in different octave registers.
Op.	Opus.
Ordered inversion	This occurs when a PC-set is inverted and transposed in such a way that the original order of the elements is unchanged.
Ordered set	A PC-set in which the order of elements is regarded as significant.
Ordered transposition	This occurs when a PC-set is transposed in such a way that the original order of the elements is unchanged.
Ordering	(1) A set placed in a temporal order. (2) A set placed into some logical order.
Order number	A number assigned to a PC in a linear set to indicate its order in the series. The first order number is zero (0).
Ordinal number	A catalog number following a cardinal number in the Table of Set Classes (see the Appendix).
P	Abbreviation for "prime" or "prime set".
PA	Pitch Axis.
Pantonality	Diverging from traditional hierarchical tonality, a pitch organization in which all PCs are treated as more or less equivalent (Schoenberg).
PC	Pitch Class. One of the 12 Pitch Classes designated by the integers 0 through 11. Pitch Class 0 refers to all notated pitches C, B-sharp, and D-double-flat. Pitch Class 1 refers to all notated pitches C-sharp, D-flat, B-double-sharp, and E-double-flat, and so on.
PCI	Pitch-Class Interval, both ordered and unordered.
PC-set	Pitch-Class Set. A set of distinct integers representing Pitch Classes.
Pentatonic scale	Usually refers to the anhemitonic five-note set $\{0,2,4,7,9\}$, Forte number 5–35, ICV 932140. (See also, e.g., set $\{0,2,5,7,10\}$, set $\{0,3,5,8,10\}$, set $\{0,2,5,7,9\}$, and set $\{0,3,5,7,10\}$.)
Primary segment	A segment determined by conventional means, such as melodic configuration.
Prime form	A set in normal order, transposed so that the first integer is 0.
Polymodality	More than one mode, occurring at the same time or in close proximity.
Polytonality	Two or more keys combined simultaneously.
Rev.	Revised.
S	Subdominant.

SA	Subdominant Axis. E.g., F–A-flat/G-sharp–B–D. Set $\{0,3,6,9\}$, Forte number 4–28 (3), ICV 004002.
SC	Set-Class.
Segment	A musical unit of fixed extent.
Segmentation	The analytical procedure by which significant musical units of a composition are determined.
Set name	The name of a PC-set, consisting of two numerals separated by a hyphen. The numeral to the left of the hyphen is the cardinal number of the set; the numeral to the right of the hyphen is the ordinal number of the set, i.e., its position on the List of Prime Forms (see the Appendix).
Similarity relation	Refers to ways in which two non-equivalent sets of the same cardinal number may be compared in terms of structural similarity and difference.
Sz	Refers to the catalogue of András Szőllősy (1956: 299–345).
T	Tonic.
TA	Tonic Axis. E.g., C–E-flat–F-sharp/G-flat–A. Set $\{0,3,6,9\}$, Forte number 4–28 (3), ICV 004002.
TC	Transpositional combination.
TE	Transpositional equivalence. Refers to two PC-sets related by the operation of transposition such that the two sets are reducible to the same prime form.
Tn	Transposition. Transposition of a PC-set S consists of the addition (modulo 12) of some integer t to each element of S.
TS	Transpositional symmetry.
Union	For two sets A and B, the union C of A and B is the set of all the elements of A and all the elements of B. This is written $C = + (A, B)$.
Unordered set	A PC-set in which the order of the elements is considered insignificant.
Whole-tone scale	Set $\{0,2,4,6,8,10\}$, Forte number 6–35 (2), ICV 060603.
Xc	The complement of set X.
X cell	Set $\{0,1,2,3\}$, Forte number 4–1, ICV 321000.
Yc	The complement of set Y.
Y cell	Set $\{0,2,4,6\}$, Forte number 4–21 (12), ICV 030201.
Zc	Z correspondent, designating one of a pair of Z-related sets.
Z-related pair	This refers to a pair of sets that have the same interval vector, but are not reducible to the same prime form.
Z cell	Set $\{0,1,6,7\}$, Forte number 4–9 (6), ICV 200022.
ω1	Omega 1, e.g., C–D–E–F-sharp–A-flat–B-flat. Set $\{0,2,4,6,8,10\}$, Forte number 6–35 (2), ICV 060603.
ω2	Omega 2, e.g., C-sharp–D-sharp–F–G–A–B). Set $\{1,3,5,7,9,11\}$, Forte number 6–35 (2), ICV 06060.

BIBLIOGRAPHY

Index of abbreviations

BBE (1976). *Béla Bartók Essays*. New York Bartók Archive Studies in Musicology. No. 8. Sel. & ed. Benjamin Suchoff. New York, NY: St. Martin's Press.

BÖI (1966). *Bartók Béla összegyűjtött írásai*. 1. kötet [*Béla Bartók's Collected Writings*. Vol. 1]. Ed. András Szőllősy. Budapest: Zeneműkiadó Vállalat.

BVZI (1956). *Bartók Béla válogatott zenei írásai* [*Béla Bartók's Selected Writings on Music*]. Sel. & ed. András Szőllősy. Budapest: Művelt Nép Tudományos és Ismeretterjesztő Kiadó.

CMPH (1951–1997). *A magyar népzene tára: Corpus musicae popularis hungaricae (CMPH)*. 1–10. kötet [*The Complete Edition of Hungarian Folksongs*. Vols. 1–10]. Ed. Béla Bartók, Zoltán Kodály et al. Budapest: Akadémiai Kiadó & Balassi Kiadó.

CMPH I (1957 [1951]). *Gyermekjátékok* [*Children's Games*]. Ed. György Kerényi. Budapest: Akadémiai Kiadó.

CMPH II (1953). *Jeles napok* [*Calendar Days*]. Ed. György Kerényi. Budapest: Akadémiai Kiadó.

CMPH III A/B (1955–1956). *Lakodalom* [*Wedding*]. Ed. Lajos Kiss. Budapest: Akadémiai Kiadó.

CMPH IV (1959). *Párosítók* [*Coupling Songs*]. Ed. György Kerényi. Budapest: Akadémiai Kiadó.

CMPH V (1966). *Siratók* [*Laments*]. Ed. Lajos Kiss & Benjámin Rajeczky. Budapest: Akadémiai Kiadó.

CMPH VI (1973). *Népdaltípusok* 1 [*Types of Folksongs* 1]. Ed. Pál Járdányi & Imre Olsvai. Budapest: Akadémiai Kiadó.

CMPH VII (1987). *Népdaltípusok* 2 [*Types of Folksongs* 2]. Járdányi Pál rendszerében szerkesztette Olsvai Imre [In the system of Pál Járdányi, ed. by Imre Olsvai]. Budapest: Akadémiai Kiadó.

CMPH VIII A/B (1992). *Népdaltípusok* 3 [*Types of Folksongs* 3]. Ed. Lajos Vargyas. Budapest: Akadémiai Kiadó & Balassi Kiadó.

CMPH IX (1995). *Népdaltípusok* 4 [*Types of Folksongs* 4]. Ed. Mária Domokos. Chief collaborator Imre Olsvai. Budapest: Balassi Kiadó.

CMPH X (1997). *Népdaltípusok* 5 [*Types of Folksongs* 5]. Ed. Katalin Paksa. Chief collaborator Imre Olsvai. Budapest: Balassi

	Kiadó.
***DocB* 1**	(1964). *Documenta Bartókiana* 1. Ed. Denijs Dille. Budapest: Akadémiai Kiadó.
***DocB* 2**	(1965). *Documenta Bartókiana* 2. Ed. Denijs Dille. Budapest: Akadémiai Kiadó.
***DocB* 4**	(1970). *Documenta Bartókiana* 4. Ed. Denijs Dille. Budapest: Akadémiai Kiadó.
***DocB* 6**	(1981). *Documenta Bartókiana* 6. Ed. László Somfai. Budapest: Akadémiai Kiadó.
IMCCBB	(1972). *International Musicological Conference in Commemoration of Béla Bartók 1971.* Ed. József Ujfalussy & János Breuer. Budapest: Editio Musica.
***Visszatekintés* 1**	Kodály, Zoltán (1974). *Visszatekintés: Összegyűjtött írások, beszédek, nyilatkozatok.* 1. kötet [*Retrospection: Collected Writings, Speeches, Interviews.* Vol. 1]. Ed. Ferenc Bónis. Budapest: Zeneműkiadó Vállalat.
***Visszatekintés* 2**	Kodály, Zoltán (1974). *Visszatekintés: Összegyűjtött írások, beszédek, nyilatkozatok.* 2. kötet [*Retrospection: Collected Writings, Speeches, Interviews.* Vol. 2]. Ed. Ferenc Bónis. Budapest: Zeneműkiadó Vállalat.

References

Aarne, Antti Amatus (1911). *Verzeichnis der Märchentypen* [*A List of Folktales Types*]. Folklore Fellows' Communications n:o 3. Helsinki: Academia Scientiarum Fennica.

—— (1987 [1961]). *The Types of the Folktale: A Classification and Bibliography.* Second revision. Folklore Fellows' Communications n:o 184. Transl. & enlarged by Stith Thompson. Helsinki: Academia Scientiarum Fennica.

Abraham, Gerard (1942). "Bartók: *String Quartet* No. 6." *The Music Review* 3 (1): 72–73.

—— (1945). "The Bartók of the *Quartets*." *Music and Letters* 4 (26): 185–194.

Adorno, Theodor W. (1973 [1949]). *The Philosophy of Modern Music* [*Philosophie der Neuen Musik*]. Transl. Anne G. Mitchell & Wesley V. Blomster. London: Sheed & Ward. Originally published in: Tübingen: Mohr-Siebeck.

—— (1982). "On the Problem of Musical Analysis." *Music Analysis* 1 (2): 169–186.

—— (1984 [1922]). "Béla Bartók." In: *Gesammelte Schriften* [*Complete Writings*]. Bd. 18: 275–278. Ed. Rolf Tiedemann & Klaus Schultz. Frankfurt am Main: Suhrkamp. Originally published in: *Neue Blätter für Kunst und Literatur* 4 (1921/1922): 126–128.

Agawu, V. Kofi (1984). "Analytical Issues Raised by Bartók's *Improvisations* for Piano, Op. 20." *Journal of Musicological Research* 5 (1–3): 131–163.

Albright, Daniel (ed.) (2004). *Modernism and Music: An Anthology of Sources.* Chicago, IL: University of Chicago Press.

Anderson, Benedict (1991 [1983]). *Imagined Communities: Reflections on the Origin and Spread of Nationalism.* Second edition. London & New York, NY: Verso.

Antokoletz, Elliott (1975). *Principles of Pitch Organization in Bartók's "Fourth String*

Quartet". Ph.D. diss. City University of New York, NY.

—— (1977). "Principles of Pitch Organization in Bartók's *Fourth String Quartet.*" *In Theory Only* 3 (6): 3–22.

—— (1981). "The Musical Language of Bartók's *14 Bagatelles* for Piano." *Tempo* 137 (June 1981): 8–16.

—— (1982a). "Pitch-Set Derivations from the Folk Modes in Bartók's Music." *Studia Musicologica Academiae Scientiarum Hungaricae* 24 (3–4): 265–274. Ed. József Ujfalussy et al. Budapest: Akadémia Kiadó.

—— (1982b). "The Music of Bartók: Some Theoretical Approaches in the USA." *Studia Musicologica Academiae Scientiarum Hungaricae* 24 (Supplementum): 67–74. Ed. József Ujfalussy et al. Budapest: Akadémia Kiadó.

—— (1984). *The Music of Béla Bartók: A Study of Tonality and Progression in Twentieth-Century Music.* Berkeley & Los Angeles, CA: University of California Press.

—— (1990). "Bartók's *Bluebeard*: The Sources of Its Modernism." *College Music Symposium* 30 (1): 75–95.

—— (1995). "Organic Development and the Interval Cycles in Bartók's *Three Studies*, Op. 18." *Studia Musicologica Academiae Scientiarum Hungaricae* 36 (3–4): 249–261. Ed. József Ujfalussy et al. Budapest: Akadémia Kiadó.

—— (1997 [1988]). *Béla Bartók: A Guide to Research.* Second edition. Composer Resource Manuals. Vol. 40. Garland Reference Library of the Humanities. Vol. 1926. New York, NY & London: Garland Publishing.

—— (2004). *Musical Symbolism in the Operas of Debussy and Bartók: Trauma, Gender, and the Unfolding Unconscious.* Oxford: Oxford University Press.

Arauco, Ingrid (1987). "Bartók's *Romanian Christmas Carols*: Changes from the Folk Sources and Their Significance." *Journal of Musicology* 5 (2): 191–225.

Ashman, Mike (1991). "Around the *Bluebeard* Myth." In: *Bartók: Stage Works.* English National Opera Guide. Vol. 44: 35–38. Ed. Nicolas John. London: John Calder Publications.

Babbitt, Milton (1949). "The *String Quartets* of Bartók." *The Musical Quarterly* 35 (3): 377–385.

—— (1986). "Order, Symmetry, and Centricity in Late Stravinsky." In: *Confronting Stravinsky: Man, Musician, and Modernist.* 247–261. Ed. Jann Pasler. Berkeley & Los Angeles, CA: University of California Press.

—— (2003 [1960]). "Twelve-Tone Invariants as Compositional Determinants." In: *The Collected Essays of Milton Babbitt.* 55–69. Ed. Stephen Peles et al. Princeton, NJ & Oxford: Princeton University Press. Originally published in: *Musical Quarterly* 46 (2): 246–259.

—— (2003 [1961]). "Set Structure as a Compositional Determinant." In: *The Collected Essays of Milton Babbitt.* 86–108. Ed. Stephen Peles et al. Princeton, NJ & Oxford: Princeton University Press. Originally published in: *Journal of Music Theory* 5 (1): 72–94.

Babits, Mihály (1997 [1939]). *Keresztül-kasul az életemen* [*Through and Around my Life*]. Szentendre: Kairosz. Originally published in: Budapest: Nyugat Kiadó.

Bachmann, Tibor & Peter J. Bachmann (1979). "An Analysis of Béla Bartók's Music Through Fibonaccian Numbers and the Golden Mean." *The Musical Quarterly* 65 (1): 72–82.

Balassa, Iván & Gyula Ortutay (1984). *Hungarian Ethnography and Folklore.* Text transl. Maria Bales & Kenneth Bales. Poems transl. László T. András. Budapest: Corvina Press.

Balázs, Béla (1908). "A tragédiának metafizikus teóriája a német romantikában és Hebbel Frigyes" ["Friedrich Hebbel and the Metaphysical Theory of Tragedy in the German Romantics"]. *Nyugat* 1 (1): 87–90.

—— (1968 [1913]). *"A kékszakállú herceg vára*: Megjegyzések a szöveghez" [*"Duke Bluebeard's Castle*: Notes on the Text"]. In: *Balázs Béla: Válogatott cikkek és tanulmányok [Béla Balázs: Selected Articles and Studies]*. Esztétikai Kiskönyvtár. 34–37. Ed. Magda Nagy. Budapest: Kossuth Könyvkiadó.

—— (1976 [1912]). *"The Wooden Prince"* [*"A fából faragott királyfi"*]. In: *Bartók Studies*. 101–110. Transl. István Farkas. Comp. & ed. Todd Crow. Detroit, MI: Information Coordinators. Originally published in: *Nyugat* 5 (24): 879–888.

—— (1979 [1910]). *A Kékszakállú herceg vára*. Kass János rajzaival, Kroó György utószavával [*Duke Bluebeard's Castle*. Illustrations by János Kass. Epilogue by György Kroó]. Budapest: Zeneműkiadó. Originally published in: *Színjáték [Stageplay]* 1 (16–17): 124–133.

—— (1982 [1922]). *Balázs Béla: Napló*. 1–2. kötet. Tények és tanúk [*Béla Balázs: Diary*. Vols. 1–2. Facts and Witnesses]. Sel. & ed. Anna Fábry. Budapest: Magvető Könyvkiadó.

—— (1994 [1908]). "Maeterlinck" ["Maurice Maeterlinck"]. In: *Inside Bluebeard's Castle: Music and Drama in Béla Bartók's Opera*. 332–339. Transl. Carl Stuart Leafstedt. New York, NY & Oxford: Oxford University Press. Originally published in: *Nyugat* 1 (1): 446–454.

Bárdos, Lajos (1974). *Tíz újabb írás, 1969–1974 [Ten Recent Essays, 1969–1974]*. Budapest: Zeneműkiadó.

Bartha, Dénes (1963). "La musique de Bartók" ["The Music of Bartók"]. In: *La résonance dans les échelles musicales*. 279–290. Ed. Edith Weber. Paris: Centre National de la Recherche Scientifique.

—— (ed.) (1974). *A zenetörténet antológiája [Anthology of Music History]*. Budapest: Zeneműkiadó.

Bartók, Béla (1913). *Cântece popolare românești din comitatul Bihor [The Romanian Folksongs from Bihor County]*. București: Academia Româna.

—— (1932). "Neue Ergebnisse der Volksliederforschung in Ungarn" ["New Results of Folk Song Research in Hungary"]. *Musikblätter des Anbruch* 14 (2–3): 37–42.

—— (1935a). "Magyar népzene" ["Hungarian Folk Music"]. In: *Révai Nagy Lexikona*. Vol. 21: 571–572. Ed. Elemér Varjú. Budapest: Révai Testvérek Irodalmi Intézet Rt.

—— (1935b). *Melodien der rumänischen Colinde [Melodies of the Romanian Colinde]*. UE XLVI. Vienna: Universal Edition.

—— (1949 [1921]). *Der hölzerne Prinz* (Op. 13). Klavierauszug [*The Wooden Prince* (Op. 13). Piano Score]. UE 6638. Vienna: Universal Edition.

—— (1952 [1925]). *Herzog Blaubarts Burg*. Partitur [*Duke Bluebeard's Castle*. Score]. Transl. Christopher Hassall. UE 13641. Vienna: Universal Edition.

—— (1956). *Bartók Béla válogatott zenei írásai (BVZI) [Béla Bartók's Selected Writings on Music]*. Sel. & ed. András Szőllősy. Budapest: Művelt Nép Tudományos és Ismeretterjesztő Kiadó.

—— (1956 [1936]). "Ferenc Liszt" ["Liszt a miénk!"]. In: *BVZI*. 220–234. Originally published in: *Magyar Tudományos Akadémiai Értesítő* 46 (462): 29–34.

—— (1963 [1921]). *Herzog Blaubarts Burg*, Op. 11. Klavierauszug [*Duke Bluebeard's Castle*, Op. 11. Piano Score]. Transl. Wilhelm Ziegler. UE 7026. Vienna: Universal Edition.

—— (1963 [1939]). "The *Second Piano Concerto.*" *Tempo* 65 (Summer 1963): 5–7.

—— (1966). *Bartók Béla összegyűjtött írásai (BÖI).* 1. kötet [*Béla Bartók's Collected Writings.* Vol. 1]. Ed. András Szőllősy. Budapest: Zeneműkiadó.

—— (1966 [1905]). "Strauss: *Sinfonia Domestica* (Op. 53)." In: *BÖI.* 707–714. Originally published in: *Zeneközlöny* 3 (10): 137–143.

—— (1966 [1908]). "Székely balladák" ["Székely Ballads"]. In: *BÖI.* 15–50. Originally published in: *Ethnographia* 19 (12): 43–52.

—— (1966 [1917]). "A Biskra-vidéki arabok népzenéje" ["Arab Folk Music in the Biskra District"]. In: *BÖI.* 518–561, 849–851. Originally published in: *Szimfónia* 1 (12–13): 308–323.

—— (1966 [1934]). "Népzenénk és a szomszéd népek népzenéje" ["Folk Music of the Hungarians and Folk Music of Their Neighboring Peoples"]. In: *BÖI.* 403–461. Originally published in: *Népszerű Zenefüzetek* 3: 36–68. Ed: Antal Molnár. Budapest: Somló Béla Könyvkiadó.

—— (1967 [1932]). *Rumänische Volkslieder aus dem Komitat Bihor* [*Romanian Folk Songs from the District of Bihor*]. Budapest: Editio Musica.

—— (1967a). *Rumanian Folk Music.* Vol. 2: Vocal Melodies. The New York Bartók Archive Studies in Musicology. No. 3. Ed. Benjamin Suchoff. Transl. E. C. Teodorescu et al. The Hague: Martinus Nijhoff.

—— (1967b). *Rumanian Folk Music.* Vol. 3: Texts. The New York Bartók Archive Studies in Musicology. No. 4. Ed. Benjamin Suchoff. Transl. E. C. Teodorescu et al. The Hague: Martinus Nijhoff.

—— (1970 [1920]). "Romanian Peasant Music." In: *DocB* 4: 107–111.

—— (1970 [1921]). "Die Volkmusik der Völker Ungarns" ["The Folk Music of Hungary's Nationalities"]. In: *DocB* 4: 112–115.

—— (1974 [1930]). *Cantata Profana: A kilenc csodaszarvas.* Kroó György előszavával, Réber László rajzaival [*Cantata Profana: The Nine Miraculous Stags.* Preface by György Kroó. Illustrations by László Réber]. Budapest: Zeneműkiadó.

—— (1976). *Béla Bartók Essays (BBE).* The New York Bartók Archive Studies in Musicology. No. 8. Sel. & ed. Benjamin Suchoff. New York, NY: St. Martin's Press.

—— (1976 [1904]). "*Kossuth Szinfóniai költemény*" ["*Kossuth Symphonic Poem*"]. In: *BBE.* 399–403. Originally published in: *Zeneközlöny* 11 (6): 82–87.

—— (1976 [1910]). "*Elektra:* Strauss Richard operája" ["*Elektra:* Opera by Richard Strauss"]. In: *BBE.* 446. Originally published in: *A Zene* 2 (4): 57–58.

—— (1976 [1912]). "Az összhasonlító zenefolklore" ["Comparative Music Folklore"]. In: *BBE.* 155–158. Originally published in: *Új Élet Népművelés* 1 (1–2): 109–114.

—— (1976 [1917]). "*The Wooden Prince* (Op. 13): The Composer About His Piece I" ["*A fából faragott királyfi* (Op. 13): A szerző a darabjáról I"]. In: *BBE.* 406. Originally published in: *Magyar Színpad* 20 (105): 2. Ed. Artúr Bárdos. Budapest: Sziklai Jenő.

—— (1976 [1918]). "*Duke Bluebeard's Castle*: The Composer About His Piece II" ["*A kékszakállú herceg vára:* A szerző a darabjáról II"]. In: *BBE.* 407. Originally published in: *Magyar Színpad* 21 (143): 1. Ed. Artúr Bárdos. Budapest: Sziklai

Jenő.

—— (1976 [1920a]). "Arnold Schoenberg's Music in Hungary" ["Arnold Schönbergs Musik in Ungarn"]. In: *BBE*. 467–468. Originally published in: *Musikblätter des Anbruch* 2 (20): 647–648.

—— (1976 [1920b]). "The Influence of Folk Music on the Art Music of Today" ["Der Einfluss der Volkmusik auf die heutige Kunstmusik"]. In: *BBE*. 316–319. Originally published in: *Melos* 1 (17): 384–386.

—— (1976 [1920c]). "The Problem of the New Music" ["Das Problem der neuen Musik"]. In: *BBE*. 455–459. Originally published in: *Melos* 1 (5): 107–110. Also available in: *BÖI*. 718–722.

—— (1976 [1920d]). "Hungarian Peasant Music" ["Ungarische Bauernmusik"]. In: *BBE*. 304–315. Originally published in: *Musikblätter des Anbruch* 2 (11–12): 422–424.

—— (1976 [1921a]). "Autobiography" ["Önéletrajz"]. In: *BBE*. 408–411. Originally published in: *Musikblätter des Anbruch* 3 (5): 87–90.

—— (1976 [1921b]). "On Modern Music in Hungary" ["Della musica moderna in Ungheria"]. In: *BBE*. 193–197. Originally published in: *Il Pianoforte* 2 (7): 193–197.

—— (1976 [1921c]). "Hungarian Folk Music" ["La musique populaire hongroise"]. In: *BBE*. 58–70. Originally published in: *La Revue Musicale* 2 (1): 8–22.

—— (1976 [1921d]. "On Modern Music in Hungary" ["A magyarországi modern zenéről"]. In: *BBE*. 474–478. Originally published in: *The Chesterian* 20 (145): 101–107.

—— (1976 [1921e]). "The Relation of Folk Song to the Development of the Art Music of Our Time." In: *BBE*. 320–330. Originally published in: *The Sackbut* 2 (1): 5–11.

—— (1976 [1928]). "The Folk Songs of Hungary." In: *BBE*. 331–339. Originally published as: "Magyar népzene és új magyar zene" ["Hungarian Folk Music and New Hungarian Music"]. In: *Zenei Szemle* 12 (3–4): 55–58. Also available in: *BVZI*. 203–214.

—— (1976 [1929]). "Structure of the *Fourth String Quartet*." In: *BBE*. 412–413. Originally published in: *Fourth String Quartet*. ii–iv. UE 9788. Vienna: Universal Edition.

—— (1976 [1931a]). "Gypsy Music or Hungarian Music?" ["Cigányzene? Magyar zene?"]. In: *BBE*. 206–223. Originally published in: *Ethnographia* 42 (2): 49–62.

—— (1976 [1931b]). "The Influence of Peasant Music on Modern Music" ["A parasztzene hatása az újabb műzenére"]. In: *BBE*. 340–344. Originally published in: *Új Idők* 37 (23): 718–719.

—— (1976 [1931c]). "What is Folk Music?" ["Mi a népzene?"]. In: *BBE*. 5–8. Originally published in: *Új Idők* 37 (20): 626–627.

—— (1976 [1933]). "Hungarian Peasant Music" ["Magyar parasztzene"]. In: *BBE*. 80–102. Originally published in: *Musical Quarterly* 19 (3): 267–289.

—— (1976 [1936]). "Why and How Do We Collect Folk Music?" ["Mért és hogyan gyűjtsünk népzenét?"]. In: *BBE*. 9–24. Originally published in: *Válasz* 2 (7–8): 397–400.

—— (1976 [1937a]). "Folk Song Collection in Turkey" ["Népdalgyűjtés Törökországban"]. In: *BBE*. 137–147. Originally published in: *Nyugat* 30 (3): 173–181.

—— (1976 [1937b]). "Folk Song Research and Nationalism" ["Népdalkutatás és nacionalizmus"]. In: *BBE*. 25–28. Originally published in: *Tükör* 5 (3): 166–168.

—— (1976 [1938]). "The Influence of Debussy and Ravel in Hungary" ["Hongrie"]. In: *BBE*. 518. Originally published in: *La Revue Musicale* 19 (187): 436.

—— (1976 [1941]). "The Relation between Contemporary Hungarian Art Music and Folk Music." In: *BBE*. 348–353.

—— (1976 [1943]). "Harvard Lectures." In: *BBE*. 354–392. Originally published in: *Journal of the American Musicological Society* 19 (2): 232–243.

—— (1976 [1945]). "Introduction to Béla Bartók Masterpieces for the Piano." In: *BBE*. 432–433. Originally published in: *Seven Sketches, Op. 9b. 3. New York, NY: Edward B. Marks Music Corp.

—— (1980). *A kékszakállú herceg vára, Op. 11 [Duke Bluebeard's Castle, Op. 11]*. Sylvia Sass, as Judith; Kolos Kováts as Bluebeard; István Sztankay, as the Bard. London Philharmonic Orchestra. Conducted by György Solti. Sound Recording. CD 433 082-2. London: Decca.

—— (1981 [1924]). *The Hungarian Folk Song [A magyar népdal]*. The New York Bartók Archive Studies in Musicology. No.13. Ed. Benjamin Suchoff. Transl. Michel D. Calvocoressi. Albany, NY: State University of New York Press. Originally published in: Budapest: Rózsavölgyi és Társa.

—— (1991 [1956]). *A kékszakállú herceg vára, Op. 11 [Duke Bluebeard's Castle, Op. 11]*. Historical Recording. Mihály Székely, bass, as Bluebeard; Klára Palánkay, mezzo-soprano, as Judith. A Budapesti Filharmóniai Társaság Zenekara [Budapest Philharmonic Orchestra]. Conducted by János Ferencsik. Sound Recording. CD 511 001. Budapest: Hungaroton Classics. Originally published on LP as: LPX 1001. Budapest: Magyar Hanglemezgyártó Vállalat.

—— (1992 [1962]). *A kékszakállú herceg vára, Op. 11 [Duke Bluebeard's Castle, Op. 11]*. Mihály Székely, bass, as Bluebeard; Olga Szőnyi, soprano, as Judith. London Symphony Orchestra. Conducted by Antal Doráti. Sound Recording. SR 90311. New York, NY: Mercury.

—— (1992 [1981]). *A kékszakállú herceg vára, Op. 11 [Duke Bluebeard's Castle, Op. 11]*. Opera Film. Directed by Miklós Szinetár. Producers: Anikó Kovács & László Steiner. Kolos Kováts as Bluebeard; Sylvia Sass, as Judith; István Sztankay, as Bard. London Philharmonic Orchestra. Conducted by György Solti. With English subtitles by Kenneth Chalmers. Videodisc. London: Decca. Originally published in: Budapest: Unitel Film- und Fernsehproduktionsgesellschaft mbH & Magyar Televízió Coproduction.

—— (1997). *Béla Bartók Studies in Ethnomusicology*. Sel. & ed. Benjamin Suchoff. Lincoln, NB & London: University of Nebraska Press.

—— (1998 [1908]). *14 Bagatell zongorára, Op. 6 [14 Bagatelles for piano, Op. 6]*. New, revised edition. Ed. Péter Bartók. Z. 934. Budapest: Editio Musica.

—— (1999 [1965]). *A kékszakállú herceg vára, Op. 11 [Duke Bluebeard's Castle, Op. 11]*. Walter Berry, bass-baritone, as Bluebeard; Christa Ludwig, mezzo-soprano, as Judith. London Symphony Orchestra. Conducted by István Kertész. Sound Recording. CD 466377-2. London: Decca.

—— (2004). *A kékszakállú herceg vára [Duke Bluebeard's Castle]*. Opera Film. Directed by Sándor Silló. István Kovács as Bluebeard; Klára Kolonits as Judith; Tamás Jordán as the Bard. Symphonic Orchestra of Hungarian Radio. Conducted by

György Selmeczy. Budapest: EPS.

Bartók, Béla & Zoltán Kodály (1913). "Az új egyetemes népdalgyűjtemény tervezete" ["Draft of the New Universal Folk Song Collection"]. *Ethnographia* 24 (5): 313–316.

—— (1921). *Folksongs*. Budapest. Popular Literary Society.

—— (1970 [1906]). *Hungarian Folksongs [Magyar népdalok]*. Reprint of the original manuscript with commentaries by Denijs Dille. London: Boosey & Hawkes. Originally published in: Budapest: Rozsnyai Károly.

Bartók, Béla & Zoltán Kodály et al. (eds.) (1951–1997). *A magyar népzene tára: Corpus musicae popularis hungaricae (CMPH)*. 1–10. kötet [*The Complete Edition of Hungarian Folksongs*. Vols. 1–10]. Budapest: Akadémiai Kiadó & Balassi Kiadó.

Bartók, Béla & Albert Bates Lord (1951). *Serbo-Croatian Folk Songs: Texts and Transcriptions of Seventy-Five Folk Songs from the Milman Parry Collection and a Morphology of Serbo-Croatian Folk Melodies*. Columbia University Studies in Musicology. No. 7. With a forward by George Herzog. New York, NY: Columbia University Press.

Bartók, Béla, Jr. (ed.) (1981a). *Apám életének krónikája*. Napról napra [*Chronicle of my Father's Life*. Day-by-Day]. Budapest: Zeneműkiadó Vállalat.

—— (ed.) (1981b). *Bartók Béla családi levelei [Family Letters of Béla Bartók]*. Co-ed. Adrienne Gombócz–Konkoly. Budapest: Zeneműkiadó Vállalat.

Bartók, János (1955). "Bartók, pionieer de la musique" ["Bartók, the Pioneer of Music"]. *La Revue Musicale. Béla Bartók: L'homme et l'œuvre 1881–1945*. Numéro special 224: 41–57.

Batta, András (1982). "Gemeinsames Nietzsche-Symbol bei Bartók und bei R. Strauss" ["Common Nietzschean Symbols in Bartók and R. Strauss"]. *Studia Musicologica Academiae Scientiarum Hungaricae* 24 (3–4): 275–282. Ed. József Ujfalussy et al. Budapest: Akadémia Kiadó.

—— (1984). *Richard Strauss*. Szemtől szembe [*Richard Strauss*]. Budapest: Gondolat Kiadó.

—— (ed.) (1999). *Opera: Komponisten, Werke, Interpreten [Opera: Composers, Works, Performers]*. Köln: Könemann.

Bausch, Pina (1977). *Blaubart: Beim Anhören einer Tonbandaufnahme von Béla Bartóks Oper "Herzog Blaubarts Burg" [Bluebeard: While Listening to a Taped Recording of Béla Bartók's "Bluebeard's Castle"]*. Videorecording. Dir. & chor. Pina Bausch. Music: Béla Bartók. Soloists: Beatrice Libenati & Jan Minarek. Company Wuppertal Tantztheatre. Frankfurt am Main: Suhrkamp.

Bellman, Jonathan (2001). "Verbunkos." In: *The New Grove Dictionary of Music and Musicians*. Second edition. Vol. 26: 425–426. Ed. Stanley Sadie & John Tyrrell. London: MacMillan Publishers.

Bent, Ian (1987 [1980]). "Analysis." In: *The New Grove Dictionary of Music and Musicians*. Revised edition. Vol. 1: 340–388. Ed. Stanley Sadie. London: MacMillan Publishers.

Berény, Róbert (1978 [1911]). "Új magyar zene egyesület" ["New Hungarian Musical Society"]. In: *Zenei írások a "Nyugatban" [Musical Writings in the "Nyugat"]*. 73–76. Ed. János Breuer. Budapest: Zeneműkiadó. Originally published in: *Nyugat* 4 (24): 1113–1114.

Bergson, Henri (1941 [1909]). *Creative Evolution [L'Évolution créatrice]*. Transl.

Arthur Mitchell. New York, NY: Modern Library. Originally published in: Paris: Félix Alcan.

Bernard, Jonathan W. (1986). "Space and Symmetry in Bartók." *Journal of Music Theory* 30 (1): 185–201.

Bettelheim, Bruno (1976). *The Uses of Enchantment: The Meaning and Importance of Fairy Tales.* New York, NY: Alfred Abraham Knopf.

Birnbaum, Marianne D. (1987). "Bartók, Kodály and the *Nyugat.*" In: *Bartók and Kodály Revisited.* Indiana University Studies on Hungary. No. 2: 55–67. Ed. György Ránki. Budapest: Akadémiai Kiadó.

Bodnár, György (1963). "Bartók et le mouvement *Nyugat*" ["Bartók and the *Nyugat* Movement"]. *Studia Musicologica Academiae Scientiarum Hungaricae* 5 (1–4): 437–354. Ed. József Ujfalussy et al. Budapest: Akadémia Kiadó.

Bónis, Ferenc (1960). *Mosonyi Mihály* [*Mihály Mosonyi*]. Budapest: Gondolat Kiadó.

—— (1963). "Quotations in Bartók's Music: A Contribution to Bartók's Psychology of Composition." *Studia Musicologica Academiae Scientiarum Hungaricae* 5 (1–4): 355–382. Ed. József Ujfalussy et al. Budapest: Akadémiai Kiadó.

—— (1972). "Bartók und der *Verbunkos*" ["Bartók and the *Verbunkos*"]. In: *IMCCBB.* 145–153.

—— (1981). "Bartók und Wagner: Paul Sacher zum 75. Geburtstag" ["Bartók and Wagner: For Paul Sacher's Seventy-Fifth Birthday"]. *Österreichische Musikzeitschrift* 36 (3): 134–147.

Boulez, Pierre (1975 [1963]). *Boulez on Music Today* [*Penser la musique aujourd'hui*]. Transl. Susan Branshaw & Richard Rodney Bennett. London: Faber & Faber. Originally published in: Paris: Gonthier.

Brelet, Gisèle (1955). "L'esthétique de Béla Bartók" ["Béla Bartók's Aesthetics"]. *La Revue Musicale. Béla Bartók: L'homme et l'œuvre 1881–1945.* Numéro special 224: 21–39.

Breuer, János (1973). "Népzene és modern zene: Adorno és a magyar zene" ["Folk Music and Modern Music: Adorno and Hungarian Music"]. *Világosság* 14 (7): 418–424.

—— (1974a). "Adorno und die ungarische Musik" ["Adorno and Hungarian Music"]. *Zeitschrift für Musiktheorie* 5 (2): 23–28.

—— (1974b). "Bartók és Kodály" ["Bartók and Kodály"]. *Világosság* 15 (2): 78–85.

—— (1975a). "Bach és Bartók" ["Bach and Bartók"]. *Muzsika* 18 (9): 20–24.

—— (1975b). "Kolinda Rhythm in the Music of Bartók." *Studia Musicologica Academiae Scientiarum Hungaricae* 17 (1–4): 39–58. Ed. József Ujfalussy et al. Budapest: Akadémia Kiadó.

Browne, Arthur G. (1931). "Béla Bartók." *Music and Letters* 12 (1): 35–45.

Burlas, Ladislav (1972). "The Influence of Slovakian Folk Music on Bartók's Musical Idiom." In: *IMCCBB.* 181–187.

Carter, Angela (1993 [1979]). "*The Bloody Chamber.*" In: *The Bloody Chamber and Other Stories.* 7–40. New York, NY: Penguin Books.

Castrén, Marcus (1989). *Joukkoteorian peruskysymyksiä* [*The Basic Questions of Set Theory*]. Musiikin tutkimuslaitoksen julkaisusarja, nro 1 [Series of Music Research Institute Publications. No. 1]. Helsinki: Sibelius-Akatemia.

—— (1997). "Joukkoluokitukseen perustuva sointuluokitus: Perusperiaatteet ja esimerkkejä sovellusmahdollisuuksista" ["Chord Classification Based on Set

Classification: Basic Principles and Examples of Applicational Possibilities"].
Sävellys ja musiikinteoria 7 (1): 6–25.

Castrén, Marcus & Mikael Laurson (1989). "Introduction to MacSet, an Analysis
Program for Pitch-Class Set Theory." *Musiikki* 19 (1–4): 436–445.

Chalmers, Kenneth (1995). *Béla Bartók*. London: Phaidon Press.

Chaplin, Charles (1947). *Monsieur Verdoux* [*Mister Verdoux*]. Film. Screenwriter,
producer, composer (music score), editor, and director: Charles Chaplin.
Hollywood, CA: Charles Chaplin Productions.

Cohn, Richard (1988). "Inversional Symmetry and Transpositional Combination in
Bartók." *Music Theory Spectrum* 10 (Spring 1988): 19–42.

—— (1991). "Bartók's Octatonic Strategies: A Motivic Approach." *Journal of the
American Musicological Society* 44 (2): 262–300.

Collaer, Paul & Joseph Weterings (1989 [1935]). "Une nouvelle œuvre d' Alban
Berg: *Loulou*" [Alban Berg's New Piece: *Lulu*"]. *Arnold Schönberg et l'école de
Vienne* [*Arnold Schoenberg and the Viennese School*]. *La Revue Musicale* 416–417:
117–122. Originally published in: *La Revue Musicale* 16: 169–174.

Collins, Adelan (1929). "Bartók, Schoenberg, and Some Songs." *Music and Letters* 10
(2): 177–181.

Cook, Nicholas (1987). *A Guide to Musical Analysis*. New York, NY: George Braziller.

Cooper, David (2001). "Béla Bartók and the Question of Race Purity in Music." In:
*Musical Constructions of Nationalism: Essays on the History and Ideology of
European Musical Culture 1800–1945*. 16–33. Ed. Harry White & Michael Murphy.
Cork: Cork University Press.

Cross, Anthony (1967). "Debussy and Bartók." *Musical Times* 108 (1488): 125–127,
129–131.

Csanak, Dóra (ed.) (1966). *Balázs Béla hagyatéka az akadémiai könyvtár
kézirattárában (Ms 5009–Ms 5024)* [*Béla Balázs's Estate in the Manuscript
Department of the Academy Library (Ms 5009–Ms 5024)*]. Budapest: Magyar
Tudományos Akadémia Könyvtára.

Dahlhaus, Carl (1980 [1974]). *Between Romanticism and Modernism: Four Studies in
the Music of the Later Nineteenth Century* [*Zwischen Romantik und Moderne: Vier
Studien zur Musikgeschichte des späteren 19. Jahrhunderts*]. Transl. Mary Whittall.
Berkeley & Los Angeles, CA: University of California Press. Originally published
in: München: Berliner Musikwissenschaftlichen Arbeiten.

—— (1987 [1968]). "Emancipation of the Dissonance" ["Die Emanzipation der
Dissonanz"]. In: *Schoenberg and the New Music*. 120–127. Transl. Derrick Puffett
& Alfred Clayton. Cambridge & New York, NY: Cambridge University Press.
Originally published in: *Aspekte der Neuen Musik*. 232–240. Ed. Wolfgang Burde.
Kassel & New York, NY: Bärenreiter.

—— (1987a [1978]). "Expressive Principle and Orchestral Polyphony in Schoenberg's
Erwartung" ["Ausdrucksprinzip und Orchesterpolyphonie in Schönbergs
Erwartung"]. In: *Schoenberg and the New Music*. 149–155. Transl. Derrick Puffett
& Alfred Clayton. Cambridge & New York, NY: Cambridge University Press.
Originally published in: *Schönberg und andere* [*Schoenberg and Others*]. 189–194.
Mainz & New York, NY: Schott.

—— (1987b [1978]). "Schoenberg's Poetics of Music" ["Schoenbergs musicalisches
Poetik"]. In: *Schoenberg and the New Music*. 73–80. Transl. Derrick Puffett &

Alfred Clayton. Cambridge & New York, NY: Cambridge University Press.
Originally published in: *Schoenberg und andere* [*Schoenberg and Others*]. 123–
130. Mainz & New York, NY: Schott.

—— (1989). *Nineteenth-Century Music* [*Die Musik des 19. Jahrhunderts*]. California
Studies in Nineteenth-Century Music. No. 5. Transl. J. Bradford Robinson.
Berkeley & Los Angeles, CA: University of California Press. Originally published
in: Wiesbaden: Akademische Verlagsgesellschaft Athenaion & Laaber.

Deák, István (1991). "Hungary: A Brief Political and Cultural History." In: *Standing
in the Tempest: Painters of the Hungarian Avant-Garde, 1908–1930*. 21–45.
Ed. Steven A. Mansbach & Richard V. West. Santa Barbara, CA: Santa Barbara
Museum of Art.

Demény, János (1946). *Bartók*. Budapest: Egyetemi Nyomda.

—— (1954). "Bartók Béla tanulóévei és romantikus korszaka (1899–1905)" ["Béla
Bartók's Student Years and Romantic Period (1899–1905)"]. In: *Zenetudományi
Tanulmányok 2: Erkel Ferenc és Bartók Béla emlékére* [*Musicological Studies 2: In
Memory of Ferenc Erkel and Béla Bartók*]. 323–487. Ed. Bence Szabolcsi & Dénes
Bartha. Budapest: Akadémiai Kiadó.

—— (ed.) (1955a). *Bartók Béla levelei: Magyar, román, szlovák dokumentumok* [*Béla
Bartók's Correspondence: Hungarian, Romanian, Slovak Documents*]. Budapest:
Zeneműkiadó Vállalat.

—— (1955b). "Bartók Béla művészi kibontakozásának évei: I. Találkozás a népzenével
(1906–1914)" ["The Years of Bartók's Artistic Evolution: I. Encounter with Folk
Music (1906–1914)"]. In: *Zenetudományi Tanulmányok 3: Liszt Ferenc és Bartók
Béla emlékére* [*Musicological Studies 3: In Memory of Ferenc Liszt and Béla
Bartók*]. 286–459. Ed. Bence Szabolcsi & Dénes Bartha. Budapest: Akadémiai
Kiadó.

—— (1967). "A szecesszió zenében" ["Secession in Music"]. *Filológiai Közlöny* 13
(1–2): 221–226.

—— (ed.) (1971). *Béla Bartók Letters*. Transl. Péter Balabán & István Farkas. Transl.
rev. Elizabeth West & Colin Mason. New York, NY: St. Martin's Press.

—— (1974). "Bartók és Balázs Béla kapcsolatáról" ["The Connection between Bartók
and Béla Balázs"]. *Tiszatáj* 28 (11): 72–76.

—— (ed.) (1976). *Bartók Béla levelei* [*Béla Bartók's Letters*]. Budapest: Zeneműkiadó.

—— (1977). "Adatok Balázs Béla és Bartók Béla kapcsolatához" ["Data on the
Relationship of Béla Balázs and Béla Bartók"]. In: *Magyar Zenetörténeti
Tanulmányok 4: Kodály Zoltán emlékére* [*Essays in the History of Hungarian
Music 4: In Memory of Zoltán Kodály*]. 361–374. Ed. Ferenc Bónis. Budapest:
Zeneműkiadó.

Descartes, René (1954 [1637]). *The Geometry of René Descartes* [*La géométrie*].
Transl. David Eugene Smith & Marcia L. Lantham. New York, NY: Dover.
Originally published in: Leyden: Joannes Maire.

—— (2000 [1637]). *Discours de la méthode pour bien conduire sa raison, et chercher
la verité dans les sciences* [*Discourse on the Method of Rightly Conducting the
Reason in the Search for Truth in the Sciences*]. Paris: Garnier-Flammarion.
Originally published in: Leyden: Joannes Maire.

Deutsch, Diana & John Feroe (1981). "The Internal Representation of Pitch
Sequences in Tonal Music." *Psychological Review* 88 (6): 503–522.

Dille, Denijs (1965). "Die Beziehungen zwischen Bartók und Schönberg" ["The Connections between Bartók and Schoenberg"]. In: *DocB* 2: 53–61.

—— (1974). *Thematisches Verzeichnis der Jugendwerke Béla Bartók, 1890–1904* [*Thematic Catalogue of Béla Bartók's Youthful Works, 1890–1904*]. Kassel: Bärenreiter.

—— (1981). "Bartók et Ady" ["Bartók and Ady"]. *Studia Musicologica Academiae Scientiarum Hungaricae* 23 (1–4): 125–153. Ed. József Ujfalussy et al. Budapest: Akadémia Kiadó.

—— (1990). "La rencontre de Bartók et de Kodály" ["The Meeting of Bartók and Kodály"]. In: *Béla Bartók: regard sur le passé*. 199–212. Ed. Yves Lenoir. Louvain-la-Neuve: Institut Supérieur d'Archéologie et d'Histoire de l'Art, College Érasme.

—— (1996 [1977]). *Bartók Béla családfája* [*Concise Genealogy of the Bartók Family*]. Transl. Dóra Csanak. Budapest: Balassi Kiadó. Originally published in: Antwerpen: Metropolis.

Dobszay, László (1982). "The Absorption of Folksong in Bartók's Composition." *Studia Musicologica Academiae Scientiarum Hungaricae* 24 (3–4): 303–313. Ed. József Ujfalussy et al. Budapest: Akadémia Kiadó.

—— (1983). *A siratóstílus dallamköre zenetörténetünkben és népzenénkben* [*The Melodic Sphere of the Lament-Style in Hungarian Music History and Folk Music*]. Budapest: Akadémiai Kiadó.

—— (1984). *Magyar zenetörténet* [*The History of Hungarian Music*]. Budapest: Gondolat Kiadó.

Dobszay, László & Janka Szendrei (1992). *Catalogue of Hungarian Folksong Types: Arranged According to Styles*. Vol. 1. Budapest: Magyar Tudományos Akadémia Zenetudományi Intézet.

Domokos, Mária (1982). "Bartók's Systeme zum Ordnen der Volkmusik" ["Bartók's System of Classification of Folk Music"]. *Studia Musicologica Academiae Scientiarum Hungaricae* 24 (3–4): 315–325. Ed. József Ujfalussy et al. Budapest: Akadémia Kiadó.

Dunsby, Jonathan & Arnold Whittall (1988). *Music Analysis in Theory and Practice*. London: Faber & Faber.

Eősze, László (1987 [1980]). "Zoltán Kodály." In: *The New Grove Dictionary of Music and Musicians*. Revised edition. Vol. 10: 137–145. Ed. Stanley Sadie. London: MacMillan Publishers.

Erdely, Stephen (1965). *Methods and Principles of Hungarian Ethnomusicology*. Uralic and Altaic Series. Vol. 52. Bloomington, IN: Indiana University Publications.

—— (1987). "Complimentary Aspects of Bartók's and Kodály's Folk Song Researches." In: *Bartók and Kodály Revisited*. Indiana University Studies on Hungary. No. 2: 69–83. Ed. György Ránki. Budapest: Akadémiai Kiadó.

—— (2001). "Bartók and Folk Music." In: *The Cambridge Companion to Bartók*. Cambridge Companions to Music. 24–42. Ed. Amanda Bayley & Jonathan Cross. Cambridge, MA: Cambridge University Press.

Estes, Clarissa Pinkola (1992). *Women Who Run with the Wolves: Myths and Stories of the Wild Woman Archetype*. New York NY: Ballentine Publishing Group.

Falk, Zsigmond (1964 [1904]). "Új magyar zenei lángész" ["New Hungarian Musical Genius"]. In: *DocB* 1: 55–56. Originally published in: *Ország-Világ* 25 (3): 51.

Fassett, Agatha (1958). *Béla Bartók's American Years: The Naked Face of Genius*.

Boston: Houghton Mifflin.

Ferge, Zsuzsa (1986). *Fejezetek a magyar szegénypolitika történetéből* [*Chapters from the History of Hungarian Politics Concerning the Poor*]. Budapest: Magvető Könyvkiadó.

Fischer, Victoria (2001). "Piano Music: Teaching Pieces and Folksong Arrangements." In: *The Cambridge Companion to Bartók.* Cambridge Companions to Music. 92–103. Ed. Amanda Bayley & Jonathan Cross. Cambridge, MA: Cambridge University Press.

Fodor Géza (1999). "Hallgatjuk és csodálkozunk" ["We Listen and Wonder"]. *Muzsika* 42 (5): 26–34.

Fodor, Ilona (1970). "Bartók magyarságélményének gyökerei" ["Origins of Bartók's Patriotism"]. *Kortárs* 14 (9): 1370–1378.

Forte, Allen (1955). "Béla Bartók Number VIII from *Fourteen Bagatelles,* Op. 6." In: *Contemporary Tone-Structures.* 74–79, 167–170. New York, NY: Columbia University Press.

—— (1960). "Bartók's 'Serial' Composition." *The Musical Quarterly* 46 (2): 233–245.

—— (1973). *The Structure of Atonal Music.* New Haven, CT: Yale University Press.

—— (1986). "Letter to the Editor." *Music Analysis* 5 (2–3): 335.

—— (1988a). "New Approaches to Linear Analysis." *Journal of the American Musicological Society* 41 (2): 315–348.

—— (1988b). "Pitch-Class Set Genera and the Origin of Modern Harmonic Species." *Journal of Music Theory* 32 (2): 187–270.

—— (1993). "Foreground Rhythm in Early Twentieth-Century Music." In: *Models of Musical Analysis: Early Twentieth-Century Music.* 132–147. Ed. Jonathan Dunsby. Oxford & Cambridge, MA: Basil Blackwell.

Forte, Allen & Steven E. Gilbert (1982). *Introduction to Schenkerian Analysis.* New York, NY & London: W. W. Norton.

Fosler-Lussier, Danielle (2001). "Bartók Reception in Cold War Europe." In: *The Cambridge Companion to Bartók.* Cambridge Companions to Music. 202–214. Ed. Amanda Bayley & Jonathan Cross. Cambridge, MA: Cambridge University Press.

Franklin, John Curtis (2002). "Diatonic Music in Ancient Greece: A Reassessment of Its Antiquity." *Mnemosyne* 56 (1): 669–702.

Frenzel, Elisabeth (1970). "Blaubart" ["Bluebeard"]. In: *Stoffe der Weltliteratur: Ein Lexikon Dichtungsgeschichtlicher Längsschnitte* [*Themes of World Literature: A Lexicon of Profiles in the History of Poetry*]. Fourth edition. 101–105. Stuttgart: Alfred Kröner.

Frigyesi, Judit (1982). "Between Rubato and Rigid Rhythm: A Particular Type of Rhythmical Asymmetry as Reflected in Bartók's Writings on Folk Music." *Studia Musicologica Academiae Scientiarum Hungaricae* 24 (3–4): 327–337. Ed. József Ujfalussy et al. Budapest: Akadémia Kiadó.

—— (1989). *Béla Bartók and Hungarian Nationalism: The Development of Bartók's Social and Political Ideas at the Turn of the Century (1899–1903).* Ph.D. diss. University of Pennsylvania. Philadelphia, PA.

—— (1993a). "Jews and Hungarians in Modern Hungarian Musical Culture." In: *Studies in Contemporary Jewry.* Vol. 9: 40–60. Ed. Ezra Mendelsohn. New York, NY & Oxford: Oxford University Press.

—— (1993b). "Maramaros: The Lost Jewish Music of Transylvania." *The Hungarian*

Journal of Jewish Culture 4 (1): 64–67.

—— (1994). "Béla Bartók and the Concept of Nation and *Volk* in Modern Hungary." *Musical Quarterly* 72 (2): 255–287.

—— (1998). *Béla Bartók and Turn-of-the-Century Budapest*. Berkeley & Los Angeles, CA: University of California Press.

Gál, István (1974). "Béla Balázs, Bartók's First Librettist." *New Hungarian Quarterly* 55 (Autumn 1974): 204–208.

Gal, Susan (1991). "Bartók's Funeral: Representations of Europe in Hungarian Political Rhetoric." *American Ethnologist* 18 (3): 440–458.

Galántai, József (1985). *A Habsburg monarchia alkonya: Osztrák-Magyar dualizmus 1867–1918* [*The Twilight of the Hapsburg Monarchy: Austro-Hungarian Dual Monarchy*]. Budapest: Kossuth Könyvkiadó.

Gárdonyi, Zoltán (1984). "Liszt Ferenc." In: *Brockhaus Riemann Zenei Lexikon*. Vol. 2: 427–439. Ed. Antal Boronkay. Budapest: Zeneműkiadó Vállalat.

Gauss, Carl Friedrich (1965 [1801]). *Disquisitiones Aritmeticae* [*Discourses on Arithmetic*]. Transl. Arthur A. Clarke. New Haven, CT: Yale University Press. Originally published in: Leipzig: Gerhard Fleischer.

Gellner, Ernest (1983). *Nations and Nationalism*. Ithaca, NY: Cornell University Press.

Gergely, András & Szász Zoltán (1978). *Kiegyezés után: Magyar história* [*After the Compromise: Hungarian History*]. Budapest: Gondolat Kiadó.

Gergely, Jean (1975). *Béla Bartók compositeur hongrois* [*Béla Bartók Hungarian Composer*]. Ph.D. diss. University of Strasbourg.

Gervais, Françoise (1971). "Étude comparée des langages harmoniques de Fauré et de Debussy" ["Comparative Study on the Harmonic Language of Fauré and Debussy"]. *La Revue Musicale*. Numéro special 272. Paris: Richard-Masse Editeurs.

Gervers, Hilda (1969). "Béla Bartók's *Five Songs* [*Öt dal*], Op. 15." *The Music Review* 30 (4): 291–299.

Gilbert, Steven E. (1970). *The Trichord: An Analytic Outlook for Twentieth-Century Music*. Ph.D. diss. Yale University. New Haven, CT.

Gillies, Malcolm G. W. (1982). "A Theory of Tonality and Modality: Bartók's Last Works." *Musicology* 7: 120–130.

—— (1983). "Bartók's Notation: Tonality and Modality." *Tempo* 145 (June 1983): 4–9.

—— (1986). *Notation and Tonal Structure in Bartók's Later Works*. Ph.D. diss. University of London.

—— (2000). "Canonization of Béla Bartók." In: *Bartók Perspectives: Man, Composer, and Ethnomusicologist*. 289–302. Ed. Elliott Antokoletz, Victoria Fischer & Benjamin Suchoff. Oxford & New York, NY: Oxford University Press.

—— (2001). "Béla Bartók." In: *The New Grove Dictionary of Music and Musicians*. Second edition. Vol. 2: 787–818. Ed. Stanley Sadie & John Tyrrell. London: MacMillan Publishers.

Glatz, Ferenc (1987). "Music, Political Thinking, National Ideas: The Social and Cultural Background to the *Kossuth Symphony*." In: *Bartók and Kodály Revisited*. Indiana University Studies on Hungary. No. 2: 69–78. Ed. György Ránki. Budapest: Akadémiai Kiadó.

Gluck, Mary (1985). *George Lukács and His Generation, 1900–1918*. Cambridge,

MA: Harvard University Press.

—— (1987). "The Intellectual and Cultural Background of Bartók's Work." In: *Bartók and Kodály Revisited*. Indiana University Studies on Hungary. No. 2: 9–23. Ed. György Ránki. Budapest: Akadémiai Kiadó.

Gombosi, Ottó (1978 [1931]). "Edwin von der Nüll: Béla Bartók." In: *Zenei írások a "Nyugatban"* [*Musical Writings in the "Nyugat"*]. 383–385. Ed. János Breuer. Budapest: Zeneműkiadó. Originally published in: *Nyugat* 24 (10): 694–695.

Gratz, Gusztáv (1934). *A dualizmus kora: Magyarország története 1867–1918*. 1. kötet [*The Era of Dualism: A History of Hungary, 1867–1918*. Vol. 1]. Budapest: Magyar Szemle Társaság.

Grayson, David A. (1986). *The Genesis of Debussy's "Pelléas et Mélisande"*. Ann Arbor, MI & London: UMI Research Press.

Griffiths, Paul (1984). *Bartók*. Master Musicians Series. London: J. M. Dent & Sons.

Gyergyai, Albert (1978 [1935]). "Paul Dukas." In: *Zenei írások a "Nyugatban"* [*Musical Writings in the "Nyugat"*]. 430–431. Ed. János Breuer. Budapest: Zeneműkiadó. Originally published in: *Nyugat* 25 (10): 308.

Hailey, Christopher (1993). *Franz Schreker, 1878–1934: A Cultural Biography*. Music in the Twentieth Century. Cambridge & New York, NY: Cambridge University Press.

Hanák, Péter (1971). *A dualizmus korának történeti problémái* [*Historical Problems of the Era of Dualism*]. Budapest: Tankönyvkiadó.

Hanslick, Eduard (1950 [1892]). "Richard Strauss's *Don Juan*" ["*Don Juan* von Richard Strauss"]. In: *Vienna's Golden Years of Music: 1850–1900*. 308–309. Transl. & ed. Henry Pleasants. New York, NY: Simon & Schuster.

Hanson, Howard (1960). *Harmonic Materials of Modern Music: Resources of the Tempered Scale*. New York, NY: Appleton-Century-Crofts.

Haraszti, Emil (1938). *Béla Bartók, His Life and Works*. Paris: L'Oiseau-Lyre.

Hartland, Edwin Sidney (1885). "The Forbidden Chamber." *The Folk-Lore Journal* 3 (3): 193–242.

Heath, Mary Joanne Renner (1988). *A Comparative Analysis of Dukas's "Ariane et Barbe-Bleue" and Bartók's "Duke Bluebeard's Castle"*. Ph.D. diss. University of Texas. Austin, TX.

Heckman, Emil (1930). *Blaubart: Ein Beitrag zur vergleichenden Märchenforschung* [*Bluebeard: A Contribution to the Comparative Study of Tales*]. Ph.D. diss. Ruprecht-Karl-Universität zu Heildelberg.

Heinichen, Johann David (1967 [1728]). *Der Generalbaß in der Composition* [*Thoroughbass in Composition*]. Facsimile edition. Hildesheim & New York, NY: Georg Olms. Originally published in: Dresden: Johann David Heinichen.

Heiniö, Mikko (1989). "Lähtökohtia oopperatutkimukseen" ["Some Starting Points for Opera Research"]. *Musiikkitiede* 19 (2): 66–94.

Helm, Everett (1953). "Bartók's *Musik für Saiteninstrumente*" ["Bartók's *Music for String Intruments*"]. *Melos* 20 (January 1953): 245–249.

Hempen, Daniela (1997). "Bluebeard's Female Helper: The Ambiguous Role of the Strange Old Woman in the Grimms' 'Castle of Murder' and 'The Robber Bridegroom'." *Folklore* 108: 45–48.

Herzog, George (1938). "A Comparison of Pueblo and Pima Musical Styles." *Journal of American Folklore* 49 (194): 283–417.

—— (1950). "Song." In: *Standard Dictionary of Folklore, Mythology, and Legend.* Vol. 2: 1046–1050. New York, NY: Funk & Wagnall.

Hindemith, Paul (1942 [1937]). *The Craft of Musical Composition.* Vol. 1 [*Unterweisung im Tonsatz.* Bd. 1]. Transl. Arthur Mendel. New York, NY: Associated Music Publishers for B. Schott's Söhne. Originally published in: Mainz: B. Schott's Söhne.

Hobsbawm, Eric J. (1990). *Nations and Nationalisms since 1780: Programme, Myth, Reality.* Cambridge: Cambridge University Press.

Hodeir, André (1961). *La musique depuis Debussy* [*Music Since Debussy*]. Paris: Presses Universitaires de France.

Honti, Rita (2004a). *Béla Bartók: "A kékszakállú herceg vára": Tone Patches, Mosaics, and Motives in 'The Lake of Tears'.* Unpublished Licentiate's thesis. University of Helsinki. Faculty of Arts. Department of Musicology.

—— (2004b). "Tone Patches, Mosaics, and Motives in Béla Bartók's *Duke Bluebeard's Castle*'s 'Sixth Door' Scene 'The Lake of Tears'." *Semiotica* 150 (4): 307–332. Ed. Jean Umiker-Sebeok & Eero Tarasti. Berlin & New York, NY: Mouton de Gruyter.

—— (2004c). "What Are the Signs of Narrativity? Models in General Semiotics." *Semiotica* 150 (4): 515–535. Ed. Jean Umiker-Sebeok & Eero Tarasti. Berlin & New York, NY: Mouton de Gruyter.

—— (2006). "Bartók's Harmonic Language." In: *Music and the Arts : Proceedings from ICMS 7.* Acta Semiotica Fennica XXIII. Approaches to Musical Semiotics 10. Vol. 2: 698–711. Ed. Eero Tarasti. Imatra & Helsinki: Finnish Network University of Semiotics, International Semiotics Institute & Semiotic Society of Finland.

Horváth, Béla (1974). "Bartók és a Nyolcak" ["Bartók and the Eight"]. *Művészettörténeti Értesítő* 2–4: 328–332.

Horváth, Zoltán (1961). *Magyar századforduló: A második reformnemzedék története, 1896–1914* [*Turn-of-the-Century Hungary: The History of the Second Reform Generation, 1896–1914*]. Budapest: Gondolat Kiadó.

Howat, Roy (1977). "Debussy, Ravel, and Bartók: Towards some New Concepts of Form." *Music and Letters* 58 (3): 285–293.

—— (1983a). "Bartók, Lendvai, and the Principles of Proportional Analysis." *Music Analysis* 2 (1): 69–96.

—— (1983b). *Debussy in Proportion: A Musical Analysis.* Cambridge: Cambridge University Press.

Hutchinson, John (1987). *The Dynamics of Cultural Nationalism: The Gaelic Revival and the Creation of the Irish Nation State.* London: George Allen & Unwin.

Ignotus, Paul (1972). *Hungary.* Nations of the Modern World Series. New York, NY & Washington, DC: Praeger Publishers.

Illyés, Gyula (1967 [1936]). *A puszták népe* [*The People of the Puszta*]. Budapest: Corvina Kiadó.

Járdányi, Pál (1961). *Magyar népdaltípusok.* 1–2. kötet [*Hungarian Folk Song Types.* Vols. 1–2]. Budapest: Editio Musica.

—— (1963). "Bartók und die Ordnung der Volkslieder" ["Bartók and the Classification of Folksongs"]. *Studia Musicologica Academiae Scientiarum Hungaricae* 5 (1–4): 435–439. Ed. József Ujfalussy et al. Budapest: Akadémia Kiadó.

Jász, Dezső (1978 [1910]). "Strauss Richárd *Elektrája*" ["Richard Strauss's *Elektra*"]. In: *Zenei írások a "Nyugatban"* [*Musical Writings in the "Nyugat"*]. 39–43. Ed.

János Breuer. Budapest: Zeneműkiadó. Originally published in: *Nyugat* 1 (8):
536–538.

Joutsenvirta, Aarre (1989). *Johdatus sävelverkkoanalyysiin [Introduction to Pitch-
Web Analysis]*. Musiikin tutkimuslaitoksen julkaisusarja 3 [Series of Music
Research Institute Publications 3]. Helsinki: Sibelius-Akatemia.

Kadarkay, Arpad (1991). *George Lukács: Life, Thought, and Politics*. Oxford &
Cambridge, MA: Basil Blackwell Publishers.

Kandinsky, Wassily (1970 [1926]). *Point, ligne, plan: Contribution à l'analyse
des elements picturaux [Point, Line, Plane]*. Ed. Philippe Serres. Transl. S. & J.
Leppien. Paris: Editions Denoël & Gonthier. Originally published as: *Punkt und
Linie zu Fläche*. München: Albert Langen.

—— (1982 [1912]). *"Der gelbe Klang: Eine Bühnenkomposition von Kandinsky"* [*"The
Yellow Sound: A Stage Composition"*]. In: *Kandinsky: Complete Writings on Art*.
Vol. 2: 2257–2284. Ed. & transl. K. C. Lindsay & P. Vergo. London: Faber & Faber.
Originally published in: *Der Blaue Reiter Almanach [The Blue Rider Almanac]*.
115–131. Ed. Wassily Kandinsky & Franz Marc. München: Piper.

Kapst, Erich (1972). "Zum Tonalitätsbegriff bei Bartók" ["Bartók's Concept of
Tonality"]. In: *IMCCBB*. 31–40.

Karlinger, Felix (ed.) (1973). *Das Motiv des "Blaubart" in europäischen Märchen
[The "Bluebeard" Motif in European Tales]*. Abruzzi: Edizioni Accademiche.

Kárpáti, János (1956). "Az arab népzene hatásának nyomai Bartók *II.
Vonósnégyesében*" ["Arab Folk Music Influences in Bartók's *Second String
Quartet*"]. *Új Zenei Szemle* 7 (7–8): 8–15.

—— (1962). "Béla Bartók et la Musique arabe" ["Béla Bartók and the Arab Music"].
In: *Musique Hongroise [Hungarian Music]*. 92–105. Ed. Maurice Fleuret. Paris:
L'Association France-Hongroie.

—— (1966). "Bartók, Schoenberg, Stravinsky." *The New Hungarian Quarterly* 7 (24):
211–216.

—— (1969a). *"Cantata Profana."* In: *Bartók Béla összkiadás: Vokális művek 6 [Béla
Bartók: Complete Edition: Vocal Works 6]*. Sound recording. 9–11. József Réti,
tenor; András Faragó, baritone. Budapest Symphony Orchestra & Budapest Chorus.
Conducted by János Ferencsik. Booklet. Sound Recording. SLPX 11510. Budapest:
Magyar Hanglemezgyártó Vállalat.

—— (1969b). "Les gammes populaires et le système chromatique dans l'œuvre de
Béla Bartók" ["Folk Music and the Chromatic System in Bartók's Works"].
Studia Musicologica Academiae Scientiarum Hungaricae 11 (1–4): 227–240. Ed.
József Ujfalussy et al. Budapest: Akadémia Kiadó. Available aslo as: "Népzene és
tizenkétfokúság Bartók zenéjében." *Magyar Zene* 10 (1969): 21–35.

—— (1971). "Polimodális kromaticizmus" ["Polymodal Chromaticism"]. *Muzsika* 14
(3): 4–8.

—— (1972 [1971]). "La désaccordage dans la technique de composition de
Bartók" ["Mistuning in Bartók's Compositional Technique"]. In: *IMCCBB*.
41–51. Originally published as: "Az elhangolás jelensége Bartók kompozíciós
technikájában." *Magyar Zene* 12: 120–131.

—— (1975 [1967]). *Bartók's String Quartets [Bartók vonósnégyesei]*. Transl.
Fred Macnicol. Budapest: Corvina Press. Originally published in: Budapest:
Zeneműkiadó.

—— (1978). "Art Music and Folk Music in Bartók's Works." *The Hungarian Quarterly* 19 (69): 212–217.

—— (1982). "Tonal Divergences of Melody and Harmony: A Characteristic Device in Bartók's Musical Language." *Studia Musicologica Academiae Scientiarum Hungaricae* 24 (3–4): 373–380. Ed. József Ujfalussy et al. Budapest: Akadémia Kiadó.

—— (1990). *"A kékszakállú herceg vára, Cantata Profana, Szonáta két zongorára és ütőhangszerekre"* [*"Duke Bluebeard's Castle, Cantata Profana, Sonata for Two Pianos and Percussion"*]. In: *Szemelvégyek a zenehallgatáshoz* [*Selections for Music Listening*]. 205–239. Ed. Sándor Kovács. Budapest: Tankönyvkiadó.

—— (1991 [1976]). *Bartók's Chamber Music* [*Bartók kamarazenéje*]. Transl. Fred Macnicol & Mária Steiner. Stuyvesant, NY: Pendragon Press. Originally published in: Budapest: Zeneműkiadó.

—— (1997). "From the *Ungaresca* to the *Allegro Barbaro*: Responses to Hungarian Music Abroad." *The Hungarian Quarterly* 38 (Autumn 1997): 124–132.

—— (2000). "A Bartók-analitika kérdései: Még egyszer Lendvai Ernő elméletéről" ["Questions of the Bartók Analysis: Once Again about Ernő Lendvai's Theories"]. *Muzsika* 43 (4): 11–16.

—— (2004 [1963–1964]). "Bartók és Schönberg" ["Bartók and Schoenberg"]. In: *Bartók analitika: Válogatott tanulmányok* [*Bartók Analytics: Selected Studies*]. 27–77. Budapest: Rózsavölgyi és Társa. Originally published in: *Magyar Zene* 4 (1963): 563–585, and *Magyar Zene* 5 (1964): 15–30, 130–142.

—— (2004 [1977]). "Alternatív struktúrák Bartók *Kontrasztok* című művében" ["Alternative Structures in Bartók's *Contrasts*"]. In: *Bartók analitika: Válogatott tanulmányok* [*Bartók Analytics: Selected Studies*]. 201–206. Budapest: Rózsavölgyi és Társa. Originally published in: *Zeneelmélet, stíluselemzés: A Bárdos Lajos 75. születésnapjára alkalmából rendezett zenetudományi konferencia anyaga* [*Music Theory, Style Analysis: Papers Presented at the Conference of Musicologists Held in Celebration of the Seventy-Fifth Birthday of Lajos Bárdos*]. 103–108. Budapest: Zeneműkiadó.

—— (2004 [1995]). "Tiszta és elhangolt struktúrák Bartók zenéjében" ["Perfect and Mistuned Structures in Bartók's Music"]. In: *Bartók analitika: Válogatott tanulmányok* [*Bartók Analysis: Selected Studies*]. 140–155. Budapest: Rózsavölgyi és Társa. Originally published in: *Magyar Zene* 36: 129–140. Also published in English in: *Studia Musicologica Academiae Scientiarum Hungaricae* 36 (3–4): 365–380. Ed. József Ujfalussy et al. Budapest: Akadémia Kiadó.

—— (2004 [2000]). "Bartók Észak-Afrikában: Egy rendkívüli gyűjtőút és annak zenéjére való hatása" ["Bartók in North Africa: A Unique Fieldwork and Its Impact on His Music"]. In: *Bartók analitika: Válogatott tanulmányok* [*Bartók Analysis: Selected Studies*]. 81–98. Budapest: Rózsavölgyi és Társa. Originally published in: *Bartók Perspectives: Man, Composer, and Ethnomusicologist*. 171–184. Ed. Elliott Antokoletz, Victoria Fischer & Benjamin Suchoff. Oxford & New York, NY: Oxford University Press.

—— (2004). "Bartók analízis az óceánon túl" ["Bartók Analysis across the Ocean"]. In: *Bartók analitika: Válogatott tanulmányok* [*Bartók Analysis: Selected Studies*]. 168–198. Budapest: Rózsavölgyi és Társa.

Kerman, Joseph (1985). *Contemplating Music: Challenges to Musicology*.

Cambridge, MA: Harvard University Press.

—— (1988 [1956]). *Opera as Drama*. Second and revised edition. Berkeley & Los Angeles, CA: University of California Press.

—— (1994 [1980]). "How We Got into Analysis, and How to Get Out." In: *Write All These Down: Essays on Music*. 12–32. Berkeley & Los Angeles, CA: University of California Press. Originally published in: *Critical Inquiry* 7 (2): 311–331.

Kodály, Zoltán (1906). *A magyar népdal strófa-szerkezete [The Stanza Structure of Hungarian Folksong]*. Ph.D. diss. University of Budapest. First published in: *Nyelvtudományi Közlemények* 36: 95–136.

—— (1957 [1918]). "Bartók Béla első operája: A *Kékszakállú herceg vára* bemutató előadása alkalmából" ["Béla Bartók's First Opera: On the Première of *Duke Bluebeard's Castle*"]. In: *Béla Bartók: Weg und Werk, Schriften und Briefe [Béla Bartók: Life and Work, Writings and Letters]*. 60–63. Ed. Bence Szabolcsi. Leipzig: Breitkopf & Härtel. Originally published in: *Nyugat* 9 (1): 937–939.

—— (1971 [1960]). *A magyar népzene [Hungarian Folk Music]*. Budapest: Zeneműkiadó. Originally published in: London: Barrie & Jenkins.

—— (1974). *Visszatekintés: Összegyűjtött írások, beszédek, nyilatkozatok. 1–2. kötet [Retrospection: Collected Writings, Speeches, Interviews. Vols. 1–2]*. Ed. Ferenc Bónis. Budapest: Zeneműkiadó Vállalat.

—— (1974 [1918]). "Claude Debussy." In: *Visszatekintés* 2: 379–381. Originally published in: *Nyugat* 11 (11): 640–642.

—— (1974 [1920]). "Árgirus nótája" ["The Song of Árgirus"]. In: *Visszatekintés* 2: 79–90. Originally published in: *Ethnographia* 31: 25–36.

—— (1974 [1921]). "Bartók Béla" ["Béla Bartók"]. In: *Visszatekintés* 2: 426–434. Originally published in: *La Revue Musicale* 2: 205–217.

—— (1974 [1923a]). "A máramarosi román népzene" ["The Roman Folk Music of Maramureş"]. In: *Visszatekintés* 2: 436–439. Originally published in: *Napkelet* 1: 657–659.

—— (1974 [1923b]). "A zenei folklore fejlődése" ["The Development of Musical Folklore"]. In: *Visszatekintés* 2: 97–98. Originally published in: *Esti Kurír* 1 (84): 26.

—— (1974 [1934]). "Sajátságos dallamszerkezet a cseremisz népzenében" ["Special Structures in Cheremis Folk Music"]. In: *Visszatekintés* 2: 145–154. Originally published in: *Emlékkönyv Balassa Józsefnek, a "Magyar Nyelv" szerkesztőjének 70. születésnapjára*. 181–193. Eds. Ödön Beké, Marcell Benedek & József Turóczi-Trostler.) Budapest: Ranschburg.

—— (1974 [1943]). "A szerzők megjegyzései a *Szó–mi* népiskolai énektankönyv bíráltára" ["The Authors' Remarks on the Critical Comments of the *Sol–mi* Song Book"]. In: *Visszatekintés* 1: 137–146.

—— (1974 [1943–1944]). "Iskolai énekgyűjtemény I–II" ["Song Collection for Schools I–II"]. In: *Visszatekintés* 1: 131–136. Originally published in: *Nemzetnevelők Könyvtára* 5 (14–15): 3–8, 263–264.

—— (1974 [1946a]). "Az Opera körül" ["Around the Opera"]. In: *Visszatekintés* 1: 180–181. Originally published in: *Opera* 1: 1.

—— (1974 [1946b]). "Bartók Béla, az ember" ["Béla Bartók, the Man"]. In: *Visszatekintés* 2: 442–446. Originally published in: *Zenei Szemle* 1: 2–5.

—— (1974 [1950]). "A folklorista Bartók" ["Bartók, the Folklorist"]. In: *Visszatekintés*

2: 450–455. Originally published in: *Új Zenei Szemle* 1 (4): 33–38.

—— (1974 [1951]). "Magyar táncok 1729-ből" ["Hungarian Dances from 1729"].
In: *Visszatekintés* 2: 274–281. Originally published in: *A Magyar Tudományos Akadémia Nyelv- és Irodalomtudományi Osztályának Közleményei* 2 (1–4): 17–22.

—— (1974 [1960]). "Erkel Ferencről" ["About Ferenc Erkel"]. In: *Visszatekintés* 2:
412–413. Originally published in: *A Magyar Tudományos Akadémia Nyelv- és Irodalomtudományi Osztályának Közleményei* 17 (1–4): 5–6.

—— (1974 [1961]). "A *333 olvasógyakorlat*-hoz" ["On the *333 Reading Exercises*"]. In:
Visszatekintés 1: 127–130. Originally published in: *333 olvasógyakorlat*. Budapest:
Zeneműkiadó.

—— (1976). *A magyar népzene* [*Hungarian Folk Music*]. Ed. Lajos Vargyas. Budapest:
Zeneműkiadó.

—— (1984 [1939]). *Magyarság a zenében* [*Hungarianism in Music*]. Budapest:
Magvető Könyvkiadó. Originally published in: *Mi a magyar?* [*What Is Hungarian?*]. 379–418. Ed. Gyula Szekfű. Budapest: Magyar Szemle Társaság.

Kohn, Hans (1945). *The Idea of Nationalism: A Study in Its Origins and Background*.
New York, NY: MacMillan Publishers.

Kosáry, Domokos G. (1944 [1941]). *Ungerns Historia* [*A History of Hungary*].
Acta Instituti Hungarici Universitatis Holmiensis. Series A: Monographiae
Hungarologicae 1. Stockholm: Ungerska Instituet. Originally published in:
Cleveland & New York, NY: Benjamin Franklin Bibliophile Society.

Kovács, Sándor (1993). "Ethnomusicologist." In: *The Bartók Companion*. 51–63. Ed.
Malcolm Gillies. Portland, ME: Amadeus Press.

Kramer, Jonathan (1973). "The Fibonacci Series in Twentieth-Century Music."
Journal of Music Theory 17 (1): 110–150.

Kring, Walter Donald (1991). *Safely Onward: The History of the Unitarian Church of
All Souls, New York City, 1882–1978*. Vol. 3. New York, NY: Unitarian Church of
All Souls.

Kroó, György (1961). "*Duke Bluebeard's Castle*." *Studia Musicologica Academiae
Scientiarum Hungaricae* 1 (3–4): 251–340. Ed. József Ujfalussy et al. Budapest:
Akadémia Kiadó.

—— (1962). *Bartók Béla színpadi művei* [*The Stage Works of Béla Bartók*]. Budapest:
Zeneműkiadó Vállalat.

—— (1963). "Monothematic und Dramaturgie in Bartók's Bühnenwerken"
["Monothematicism and Dramaturgy in the Stage Works of Béla Bartók"]. *Studia
Musicologica Academiae Scientiarum Hungaricae* 5 (1–4): 449–467. Ed. József
Ujfalussy et al. Budapest: Akadémia Kiadó.

—— (1972). "On the Origin of *The Wooden Prince*." In: *IMCCBB*. 97–101.

—— (1975 [1971]). *Bartók kalauz* [*A Guide to Bartók*]. Second edition. Budapest:
Zeneműkiadó.

—— (1981 [1969]). "Some Data on the Genesis of *Duke Bluebeard's Castle*" ["Adatok
A Kékszakállú herceg vára keletkezéstörténetéhez"]. *Studia Musicologica
Academiae Scientiarum Hungaricae* 23 (1–4): 79–123. Ed. József Ujfalussy et
al. Budapest: Akadémia Kiadó. Originally published in: *Magyar Zenetörténeti
Tanulmányok Szabolcsi Bence 70. Születésnapjára* [*Essays in the History of
Hungarian Music in Honor of Bence Szabolcsi's 70th Birthday*]. 333–337. Ed.
Ferenc Bónis. Budapest: Akadémia Kiadó.

—— (1993). "Opera: *Duke Bluebeard's Castle.*" In: *The Bartók Companion.* 349–359.
Ed. Malcolm Gillies. Portland, ME: Amadeus Press.

—— (1995). "Bartók and Dukas." *The Hungarian Quarterly* 36 (139): 114–123.

Kuokkala, Pekka (1979). "Sectio aurea Joonas Kokkosen oopperassa *Viimeiset kiusaukset*" ["Section Aurea in Joonas Kokkonen's Opera *Last Temptation*"]. In: *Ihminen musiikin valtakentässä.* Juhlakirja professori Timo Mäkiselle 6.6.1979. 190–202. Jyväskylä Studies in the Arts 11. Ed. Reijo Pajamo. Jyväskylä: Jyväskylän yliopistopaino.

—— (1992). *Ooppera "Viimeiset kiusaukset" Joonas Kokkosen säveltäjäkuvan heijastumana* [*Joonas Kokkonen's Composer-Portrait through His Opera "The Last Temptations"*]. Jyväskylä Studies in the Arts 39. Jyväskylä: Jyväskylän yliopistopaino.

Lackó, Miklós (1987). "The Intellectual Environment of Bartók and Kodály, with Special Regard to the Period between the Two World Wars." In: *Bartók and Kodály Revisited.* Indiana University Studies on Hungary. No. 2: 25–44. Ed. György Ránki. Budapest: Akadémiai Kiadó.

Lampert, Vera (1976). *Béla Bartók (1881–1945).* Budapest: Akadémiai Kiadó.

—— (1981). "Contribution to the Dating of Some Bartók Folk-Song Arrangements." *Studia Musicologica Academiae Scientiarum Hungaricae* 23 (1–4): 323–327. Ed. József Ujfalussy et al. Budapest: Akadémia Kiadó.

—— (1982). "Bartók's Choice of Themes for Folk-Song Arrangement: Some Lessons of the Folk-Music Sources of Bartók's Works." *Studia Musicologica Academiae Scientiarum Hungaricae* 24 (3–4): 401–409. Ed. József Ujfalussy et al. Budapest: Akadémia Kiadó.

—— (1993). "Works for Solo Voice with Piano." In: *The Bartók Companion.* 387–412. Ed. Malcolm Gillies. Portland, ME: Amadeus Press.

—— (1995). "*The Miraculous Mandarin*: Melchior Lengyel, His Pantomime, and His Connections to Bartók." In: *Bartók and His World.* 149–171. Ed. Peter Laki. Princeton, NJ: Princeton University Press.

—— (2005 [1980]). *Népzene Bartók műveiben: A feldolgozott dallamok forrásjegyzéke: Magyar, szerb, román, rutén, szerb és arab népdalok és táncok* [*Folk Music in Bartók's Works: Source Catalogue of Bartók's Folk-Song Arrangements: Hungarian, Romanian, Ruthen, Serbian, Arab Folk Songs and Dances*]. Second corrected and enlarged edition. Budapest: Helicon Kiadó. Originally published as: *Bartók népdalfeldolgozásainak forrásjegyzéke* [*Source Catalogue of Bartók's Folk Song Arrangements*]. Budapest: Zeneműkiadó.

Lampert, Vera & László Somfai (1980). "Béla Bartók." In: *The New Grove Dictionary of Music and Musicians.* Vol. 2: 197–225. Ed. Stanley Sadie. London: MacMillan Publishers.

Lányi, Viktor (1978 [1916]). "A *Csongor és Tünde*" ["*Csongor and Tünde*"]. In: *Zenei írások a "Nyugatban"* [*Musical Writings in the "Nyugat"*]. 138–140. Ed. János Breuer. Budapest: Zeneműkiadó. Originally published in: *Nyugat* 9 (2): 895–896.

László, Ferenc (1978). "Megjegyzések a Bartók-életrajz Dósa Lili-epizódjához" ["Observations on the Lidi Dósa Episode in the Life of Bartók"]. *Muzsika* 21 (2): 1–8.

—— (1980). "A *Cantata Profana* keletkezéstörténetéhez" ["On the Genesis of *Cantata Profana*"]. In: *Bartók Béla: Tanulmányok és tanúságok* [*Béla Bartók: Sudies and*

Testimonies]. 213–254. Bukarest: Kriterion Könyvkiadó.

—— (1981). "Bihar és Máramaros között: Bartók Béla bánsági román gyűjtéséről" ["Between Bihar and Máramaros: Béla Bartók's Roman Collecting Tour in Bánság"]. *Korunk* 40: 94–101.

—— (2005). "Bartók és a román kolindák." *Magyar Zene* XLIII: 259–272.

László, Zsigmond (1961 [1955]). "A prozódiától a dramaturgiáig – Bartók Béla" ["From Prosody to Dramaturgy – Béla Bartók"]. In: *Ritmus és dallam: A magyar vers és ének prozódiája* [*Rhythm and Melody: The Prosody of Hungarian Verse and Melody*]. 233–276. Budapest: Zeneműkiadó Vállalat. Originally published as: "*A kékszakállú herceg vára* prozódiájáról" ["On the Prosody of *Bluebeard's Castle*"]. *Új Zenei Szemle* 6 (9): 48–61.

—— (1985). "A prozódiától a dramaturgiáig – Bartók Béla" ["From Prosody to Dramaturgy – Béla Bartók"]. In: *Költészet és zeneiség: Prozódiai tanulmányok* [*Poetry and Music: Studies on Prosody*]. 100–129. Budapest: Akadémiai Kiadó.

Leafstedt, Carl Stuart (1990). "Structure in the 'Fifth Door' scene of Bartók's *Duke Bluebeard's Castle*: An Alternative Viewpoint." *College Music Symposium* 30 (1): 96–102.

—— (1994). *Music and Drama in Béla Bartók's Opera "Duke Bluebeard's Castle".* Ph.D. diss. Harvard University. Cambridge, MA.

—— (1995a). "*Bluebeard* as Theater: The Influence of Maeterlinck and Hebbel on Balázs's *Bluebeard* Drama." In: *Bartók and His World.* 119–148. Ed. Peter Laki. Princeton, NJ: Princeton University Press.

—— (1995b). "Judith in *Bluebeard's Castle*: The Significance of a Name." *Studia Musicologica Academiae Scientiarum Hungaricae* 36 (3–4): 429–447. Ed. József Ujfalussy et al. Budapest: Akadémia Kiadó.

—— (1999). *Inside Bluebeard's Castle: Music and Drama in Béla Bartók's Opera.* New York, NY & Oxford: Oxford University Press.

—— (2000). "*Pelléas* Revealed: The Original Ending of Bartók's Opera, *Duke Bluebeard's Castle*." In: *Bartók Perspectives: Man, Composer, and Ethnomusicologist.* 226–244. Ed. Elliott Antokoletz, Victoria Fischer & Benjamin Suchoff. Oxford & New York, NY: Oxford University Press.

Lendvai, Ernő (1947). "Bartók *Improvisations* sorozatáról (1920)" ["On Bartók's *Improvisations* (1920)"]. *Zenei Szemle* 3 (20): 151–167.

—— (1955). *Bartók stílusa* [*Bartók's Style*]. Budapest: Zeneműkiadó.

—— (1957). "Einführung in die Formen- und Harmoniewelt Bartóks" ["Introduction to Bartók's World of Form and Harmony"]. In: *Béla Bartók: Weg und Werk, Schriften und Briefe* [*Béla Bartók: Life and Work, Writings and Letters*]. 91–137. Ed. Bence Szabolcsi. Leipzig: Breitkopf & Härtel.

—— (1960–1961). "*A Kékszakállú herceg vára*" [*"Duke Bluebeard's Castle"*]. *Magyar Zene* 1: 339–387.

—— (1964). *Bartók Dramaturgiája: Színpadi művek és a "Cantata Profana"* [*Bartók's Dramaturgy: Stage Works and the "Cantata Profana"*]. Budapest: Zeneműkiadó.

—— (1966a). "Bartók und der Goldene Schnitt" ["Bartók and the Golden Section"]. *Österreichische Musikzeitschrift* 21: 607–614.

—— (1966b [1962]). "Duality and Synthesis in the Music of Béla Bartók." In: *Module, Proportion, Symmetry, Rhythm.* 174–193. Ed. György Képes. New York, NY: George Braziller. Originally published in: *The New Hungarian Quarterly* 3 (7):

91–114.

—— (1968). "Introduction aux formes et harmonies Bartókiennes" ["Introduction to Bartókian Forms and Harmonies"]. In: *Bartók, sa vie et son œuvre* [*Bartók, His Life and Work*]. 99–137. Ed. Bence Szabolcsi. Paris: Boosey & Hawkes.

—— (1971). *Béla Bartók: An Analysis of His Music*. London: Kahn & Averill.

—— (1974). "*Allegro barbaro:* Az új magyar zene bölcsőjénél" ["*Allegro barbaro:* In the Cradle of the New Hungarian Music"]. In: *Magyar Zenetörténeti Tanulmányok 3: Mosonyi Mihály és Bartók Béla emlékére* [*Essays in the History of Hungarian Music 3: In Memory of Mihály Mosonyi and Béla Bartók*]. 257–269. Ed. Ferenc Bónis. Budapest: Akadémia Kiadó.

—— (1980). *Polimodális kromatika* [*Polymodal Chromaticism*]. Budapest: Editio Musica.

—— (1983). *The Workshop of Bartók and Kodály*. Budapest: Editio Musica.

—— (1988). *Verdi and Wagner*. Budapest: International House.

—— (1993). *Symmetries of Music: An Introduction to the Semantics of Music*. Kecskemét: Kodály Institute.

—— (2000 [1971]). *Bartók költői világa* [*The Poetic World of Bartók*]. Budapest: Akkord Zenei Kiadó.

Lengyel, Menyhért (1963 [1917]). "*The Miraculous Mandarin.*" *The New Hungarian Quarterly* 4 (11): 30–35.

Lerdahl, Fred (1992). "Cognitive Constraints on Compositional Systems." *Contemporary Music Review* 6 (2): 97–121.

—— (2001). *Tonal Pitch Space*. Oxford: Oxford University Press.

Lerdahl, Fred & Ray Jackendoff (1983). *A Generative Theory of Tonal Music*. Cambridge, MA: MIT Press.

Lesznai, Lajos (1973 [1961]). *Béla Bartók: His Life and Work* [*Béla Bartók: Sein Leben, Seine Werke*]. Transl. Percy M. Young. New York, NY: Octagon Books. Originally published in: Leipzig: Deutscher Verlag für Musik.

Lindlar, Heinrich (1984). *Lübbes Bartók Lexikon* [*The Bartók Lexicon of Lübbe*]. Bergisch Gladbach: Gustav Lübbe.

Liszt, Franz (1861 [1859]). *A cigányokról és a cigányzenéről* [*Gypsies and Gypsy Music in Hungary*]. Transl. Székely József: Pest: Heckenast. Originally published as: *Des Bohémiens et de leurs musique en Hongrie*. Paris: A. Bourdilliat.

Little, Jean (1971). *Architectonic Levels of Rhythmic Organization in Selected Twentieth-Century Music*. Ph.D. diss. Indiana University. Bloomington, IN.

Lukács, György (1918). *Balázs Béla és akiknek nem kell: Összegyűjtött tanulmányok* [*Béla Balázs and Those Who Do Not Need Him: Collected Studies*]. Gyoma: Kner Izidor.

—— (1971). "Béla Bartók: On the Twenty-Fifth Anniversary of His Death." *The New Hungarian Quarterly* 12 (41): 42–55.

—— (1972). "Bartók und die ungarische Kultur" ["Bartók and Hungarian Culture"]. In: *IMCCBB*. 11–12.

—— (1974 [1911]). "The Metaphysics of Tragedy" ["A tragédia metafizikája"]. In: *Soul and Form*. 152–174. Transl. Anna Bostoc. Ed. Paul Ernst. Cambridge, MA: MIT Press.

Lukács, John (1988). *Budapest 1900: A Historical Portrait of a City and Its Culture*. New York, NY: Grove Weidenfeld.

Macartney, Carlisle Aylmer (1937). *Hungary and Her Successors: The Treaty and Its Consequences, 1919–1937.* London: Oxford University Press.

Maeterlinck, Maurice (1910). *"Sister Beatrice'"and "Ariane et Barbe-Bleue":* Two *Plays.* Transl. Bernard Miall. New York, NY: Dodd & Mead.

Markowsky, Liesel (1970). "Béla Bartók – ein grosser Humanist und Demokrat" ["Béla Bartók – a Great Humanist and Democrat"]. *Musik und Gesellschaft* 20 (9): 577–585.

Mason, Colin (1949). "Bartók's *Rhapsodies." Music and Letters* 30 (1): 26–36.

—— (1950). "Bartók and Folksong." *The Music Review* 11 (4): 292–302.

—— (1957). "An Essay in Analysis: Tonality, Symmetry, and Latent Serialism in Bartók's *Fourth Quartet." The Music Review* 18 (3): 189–201.

—— (1958). "Bartók's Early *Violin Concerto." Tempo* 49 (Autumn 1958): 11–16.

Mathieu, William Allaudin (1997). *Harmonic Experience: Tonal Harmony from Its Natural Origins to Its Modern Expression.* Rochester, VT: Inner Traditions International.

Mauser, Siegfried (1981). "Die musikdramatische Konzeption in *Herzog Blaubarts Burg*" ["The Musical-Dramatic Conception in *Duke Bluebeard's Castle*"]. *Musik-Konzepte* 22: 66–82. Ed. Heinz-Klaus Metzger & Rainer Riehn. München: Richard Boorberg.

May, Arthur James (1951). *The Hapsburg Monarchy, 1867–1914.* Cambridge, MA: Harvard University Press.

McCagg, Willam O. (1972). *Jewish Nobles and Geniuses in Modern Hungary.* East European Monographs. No. 3. New York, NY: Columbia University Press.

McGlathery, James M. (1993). *Grimms' Fairy Tales: A History of Criticism on a Popular Classic.* Columbia, SC: Camden House.

Merényi, László (1978). *Boldog békeidők... Magyarország 1900–1914.* Magyar história [*Happy Peace Times... Hungary 1900–1914.* Hungarian history]. Budapest: Gondolat Kiadó.

Messiaen, Olivier (1966 [1944]). *Technique de mon langage musical* [*The Technique of My Musical Language*]. Paris: Alphonse Leduc.

Meyer, Leonard B. (1973). *Explaining Music: Essays and Explorations.* Chicago, IL: University of Chicago Press.

Milloss, Aurél (1972). "Stravinsky és a balett" ["Stravinsky and Ballet"]. In: *In memoriam Igor Stravinsky.* 77–82. Budapest: Zeneműkiadó.

Mitchell, Donald (1987). *The Language of Modern Music.* New York, NY: St. Martin's Press.

Molnár, Antal (1931a). "Modern és *Modern*" ["Modern and *Modern*"]. In: *Bevezetés a zenekultúrába* [*Introduction to the Culture of Music*]. 93–112. Budapest: Dante Könyvkiadó.

—— (1931b). "Operakultúra" ["The Culture of Opera"]. In: *Bevezetés a zenekultúrába* [*Introduction to the Culture of Music*]. 229–248. Budapest: Dante Könyvkiadó.

—— (1948). *Bartók művészete, emlékezésekkel a művész életére* [*Bartók's Art with Recollections of the Artist's Life*]. Budapest: Rózsavölgyi és Társa.

—— (1961 [1918]). "Bartók operája: *A kékszakállú herceg vára*" ["Bartók's Opera: *Duke Bluebeard's Castle*"]. In: *Írások a zenéről* [*Writings on Music*]. 27–35. Ed. Ferenc Bónis. Budapest: Zeneműkiadó Vállalat.

Molnár, Géza (1964 [1904]). "Musica Militans." In: *DocB* 1: 53. Originally published in: *A Hét* 14 (3): 42.

Monelle, Raymond (1968). "Notes on Bartók's *Fourth Quartet.*" *The Music Review* 29 (2): 123–129.

—— (1970). "Bartók's Imagination in the Later *Quartets.*" *The Music Review* 31 (1): 70–81.

Moreaux, Serge (1949). *Béla Bartók: His Life, His Works, His Language* [*Béla Bartók: sa vie, ses œuvres, son langage*]. Preface by Arthur Honegger. Transl. George Sutherland Fraser & Erik de Mauny. London: Harvill Press. Originally published in: Paris: Richard-Masse.

Morgan, Robert P. (1991). *Twentieth-Century Music: A History of Musical Style in Modern Europe and America.* Norton Introduction to Music History Series. New York, NY: W. W. Norton.

Morris, Robert D. (1987). *Composition with Pitch-Classes: A Theory of Compositional Design.* New Haven, CT & London: Yale University Press.

Mosley, David L. (1990). *Gesture, Sign, and Song: An Interdisciplinary Approach to Schumann's "Liederkreis" Opus 39.* New York, NY: Peter Lang Publishing.

Németh, Amadé (1967). *Erkel Ferenc* [*Ferenc Erkel*]. Budapest: Gondolat Kiadó.

Nettl, Bruno (1958). "Transposition as a Composition Technique in Folk and Primitive Music." *Ethnomusicology* 2 (2): 56–65.

—— (1964). *Theory and Methodology in Ethnomusicology.* London: Collier MacMillan Publishers.

—— (1965). *Folk and Traditional Music of the Western Continents.* Prentice Hall History of Music Series. Englewood Cliffs, NJ: Prentice-Hall.

Nordwall, Ove (1965). "The Original Version of Bartók's *Sonata for Solo Violin.*" *Tempo* 74 (Autumn 1965): 2–4.

—— (1972). *Béla Bartók: Traditionalist / Modernist.* Stockholm: Svenska Musikförlaget.

Norris, Geoffrey (1980). "Slavonic and Nationalist Opera." In: *The New Grove Dictionary of Music and Musicians.* Vol. 13: 599–603. Ed. Stanley Sadie. London: MacMillan Publishers.

Nüll, Edwin von der (1930). *Béla Bartók: Ein Beitrag zur Morphologie der neuen Musik* [*Béla Bartók: A Contribution to the Morphology of the New Music*]. Halle: Mitteldeutsche Verlagsanstalt.

—— (1932). *Moderne Harmonik* [*Modern Harmony*]. Ed. Georg Schünemann. Leipzig: Friedrich Kistner & C. F. W. Siegel Musikverlag.

Oettingen, Arthur Joachim von (1913 [1866]). *Das Duale Harmoniesystem* [*The Dual Harmony System*]. Leipzig: C. F. W. Siegel. Originally published as: *Harmoniesystem in dualer Entwickelung: Studien zur Theorie der Musik.* Leipzig: W. G. Gläser.

Oláh, Gusztáv (1949–1950). "Bartók and the Theater." *Tempo* 13–14: 4–8.

Oramo, Ilkka (1976). "Tonaalisuudesta Bartókin *Bagatellissa* op. 6, nro 1" ["Tonality in Bartók's *Bagatelle,* Op. 6, No. 1"]. In: *Festskrift till Erik Tawaststjerna.* Acta Musicologica Fennica 9. 198–220. Ed. Erkki Salmenhaara. Helsinki: Suomen Musiikkitieteellinen Seura.

—— (1977a [1976]). "Marcia und Burletta: Zur Tradition der Rhapsodie in zwei Quatettsatzen Bartóks" ["Marcia and Burletta: On the Tradition of Rhapsody in Two of Bartók's Quartet Movements"]. *Musikforschung* 30 (1): 14–25. Originally published as: "Marcia ja Burletta. Rapsodian perinteestä kahdessa Bartókin kvartetto-osassa." *Musiikki* 6 (3): 14–32.

—— (1977b). *Modaalinen symmetria: Tutkimus Bartókin kromatiikasta* [*Modal Symmetry: A Study of Bartók's Chromaticism*]. Acta Musicologica Fennica 10. Helsinki: Suomen Musiikkitieteellinen Seura.

—— (1980). "Modale Symmetrie bei Bartók" ["Modal Symmetry in Bartók"]. *Die Musikforschung* 33: 450–464.

—— (1982a). "Die notierte, die wahrgenommene und die gedachte Struktur bei Bartók" ["The Notated, the Perceived and the Intended Structure of Bartók"]. *Studia Musicologica Academiae Scientiarum Hungaricae* 24 (3–4): 439–449. Ed. József Ujfalussy et al. Budapest: Akadémia Kiadó.

—— (1982b). "Kultainen leikkaus musiikissa: Kriittinen katsaus esteettisen normaalisuhteen teoriaan" ["Golden Section in Music: A Critical Review of Aesthetic Norm Theory"]. *Musiikki* 12 (4): 247–292.

Orvis, Joan (1974). *Technical and Stylistic Features of the Piano Etudes of Stravinsky, Bartók, and Prokofiev.* D.M.A. diss. Indiana University. Bloomington, IN.

Olsvai, Imre (1997). "Vikár Béla népzenegyűjtésének és *Kalevala*-fordításának hatása Bartók Béla, Kodály Zoltán és József Attila művészetére" ["The Impact of Béla Vikár's Folk Music Collection and *Kalevala* Translation on the Art of Béla Bartók, Kodály Zoltán and Attila József"]. In: *Néprajzi Értesítő: Annales Musei Ethnographiae* 79: 91–99. Ed. Attila Selmeczi Kovács. Transl. of the summaries by Gábor Komáromy. Budapest: Néprajzi Múzeum.

Parker, Mary Elizabeth (1987). *Bartók's "Mikrokosmos": A Survey of Pedagogical and Compositional Techniques.* D.M.A. diss. University of Texas. Austin, TX.

Parks, Richard (1981). "Harmonic Resources in Bartók's 'Fourths'." *Journal of Music Theory* 25 (2): 245–274.

—— (1989). *The Music of Claude Debussy.* New Haven, CT & London: Yale University Press.

Perle, George (1955). "Symmetrical Formations in the *String Quartets* of Béla Bartók." *The Music Review* 16 (November 1955): 300–312.

—— (1962). *Serial Composition and Atonality: An Introduction to the Music of Schoenberg, Berg, and Webern.* London: Faber & Faber.

—— (1977). "Berg's Master Array of the Interval Cycles." *The Musical Quarterly* 63 (1): 1–30.

—— (1990a). *The Listening Composer.* Ernst Bloch Lectures no. 7. Berkeley & Los Angeles, CA: University of California Press.

—— (1990b). "Pitch-Class Set Analysis: An Evaluation." *Journal of Musicology* 8 (2): 151–172.

—— (1996 [1977]). *Twelve-Tone Tonality.* Second edition. Berkeley & Los Angeles, CA: University of California Press.

Perrault, Charles (1920 [1697]). *The Fairy Tales of Charles Perrault.* Illustrated by Harry Clarke. Ed. Thomas Bodkin. New York, NY: Dodge Publishing. Originally published as *Histoires ou contes du temps passé avec des Mortalités: Contes de ma mère l'Oye* [*Stories or Tales from Times Past, with Morals: Tales of Mother Goose*]. Paris: Claude Barbin.

Persichetti, Vincent (1949). "Current Chronicle." *The Musical Quarterly* 35 (1): 122–126.

—— (1961). *Twentieth-Century Harmony: Creative Aspects and Practice*. London: Faber & Faber.

Petersen, Peter (1971). *Die Tonalität im Instrumental-Schaffen von Béla Bartók* [*Tonality in the Instrumental Works of Béla Bartók*]. Hamburger Beiträge zur Musikwissenschaft. Bd. 6. Hamburg: Karl Dieter Wagner.

Proctor, Gregory (1978). *Technical Bases of Nineteenth-Century Chromatic Tonality: A Study in Chromaticism*. Ph.D. diss. Princeton University. Princeton, NJ.

Propp, Vladimir Yakovlevich (1958 [1928]). *Morphology of the Folktale*. Transl. Laurence Scott. Bloomington, IN: Indiana University Press.

Prunières, Henry (1989 [1936]). "Nécrologie: Alban Berg" ["Necrology: Alban Berg"]. *Arnold Schönberg et l'école de Vienne* [*Arnold Schoenberg and the Viennese School*]. *La Revue Musicale* 416–417: 123.

Puchner, Walter (2000 [1995]). "Mädchenmörder" ["Girl's Killer"]. In: *Enzyklopädie des Märchens* [*Encyclopaedia of the Folktale*]. Vol. 8: 1407–1413. Ed. Kurt Ranke, Rolf Wilhelm Brednich et al. Berlin & New York, NY: Walter de Gruyter.

Purswell, Joan (1981). "Bartók's Early Music: Forecasting the Future." *Clavier* 20 (8): 23–27.

Pütz, Werner (1968). *Studien zum Streichquartettschaffen bei Hindemith, Bartók, Schönberg und Webern* [*Studies on the String Quartets of Hindemith, Bartók, Schoenberg and Webern*]. Ph.D. diss. University of Köln.

Pyrhönen, Heta (2004). "Kaunokirjallisuuden temaattisesta tutkimuksesta" ["On the Thematic Study of Literature"]. *Synteesi* 23 (1): 28–52.

Rahn, John (1980). *Basic Atonal Theory*. New York, NY: Longman.

Rameau, Jean-Philippe (1971 [1722]). *Traité de l'harmonie reduite à ses principes naturels* [*Treatise on Harmony Reduced to Its Natural Principles*]. Transl., with introduction and notes, by Philip Gossett. New York, NY: Dover Publications. Originally published in Paris: Ballard.

Rátz, Ilona (1972). "Béla Bartók Csík megyei pentaton gyűjtése 1907-ben" ["Béla Bartók's Collection of Pentatonic Tunes in Csík County, 1907"]. In: *Népzene és zenetörténet*. 1. kötet [*Folk Music and Music History*. Vol. 1]. 9–62. Ed. Lajos Vargyas. Budapest: Zeneműkiadó.

Reaves, Florence Ann (1983). *Bartók's Approach to Consonance and Dissonance in Selected Late Instrumental Works*. Ph.D. diss. University of Kentucky. Lexington, KN.

Réti, Rudolph Richard (1951). *The Thematic Process in Music*. New York, NY: MacMillan Publishers.

—— (1958). *Tonality, Atonality, Pantonality: A Study of Some Trends in Twentieth-Century Music*. London: Barrie & Rockliff.

Révész, Géza (1954 [1913]). *Introduction to the Psychology of Music* [*Zur Grundlegung der Tonpsychologie*]. Transl. G. I. C. De Courcy. Norman, OK: University of Oklahoma Press. Originally published in: Leipzig: Veit.

Roiha, Eino (1956). *On the Theory and Technique of Contemporary Music*. Suomalaisen tiedeakatemian toimituksia sarja B, nide 95: 2. Helsinki: Suomen Tiedeakatemia.

Romsics, Ignác (1982). *Ellenforradalom és konszolidáció* [*Counterrevolution and Consolidation*]. Budapest: Gondolat Kiadó.

Rothe, Friede F. (1941). "The Language of the Composer: An Interview with Béla

Bartók, Eminent Hungarian Composer." *The Etude* 59 (5): 83, 130.

Samson, Jim (ed.) (2001). *The Cambridge History of Nineteenth-Century Music.* Cambridge Studies in Early Modern History. Cambridge, MA: Cambridge University Press.

Sárosi, Bálint (1978). *Gypsy Music.* Budapest: Corvina Press.

—— (1986). *Folk Music: Hungarian Musical Idiom.* Budapest: Corvina Press.

Saygun, Ahmed Andan (1976). *Béla Bartók's Folk Music Research in Turkey.* Ed. László Vikár. Transl. Samira B. Byron. Budapest: Akadémiai Kiadó.

Scheiber, Alexander (1985 [1971]). "Alte Geschichten in neuem Gewande" ["Old Stories in New Garment"]. In: *Essays on Jewish Folklore and Comparative Literature.* 307–397. Budapest: Akadémiai Kiadó. Originally published under the title: "Old Stories in New Garment." *Fabula* 12: 90–96, 248–256.

Schenker, Heinrich (1956 [1935]). *Free Composition [Der freie Satz].* Transl. & ed. Ernst Oster. New York, NY: Longman. Originally published in: Wien: Universal Edition.

Schneider, David E. (1995). "Bartók and Stravinsky: Respect, Competition, Influence, and the Hungarian Reaction to Modernism in the 1920s." In: *Bartók and His World.* 172–199. Ed. Peter Laki. Princeton, NJ: Princeton University Press.

—— (1997). *Expression in the Time of Objectivity: Nationality and Modernity in Five Concertos by Béla Bartók.* Ph.D. diss. University of California. Berkeley, CA.

Schoenberg, Arnold (1975 [1947]). "Folkloristic Symphonies" ["Symphonien aus Volksliedern"]. In: *Style and Idea: Selected Writings of Arnold Schoenberg [Arnold Schönberg: Stil und Gedanke].* 161–166. Ed. Leonard Stein. London: Faber & Faber. Originally published in: *Musical America* 67 (February 1947): 7, 370.

—— (1978 [1911]). *Harmonielehre [Theory of Harmony].* Transl. Roy E. Carter. Berkeley & Los Angeles, CA: University of California Press. Originally published in: Leipzig & Vienna: Universal Edition.

—— (1984). *Style and Idea: Selected Writings of Arnold Schoenberg [Arnold Schönberg: Stil und Gedanke].* Ed. Leonard Stein. Transl. Leo Black. London: Faber & Faber. Originally published in: Frankfurt am Main: Fischer Taschenbuch.

—— (1987 [1958]). *Arnold Schoenberg Letters [Arnold Schoenberg: Ausgewählte Briefe].* Sel. & ed. Erwin Stein. Transl. Eithne Wilkins & Ernst Kaiser. Berkeley & Los Angeles, CA: University of California Press. Originally published in: Mainz: B. Schott's Söhne.

Sebestyén, Gyula (1902a). *A regösök: Magyar Népköltési Gyűjtemény.* V. kötet [*Regös Singers: Hungarian Folk Collection.* Vol. V]. Ed. Gyula Vargha. Budapest: Kisfaludy Társaság.

—— (1902b). *Regös-énekek: Magyar Népköltési Gyűjtemény.* IV. kötet [*Regös Songs: Hungarian Folk Collection.* Vol. IV]. Ed. Gyula Vargha. Budapest: Kisfaludy Társaság.

Seiber, Mátyás (1945). *The "String Quartets" of Béla Bartók.* London: Boosey & Hawkes.

Shepard, Roger N. (1962). "The Analysis of Proximities: Multidimensional Scaling with an Unknown Distance Function. II." *Psychometrika* 27 (3): 219–246.

—— (1982). "Geometrical Approximations to the Structure of Musical Pitch." *Psychological Review* 89 (4): 305–333.

Shepard, Roger N., Dan W. Kilpatrick & James P Cunningham (1975). "The

Internal Representation of Numbers." *Cognitive Psychology* 7 (1): 82–138.

Smith, Anthony D. (1991). *National Identity*. London: Penguin Books.

—— (1994). "Gastronomy or Geology? The Role of Nationalism in the Reconstruction of Nations." *Nations and Nationalism* 1 (1): 3–23.

—— (2000). *The Nation in History: Historiographical Debates about Ethnicity and Nationalism*. The Menahem Stern Jerusalem Lectures. Cambridge, UK: Polity Press.

—— (2001). *Nationalism: Theory, Ideology, History*. Cambridge, UK: Polity Press.

Solomon, Larry Joseph (1973). *Symmetry as a Determinant of Musical Composition*. Ph.D. diss. West Virginia University. Morgantown, WV.

—— (1982). "The List of Chords, Their Properties and Use in Analysis." *Interface* 11 (2): 61–107.

Somfai, László (1973). "Bartók rubato játékstílusáról" ["Rubato Style in Bartók's Own Interpretation"]. In: *Magyar Zenetörténeti Tanulmányok 3: Mosonyi Mihály és Bartók Béla emlékére* [*Essays in the History of Hungarian Music 3: In Memory of Mihály Mosonyi and Béla Bartók*]. 225–235. Ed. Ferenc Bónis. Budapest: Akadémiai Kiadó.

—— (1981a). "Die *Allegro barbaro* – Aufnahme von Bartók textkritisch Bewertet" ["The *Allegro barbaro* – Textual Source Value of the Recording by Bartók"]. In: *DocB* 6: 259–275.

—— (1981b). "Manuscript Versus Urtext: The Primary Sources of Bartók's Works." *Studia Musicologica Academiae Scientiarum Hungaricae* 23 (1–4): 17–66. Ed. József Ujfalussy et al. Budapest: Akadémia Kiadó.

—— (1981c). *Tizennyolc Bartók-tanulmány* [*Eighteen Bartók Studies*]. Budapest: Zeneműkiadó.

—— (1995). "Perspectives of Bartók Studies in 1995." *Studia Musicologica Academiae Scientiarum Hungaricae* 36 (3–4): 241–247. Ed. József Ujfalussy et al. Budapest: Akadémia Kiadó.

—— (2000 [1996]). *Bartók kompozíciós módszere* [*Béla Bartók: Composition, Concepts and Autograph Sources*]. Budapest: Akkord Zenei Kiadó. Originally published in: Berkeley & Los Angeles, CA: University of California Press.

Soriano, Marc (1968). *Les Contes de Perrault: Culture savant et tradition populaire* [*The Fairy Tales of Perrault*]. Paris: Gallimard.

Starr, Lawrence (1973). *"Mikrokosmos": The Tone Universe of Béla Bartók*. Ph.D. diss. University of California. Los Angeles, CA.

—— (1985–1986). "Melody-Accompaniment Textures in the Music of Bartók, as Seen in His *Mikrokosmos*." *Journal of Musicology* 4 (1): 91–104.

Stein, Erwin (1989 [1928]). "Idées d'Arnold Schoenberg sur la musique" ["Arnold Schoenberg's Ideas on Music"]. *Arnold Schönberg et l'école de Vienne* [*Arnold Schoenberg and the Viennese School*]. *La Revue Musicale* 416–417: 73–78.

Stevens, Halsey (1964). *The Life and Music of Béla Bartók*. London & New York, NY: Oxford University Press.

Straus, Joseph N. (1990). *Remaking the Past: Musical Modernism and the Influence of the Tonal Tradition*. Cambridge, MA: Harvard University Press.

—— (2000). *Introduction to Post-Tonal Theory*. Englewood Cliffs, NJ: Prentice-Hall.

Stravinsky, Igor (1962 [1935]). *An Autobiography* [*Chroniques de ma vie*]. New York, NY: W. W. Norton. Originally published in: Paris: Denoël.

Stravinsky, Igor & Robert Craft (1981). *Expositions and Developments*. Berkeley & Los Angeles, CA: University of California Press.

Suchoff, Benjamin (1977). "Bartók's Musical Microcosm." *Clavier* 16 (5): 18–25.

—— (1987). "Ethnomusicological Roots of Béla Bartók's Musical Language." *The World of Music* 29 (1): 43–65.

—— (1993). "Fusion of National Style: Piano Literature, 1908–11." In: *The Bartók Companion.* 124–145. Ed. Malcolm Gillies. Portland, ME: Amadeus Press.

—— (1995). *Bartók: "Concerto for Orchestra": Understanding Bartók's World.* Monuments of Western Music. New York, NY: Schirmer.

—— (2000). "Bartók's Odyssey in Slovak Folk Music." In: *Bartók Perspectives: Man, Composer, and Ethnomusicologist.* 15–27. Ed. Elliott Antokoletz, Victoria Fischer & Benjamin Suchoff. Oxford & New York, NY: Oxford University Press.

—— (2002). *Béla Bartók: Life and Work.* Lanham, MD & Oxford: Scarecrow Press.

Suhrbier, Hartwig (ed.) (1987 [1984]). *Blaubarts Geheimnis: Märchen und Erzählungen, Gedichte und Stücke* [*Bluebeard's Secret: Tales and Explanations, History and Pieces*]. Second edition. Cologne: Eugen Diederich.

Szabolcsi, Bence (1951). *A XIX. század magyar romantikus zenéje* [*Hungarian Romantic Music in the Nineteenth Century*]. Budapest: Zeneműkiadó.

—— (1955). "*A csodálatos mandarin*" [*"The Miraculous Mandarin"*]. In: *Zenetudományi Tanulmányok 3: Liszt Ferenc és Bartók Béla emlékére* [*Musicological Studies 3: In Memory of Ferenc Liszt and Béla Bartók*]. 519–535. Ed. Bence Szabolcsi & Dénes Bartha. Budapest: Akadémia Kiadó.

—— (ed.) (1956). *Bartók, sa vie et son œuvre* [*Bartók, His Life and Work*]. Budapest: Corvina Press.

—— (ed.) (1957). *Béla Bartók: Weg und Werk, Schriften und Briefe* [*Béla Bartók: Life and Work, Writings and Letters*]. Leipzig: Breitkopf & Härtel.

—— (1960). "Liszt és Bartók" ["Liszt and Bartók"]. *Élet és Irodalom* 4: 51–52.

—— (1976a). "Bartók's Principles of Composition in the Light of an Interview" ["Béla Bartók kompozíciós elvei, egy nyilatkozata tükrében"]. In: *Bartók Studies.* 19–21. Comp. & ed. Todd Crow. Detroit, MI: Information Coordinators.

—— (1976b). "Man and Nature in Bartók's World." In: *Bartók Studies.* 63–75. Comp. & ed. Todd Crow. Detroit, MI: Information Coordinators.

Szalay, Miklós (1974). "A sötétség és a fény zenéje" ["The Music of Darkness and Light"]. In: *Bartók-dolgozatok* [*Bartók Studies*]. 19–27. Ed. Ferenc László. Bukarest: Kriterion Könyvkiadó.

Szekfű, Gyula (1939). *Magyar történet. V. kötet* [*Hungarian History.* Vol. V]. Budapest: Királyi Magyar Egyetemi Nyomda.

Szentkirályi, András (1976). *Bartók's "Second Sonata for Violin and Piano" (1922).* Ph.D. diss. Princeton University. Princeton, NJ.

—— (1978). "Some Aspects of Béla Bartók's Compositional Techniques." *Studia Musicologica Academiae Scientiarum Hungaricae: Incohata a Zoltán Kodály* 20 (1–4): 157–182. Ed. József Ujfalussy et al. Budapest: Akadémia Kiadó.

Szerb, Antal (1982 [1934]). *Magyar irodalomtörténet.* Hetedik kiadás [*History of Hungarian Literature.* Seventh edition]. Budapest: Magvető Könyvkiadó. Originally published in: Cluj-Kolozsvár: Erdélyi Szépmíves Céh.

Szerző, Katalin (1979). "A *Kékszakállú herceg vára* szöveges forrásai – Újabb adatok a Bartók-mű keletkezéstörténetéhez" ["*Bluebeard's Castle* Text Research

– Recent Data on the Composition History of Bartók's Work"]. In: *Zenetudományi Dolgozatok*. 19–33. Ed. Melinda Berlász & Mária Domokos. Budapest: Magyar Tudományos Akadémia Zenetudományi Intézet.

Szigeti, Joseph (1967). *With Strings Attached: Reminiscences and Reflections.* New York, NY: Knopf.

Szőllősy, András (1956). "Bibliographie des œuvres musicales et écrits musicologiques de Béla Bartók" ["Bibliography of Musical Works and Musicological Writings of Béla Bartók"]. In: *Bartók, sa vie et son œuvre* [*Bartók, His Life and Work*]. 299–345. Ed. Bence Szabolcsi. Budapest: Corvina Press.

Tallián, Tibor (1981a). *Béla Bartók: The Man and His Work.* Transl. Gyula Gulyás. Budapest: Corvina Press.

—— (1981b). "Die *Cantata Profana* – ein Mythos Über des Übergangs" ["The *Cantata Profana* – A Myth of Transition"]. *Studia Musicologica Academiae Scientiarum Hungaricae* 23 (1–4): 135–200. Ed. József Ujfalussy et al. Budapest: Akadémia Kiadó.

—— (1983a). "Bartók Béla." In: *Brockhaus Riemann Zenei Lexikon*. Vol. 1: 129–144. Ed. Antal Boronkay. Budapest: Zeneműkiadó Vállalat.

—— (1983b). *"Cantata Profana" – az átmenet mítosza* [*The "Cantata Profana" – A Myth of Transition*]. Ph.D. diss. Liszt Academy of Music. Budapest: Magvető Könyvkiadó.

—— (ed.) (1989). *Bartók Béla írásai.* 1 kötet [*Béla Bartók's Writings*. Vol. 1]. Budapest: Editio Musica.

Tarasti, Eero (1994 [1978]). *Myytti ja musiikki: Semioottinen tutkimus myytin estetiikasta.* Helsinki: Gaudeamus. Originally published as: *Myth and Music: A Semiotic Approach to the Aesthetics of Myth in Music, Especially That of Wagner, Sibelius and Stravinsky.* Acta Musicologica Fennica 11. Helsinki: Finnish Musicological Society.

Taruskin, Richard (1986). "Letter to the Editor." *Music Analysis* 5 (2–3): 313–320.

—— (2001). "Nationalism." In: *The New Grove Dictionary of Music and Musicians.* Second edition. Vol. 17: 689–706. Ed. Stanley Sadie & John Tyrrell. London: MacMillan Publishers.

Tatar, Maria (2003 [1987]). *The Hard Facts of the Grimms' Fairy Tales.* Expanded second edition. Princeton, NJ: Princeton University Press.

Tenney, James (1993 [1983]). "John Cage and the Theory of Harmony." In: *Writings about John Cage*. 136–161. Ed. Richard Kostelanetz. Ann Arbor, IN: University of Michigan Press. Originally published in: *The Music of James Tenney*. 55–83. Ed. Peter Garland. Santa Fe, NM: Soundings Press.

Tenzer, Michael (2000). *Gamelan Gong Kebyar: The Art of Twentieth-Century Balinese Music.* Chicago Studies in Ethnomusicology. Chicago, IL: University of Chicago Press.

Tóth, Aladár (1920). "Kodály és *Vonóstriója*" ["Kodály and His *String Trio*"]. *Nyugat* 13 (13–14): 743–744.

—— (1930). "Bartók Béla." In: *Zenei Lexikon*. Vol. 1: 75–79. Ed. Bence Szabolcsi & Tóth Aladár. Budapest: Győző Andor Kiadása.

Travis, Roy (1970). "Tonal Coherence in the First Movement of Bartók's *Fourth String Quartet*." *Music Forum* 2: 298–371.

Treitler, Leo (1959). "Harmonic Procedure in the *Fourth Quartet* of Béla Bartók."

Journal of Music Theory 3 (November 1959): 292–297.

Ujfalussy, József (1959). *Debussy*. Budapest: Gondolat Kiadó.

—— (1962). "A hídszerkezetek néhány tartalmi kérdése Bartók művészetében" ["Some Inherent Questions of Arch Symmetry in Bartók's Works"]. In: *Zenetudományi Tanulmányok 10: Bartók Béla emlékére [Musicological Studies 10: In Memory of Béla Bartók]*. Vol. 10: 15–30. Ed. Bence Szabolcsi & Dénes Bartha. Budapest: Akadémia Kiadó.

—— (1969). "Az *Allegro barbaro* harmóniai alapgondolata és Bartók hangsorai" ["The Basic Harmonic Conception of *Allegro barbaro* and Bartók Scales"]. In: *Magyar Zenetörténeti Tanulmányok Szabolcsi Bence 70. Születésnapjára [Essays in the History of Hungarian Music in Honor of Bence Szabolcsi's 70th Birthday]*. 323–331. Ed. Ferenc Bónis. Budapest: Akadémia Kiadó.

—— (1971 [1970]). *Béla Bartók [Bartók Béla]*. Transl. Ruth Patkai. Budapest: Corvina Press. Originally published in: Budapest: Gondolat Kiadó.

—— (1972). "Gemeinsame Stilschicht in Bartóks und Kodálys Kunst" ["Common Layer in the Art of Bartók and Kodály"]. In: *IMCCBB*. 155–157.

—— (1976). "Bartók Béla: *A kékszakállú herceg vára*, Op. 11" ["Béla Bartók's *Duke Bluebeard's Castle*, Op. 11"]. *A Hét Zeneműve* 2: 32–38.

—— (ed.) (1980 [1958]). *Bartók breviárium: Levelek, írások, dokumentumok [Bartók Breviary: Correspondences, Essays, and Documents]*. Budapest: Zeneműkiadó.

—— (1982). "1907–1908 in Bartók's Entwicklung" ["The Years 1907–1908 in Bartók's Development"]. *Studia Musicologica Academiae Scientiarum Hungaricae* 24 (3–4): 519–525. Ed. József Ujfalussy et al. Budapest: Akadémia Kiadó.

Ujfalussy, József & János Breuer (eds.) (1972). *International Musicological Conference in Commemoration of Béla Bartók 1971 (IMCCBB)*. Budapest: Editio Musica.

Uther, Hans-Jörg (2004). *The Types of International Folktales: A Classification and Bibliography Based on the System of Antti Aarne and Stith Thompson. Parts I–III.* Folklore Fellows' Communications nos. 284–286. Ed. Sabine Dinslage, et al. Helsinki: Suomalainen Tiedeakatemia.

Valkó, Arisztid (1977). "Adatok Bartók színpadi műveihez" ["Data Concerning the Stage Works of Bartók"]. *Magyar Zene* 18: 433–439.

Vargyas, Lajos (1976). *A magyar népballada és Európa [The Hungarian Folk Ballad and Europe]*. Budapest: Zeneműkiadó.

—— (1982). "Sophisticated Contemporary Music Derived from the Music of Peasants." *Cultures* 8 (2): 43–52.

Várnai, Péter (1969 [1967]). *Székely Mihály [Mihály Székely]*. Second edition. Budapest: Zeneműkiadó.

—— (1978 [1956]). "*A kékszakállú herceg vára*, Op. 11." ["*Duke Bluebeard's Castle*, Op. 11"]. In: *Béla Bartók: "A kékszakállú herceg vára, Op. 11" [Béla Bartók: "Duke Bluebeard's Castle, Op. 11"]*. Historical Recording. Booklet. 1–2. LPX 11001. Budapest: Magyar Hanglemezgyártó Vállalat.

Vázsonyi, Nicholas (2005). "*Bluebeard's Castle*: The Birth of Cinema from the Spirit of Opera." *The Hungarian Quarterly* 46 (178): 214–236.

Veress, Sándor (1949). "*Bluebeard's Castle*. Part 1." *Tempo* 13 (Autumn 1949): 32–37.

—— (1949–1950). "*Bluebeard's Castle*. Part 2." *Tempo* 14 (Winter 1949–1950): 25–35.

Vinton, John (1966). "Bartók on His Own Music." *Journal of the American*

Musicological Society 19 (2): 232–243.

Vogel, Martin (1966). "Arthur v. Öttingen und der harmonische Dualismus" ["Arthur von Öttingen and the Harmonic Dualism"]. In: *Beiträge zur Musiktheorie des 19. Jahrhunderts*. 103–132. Ed. Martin Vogel. Regensburg: Bosse.

Voigt, Vilmos (1976). "Bevezetés: Az etnoszemiotikáról" ["Introduction: On Ethnosemiotics"]. *Ethnographia* 87 (3): 321–326.

—— (1979). "Folklore and Folklorism Today." *Folklorismus Bulletin* 1 (April 1979): 21–29.

—— (1981 [1980]). "A történeti magyar mesekutatás kérdései" ["Some Questions on Historical Hungarian Tale Research"]. In: *A Janus Pannonius Múzeum Évkönyve* 25: 253–257. Pécs: Janus Pannonius Múzeum.

—— (1982). "Baltic Problems of Hungarian Prehistory." *Études finno-ougriennes* 15 (1978–1979): 447–453.

—— (1983) "Az érzelmek és a fájdalom eltávolítása (Menyasszonysiratók)" ["Removing Feelings and Pains (Bridal Laments)"]. In: *Lakodalom* [*Wedding*]. 397–407. Ed. László Novák & Zoltán Ujváry. Debrecen: Kossuth Lajos Tudományegyetem Néprajzi Tanszéke.

—— (1984). "Van-e határa egy népi kultúrának?" ["Is There Any Border for Folk Culture?"]. In: *Interetnikus kapcsolatok Északkelet-Magyarországon*. A Herman Ottó Múzeum néprajzi kiadványai 14: 75–89. II. Kiegészítő kötet. Ed. Ernő Kunt, József Szabadfalvi & Gyula Viga. Miskolc: Herman Ottó Múzeum.

—— (1986). "Honti János összehasonlító filológiája ma" ["János Honti's Comparative Philology Today"]. *Ethnographia* 97 (2–3): 368–376. Ed. Vilmos Voigt. Budapest: Akadémiai Kiadó.

—— (1988). "Bartók találkozik a folklórral" ["Bartók Meets Folklore"]. In: *Urálisztikai tanulmányok: Bereczki-Emlékkönyv*. Vol. 2: 391–396. Ed. Domokos Péter & Pusztay János. Budapest: ELTE.

—— (1990a). *A folklorizmusról* [*On Folklorism*]. Néprajz egyetemi hallgatóknak 9. Debrecen: Kossuth Lajos Tudományegyetem Néprajzi Tanszéke.

—— (1990b). "A nemzetközi folklorisztika ma" ["International Folklorism Today"]. In: *Folklór, Folklorisztika és Etnológia* 196: 3–36. Ed. Vilmos Voigt. Budapest: Akadémiai Kiadó.

—— (1990c). "Mesék és értelmezésük" ["Tales and Understanding Them"]. In: *Folklór, Folklorisztika és Etnológia* 200: 100–109. Ed. Vilmos Voigt. Budapest: Akadémiai Kiadó.

—— (1990d). "Sur les niveaux des variantes de contes" ["On the Levels of Variations in Tales"]. In: *D'un conte... a l'autre: La Variabilité dans la littérature orale* [*From One Tale... to Another: The Variability in Oral Literature*]. 403–414. Paris: Editions du CNRS.

—— (1991 [1987]). "Not a Simple Pan-Slavic Genre (The Bride's Lament in Hungarian Folklore)." In: *Finnish-Hungarian Symposium on Music & Folklore Research 15–21.11.1987*. 96–103. Ed. Antti Koiranen. Tampere: Tampereen yliopiston kansanperinteen laitos.

—— (1997). "Megoldott és megoldatlan kérdések hangrögzítésünk kezdetei körül: A kép- és hangrögzítés változó módszerei a népi kultúrában" ["Solved and Unsolved Problems Concerning the Beginnings of Sound Recording: The Changing Techniques of Audio and Video Recording in Ethnographical Research"]. *Néprajzi*

Értesítő: Annales Musei Ethnographiae 79: 103–107. Ed. Attila Selmeczi Kovács. Transl. of the summaries by Gábor Komáromy. Budapest: Néprajzi Múzeum.

—— (1993a). "Az új magyar népmesekatalógus kérdései" ["Problems of the New Hungarian Tale-Type Index"]. *Ethnographia* 104 (1): 167–180.

—— (1993b). "Neofolklorism: Why It Is a Neglected Topic in the Study of Counter-Culture in Nordic Literatures." In: *Literature as Resistance and Counter-Culture*. Papers of the 19th Study Conference of the International Association for Scandinavian Studies. 339–345. Ed. András Masát & Péter Mádl. Budapest: Hungarian Association for Scandinavian Studies.

—— (1999 [1990]). "Modern Storytelling – *Stricto sensu*." In: *Suggestions Towards a Theory of Folklore*. 211–219. Preface by Alan Dundes. Budapest: Mundus Hungarian University Press. Originally published in: *Storytelling in Contemporary Societies*. 23–31. Ed. Lutz Röhrich & Sabine Wienker-Piepho. Tübingen: Gunter Narr.

—— (1999 [1972]). "Some Problems of the Narrative Structure Universals in Folklore." In: *Suggestions Towards a Theory of Folklore*. 76–91. Preface by Alan Dundes. Ed. Szilárd Biernaczky. Budapest: Mundus Hungarian University Press. Originally published in: *Acta Ethnographica Academiae Scientiarum Hungaricae* 21 (1–2): 55–72.

—— (2005 [1970]). "Vom Neofolklorismus in der Kunst" ["On Neofolklorism in Art"]. In: *Europäische Linien: Studien zur Finnougristik, Folkloristik und Semiotik* [*European Lines: Studies on Finn-Urgrism, Folklorism and Semiotics*]. Studies in Ethnology 2. 179–206. Ed. Gábor Barna. Budapest: Akadémiai Kiadó. Originally published in: *Acta Ethnographica Academiae Scientiarum Hungaricae: Gyula Ortutay Sexagenario* 19 (1–4): 401–424. Ed. Tibor Bodrogi, Béla Gunda & István Tálasi. Budapest: Akadémiai Kiadó.

Voigt, Vilmos & Szemerkényi, Ágnes (1984). "A 'hatos' a magyar közmondásokban" ["Number 'Six' in Hungarian Proverbs"]. In: *Folklór, Folklorisztika és Etnológia* 88: 470–477. Ed. Vilmos Voigt. Budapest: Akadémiai Kiadó.

Vonnegut, Kurt, Jr. (1988). *Bluebeard.* New York, NY: Delacorte Press.

Wagner, Richard (1984 [1852]). *Oper und Drama* [*Opera and Drama*]. Ed. Klaus Kropfinger. Stuttgart: Philipp Reclam Jr. Originally published in: Leipzig: Verlagsbuchhandlung J. J. Weber.

—— (1993 [1949]). "The Art-Work of the Future." In: *The Art-Work of the Future and Other Works*. 69–213. Transl. William Ellis. Lincoln, NB, and London: University of Nebraska Press.

Waldbauer, Iván F. (1996). "Theorists' Views on Bartók from Edwin von der Nüll to Paul Wilson." *Studia Musicologica Academiae Scientiarum Hungaricae* 37 (1): 93–121. Ed. József Ujfalussy et al. Budapest: Akadémia Kiadó.

Webern, Anton (1975 [1960]). *The Path to the New Music* [*Der Weg zur neuen Musik*]. Transl. Leo Black. New Jersey: International Edition. Originally published in: Wien: Universal Edition.

Weiss-Aigner, Günter (1982). "Tonale Perspektiven des jungen Bartók" ["Tonal Perspectives in the Young Bartók"]. *Studia Musicologica Academiae Scientiarum Hungaricae* 24 (3–4): 537–548. Ed. József Ujfalussy et al. Budapest: Akadémia Kiadó.

Weissmann, John S. (1980). "Verbunkos." In: *The New Grove Dictionary of*

Music and Musicians. Vol. 18: 629–630. Ed. Stanley Sadie. London: MacMillan Publishers.

Wellesz, Egon Joseph (1989 [1923]). "Arnold Schönberg et son œuvre" ["Arnold Schoenberg and His Works"]. *Arnold Schönberg et l'école de Vienne* [*Arnold Schoenberg and the Viennese School*]. *La Revue Musicale* 416–417: 11–28.

—— (1989a [1926]). "La voie nouvelle – I" ["The New Voice – I"]. *Arnold Schönberg et l'école de Vienne* [*Arnold Schoenberg and the Viennese School*]. *La Revue Musicale* 416–417: 29–42.

—— (1989b [1926]). "La voie nouvelle – II" ["The New Voice – II"]. *Arnold Schönberg et l'école de Vienne* [*Arnold Schoenberg and the Viennese School*]. *La Revue Musicale* 416–417: 43–55.

—— (1989c [1926]). "La doctrine – III" ["The Doctrine – III"]. *Arnold Schönberg et l'école de Vienne* [*Arnold Schoenberg and the Viennese School*]. *La Revue Musicale* 416–417: 56–62.

—— (1989d [1926]). "La doctrine – IV" ["The Doctrine – IV"]. *Arnold Schönberg et l'école de Vienne* [*Arnold Schoenberg and the Viennese School*]. *La Revue Musicale* 416–417: 63–72.

Whittall, Arnold (1983). "Analysis." In: *The New Oxford Companion to Music.* Vol. 1: 58. Oxford: Oxford University Press.

Wilcox, Howard (1992). "Generating Fibonacci Sequences of Pitch-Classes." *Sonus: A Journal of Investigations into Global Musical Possibilities* 12 (2): 44–47.

Wilson, Paul Frederick (1982). *Atonality and Structure in Works of Béla Bartók's Middle Period.* Ph.D. diss. Yale University. New Haven, CT.

—— (1984). "Concepts of Prolongation and Bartók's Opus 20." *Music Theory Spectrum* 6: 79–89.

—— (1986). "Review of *the Music of Béla Bartók: A Study of Tonality and Progression in Twentieth-Century Music* by Elliott Antokoletz." *Journal of Music Theory* 30 (1): 113–121.

—— (1992). *The Music of Béla Bartók.* New Haven, CT & London: Yale University Press.

—— (1993). "Approaching Atonality: *Studies* and *Improvisations*." In: *The Bartók Companion.* 162–184. Ed. Malcolm Gillies. Portland, ME: Amadeus Press.

Wittlich, Gary E. (1969). *An Examination of Some Set-Theoretic Applications in the Analysis of Non-Serial Music.* Ph.D. diss. University of Iowa. Iowa City, IA.

Woodward, James E. (1981). "Understanding Bartók's *Bagatelle*, Op. 6/9." *Indiana Theory Review* 4 (2): 11–32.

Yeomans, David (2000). "Background and Analysis of Bartók's *Romanian Christmas Carols for Piano*." In: *Bartók Perspectives: Man, Composer, and Ethnomusicologist.* 185–195. Ed. Elliott Antokoletz, Victoria Fischer & Benjamin Suchoff. Oxford & New York, NY: Oxford University Press.

Zsuffa, Joseph (1987). *Béla Balázs: The Man and the Artist.* Berkeley & Los Angeles, CA: University of California Press.

APPENDIX

List of Prime Forms and Interval Class Vectors

	Forte number	PCs	IC-Vector
1.	3 – 1 (12)	0,1,2	210000
2.	3 – 2	0,1,3	111000
3.	3 – 3	0,1,4	101100
4.	3 – 4	0,1,5	100110
5.	3 – 5	0,1,6	100011
6.	3 – 6 (12)	0,2,4	020100
7.	3 – 7	0,2,5	011010
8.	3 – 8	0,2,6	010101
9.	3 – 9 (12)	0,2,7	010020
10.	3 – 10 (12)	0,3,6	002001
11.	3 – 11	0,3,7	001110
12.	3 – 12 (4)	0,4,8	000300
13.	4 – 1 (12)	0,1,2,3	321000
14.	4 – 2	0,1,2,4	221100
15.	4 – 3	0,1,3,4	212100
16.	4 – 4	0,1,2,5	211110
17.	4 – 5	0,1,2,6	210111
18.	4 – 6 (12)	0,1,2,7	210021
19.	4 – 7 (12)	0,1,4,5	201210
20.	4 – 8 (12)	0,1,5,6	200121
21.	4 – 9 (6)	0,1,6,7	200022
22.	4 – 10 (12)	0,2,3,5	122010
23.	4 – 11	0,1,3,5	121110
24.	4 – 12	0,2,3,6	112101
25.	4 – 13	0,1,3,6	112011
26.	4 – 14	0,2,3,7	111120
27.	4 – Z15	0,1,4,6	111111
28.	4 – 16	0,1,5,7	110121
29.	4 – 17 (12)	0,3,4,7	102210
30.	4 – 18	0,1,4,7	102111
31.	4 – 19	0,1,4,8	101310
32.	4 – 20 (12)	0,1,5,8	101220
33.	4 – 21 (12)	0,2,4,6	030201

34.	4 – 22	0,2,4,7	021120
35.	4 – 23 (12)	0,2,5,7	021030
36.	4 – 24 (12)	0,2,4,8	020301
37.	4 – 25 (6)	0,2,6,8	020202
38.	4 – 26 (12)	0,3,5,8	012120
39.	4 – 27	0,2,5,8	012111
40.	4 – 28 (3)	0,3,6,9	004002
41.	4 – Z29	0,1,3,7	111111
42.	5 – 1 (12)	0,1,2,3,4	432100
43.	5 – 2	0,1,2,3,5	332110
44.	5 – 3	0,1,2,4,5	322210
45.	5 – 4	0,1,2,3,6	322111
46.	5 – 5	0,1,2,3,7	321121
47.	5 – 6	0,1,2,5,6	311221
48.	5 – 7	0,1,2,6,7	310132
49.	5 – 8 (12)	0,2,3,4,6	232201
50.	5 – 9	0,1,2,4,6	231211
51.	5 – 10	0,1,3,4,6	223111
52.	5 – 11	0,2,3,4,7	222220
53.	5 – Z12 (12)	0,1,3,5,6	222121
54.	5 – 13	0,1,2,4,8	221311
55.	5 – 14	0,1,2,5,7	221131
56.	5 – 15 (12)	0,1,2,6,8	220222
57.	5 – 16	0,1,3,4,7	213211
58.	5 – Z17 (12)	0,1,3,4,8	212320
59.	5 – Z18	0,1,4,5,7	212221
60.	5 – 19	0,1,3,6,7	212122
61.	5 – 20	0,1,3,7,8	211231
62.	5 – 21	0,1,4,5,8	202420
63.	5 – 22 (12)	0,1,4,7,8	202321
64.	5 – 23	0,2,3,5,7	132130
65.	5 – 24	0,1,3,5,7	131221
66.	5 – 25	0,2,3,5,8	123121
67.	5 – 26	0,2,4,5,8	122311
68.	5 – 27	0,1,3,5,8	122230
69.	5 – 28	0,2,3,6,8	122212
70.	5 – 29	0,1,3,6,8	122131
71.	5 – 30	0,1,4,6,8	121321
72.	5 – 31	0,1,3,6,9	114112
73.	5 – 32	0,1,4,6,9	113221
74.	5 – 33 (12)	0,2,4,6,8	040402
75.	5 – 34 (12)	0,2,4,6,9	032221
76.	5 – 35 (12)	0,2,4,7,9	032140
77.	5 – Z36	0,1,2,4,7	222121

78.	5 – Z37 (12)	0,3,4,5,8	212320
79.	5 – Z38	0,1,2,5,8	212221
80.	6 – 1 (12)	0,1,2,3,4,5	543210
81.	6 – 2	0,1,2,3,4,6	443211
82.	6 – Z3	0,1,2,3,5,6	433221
83.	6 – Z4 (12)	0,1,2,4,5,6	432321
84.	6 – 5	0,1,2,3,6,7	422232
85.	6 – Z6 (12)	0,1,2,5,6,7	421242
86.	6 – 7 (6)	0,1,2,6,7,8	420243
87.	6 – 8 (12)	0,2,3,4,5,7	343230
88.	6 – 9	0,1,2,3,5,7	342231
89.	6 – Z10	0,1,3,4,5,7	333321
90.	6 – Z11	0,1,2,4,5,7	333231
91.	6 – Z12	0,1,2,4,6,7	332232
92.	6 – Z13 (12)	0,1,3,4,6,7	324222
93.	6 – 14	0,1,3,4,5,8	323430
94.	6 – 15	0,1,2,4,5,8	323421
95.	6 – 16	0,1,4,5,6,8	322431
96.	6 – Z17	0,1,2,4,7,8	322332
97.	6 – 18	0,1,2,5,7,8	322242
98.	6 – Z19	0,1,3,4,7,8	313431
99.	6 – 20 (4)	0,1,4,5,8,9	303630
100.	6 – 21	0,2,3,4,6,8	242412
101.	6 – 22	0,1,2,4,6,8	241422
102.	6 – Z23 (12)	0,2,3,5,6,8	234222
103.	6 – Z24	0,1,3,4,6,8	233331
104.	6 – Z25	0,1,3,5,6,8	233241
105.	6 – Z26 (12)	0,1,3,5,7,8	232341
106.	6 – 27	0,1,3,4,6,9	225222
107.	6 – Z28 (12)	0,1,3,5,6,9	224322
108.	6 – Z29 (12)	0,1,3,6,8,9	224232
109.	6 – 30 (12)	0,1,3,6,7,9	224223
110.	6 – 31	0,1,3,5,8,9	223431
111.	6 – 32 (12)	0,2,4,5,7,9	143250
112.	6 – 33	0,2,3,5,7,9	143241
113.	6 – 34	0,1,3,5,7,9	142422
114.	6 – 35 (2)	0,2,4,6,8,10	060603
115.	6 – Z36	0,1,2,3,4,7	433221
116.	6 – Z37 (12)	0,1,2,3,4,8	432321
117.	6 – Z38 (12)	0,1,2,3,7,8	421242
118.	6 – Z39	0,2,3,4,5,8	333321
119.	6 – Z40	0,1,2,3,5,8	333231
120.	6 – Z41	0,1,2,3,6,8	332232
121.	6 – Z42 (12)	0,1,2,3,6,9	324222

122.	6 – Z43	0,1,2,5,6,8	322332
123.	6 – Z44	0,1,2,5,6,9	313431
124.	6 – Z45 (12)	0,2,3,4,6,9	234222
125.	6 – Z46	0,1,2,4,6,9	233331
126.	6 – Z47	0,1,2,4,7,9	233241
127.	6 – Z48 (12)	0,1,2,5,7,9	232341
128.	6 – Z49 (12)	0,1,3,4,7,9	224322
129.	6 – Z50 (12)	0,1,4,6,7,9	224232
130.	7 – 1	0,1,2,3,4,5,6	654321
131.	7 – 2	0,1,2,3,4,5,7	554331
132.	7 – 3	0,1,2,3,4,5,8	544431
133.	7 – 4	0,1,2,3,4,6,7	544332
134.	7 – 5	0,1,2,3,5,6,7	543342
135.	7 – 6	0,1,2,3,4,7,8	533442
136.	7 – 7	0,1,2,3,6,7,8	532353
137.	7 – 8	0,2,3,4,5,6,8	454422
138.	7 – 9	0,1,2,3,4,6,8	453432
139.	7 – 10	0,1,2,3,4,6,9	445332
140.	7 – 11	0,1,3,4,5,6,8	444441
141.	7 – Z12	0,1,2,3,4,7,9	444342
142.	7 – 13	0,1,2,4,5,6,8	443532
143.	7 – 14	0,1,2,3,5,7,8	443352
144.	7 – 15	0,1,2,4,6,7,8	442443
145.	7 – 16	0,1,2,3,5,6,9	435432
146.	7 – Z17	0,1,2,4,5,6,9	434541
147.	7 – Z18	0,1,2,3,5,8,9	434442
148.	7 – 19	0,1,2,3,6,7,9	434343
149.	7 – 20	0,1,2,4,7,8,9	433452
150.	7 – 21	0,1,2,4,5,8,9	424641
151.	7 – 22	0,1,2,5,6,8,9	424542
152.	7 – 23	0,2,3,4,5,7,9	354351
153.	7 – 24	0,1,2,3,5,7,9	353442
154.	7 – 25	0,2,3,4,6,7,9	345342
155.	7 – 26	0,1,3,4,5,7,9	344532
156.	7 – 27	0,1,2,4,5,7,9	344451
157.	7 – 28	0,1,3,5,6,7,9	344433
158.	7 – 29	0,1,2,4,6,7,9	344352
159.	7 – 30	0,1,2,4,6,8,9	343542
160.	7 – 31	0,1,3,4,6,7,9	336333
161.	7 – 32	0,1,3,4,6,8,9	335442
162.	7 – 33	0,1,2,4,6,8,10	262623
163.	7 – 34	0,1,3,4,6,8,10	254442
164.	7 – 35	0,1,3,5,6,8,10	254361
165.	7 – Z36	0,1,2,3,5,6,8	444342

166.	7 – Z37	0,1,3,4,5,7,8	434541
167.	7 – Z38	0,1,2,4,5,7,8	434442
168.	8 – 1	0,1,2,3,4,5,6,7	765442
169.	8 – 2	0,1,2,3,4,5,6,8	665542
170.	8 – 3	0,1,2,3,4,5,6,9	656542
171.	8 – 4	0,1,2,3,4,5,7,8	655552
172.	8 – 5	0,1,2,3,4,6,7,8	654553
173.	8 – 6	0,1,2,3,5,6,7,8	654463
174.	8 – 7	0,1,2,3,4,5,8,9	645652
175.	8 – 8	0,1,2,3,4,7,8,9	644563
176.	8 – 9	0,1,2,3,6,7,8,9	644464
177.	8 – 10	0,2,3,4,5,6,7,9	566452
178.	8 – 11	0,1,2,3,4,5,7,9	565552
179.	8 – 12	0,1,3,4,5,6,7,9	556543
180.	8 – 13	0,1,2,3,4,6,7,9	556453
181.	8 – 14	0,1,2,4,5,6,7,9	555562
182.	8 – Z15	0,1,2,3,4,6,8,9	555553
183.	8 – 16	0,1,2,3,5,7,8,9	554563
184.	8 – 17	0,1,3,4,5,6,8,9	546652
185.	8 – 18	0,1,2,3,5,6,8,9	546553
186.	8 – 19	0,1,2,4,5,6,8,9	545752
187.	8 – 20	0,1,2,4,5,7,8,9	545662
188.	8 – 21	0,1,2,3,4,6,8,10	474643
189.	8 – 22	0,1,2,3,5,6,8,10	465562
190.	8 – 23	0,1,2,3,5,7,8,10	465472
191.	8 – 24	0,1,2,4,5,6,8,10	464743
192.	8 – 25	0,1,2,4,6,7,8,10	464644
193.	8 – 26	0,1,2,4,5,7,9,10	456562
194.	8 – 27	0,1,2,4,5,7,8,10	456553
195.	8 – 28	0,1,3,4,6,7,9,10	448444
196.	8 – Z29	0,1,2,3,5,6,7,9	555553
197.	9 – 1	0,1,2,3,4,5,6,7,8	876663
198.	9 – 2	0,1,2,3,4,5,6,7,9	777663
199.	9 – 3	0,1,2,3,4,5,6,8,9	767763
200.	9 – 4	0,1,2,3,4,5,7,8,9	766773
201.	9 – 5	0,1,2,3,4,6,7,8,9	766674
202.	9 – 6	0,1,2,3,4,5,6,8,10	686763
203.	9 – 7	0,1,2,3,4,5,7,8,10	677673
204.	9 – 8	0,1,2,3,4,6,7,8,10	676764
205.	9 – 9	0,1,2,3,5,6,7,8,10	676683
206.	9 – 10	0,1,2,3,4,6,7,9,10	668664
207.	9 – 11	0,1,2,3,5,6,7,9,10	667773
208.	9 – 12	0,1,2,4,5,6,8,9,10	666963

INDEX